HANNAY
SAMPSON
· EX LIBRIS ·

For detailed map of shaded
area see inside back cover

Barrier of Spears

To
My Climbing Companions
Down the Years

R. O. PEARSE

Barrier of Spears

DRAMA OF THE DRAKENSBERG

Illustrated by
MALCOLM L. PEARSE

Emm.
Mont-Aux-Sources Hotel
The Drakensberg
Kwazulu-Natal
April 1999

HOWARD TIMMINS
1973

ISBN 0 86978 050 6

"*When my eldest boy was eight years old he went with his mother up the North ridge of Tryfan on a day when a wild Westerly was driving cloud and soft rain over the ridge. They were alone, and on a ledge near the top he stopped and said thoughtfully : 'Mummy, these are the wild and lonely places.'* "

Charles Evans, in his Valedictory
Presidential Address to the Alpine
Club, 7th December, 1970.

ACKNOWLEDGMENTS

Grateful acknowledgement is made by the author to the following authors and publishers for their courtesy in allowing certain copyright passages to be included in this book:

Messrs. Maskew Miller for the verse by Mary Boyd on page 211.

The Editor of *The Journal of the Mountain Club of S.A.* for the poem on page 83, and for the account of Richard Barry's death, commencing on page 140.

Professor Walter Battiss for the passage on page 37.

Mr. A. R. Willcox for the passage on page 255.

Mr. Martin Winter for the passage from his Log Book, on page 118.

The Editor of the *Alpine Journal* for permission to reproduce the map on page 53.

Professor P. J. Schoeman for the passages on pages 3, 6 and 30.

The Cambridge University Press for the quotation from Mr. Arthur R. Hinks on page 52.

The Literary Trustees of Walter de la Mare and the Society of Authors as their representative for the two lines of poetry on page 39.

Owing to the high costs of colour reproduction it would have been impossible to publish this book at a moderate price without the generous help of a number of people. The author wishes to express his gratitude to the following individuals and organisations, all of whom have offered either generous financial assistance, or help in other ways:

Human Sciences Research Council
Natal Building Society
Cathedral Peak Hotel
Mountain Club of S.A., Natal Section
Estcourt High School
Drakensberg Boys Choir School
Estcourt and District Rotary Club
G.D.B. Forder Esq.

The financial assistance of the Human Sciences Research Council is particularly appreciated. It is to be noted that all opinions expressed in this work, or any conclusions reached, are those of the author, and must in no instance be regarded as a reflection of the opinions or conclusions of the Human Sciences Research Council. The book is No. 40 in the Council's Publication Series.

CONTENTS

Page

Foreword by the Hon. S. P. Botha, Minister of Forestry

Preface i

Prelude: How It All Began iii

PART I

CHAPTER I   The Little Yellow Hunters 3

CHAPTER II   The Black Man 12

CHAPTER III   The Coming of the White Man 24

CHAPTER IV   Early Travellers in the Drakensberg 39

CHAPTER V   Of Maps and Mapping 52

CHAPTER VI   Climbers All 63

CHAPTER VII   George Thomson 77

PART II

CHAPTER VIII   Ghost Hotel 87

CHAPTER IX   Mont-aux-Sources and the Royal Natal National Park . . 95

CHAPTER X   The Lovely Mnweni 109

CHAPTER XI   Cathedral of the Skies 119

CHAPTER XII   Cathkin 131

CHAPTER XIII   The Giant's Castle Game Reserve 147

CHAPTER XIV   The Silent Snow 159

PART III

CHAPTER XV   The Geography of Hope—1 173

CHAPTER XVI   The Geography of Hope—2 184

CHAPTER XVII   Lammergeyer 194

CHAPTER XVIII   The Wild Ones 204

CHAPTER XIX   The Men Who Guard the Trees 214

CHAPTER XX   Smoke on the Pass—1 226

CHAPTER XXI   Smoke on the Pass—2 237

CHAPTER XXII   Aftermath 246

CHAPTER XXIII   What of the Future 255

L'ENVOI   266

APPENDIX 1   The Langalibalele Rebellion and the Hlatimba Pass . . . 269

			Page
APPENDIX 2	Climbing Techniques	. . . .	272
APPENDIX 3	Drakensberg Maps	. . . .	274
APPENDIX 4	Heights of Drakensberg Peaks and Record of First Ascents	.	283
BIBLIOGRAPHY		. . . .	289
INDEX		. . . .	295

MAPS AND DIAGRAMS

Profile through Drakensberg, showing geological features	viii
Map of Drakensberg, A. H. Stocker, 1888	53
Map of Mont-aux-Sources Area	88
Sketch of Mont-aux-Sources Area	96
Map of Mnweni Area	110
Map of Cathedral Area	120
Map of Cathkin Area	132
Sketch of Cathkin Area	137
Map of Giant's Castle Game Reserve	148
Map showing plan of Military Operations against Langalibalele	231
Map showing pursuit of Langalibalele	247
Map showing Drakensberg Bantu Locations, Government Forestry Areas, and Natal Parks Board Areas	260
Code Index of 1:50 000 Maps	281

ILLUSTRATIONS

facing page

Autumn Evening. From the garden of the author's home iv

The Timeless Drakensberg . . . . *between* iv *and* v

Home of the Bushmen. The Great Injasuti Valley v

From the lip of the Tugela Falls. A winter's morning 120

Sunrise from the summit of Gray's Pass 120

Barrier of Spears. From the summit of Cleft Peak 121

Monk's Cowl, with Cathkin Peak to the left and the cliffs of Champagne Castle to the
right 136

Winter idyll. The summit of the Amphitheatre 137

The Mountain Club Hut, summit of Amphitheatre 137

Ice-pinnacles below Mponjwana 144

Light floods into the great Ntonjelane valley as the sun begins to rise 144

Tranquillity. Cathkin Peak and Sterkhorn . . . . *between* 144 *and* 145

The Cathedral Range reflected in a mountain vlei 145

A strange rock pinnacle in Organ Pipes Pass 145

The Northern Ifidi Pinnacle 152

The fury of the storm 152

Giant's Castle 153

The soaring pinnacle of the Western Injasuti Triplet 153

The mighty face of the Amphitheatre Wall and the Tugela Falls 168

The Silent Snow 168

Winter sparkle. Snow cameo in the Mnweni area 169

After the blizzard. From the Upper Injasuti Cave 169

The African Lammergeyer 200

Wild Flowers of the Drakensberg 201

The sound of many waters. The Mnweni River 264

Sunrise over the distant Cathedral Range, from Mponjwana 264

Evening clouds gather around the face of Cathkin Peak 265

*The photographs of the Lammergeyer, which
appear in Chapter XVII, were taken by
H. G. Symons, P. R. Barnes, D. D. Morrison
and R. O. Pearse.*

FOREWORD BY
THE HONOURABLE S. P. BOTHA, MINISTER OF FORESTRY

Ever since the Voortrekkers wound their perilous way down the passes of the Drakensberg, this magnificent mountain range has played an important part in our history. But the author goes further back than this. He traces the story of this mountain land down the years from primeval times to the present day and into this already rich tapestry he weaves an absorbing account of its flora, its fauna, and of the men who climb its high peaks. He ends with a passionate plea for its preservation and outlines a bold plan to achieve this.

He could not have known, when he wrote his book, that my Department was busy planning for the very thing he advocates. The Department of Forestry is charged with the responsibility of looking after the nation's catchment areas, and it is something to be thankful for that the scientific aspects of managing wilderness areas, nature reserves and mountain catchments are basically the same and not incompatible with outdoor recreation. Planning for multiple use of our mountain land is receiving high priority.

"Our Green Heritage" campaign currently under way is designed to create an appreciation amongst South Africans of the importance of trees, a love for our country's flora, and an awareness of our mountain areas, especially for recreational purposes, and to develop a strong desire amongst our people for the conservation and preservation of these areas.

It is my intention this year to declare large parts of the Natal Drakensberg as Wilderness Areas. Wilderness Areas may be a new concept to many South Africans, but we are going to hear more and more about them. The demarcation and setting aside of these areas will be done in terms of section 7A of the Forest Act, 1968 as amended.

I welcome and commend this worthy contribution to South Africa's Green Heritage Year.

Hon. S. P. Botha, Minister of Forestry

3rd April, 1973

PREFACE

The Drakensberg Range forms the eastern escarpment of South Africa. It is actually a mountain chain of some 960 km in length. In the north it separates the Transvaal Lowveld from the Highveld, and, commencing at about Lat. 23 degrees, runs south to Laing's Nek, at the point where the three Provinces, Natal, the Transvaal and the Free State meet. From that point it swings south-west, forming the boundary between Natal and the Free State. At *Mont-aux-Sources* it turns south-east, and forms the boundary between Natal and Lesotho, veering south-west again at *Giant's Castle*. Soon after this it enters the Cape Colony, and gradually merges into the Stormberg Mountains.

In this book I have limited myself to the 95 kilometres between *Mont-aux-Sources* and *Giant's Castle*, with only occasional references to those portions lying north and south of this stretch. Here it is at its finest, the average height being 3 050 metres, and the highest peaks rising to over 3 350 metres. North and south of this area, especially north, it is nothing like so impressive.

How the name "Drakensberg", meaning the Dragon Mountains, came to be given, is not known. It was in use well before the Voortrekkers came to Natal in 1837. In those early days it was sometimes spelt "Drakenberg", sometimes "Draaksberg", while a map published in 1847 by James Wyld, Geographer to the Queen, calls it "Drache Berg or Quathlamba Mountains". By 1850, however, the present spelling of *Drakensberg* appears to have been well established. About 48 km west of Matatiele is an isolated peak called *Drakensberg*, or *Dragon's Rock*. It is possible that the name of the whole Range was derived from this peak. The Zulu name is Quathlamba, meaning "A barrier of up-pointed spears".

I have devoted three Chapters and an Appendix to the Langalibalele Rebellion, and to the action of November 4, 1873 on the summit of the Drakensberg. Apart from several widely-accepted errors which I wished to clear up, this is a story of matchless endurance and courage (and of bitter shame), which deserves to be told in full and recorded. It has never been told fully before, and of course it had a profound influence on events in South Africa, and, to a lesser extent, overseas as well.

Zulu Orthography

One of the charming features of Natal is that in so many cases the old Zulu place-names have been retained. These are always descriptive, sonorous, and often beautiful. It is good to see that so many of our Drakensberg rivers have retained these Zulu names. Unfortunately we cannot say the same for the peaks. Many of these names have been lost or discarded in favour of English names. Wherever possible I have given the original Zulu name as well as the English name.

The spelling of Zulu place-names, however, is always a difficulty in books of this nature. Many of these are, to-day, incorrectly spelt, but by now this spelling has become generally accepted. Some writers have attempted to use the correct Zulu spelling for place-names, and thus spell Tugela *uThukela*. This, I claim, can be irritating to the general reader. To be consistent, had I done this I would have had to spell Umkomaas *emKhomazi*, Umzimkulu *emZimkhulu*, Umgeni *emNgeni*, and so on, while if I had used the form *eXobho*, the reader would have not only been irritated: he would have been frankly mystified, for I doubt whether he would have recognised it as the correct form for Ixopo! I have, therefore, retained the spelling of all generally-accepted names, even though many of these are incorrect, but in the case of lesser-known names I have attempted to establish the correct spelling.

Similarly, in the case of tribal names, the correct spelling would be *amaZizi, amaHlubi*, for the plural, i.e. the amaZizi people, the amaHlubi people, but *iZizi* and *iHlubi* for the singular, i.e. an iZizi man, an iHlubi woman. Again this can be irritating. Here I have adopted the more westernized spelling of *Amazizi* and *Amahlubi* for the plural, and simply Zizi and Hlubi for the singular.

In the case of the people of Lesotho (the former Basutoland) I have used the Zulu name for the plural, *Basutho* (the shortened form of the Zulu *abaSutho*), and for the singular the Sotho form *Mosutho*, which is better known than the Zulu *umSotho*.

I have applied the same principle of simplification to words such as *iNduna* (which I have spelt *Induna*), *iMfe* (spelt *Imfe*), *iMpe* (spelt *Impi*), and so on. I have also retained the westernized form *Quathlamba*, instead of the more correct *uKhahlamba*.

In all matters concerning Zulu orthography I have been guided by Mr. Sigurt Bourquin, Director of Bantu Administration, Durban, a noted authority on Zulu language and customs. To him I am greatly indebted, for he has not spared himself in the task I asked him to undertake, often at great cost to himself. I must make it clear, however, that where I have departed from the correct and orthodox spelling, as supplied by him, the decision has been mine, and mine alone.

Readers who are unacquainted with climbing techniques and terms, and who wish to follow the stories of Drakensberg climbs which are told in this book, should make a point of reading Appendix 2.

"Emkhizweni"
Loskop, Natal.   R.O.P.
September 1972.

HOW IT ALL BEGAN

For some reason my pipe was not drawing properly. But that did not matter. I was sitting in my deck-chair, on the lawns of *Emkhizweni*, our new home. Over to the left the plane trees were just beginning to turn brown. To the right, a single Liquidamber tree flamed in a blaze of red and gold. In front, soaring up into the clouds, was *Cathkin Peak*, and I watched it slowly turning from the translucent blue of afternoon to the deep purple of twilight. Suddenly, as the sun began to set over Hlatikulu Nek, a blazing sword struck sharply and obliquely through the gap between *Cathkin* and *Sterkhorn*, and the rocks of *Wostyn* glowed for a brief moment with a gold that rivalled the gold of the Liquidamber. Then it was gone. The night was coming.

It was autumn, 1966. Five months previously the farewells had been said after my twenty five years as Headmaster of a large co-educational High School, our boxes had been packed, we had torn up the roots of many years, and had headed for our new home, *Emkhizweni*, the Place of the Misty Rain, in the foothills of the Drakensberg. Over those twenty five years I had grown to love the mighty Drakensberg mountains, for we could see their blue spires from the front door of our home in the school grounds, and access to them was easy. In fair weather and wild storm I had roamed the pleasant valleys of the Little Berg, climbed the rugged pinnacles of the High Berg, and slept among the peaks, sometimes on snow-clad slopes. And when the inevitable prospect of retirement had loomed up, and I knew I would have to leave the School I had loved, what more natural home for myself and my wife than the Drakensberg. Five years before we were due to go we had bought a fifteen-acre plot on the slopes of *Wostyn*, in the Cathkin area, with one of the most wonderful views I have ever seen. For five years we had spent our holidays there, in our Gypsey caravan, slowly converting wild and virgin veld (there was not a single tree on it when we bought) into a pleasant garden. Slowly, over the years, we had imposed some sort of order on the rolling slopes and the wild grasses. Terraces were levelled and grassed, trees planted, a swimming bath built, and finally had come the white walls of our home and the bright flame of the bougainvilleas clambering over them.

Now most of the work had been done, it was autumn, and we had been five months in our new home. I could relax, with a pipe and a glass of beer, and the leaves dropping slowly from the autumn trees.

And in front, peer amongst Drakensberg peaks, *Cathkin*, red in the dawn, purple in the late afternoon, enigmatic, pearl-grey and aloof as the clouds built up around it, and the summer storms swept across its changing face. And on each side, though we could not see them, for they were hidden by the spurs of the Little Berg, mile upon mile of blue peaks, marching proudly in the sunlight of their million years – the mighty Drakensberg range.

How had it all started, these enigmatic, snow-crowned peaks, soaring up into the sky? What was their story, hidden in the mists of time? How had it all begun?

Actually the scientist to-day has a pretty shrewd idea of how it all started. Over the years he has probed, analysed, and studied the record of the rocks. He has turned his telescope to the stars, and has penetrated the depths of space, first by sight, then by radio waves, and finally, since 1969, in person (albeit by proxy) as his space-ships have taken off on their first hesitant, but breathless, journeys into the solar system. Slowly the doors of our knowledge are being unlocked one by one.

But should he go still further back? Are the facts and figures of the scientist the last word, or is there an intelligence behind all this, directing, controlling, guiding?

This, of course, lies outside the realm of the scientist. The scientist is concerned only with physical, measurable, reproducible facts and events. Philosophical speculation is not his sphere.

When the French mathematician and cosmologist, Laplace, was asked by Napoleon whether his study of astronomy had proved the existence of God, he replied, "Sire, in my science I have no need of such an hypothesis". I do not think he was thereby denying the existence of God. His reply was actually a very reasonable one, indicating, as it did, merely the limitations of his field of study. It was just not his business.

But man is more than a scientist. He is also a dreamer, and the dark mystery of the beginning of all things has always held his imagination. Ever since the untutored Bushman looked up into the night sky and decided that the stars were the camp fires of the souls of the departed, man has dreamed, and speculated. The intellectual excitement of trying to decipher the meaning of the universe is a challenge that the mind of man will never fail to respond to. "Seek for some sort of answers we must," says Theodosius Dobzhansky, "because it is the highest glory of man's humanity that he is capable of searching for his own meaning and for the meaning of the Cosmos." The scientist, when he leaves his laboratory, dreams. He would be a poor scientist if he did not! Sir James Jeans allowed himself to dream, and called Astronomy the most poetical of all the sciences.

Is there, behind it all, a purpose, a guiding intelligence? I believe that the evidence of planned order, of inexorable law, of careful thought, of divine imagination is far too overwhelming to permit of any other explanation. I believe this vast universe, which is our home, "with all its mighty throng", as the New English Bible puts it, down to the tiny gnat which buzzes round your candle flame, started as an idea in the mind of God.

And what more majestic or noble language could one find to describe those mighty cosmic events in the dawn of time than the sonorous organ notes of the first chapter of Genesis. "In the beginning . . . the earth was without form, and void, and darkness was upon the face of the deep, and the Spirit of God moved upon the face of the waters."

"In the beginning . . . God."

How many countless aeons of time fled slowly by as the earth pursued its endless journey round the sun, no-one knows. But eventually the earth as we know it began to emerge. We must assume that the flaming mass of gas and vapour slowly cooled to molten rock and then to vast, steaming seas, of which we read in the record of the rocks. Then, strange and terrible as it must have appeared at first, the dry land began to emerge. The cooling process continued, and as the rocks cooled they contracted, and vast lateral pressures were set up, producing surface movements, so that mountains, hills and valleys began to take shape. Amongst the oldest known rocks in the world are some G4 granite rocks discovered in Swaziland, only some 325 kilometres from our Drakensberg. Dated by the rubidium-strontium radio-dating method, they work out at between 3 010 and 3 130 million years old.

Our rocks in the Drakensberg area are younger than this. Here the bed of the seas was made up of what is known as Table Mountain Sandstone, originally laid down as a sediment on the floor of this vast ocean. As these sediments grew too heavy, they collapsed into troughs on the bed of the sea. Then lateral pressures produced a general up-rising, and so the dry land appeared. All this took place about 300 000 000 years ago.

Then slowly, over a great part of what is now Central and Southern Africa, a vast lake appeared, and it is probably here, in the warm waters of this sea, as in seas elsewhere, that life first appeared. It included the area now occupied by the Drakensberg Mountains.

During this time Southern Africa, India, Australia, South America and Antarctica formed a vast land mass which we to-day name Gondwanaland, a huge continent over which climatic conditions were fairly constant.

Then the eternal erosion cycle set in. Soil was washed down from these up-thrust surrounding hills, and the Great Lake began to fill up. It became a huge marsh, a vast, steaming swamp, and it was here, as in similar swamps all over the face of the earth, that life developed. It started, from its dim beginnings, to teem, to differentiate, to breed, to struggle and toil, endlessly,

Autumn evening

*From the garden of the
author's home.*

"*The Timeless Drakensberg.*"

Home of the Bushmen.
The Great Injasuti Valley.

ever upwards and outwards, on a journey that was to take it from the primordial slime to the stars. And to what purpose, the travail, the bitter toil, the mindless agony, the long upward surge? What was the ultimate goal? Ask of the stars, for I cannot tell you. And it matters little, for whatever the distant goal, it is the toil and the travail that counts.

Here, in this steaming marsh, plant life began to flourish. It was here that the huge reptiles of the slime floundered, and lived, and fought, and died. Some were small but some were great, big stupid inoffensive creatures, feeding on the rank vegetation, the giant ferns and cycads of the swamps. Others were fearsome creatures feeding on each other, with huge teeth and terrible jaws, ripping and tearing in the mud and slime. Monsters up to 18 metres in length were not unknown. When they died their bodies sank into the mud of the Great Swamp, and the mud turned to rock, enclosing the fossilised skeletons of these huge beasts for all time. To-day we call these rocks, geologically, the Ecca and Beaufort series. You will not find them in the Drakensberg, for they have been overlaid by the basalt, the sandstone, the Red Beds and the Molteno Beds of the Stormberg Series, as we shall show. Only a few miles away from the High Drakensberg, however, at Bergville, at Estcourt, and in the Midlands of Natal, down to about the 600 metre level, these rocks have been exposed, and it is here that traces of these primordial reptiles appear.

Now the Great Swamps began to dry out, and the reptiles, the dinosaur and the stegosaurus began to disappear. Some died out slowly. Others seemed to disappear suddenly. Unable to adapt to changing conditions, they ceased to exist. Perhaps it was the coming of one of the great Ice Ages that spelt their doom. Perhaps it was the approach of desert conditions. Whatever it was, their fate was sealed.

By this time some 8 500 metres of mud and sand had accumulated in the Great Marsh. This indicates clearly that the bottom of the lake must have been slowly sinking, for no lake could have been 8 500 metres deep to start with.

It is also quite clear that by now a period of steadily increasing aridity had set in. This arid period resulted directly in the formation of the Red Beds and the Molteno Beds, which overlaid the hardening mud of the swamp, for these coloured muds and shales, red, yellow, purple and blue, always resulted from arid conditions. To-day they form the lowermost strata of what geologists call the Stormberg Series in the Drakensberg. This is part of the Karoo System. You will find these beds on the slopes of the Little Berg, between the 1 370 metre and the 1 830 metre levels, just below the Sandstone rock bands. When we dug the holes for our fruit trees at *Emkhizweni*, which is at an altitude of 1 463 metres, we found clear evidence of the Molteno Beds. In quite a small area deposits of yellow, red, brown, purple and blue gravels and clays were dug up. Above these Molteno Beds, on the slopes of the Little Berg, the dark, purplish-red shales of the Red Beds can be clearly seen, where erosion has stripped the slopes of their ground cover.

It was the laying down of these two drier layers, the Molteno Beds and the Red Beds, that spelt the final end of the great reptiles. The Molteno Beds were laid down in shallow water, under climatic conditions of intermittent rainfall. Swamps were now isolated, not very extensive, and in process of drying up. Many of the hardier reptiles lasted on into this period. But by the time the Red Beds were laid down, most of the swamps had gone, and so, too, had most of the reptiles.

That these huge beasts once roamed in the area now occupied by the Drakensberg is clear. They have left their footprints, and sometimes their bones, behind. Partial skeletons and portions of skulls are not uncommon. None have been found on the Natal side of the Drakensberg, but they have been found in the Molteno Beds in Lesotho, notably by Mr. G. M. Stockley, and Dr. L. D. Boonstra. Rev. S. S. Dornan collected dinosaurian bones of *Massospondylus* in Lesotho in 1908.

Dinosaur footprints have been frequently found in Lesotho. Rev. S. S. Dornan was the first to record these, at Tsikoane, Qalo, Morija and Teyateyaneng. Some even showed skin corrugations. At Tekoane he found more than 50 altogether, some as long as 36 cm. All were three-toed, and very clear. One set of footprints of a small reptile has been found in the Giant's Castle Game Reserve on the Natal side of the Drakensberg.

After the Molteno Beds and the Red Beds had been laid down, the winds began to blow, great, howling, shrieking desert winds, such as the earth had rarely known, blowing timelessly and endlessly over these arid plains. The topmost layers of the surrounding hills were stripped off by these scything gales, carried long distances, and deposited in the form of sheets of sandstone on top of the shales of the Red Beds and the Molteno Beds, making a new layer. It is these sandstone rock layers, exposed now in the form of horizontal rock bands, 70 to 80 metres high (on *Ntabamhlope* they are 244 metres high!) that form such a prominent feature of the Little Berg to-day. Prevailingly cream-coloured or white, they sometimes appear pink, brown, deep red, pale blue, or grey. The sheer cliffs are often accompanied by rock pinnacles carved into fantastic shapes and sizes. This rock band is called Cave Sandstone, because of the many caves formed in it by the faster weathering of softer layers. It is these caves, so common in the Little Berg, which delight the heart of the mountaineer to-day, caught out in the open with no shelter, when the storms sweep down upon him from the high peaks.

By this time, of course, the original primal vegetation, and the huge animals of the slime, had disappeared completely. The earth was drier. Smaller, hardier, more agile types of animals began to appear, as life battled for survival in the face of changing conditions. The foundation rocks of what we call to-day the Little Berg were being laid down, the Great Sculptor hard at work, his tools the wind and the rain, sandstone, gravel and time. The stage was being set for the world as we know it to-day and for the emergence of man.

One mighty cataclysm still remained before the Drakensberg which we know to-day could appear. The depressions, which we have already noted, formed by folding of the earth's crust, became the weakest portion of the crust. Eventually, these depressions fractured, aided perhaps by bursting pressures from below, for underneath the bed of what had been the Great Lake lay mighty, smouldering fires, mile upon deep mile of white-hot molten rock. And then with a roar which must have shaken the very heavens, these huge imprisoned forces broke free, and burst through, forcing their way between fissures in the muds and shales of the Molteno and Red Beds, roaring through the vast sheets of sandstone, and pouring out on to the waiting plains. Over vast areas of land the sky steamed and flamed, and always the shattering roar of the lava floods as they raced over the arid plains.

Behind it all was still the governing intelligence, the guiding will, but now the Great Sculptor had taken unto himself a new and a mighty tool!

Layer after layer of the lava was laid down on top of the sandstone, hardening into basalt, varying in thickness from a few centimetres to hundreds of metres. These layers may be traced to-day in the basalt cap of the High Drakensberg, in the highlands of Lesotho, in the eastern districts of the Orange Free State, and on into the Lebombo Range and the mountains of the Eastern Transvaal. In the Drakensberg these periodic layers are particularly noticeable. They form long, horizontal rock ledges, stretching often for several kilometres, with a total thickness of between 1 220 to 1 525 metres. They stand out very clearly indeed after a fall of snow. This was probably the largest eruption in the long history of the earth. Its southern limit stretched to beyond Port Elizabeth, its western beyond Kimberley, its northern close to the Limpopo River, and its eastern to an unknown distance beyond the present coast-line.

To-day pebbles of agate are often found in the beds of most Drakensberg streams, and on the flat areas on the summits of the Little Berg. These come from this lava, and are formed in an interesting way. As volcanic material solidifies, gas bubbles are trapped in it. Mineral-rich liquids percolate through the rock, and get into these holes, and thus form concentric layers of beautifully coloured agates, quartz and chalcedony. To-day one can collect hundreds of them in a day's walk over the Little Berg.

It was towards the end of this volcanic period that the ancient land-mass of Gondwanaland began to disintegrate. Huge sections began to break off to form Madagascar, India, Australia, Antarctica and South America. Once again the seas broke in, and made more humid conditions possible.

We have now reached this position: superimposed on top of the older rocks and the dried-out deposits of the Great Lake, we have, firstly, the layer we call the Molteno Beds, and above that another layer, the softer Red Beds. Superimposed on this is a third layer, vast sheets of wind-blown sandstone. Lastly, there is a final capping of lava, 1 525 metres thick, which to-day we call basalt.

This vast "sandwich" covered most of what we know to-day as South Africa – the whole of the Free State, most of the Transvaal, the Northern and Central Cape, and all Natal. It is known as the Karoo System. It almost certainly stretched over the whole of Gondwanaland far beyond the present coastline and was probably a dreary, grim, horrifying wasteland, more horrifying than any desert of to-day. Gone were the lush forests, the steaming swamps, the creatures of the slime. Could any sort of life possibly exist on these arid, burnt plains of hardening lava?

Actually, geologists tell us, some sort of life must have existed, for the evolutionary chain continued uninterrupted. Life certainly continued to flourish in the northern hemisphere, and almost certainly continued even in Gondwanaland. Evidence from the sites of modern volcanoes indicates that lava flows can be colonised by vegetation taking advantage of the enriched soils derived from ash and the lava itself. It is possible that the lava flows in Gondwanaland left islands of exposed land masses that remained uncovered, and of course marine life must have existed and was probably abundant. To be honest, however, we must admit that we know very little as to what conditions were like in South Africa during and immediately after these great outpourings of lava.

But still there was no Drakensberg.

Now, for the last time, the Great Sculptor took up his tools of wind and rain, of heat and cold, and the Drakensberg began to emerge. First the warm Moçambique current changed its course, and it flowed swiftly down the east coast of Natal, bringing with it masses of warm, humid air, and teeming torrents of rain. The rain poured down from the lowering heavens on to these dry, arid plains. The land was drenched with it. Erosion set in, persistent, urgent, remorseless. Slowly the basalt began to crumble, retreating westwards, and after it came the sandstone, swept away by the torrential floods. Sometimes harder deposits of sandstone would be left behind, and so we have *Table Mountain*, near Pietermaritzburg, and *Ntabamhlope* in the Estcourt district. Professor L. C. King has computed the rate of retreat at about 30 centimetres every two hundred years. Steadily, remorselessly, through the Middle and Late Mesozoic periods, year after year, century after century, the slow erosion went on. The escarpment has retreated about 45 centimetres since Van Riebeeck landed at the Cape, 6½ metres since earliest recorded history, and about 1½ kilometres since man made his first appearance on earth. The topography of the Drakensberg is thus substantially the same as that which the first man would have seen a million years ago.*

Eventually the escarpment reached its present position. The edge of the sandstone became the Little Berg, and the edge of the basalt, superimposed on top of the sandstone, and a little further back, became the main Drakensberg Range of to-day. Over southern and eastern Natal much of the Karoo System rock and of the Beaufort Series was almost totally stripped off by this westward-marching erosion, and we see exposed the older, underlying formations, the

*Some recent authorities even put the date as far back as 3 000 000 years.

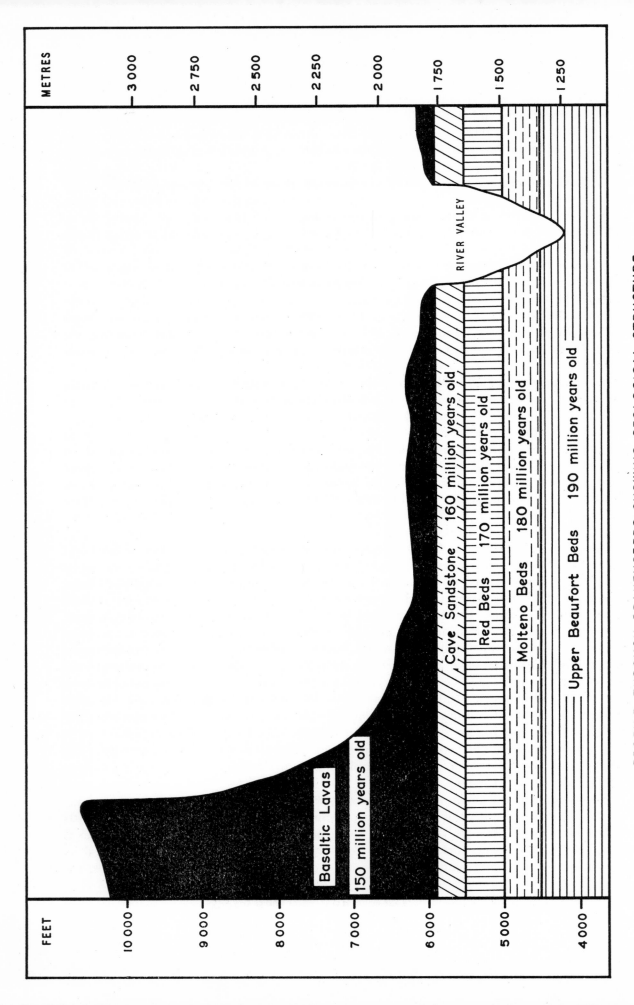

PROFILE THROUGH DRAKENSBERG SHOWING GEOLOGICAL STRUCTURE

METRES

3 000
2 750
2 500
2 250
2 000
1 750
1 500
1 250

FEET

10 000
9 000
8 000
7 000
6 000
5 000
4 000

RIVER VALLEY

Basaltic Lavas   150 million years old

Cave Sandstone   160 million years old

Red Beds   170 million years old

Molteno Beds   180 million years old

Upper Beaufort Beds   190 million years old

Ecca and Dwyka Series, and the original Table Mountain Sandstone. To the north and the west, however, we still have the rolling grasslands of the Beaufort and Ecca Series, sweeping up to the sandstone-topped faces of the Little Berg, and the towering basalt cliffs of the High Drakensberg.

One important point follows from all this, which it is important to remember. There is no "other side" of the Drakensberg. When you climb to the summit from the Natal side, at 3 050 metres, you do not go down the other side. You are on top of a lofty plateau, stretching westwards far into Lesotho.

All this time, patiently, timelessly, the Great Sculptor worked away at the face of the Drakensberg. In gentle mood he carved the lovely valleys of the Little Berg, and caused the rivers to flow softly through them, and the grass to grow, and the forests to take shape. And still the rains poured down, but gently now; from the valleys came the sound of many waters; the rich, black earth, deep with humus, began to appear, and the wild animals and the flowers of the high places found there a home.

In sterner mood he carved, above the Little Berg, the mighty face of the Drakensberg itself. Isolated peak upon peak, deeply-etched channels, tremendous gorges, dark eerie chasms, knife-like ridges, minarets, towers, citadels, began to appear. It was a grim, and often a hard world, this world of the high peaks. For long months the ice would bind the rocks in a grip of iron, the snows would block the passes, and about the soaring spires the winds would cry endlessly in the silence of the night. But it is a world I have grown to love, and I would like to tell you something about it.

First, however, came man.

Just when, or where, he emerged we are not quite sure. The date is usually put at about one million years ago, and the place, in all probability, was somewhere in what is to-day called Central or Southern Africa. It is even possible to speculate that it might not have been far from our own Drakensberg, but this is only pure speculation.

First came the man-apes, brutish creatures with low foreheads and prognathous jaws, but in the dim recesses of their minds was already hidden the promise of humanity. Like the great creatures of the slime, Prognathous Man also fought and struggled and died, but unlike these creatures his destiny was not extinction but an endless road ahead.

There came a day when his fingers closed for the first time on a gnarled stick, and blindly, unthinkingly, he struck, and he knew power, and a new dimension to his puny strength. He had used, for the first time, a tool, and from now on he was for ever separated from the beasts of the field. He had discovered the potential to change his world and to become its master.

Then, in the dim recesses of his mind, he began to know discontent and dissatisfaction, desire and wonder. He started to change. He stood more erect. The long prognathous jaw began to recede, the flattened forehead grew and expanded and his brain stirred in its long sleep, and awoke. His hands, as they practised on the rounded stick, became more flexible, especially his thumb, and he was able to devise new and better tools. At some time, hidden deep in the shadowy centuries, the lines of his face softened, the muscles of his jaw relaxed and became mobile, and he knew speech. He mastered the mysteries of fire. And then God breathed into his nostrils the breath of life, and man became a living soul.

South Africa's past has been described as "the greatest silence in history". Even so, impressive finds of the early precursors of man have been made in the Transvaal, the Free State, the Cape and Rhodesia. In 1924 Professor Raymond Dart discovered the Taungs skull in the north-western Cape, with a geological age of about a million years. This was the skull of a man-like ape, in contradistinction to the Java and Pekin finds, which were of ape-like men. Professor Dart christened it *Australopithecus africanus*, which means "Southern Ape of Africa". In 1936 Dr. Robert Broom, a medical practitioner until the late J. H. Hofmeyr made it possible for him to devote his full time to palaeontology, investigated the Sterkfontein finds of man-apes, and Makapansgat was the scene of yet another discovery investigated by Professor Philip V. Tobias. Swartkrans and Kromdraai added their names to the tally, while the whole of the Vaal River Basin proved an important area for the study of prehistoric man. Dr. Robert Broom, regarded in his time as the world's most distinguished comparative anatomist, believed that Africa was the cradle of the human race, and that it was probably in South Africa that man first emerged.

No skeletal remains of man earlier than the Late Stone Age have been found in Natal, but he certainly lived here, as Middle Stone Age and Earlier Stone Age tools are found in great abundance all the way from the mountains to the sea. His skeletal remains were no doubt swept away by the heavy erosion of the Late Pleistocene period.

But as far as the Drakensberg itself is concerned, nothing has been found here dating back to a period earlier than a few centuries ago. A careful plotting of Middle Stone Age sites in Natal indicates clearly that they ended at about the 1 220 metre contour level (4 000 ft.). It might be thought that the heavy erosion to be expected in a mountain region had obliterated all signs of early man in the Drakensberg, and that he might have lived here in spite of the lack of evidence, but even in sheltered caves protected from erosion not a single sign of early man has ever been found. Professor O. Davies is of the opinion that "the rarity of older remains in the Drakensberg foothills suggests that man moved into them recently". He gives no reason for this late arrival, but A. R. Willcox believes that early man did not inhabit the Drakensberg because it was so heavily forested in those days.

But no-one really *knows*.

Before we move on to the first recorded inhabitants of the Drakensberg, let us try and get all that we have said in this chapter into perspective, and summarise our figures. According to the latest computation, when man first appeared on the scene, a million years ago, the oceans had already swarmed with living creatures for more than 500 million years, although the first signs of life had appeared immeasurably earlier than this. The subsequent figures are as follows:

Land animals and green plants appeared 490 million years ago
Reptiles appeared 270 million years ago
The Molteno Beds were laid down 180 million years ago
The Red Beds were laid down 170 million years ago
The Sandstone layers were laid down 160 million years ago
The great lava flows occurred 150 million years ago
The Drakensberg became recognisable as a mountain chain 1½ million years ago (very approximate)
Man appeared one million years ago.*

Unfortunately the human mind is unable to grasp the significance of figures as huge as these. Let us reduce them proportionately to more manageable form. Let us imagine that the land animals and the green plants appeared 68 days ago, just over two months back. Then the other figures would be as follows:

The reptiles would have appeared one month later, i.e. 37 days ago.
The Molteno Beds would have been laid down 25 days ago
The Red Beds would have been laid down 23 days ago
The Sandstone layers would have been laid down 22 days ago
The volcanic lavas would have been poured out 21 days ago
The Drakensberg would have appeared as a recognisable mountain chain about 5 hours ago
Man would have appeared on the scenes only a little over three hours ago
His whole recorded history would have started only one minute ago!

*See footnote on page vii.

These figures stagger the imagination. But what a call they are to optimism and the larger vision, especially when one realises that all man's recorded progress is but one minute of time as against the three hours since he first appeared on this earth. There are some who doubt the validity of reading into the future the progress observable as we look into the past. Evolution, it is claimed, is passing more and more into the hands of man himself, and if this is so, then, so the argument goes, there is nothing pre-destined about it, and it is possible that only disaster lies ahead. I cannot believe this. For one thing, it takes no account of the directing intelligence behind it all. When one contemplates man's spiritual progress during the *apparently* long period of his recorded history, one is sometimes tempted to despair: how slow it has all been, and how slight the advance! He seems almost to have been standing still. But compared with his infinitely longer past, this is but one short minute of time.

And if this is so, what tremendous and exciting possibilities open out to his future, stretching away into the centuries ahead! General Smuts believed this. "To those who have asked me whether I am a pessimist or an optimist," he once said, "I have replied that when I look merely at history I am tempted to be a pessimist about man, but when I look at pre-history, I am an optimist. The case for progress on the evidence of pre-history is simply overwhelming. For us, children of to-day, pre-history is . . . a message, a call to good cheer and faith in our future, an inspiration for the march, the endless march, and the road stretching before us."

PART 1

In which the reader having watched the setting of the stage,
meets some of the actors

CHAPTER I

THE LITTLE YELLOW HUNTERS

"I am as old as my disappointments in life, and as young as my naughtiest thought".

—XAMEB THE BUSHMAN, TO
PROFESSOR P. J. SCHOEMAN

Xan-xeib the Bushman sat at the entrance of his sandstone cave, shaping the rounded stone which he was making for his *qibi*, the digging-stick. To-morrow Xos, his wife, would use it to dig up the ants' nest they had found down in the valley. Behind him the mountains were a bright splendour of shimmering blue, topped with the massive face of Ngonomateng, or Mdedelelo, as the Amazizi down in the plains called it, and which in time to come the white man would call *Cathkin Peak*. Below him the sunlight slept in the green valley, and in the sky above the great cloud caravans moved silently across an azure plain. Behind him Xos, his wife, was preparing the bulbs and the roots they had gathered that morning for the stew-pot, while in the far corner Son-eib, the old man of the tribe, was busy painting an oribi on the wall of the cave.

Below, in the valley, he could see his two sons, Kaang and Kibike, stalking an eland, while away off, down in the plains, he could see the bee-hive huts of the Amazizi, and the smoke from their fires curling drowsily in the pale sunlight. Many, many moons had the Amazizi dwelt there, how long he could not remember. Son-eib, the old man of the cave, who was so old that the wrinkled skin of his stomach hung down in massive folds almost to his thighs, claimed to remember when they had first arrived with their chief Langa, from where the sun rose in the east. But the land was big, there was plenty for all. The Amazizi lived apart with their flocks and their herds, and had no liking for the mountains, preferring the long, rolling plains, while Xan-xeib and his people loved to roam the warm, sun-filled valleys of the Little Berg, and climb the rock-girt peaks. They lived by hunting, and knew little of domestic animals, let alone vast herds of cattle. There was no clashing of interests, and there was peace between the people of Xan-xeib and the Amazizi.

How long he, Xan-xeib, and his people had lived in this pleasant land, was lost in the mists of time. Ngangngang the aged one, who had died a long time ago, used to tell of how the Bushmen crossed the ocean in a great basket in the earliest of times, and so came to the happy hunting grounds of the Drakensberg. But he, Xan-xeib, neither knew nor cared, for the game was fat, life was good, and below the whole valley slept in the soft afternoon sunlight.

From where had he come, the little yellow hunter, and why was he dwelling here in the high Drakensberg? At one time it was thought that the Bushmen were the earliest inhabitants of South Africa, a view held by Stow in his *Native Races of South Africa*, first published in 1905. Very few anthropologists hold this view to-day. The remains of Stone Age man in South Africa are clearly differentiated into three distinct periods, Early Stone Age, Middle Stone Age and Later Stone Age. The Bushmen belong to the Later Stone Age. There are no skeletal remains of Bushmen in the first two cultures. While the Middle Stone Age developed out of the Early Stone Age, it could not have given rise to the Later Stone Age. There is a lack of continuity of type between the two, and archaeologists to-day are almost unanimous in saying that the Later Stone Age culture invaded South Africa from the north, and superseded the two existing Stone Age cultures. Bleek and Lloyd both state that the Bushmen themselves definitely believed in an earlier race that preceded them.

These people coming down from the north were known to the Zulus as *abatwa*, "castaways",

3

or "abandoned people", though Molema states that *Batwa* means "Men of the South". The Basutho knew them as *Baroa*. To-day it is generally agreed that they arrived in South Africa about 7 000 or 8 000 years ago, though Ellenberger gives the date as only two thousand years before the arrival of the Bantu.

Some anthropologists have held that they are connected with the pygmies of Central Africa. According to H. M. Stanley these pygmies were also known as *Batwa*, or *Watwoa*, and both races exhibited the phenomenon known as steatopygia. This is an accumulation of fat on the buttocks, especially in the case of women.* But the shape of the head and the build of the body both preclude this: there is no racial similarity between the two races.

There are, however, clear evidences of the former existence of Bushmen in East and Central Africa. Characteristic physical features keep cropping up, there are traces of language similarity, and above all, the rock paintings so richly displayed in our own Drakensberg appear, though more sparsely, throughout East and Central Africa.

Most interesting of all is the fact that these paintings also occur in France and Spain. Is it possible that the cave artists of these two countries migrated south and became ultimately the Bushmen of the Drakensberg? Many anthropologists have held that this is possible. A more likely theory would seem to be the one held by Mr. A. R. Willcox.

Willcox believes that the original home of both sets of artists was in the Sahara. It is generally accepted that during the Great Ice Age the Sahara was a well-watered stretch of country with rolling grass-lands and plentiful game. Even down to early Roman times wheat was grown there extensively. As the ice melted and temperatures rose, desert conditions began to set in, and gradually the hunters of the plains were driven out, some to go north into France and Spain, and some south.

It is a fascinating problem, and many other ingenious theories have been advanced in an effort to explain the origin of this strange people. Ellenberger, in 1912, put forward the idea that the Bushmen were originally the Horites (or Hurrians) of the Bible, who were driven out of Edom by Esau into North Africa. It is known that the Horites were cave dwellers, that their physical characteristics were very similar to those of the Bushmen, and that their language was "like the squeaking of bats". But did they ever become the Bushmen of the 19th century? Ask of the wheeling vulture in these lonely skies, for only he knows.

Another theory, also discounted to-day, is that they were brought down by the Phoenicians to work in their gold mines, as slaves. As the mines petered out, they were left behind, and this would, so the theory goes, account for their Zulu name "abandoned" or "castaways".

Are the Bushmen connected in any way with the Hottentots? Schapera points out that there *are* similarities between the two races. Bodily characteristics, even to the typical steatopygia, are similar, except for the fact that Hottentots are tall while Bushmen are short. Their languages are dissimilar, except that they share the clicks. The Hottentot language is akin to an early Egyptian language, ancient Coptic. The Bushman language is not. And there are even bigger differences, particularly cultural. Bushmen are hunters and cave-dwellers, while Hottentots are pastoralists. It would appear that there is little, if any, connection.

Set apart, a race unique, neither Semitic, Mongolian, Caucasian or Negroid, with a language having no relation to that of any other, their origins hidden in the mists of time, the Bushmen are one of the great enigmas of history. Even the date of their arrival in Southern Africa is unknown. The only certain date we have is 1655, for it was in that year that the first recorded contact took place between the Bushmen and a party of Burghers under a Dutch official, Wintervogel, on the banks of the Berg River. The only certain fact is that round about 1800 A.D. and for many years prior to that, the only inhabitants of the Drakensberg were Bushmen.

* The name was suggested by the traveller Burchell to describe the enlarged buttocks of Hottentot women. He concocted the word from two Greek words meaning fat and buttocks.

The rest is all conjecture. We just do not know. We peer into the dim and distant past, "as through a glass darkly", and all we see is shadowy figures moving across the stage. The Archaeologist probes, and unravels, and feels his way, and bit by bit his knowledge increases as some of the pieces fall into place. The mists clear for a brief moment, only to close in again. "It is good," says William Beebe, the great oceanologist, "that man should continue to explore and to search, even though final knowledge will for ever elude him. The mysteries and the wonders of the Universe are without end."

They were small in stature, these Bushmen, the average height being about 122 cm to 137 cm. Their general build was slim and lean, and even their young people showed little of the rounded outlines of youth. The amount of fat under the skin was remarkably small, with the result that the skin became as dry as leather, falling into strong folds around the stomach. The back was hollowed, the stomach often protruding. Their colour was light brown, lips thick, the nose small, depressed and flat. The chin was receding, as also the forehead. There was little body hair, the eyes were bright, the mouth smiling, often impishly.

One of the most prominent features of their anatomy was the phenomenon we have already referred to, that of steatopygia (the accumulation of fat on the buttocks). Steatopygia is not exclusive to the Bushman, however. As we have seen, it is found also among the Hottentots, and the Pygmies of Central Africa. The discovery in certain caves in the south of France of ivory figurines also exhibiting this peculiar abnormality gives weight to the theory we have already noted of a possible cultural connection between the Stone Age people who lived and painted in these caves, and our own Bushmen.

They were essentially children, children in their simplicity, children in their gay, cheerful disposition, in their lack of inhibitions, and their irresponsibility. They were averse to work, fond of dancing, of acting, of dressing up, and of telling stories. Their folklore and their mythology are only equalled by the scope and the extent of their famous rock paintings. Some idea of the astonishing wealth of this folklore may be formed when we realise that the material collected by the late Dr. W. H. Bleek, and housed in the Sir George Grey library at Cape Town, forms 84 stout MS volumes of 3 600 pages. They were honest. No matter with what crime a Bushman was charged, it was well-known in the law-courts that if he denied having committed it, he could be believed. They were a happy, laughter-loving race, with time after the chase for some of the gentler arts – painting; singing; dancing, especially by moonlight, to the beat of a drum. They had no fear of death, and never asked for mercy. Above all, they had a passionate love of liberty, and many are the stories told of Bushmen, locked up in jail, who pined away and died for no apparent cause, and of others who preferred liberty and hunger to a life of servitude and a full belly. George William Stow tells of an aged Bushman he once found on the banks of the Orange River. He had seen the coming of the white man, the rape of his fair land, the loss of his happy hunting grounds, the decimation of his kin. "But," says Stow, "he drew himself up proudly. 'We are free men,' the Bushman said, 'we love the sun'."

It used to be the practice, in early Settler days, to malign the Bushman. He was dirty, cruel, vindictive and degenerate, little better than an animal. He was a barbarian, untaught and unteachable. A French missionary once said that they clucked like turkeys, while a man as enlightened as Livingstone remarked that they were as baboon-like as baboons were Bushman-like. But the cruelties attributed to him were the result of equal barbarities practised on him by early Settler and African alike. And if he was a savage, let us not forget that even a savage can be "noble". In 1846 Mr. John Shepstone, brother of the famous Sir Theophilus Shepstone, reported that the Bushman had been much maligned. He was intelligent, kindly, hospitable, generous, and certainly not vicious or depraved, as he had so often been represented. He frankly admitted, however, that the Bushman was a born thief!

And I cannot believe that a people who loved the gentler arts of life, who excelled so

5

brilliantly in painting, whose hearts were so moved by the tides of beauty, as their poetry so obviously showed they were, could have been vicious or depraved.

And they *were* poets, as well as painters. "A woman's heart," said Xameb the Bushman to Professor Schoeman, "is like the flush of dawn. It conquers every dark night. Give her rest, and the marrow of every buck you shoot, and her heart soars up above all the dusty trails of everyday life." And on another occasion: "The paths on which the youthful heart seeks fulfilment of its dreams are long paths, but they are very beautiful. Along those paths you walk with eyes raised to the far-away mountains. You will not trip over any stone, nor will you tread on any thorns. There, no snake lurks in the grass; there, no tired voice of a mother calls you to soothe the crying baby, or wash a pot. Beautiful paths, these, on which a young heart lingers with its dreams." And how do you like this description of the dawn: "When the white bull tears the black blanket of the night with his red horns"? This is poetry of a high order.

Like their characters, their social system was simple and uncomplicated. They lived a roving life, and never drove their roots deep. Scattered families would live together in caves in the Drakensberg, and it would seem that any tribal system was almost completely lacking, although occasionally different family groups would meet together for a game drive, or a moonlight dance. On the whole they were monogamous, and unfaithfulness in marriage was almost unknown. The erring wife, when this rarely happened, would always receive a sound beating from her wrathful husband! They had no objection, however, to polygamy. The men were the hunters, while the women did all the domestic work – caring for the children (of whom, by the way, they were inordinately fond), fetching water, digging for roots and bulbs, and seeing to the cooking.

Down in the river valleys and the approaches to the Berg lived the Amazizi, a tribe of the Embo Nguni group, and between the two peoples there was peace. The Amazizi were pastoralists and agriculturists: the Bushmen were hunters, and never tilled the ground or kept cattle, so why fight? It must have been an idyllic age – the Bushmen at peace with one another and with their Bantu neighbours, their only enemies the beasts of prey. It is only in their later paintings that scenes of battle and of war occur.

And they must have seen the Drakensberg at its best, in all its early glory, before the white man came with his hunting rifles, his plough-shares, his tree-felling and his grass-burning. Here the grass stood rich and green, the forests filled the deep river-valleys, the only sound was the splash of water, and the well-fed buck drank deep from the coldest and clearest of mountain pools.

And here he dreamed, while the ages came and went. Here he spun his timeless stories of N'go the mantis, of Quap, the elephant, of Kauru, the dassie, of Xo, the porcupine, and of Kaang, the Lord of Life and Death. N'go the mantis, was the favourite hero of Bushman folklore. He was gifted with supernatural powers, yet showed great foolishness. He was mischievous, kind, and very human. There seems to be some doubt as to whether the Bushmen actually worshipped the mantis. They certainly did worship a Supreme Being, whom they called Kaang, or Qhang. They invoked his aid in times of drought and distress. Only the eland knew where Qhang dwelt. Every animal had been given a special mark by Qhang, somewhere on its body, though only a Bushman could find it. They buried their dead with an implicit faith in a return to life. To the Bushman the stars were the camp-fires of the departed. Myths, fables, legends, poetry, tales about the sun and the moon, histories, tribal customs, traditions, all came tumbling out of the fertile brains and the teeming imaginations of the little brown men and women. And occasionally, in all this mass of myth and fable, you come across something that startles you with its old, old wisdom, the wisdom of forgotten ages. "When the world was still in twilight," starts one of their stories, "When the world was still in twilight, and full of marshes." How did he know that, the little yellow hunter?

How did he know a great many things, known to only a few to-day. How did he find his way from point to point? Early investigators have told of his amazing ability to make his way, in a straight line, for hundreds of kilometres, to any place he had been in before – and he could never explain how he did it! Even children, of nine or ten years of age, could do this after a lapse of many months.

William Bazley, the Byrne immigrant and founder of the town of Port Shepstone, discovered last century that the Bushmen had found a method of inoculating themselves against snake-bite, a secret which modern man only discovered much later. A snake would be held by the head so as to pull back the upper lip. The exposed fangs were then drawn across the upper arm, making two fine scratches, into which a drop of venom would be rubbed. Another discovery, made this time by Dr. W. H. Bleek last century, was that the Bushmen had been observing four of the moons of Jupiter long before astronomers had discovered them with the aid of telescopes.

Actually, the Bushmen can almost be regarded as a link between man and the animal world. Man acts largely on pure reason: the animal world relies on blind instinct. The Bushman was midway between the two, often more animal than man, and many of his actions can only be explained on the basis of instinct. He certainly had a profound knowledge of wild animals and their ways, and was almost one of them. Eugene Marais, of *Soul of the White Ant* fame, tells in one of his books of a farmer who kept a tame baboon in his backyard, on a length of chain tied to a pole. The farmer's wife had a baby, and the farmer once showed the baby to the baboon. The baboon was immensely interested, so much so that he would stand upright on his box and look through the bedroom window at the child sleeping in its cot. One day, when the farmer was away, the woman heard her baby crying from the bedroom. She went in to the room, and was horrified to find that the baboon had broken free from his chain, had entered the bedroom, seized the child, and, with teeth bared, was sitting on the window-ledge with the child in his arms. Frantically the woman made a wild lunge for the child, whereupon the baboon climbed up a creeper on the outside wall, from there to the roof, and thence to the upper branches of a tall tree. The mother screamed, and sent her maid to the neighbouring farm for help. Several men arrived, and various efforts were made to induce the baboon to come down – sweets and tit-bits laid out on plates, and so on. All to no purpose. The baboon remained sitting on one of the top branches, holding the child. Various suggestions were made – shoot the baboon and catch the child as it fell, was one. This was rejected as being far too dangerous. All they could do was to hold a blanket open below the baboon, in the hope that if he should let the child drop, they would be able to catch it as it fell.

Then someone had a brainwave. On one of the neighbouring farms was an old Bushman. He was sent for. As soon as he arrived, he immediately rejected the idea of trying to entice the baboon down with sweetmeats. That would only make the animal suspicious, he said. Instead, he told everyone to go inside the house, and to close all the windows and doors. Then he "spoke" to the baboon, in what he said was baboon language. To the amazement of everyone inside, the baboon started to climb down the tree, and then docilely handed the child over to the Bushman.

His knowledge (or should we say instinct?) extended to other fields as well. He never cultivated a single plant, but he had an intimate knowledge of their properties, edible, medicinal and poisonous. He had an equally intimate knowledge of the heavens. He was able to differentiate all the major stars, and understood the movements of the planets in their courses. He had amazing speed and stamina. A recent Botswana Government report told of a Bushman who had run 55 km, through heavy sand, in five hours, in midsummer. His hearing was as acute as his eyesight. In the Kalahari a Bushman has been known to hear a single-engined aircraft at a distance of 115 km. Completely at home with nature and with his environment, he was at his best, perhaps, as a hunter. Capt. A. W. Drayson, who hunted in the area between Pietermaritzburg and the Bushman's River in 1850, said that a Bushman could hit a running buck at a distance of 75 metres, and could deliver ten arrows in twice as many seconds.

He certainly lived on the fat of the land. Venison, of course, was always available in quantity, and it was supplemented by a variety of other sources. "Bushman rice" was a favourite item. This consisted of termites' eggs, fried in a pot made of baked earth. Locusts were considered a great delicacy, and lizards, frogs, worms, and caterpillars all added variety, while of course bulbs, roots and berries gave a welcome addition to their diet. Sometimes they would take the thick part of an eland's hide, and throw it on the fire. When it was burnt quite crisp, it would be taken off and left to cool. It was then pounded with a stone into a powder, thrown into a pot with water, and boiled. It soon became a thick jelly, and this was used for food when game was scarce. They ate voraciously. It is said that five Bushmen would eat a whole zebra in a few hours, while conversely, they could go for long periods without food.

Honey was greatly esteemed. To reach the bees' nest, they often used leather thongs as ropes, and sometimes wooden pegs as pitons. Within a couple of kilometres of my home, in the Valley of the Makuruman, I discovered one day, deep in the forest, the remains of a wooden ladder, very old, tied together with riempies, almost completely rotted away, leaning against a huge yellow-wood tree. It might, of course, have been of Bantu origin, but from their paintings the Bushmen are known to have constructed ladders of this type, and it certainly was very old. In 1930 Professor Sweeney and his wife, crossing over from the Ntonjelane Valley to the Mhlwazini, made a similar discovery in the Oqalweni forest – an old, almost rotten ladder leaning against a rock wall, with an obvious beehive in a high crack in the rock above it. Again, it might have been of Bantu origin, but, like the one I found, it had been made without nails.

The Bushmen were essentially Stone Age men, and a great deal of their interest lies in the fact that they have survived right into the Space Age without going through the intermediate stages of Bronze and Iron. Only in recent times have they learnt to work in iron. But they were expert stone-workers – digging sticks, (the *qibi*, a long stick passed through a stone with a hole in it, used for digging, breaking ants' nests, etc.), pipe-bowls (they were avid smokers), stone knives, arrow-heads, etc. There is actually a wealth of stone implements in the caves of the Drakensberg. At first these were not understood. They were supposed to have been fragments dropped from the sky. Then, about the middle of last century, scientists began to take an interest in them. In 1855 Colonel T. H. Bowker recognised them for what they were, and made a collection of them from caves in the Cape. Boucher de Perthes, a French archaeologist, interpreted them correctly, and Sir Langham Dale, Superintendent General of Education for the Cape, also became interested, and was amongst the first to link these stone implements with the Bushmen.

They were skilful in making musical instruments – drums made by stretching a skin over a clay pot; tambourines, with earthenware resonators; a bow-type instrument, with gourds or tortoise-shell resonators.

Their arrow-heads were especially interesting. They were pointed with ivory, bone or quartzite, (not flint: flint is not found in South Africa. They were sometimes, however, made of indurated shale, as well as of quartzite). These were kept carefully in a quiver made of buckskin. The arrow-heads were tipped with a virulent poison, the nature of which is still something of a mystery. It is possible that the venom of a snake or a scorpion, or perhaps a black spider of the genus *Mygale*, was used. Lawrence Green, in one of his books, however, tells of an officer in the South African forces which invaded German South-West Africa in 1915. He went over to England after the campaign, taking with him a number of Bushman arrows with the poison still on them. These he handed to a toxicologist at London University for analysis. The report: deadly dangerous, but the poison defied analysis. It was not snake venom, but a vegetable poison unknown to science. Some bulbs are certainly known to be poisonous, and may have been used. The bulb of *Boophane disticha* contains a virulent poison, the nature of which has not yet been identified. *Moraea spathulata*, the yellow Iris, which is common on the summit of the Drakensberg, is also known to be poisonous, but again the nature of the poison has eluded scientists. This does not mean, of course, that it could not have been used by the Bushmen. But the poison would have had to be mixed with some sort of medium, and here we are on even less certain ground. It seems possible that the milky juice of *Amaryllis toxicaria*, or of *Euphorbia arborescens*, may have been used. Xameb the Bushman told Professor Schoeman that the venom of snakes was used, but admitted that there was another ingredient, the details of which he refused to divulge.

But it is by their rock paintings that they will chiefly be remembered. These are far more extensive than is generally realised. The rock paintings of Southern Africa probably exceed in number those in all other parts of the world combined. And in all South Africa, no area is richer than the Natal Drakensberg. Curiously, there are hardly any Bushman paintings in Zululand. The only one I know of is at Qudeni, in the Nkandhla district. Not only are they extensive, but they are far superior to the cave art of France and Spain.

Our own Drakensberg paintings show a wide range of development, from early monochromes to true shaded polychromes, where carefully graduated washes have been used to achieve the desired result. Experiments are even made in foreshortening and perspective. Walter Battiss has pointed out how excellent is the portrayal of the human figure. This is usually portrayed in animated action. Animals are usually portrayed in repose. There is a keen perception of line and form and graceful curve, even to the drawing of muscles and sinews, and a concentration on essentials, all else being left out. Our art is obsessed with complicated backgrounds and foregrounds. The Bushman artist left all this out, concentrating starkly on one single theme, animated action, or calm repose. "No artist," says Walter Battiss, "has said more, saying less."

One interesting feature of their paintings is that they never portrayed the human face. The head is usually painted simply as a single line or blob. It is possible that this is part of the savage superstition that if you have the portrait of someone you can cause him harm. But some authorities, including Ellenberger, go even further, and suggest that this is yet another indication that the Bushmen may have been connected with the early Israelites, for the Israelites were forbidden, by the law of Moses, to depict a human face.

Sometimes they give their human figures animal and insectlike heads. It is worth noting that this feature also appears in Egyptian art. In the case of the Bushmen, they may have been illustrating some of their myths, in which animals are regarded as human-like. Or it may be connected with some of their dances and religious ceremonies, where animal-headed masks were used. Stow considered that it was linked with the well-known Bushman practice of disguising themselves when hunting, in order to approach more closely to their quarry. Qing, the Bushman, told J. M. Orpen in 1874 that Bushman paintings of men with rhebok heads were people who had died, and who now lived in rivers.

The material used for their paint is still largely a matter of conjecture. It is fairly certain that most of their actual colours were of natural rock-mineral origin. Since the days of Pompeii it has been known that ochre (iron oxide) will change colour if heated. A range of bright colours results – from yellow to claret, dark red, deep purple, browns and chocolates. A small quantity of this reddish-brown paint was analysed some years ago by the C.S.I.R. and found to consist of haematite and mixed hydrated iron oxides. Similarly, manganese ores were used for purple and purplish-black. Charcoal or graphite was used for black, while kaolin clay, bird droppings and lime deposits supplied the white pigment. There appeared to be three different kinds of white. When wet, one remains the same, one tends to go black, and the other disappears completely until it dries again. The commonest colours used appear to be browns and reds, whites and blacks. Pure yellow, green, blue and purple are practically never used.

But what is still a mystery is, like their poisons, exactly what media they used to mix their paints with. The permanence of their paintings is quite phenomenal. Specific paintings have been known for between 70 and 100 years, and practically no fading can be detected. What was the secret? No-one really knows. These little painters solved successfully the problems of the eroding action of sun and wind, the cold of snow and frost, and even to some extent rain, though water does have some effect on the permanence of the paintings. (That is why one should never spray paintings with water when one photographs them, in an attempt to bring the colours out more brightly.)

What, then, did they use? A number of suggestions have been made. Tree gums, animal fat, bees-wax, gall from gall-bladders and honey are all possibilities. Blood is known to have been used, especially for the red colours, and also hyracium (rock-rabbit urine), and the white of eggs. Many shelters which contain paintings have a wealth of ostrich-egg shells in them. The thick white juice of plants such as *Asclepias gibba*, *Eulophia hians*, *Parapodium castatus*, *Euryops multifidus* and *Cotyledon paniculata* are also known to have been used. But none of these entirely answers the question of the permanence of the paintings. Townley Johnson and C. K. Cooke have made extensive experiments with all these media, but none would seem to be entirely satisfactory, egg-tempera appearing to be the best.

Hunting scenes form the bulk of the subjects portrayed. Leopards, rhino, buffalo, eland, antelopes are all common and rarely, elephants. Snakes and frogs are also rare. The Main Caves at Giant's Castle have a fine painting of a snake. Trees, landscape and fish are very rare. No pre-historic or extinct animals are shown except the quagga. Sheep, oxen and horses appear in the later paintings. Very common are the hunters with their bows and arrows. These are usually portrayed very vividly in animated action. Animals are usually portrayed in repose, sometimes trotting.

These paintings are of absorbing interest, the only open window that we have into the life and customs of Stone-Age man. The interpretation of many of them is extremely difficult, and puzzles abound. Near Bethlehem, in the Orange Free State, is a picture of a red and yellow painted disc with a long tail streaking behind it. Could this be Halley's Comet? Rainbows appeared to be common in many paintings, but then a difficulty arose: some of the rainbows were upside-down! Then along came a bee-keeper from Empangeni, Robin Guy; his verdict – that the upside-down rainbows were really combs of wild honey, to which, as we have seen, the Bushmen were very partial. On closer examination it even looked as if there really were bees flying around as well! Harald Pager has definitely identified bees and honey-combs in a painting in a cave in the Ndedema Valley, near Cathedral Peak.

It is also fascinating to watch how the technique of the artist improves with the passage of time. At first animals are painted from the side, in one colour only. These are called monochromes. Then bichromes and polychromes are introduced, animals are painted in different positions, and finally attempts are made at shading, foreshortening, and even perspective. It is the introduction of shading, modelling and foreshortening, say Lee and Woodhouse, that sets South African rock art in a category of its own.

Can we say with any certainty how old these paintings are? Unfortunately, no. Some we accept as fairly recent. They portray the white man's sheep and cattle, his horses, and even red-coats with guns. Some depict ships with sails. These are all obviously fairly recent. But how far they go back, we do not know. Bushman painters loved to superimpose one picture on another. It has been noticed that the lower layers never contain Bantu figures. This is a partial clue. Unfortunately there is insufficient carbon in the paintings to enable carbon-dating methods to be employed.

And finally, we might ask ourselves, why did the Bushman artist paint these magnificent paintings? Many answers have been suggested – that he painted to record events and recent happenings, to illustrate folk tales, to denote ownership of a cave. Some have suggested that there was some sort of magic involved, to ensure a successful hunt. Perhaps the paintings were designed to explain ceremonies, such as initiations. But of them all, I like the suggestion of the late Abbé Breuil. The Abbé was sure that the little fellow painted for sheer *joie de vivre* — the delight of being young and agile, fleet of foot and supple of joint, deft in shooting arrows. They painted for the sheer joy of it.

Whatever the motive, whatever their secrets, these Stone Age artists have left us an imperishable monument to their artistic ability, and a complete picture of their way of life.

To-day some three to four hundred of these painted caves and rock shelters are to be found in the Drakensberg. Many others await discovery. They form an incalculable art treasure, for this and future generations. Will you not help to protect them? To scrawl your name across a painting, as has been done so often in the past, is sheer vandalism, and unforgiveable. To-day serious workers in the field are not announcing their discoveries to the general public. They are keeping them to themselves. The Natal Provincial Administration is finding it necessary to fence in their better-known caves. What a dreadful indictment this is of our modern civilisation! We do not deserve that such priceless works of art should have been given into our safe-keeping. Let us recall the words of Lawrence Green. These caves and their exquisite paintings, he said, "are a staging post in man's long journey from the vast blackness of the silent past into the light of recorded history".

*   *   *   *

There came a day when Xan-xeib the Bushman, sitting at the entrance of his cave, heard from afar a strange sound, a vague and menacing clamour as of men in turmoil, and looking up, he saw, away in the distance, a yet stranger sight – the bee-hive huts of the Amazizi going up in flame and smoke.

The red fires of invasion had come to his happy hunting grounds, and his days were numbered.

CHAPTER II

THE BLACK MAN

"I am black, but comely, O ye daughters of Jerusalem"
SONG OF SOLOMON

Just when the Amazizi settled in the foothills of the Drakensberg we are not quite sure. They were a tribe of the Embo Nguni group of Bantu, which arrived in southern Africa soon after 1200 A.D. Of the origin of the Bantu we are also, as in the case of the Bushmen, not sure. Like the Bushmen, we are dealing again with shadowy figures, moving darkly against a still more shadowy background. It is conjectured that something like 2 000 years ago African negroes fused with a Hamitic or Semitic stock from Asia, and that from this fusion came the Bantu, their homeland being in the region of southern Sudan.

About the dawn of the Christian era they started drifting southwards, a strange, unaccountable mystical urge that again and again, down the ages, has seized on a particular people – just why, we do not know. As they travelled southwards, they became intermingled with other people, some of whom they absorbed. When they reached the neighbourhood of the East Coast they mixed their blood with Arab and Asiatic traders. They probably reached Rhodesia about 400 A.D., and by about 1200 A.D. were ready to enter South Africa.

Recent research has shown that their arrival in this country must now be put back much further in time than was originally thought. It used to be held that their arrival coincided roughly with that of the European. We know now that when Van Riebeeck arrived at the Cape in 1652 the greater part of South Africa was already occupied by Bantu-speaking people. Brookes and Webb give the date as 1400 A.D. or earlier. Professor Monica Wilson gives it as 1200 A.D.

To the pleasant foothills of the Drakensberg came the Amazizi. Their own tradition tells us that they arrived about 1700 A.D., under their Chief Langa, but Professor Monica Wilson is of the opinion that the advance guard of the Embo Nguni invasion of Natal reached the foothills of the Drakensberg much earlier, about 1300 A.D. It is possible that the Amazizi were not the first to arrive, but that other related tribes preceded them, and then passed on southwards into Pondoland. Whatever the exact date may be, we do at least know that prior to the white man's arrival the Amazizi had inhabited the foothills of the Drakensberg in peace and contentment for many, many years. Pushing up the river valleys which cut westwards into these mountain solitudes, they had come with their wives and their families, their herds and their cattle, and soon the broad valley of the Bushman's, the heavily-forested Injasuti, the smiling valley of the Sterkspruit, the Mhlwazini and the Umlambonja, the Mnweni and the Singati, knew their bee-hive huts and the lowing of their cattle.

Their lives were as tranquil and serene as the lazy smoke of their cooking fires. Next to them, higher up in the mountains, dwelt the Bushmen, the little yellow hunters, but there was peace between the Amazizi and the Bushmen. The Amazizi were pastoralists and herdsmen: the Bushmen were hunters. There was no clash of interests. In fact, there was a good deal of intermingling and inter-marriage. Amongst the Amazizi who remain to-day in the Drakensberg clear Bushman characteristics may often be seen. Burial sites of the Amazizi have been discovered and excavated in rock shelters near the present Cathkin Park Hotel and on the farm *Brotherton* in the Cathedral area, the skeletons all showing Bush characteristics. A. T. Bryant, in an unpublished MS in the Killie Campbell Library, refers to the "remarkable, intimate relationship" which existed for a time between the Ngunis and the Bushmen. Alone amongst the Bantu, the Amazizi used bows and arrows. They must have learnt their use from their Bushman neighbours.

One by one the years drifted by, and nothing occurred to disturb the tranquillity of their idyllic existence. Round about 1700 A.D. the Amatheza, a small clan of the Amazizi living in the Valley of the Upper Bushman's, underneath the hill Sandlulube, hived off and trekked north. They travelled through the foothills of the Mnweni into the Mont-aux-Sources area, and from there crossed over the Drakensberg by the Pass known to-day as Basuto Gate (previously known as Gordon's Pass) and so into the Witzieshoek area. After a brief stay there, they passed on into the valley of the Caledon, and so into Lesotho. This small clan came to be known as the Maphetla, or Pioneers, for these were the first Bantu to settle in Lesotho, hitherto the undisputed domain of the Bushmen. They had opened up a road into a new country. With later accretions, they form the real origin of the Sotho nation, the Basutho of to-day.

But the bulk of the tribe stayed on in the beautiful valleys of the Little Berg, for here life was good, the sun shone day after day, the grass was green, and many streams flowed down from the mountains and watered this pleasant land.

Their life was the very apotheosis of simplicity. We, to-day, are never free from the burden of our possessions. We clutter our lives up with irrelevancies; "we look before and after and pine for what is not". The Amazizi had learnt how to make of simplicity a way of life, and therein they found peace, tranquillity, happiness and contentment.

What, for instance, could be more simple than their bee-hive huts, nestling under the blue peaks of the Drakensberg? Together with their cousins in the other Embo Nguni tribes, they had evolved a simple dwelling, only a rough binding together of saplings and grass, and yet architecturally and aesthetically, it was well-nigh perfect – strong, cosy, beautifully proportioned and well-ventilated. The thatch of both walls and roof kept an even temperature, warm in winter and cool in summer. There were no draughts: the circulation was pleasant – a perpetual stream of gentle air, moving the whole time. The doorway was just the right height, big enough to admit light and small enough to keep out wind. The hut itself, outwardly, had a surprising beauty, blending naturally into its surroundings. It combined strength and perfect symmetry, the strength lying in the application of the "arch" principle. It was able to withstand the severest storms: the wind just glided over it.

Inside it was well kept. Do not judge the Zizi hut of the early nineteenth century by the dilapidated and dirty hovels we sometimes see to-day. Civilisation, I am afraid, has not been kind to the Bantu. The Amazizi took a pride in their dwellings. Their huts were always kept scrupulously clean and tidy. There was a place for everything. Any form of disorder was distasteful to them. The floor was always carefully levelled, smeared with cow-dung, and in the better huts beef-fat was also carefully rubbed in and polished until the floor looked almost like deep black marble. It was swept out at least once a day, and the whole hut had the pleasant milky aroma of a dairy.

As simple as their huts was the smooth tenor of their daily lives. The Amazizi, like most of the Bantu tribes, practised polygamy. Each wife had her own hut, where she lived with her children. These huts, together with others occupied by married children of the family head, would be grouped together in a simple kraal, all its occupants bound together by family ties. There were no villages, no towns, no roads, no rents to pay or to collect, no fences, no private occupation of land. To the Amazizi, the good things of this world belonged to all men. It is in this respect that he and his other Embo Nguni cousins have found it most difficult to adjust to modern civilisation, with its idea of private ownership. This is quite incomprehensible to the African mind. To the African a man is no more justified in claiming a piece of land or a stretch of water for himself, than he would be to claim the air around him and the light of heaven as his private property.

Each kraal would have a kraal head, whose authority was absolute and whose word was law. It was the kraal head who dispensed justice, again a very simple matter, for there was no written law – and no lawlessness. There was a certain body of customary law (actually very little) and there was common sense. It was, no doubt, a benevolent despotism, but with the accent on benevolence. A number of kraals would be grouped together under a superior kraal-head, the *Umnumzane*. These, in turn, would be grouped together under an *Induna*, and over all was the Chief. It was as simple as that. There were no elections, no constituted Councils, no Parliaments, no police force. The *Indunas* would act as a casual Advisory Council for the Chief, and that was all. The rule of life and law seemed to be: do as you like, work when you will (but don't kill yourself!) and don't infringe on the rights of others. The general code was simply a respect for honour and decency. All had been trained to discipline and self-restraint.

Life was indeed happy and carefree. There was no living to earn, no fortune to make, no dignities to aspire to, no ambitions, few disappointments and fewer worries. There were neither shops nor taxes, and no money. There were no court-houses, no jails, and no churches – no fearsome penalties threatening in another world. There was only the sun's hand resting lightly on the mountain side, the lowing of their cattle, and at the end of the day a pot of beer and a pipe-full of *ugwayi**.

Kingpin of the whole system was *paterfamilias*, the head of the family. The one great law was complete and absolute submission to paternal authority. The head of the household demanded, and received, unquestioning and instant obedience, from wives, daughters, sons, even from grown-up sons with families of their own. A. T. Bryant says of the Zulu home that it "was a model to civilized man of stern family discipline and refined manners". And he could have said the same of the Zizi home. Going hand in hand with this stern discipline was a very genuine affection for the children, and a desire to see them happy. Respect and submission to all in authority over him came to be ingrained in the character of every Zizi. The head of the family had drastic powers, even to the infliction of death in cases of gross insubordination. But although his powers were extreme, he had to exercise these powers with discretion. If he killed, there had to be adequate reason for the killing. The sanction here was simply public disgrace, but it was a very powerful sanction, to which the Amazizi were very sensitive.

There were, as we have said, no shops, no bazaars, no markets. The Amazizi never bought or sold for money. Indeed, there were no words for these in his language. Everything was done by barter. As far back as the year 2000 B.C. the Chinese were using money. By 200 B.C. the Romans had already struck their first coins. At the beginning of the nineteenth century A.D. the Amazizi were still bartering a pot of millet for the head of an assegai. Their wealth consisted solely in their wives, their marriageable daughters, their cows, their sheep and their goats.

There were no schools. The young Zizi boy was instructed in the simple usages of the tribe by his father, the girls by their mother. The girls learnt the arts of cooking and home care by doing the daily chores around the hut, and by caring for the younger children. The boys grew to manhood by herding the cattle in the open fields, coping with wild animals, and joining with their fathers in the occasional hunt. They soon became wise in all the ways of nature – the names and properties of grasses, trees and plants, their medicinal properties, the habits of wild game, animal and bird physiology, the ways of insects. They watched the clouds building up against the faces of the peaks, the mists settling softly over the valleys, the storms which swept across the land, the snows which etched the slopes of Quathlamba in purest white, and they learnt thereby to interpret the signs of the weather. They learnt other things, too – how to carry their full share of responsibility, how to be self-reliant and trustworthy. They learnt loyalty to family and to clan, a love of freedom, and the art of self-defence.

In dress and physique the Zizi was a fine fellow. Clothing was again of the simplest. He had no knowledge of any kind of cloth. When the Zizi gentleman stepped out into society he wore

* ugwayi: tobacco (Zulu).

behind only a short and loosely hanging apron of supple hide from his waist, in front a bunch of furry tails, the *umutsha* of his cousins, the Zulus. It was, perhaps, a somewhat airy style of trousers, but it sat on his lower limbs far more gracefully than the finest tailor-made garment he might purchase in Savile Row! And was it not cool, breezy, hygienic and perfectly decent! On one side he would hang a small bag of weasel or polecat skin in which to carry his snuffbox. Then, a few armlets of brass wire, his *umncedo* suitably affixed, and our Zizi gentleman was ready to step out into the world.

He took tremendous pride over his person, too. He was clean and careful of his appearance. He bathed frequently, and after his bathe he would anoint his body with a mixture of fat and red clay, which he would rub into his skin until it positively shone with health and beauty. The whole Zizi family washed their hands, both before and after a meal, and always cleaned their teeth after eating. The men were tall, robust and muscular, "the comeliest development of the true Negro," said Sir Harry Johnston of their close cousins, the Zulus, and the Amazizi were no whit behind. Their carriage was graceful, they held themselves erect, head well thrown back, bearing themselves proudly, and they looked you straight in the face. Respectful to superiors, the Zizi was never subservient. He never bowed and scraped, even to a king. He never cringed, as they do in the East. If ever there was a born democrat, in the truest sense of the word, it was our Zizi gentleman.

They were courteous, too, and hospitable. Refinement of manners counted highly amongst them. One December my son, Malcolm, and I spent several weeks in the higher reaches of the Great Mnweni Valley, below *Ifidi Buttress*. On our way there we passed through Makopo's kraal, and stopped for an hour or so to pass the time of day and to make our presence known, as one always does when one encounters a Zizi kraal in these parts. We passed on our way and established our camp eight kilometres on, higher up the valley, and forgot the incident. But on Christmas morning a messenger arrived from the kraal bearing greetings from the Chief, and a gift of sour milk and a shoulder of mutton for the strangers in their land.

Their code of etiquette was equal to anything in our modern civilisation. There was a proper way to greet strangers, and a proper way to take leave of them; a proper way to enter a hut, and a proper way to leave it; a proper way to treat parents; a proper way to sit in a hut – men and boys on one side, women and girls on the other. There were correct procedures for eating food, for placing spoons against a dish, for washing the hands, for handling a pot of beer. There were rules for walking across the veld, rules for regulating the behaviour between the sexes, and very strict rules for the art of courtship. Good taste and consideration for others, they thought, were the hall-marks of good behaviour. Uncouthness of behaviour was practically unknown.

Their daily life was simplicity itself. Each kraal was self-contained and self-supporting. There was a clear division of labour between the various members of the family. The men saw to the building and repair of the huts, the maintenance of cattle kraals, the clearing of bush, the milking, and the tending of the cattle. Boys were taught and instructed in these tasks from an early age, and expected to play their full part, especially as herd boys. To the women fell the tasks of keeping the home clean and tidy, of preparing the food, fetching water and collecting wood, and above all, of working in the fields. The girls cared for the younger children, and helped their mothers. It was a co-operative effort, and a healthy open-air life, with few cares and worries. For recreation there was always the occasional hunt, or perhaps a beer-drink or a wedding to attend. In the afternoons the young men would dress up in all their finery, and go courting, while the older men would sit in the sun with their pipes and their beer. Of dancing they were inordinately fond, and anyone who has seen one of these organised dances, with the men dressed in feathers and ox-tails, stamping out the rhythm in thunderous unison, their feet pounding the dust, and the women clapping and "ululating" with their high-pitched voices, will never forget it.

The simplicity of their life extended even to their meals and to their food. Only two meals made up their day, the first at about 11 a.m., when the main tasks of the day had been completed, and the second at dusk. Their staple food was maize or millet. An old Zulu myth describes how the wife of Nkulunkulu (the first man and procreator of the rest of mankind) after bearing him a child, found it such a nuisance that she determined to rid herself of it by feeding it on a certain poisonous-looking plant. The more she fed it the fatter it grew, and so the nutritive value of millet was discovered.

All they had in addition to their millet and maize was pumpkin, sweet potatoes and melons. Usually these were simply boiled. Maize was sometimes roasted on the cob. Meat, though greatly relished, was rare. It was only available after a hunt (which was not often: the Amazizi were not great hunters, like their neighbours, the Bushmen) or on a special occasion, like a wedding, when a beast would be slaughtered. Sour milk was a staple article of food, and so was beer, made from fermented sorghum, or kaffir-corn. There were no condiments, and no salt. Their only form of sugar was the sweet stalk of the *Imfe*.

Life, certainly, could hardly have been more delightful. But there was another side to the picture. In their striving for simplicity they went to extremes, and life became impoverished. It became stagnant, destitute of all progress, of all improvement, of all advance. Intellectually and spiritually it became completely bankrupt. The Amazizi never travelled. The great majority of them grew up, lived and died within sight of the ancestral family hut. Their world was only a few kilometres in circumference, and they knew nothing of the world outside. All their joys and sorrows, their interests and their desires, their thoughts and their activities, were bounded by the blue wall of the Drakensberg on the one side, and the untrodden hills and valleys of Natal on the other. So halcyon and easy was their life on these warm, golden plains, that it engendered indolence, mental lethargy, and inertia. For man's mental and spiritual qualities to evolve he must have battle and hardship and bitter toil – the long, unending endeavour to grow upwards and outwards. The Amazizi lacked this. They left behind no great inventions, no written language, no art, no literature. They had, in fact, a complete lack of any inventive power. They took over the bow and arrow from the Bushman: otherwise their only weapon was the iron-tipped spear, indicating merely the first emergence from the Stone Age. They knew a little bit about iron smelting, but not much. Artistically they were immeasurably poorer than their neighbours, the Bushmen. Spiritually they seemed to have lacked any religious sense, and they left no great myths behind. Their intellectual poverty was abysmal. They had only the simplest of tools. They knew nothing about building in stone. They could not measure distances: the distance between two places was always given as the time you took to travel it, and time could only be measured by the sun. The ease of their life, where nature supplied their every want, resulted in a thriftlessness and an inability to plan and provide for the future which to this day has meant that they are still largely a helot race, hewers of wood and drawers of water. Depending for their food to a large extent on agriculture, they knew nothing of artificial irrigation, or of the purposeful fertilization of their fields. Though familiar with cow-dung, they had failed completely to realise its fertilising potentialities. Their soft, easy-going life had sapped them of all initiative.

It is one of the great laws of life, applicable to great nations no less than to the individual: grow soft and flabby, and you will go under. They went under.

As Xan-xeib the Bushman had seen from his rock cave high in the mountains, the Amahlubi one day swept down upon them from the north-east. It was 1818. Their pleasant life under the shadow of the Drakensberg was to end in fire and rapine. What had happened?

Although the events which triggered off the great invasions of the Drakensberg from 1818 to 1828 took place 260 kilometres away, we must glance briefly at them if we are to understand what happened.

Away to the north-east, in far-off Zululand and on the plains of Northern Natal, a number

16

of other Nguni tribes had settled at about the same time that the Amazizi had reached the Drakensberg. Amongst them were the Amahlubi, under their chief Mtimkulu, one of the largest of the Nguni tribes; the Amangwane under their chief Matiwane; the Mthethwa, under Dingiswayo; the Ndwandwe under Zwide; and the Zulus, a rather small, insignificant tribe which had submitted to the authority of the Mthethwa. For something like five hundred years these tribes had flourished and multiplied on the plains of one of the finest areas in all South Africa, and by the commencement of the nineteenth century there were clear signs of over-population. Sir Theophilus Shepstone estimated their numbers at a million, and this figure is borne out by Major Charters, the commander of the military force sent to Port Natal in 1838, who estimated the number of human beings destroyed by Shaka at about the same figure. When Charles Barter visited the area around the Tugela River in 1852 he remarked that the country bore clear signs of once having been very thickly populated. It was now denuded of people, but ruins of old cattle kraals abounded everywhere. In 1802 a disastrous famine broke out, a clear indication that the land could not carry this vast and growing population. It only needed a spark to set the dry grass of the veld ablaze. That spark occurred in 1818, and it started a blaze which was to bring ruin and desolation to the tranquil land of the Drakensberg.

Immediate neighbours of the Mthethwa were the Amangwane, living in the present Vryheid district, under a chief by the name of Matiwane. Matiwane was a savage and merciless despot. Fierce and proud, he had a short, broad build, with a pronounced stoop. He was a man of considerable ability, but his savagery in warfare had become a byword. He was the gentleman who had the delightful habit of plucking the gall-bladders from the bodies of his dying foes, and greedily downing the contents in a single gulp, believing thereby that he would add their courage and ferocity to his own! His battle-cry: "We strive for cattle only and for land! Hayi ho ho!" struck terror into the hearts of his enemies. He began to make a nuisance of himself.

In 1818 Dingiswayo, Chief of the Mthethwa, decided that Matiwane was becoming too powerful. He ordered an attack on him. Matiwane, advised by his spies, prepared for the gathering storm. He asked Mtimkulu, father of Langalibalele, and Chief of the Amahlubi, to look after his cattle, and prepared for the worst. In the event, Matiwane, confronted by overpowering forces, capitulated, but he vowed vengeance. Then, to his fury, he found that Mtimkulu was refusing to return his cattle. Mobilising his army once again, he was about to fall upon the Amahlubi, when Zwide, Chief of the Ndwandwe, attacked him in his rear. Caught unprepared, the Amangwane were utterly routed, and were driven in panic before the exultant Ndwandwe, who burnt and destroyed everything in their path.

Matiwane, deprived now of his cattle and driven from his home, decided to seek a new home. But before setting out, he thought he might as well settle scores with the Amahlubi, who were still holding on to his cattle. After a forced march, and with picked troops, he ringed the Hlubi capital by night, and, as dawn broke, he hurled his troops upon it like a thunderbolt, and slaughtered everyone in it, men, women and children, including Mtimkulu himself. The Amahlubi, under Mtimkulu's brother, Mpangazita, fled for their lives, and headed straight for the Drakensberg, only to find the Amazizi already in occupation.

That is what Xan-xeib the Bushman had seen from his lofty cave. That is why, on a day late in 1818, the peaceful Amazizi awoke to the spine-chilling battle-cry of the Amahlubi, and the peace of the valleys was shattered with the roar of battle and the screams of women and children. At night the dark precipices of the sleeping peaks glowed red with the flames of burning kraals, and Xan-xeib the Bushman, sitting at the front of his cave, looked down in wonderment and in fear.

Some of the Amazizi fled higher up into the mountains, finding a refuge in the impenetrable valleys, and thereby clashing with the Bushmen. Some turned south, along the wall of the Drakensberg, crossed the headwaters of the Umzimkulu, and finally disappeared for ever, absorbed by the Pondos of the eastern Cape. And a few turned northwards, crossed the

Drakensberg at Basuto Gate along the path the Amatheza had taken a hundred and twenty years before, and joined their clansmen in Lesotho and the north-eastern Free State.

But worse was to come. For hard upon the heels of the Amahlubi came the avenging hordes of the Amangwane, under Matiwane, hacking their way westwards in their search for their new home. Once again the valleys and the foothills of the Drakensberg rang to the sound of battle, and night after night the leaping flames roared up into the night sky, as Matiwane and his men fell upon the Amahlubi.

The Amahlubi, in their turn, fled. "There was a white mark from the Tugela to Thaba Ntshu", said an aged member of the Amahlubi tribe, "and that mark was our bones." In their blind terror some, like the Amazizi, forced their way deeper into the recesses of the Drakensberg. The bulk of them, those whose corpses did not lie whitening in the long grass, fled northwards under Mpangazita, in the tracks of the fleeing Amazizi, and, in their turn, entered the wide lands of the eastern Free State and the mountains of Lesotho.

And then for ten long years the whole of this lovely country, the country of the Malutis and the Caledon River in the north-eastern Free State, was ravaged by war after war, the Wars of the Mfecane, when Amahlubi fought Amazizi, Amazizi fought the Bafukeng, the Bafukeng fought the Bakwena, and all together fought the local Batlokwa under Queen Mantatisi.

Down in the Drakensberg the fires still burned. The whole stretch of country from *Mont-aux-Sources* to *Giant's Castle* was ravaged and looted – the smiling Valley of the Mnweni, where the Ntonjelane dances in the sunlight, the broad uplands of the Mhlwazini, and the green Valley of the Sterkspruit, under the shadow of *Cathkin Peak*. And it was here, in the Valley of the Sterkspruit, in front of brooding *Cathkin*, that Matiwane, sated with slaughter, paused, saw the shining valley and found therein his new home.

But only for four short years. It was Matiwane, this time, who was to have his peace disturbed. Once again from the plains to the north-east came the same terrifying sound, the thunder of marching men, and for the third time in five years the turmoil of invasion came to the Drakensberg. This time it was Shaka!

When, four years previously, Dingiswayo had set out to destroy Matiwane, his armies had been under the command of a young chief of the Zulus. His name was Shaka. Dingiswayo died late in the year 1818, and by 1822 Shaka had absorbed the Mthethwa into his own tribe. The curtain had rung up on a new act in the great drama.

Shaka is certainly one of the most remarkable characters ever to be thrown up in the troubled waters of South African history. He can only be described as a savage, if brilliant, conqueror, one of the greatest military geniuses Africa has ever known. He re-organized, first, his small Zulu army, and later the army of the whole Mthwetha tribe. One of his first innovations was to change the long throwing spear for the short, stabbing assegai, and to provide his men with a larger shield. Thus equipped, the Zulu warrior would rush up to his enemy, hook the left side of his own shield round the left side of his opponent's, and wrench it aside, thus exposing the left arm-pit. Into this he would plunge his spear, right to the heart, and then withdraw it as his enemy fell. He was then ready for the next man. To return from battle without his spear meant instant death. Shaka adapted the well-known encircling movement, used in hunting game, as his major tactic – the dreaded encircling horns. He also developed a much fiercer type of warfare, where no quarter was given. In the past, tribal warfare in Zululand had been a rather pleasant affair, very similar to the Medieval jousts and tournaments in Europe. Neither side wished to inflict serious damage on their respective opponents. After a lot of shouting and clashing of sticks, with a few warriors tumbled in the dust, honour was satisfied, and each side would withdraw. Shaka changed all this. It was now war to the death, the sudden unannounced strike in the night, the wholesale massacre of men, women and children. He made his men fight barefoot, for greater mobility. Like all great commanders, he gave tremendous care and thought to the comfort and well-being of his men. They were well-supplied with meat. Boys of 14 and 15 were enrolled in a special corps of *udibi*, military orderlies or batmen, one for every three fighting men. It was their task to carry the sleeping mats, dry fuel, and food for the troops, so that, unlike others, Shaka's men were always warm and well-fed. Their morale was consequently high. The devotion of his men exceeded that of the Roman legions, while their ferocity outstripped that of the Goths and Huns. Shaka appointed as their commanders only men whom he could trust implicitly. As an architect of victory, he was incomparable.

But he was savage and merciless. The penalty for failure in battle was instant death. To test the devotion of his men on one occasion, he ordered a whole regiment to hurl themselves over a cliff. To a man, they obeyed. Giving the royal salute, "Bayete!" they leapt to destruction. At his audiences, he would look around, fix his eyes on some unfortunate individual, and say, "That man's face makes me sick. Take him away and kill him." On one occasion it was reported to him that some of the young boys of the royal kraal had been found peeping through the door of the harem hut. "Kill them," he said. But the guards couldn't find the particular culprits. "Kill the whole lot of them then," said Shaka nonchalantly. Sometimes he caused the eyes of his men to be forced out of their sockets with pointed stakes, and allowed the blinded victims to roam about as objects of ridicule. Fathers stabbed children, sons choked mothers at his command without a moment's hesitation. Fynn, who was staying at the royal kraal at the time, gives a vivid description of the slaughter that went on on the occasion of the death of his mother, Nandi, simply because Shaka thought his people were not showing sufficient grief. On the first day alone Fynn estimated that 7 000 men, women and children had been butchered – and it went on for days.

Shaka had never forgotten Matiwane, now living peacefully in the Cathkin area. There came a day in 1822 when he decided to wipe Matiwane from the face of the earth. The order was issued from the Royal Kraal of Dukuza to march.

The impis,* under Shaka's general Mdlaka, assembled with their long cow-hide shields and their magnificent feathered head-dresses, their stabbing assegais and their heavy knob-kerries. Slowly at first, and then with increasing speed, they streamed out of the royal gates, westwards, with their long loping tread.

Matiwane looked up one day, from under the shadow of *Cathkin Peak*. Away in the distance he saw the long slopes of the rising ground beyond the Injasuti River. They were black with moving men. The noise of their coming was as the rustling sound of a swarm of locusts, menacing, terrifying. And for the third time the dark peaks of Quathlamba were etched black against a flaming sky.

Matiwane fled. No man could withstand the mighty hammer-blows of Shaka's impis. He fled, first of all, into the Mnweni area, and there gathered his forces. He thought his front would be well-protected by the Tugela and Umlambonja Rivers. In an emergency he would be able to escape over the Drakensberg into Lesotho via the headwaters of the Mhlwazini and Ndedema Rivers. Mdlaka, however, came up behind *Arthur's Seat* (*Mpimbo*), with another arm of his forces over the *Rockeries*, and down the Magangangozi, thus cutting off his escape route. In the ensuing battle Matiwane just managed to escape, still northwards. Once again the Pass at Basuto Gate saw the long line of fleeing men making for Witzieshoek and the plains of the eastern Free State, and the armies of Matiwane were now flung into the already vast cauldron of the Mfecane.

The resulting chaos staggers the imagination. Says E. A. Ritter, in *Shaka Zulu*, "The pitiless cruelty and unspeakable brutality of these inter-tribal wars of annihilation baffle description". Ellenberger said, "The ruin and devastation that spread over the north-eastern Free State and northern Lesotho was one of the greatest in the history of the world." And

* Impi: Army (Zulu).

19

Makonosoang, then an old man, told Ellenberger: "I lived on roots, grass seed, and even ate pot-clay to try thereby to stay my hunger. The hand of the Amangwane was heavy on the land. All the tribes were at war with each other."

Down in the Drakensberg it was nearly as bad. Shaka's impis went on the rampage. Tribe after tribe was driven westwards, came up against the impenetrable wall of the Drakensberg, and there either perished, or were deflected north or south. Those who went north were swallowed up in the Wars of the Mfecane, and disappeared from sight. Those who turned south followed the wall of the Drakensberg, crossed the headwaters of the Umkomaas, the Umzimkulu and the Umzimvubu, and finally ended up in Pondoland and the north-eastern Cape. In this way the Thembu arrived, spent a brief while in the valleys and gorges of the Drakensberg, were driven out, and headed south. They were followed by the Amachunu, under Macingwane. With the Thembu they ultimately formed part of the Pondo nation. Their descendants may be found to-day in the Transkei. Year after year a flood of terrified humanity rolled south-westwards towards the hills and valleys of the Drakensberg. The whole of this lovely country was in an uproar.

Some decided to stay on and fight it out from their tenuous refuges in the deep-cut valleys of the Little Berg. There were still a few of the Amazizi left, and these were joined by scattered remnants of the Amahlubi and the Amangwane. The Fern Forest, in the Cathedral area, was one such hide-out. To this day the forest is still known to Africans as Magwaleni, "Cowards Bush".

Climbing one day in the Mont-aux-Sources area, I found myself on a narrow ledge, half way up one of the sandstone rock faces of the Little Berg. Here I found a whole collection of grinding stones and clay pots, similar to those made by the Amangwane. Some were grouped around what must once have been a fireplace. By digging I managed to uncover several more. This must have been one of the hide-outs of a group of either Amazizi or Amangwane. They could not have chosen a better position. In front was a screen of small trees. There was only one way up to the ledge – the chimney up which I had climbed, and the whole position commanded a magnificent view of the whole valley, 300 metres below. As a defensive position it was completely impregnable. I brought one of the pots down with me, and it was later identified by the Natal Museum as being almost certainly of Amangwane origin, and about 130 years old.

By 1823 the whole of Natal was completely devastated. From a population of about a million it had shrunk to less than 3 000. Farewell went even further. In 1824 he described the territory made over to him by Shaka as containing "not more than three or four hundred souls". Theal states that when Retief and his Voortrekkers came down the passes of the Drakensberg in 1837 they encountered no sign of human habitation between the Drakensberg and Port Natal, a distance of 240 kilometres. "The ten years of Shaka's reign," says Professor Hattersley, "represent a period of ruin and disaster in south-eastern Africa."

And then, to add to the horrors of that dread time, the few remaining Bantu in this once lovely land took to cannibalism. Their main stronghold was in the mountain fastness of *Job's Kop*, or *Elenge*, in the Wasbank district. Some historians have conjectured that it was only here that this grim practice flourished, but there is ample evidence that by 1825 it had spread throughout western Natal, into the Drakensberg, and on into the eastern Free State and northern Lesotho. In the Drakensberg the Duga clan, under Mdavu, had sought refuge in the more inaccessible caves, and cannibalism was rife amongst them. The Amazizi, the Amahlubi and the Amangwane all followed suit. The Bele tribe was especially noted for this practice. Renowned cannibal leaders were Mahlaphahlapha at the dreaded *Job's Kop*: even he eventually found his way into the pot. Chief Sidinane had his headquarters close to the present Royal Natal National Park, and visitors are still taken to the famed Cannibal Caves, where he lived.* Luphalule had his stronghold in a cave on the farm Freiburg, near Helpmekaar. Here,

_____

* He was still alive in 1870, when Dr. J. W. Matthews visited the area. See page 97.

to this day, you can see a huge, flat stone on which victims were slaughtered after having been ham-strung, and the marks on the stone where the knives were sharpened. People dared not move about except in large, armed parties, and preferably at night. Lonely strangers had hardly any chance at all. Victims would first be ham-strung, and kept in the "pantry" until needed. Then they would be killed, often with a twist of the neck, cut up, skinned and roasted or grilled. The cannibals had a grisly song which they would sing in front of their victim while he lay bound before them:

> We are cannibals, we eat people.
> We eat thee, we eat people.
> We eat the brain of a dog,
> And that of a little child.
> We eat the fingers of people,
> We eat the fat of mankind,
> Thou toy of the man-eaters,
> Thou delicious morsel –
> Strike! Strike him down, my comrades!

After having devoured the flesh, they emptied the skull and made a cup of it. They melted the fat by the sun or the heat of a fire, and either drank it, or anointed their hair with it. If no other victims could be found, they ate their own wives and children, and exchanged them with each other.

As late as 1836 Chief Balule, son of Mahlaphahlapha, who went into the pot at *Job's Kop*, still ate human flesh in his lair on the Upper Tugela River, and in the same year, when M. Arbousset, the French missionary, came to Lesotho, he found cannibalism still rife there. Mokapakapa, a Mosutho, was quite open about it. He told M. Arbousset how he, his three wives, his children and his servants had been captured by a cannibal tribe. They were driven like sheep to the slaughter. "They called my children two pretty lambs, their mothers they denominated three cows, my servants three oxen, and myself an eland. These words were our death warrant. My mother, my wives, my children and my servants were killed before my eyes, cut into pieces, cooked in dishes, or roasted on the coals, until the last morsel of them was devoured. It was only to my leanness that I owed my life."

Sikwate, a native of the Cathkin area, told the Witwatersrand University Archaeological Expedition in 1931 that his grandfather had left his four wives concealed in a cave in the area when he set out on a military expedition. On his return he found that all four had been discovered and eaten!

How can one account for such a strange and unnatural aberration in human nature? It is to be noted that many historians attribute this particular outbreak to the wars of Shaka, but although cannibalism reached its height during this period, these wars were not the cause of it. It first raised its ugly head during the great famine of 1802. Even this is not a complete answer. It has been proved elsewhere that cannibalism is not always accompanied by an absence of food. Torday and Joyce have pointed out that many of the tribes of the western Congo which were particularly addicted to cannibalism, came from districts where food, both animal and vegetable, was particularly abundant. And why cannibalism, when vast herds of game were still roaming the plains of Natal and the hills and valleys of the Drakensberg? It would almost seem as if periodically a strange, unaccountable madness seizes on races low down in the scale of human life, a madness which suppresses all decent human instincts, all reason, all natural desire for fellowship, all intellect and compassion, everything which raises a human being above the brute beast. It is cruelty practised for its own sake, and delighted in – children butchered and roasted under the eyes of their parents, women in the presence of their husbands. It is a strange, strange world in which we live!

We might also ponder briefly here another curious fact. Why is it that practically all the great migrations in human history, all the savage invasions, from Jengis Kahn, the Goths, the Huns, down to the vast Bushman and Bantu migrations, the wars of Shaka, the invasions of the Drakensberg, why have they all been in a southerly and westerly direction, and practically never in a northerly and easterly direction? The colonization of America, the irruption west-wards into the Indian Ocean by Japan in 1942 (why did she not strike *east* and attack the western coast of America?) all follow the same pattern. Even to-day the greatest external threat to western civilisation is looming up over the eastern horizon! In truth, the call has always been: "Go west, young man!"

And what is it, in any case, that, down through the ages, has triggered off periodically these vast irruptions? Some would say over-population, and we have already noted that it was probably this that started off the chain-reaction of the Drakensberg invasions. But it would seem to go deeper than that. It would seem that, deep down below the surface of humanity, is a compulsive force, long battened down, which every now and then bursts forth, and the world stands appalled at the fury unleashed. And afterwards? Desolation, ruin, but in a strange way there is an ultimate cleansing, a cathartic re-generation, as humanity renews its upward march. The boil, long suppressed, suddenly bursts through the resisting flesh. But that is not the important thing. What *is* important is the renewed health of the body that follows. And so the long agony of Shaka's wars was eventually woven into the warp and woof of a new South Africa.

And the long agony was almost over. Amidst the vast turmoil of the Mfecane, in the lands that lay beyond the Drakensberg, one man emerged as a rock in turbulent seas. Moshoeshoe, of the Bakoni clan, son of an insignificant chieftain, Peete, determined to bring peace to his people by uniting all the warring clans, welding them into a nation and expelling the invaders. A man of vision and of statesmanship, all he lacked was the power. But he had heard of the mighty Shaka, beyond the peaks of the Drakensberg, and his impis. He would appeal to him for help.

And so, on a winter's day in 1823, a group of horsemen might have been seen making their way down the Pass of the Qola la Masoja, which we to-day call the Organ Pipes Pass, in the Cathedral area. The snows had been heavy that year, and the going was hard. They carried with them gifts of ostrich plumes, and feathers of crane and finch, and otter and jackal skins. In command was Khoho, the special emissary of Moshoeshoe, and he was on his way to Shaka to ask for help.

Slowly they made their way down the Pass, and then more swiftly through the foothills and across the rolling plains that led to Dukuza, the Royal Kraal in Zululand. Three months later they were back, with a present of 50 head of cattle for Moshoeshoe, and a promise that Shaka would march.

Early in 1826 the army set off, under Dingane and Mhlangana, and soon the Pass they ascended, which we call to-day Van Reenen's Pass, heard the tramp of marching feet, as the impis, company upon company, streamed relentlessly up and over the mountains. Line upon line they came, endlessly, and the noise of their coming startled the Martial Eagle high on his lonely crag. Then on, through Witzieshoek, into the eastern Free State, across the Caledon, to their first confrontation with Matiwane, at Likhoele.* Again they met, at Kolonyama, and yet again near the present Ladybrand. In this last battle Dingane and Matiwane met face to face for a brief moment, and Matiwane inflicted a near-fatal wound near Dingane's left armpit.

But by this time Matiwane had had enough, and he fled with all his men and with what cattle he was able to save, southwards. Through Mohaleshoek they went, and then down into the north-eastern Cape. Here he was turned back by the guns of the white man, under Colonel Somerset. For Matiwane it was the end of the road: he was utterly routed. He had trekked nearly a thousand kilometres from his old home in the hills of Zululand. Now, broken in heart,

---

* There is some little doubt as to whether it was the armies of Shaka or Mzilikazi which finally defeated the Amangwane. I have followed Ellenberger, Ritter and Bryant, the latter admitting to a small doubt in his mind.

weary, and sick for home, he and the remaining handful of his followers turned and headed north again. Threading his way once more down the Pass at Basuto Gate, which he had climbed so confidently six years before, he passed again, for the last time, under the shadow of the *Amphitheatre*, and so out into the plains of Natal. Early in 1829 he reached home.

Here he found Shaka dead, and Dingane, his old foe, on the throne. Dingane kept him waiting for a few days, and then he sent for him. Suspecting the worst, he removed his brass arm-ring and handed it to his fourteen-year old son, Zikhali, whom he instructed to remain at home. "Where are your people?" asked Dingane. "Here they are, all that are left of them," was the reply. "Then take them away," Dingane ordered. They were led away, and each man had his neck broken by a violent twist of the head.

Then, turning to Matiwane, baring his breast and pointing to the old wound near his left armpit, Dingane said gently, "Knowest thou that wound, son of Masopha?" "Yes, Chief," came the answer, "it is mine." These were his last words. They first put out his eyes, and then killed him by forcing sticks up his nostrils into the brain.

So died Matiwane, son of Masopha, annihilator of the Amahlubi and the Amazizi, and scourge of the Drakensberg. We need not mourn his passing. "During his lifetime," says Ellenberger, "he had brought ruin and devastation and death to many thousands of people over a vast tract of country, and it is hard to feel much pity for him."

The subsequent history of the main actors in this drama need not detain us long. Moshoeshoe went on to become the father of his people, to weld the various Sotho tribes into a great nation in the mountain country of Lesotho, where they live in peace and contentment to this day. Shaka, as we have seen, was dead, assassinated by his two brothers, Dingane and Mhlangana, on 22 September 1828, only a few short months before the return of Matiwane. In the kraals of Zululand men still speak his name with awe. Zikhali, the young man to whom Matiwane handed his brass arm-ring, we shall meet again, and we shall also meet again another young man, Langalibalele, son of Mtimkulu, Chief of the Amahlubi.

In the Drakensberg, after the vast devastation, with the long agony over at last, life began once more to emerge. Men came down again from the heights into the valleys and the plains, and started to cultivate anew the ruined fields. The "cowards" came out of the Magwaleni forest, once again built their huts in the Valley of the Umlambonja, and looked every man in the face. The Amazizi and the Amangwane, what was left of them, came out of their hiding places and settled in the Mnweni and the Singati and the Injasuti, and no man's hand was against them. You may see their descendants to-day in the Upper Tugela Location and in Drakensberg Location No. 2. We shall see in a later Chapter how Zikhali, son of Matiwane, returned to his people and rebuilt much of their later power, and of how Langalibalele, son of Mtimkulu of the Amahlubi, re-established his people in the area north of *Giant's Castle*, the present Drakensberg Location No. 1. Slowly the bee-hive huts were rebuilt, and the smoke from the cooking fires curled up lazily again in the still mountain air, and the valleys echoed once again to the calls of the herd-boys as they tended their cattle on the green hillsides.

And what of the little yellow hunters all this time? Hemmed in by the anvil of the iron wall of the Drakensberg behind them, and the mighty hammer-blows of the Zulu impis in front, they fought a grim and desperate battle for life. But worse was to come. To these two pressures, two more were to be added, two lateral thrusts this time, one from the north as the Voortrekkers wound their way down the slopes of the Drakensberg, and one from the south, as the English settlers pressed up from Port Natal, hemming them in yet closer. Their doom was sealed.

CHAPTER III

THE COMING OF THE WHITE MAN

"Say not the struggle naught availeth,
The labour and the wounds are vain."
—A. H. CLOUGH

On 14th November 1837, the first creaking wagons of the Voortrekkers began their slow and lumbering descent of the Drakensberg.

After months of trekking across the arid plains of the Free State, they had crossed the Eland's River, and had come to a land "rich in water and grass and very fruitful". Eyes which had grown weary with gazing on the winter plains saw with delight the new green grass of spring, the rushing mountain streams, and the mountains themselves, standing in silent majesty on the edge of the great escarpment. Huge kopjies, isolated and boulder-strewn, with their sandstone pinnacles, stretched as far as the eye could see. And everywhere were the flowers, dew-drenched and swaying softly in the cool air – red, blue, yellow and white. Especially notable was a large red one they had never seen before, probably one of the Brunsvigias. The scent of the flowers invaded even their laager, and in their joy they called their camping site *Bloemendal*.

Firewood was plentiful, and here they collected all their scattered wagons, 54 of them altogether, deciding to remain for several months while Piet Retief, their leader, set out to explore the route to Port Natal. They had arrived at a spot 40 km north-east of *Mont-aux-Sources*, midway between this latter point and Van Reenen's Pass.

Retief set out on Friday, 6th October, with four wagons and fourteen men, riding steadily for the plains of Natal. Standing on the edge of the escarpment, before commencing the descent, he gazed down on what he described as "the fairest view in Africa he had ever seen". To his right stretched the long cloud-capped line of the Drakensberg, culminating in the mighty precipices of *Sentinel Peak* and the *Amphitheatre*. To his left the slopes were gentler, in all their spring glory, and in front, 700 metres below him, like a crumpled carpet, lay the hills and valleys of Natal.

Retief was away for seven weeks altogether. He arrived at Port Natal, a squalid little place with only one stone building, another of wood, and a few rude hovels and African huts, on 20th October. In the meantime the rest of the Voortrekkers spent their time hunting, exploring the countryside, and searching for possible passes down the mountains. On Saturday, 21st October, they shifted their laager to Kerkenberg, nearer the edge of the escarpment, and here, on Sunday, 12th November, Retief's twenty-two year old daughter, Deborah, painted his name on a large rock in green paint. It was her father's 57th birthday. You can still see the name there to this day.

The next day they started to move, leaving Kerkenberg and outspanning three hours later on the edge of the Drakensberg. An air of suppressed excitement pervaded the whole camp, and that night, at evening prayers, Erasmus Smit, the Dominee, in his enthusiasm expounded no less than five Psalms! Next day, Tuesday, 23 wagons inspanned and descended the face of the Drakensberg, using chains on each wheel to brake the wagons. By sunset 18 wagons were down. One wagon was badly damaged, and four others had been unable to make it, but there had been no injury to man or beast. Next day several Trekkers returned to the summit and helped these five wagons down, and in the late afternoon six more wagons arrived.

It was an epic undertaking. North-east of *Mont-aux-Sources*, of course, the Drakensberg is nothing like as terrifying as it is further south. Here the sheer precipices give place to rolling slopes and deep-cut valleys, but even so it was enough to appal the stoutest heart.

The pass they had discovered is the one a kilometre or so south-west of Bezuidenhout Pass, known as Step Pass. The news soon spread, and within a few days wagons from all directions were converging on this and on two other suitable passes discovered later, Bezuidenhout Pass and De Beer's Pass.

With back wheels locked, men heaved and strained and battled on long ropes and trek chains to act as brakes and to prevent the wagons from toppling over. The green slopes and the krantzes rang to the shouts of men, the cries of the drivers and the "voorlopers", the whip-lash crack of the "voorslae", and the creaking and groaning of the wagons as they snaked their way down the long slopes. Baggage and chests were all lashed fast to the wagons. Women and children walked down, the old, the sick and the decrepit carried on rough stretchers, friends walking alongside them. They were an exultant and joyous crowd of men and women, entering upon a new and unexplored world of mountain, stream and valley. Every step was a discovery.

All that week and the next they poured down into Natal. Sometimes as many as 100 wagons went down in a day. By the time Retief rejoined them at the end of November close on 1 000 wagons were spread out along the Tugela and its tributaries.

Only one aged Boer doubted. Looking out late one afternoon he watched the long shadows of the *Sentinel* and of the *Amphitheatre* sweeping over the hills and valleys of Natal as the sun went down behind them. Lifting up his aged head he said in solemn tones: "Woe to the land that has shadows on its borders!" And the shadows *were* there. In a few short months Retief and his men would be dead, and Weenen, Vegtlaager, Blaaukrantz would be written in tears across the pages of South African history. With happier prophetic insight, as he looked at the green slopes and the toppling crags down which the wagons were coming, he might have seen in the blue sky above his own descendants in their silver survey aircraft, flying back and forth over the mountains searching for a Pass to carry the mighty four-lane tarred Freeway from the Midlands of Natal into the plains of the Free State, and so on to the teeming metropolis of the Witwatersrand.

And so the Trekkers came to the well-watered country and the pleasant hills and valleys of north-western Natal, and here they played out their drama to the magnificent backdrop of the Drakensberg Mountains. Slowly the white-tented wagons began to fan out, southwards and eastwards and westwards. Many turned west to the beckoning mountains of Quathlamba, and soon parties of mounted Trekkers must have ridden up into the valleys of the Little Berg, and gazed in awe at the mountain splendour which opened out before their astonished eyes. By the end of 1837 several hundred wagons had spread out along the upper waters of the Tugela and its tributaries. By February 1838 the Blaaukrantz and the Bushman River valleys had been occupied.

In June 1838 Gert Maritz established his laager on the left bank of the Injasuti, or Little Tugela River, at the point where the present Loskop road crosses it. The site is occupied to-day by the Bantu Affairs Department Depot. I think it must have been this party of Trekkers who were amongst the first to explore this section of the Drakensberg, for from Maritz's laager it was nothing more than a pleasant day's ride up the broad valley of the Injasuti into the heart of this magnificent mountain area. Maritz still had the padre, Erasmus Smit, with him. I hope the good Dominee had the wit, and the grace, to preach at least one sermon from the text: "I will lift up mine eyes unto the hills from whence cometh my help".

Then the Trekkers settled down to their long task of taming a savage land. With a purpose "ribbed and edged with steel", they set their faces to the upward slope. They had a goal which none would live to see, nothing less than the building of a nation, but their very striving was part of the goal, for it is the unending endeavour, the long march upwards, that builds character.

Without a goal, without a purpose, man is lost. Fortunate, indeed, were these hardy Trekkers in the Holy Grail they held before their eyes.

A considerable number of them settled in the deserted foothills of the Drakensberg, mainly between the Tugela and the Bushman rivers, and to this day most of the farms in this area carry Afrikaans names. It is generally thought, for instance, that David Gray was the first to farm in the Cathkin area, on the site of the present Nest Hotel. This is not so. The farm was originally owned by a Mr. Opperman, a Voortrekker, and was called *Opperman's Kraal*. It changed its name only when David Gray bought it in 1855. The farm *Arthur's Seat*, on which the prominent mountain *Arthur's Seat* (*Mpimbo*) is situated, was originally called *Buffelshoek*.

At first it was all a very casual affair. Farms were laid out with very ill-defined boundaries. Little attempt was made to establish attractive homesteads. The Dutch farmers were essentially nomads, and never sent their roots really deep. As late as 1850 many of them were still living in their wagons, or in what were known as simple "hardbies" huts. They dressed in moleskins and veldskoens, with enormous hats, a metre across, made of wheat straw, and lined with some green material. The weight of the finished article was considerable. Their guns were still of the flint and steel type. The women all wore voluminous skirts and the traditional "kappie". So great was their dread of the Africans that all, men and women, went to bed in their clothes, ready for any emergencies that might arise during the course of the night.

It was a hard and dour life they lived, their only contact with civilisation and the larger world outside the occasional itinerant "smous". The *smous* was a sort of wandering trader, bringing to isolated farmhouses his wares – cheap jewellery, pots and pans, coarse materials, and all the gossip of the towns. It was all done by barter, the *smous'* goods being exchanged for grain, ivory and skins. The *smous* was the link between the growing towns and the far interior. He must have often visited the Drakensberg areas.

So great was the confusion in the matter of farms that one of the first tasks of the Government in the 1840's was to try and regularise the boundaries. Farms of 243 ha (600 acres) were allotted to all Trekkers who had settled in Natal prior to 1840.

But now a new problem arose. With the death of Shaka and the defeat of Dingane by the Boers, Natal was flooded by a large influx of returning Bantu refugees. By 1846 nearly 100 000 Africans were wandering up and down Natal. Something had to be done, and it was then that the Government established seven Native Reserves, one of which, the Quathlamba Reserve, was in the Drakensberg. But again, there were no defined boundaries. A map of Natal, prepared in 1853 by C. J. Cato, marks the whole of the area between *Giant's Castle* and *Mont-aux-Sources* along the line of the Berg simply as "Quathlamba Location", with no boundaries, but, as we have already seen, there were already a number of Trekker farms in the area. This resulted in a good deal of dissatisfaction amongst the Trekkers, and a mass exodus into the Transvaal occurred, where land was free, and where 3 240 ha (8 000 acre) farms could be laid out. Many trekker farms were sold to English colonists.

In 1848 Sir Harry Smith promised to investigate Trekker grievances, and in the ensuing years an attempt was made to stabilise the position. A proper police force was established to check Bushman raids, and an attempt made to define properly the Native Reserves. In 1849 the ill-defined "Quathlamba Location" was split up into three well-defined Reserves, which exist to this day, and which are discussed later in this Chapter and in Chapter XXIII.

The first English settlers had come to Port Natal thirteen years before the Voortrekkers descended the Drakensberg. Slowly they began to spread inland, but it was not until the 1840's that they began to arrive in the Drakensberg. In contrast to the somewhat rootless Boer occupation, these English settlers began to establish themselves much more securely. Farms were laid out with a sense of permanence, and many are still occupied to-day by the descendants of these same hardy pioneers. Then, in the years 1849–51 came an influx of nearly 5 000 settlers of British origin, and Natal was transformed from a simple rural community of Afrikaans farmers into a far more complex and varied community.

We cannot, of course, follow in detail this steady progress throughout Natal. It will be sufficient if we trace the origin of some of the men and women who have left their mark on the Drakensberg.

Much of the early settlement took place on the coast, around Pietermaritzburg, and at York, Byrnetown, Richmond, and so on. But early on the lovely country around Lidgetton and the Dargle and from there towards the Drakensberg, attracted the attention of many of the early settlers. This is magnificent country, a country of soft meadowlands, of deep forests, and of clear, bubbling mountain streams. John Shedden Dobie, in his *Journal*, talks of yellow-woods five feet in diameter in this area. Winters were cold and brisk, but in the summer the sun shone day after day in a cloudless sky, and the land was content. As a boy I used to spend my summer holidays in this lovely land, on my uncle's farm next to *Kilgobbin*, ancestral home of the Fannins, and I have never forgotten those care-free days, the soft rolling downs, the gloom of the forests, and the mists that crept silently up in the night-time, and shrouded the forest trees in mystery. The area was given the name "Dargle" by Thomas Fannin, after the Dargle stream south of Dublin, from where he came.

He had left England with his wife and family in June 1845. After spending two years in the Cape and prospecting for a time in South-West Africa, he and the rest of his family sailed for Natal in the *Flora*, arriving at Port Natal in December 1847. After two days at the Port they set out for Pietermaritzburg, the journey taking them six days. In February 1848 they arrived in the area we have already described.

It was wild and unknown country. On their way up from Pietermaritzburg they only passed two deserted Dutch farmsteads. Though there was a drift of sorts over the Umgeni, Howick had not yet been laid out. But the country was lovely beyond telling.

Here Thomas and his young wife settled, found their roots, and started the business of raising a family. They bought a 2 428 ha farm, *Buffels Bosch*, from a Methodist missionary, and renamed it *Kilgobbin*. Wherever you went on the farm you were never out of the sound of splashing water, and it was surrounded by indigenous yellow-wood and sneeze-wood forests. The country between them and the Drakensberg was No-man's Land.

Thomas and his wife had eleven children altogether, and for a hundred years and more this gifted family served Natal in a variety of ways. John Eustace, the third son, became a Land Surveyor and ultimately a Magistrate and a J.P. In December 1873 he was employed by the Government, after the Langalibalele Rebellion, to report on the passes of the Drakensberg, with a view to blowing them up and rendering them impassable. He was accompanied by 40 Africans and 6 white volunteers for his protection, and was one of the first Europeans to make a thorough exploration of the Drakensberg. He died in 1905.

George Fox, the second son, became a noted plant collector and pioneer botanist in Natal. The lovely creamy-white Drakensberg Anemone, *Anemone fanninii*, and the little ground orchid, *Disperis fanninii*, so common in our Drakensberg forests, are both named after him.

Meredyth, the fourth son, took over *Kilgobbin* after the death of his father in 1862, and farmed there for the rest of his life. We shall meet Meredyth again later in this book, for he was one of the Carbineers who took part in the Langalibalele Rebellion.

The fifth daughter, Marianne, married the Ven. Archdeacon Roberts. They had a son, Dr. Austin Roberts, author of that well-known classic, *Birds of South Africa*. Emily, the sixth daughter, married Henry Bucknall, another pioneer settler, whom we shall also meet again. Later he and Emily returned to Australia, from where Henry had originally emigrated.

Thomas died on September 17, 1862. His widow survived him for 30 years, dying at *Kilgobbin* in 1892. Both are buried in the churchyard at Dargle.

Three years after Thomas Fannin bought *Kilgobbin* he was joined by Robert Speirs. Born in 1802, he had come out to Natal in the *Conquering Hero*, with his brother James, in 1850. Fortunately he had brought with him material for a saw-mill, and on his arrival he bought a farm on the banks of the Lions River, near the present Lidgetton, from Carl Preller. In 1855 he moved to a new farm, *Mount Park* nearer to the Drakensberg. The land between him and the Berg, where the Bushmen lurked, was completely uninhabited. He had three sons, Charles, the eldest, Bob and Alexander. He died in 1879. We shall meet this family again also, for all played a notable part in the opening up of the Drakensberg.

Further north we must notice the arrival, in 1847, of Rev. C. W. Posselt and Mr. W. Gulden Pfenning, of the Berlin Missionary Society, in what is known to-day as the Cathedral area of the Drakensberg. They established the Emmaus Mission Station and Hospital for the Amangwane tribe, and were actually the first Europeans to settle there.

In 1850 they were joined by Rev. Karl Edward Zunckel, and for the first time the name Zunckel was associated with the Drakensberg. No-one has done more to open up this mountain region, and for the Drakensberg Hotel industry, than the Zunckel family. Rev. K. E. Zunckel had emigrated to Natal from Berlin as a Lutheran Missionary. His son Wilhelm farmed in the foothills of the Drakensberg for many years. Wilhelm had seven children, one of whom was the famous Otto Zunckel.

Otto never entered school. All his schooling came from his parents. As a boy he often helped his father, herding sheep and goats, and sleeping in a huge cave in the Cathkin area, known to-day as Zunckel's Cave. He married Mathilda Posselt, quiet, smiling and lovely, and they had four children, Walter, Gerald, Udo, and a daughter, Ruth, the youngest. It was Otto and his three sons who did so much for the Hotel industry in the Drakensberg, and who took part in many of the dramatic Berg rescues. Time and again they were called out of their beds in the early hours of the morning to go to the help of stranded mountaineers, or to bring back the body of a climber who had fallen to his death. Udo was the first head boy, and first Dux, of my old school, Estcourt High School.

Rev. Karl Zunckel, the original pioneer, died in 1899. Otto, his grandson, retired from the Hotel business in 1940, and bought a farm at the summit of Oliviershoek Pass, where he died in 1947. Three months later Mathilda was killed tragically in a motor-car accident. Udo's son, Anton, until recently still carried on the old Zunckel tradition as mine host at Cathkin Park Hotel.

On 21st September 1849 the barque *Aliwal*, 425 tons, left London, bound for Port Natal. On board were a Mr. and Mrs. David Gray and their four children. Mrs. Gray had been a Miss Isabella Park. The voyage was uneventful until they neared their destination, when, just south of the Umkomaas River, the ship was nearly wrecked on a dangerous shoal. It has since been named the Aliwal Shoal, after the name of David Gray's ship.

David first of all inspected the plot of ground offered him at Richmond, found it worthless, and decided to trek up-country. They arrived at a farm *Greystone*, eight kilometres west of Bushman's River Drift (later Estcourt), towards the Drakensberg. It was owned by Mr. Henry Ogle, who had accompanied Fynn in the *Julia* in 1824, the first white men to settle at Port Natal. Later it was bought by Sir Frederick Moor, the last Prime Minister of Natal before Union, and retained by his sons and grandsons for many years. In 1967 the farm was taken over by the Natal Provincial Administration as a Game Reserve, and named Moor Park. The old homestead was bought by the Veld and Vlei Organisation, (based on the famous Outward Bound Schools) as their South African Headquarters.

David Gray and his family lived there for about a year, and then moved to Weston, near Mooi River, where they established an Hotel (later known as the Bridge Hotel) at the drift where the old main road to the north crossed the Mooi River. Motorists of an older generation, who used to travel the Mooi River-Pietermaritzburg road on their way to Durban, before the building of the present road, will recall, with nostalgic memories, this quiet spot, the old Hotel, the Bridge, and the willow trees.

Finding Hotel life uncongenial, David moved, in 1858, with his wife and now eight children, to the Cathkin area, and there bought a farm from Charles Green which Green had acquired from Opperman the Voortrekker in 1854. This farm, then known as *Opperman's Kraal*, and now as the *Nest*, was owned by David Gray and his descendants for many generations, and was eventually converted into the present Nest Hotel. It has been the Mecca for bowlers and mountaineers for many years. In 1863 Gray moved his homestead a couple of kilometres away to a new site, which he named Cathkin, after Cathkin Braes near Paisley, his home town in Scotland. The site of this old homestead is on Ivan Driemeyer's farm, but all that remains of it now are a few ancient oak trees, and the marks of almost obliterated foundations in the long grass.

The Gray family are synonymous with the Cathkin area; they gave the name of their farm to *Cathkin Peak*, and David's grandsons and great-grandsons still farm in the area. Many of his ten children played a notable part in the opening up of Natal.

Closely associated with David Gray was Patrick Campbell Sclanders. He arrived in Durban on the *Lord Haddo* on 17 November 1861. After an unsuccessful sheep-farming venture near Weston, on the Mooi River, he too moved to the Cathkin area, took over the *Nest*, and married David Gray's eldest daughter, Mary, on 30th September 1864. According to Andrew Sclanders, Patrick's son, they had to drive the stock into a stone-walled corral every night and stand guard over them because of the lions. To-day the name Sclanders, in the Drakensberg areas, is as well-known as that of the Grays and the Zunckels.

One other family is worth noting. In 1860 John Coventry came out to South Africa. Bound actually for Australia, he landed at Cape Town, and finding no boat available for Australia, and liking the country, he decided to stay. After caring for mental patients on Robben Island for a while, and farming in the Eastern Cape and the Free State, he came to Natal in 1870. He settled in a broad and lovely valley midway between Ladysmith and Bergville. He called it *Acton Homes*, after his original home at Iron Acton, near Bristol, and with his five strong sons, started farming there. To the east of this valley ran the road over into the Free State, with Dew Drop Inn only a few kilometres away from *Acton Homes*, where weary travellers were sure of a bed and a cheery yarn from the innkeeper, a Mr. Dodds. Dodds kept a tame baboon, who caused immense hilarity to his guests by quaffing beer from a tankard in the pub. After Dew Drop Inn came another Inn, Tent Hotel, at the foot of the Pass and then came the long climb up the slopes of the Drakensberg.

To return briefly to the Coventry's. John's descendants still farm at *Acton Homes*. In 1903 his grandson Walter bought the farm *Goodoo*, in the Mont-aux-Sources area, and it was he who first conceived the idea of using his farm to attract holiday-makers into the Drakensberg. He started taking in paying guests, and later the farm developed into the present National Park Hotel.

And so those early Colonists strove and struggled and battled their way upwards, subduing untamed nature to their purposes. They believed, to start with at least, that their motive was only trade, or, in the case of the Trekkers, a love of freedom. They toiled better than they knew. For actually they were obeying, albeit unwittingly, one of the great laws of nature: progress or die. If you remain static, you perish. It matters not one whit the goal, even if there *is* a goal – some "far-off, divine event towards which the whole creation moves" – that matters little. What *does* matter is the struggle. Britain's finest hour was not the hour of fulfilment on Luneberg Heath in 1945, but the hour in 1940, when she stood alone against the might of Nazi Germany, and decided to fight. Dr. W. J. Steenkamp, politician, author, big game hunter, tells in one of his books, with engaging frankness, how, as a young man, he struggled to achieve purity and complete chastity. He never quite succeeded, never reached his goal, but he realised in later life how this struggle, which had seemed so unavailing at the time, had put steel into his character, and had enabled him later to face successfully the demands of a hard life.

And all the time, high up in his rocky eyrie, the little yellow hunter watched . . . and wondered . . .

Trouble between the Bushmen and the settlers started early, and was inevitable. It was the clash of two irreconcilable cultures. The Bushmen did not recognise private ownership. The game belonged to all men. So did the white man's cattle – the Bushman had as much right to shoot these strange new animals as the buck that roamed the mountain sides. But what the Bushman *did* recognise was territorial rights over the hunting lands. Each band of Bushmen had its own hunting ground, and these rights were absolute. For one Bushman group to hunt in the territory of another group was tantamount to a declaration of war, and everyone recognised it as such. So that when the white man forbade the Bushman to shoot the white man's cattle, and yet went shooting game himself in the Bushman's territory, it meant war! Not only so: the Bushman only hunted for food: the white man hunted and killed indiscriminately, for sport or trophies, and this made matters much worse. Finally, as the white man began to shoot out the game, the Bushman found his very livelihood threatened, and there was only one answer to that! "All the game on the plains and on the mountains were ours," said Xameb the Bushman to Professor Schoeman. "They were our food, our clothes, and the price with which we won our wives. But then you came, and began shooting until even the vultures could not eat up everything. In those days the law of my people said 'a buck for a buck, a hide in exchange for another hide'. When you thus exterminated our cattle, when we saw our children getting thinner from eating puff-adders, then we began to aim our arrows at *your* cattle . . . because we wanted to live."

And let us admit frankly that there was, almost certainly, another motive: it *was* grand sport, you couldn't get away from it! Did not our own forbears, in the Highlands of Scotland and Wales indulge in the same sport?

"*The mountain sheep are sweeter,*
But the valley sheep are fatter;
We therefore deemed it meeter
To carry off the latter.

As we drove our prize at leisure
The king marched forth to catch us;
His rage surpassed all measure,
*But his people could not match us!**

So who are we to cast the stone!

Day after day, year after year, the little yellow hunters sallied forth from their mountain caves, and raided the lowland pastures of the white man. Always the pattern was the same. At dawn a farmer would discover that his stock had been raided during the night. He would report it to the nearest Magistrate's office, who would order out a few police, or perhaps the Carbineers. These, together with a small commando raised from the farmer's neighbours, would set out and follow the spoor. But success in recovering the stolen cattle was rare. All too often, when the pursuit was too hot, the Bushmen would slaughter the animals rather than let them fall into the hands of their rightful owners.

Autumn and winter were their favourite periods. The cattle were at their best in the autumn, and better able to endure a long journey, while the harsh winters made pursuit difficult. Cattle would be driven up into the mountains by the steepest and most precipitous paths. A favourite trick was to smear cow-dung on the rocks in front of the leading animals, so

* T. L. Peacock: *The War Song of Dinas Vawr*

30

as to persuade them that others had gone that way before them, and that therefore the route must be practicable. The slaughtering of the animals, plus the poisoned arrows the Bushmen used, infuriated the settlers, and soon it was war to the death. In fact the Bushmen were hunted into their lairs like wild animals, and shot down without compunction. None were exempt from slaughter – pregnant women, and babies in arms, young and old. Hunted down with dogs like wild beasts, they never surrendered. Cave entrances would be blocked up with brushwood and fired, children flung back into the flames. Still they fought on. Quarter was neither asked, nor given.

Every man's hand was against them. In 1852 Charles Barter said of the Bushman raids: "There is but one remedy for this evil – the entire extermination of these Children of the Mist, whom it is impossible to reclaim and difficult to hold in any check." J. Forsyth Ingram said of them: "They were, and are, in almost every respect, beyond the pale of the lowest class of humanity." While there was much talk in Natal in those early days of the white man's duty towards the Bantu people, and a very genuine desire to uplift and to civilise, not one voice was raised in defence of the Bushman.

It was in the 1840's, it will be remembered, that the country between the main road to the Transvaal and the Drakensberg began to fill up. Scattered farms began to appear in the Dargle, and all along the line of the Berg. By 1846 the depredations were so bad that it was decided to station a party of mounted men in constant readiness to pursue cattle thieves. The Post was to be situated on the farm of a Mr. Stephanus van Vuuren, in the Elandskop district, near Boston, who had been heavily raided in March of that year. The post would be manned by one N.C.O. and ten privates of the Cape Mounted Rifles. It was opened in April 1847.

By then the first confrontation between the raiders and the authorities had already taken place. On the night of 5th December, 1846, 15 cattle had been stolen from P. G. Pretorius' farm, near Otto's Bluff. The Government decided to act. On 14th December Walter Harding was instructed to take charge of a party of Cape Mounted Rifles and burghers, and to capture the robbers. It was a properly organized expedition, under command of a senior Government official. Soon after they left Pietermaritzburg, an express message was received that Bushmen had just raided C. P. R. Lotter, on the Mooi River. This was a golden opportunity to get between the raiders and the Drakensberg. Patrols were sent out to watch the passes south of *Giant's Castle*, and camp was set up in the Loteni Valley. In the event, the Bushmen were intercepted, and 15 out of 16 of Lotter's cattle were recovered.

In that same year the Government sent John Shepstone, brother of Sir Theophilus Shepstone, into East Griqualand in an attempt to induce the Bushmen there to submit to a more settled form of life. He failed. The reply of the Bushmen was that their roving life was a happy one, and they did not wish to change it.

On 30th July, 1847, a long letter appeared in the *Natal Witness* from A. W. J. Pretorius, the Trekker leader, who was now farming an hour's ride north of Pietermaritzburg, complaining bitterly of the imbecility of the Government in not putting a stop to the raids. The Fannin and the Speirs families, being right on the frontier, were in the thick of it all.

Up to the end of 1847 most of the raids had been in the Pietermaritzburg-Karkloof area, but towards the end of 1847 they shifted to the Bushman's River area. In December 1847 a new military post was established at Bushman's River Drift, which eventually, in 1874, became Fort Durnford, on the outskirts of Estcourt.

That same month, December 1847, 63 horses were stolen in the Bushman's River area. Four Cape Corps men and Mr. G. Rudolph set off in pursuit. The raiders were followed up the Bushman's River into the Drakensberg. There the Bushmen turned south, crossed the Umkomaas, and headed for the Umzimkulu. Only six dead horses were recovered, and the men were away a whole week.

A year later 200 head of cattle and several horses were stolen from Philip Nel, at Bushman's

River. Lieut. Melville, in command of the new Post, together with a large force from the Post and Nel himself, set off in pursuit. They followed the spoor right up to the summit of the Drakensberg. We might note this. It is the first recorded ascent of the Drakensberg from the Natal side by white men. From Melville's description, it looks as if they ascended Langalibalele Pass, but we cannot be sure of this. They went over into Lesotho, in the direction of Mokhotlong. Here Melville had to be left behind as he was ill. The rest of the party pursued the Bushmen through unknown country, along the summit to the source of the Umzimkulu, down the Drakensberg, and then in a northerly direction, back to the Umkomaas, the Loteni and *Giant's Castle*. They were away three weeks and recaptured a number of horses and cattle.

But the raids continued.

The following March the area was again raided, the target this time being Henry Ogle's farm, *Greystone*.

By 1849 it was obvious that the policy of establishing military Posts at Van Vuuren's and Bushman's River Drift, and of following up individual raids with police and commandos, was failing. The Government therefore decided to implement a long-suggested policy of establishing buffer native locations between the settlers and the Drakensberg. In April 1849 Langalibalele and Putini were established in the area between *Giant's Castle* and *Cathkin Peak*. Further north were the Amangwane, under Zikhali, son of Matiwane. Hence arose the three Drakensberg Locations, Nos. 1 and 2, and the Upper Tugela Location.

At first it might seem somewhat cynical to expose African tribes to these raids, in place of the settlers, but there was a good reason for the move. With the settlers there was always a long delay in raising a commando with which to pursue the raiders. With the Amahlubi and the Amangwane this was different. They lived a close-knit, disciplined communal life, and were able to move swiftly against any possible raiders. The system worked well, Zikhali, in the north, being particularly successful.

In August 1850 a new military Post was established at Spioenkop, near the source of the Umgeni (not to be confused with the more celebrated Spioenkop, on the banks of the Tugela, of Boer War fame). Six years later this post was re-built and enlarged by the men of the 45th, or Nottingham, Regiment, and named Fort Nottingham.

In 1851 Robert Speirs reported that his best herd had been carried off, from his Lidgetton farm, and that two herd boys had been killed.

From 1852 to 1856 the raids ceased almost entirely in the Bushman's River area, due largely to the success of the Locations system, and the centre of interest again shifted further south. In 1852 it was the turn of the Cedara district. Fifteen head of cattle were stolen from the farm *Boschoek*, near the present Cedara College of Agriculture. In 1859 the Government settled Chief Lugaju at Impendhle to act as a buffer between these raiders and the colonists, and a system was also inaugurated whereby young farmers could be called out on commando.

In 1855 the Volunteer movement was started in Natal, to help in the defence of the infant Colony. Two regiments were founded, the Durban Volunteer Guard, and the Natal Carbineers. From that time these two regiments, and especially the Carbineers, were used increasingly in checking Bushman raids, in spite of the *Natal Mercury's* caustic reference to "playing at soldiers".

In 1856 the Carbineers had their first "blooding". In March of that year a particularly big raid occurred in the Dargle district. No less than 460 head of cattle were stolen. On 5th March a party of nine troopers, under Lieut. Col. St. George, set out from Pietermaritzburg in pursuit of the raiders. They spent the first night at Tom Fannin's farm, and from there Fannin accompanied them as guide, and they proceeded on to Fort Nottingham. After that they were in what they described as "dreary, desolate and inhospitable country", and they were glad to have Tom Fannin with them. They reached the main Drakensberg, but there had to turn back for lack of supplies. Fifty head of cattle had been found butchered on the track.

32

Eight days later a second patrol of ten men was sent out under Captain Allen. From Fort Nottingham they headed for the Loteni. They were hampered for most of the way by dense mist and heavy rain, but managed to penetrate well into the Loteni and up the eastern spur of *Giant's Castle*. From there they looked down into the deep-cut valley of the Upper Loteni. Descending this, they followed the river up to its source under the southern precipices of *Giant's Castle*, a spot which they named Sunday's Kloof, as they had reached it on a Sunday. Then, according to them, they "accomplished the climb to the summit of the hill before dark". Was this the summit of the Drakensberg? It is not clear. They then returned home without having contacted the raiders, after a very wet and exhausting foray.

On one occasion Captain Lucas and a party of Cape Mounted Rifles had a very narrow escape. They had pursued a gang of Bushmen deep into the mountains. That night the men bivouacked round the fire, in a circle with their saddles arranged round them as a laager. Before finally turning in, Capt. Lucas strolled outside for a last quiet smoke. Though he could neither see nor hear anything, he felt that eyes were watching him, and he had a queer presentiment of evil. He returned to his men, and ordered them to move out of the circle of the firelight, and to sleep a little away from the fire. This they did. Next morning 25 poisoned arrows were found within the circle, delivered in the silence and the darkness of the night.

Captain G. A. Lucas, incidentally, was one of those colourful characters that seem to adorn Natal's early history. He was the son of the Rt. Hon. Edward Lucas, Under Secretary of State for Ireland, and, as a Cornet in the 73rd Regiment, had been a survivor of the wreck of the *Birkenhead*. He came to Natal and bought the farm *Upper Hilton*, and then joined the Civil Service, selling his farm to Rev. W. O. Newnham, who was looking for a site for the present Hilton College. Lucas became a Magistrate, and was known as "Thula, damn you" (Thula: Zulu for "shut up") because of his habit of saying this to witnesses from the Bench!

In May 1868 the Cathkin area was raided, and the local tribespeople lost heavily. This time the raiders were pursued to the summit of the Drakensberg, and many cattle were recovered, near the source of the Orange River, it was said.

The following June it was the turn of the Cathedral area. On the 15th of that month Mondisa, an Amangwane chief living near the source of the Umlambonja, reported that he had had all his cattle stolen. Captain Allison, the Border Agent at Oliviershoek, set out immediately with ten mounted Africans to recover the cattle. They climbed the Drakensberg and followed the spoor well into Lesotho, but failed to catch up with the raiders.

Subsequent raids showed that this district was now to be the target, and that a considerable force of Bushmen had been gathered for the job. The anger of the colonists was exacerbated by another big raid in July 1869. On the 24th of that month 120 cattle and 30 horses were stolen from William Popham's farm, *Meshlynn*, near the source of the Little Mooi. The raiders escaped along a well marked trail up a pass south of *Giant's Castle*, almost certainly the Hlatimba Pass. It was decided to deal once and for all with the menace, and plans were made to assemble the largest expedition ever to take the field against the Bushmen.

John Macfarlane, the Magistrate at Estcourt, was informed, given over-all command of operations, and told to *liaise* with Captain Allison. (Macfarlane was known to the Africans as *Ndabandhlevu*, which means "The Law with a Beard", because of the magnificent beard, magnificent even for those days, which he possessed. He subsequently owned the farm on which the township of Mooi River now stands.) As soon as he heard the news he wrote a jubilant note to Allison: "Hooray! Hooray! Hooray! Good news for the Border Agent!" and immediately hurried up to Oliviershoek to confer with Allison.

It was arranged that two separate columns, totalling 11 Europeans and 200 Africans, should set out in pursuit of the raiders, one under Major Giles and one under Captain Allison. Major Giles' party, consisting of 100 Africans and four European volunteers went up the Pass south of *Giant's Castle* taken by the raiders, after having been delayed by a tremendous snow-storm. Once on top of the Drakensberg they headed north to a point not far from *Champagne Castle*, and then turned south again. The second column, under Captain Allison, was to rendezvous with them on the summit. This column ascended the Namahadi Pass, at *Mont-aux-Sources*, and travelled south down one of the tributaries of the Orange River.

The two parties met on the eastern highlands of Lesotho on 22nd September, well south of the Hlatimba Pass. Soon after that they intercepted the Bushmen, and a sharp engagement ensued, in which 17 Bushmen were killed, together with, unfortunately, seven women and children. 60 horses were re-captured. According to one Basutho writer, the spot was at the confluence of the Orange and the Sinqunyana Rivers. This is the first occasion when an officially organized force from Natal succeeded in completely overpowering a band of Bushmen.

After the engagement the two columns continued still further south, and found their way back into Natal by a pass down the Drakensberg near the source of the *Umzimvubu River*.

This expedition deserves to be better known for its courage and daring. The men were away for two months, travelled most of the time through unknown and hostile country, covered nearly a thousand kilometres, and only lost one man through sickness.

On their return Captain Allison sent in a full report to Shepstone, in which he paid high tribute to his African levies. "Scantily clothed," he says, "and exposed at times to severe cold and storms, without cover of any kind, except such temporary shelter as could only now and then be obtained, weary, and with their feet cut and bruised by the continual fording of rivers, marching by day and watching by night, these men have held on without a murmur through a march of more than 600 miles, through difficult and all but impassable country, giving an exhibition of courage, endurance, loyalty and obedience not to be surpassed by the best-disciplined troops."

We give now in full the story of another of these raids, for it includes the first fatal accident in the Drakensberg that we know of, and also gives a very vivid idea of the dangers and hardships experienced by these pioneer colonists of the infant Colony, and of the hazards of travel in the Drakensberg in those days.

In March 1862 the Bushmen made a daring raid on the Dargle district. James Speirs, brother of Robert, lost 75 cattle and 15 horses, and Bob Speirs, his nephew, lost a horse that had cost £40. Charles also had been raided. The neighbours were summoned and they set off immediately, following a clear spoor round the shoulder of the *Inhluzana* and up the Umgeni River to its source. By evening they had reached the Insinga River, and here they camped for the night. Next morning they set off again, but soon they came across animal after animal, stabbed to death instead of being abandoned to their rightful owners. Then, just past the Loteni River came the climax – the rest of the cattle lying in a ghastly heap of mutilated carcasses. Obviously, the Bushmen had found the pace too hot, and had decided to rid themselves of the encumbrance. Infuriated, the farmers returned home, but agreed to meet in ten days' time at Lugaju's kraal, with a much larger force, and then to wipe out the marauding Bushmen.

On the appointed day ten Carbineers assembled at the kraal together with ten farmers and fourteen Africans, all under the command of Captain Proudfoot. Captain Proudfoot was another of these colourful characters in the early days of the Colony. He was an imposing man of great physical strength, and came to be known as "the Garibaldi of Natal". He settled at Riet Vlei on his farm *Craigieburn*, named after his home in Scotland. He played a prominent part in the Volunteer movement in Natal, and commanded the Carbineers in the 50's and 60's. He lived in great simplicity in his bachelor establishment, and died there in 1890. He was said to be the cousin of the Empress Eugenie.

This time the men climbed to the summit of the Drakensberg, almost certainly up the Pass climbed by Giles in 1869, known as Proudfoot's Pass, a Pass about which we shall have a good deal to say in the closing chapters of the book. It is known to-day as the Hlatimba Pass. At first heavy mist held them up (they named the area at the Pass "Mount Misery") and then they rode on for eight days along the summit in a wide circle, coming out eventually at the source of the Umzimkulu River, 40 km south-west of where they had ascended the Berg. This was almost exactly the route taken by Lieut. Melville's party, fourteen years previously, in 1848. They had just off-saddled when, on the slope of a hill, they spotted a young Bushman galloping away on a horse. Robert Speirs (Jnr.) and Henry Dicks gave chase, the Bushman abandoned his horse, tripped and fell, and Speirs (Snr.) was on him in a flash, pinioning him to the ground and capturing him. He was brought back to Natal under the charge of Captain Proudfoot, and kept at his farm *Craigieburn*, but three years later he died of tuberculosis. He was buried, and twenty six years later, in 1888, Dr. Sutherland, Surveyor General of Natal, came to hear of it. He obtained permission for the body to be exhumed, and sent it over to Edinburgh University. The story of how it was smuggled over to England in a lady's cabin-box, unknown to the good lady herself, is one of the more bizarre stories of these early times, and may be read in A. F. Hattersley's *Oliver the Spy*. The hole from which the skeleton was exhumed is still to be seen on *Craigieburn* farm.

During this chase Thomas Hodgson,* one of the farmers, had been accidentally, but seriously, wounded in the thigh by the man who was riding next to him. It was a gaping wound, the whole thigh being shattered. It was decided that four of the party, Proudfoot, Speirs (Snr.), Willie Speirs and Fred Bucknall, should remain behind to care for the wounded Hodgson, while the rest returned home for help and medical aid. They set out, Robert Speirs going with them a short way to show them the head of the Pass, down which they would descend the Drakensberg. Before returning to the others, Speirs decided to visit a cave where some Bushmen had been seen sheltering the previous day. He travelled some eight to ten kilometres, and then, hot, weary and tired, he sat down in the shade of some rocks to rest. When he got up he was overtaken by violent cramp, and, with a heavy thunderstorm almost upon him, he just managed to reach the cave. Here, with the rain continuing, he decided to spend the night. Fortunately there was plenty of firewood, so he had a good fire.

Meanwhile, back at the camp, Hodgson was in a bad way. In fact, he was obviously dying. The mist and the rain came down, and the three men, surrounded by Bushmen with their poisoned arrows, in the loneliness and silence of the high peaks, and with a dying man on their hands, lost their nerve and panicked. As soon as Hodgson was dead (there was even a doubt whether he *was* dead!) they buried him under a pile of stones and, assuming that Speirs had gone ahead with the others, they fled down the mountain pass, taking Speirs' horse and all the food with them.

Next morning, in pouring rain, Speirs returned to the camp to find it deserted, and only a pile of stones to mark the spot. He prised off a few of the stones, and found, to his horror, Hodgson's body. Everything else was gone, including his own horse. The only thing he found in the camp was a tin, which he thought was a tin of gun-powder he had left there. He took this with him, and then set off to follow the spoor of his comrades.

He walked all day through pouring rain, and then all through the night to avoid freezing to death. During the night he came to the head of the Pass, descended it, and in the morning found himself at the foot of the Berg. Here, with the sun shining, he rested awhile in its warmth. His matches were wet through, but, tearing off a piece of the lining of his coat sleeve, he set it alight with a shot from his gun, and managed to make a fire. He also managed to shoot three small birds, which he cooked and ate. This was Wednesday, and it was the first food he had had since the previous Monday morning. He stayed there all day and the next night, keeping a good fire going as a signal, and firing an occasional shot.

The next morning he decided to set out again, but in coming down the Pass he had lost the trail, and soon he was completely lost. He reached the Umzimkulu without finding the spoor.

* His name has been variously given, incorrectly, as Hudson and Hodson.

Here he shot a small bird, and took the tin out of his pocket to light his powder-flask, but to his horror he found that instead of gunpowder it contained only salt. This left him with just enough powder for two and a half shots, and after that he would be unable to light a fire, and would have to eat whatever he killed raw. He was 80 kilometres away from home (when telling the story later Speirs claimed, wrongly, to have been 100 miles – 160 km – from home!) in wild and mountainous country, weak from want of food, and weary from lack of sleep. But still he kept walking. He decided to strike north, in the hope of finding the tracks of their outward journey, and the carcasses of the slaughtered cattle. As long as his powder lasted he was able to light fires, both for cooking and as signals, but soon this was finished.

On one day heath blossoms were all he could find to eat. On another he killed a dassie which he ate raw, and then he lived on bulbs and insects. Grasshoppers he found not bad, but they were scarce and hard to catch. For four days he fed on the ants from an ants' nest, crushing the nest in his handkerchief. But they still stung his mouth and throat. On one day he scratched his will on the walls of a small cave. He eventually found the hill on which the cattle had been slaughtered, but was too weak to climb it.

At last, on the fourteenth day, he staggered into Dumisa's kraal at Impendhle, and a messenger was immediately sent on horseback to his farm with the news of his arrival.

In the meantime the Speirs family had not been idle. As soon as they learned that their father had been left behind, Bob and Charles set out with George Fox Fannin to find him. They were not unduly alarmed. They did not know that no food had been left behind for him, and thought that possibly he might be enjoying a little pleasant hunting on his own. It turned out later that they must have been very close together at one stage, each on opposite sides of a small hill. The young men then returned home, and there the natives reported seeing fires burning on the mountains for four days. Charles immediately set out again. On the way he met Dumisa's messenger, and hastened to the aid of his father.*

To-day Thomas Hodgson still lies buried close to the highest of the twin peaks that bear his name, where the only sounds are the rustling of the wind in the grass and the lonely cry of the wheeling vultures.

After 1870 the Bushman raids fell off sharply. None at all were reported in 1871, and in August 1872 the last recorded raid in Natal took place. In that month the Upper Polela was raided, and 17 horses were taken. Counter-measures were swift: five Bushmen, two women and a girl were killed, and two women with babies captured.

And then, *just* too late, comes the first hint of sympathy for these little people. In reporting the raid, the *Natal Mercury* said:

> "Could nothing be done to bring these unfortunate creatures – thorough outcasts of
> humanity, shot down as dogs whenever the opportunity offers – to live the quiet
> pastoral life of the kaffir? By educating a few of these people, in time they might
> become messengers of good to the last of the race of the once formidable and numerous
> Bushmen."

But it was too late. In 1871 the last remnants of the Lesotho Bushmen were destroyed by Jonathan and Joel Molapo, grandsons of Moshoeshoe. It is doubtful whether any remained in the Drakensberg after 1875, though as we shall show in Chapter IX, a small band was seen in the Mont-aux-Sources area in 1878. There are still a few stories current amongst Natal farmers of individual Bushmen having been seen in the Little Berg in the early 1900's, but little credence

* I have told this story as it was told in later years by Robert Speirs himself, but I must admit to a certain amount of scepticism. That something happened I have no doubt, but to me it is incomprehensible that a man who had farmed in the area for 11 years, and had hunted there, could have been lost in this way for two whole weeks. If it had been on the summit of the Drakensberg I might have believed it, but he got down without difficulty. From there he had only to follow any one of a hundred streams to come out eventually (two days at the most) into civilisation.

need be given to these. In 1910 Maurice Evans speculated that there might be a few Bushmen left between the Malutis and the Drakensberg, but this also is extremely doubtful. If only they could have survived another ten years the awakening conscience of mankind might have found a sanctuary for them, and the last remaining men of the Stone Age might have lived on into the twentieth century. A recent careful study by Professor Tobias gives the number of Bushmen remaining in the whole of the Republic as only 20. In Botswana his estimate is 31 000, and in South-West Africa, 20 311. There are some who believe that many of these are the descendants of Drakensberg Bushmen who escaped the slaughter and migrated across the Free State. I cannot believe this. I believe the Kalahari Bushmen are a separate branch of the original Bushman race, which hived off westwards during their ancient southward migration.

Here in the Drakensberg, hemmed in on all sides, they put up a magnificent stand which, if it could have been recorded, would be one of the epics of history. It is impossible not to feel a deep sympathy and a great admiration for them, in their last days. They fought against tremendous odds, and a certain and terrible fate, in an effort to retain their children, their freedom, their happy hunting-grounds, their rivers and their game. These things had belonged to their fathers, and to their fathers' fathers, since time immemorial. They would not lightly let them go.

Surrender was not in their vocabulary. Shot through one arm, the Bushman would instantly use his knee or foot to draw his bow. If his last arrow was gone, he would still go on fighting, until, finding death remorselessly upon him, he would hasten to cover his head, that no enemy might see the agony of death upon his countenance.

George William Stow tells the epic story of the last stand of one Bushman clan in the Sneeuberg. Pursued into the mountains by a commando of farmers, they were eventually cut off amongst the rocks at the edge of a precipice. Here they turned at bay for the last time. One after another they fell to the guns of the farmers, until only one Bushman remained alive. He retreated to the farthest point of an over-hanging rock, in a position where no member of the commando dared follow. From there, with his last arrow on the string, he shouted defiance at his tormentors. The commando leader called out offering to spare his life if he would surrender. "A chief knows how to die!" called out the Bushman. He released his last arrow, and leapt headlong over the precipice.

And Stow adds this final epitaph to a gallant race: "Had they been men of any other race except that of the despised and often falsely maligned Bushmen, the wrongs which were heaped upon them, the sufferings they endured, their daring and intrepidity, their unconquerable spirit, and the length of the hopeless struggle they maintained when every other race was arrayed against them, coveting their land and thirsting for their blood, would have placed them, notwithstanding the excesses into which they were betrayed, into the rank of heroes and patriots of no mean order."

And to this tribute we add one more, by Walter Battiss:

"There is no ugliness, but only beauty, in what remains of their frail existence. Nature was not destroyed, injured or warped by their proximity. As casual as the wind and water, they lived in undisturbed serenity while the ages came and went. Now they have all gone, but their art remains."

Yes, let us always remember that even though they did raid the cattle of the white man, they held the line of the Berg during those critical years when Bantu and European were invading Natal with their tree-felling, their ploughing, their over-grazing, and their burning. It is to these little yellow hunters that we owe to-day the unspoilt beauty of the Drakensberg. Without them we might have lost it forever.

To-day the pioneers have gone: and so have the Bushmen: it is we who remain. The Drakensberg to-day is a holiday resort for the white man, with many homely Berg Hotels nestling in the valleys. Visitors enjoy all the amenities that the pioneers knew not, every kind of recreation, including hiking and mountaineering. But as they ramble over the grassy slopes few are aware of the drama which played itself out on these hills only a century ago. Only the Black Man, who still inhabits these mountain valleys, remembers . . . and tells and re-tells the story of that indomitable race of little men, and the drama of their passing.

CHAPTER IV

EARLY TRAVELLERS IN THE DRAKENSBERG

"Is there anybody there?" said the Traveller,
"Tell them I came, and no-one answered."
—WALTER DE LA MARE

It was a lonely, empty land into which those first travellers came. The peaks stood remote, far, enigmatic, unknown. Only the Bushmen and the wild game lived in those grim solitudes. The foothills, once the peaceful homes of the Amazizi, had been ravaged and depopulated by the ravening hordes of Shaka and Matiwane. Only the eagle, soaring a thousand metres up into the thin air, watched, and waited.

It is not surprising that the early colonists were slow in penetrating this mountain world. To a young community, struggling to subdue nature to its needs, mountains are little more than a barrier, a hindrance to travel and to trade. With all their love of beauty and of physical fitness, the Greeks never awoke to the splendour of their own mountains. They never climbed them for pleasure. It is only later, when increasing prosperity brings leisure, and the concrete jungle begins to press hard on the spirit of man, that mountains come into their own. The golden age of the Alps had to await the climbing of the Matterhorn by Whymper in 1865 before it got under way.

There were other reasons, too, not the least being the fact that up to about 1875 the intruder was, as likely as not, liable to get a poisoned arrow in his back, if he penetrated into the shadow of the great peaks.

Then, of course, access to the Drakensberg was extremely difficult in those early days. The country was wild and broken, and wagons or horseback were the only means of transport. From Durban up to the passes of the Drakensberg ran the slender thread of the "main road", for many years merely a series of winding tracks through the long grass of the veld. Even this was thirty kilometres to the east of the Drakensberg. It was not until the fifties that a start was made on improving the track between Maritzburg and Durban. Beyond, and for many years, only the wagon tracks remained. Hardening only came in the late sixties. The Government erected a chain of straw huts along it for the use of travellers, but there were no bridges. Major rivers were crossed at drifts, with small boats and ferrymen in attendance. Often wagons would have to be taken to pieces and reassembled on the other side. When the rivers came down in flood they could not be crossed for weeks at a time. In 1852 Mr. John Bird, Acting Surveyor-General, was asked by the Government to plan a road from Maritzburg to Ladysmith, which had been founded three years previously. Bird estimated the cost of the 100 odd miles at £11 500! (To-day, based on the costs of the new Mooi River-Estcourt Highway, the figure would be £39 345 500 (R78 691 000!) As late as 1876 the journey from Pietermaritzburg to the Free State border still took six to seven days, even though all the rivers had by then been bridged, except for the Tugela. If the traveller wished to branch out on either side of this winding ribbon, for some outlying farm, or for the mountains, he simply followed his nose, and depended on local farmers for hospitality.

Transport, of course, was all by Cape Wagon, a sturdy, strongly-built vehicle that served as coach and home for the traveller often for long months at a time. The secret of a really first-class wagon was its *looseness*. It had to be made in such a way that its various parts would respond and *give* to the multitude of bumps and strains it would be subjected to. The length was from $3\frac{1}{2}$ to $5\frac{1}{2}$ metres, and the breadth about $1\frac{1}{4}$ metres. It was usually made of stinkwood, and a really first-class wagon could cost anything up to R200. In addition, a team of 12 to 14 oxen, would be required costing about R15 per head, and bringing the total cost to about R400, no mean sum in those days. The traveller, John Shedden Dobie, described wagon-travelling as "the jolliest and most independent style of travelling ever I have tried, a prolonged picnic".

But it was a lonely, empty land.

Robert Ralfe (pronounced Rayf) farming at *Bergvliet*, just beyond the Military Post at Bushman's River Drift (his descendants still farm there) went for 14 years without seeing a European woman!

William Allerston, who had been offered a position at the newly-established village of Ladysmith, as a Constable, at £4 a month, arrived there at the end of 1849 with his wife and family to find only four houses of wattle and daub. There had been a fifth, but it had fallen down the day before he arrived. In order to obtain food supplies for the family he had periodically to walk 64 kilometres to Bushman's River Drift, bringing the provisions home on his back.

When the Emmaus Mission Station was established in the Drakensberg in 1847, postal communications with Maritzburg and Durban took place only every six months.

In May 1850 Rev. James Green (later Dean Green) rode up from Pietermaritzburg to beyond Harrismith to meet Bishop Gray, who was coming to Natal overland from the Cape. From the time he left the present town of Estcourt to his return there, he did not see, or taste, bread, vegetables, sugar, coffee or any meat but game. The Dutch were still living in their wagons.

When Charles Barter, a prominent figure in early Natal days, made a similar trip the same year, he missed Ladysmith altogether, and went on into the Free State without ever finding it!

If these were the conditions in the Midlands, north of Pietermaritzburg, what of the Drakensberg itself? A map of Natal, prepared in 1853 by C. J. Cato, gives a good idea of what was known of the area in the 1850's. North of Pietermaritzburg only three rivers are named, the Mooi, the Klip and the Buffalo (on the coast no less than 66 are named!), while Weenen is placed on the Klip River instead of the Bushman's. The Drakensberg is simply shown as a straight line, though there does appear to be a slight bend, unnamed, at what would be *Giant's Castle*. Not a single peak is named. Another map, published in Holden's *History of the Colony of Natal*, in 1855, is little better. The height of the Drakensberg is given as "four to five thousand feet (1 220 to 1 524 metres) above sea level". The actual average height is 10 000 feet (3 048 metres). Well could Dr. W. H. Bleek, writing in that same year, 1855, say: "The recesses of the Kahlamba are practically unexplored."

It was more than unknown. It was a place of superstitious dread. Many were quite convinced that it was the abode of mythical dragons. Even so reputable a paper as the Bloemfontein *Express* reported in its issue of 26th April 1877 that an old farmer and his son had come back terrified from a trip into the Drakensberg, claiming to have actually seen the dragon, a fearsome monster with two wings and a forked tail, several hundred feet long, and flying very high. One cannot help wondering how many wayside pubs the two had visited on their way home!

Actually no-one quite knew what lay behind those enigmatic spires. There was a well-established rumour that the mythical unicorn was to be found there, a rumour referred to by Sir John Robinson, in his book *A Life-time in South Africa*, published in 1900. Round about 1855 a Zulu told Mr. A. Osborn, a Natal settler, that he and five other Zulus had once climbed to the summit behind *Mont-aux-Sources*. They had then gone a little distance inland, when they found a remote and fairly extensive swamp, "of the extent of one day's travelling". There they found six large animals, about the size of a blesbok, dark brown in colour, and each with a long, straight single horn on its forehead. The animals were extremely ferocious, and attacked immediately, killing five of the Zulus. The sixth only escaped by climbing a large rock. In

40

February 1866, during the Basuto War, a strong column patrolled this plateau, and discovered the vlei, but there were no unicorns!

A Mosutho in the service of Daniel Bezuidenhout, then living near Bethlehem, offered to show his master a kind of animal which, from his description, must have been exactly the same animal as the ones described to Mr. Osborn. The Mosutho added that it was so fierce that it would attack its own shadow!

The good colonists of Natal were so convinced that there was *something* there that in 1860 they seriously considered organising an expedition to hunt out the mythical unicorn. It was proposed that a Natal Unicorn Company, Ltd., should be floated, but it never came to anything, largely owing to the hostile attitude of Moshoeshoe. The area was not approachable from the Natal side, owing to a lack of knowledge of the passes. The only way up to the plateau was through Witzieshoek and up the Namahadi Pass, and Moshoeshoe was more than ordinarily suspicious of the whole idea. In any case, as one of the members pointed out, what about the Bushmen lurking in the recesses of the Malutis, with their poisoned arrows! That seemed to put a final damper on the whole scheme, and the unicorns were left in peace!

Who were the first white men actually to see the Drakensberg? Strangely enough, we can almost certainly answer that question. On 21st January 1593 (in London people were beginning to talk of a new playwright by the name of William Shakespeare), the *Santo Alberto*, a large Portuguese vessel, richly loaded, set sail from Cochin for Portugal with 347 souls on board. Two months later, on 24th March 1593, she was wrecked between the Bashee and Great Kei Rivers. Sixty-two people were drowned, but the survivors, 125 Portuguese and 160 slaves, set out for Lourenço Marques. Shipwrecks were frequent on this wild and inhospitable coast in those days. The usual procedure was for the survivors to trek overland, following the coast, and to head either for Lourenço Marques or the Cape. The great difficulty was always the broad river mouths to be crossed. On this occasion the survivors, men and women, decided to strike further inland, to avoid the broad river crossings. It must have been one of the epic journeys of history – more than a thousand kilometres of wild, unmapped country. Many died by the way, but the survivors actually reached their destination, after a journey lasting three and a half months. They crossed the Upper Umzimvubu, the Umzimkulu, the Upper Umkomaas, and the Upper Tugela. They must have passed through the midlands of Natal and Zululand, more than 200 years before the Voortrekkers arrived there. On the 2nd May, when they must have been either near the Dargle, or the Loteni, they reported seeing, towering above them to the west, a great range of snow-covered mountains. This could be no other than the Drakensberg.

It is pleasant, in an idle moment, to let one's imagination play around this simple incident from the dim and distant past. How close to the Drakensberg did they come? Did they, perhaps, pause awhile in this pleasant land, and did some of the more adventurous souls go exploring, and did they perhaps penetrate the valleys of the Little Berg? Did they even climb one of the passes to the top? We do not know, and it does not greatly matter. It is sufficient that this mighty mountain chain had at last unveiled her beauty to the eyes of the white man.

Then, as the mists close in around the peaks on a summer's day, so the mists of time close in about this lonely land. For more than two centuries all is darkness. But sometimes the mists part, and reveal for a brief moment some elusive peak or soaring pinnacle, only to close in again and leave behind an unanswered question. And so, over the years, we catch an enigmatic, tantalising glance at some lonely traveller who appears for a moment and then is swallowed up again in the darkness, the story of whose coming and going will remain for ever untold.

In February 1829 a Dr. Alexander Cowie, former surgeon from Albany in the Cape, and Benjamin Green, a merchant from Grahamstown, arrived at Port Natal. But they hardly even step on to the stage. They came with the intention of exploring the Drakensberg and discovering the source of the Orange River, for even by that early date it had challenged the curiosity of men. But they changed their minds, and tried Zululand instead, and thereby went to their deaths.

Towards the end of 1836 two deserters from a British garrison in the Cape pitched up in Zululand, after walking for 23 days across the Drakensberg. Who were they? And where, and by what passes did they descend the Drakensberg? After this brief glimpse, the mists close in on our questions, and we simply do not know. In May of the following year two more deserters made the same journey across the trackless Drakensberg, and again there is the same enigmatic silence to all our questions.

Down the years came others. They pause a moment on the stage, and pass on into the wings. In 1845 Mr. W. Stanger was appointed Surveyor-General, and with four assistants was given the task of fixing the boundaries of Natal, and preparing a trigonometrical survey of the whole Colony. We have no record of where they went and what they did, but they must have made at least a tentative survey of the Drakensberg. Did they, perhaps, climb to the summit?

In 1873 John Eustace Fannin, who by that time had joined the Civil Service, was sent by the Government to report on the passes of the Drakensberg. It must have been a dangerous and difficult task, for there were still Bushmen hiding in the innermost recesses of the Drakensberg in those days. What he did we do not know – again the mists close in after granting us one tantalising glimpse – but what adventures they must have had!

In 1874 Colonel A. W. Durnford and a detachment of the 75th Regiment spent six months in the Drakensberg, blowing up the mountain passes between Oliviershoek and *Giant's Castle*. They assembled at Estcourt, and from there proceeded first of all to David Gray's farm *Cathkin*. They then crossed the Sterkspruit and pitched camp underneath the krantzes of the Little Berg. From this point they destroyed Gray's Pass. They then crossed over the Little Berg into the Mhlwazini Valley, and camped at the foot of a hill "with a most extraordinary hole in its crest, through which the sky can be seen". Mountaineers who know the area will recognise it as *Gatberg*. They then destroyed the Organ Pipes Pass (known in those days as Old Bushman's Pass) and the Umlambonja Pass. The signs of their demolitions in Organ Pipes Pass can still be seen.

After this they returned to their base at *Cathkin Farm*, refitted, and then turned north, camping at a German Mission Station, either Emmaus or Hoffenthal, probably the latter. From there they penetrated into the Mnweni area, and blew up Rockeries Pass, which they called Amaponjwana Pass. Here the cold was so intense that huge fires had to be lit to keep the men warm, and shifts of ten minutes on and ten minutes off arranged.

Back at Gray's farm for a second refit, and this time they headed south, up the Injasuti River, and so into the Giant's Castle area, where they established their camp at the foot of Langalibalele Pass, just below the Main Caves, only a couple of kilometres from the present Hutted Camp of the Natal Provincial Administration. Here they experienced a tremendous snow-storm, and here also the regimental cook one day carved the figures "75" on a giant boulder, a relic of their stay which is still visible.

In 1896 the Rinderpest Patrol visited the Drakensberg areas. Scratched high on the walls of a cave, also in the Giant's Castle area, are their names, R. W. Wilson, who spent three years in the area, J. K. Popham, H. C. Boast and W. J. Stone.

These are merely glimpses into a fascinating past. Of much more importance are seven travellers who have left us a record of their travels, and whose story we know, often in a good deal of detail.

It was to the southern end of our mountain chain that our first traveller came. On 29 December 1834 there arrived in Natal a young man of dynamic and restless character, Captain Allen Francis Gardiner R.N. Gardiner Street in Durban is named after him. He had travelled overland from the Cape. Eight months previously his young wife had died, and, deeply affected by her death, Gardiner, now forty-one years old, had decided to resign his commission in the

42

Navy, and devote the rest of his life to missionary work. Gaunt, long-legged, and wearing an eye-glass, he was blessed with a wild impetuosity that would brook no opposition. His Zulu name was *Khamungama*, the Insatiable One, and for seventeen years he lived a roving, impatient, adventurous life, burning himself out in the service of the God he worshipped. "How much he achieved is immaterial," says Graham Mackeurtan. That did not matter. His quest gave him as richly satisfying a life as any man could wish for.

Within a couple of days of his arrival he travelled up to Zululand, and made contact with Dingane, but the Zulus were in no mood for religion, and, with a heavy heart, Gardiner returned to Port Natal, where he established the first Mission Station in Natal on the Berea, which he named, because, according to the Acts of the Apostles, the men of Berea were more noble than those of Thessalonica, because they readily received the word of God. Here he eventually played a notable part in the founding of the town of Durban.

In the meantime, he had visited the Drakensberg. Soon after he arrived at the Royal Kraal Gardiner realised that there was considerable friction between Dingane and the settlers, particularly the ivory traders. Dingane asked Gardiner to put a stop to this, and eventually Gardiner decided that his best course was to return to the Cape and ask the Cape Government to take over Natal. Eight months after his arrival he set out to return to the Cape along the coastal route through Pondoland, but at the Umzimvubu he found his way blocked by the interminable inter-tribal wars triggered off by Shaka. He had to turn back, but on 24 September 1835 he set off again from Durban, with the idea of trying to cross the Drakensberg, which of course was still completely unknown. With Dick King, Henry Ogle and two others he set off from Port Natal, travelling slightly west of true north. He crossed the Umlazi, and went via Umbumbulu and Stony Hill past the present Richmond. Fording the Umkomaas near the present Deepdale, he continued inland towards the upper reaches of the Umzimkulu, and then climbed up to the Underberg plateau near Highbury. From here he probed into the mountains in various directions, searching for a possible pass which, he hoped, would carry his loaded wagons into the hinterland, and so to the Cape. He investigated the present Sani Pass, at the head of the Umkomozana River, and found it unsuitable. Here he wrote in his Diary: "A remarkable mountain has been visible in the Quathlamba Range nearly the whole morning, bearing north-west, and from its singularly indented outline I have been induced to name it the *Giant's Cup*." Twenty-seven years later the name was changed to *Hodgson's Peak*, for it was here that Thomas Hodgson died in 1862.

Failing to find his pass here, he then turned south-west along the line of the Drakensberg. He travelled 25 km the first day, and on the second day encountered another mighty peak. We turn to his Diary: "I was . . . quite startled at the appearance of a rugged mountain which I have named *Giant's Castle* . . . It's resemblance to Edinburgh Castle . . . was so striking that, for the moment, I could almost fancy myself transported to Prince's Street." This was the present *Garden Castle*.

The name stood for many years. It was later transferred to the present *Giant's Castle*, 50 km to the north, as we shall show in Chapter XIII.

Gardiner then continued southwards, still probing into the mountains, and finding the whole country deserted. Finally, on 23 October 1835, he abandoned the search, headed south-east for the coast, and came out finally at a point just north of Port St. John's. Eventually, this gifted, energetic and impetuous man transferred his missionary activities to Chile, and died there on 6th September 1851, from exposure and starvation while on a visit to Tierra del Fuego.

The year after Gardiner explored the southern end of the chain, it was the turn of the northern end. There came a day in the winter of 1836 when two French missionaries stood spell-bound on the summit of a peak which forms the centre-knot of three diverging lines – the main Drakensberg running south, the Malutis running north-west, and the continuation of the Drakensberg at a lower level, running north-east into the Transvaal.

Two or three months earlier, on 13th March 1836, M. Thomas Arbousset and M. Francois Daumas, two French missionaries at the Mission Station of Moriah in Lesotho, had set out on an exploratory tour of the north-eastern corner of Lesotho, towards the Blue Mountains, the Quathlamba, "mountains which, so far as is known," says Arbousset, "no European foot had yet trode" (*sic*). It was, indeed, savage and unknown country. Before they left, they spent half an hour in prayer. "Many were the thoughts and feelings which crowded upon us," says M. Arbousset. "We knew not to what people, or into what regions, the Lord was sending us; we knew not what trials we might be called upon to endure; we knew not how, or when we should return, or what in the meanwhile might befall the station of Moriah, and the friends we were leaving there. Prayer calmed our anxious spirits, and alleviated the anguish of our hearts." But they were tough, hardy pioneers of the ilk of Cromwell and his men. Perhaps there is a clue to the characters of the two men in the sermons they preached on the sixth day after they set out. "I preached," says M. Arbousset, with naive frankness, "on the destruction of Sodom and Gomorrah, and in the evening M. Daumas spoke from the words of the Apostle John, 'God is love'."

Early in April they arrived at the edge of the escarpment, and gazed down in awe over the tremendous battlemented cliffs of what we call to-day the *Amphitheatre*. Three kilometres west was the mountain to which we have already referred, and which they named *Mont-aux-Sources*.

They are, admittedly, a little confused about the geography of the area. They give the height fairly accurately as "not less than 10 000 English feet" (3 048 metres), (actual height is 10 768 feet: 3 282 metres) and the height above the summit plateau, which they say the Basutho call Pofung, the Place of the Eland, as 1 400 feet (427 m). But they give the circumference of the base of *Mont-aux-Sources* as 20 miles (32 km) and describe the summit as a plateau or table-land. Neither of these is correct. In giving the circumference as 20 miles they must have been thinking of the plateau from which *Mont-aux-Sources* rises.

They gave it this name because on its summit they found the sources of four great rivers, which they give as the Orange, or Sinqu, flowing south; the Caledon, to the west; the Namagari, or Fal (Vaal?) flowing north; and the Letuele (Tugela) flowing to the east. We know that again they were not quite right, and that the four rivers are the Eland, the Tugela, the Eastern Khubedu and the Western Khubedu. The Tugela and the Eland flow side by side for a short distance, separated by a low ridge. Then they separate, the Eland to flow north into the Vaal, and the Tugela eastwards into Natal. The Western Khubedu flows into the Orange, but the true source of the Orange is 16 km to the south of *Mont-aux-Sources*. The Eastern Khubedu flows eastwards over the escarpment (the Ribbon Falls) and then joins the Tugela. Though incorrect in some of their surmises, let us salute these two lonely, intrepid travellers, the second party of white men to gaze at close quarters on the real grandeur of the *Amphitheatre*.

For they were not the first, as is generally supposed. In the same year that Arbousset and Daumas reached *Mont-aux-Sources*, Captain Allen Gardiner published an account of his own travels. He included in his book a rough map of Natal, and at the source of the Tugela is the word "*Saddleback*". It was by this name that the *Amphitheatre* was known for many years. Somebody had been there (though probably not to the summit), and named it, before Arbousset and Daumas!

About our next traveller we do not know much, but he is interesting from one point of view, for he was instrumental in the naming of *Cathkin Peak* and *Champagne Castle*. In 1861 Major Grantham was busy on a military survey of Natal. Grantham had been born in 1829, and as a young Lieutenant in the Engineers he helped to lay out Aldershot Camp. Before coming to Natal he spent a brief while in the East Indies. In the sixties, now a Major, he retired from the army and went to Australia, where he advised the authorities on railway planning. But his heart was in South Africa, and round about 1889 he returned to Natal, where he died in 1896. He was a man of splendid physique, 183 cm in height, and a tremendous walker. In the course of inspecting the Drakensberg in 1861, he made David Gray's farm, *Cathkin*, his Headquarters. It was during this visit that *Champagne Castle* and *Cathkin Peak* were named. The two peaks are very close together.

Champagne Castle is actually a rounded dome set a few hundred metres inland from the edge of the escarpment, but the precipitous cliffs of the escarpment on two sides of the mountain are usually considered part of *Champagne Castle*. Although one of the highest points in the range (3 377 m) it is very easily climbed via Gray's Pass.

Cathkin Peak is a very different proposition. It is a huge, square, free-standing block of a mountain, completely separate from the escarpment. While *Champagne Castle* is easily climbed, *Cathkin* ranks as a difficult climb. It was not conquered until 1912. Its height is 3 149 metres. When Grantham visited David Gray neither peak had been named.

There are three stories as to how the peaks were named. One, that has been current for some time, claims that Grantham and David Gray decided to climb the peak known to-day as *Champagne Castle*. In their haversack they carried a bottle of champagne which they had optimistically brought with them to celebrate their climb. The going was tough, the day was hot. They took it in turns to carry the haversack. But when they reached the top and opened the haversack, the bottle was half empty! Neither man would admit to having taken a quiet pull from the bottle on the way up, so, to settle the argument, they decided to blame it on the mountain, and to call it *Champagne Castle*.

It is a delightful story, but Charles Gray, a near neighbour of mine in the Valley of the Sterkspruit, claims that it is incorrect. Charles Gray is a grandson of the original David Gray, son of Andrew Gray, and he claims to have the true story as given him by his father, who was present as a boy when the actual events took place. According to Charles Gray, his grandfather David did not climb the peak with Grantham. Grantham climbed with his batman. During the climb, the young man slipped and fell, and in so doing broke the bottle of champagne which he was carrying in his haversack.

On his return to David Gray's farm *Cathkin* Major Grantham told Gray of the incident, and announced his intention of calling the peak *Champagne Castle*, because his servant had already christened the peak by breaking the bottle over it. David Grey showed his keen disappointment at this, saying, "I had hoped that you were going to call it after my farm, *Cathkin*". Major Grantham, sensing Gray's disappointment, but wanting to retain the name he had decided upon, compromised by saying, "Its name shall be *Cathkin Peak or Champagne Castle*".

But there is still a third story. Henry Brooks, in his *Natal*, published in 1876, states that *Champagne Castle* owes its name to "a bet between two distinguished authorities in the Colony". This story is repeated in a Guide Book, *Glimpses in Natal*, issued in 1905 in connection with the visit to Natal of the British Association. All my efforts to find out who the two "distinguished authorities" were, or what the bet was, have failed.

To return to Grantham's part in the naming of the peaks, Charles Gray points out that for many years, well into the 1900's the term *Cathkin Peak or Champagne Castle* was used on all published maps. He is not quite right here. The Stocker map, published in 1888, which we deal with in the next Chapter, clearly differentiates between the two peaks. But I think that of the three stories, Charles Gray's is more likely to be correct than the other two.

For the rest of Major Grantham's travels in the Drakensberg we are again left, as in the case of so many others, with pure speculation.

We come next to a most delightful character, John Shedden Dobie. Dobie was a pioneer sheep-farmer in this country. He came to Natal from Australia in August 1862. Soon he became tired of sheep-farming, and then he made three quite extensive journeys in Natal and the Eastern Cape. But he was obviously of a restless disposition, and in 1866, after only four years in Natal, he left for South America, where we lose all trace of him. One of his journeys brought him into the Drakensberg.

He was a shrewd observer of his fellow-men, taking in the human scene around him with tolerance, understanding, and a delightful sense of humour. He did not like Bishop Colenso. He had three dark grey kittens, whom he called *Zulu, Satan* and *Colenso*, "*Colenso* being the blackest of the lot". On two of his fellow-colonists, Alexander Gibson and Wilson Wood, his comment is: "Rum pair of pups! Wood going about in short pyjama drawers and helmet hat." He had, too, a vivid turn of phrase. Speaking of *Giant's Castle* he says, "The Giant fired the opening gun from his Castle at a quarter past 12, and after that there was an end of any hopes of seeing the Berg again. The thunder growled and the clouds gathered." He was a man of exceptionally strong physique, and a fine artist, his note-books being illustrated with a series of most delightful sketches. His *Journal*, which includes some of these sketches, has recently been published.

In April 1863 he left Frederick Moor's farm, *Greystone*, just outside Estcourt for David Gray's farm. At first there were faint tracks of a road, and then a series of wagon tracks, difficult to follow, and then he simply had to depend on his sense of direction. From an examination of his account, I think he must have ridden in a fairly direct line, over the hilly country to the south of the present Estcourt-Loskop road, probably through the present Pasture Research Station. He crossed the Little Tugela (the Injasuti) "at a good drift". The Berg was "shrouded in rain and thunder-rain". He stopped at one kraal to ask where Gray's place was, but they did not know, and he had to ride on. He discovered afterwards that he should have asked for "David's place". Eventually, towards dusk, he came out on the hills above and to the south of Ivan Driemeyer's present farm, and saw below him the cluster of gum trees which denoted a farm-stead (the present Nest Hotel). It was David Gray's "old place", and he had to go on to David Gray's new farm, *Cathkin*.

Next day, after spending a pleasant evening with David, he pushed on into the Drakensberg. He crossed the Sterkspruit, which he also called the Little Impofana, and then entered what can have been nothing else than the beautiful valley of the Sterkspruit, where my home *Emkhizweni* is situated. He described it as "a basin at the foot of one of the spurs of the mountain, which is dotted over with sugar-bushes and clumps of bush, and waterfalls in the ravines".

Here he visited Robert Hope Moncrieff, farming at *Kilfargie*. Moncrieff was living in a primitive kaffir hut, and had settled there only two months previously. He was a brother of the Colonel Moncrieff, of the British army, who had invented the Moncrieff gun. Here Dobie spent the night. It was cold, and each man had only one blanket. During the night, when Moncrieff thought Dobie was asleep, he got up and covered Dobie with his own blanket. Alas, the generous-hearted young man was not to enjoy for much longer the peace and beauty of this lovely valley. Towards the end of the year he started to build a proper house. Needing labour and materials, he rode off one day, just before Christmas, up the Sungabala Pass, a few miles east of the Royal Natal National Park. Near the summit, while resting, he was set upon by four Amangwane tribesmen, Nagazana, a son of Chief Zikhali, Lugelezana, Matsheni and Magonondo, and savagely murdered. He was about to outspan, and had put his head under the flap of his saddle to loosen the girth, when the first man hurled an assegai, which penetrated Moncrieff's back. Moncrieff tried to cross a small stream in order to place it between himself and his attackers, when he was struck by another assegai, and fell. The four men then set upon him with their knobkerries and killed him, burying the body in a hole in the ground. Later the four were arrested. Magonondo turned Queen's evidence and was pardoned. The other three were condemned to be hanged in chains at the scene of the murder, and their bodies to remain there exposed to the weather, but the Governor would not confirm this, and the three men were hanged in the Estcourt gaol. Kenneth Howard Hathorn, as a boy of 15, was in the party which was sent out to recover Moncrieff's body. Hathorn later became a puisne judge.

There is, incidentally, an interesting semantic coincidence in connection with the name of

Moncrieff's farm, *Kilfargie*. It was actually named after the Moncrieff ancestral home in Scotland, but there are still farmers in the district who will tell you that the name is really *Koelvaatjie*, the name coming from the fact that Moncrieff used to keep his milk and butter fresh by putting them into a hole in the icy Berg stream which ran past the farmhouse. It is quite a coincidence that the two names are pronounced almost exactly the same.*

The following morning, after their night in the hut, the two men rode up to "Griqua's Hoek" – "a stiff climb up the range", he calls it. I have been unable to identify this place, but it may have been Hlatikulu Nek. Dobie must have done some climbing here, for "immediately under the perpendicular cliffs of Champagne Peak" he saw the spoor of three lions.

They returned down the Impofana to *Kilfargie*, where Dobie left Moncrieff and continued down to David Gray's. Next day he struck almost due north, cross-country, arrived at Emmaus Mission Station and from there proceeded on to Ladysmith.

It is interesting to note that Dobie was the first traveller to come to the Drakensberg purely on pleasure bent, and not in the path of duty or necessity.

Most of these tentative probes into the Drakensberg had come from the east, the Natal side, and the main features of the Drakensberg were gradually becoming known. In 1887 came one from the west, the Lesotho side. On October 15 of that year Lieut. Col. Sir Marshall Clarke, K.C.M.G., High Commissioner for Basutoland, left Butha Buthe for an exploratory tour of the eastern highlands of Lesotho, or Basutoland as it was then called, and of the Drakensberg escarpment. It was a large party, consisting of 17 men and 30 horses. They planned to be away for three weeks. The country was entirely unknown, even to the Basutho, and their first difficulty was to obtain reliable guides. They headed first in the direction of *Mont-aux-Sources*, but, when about 24 km away, they turned south-east and travelled roughly parallel to the edge of the escarpment, in wild and lonely country, at an altitude of between 2 438 and 2 743 metres. After passing the Motai, at an elevation of 3 185 m (Clarke may be a little out here) they struck Mopeli's bridle path, the main highway from Witzieshoek to South Basutoland, and made rapid progress, heading now due south. This brought them to the junction of the Orange (Sinqu) and the Seate. Turning now north-east, they followed the Seate up towards the Drakensberg, and eventually came out on the edge of the escarpment. From Clarke's description it is a little difficult to make out just where he was. From an accompanying map, he would appear to have reached *Champagne Castle* and *Cathkin Peak*, but the description in his text applies more to the Mnweni area, and there are other indications which tend to confirm this. He gives no names at all, but mentions that they were at an altitude of 3 246 metres, from which they could see the *Platberg* near Harrismith, the plains of the Orange Free State, the northern portions of Natal and Zululand, and the line of the Drakensberg stretching from *Mont-aux-Sources* to the Transvaal. In the immediate foreground was a "solitary bluff, grass-topped, but inaccessible", rising to the same altitude as the cliff. "The picture was made wilder" says Clarke, "by a rift, 50 or 60 feet across, running the entire depth of the cliff, and having no visible outlet at the bottom." He mentions a swamp, about a mile in diameter, which gives rise to the Sinqu, or Orange, and also a waterfall down the escarpment, the sound of which could be clearly heard. This general description fits the Mnweni area much better than the Champagne area, although I confess to being puzzled at the waterfall.

From there they turned back into Basutoland, passed the junction of the Semena and the Orange, visited the famed Sehonghong cave, crossed the Orange and then the Mantsunyane, went down the Lesobeng Pass and so to Roma, 30 km from Maseru, and site of the present University of Botswana, Lesotho and Swaziland.

Our next travellers are important, for they were the first real mountaineers in South African climbing history, and they hold the record for the first climbs of any magnitude in the

---

* This is not the only case where an English name has been, erroneously, Africanerised. Another farm in the Cathkin area, known as *Heartsease*, is spelt *Hartsies* in some maps.

Republic. The earliest account of any serious climbing on Table Mountain, usually regarded as the birth-place of South African mountaineering, only dates from 1892, when S. B. Morgenrood and H. Bishop ascended Window Gorge, Silverstream Ravine and Kloof Corner. The Cape Mountain Club was only founded in 1891. The Stockers climbed in 1888.

Towards the end of 1887 the Rev. A. H. Stocker came out to this country, apparently on a visit to his brother, F. R. Stocker, who was managing Ben Wilkes' farm, *Wellington*, near the present Draycott. A mountaineer himself and a member of the select Alpine Club, he thrilled at the contemplation of what the Drakensberg offered. Of the majestic scenery that confronted him he says: "Of this I hardly know what to say. Word-painting cannot describe (it)." On January 23 1888, he persuaded his brother to come with him on a climbing expedition into these beckoning mountains.

They made their way to David Gray's farm, and then to Gray's Cave "on the Sterk Spruit Berg" and camped there. This cave is really a series of caves, well-known to mountaineers, just beyond the *Sphinx* on the bridle path to the summit of the Little Berg, in the Champagne-Cathkin area. To-day they are called the Basuto Caves. The luck of the two men was out however. It rained for a week, and they did nothing.

But in April they were back, and this time they succeeded in climbing *Champagne Castle*, the height of which they give as 11 355 feet (3 461 metres. Actual height 3 377 m). They camped in a lovely gorge, about five kilometres from where their climb commenced. This could easily have been Sterkspruit Gorge. From there they made their way to the base of the mountain, almost certainly up the Mhlwazini Valley. At the foot of the climb, (the present Base Camp, where the Keith Bush Hut is now situated), they turned slightly left, instead of right, up Gray's Pass, to-day's usual route, taking what mountaineers call the High Route. This is a difficult climb, involving a good deal of fairly stiff rock work. Near the top the rocks were glazed with ice, and they found the going hard. The view from here, however, was magnificent, "the grandest I know anywhere," said A. H. Stocker, "a lovely valley with four magnificent peaks at the upper end, two square blocks and two aiguilles, lying to the north of *Champagne Castle*", (known to-day as *Dragon's Back*). By 2.30 p.m. they had reached the summit, which they described as a flattened dome, extremely dull and uninteresting. They descended via Ship's Prow Pass, (which they called Champagne Castle Pass) "the stoniest and most abominable gully I ever was in", was Stocker's verdict, one which modern mountaineers would agree with, and they did not get back to their camp until 10.20 p.m., after having been out 15 hours and 50 minutes. Before leaving the summit of *Champagne Castle* they noticed to the south, and a number of kilometres inland, a peak which seemed higher than the one on which they were standing, thus anticipating by 60 years the findings of surveyors in the 1950's.*

In May, with F. L. Bridger, Rev. A. H. Stocker made a reconnaissance of *Cathkin Peak* — we have already pointed out that by now the names of the two peaks are clearly differentiated. Later that same month he was back in Gray's Cave with his brother. From there, with African porters, they transferred their camp to "a splendid little nook, sheltered by rocks and a tree", at about the 2 493 m level. (I suspect they were a little lower than this, as 2 493 metres is well above the tree line.) Here they spent three nights. On their first day (May 24) they made their first attempt on *Sterkhorn* (*Little Tetelelu*, they give as the Zulu name). They climbed to the nek between *Sterkhorn* and *Cathkin Peak*,† which they called Sterkhorn Pass. From there they descended a little on the western side, turned right, and contoured on a broad grassy ledge under the steep final rocks. They attempted to climb these final rocks, failed, and continued on in a northerly direction, until they reached the great gully between the north and middle peaks. (*Sterkhorn* has three summits, the South Summit, the highest and most difficult; the North Summit, slightly lower, and an easy climb; and Middle Summit, the lowest.) Again they tried

---

* See pages 55 *et seq*.　　　　　† See sketch page 137.

to climb the South Peak, by the north-west buttress this time, and again failed. From here they had a look at the North Peak, and did not like the look of it, but found that by contouring round on to the east side, they easily reached the summit. They gave the height of the summit as 10 093 feet (3 076 m). Again they were out, by 338 feet, for the correct height is 9 755 ft. (2 973 m).

On the following day they made yet another attempt on the South Peak, on the east face this time, and again failed.

Two months later they headed for the Mnweni area, setting out on June 12. On their way there they were particularly impressed by the Cathedral Range, which they called the Ibotwana Ridge. They first of all made their way up the left-hand tributary of the Ntonjelane. (There are two forks to the Ntonjelane River, the left-hand one to the west, called *Ntonjelan' eshonalanga*, the Ntonjelane of the Sunset; and the right-hand one, to the east, the *Ntonjelan' ephumalanga*, the Ntonjelane of the Sunrise.) Near its source they attempted to climb the North Face of *North Saddle* – they called the Saddle *Segwana Cirque* – failed, and next day made their way up the other branch of the Ntonjelane, climbed the Ntonjelane Pass to the summit, and then walked along the top, past the *Saddle* to the head of Rockeries Pass. *Mponjwana* itself is well described – a magnificent peak, cut off from the main escarpment by a huge chasm some 450 metres deep. "The rock scenery round," says the padre, "is simply magnificent, and could draw expressive remarks from the most cold-blooded." Wisely, perhaps, he adds: "I forbear. The Alpine Journal is not the place for such enthusiastic outbursts!"

They returned the way they had come – one wonders why they did not descend Rockeries Pass – and three days later were home again.

In July, back at David Gray's, Stocker and a Mr. Douglas Parker did a bit of exploring in the Little Berg in the Cathkin area, discovering a new cave, which they called Eagle Cave. This, I am sure, is the cave high up in a lateral valley above the right bank of the Spitzberg Stream (Wonder Valley). Successful climbing was out of the question, as the winter was severe and the peaks all iced up. From this cave, however, they did attempt to climb *Cathkin Peak* via the South Gully. They actually got to within 155 metres of the summit, but here they had to turn back, defeated by the ice and the sheer face of the final rock wall.

From Eagle Cave they trekked across to Gray's Cave, determined on a final attempt on the South Peak of *Sterkhorn*. Stocker gives a clear and detailed description of the peak and of their climb – the two chimneys, one with a most difficult chock-stone, the east buttress, a very tricky traverse with little in the way of hand-holds, back on to the south-east ridge, an ice-axe step to a sloping ledge, under an overhanging rock, one final chimney, and at last they were at the top, at 1.40 p.m. Not fancying the descent by the route they had climbed the peak, they decided to go down the west face. They built a small cairn, set fire to as much grass as they could, to announce their success to the watchers in the valley down below, and then roped down, not, incidentally, by abseil, but hand-over-hand.

On October 11 Stocker was back at Eagle Cave, with Andrew Gray, David's son, this time, to make a final attempt on *Cathkin Peak*. But the great prize eluded them. Unfortunately, their pack-horse and African boy never turned up, and they had to return to their respective homes. *Cathkin* remained unconquered.

These climbs are of tremendous interest. Not only were they the first serious recorded climbs in the Drakensberg: they were the first in South Africa. But more important, for our purpose, is the window they open on the state of our knowledge of the Drakensberg. We have now reached the late 1880's. From being a *terra incognita*, the Drakensberg is now obviously becoming well-known. Stocker talks familiarly of the Little Berg, of the sandstone rock layers, of the caves in the Little Berg, well-stocked with wood and water, "used by sportsmen and kaffirs". It is already realised that winter and not summer is the best climbing season, and June the best month. Although we have no records of them, a number of trips must have been made into the Drakensberg by this time. The route into the Mnweni is obviously known. Stocker knew that there was a South Gully to *Cathkin Peak*, and that this offered the best route to the summit. Someone must have been there before him, for one cannot see this gully from the farms in the valley. The map which accompanies his article in the *Alpine Journal*, will be found on page 53.

Our last journey is an epic trek along the top of the escarpment, in the winter of 1908.

In that year the dreaded East Coast Fever was raging amongst the cattle of Natal. All movement of cattle from one territory to another had to be stopped. The Governments of Natal and Lesotho arranged for a joint police patrol to carry out a reconnaissance survey along the summit of the Drakensberg, to demarcate the correct line of the border, and to pin-point the passes that would have to be fenced. The patrol consisted of Sub-Inspector Marsh of the Basutoland Mounted Police, Sgt. A. H. Openshaw and Tpr. E. R. Blackburn of the Natal Police, four Basutho Native Policemen and two Zulu Native Policemen. They covered the whole area from *Giant's Castle* to *Mont-aux-Sources*, and the complete trek took longer than a month. They were mounted on sturdy Basutho ponies, and food, blankets and tents were carried on pack-ponies. Their rations consisted of army biscuits, bully beef, mealie-meal, coffee, and an occasional buck shot for the pot. Communication with the outside world was maintained by heliograph. Four successive communication points were arranged, the first on the lower slopes of *Ntabamhlope Mountain*, the second at Loskop, the third at Winterton, and the fourth at Bergville. Each morning, at a pre-arranged time, it was Trooper Blackburn's job to contact Trooper Hills of the Natal Police at the nearest of these four check points. Sgt. Openshaw was a bit of a scholar, and they had lots of fun with the heliograph. Towards the end of their journey, when Bergville was the check-point, he asked Blackburn to call up the Magistrate and to send the message in Latin. Half an hour later the reply came – in Greek!

They set off from *Giant's Castle*, where, under a cairn of stones, they found a sealed bottle. Inside was a parchment with a message of greeting, in Latin (those policemen were well-educated in those days!) from a reconnaissance patrol of the 7th Dragoon Guards to Sir Henry Bale, Chief Justice of Natal. Sir Henry was Chief Justice in 1901. What were those Dragoon Guards doing there, seven years prior to the Natal-Basutoland patrol?

At the Carbineer Memorial, at the head of Langalibalele Pass they found an old Waterbury watch, blackened with age and exposure, but it began to tick when wound up. It must have lain there for 35 years.

The trip was made in the middle of winter, and in the early stages, especially, deep snow covered the whole of the summit plateau. By the time they reached the present Cathedral area they had had enough of the bitter cold, the biting winds and the exposure, and they struck down the Tlanyaku valley to a lower altitude. Here they found a strong stream, not iced over, and plenty of fuel, and relaxed for a few days in the warm valley. Then back to the heights where bitter Berg winds, howling over miles of snowfields, beset them. By now they were opposite what they called *Cathedral Peak*, (this was probably the Mnweni, see page 123), and the bitter weather again drove them away from the escarpment. For a while they travelled along Mopeli's track, which leads down to Witzieshoek. The track was covered with snow, but well-marked with beacons.

At one point on this stretch they nearly came to grief. Openshaw and Marsh became separated from the main convoy. When at last they spotted it, it was away off on the horizon, heading rapidly northwards. It carried all the food and all the bedding, and the two men would never have survived a night out alone in the open without it. It was impossible to catch up with them, and shouting had no effect. Eventually they set fire to the grass, and that soon attracted the attention of the convoy. Finally, they reached the Namahadi Pass, and home and warmth and civilisation awaited them.

A trip of this nature would tax the strength of the strongest man, and towards the end Sgt.

Openshaw suffered a heart attack, due, almost certainly, to prolonged exposure at a high altitude. He never fully recovered, and died a few months later.

It was indeed, an epic journey, as anyone who has spent even a few days on the summit in the bitter weather of midwinter will testify. The cold saps not only your physical energy, but your very will to survive, and if they had succumbed they would not have been the first or the last.

I know of only one other summit journey to match it, indeed to surpass it. In May 1966 three men, H. G. (Godfrey) Symons, P. R. (Bill) Barnes and W. R. (Bill) Trauseld – I know them well, and have often climbed with them – walked from *Mont-aux-Sources* to *Giant's Castle*. The Openshaw-Blackburn patrol had pack-mules for their food and gear. These men carried everything on their backs. Not only so, but they kept to the escarpment edge the whole way. The police patrol used, for some little distance, the inland Mopeli track, which is infinitely easier. Others have also done the journey in this way. The edge of the escarpment is not only deeply indented, doubling the distance covered, but it is a wild jumble of hills and valleys, and I know of few more exhausting things than to travel along it, with a heavy pack, at an altitude of over 3 000 metres. These three men did the whole trip on foot in ten days, which included heavy snow, wind and rain. On May 15 Eddie Brokensha dropped them three tins of beer from his light Cessna plane, on to the summit of *Champagne Castle*. Otherwise they saw no-one.

And so the Travellers go on their way, appearing for a moment out of the mists of time to play their brief part against the magnificent backdrop of the mountains, and then to fade into oblivion. We salute them, for they played a vital part in the opening up of the Drakensberg.

CHAPTER V

OF MAPS AND MAPPING

> *"An exquisite piece of Geodesy may give as real a pleasure, and be as genuine a source of pride, as the masterpieces of art and literature."*
> —ARTHUR R. HINKS

In one of his essays Alpha of the Plough remarks that maps are the magic carpet that whisks one away to sunny lands and serener days. I would say that they are "magic casements opening on the foam of perilous seas in faery lands forlorn". To browse over a good map of a country you have known and loved is to bring back after many years nostalgic memories, while to study a map of the unknown is to excite the imagination and call up visions as few other things can do.

But maps do more than this. A careful study of early maps reveals immediately how much is known of a particular stretch of country at a particular time, although it must always be remembered that the map-maker is usually at least ten years in arrears of local knowledge.

There are no early maps of the Drakensberg. The first map of Natal showing the Drakensberg that I have been able to trace is the one included in Captain Allen Gardiner's *Narrative of a Journey to the Zooloo Country*, dated 1836. This latter is a very rough map, compiled by Gardiner himself, and it formed the basis of all future maps of Natal up to the early fifties. The Drakensberg is merely indicated by a straight line running roughly from north-east to south-west through a blank stretch of country, and no names at all are given, apart from "Saddleback", already mentioned.

In 1846 William Stanger, the Surveyor-General, complained that all available maps were full of mistakes. The coastline had been surveyed by the Admiralty, and was fairly correct. Inland topographical details were few and largely conjectural, and the Drakensberg, which was still a blank straight line, was invariably located 112 km too far to the east.

The first map of Natal to make an attempt at straightening things out was issued by Wyld in 1850. This map measures 40,6 cm x 55,9 cm and is to a scale of one inch to 8⅛ miles.

About the same time Stanger, the Surveyor-General, brought out the first official map of Natal to a scale of 1 inch to 9 miles. Again, the details as far as the Drakensberg is concerned, are meagre.

In 1861 Major Grantham, as we have seen, was engaged by the War Office on a map of Natal for military purposes. This appeared in 1863, and was a large map in four sections, each section measuring 96,5 cm x 167,6 cm and the scale was one inch to 3,8 miles. Although Grantham spent some considerable time in the Drakensberg, his map is still woefully lacking in detail. The line of the Berg is more accurate, but the only place-names given are *Cathkin Peak or Champagne Castle*, *Giant's Castle*, Bushman's River, Bushman's Pass (later known as Langalibalele Pass), Little Tugela and Tugela. Another military map, compiled by the Intelligence Branch of the Quartermaster General's Department in June 1879, is little better, its chief interest lying in the two remarks inserted on the country to the west of the Drakensberg, "Deep rocky valleys infested by Wild Bushmen", and "Very Wild and little-known Country inhabited by Bushmen".

For further information on Natal maps, and on the details they supply on the Drakensberg, the reader is referred to Appendix 3.

The first map of the Drakensberg *per se* is the one which accompanied the article in the

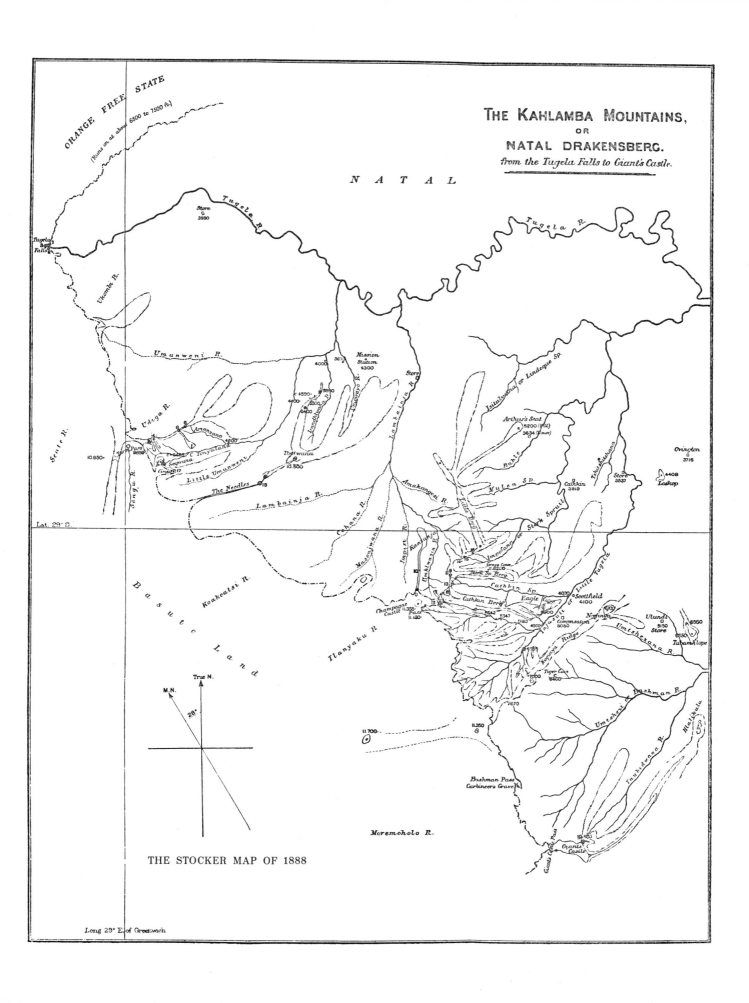

THE STOCKER MAP OF 1888

Alpine Journal of 1889, describing the Stocker climbs in the Drakensberg, to which we referred in the last Chapter. This map is a land-mark in the opening-up of the Drakensberg, and throws a flood of light on our knowledge of this mountain region at that time. It covers the whole area from *Mont-aux-Sources* to *Giant's Castle*, and though far from perfect, is a complete change from all the maps we have had so far. The map is based on the map of Alexander Mair, Land Surveyor of Natal, issued in 1875, but where the extra information comes from we are not told. The Alexander Mair map has only eight names in the Drakensberg region, Tugela Waterfall (at the *Amphitheatre*), Tugela River, Losonjo River (Umlambonja River?), *Cathkin Peak or Champagne Castle*, Injasuti or Little Tugela River, Bushman's River Pass, Bushman's River, and *Giant's Castle*.

The Stocker map has no less than 47 names. Two or three of these are a little difficult to identify to-day, but most are recognisable. As this map is such an important landmark, we give all these names, together with their modern equivalents in brackets, and the map itself is reproduced on the previous page.

Tugela Falls
Woodhouse Kop (*Sentinel?*)
South Tugela Gate (*Eastern Buttress?*)
Mont-aux-Sources
Tugela River
Ukombi River (Singati?)
Umunweni River (Mnweni River)
Udiga River (Mbundini River?)
Tarn Pass (Rockeries Pass)
Imponjwana (*Mponjwana*, or *Rockeries Tower*)
Umunweni Castle (*Rockeries*)
Two peaks of Umponqwasi (Two *Mnweni Needles*)
Amanzana River
Tonyalana River (Ntonjelan' eshonalanga)
Little Umunweni (Ntonjelan' ephumalanga)
Segwana Cirque (*Saddle*)
Ibotwana (*Cathedral Peak**)
Two peaks (*Outer* and *Inner Horns*)
The Needles (*Chessmen*)
Lambainja River (Umlambonja)
Cohana River (Ndedema River?)
Masonjwana River (Masongwana)
Impisi River (Nkosazana)
Kantunja (*Gatberg, Ntunja*)
Umhlwazin River (Mhlwazini)
Kantunja Arête (*Dragon's Back*)
Champagne Castle
Pass (Ship's Prow Pass)
Cathkin Peak
Inkosana (*Monk's Cowl*)
Sterk Horn
Umhlwazin Eland Pass (Hlatikulu Nek)
Isiwa Nimpumalanga or East Kranz (Eastern precipices of *Champagne Castle*)
Impofana or Sterk Spruit

* He may, however, be giving the Zulu name for the Chessmen, which he calls the Needles, or of the whole Cathedral range. Ibotwana in Zulu means 'children'.

Gray's Cave (Basuto Caves)
Eagle Cave (Cave in right-hand lateral stream in Wonder Valley?)
Injasuti or Little Tugela
Scottfield
Compensation
Cathkin Spruit (Spitzberg Stream – Wonder Valley)
Noginya Ridge (Negenya: Cloudland's Col)
Tiger Cave
Umtshexi or Bushman's River (Mtshezi)
Bushman's Pass
Inubidwana River (Ncibidwane)
Giant's Castle
Giant's Castle Pass

It is, indeed, a notable increase in our knowledge of the Drakensberg.

Not the least interesting feature of this map are the two peaks on a high ridge, stretching westwards into Lesotho, about 15 km south of *Champagne Castle*. They are marked 11 350 and 11 700. These two unnamed peaks are the *Injasuti* and *Makheke*. This latter peak, it will be noticed, is 345 feet higher than *Champagne Castle*, according to the figures given in the Stocker map. And yet right up to the early 1930's this fact was completely missed by subsequent cartographers, who usually gave *Champagne Castle* as the highest point in the Drakensberg area. That the Stockers knew of this still higher point 83 years ago, and gave its height with considerable accuracy, long before the days of systematic surveying, is quite remarkable. For the Stockers were right! *Makheke is* higher than *Champagne Castle*, by 276 feet.

What, then, is the highest point in the Drakensberg, and is the highest point in the Drakensberg the same as the highest point in Southern Africa?

The story of the search for this highest point is an interesting one. For many years *Mont-aux-Sources* was accorded the honour. Although mountaineers from the earliest days doubted this, the error has been perpetuated in some Geography books down to the present time. In 1922 Bassett-Smith and Cameron, two mountaineers who were amongst the first to climb in the Drakensberg after the Stockers, gave it as their opinion that the highest point in the range was "a point on a ridge a few miles north of *Champagne Castle*". They were almost certainly referring to *Cleft Peak*, in the Cathedral area.

But as time went on rumours of a high ridge west of *Injasuti* kept cropping up. This ridge forms the watershed of the Bafali and the Sanqebethu Rivers, and culminates in several particularly high peaks. In 1938 Col. Park Gray, grandson of old David Gray, and Mr. J. van Heyningen, the forester at Cathkin Peak, climbed to the top of *Champagne Castle* with a spirit level, and with this primitive instrument established the fact that at least one peak on this ridge, subsequently known to be *Makheke*, was almost certainly higher than the peak they were standing on. They proceeded on to this peak, climbed it, and built a cairn of stones on the summit, in which they left a bottle with their names and the date. They named the peak "Gray's Peak". A couple of kilometres to the north-east and north-west were two other peaks, only slightly lower than the one they were standing on. This is usually quoted as the first ascent of Gray's Peak, but it must have been climbed before 1888, for the Stockers gave its height as 11 700 ft., and heights in those days were almost invariably computed from aneroid barometer readings, taken on the spot.

In April 1945 Des Watkins and Charles Gloster visited the area, taking three days to reach the three peaks, *Makheke*, *Ubutswane* and *Mafadi*. The highest, *Makheke*, (Gray's Peak) was easily distinguished as it was capped with two layers of basalt. The other two had only one basalt rock band. They climbed *Makheke*, and estimated its height by aneroid barometer as 3 488 metres, only 27 metres higher than its subsequent official height. On their return they had a bad time. Rain set in and heavy mist blanketed the valleys. They set their course by compass for *Champagne Castle*, but compass readings in this rocky area are notoriously faulty, and they came out at *Ndedema Dome*, 30 degrees off course, two days overdue, and suffering from lack of food and exposure.

A year later Des Watkins was back again, with an Abney level this time. Assuming *Champagne Castle* to be 3 429 metres, he made *Makheke* just over 3 520 metres, slightly higher this time than his previous reading. Actually, *Champagne Castle* is only 3 377 metres, and compensating for this error, Watkins' reading should have been 3 468 metres for *Makheke*, only 7 metres out from its correct height, a remarkably accurate figure considering the instrument he was using. He also fixed the heights of *Mafadi* as 3 to 4½ metres lower than *Makheke*, and *Ubutswane* very slightly lower than *Mafadi*.

About the same time, on July 20 and 21 of 1946, with the controversy at its height, I set out with Ian Clarke of Cathkin Park Hotel, John Harwin of the University of Natal, and David Paton, son of Dr. Alan Paton. We lugged a dumpy-level to the top of *Champagne Castle*, and established definitely that there were at least two peaks on the ridge running westwards from *Injasuti*, higher than the point we were standing on. Of course we could not compute their exact heights, nor could we compensate for the curvature of the earth, but we estimated that they were between 35 m to 45 m higher.

For the next five years *Makheke* stood as the highest point in Southern Africa south of *Kilimanjaro*.

In December 1950 Des Watkins was back for the third time in a final effort to establish the exact height of *Makheke*. This time he had with him Barry Anderson, a Durban surveyor, and much more sophisticated instruments. They made the height of *Makheke* on this occasion 3 461 metres, which was dead on the mark. But to their amazement and excitement they saw another peak, 27 kilometres to the south-west, which was definitely higher than *Makheke*. No computation of its height was possible, but obviously it had to be visited.

They did this three months later. On March 24, 1951 they set out with six other men, including Roy Goodwin, a student surveyor, up the Mohlezi Pass, with proper survey instruments. They climbed to the top of the Pass, and then headed inland for 6½ kilometres to the new peak, which they climbed on Sunday, March 25. Their survey instruments established its height as 3 482 metres, 31 metres higher than *Makheke*. A Basutho chief in the area gave its name as "*Thabantshonyana*", meaning "The Little Black Mountain".

From the summit their view was breathtaking. They could see the top of the Berg from *Mont-aux-Sources* in the north to Qacha's Nek in the south, and in front almost the whole of Natal.

It only remains to add that on February 25, 1954, this peak was finally, and officially, established as the highest point in Africa south of *Kilimanjaro*. On that day Mr. Hugh Peake, Colonial Surveyor, and Mr. A. Bisschoff, Agricultural Officer for Mokhotlong District, climbed to the top of the mountain with the necessary survey instruments. They checked and cross-checked both the name of the mountain with local chiefs, and their figures. The name, they found, was not quite the same as that given to Des Watkins and Barry Anderson in 1951, *Thabantshonyana*, "The Little Black Mountain". They established it as "*Thabana Ntlenyana*", "The Beautiful Little Mountain", and so it stands to-day. They gave the height as 3 482 m, and *Makheke* as 3 461 m, confirming exactly the figures obtained by Des Watkins and Barry Anderson in 1951. The mountain lies 22 km south-west of *Giant's Castle*, and 27 km from *Makheke*. (Lat. 29° 28' 07" S., Long. 29° 16' 08" E.)

But this does not quite settle the question as to which is the highest peak in the *Drakensberg*, for neither *Thabana Ntlenyana* nor *Makheke* are on the watershed. They lie several kilometres inland. The six highest peaks in the Drakensberg, according to the latest survey figures, are as follows:

56

Injasuti	3 459 metres	
Champagne Castle	3 377 metres	
Popple Peak	3 325 metres	
Giant's Castle	3 316 metres	
Mont-aux-Sources	3 282 metres	
Cleft Peak	3 281 metres	

Four of these peaks, *Injasuti*, *Champagne Castle*, *Popple Peak* and *Mont-aux-Sources* are set inland slightly, but as they are all on the watershed they have been included.

After the Stocker map of 1888 we had to wait 40 years before the first really accurate and authentic map of the Drakensberg became available. In 1927 Mr. (later Professor) G. M. J. Sweeney produced a map of the Drakensberg which, right down to the present day, has maintained its reputation and its popularity as the most accurate and authoritative map of the Drakensberg. It was a remarkable piece of work, and was undertaken to meet the needs of the infant Natal Mountaineering Club. Mr. Sweeney based his map on the farm surveys in the Surveyor-General's office, which were incorporated in a large wall map known as Holmden's Map of Natal. The scale was half inch to the mile.

Mr. Sweeney's completed map was to the same scale, measured 52 cm x 73,5 cm, and covered the whole area from *Mont-aux-Sources* to *Giant's Castle*. It proved an immediate success, and passed through many editions, the "Bible" of Natal mountaineers for many years. It is still in use to-day.

In 1945 J. E. L. Peck and I mapped the Cathkin area by plane table, and with subsequent information extracted from aerial photographs, produced a map 51 cm x 65,5 cm, to the scale of 2 inches to the mile. This map was published by the *Cape Times* in five colours.

A year later Mr. Albert van der Riet, of the Cathedral Peak Hotel, asked me to produce a similar map of the Cathedral area, and I spent my holidays during the next couple of years on the job, finding it extraordinarily interesting and exhilarating. Added to the delight of familiarising myself with one of the most beautiful areas in the whole Drakensberg was the constant challenge of the mathematical problems which kept arising, and I am no mathematician! This map also was eventually published in five colours by the *Cape Times*, its east-west axis matching with the Cathkin Map. These two maps formed the basis of two large relief model maps which I built for Cathkin Park Hotel and Cathedral Peak Hotel, to the scale of 6 inches to the mile. In 1963 I built a similar relief model map of the Giant's Castle area for the Natal Parks, Game and Fish Preservation Board.

To give an idea of what the work involved, it may not be out of place if I close this Chapter with a few pages from my Log Book of 1947. (The map on page 110 will be found helpful.)

"Friday, October 3, 1947. Left Estcourt about 4 p.m. with the intention of mapping the line of the escarpment north and south of the *Umlambonja Buttress*, and the main peaks of the Cathedral Range. Arrived at Cathedral Peak Hotel 6 p.m. Sat up until nearly twelve o'clock with George Thomson. He has a fine set of photographs of all his famous climbs. He told me the story of his attempts, with Peter Pope-Ellis and young Henning, to recover the body of Tom Pinkney, the young Johannesburg man who had fallen to his death down the Amphitheatre Wall a few days previously. It must have been a most gruelling climb – the worst, he said, in his experience, and if George says it was bad, it must have been! Bad weather had been the cause of their failure.

"Saturday, October 4, 1947. Left Hotel 7.20 a.m. and made my way up the Umlambonja with a very heavy pack – a gruelling slog, boulder-hopping for about four hours. The view, as I climbed higher, and the *Chessmen* and the *Buttress* closed in, was magnificent. Arrived at Twins Cave about 3 p.m. Found it without difficulty on north side of the *Twins*, very roomy and snug. Altitude must have been close on 9 000 feet. Unfortunately on the way up I had slipped and

fallen, and I found I had broken eight of the dozen eggs I was carrying in a billy-can. After extracting egg-shells, made egg-flip out of the sticky mess which remained at the bottom of the can. Then sat outside on a ledge, very tired, smoked my pipe and admired the view, one of the finest I have seen. Full in front, *South Saddle Peak, Outer Mnweni Needle, Devil's Tooth* and *Eastern Buttress*. Ground dropped sharply from cave mouth to valley of the Ntonjelane, and from there simply a mass of jumbled hills, valleys and minor peaks stretching across to the Free State. Watched the shadows lengthen – blue and purple in the gorges, fading to softer hues in the distance, the whole capped with a quietly-tinted sunset. Then went in to cook supper and prepare for the night. Found fair amount of timber about, but not enough to indulge in the luxury of a camp fire. Water the main difficulty. There is a slight drip in the cave, enough to fill a billy-can overnight, and that was all. Slept well.

"*Sunday, October 5, 1947.* Up at dawn, breakfast, and started climbing by 6 a.m. Fairly stiff but short climb brought me to the summit of the escarpment. Established the first flag-beacon by 7 a.m. Thereafter established a further five along the escarpment, including the final control-beacon, the latter at the summit of an unnamed peak. Very tired by 11 a.m., so had lunch at the top of this peak, boiling some Oxo. Returned along beacon route, and took shots from each one, thus mapping in some three to four miles of escarpment. Back at cave soon after 3 p.m. to find baboons had been busy in my absence. The camp looked as if it had been well-nigh wrecked – paper and cardboard packages ripped to pieces and strewn all over the place. Every package had been torn open, three packets of biscuits and four remaining eggs wolfed. The only things that had escaped were the tinned stuff and a few other items tied up in bags. Raisins strewn all over the floor. I shall be short of food before the end of the trip. Pipe outside and watched sunset. Read till fairly late. During the night the wind changed and moaned eerily about the rock pinnacles. It looked as if mist was banking up.

"*Monday, October 6, 1947.* Woke once during the night, at 1.30 a.m., to find heavy mist. Morning dawned clear, but mist filled all the valleys below. Unforgettable sight – high above the clouds, sun rising above them, isolated peaks rising sharply black through white wool. After breakfast attempted to climb the *Twins*. Actually there are three peaks, the south-west one, the highest; the north-east; and a central one. The north-east one was easy. I attempted the south-west one first of all from the west face. This attempt failed completely. I then tackled the north face, and got to within 20 feet of the summit, but was forced back: it was too risky without a second man. Then tried the east face, and an easy but exhilarating climb brought me to the summit at about 8.30 a.m. Back to camp, and read until lunch time.

"After lunch took the plane-table and tripod up to the summit of *N.E. Twin* for a few readings. The summit was only a few feet square, and already contained the usual cairn of stones. There was just room for myself and the tripod. I have never before worked on such a lonely spot, and with such a sense of isolation and exposure. On the one side, a sheer 2 000 feet drop, was the Umlambonja. On the other, not quite so sheer, the Ntonjelane glittered like a steel thread at the bottom of the valley. I seemed to be not of the earth, detached, remote, suspended in mid-air. Clouds were gathering, and the mutter of distant thunder drove me down in a hurry. Back to camp, to watch the storm break over *South Saddle*. Remembered the cheese at supper but could not find it. Hell, but those baboons were real connoisseurs! They must have finished their meal with biscuits and cheese!

"*Tuesday, October 7, 1947.* Up early, and off to the summit again. Making for my first beacon of Sunday, I worked in a northerly direction this time, fixing plane-table points along the escarpment edge. Reached head of Ntonjelane Pass, and met a cavalcade of 13 pack-horses carrying mealies, and three Basutho in pink balaclavas and red and green blankets. The Ntonjelane Pass is one of the main routes between Natal and Basutoland. This party was probably taking mealies, purchased in Bergville or Winterton, back into the kraals of Basutoland, in exchange for their wool. I descended half-way down the Pass in order to get some cross-shots on to the Cathedral Range, now to the south of me. This is a view seldom seen by the ordinary tourist, and was grand beyond all telling – *Cathedral* and the *Bell* heaving themselves up into the sky; *Outer Horn* and *Inner Horn*, grim and forbidding; the *Chessmen*, peak on minor peak; the *Mitre* and the *Twins*. I could just see the cave in the distance, across the valley. There are two Ntonjelanes, Ntonjelan' ephumalanga, and Ntonjelan' eshonalanga (Ntonjelane of the Dawn and Ntonjelane of the Sunset) i.e. East and West. I was at the head of the former, and a lovely valley it looked, green and beautifully wooded. I had never been into it before. I was able to map all the headwaters and tributaries of this stream – a good day's work – and was back in camp, pretty tired, by midday.

"In the afternoon I climbed up to a narrow ledge, half-way up the south-west *Twin*, with my book, a pocket edition of Izaak Walton's *Compleat Angler*, and all the world laid out below me. Here for a brief while I sat as quietly and as free from care as ever old Izaak used to do under his sycamore tree, and wandered with him the pleasant meadows and the scented cowslip banks beneath Amwell Hill. I have finished my work on the summit, and I think I shall drop down into the Ntonjelane of the Dawn tomorrow, a day earlier than I had planned. I don't want to be caught up here in bad weather, and it might change at any moment. It is a glorious afternoon, the only sound being the sighing of the wind in the crags. Down below, miles it seems, but really only a few thousand feet, the Ntonjelane threads its way through the valley. Beyond, range upon range of smoke-blue hills stretch away into the Free State, with *South Saddle*, noble peak, standing guard over it all. I have just watched an eagle having a bit of sport with a dassie. The eagle swooped by with a "whoosh" of its wings, the dassie struggling in its claws. Suddenly the dassie broke loose and fell, but the eagle wheeled and dived, caught it again, and was off.

"After supper that night I took my pipe and coffee out as usual on to the slope in front of the cave for the last time, to watch the sunset. A storm was brewing, thunder was growling and muttering amongst the crags to the north. I don't think I have ever seen more remarkable colouring. A queer, greenish light seemed to pervade everything. Away in the distance *Eastern Buttress* and *Devil's Tooth* glowed a rich ultramarine. The *Outer Mnweni Needle* and its attendant foothills were draped in a paler green, while nearer, *South Saddle* and the whole line of the Berg gleamed a dark jade, unearthly and macabre. I watched breathlessly when suddenly one single peak, far-off *Mponjwana* jutting up above *South Saddle*, shone out a fiery, smoky red, as if lit by internal fires, a crimson finger in a world of green. It must have just caught the last rays of the setting sun. For two minutes it seemed to throb and glow with red heat. Then the scene darkened. The nearer peaks turned jet black; the Mnweni Mountains and the far *Amphitheatre* still burned blue, while the sky turned a dull, angry red. Then, as if a gigantic hand had moved across the scene, all colour was wiped away. The reds and the blues and the greens drained off, and the stars were shining in a jet-black sky.

"*Wednesday, October 8, 1947.* The afternoon of a strenuous morning. I am sitting at the entrance of my new home, the Ntonjelane Caves. I am not sorry to reach this pleasant land. The top is grand beyond all telling, but it is an austere grandeur, and life there is always a battle, a battle for warmth, a battle for water, a battle for firewood, a battle against fatigue, sometimes a battle for life itself. The air is thin, and you use up energy at a terrific rate, living at twice the pace you do at lower altitudes. You do not sleep much: you do not need much sleep. Around are bare rocks, no trees, and little grass. Stunted bushes, six inches high, provide variety and firewood. Life is lean and streamlined. Down here, in the valleys of the Little Berg, the air is mild, the grass is lush; there are flowers and the sound of running water, and trees with cool shade, and the glow of your camp fire at night is warm and relaxing. I think I know what Abraham must have felt when he reached the Promised Land after his long trek across the desert.

"I had left Twin Cave at 7.15 a.m., again with a heavy pack, and had entered what was new country to me, with only the map to guide me. I headed straight down from the cave into the valley below, five thousand feet, taking it easily, and reaching the bottom in a couple of hours. Then a pleasant walk of an hour over gentle grass slopes brought me to the Caves. Their position was marked roughly on Sweeney's map, and I found them without much difficulty. They are in a lateral valley of the Ntonjelane, a tiny, wooded gorge, a truly lovely spot. The caves are high up in the gorge, very roomy, with a large waterfall flowing over at one end, right under the south face of *South Saddle*. In front one looks out over the yellow-woods and down into the gorge, where the stream murmurs. *Saddle Peak* dominates all. The continuous sound of the waterfall is like music after the monotonous drip-drip-drip at Twins Cave, into the billy-can, regularly every ten seconds. I can see the white flash of the waterfall through the green as I write.

"I celebrated my arrival by going down into the stream for a plunge. Water was far too precious up on top to waste on washing. I found a lovely pool of frothing water, and it was icy cold. It was the first time I had had my clothes off since leaving the Hotel. I spent the afternoon getting the cave ship-shape, building a fireplace, checking supplies and writing up my Log. Later on a storm broke, but it soon cleared, and the night was clear and starlit. I sat by a roaring fire with Izaak Walton, and had a grand evening.

"*Thursday, October 9, 1947*. After breakfast at 6 a.m. I left the cave and set off up the slope. The job was to map the whole of the Cathedral Range, from the *Twins* to the *Three Puddings*. I first of all climbed half way up *South Saddle*, where I took my first shots. I then made my way eastwards along the crest of the ridge between Saddle Stream and Ntonjelan' ephumalanga, running parallel to the Cathedral Range. This was the ridge which John Peck had climbed in July 1945, when he was mapping the Rockeries area, the day we sub-camped in Saddle Stream. To the north I could see the spot where we had camped, away down in the valley. Above it was the ridge in which our cave had been situated, and *North Saddle*, and the two *Mnweni Needles* and *Rockeries Tower*, and the Pass we had struggled up in a howling gale, two years previously. In the other direction, the Cathedral Range, steel-blue in the early morning light. I should imagine that this ridge, on which I was working, would give one one of the finest panoramas in the whole of the Drakensberg. I finished the job by midday, including a complete photographic record, and then made off up the ridge and so back to the cave. I arrived home pretty well all in, and slept most of the afternoon. The heat had been terrific during the day, and I had been at it for six days with hardly a break. I woke up at 5 p.m. to the crash of thunder reverberating through the gorge. It was the biggest storm we had had so far. Spent the evening again by the fire with my book. Still pretty tired – I shall have to have a couple of days off.

"*Friday, October 10, 1947*. Woke up this morning to find the gorge blanketed in mist. Luckily I had decided to take at least one day off, so it doesn't matter. Lazed in bed, and had a late breakfast. (By late I mean 6.30 a.m. instead of 5.30!) Spent an hour or so checking over the map, and then snuggled down with my book.

"I have been trying to work out why I do this sort of thing. Here am I, a fairly respectable member of society, living in a cave miles away from civilisation, in unknown country, doing my own cooking, getting tired, and hot, and dirty, and enjoying it. It is too easy to say I needed a change, or that the peace of nature drew me, or that I had a job of mapping to do. Why do it at all? I don't think it is entirely because of a love of nature. It goes deeper than that. I have a theory that it is a deep-seated, subconscious protest against all the artificiality and ease of modern civilized life. We lead such superficial lives, in square houses, in regimented streets, where the procuring of the essentials of life – food, clothing, shelter – is no problem at all. These things are no further off than the nearest telephone. Life was not meant to be like this. Here I have only myself to depend on. I have to find shelter, I have to carry my own food and bedding with me, I have to find my own way without any sign-posts. If I conk in or get lost, or the weather changes, I have only myself to rely on to get me out of the mess. If I sprain my ankle, I can't telephone the nearest doctor. There is no-one to help me. And life is reduced to its essentials – food, warmth, shelter. It is simplified. I believe it is good for a man that he should sometimes break loose and go primitive once again. And all this does not mean to say that I shall not appreciate a soft bed, a decent meal, my wife and my children, my books and my job, when I get back!

"Mist lifted at about 11 a.m. Went out photographing, back for lunch, read and slept during the afternoon. By supper time I was really hungry: during the last few days I have had to ration myself very carefully in order to come out, and the food position is quite a problem. I shall probably have enough if I go carefully, but the monotony of the diet is beginning to tell. I am trying experiments to vary it. Yesterday, for instance, I made a pudding for lunch out of the powdered rusks I had left, chocolate, sugar and dried milk, boiled up into a mush and seasoned with raisins. To-day, stewed prunes and apples, (usually eaten dry), served with cream (dried milk at double strength). My mouth fairly waters when I think of the cheese and the biscuits and the eggs those baboons wolfed. May the dirty blighters rot in hell for it! I am still pretty tired, and shall take tomorrow off. It is going to be a long march home. I shall leave here the day after tomorrow. I calculate I am about one and a half days march off from the Hotel (I intend making my way down the Ntonjelane, up the Cathedral Ridge, past the *Three Puddings*, and so home via Ganapu Ridge.) That should get me in about midday Monday, but I think I shall try and do it in one day. (The reason for this is *not* the vision of a nice, juicy steak awaiting me when I get in!). The only thing that worries me is the possibility of mist. Then I should be in real trouble. I shall be travelling through unknown country. I could find my way on a clear day, but not in mist, through the maze of ridges and valleys that lie between me and the Hotel. If the mist comes down, I shall have to 'stay put' until it clears, in which case a long-suffering Education Department will give me the sack for not being back on time – unless I die of starvation meanwhile!

"The usual storm in the afternoon, and then dusk, and time to light the fire for the evening. I have been sitting at the cave entrance with my usual pipe. What a contrast between this view and the one from Twins Cave! Here, massed green foliage of ageless yellow-woods, a flashing waterfall, and only fifty yards away, the brown, enclosing walls of the gorge. There, limitless miles of mountain, hill, valley, crag and stream laid out, a patch-work quilt, six thousand feet below, sweeping into the distance. The cosiness of a world in miniature, and the grandeur of limitless horizons.

"*Saturday, October 11, 1947.* Opened the fourth tin of meat for breakfast. I brought five with me. The previous three were incidents: this was an event! I lingered long and lovingly over it. After breakfast, went down to the Ntonjelane. It was a grand day, a day of bracing wind and clear sunlight. Throughout the long hours of the morning endless battalions of massed white clouds marched steadily south along the ramparts of the Berg. The bottle-brushes were out in bloom, and the scarlet flame of their flowers, the green trees of the valley, the rippling stream and the steel-blue peaks crowned with the blue sky and the racing clouds, made a picture I shall long remember. It was a photographic paradise, but I had finished my last spool the previous day.

"I found a shady tree beside a suitable pool, stripped, and washed my one and only shirt and pants. Then lay out on the grass with a book while they were drying. When they were dry, a plunge myself in the cold water, and for the first time in a week I felt really clean. Back to the cave for lunch, and then I spent the afternoon on the slope of the hill above the gorge. Never have I so wanted a roll of film, but I consoled myself after a while, for I knew that no mere nitrate of silver could ever fix these changing lights and colours, these blue shadows that chased over the long green hills, and the far peaks.* On three sides they rose, peak after peak, in changing hourly beauty, and on the fourth the broadening Valley of the Ntonjelane, green and lovely beyond telling, stabbed with the flame of the bottle-brushes. And still those piled, fantastic masses of shining cumulus cloud, massed battalions of them, marched inexorably southwards over a prussian-blue parade ground. Only a painter could have caught the glory and the majesty of it.

"Back in the twilight, by a circuitous route, discovering another set of caves on the way, to supper, and the cosy glow of the camp fire flickering on the walls of the cave. At dusk the cohorts of the clouds were still streaming south, but each one now was a golden glow of fire in the light of the setting sun.

"*Sunday, October 12, 1947.* I was early astir, cooked breakfast, and then packed. By 6.45 a.m. I was on my way. I first of all followed the Ntonjelane down the valley for a couple of miles, then struck right up the bed of the main Cathedral stream, and so up on to the ridge which carried me right up under the crags of the *Outer Pudding*. It was another glorious day. The mist was lifting from the peaks. The grass was crisply green under foot, and the slopes alive with the first flowers of spring. Every little gully was crowded with the blue *Scilla natalensis* and the creamy-white *Anemone fanninii*, while every now and then I came across great patches of red everlastings. But it was the grass which was so lovely. It was like a green flame. The climb up from the valley was really exhilarating, my pack easy, my heart light, and by eleven o'clock I was topping the hills that look down into the shy Nxaye, and had linked up with the area I had mapped last July. Down into the Nxaye, where I stripped and plunged and had lunch, and then up on to Ganapu Ridge, and home by way of Baboon Rock (Memo: must get Albert† to change the name of this lovely rock!) Hotel was reached about 4 p.m. where a hot bath, dinner, and a sixty-mile drive home under the stars awaited me.

"*POSTSCRIPT:* I think I know the answer to the little problem I considered on page 60. I can best explain it by the story of the lunatic who spent his time bashing his head against a stone wall. A visitor stood watching him for some time, and then said, 'My good man, why are you doing this? You surely can't like it!' 'Ah,' said the lunatic, 'perhaps not. But you've no idea how lovely it is when you stop!'"

*This was before colour film became generally available.
† Mr. Albert van der Riet, proprietor of the Cathedral Peak Hotel.

CHAPTER VI

CLIMBERS ALL

*Great things are done when men
and mountains meet.*
—WILLIAM BLAKE

The Natal Mountain Club was formed on 15th April 1919.

Actually, this was not the first attempt at starting organised climbing in the Drakensberg. In 1910 a Drakensberg Club had been formed, with Judge Broome as President. But the war had intervened, the Club had ceased to function, and the only reminder that we have of it to-day is *Broome Hill* in the Royal Natal National Park.

But by 1919 the war was over. The Drakensberg was now much more accessible, spirits were high, and a small group of enthusiasts had already penetrated into the unknown recesses of the mountains, and had found them full of promise. The year 1919 marks the beginning of a new era in Drakensberg climbing history.

On Tuesday evening, 15th April of that year a public meeting was held in the Town Hall, Pietermaritzburg, with the Hon. G. T. Plowman, Administrator of Natal, in the chair. On the motion of Col. J. Fraser, seconded by Mr. (later Dr.) J. S. Henkel, it was decided to found a Mountaineering Club, with Sir George Plowman as its first President and D. W. Bassett-Smith as its Secretary. The Natal Mountaineering Club was off to a good start. Its initial membership stood at 37, but within a year had increased to nearly 150.

The moving spirit behind the formation of the Club was Hubert Botha-Reid. He gathered round him a band of enthusiastic climbers, amongst them D. W. Bassett-Smith, R. G. Kingdon, Dr. Park Ross, W. E. Marriott, "Doc" Ripley, Maurice Sweeney, and the systematic exploration of the Drakensberg began. Gradually the infant Club grew from sturdy and adventurous youth to full maturity. By 1937 the standard of its climbers was so high that in that year all parties at the July Camp in the Injasuti were led by Natal men. In 1953, after an independent existence of 34 years, the Club merged with the Mountain Club of South Africa, and in 1969, on Friday, October 31st, it celebrated its Jubilee at a magnificent banquet at the Imperial Hotel, Pietermaritzburg.

A strict, but unwritten, code of ethics was soon developed, respected by all members of the Club. No climb involving any unjustifiable risk was ever to be undertaken. Every climber had a strong sense of responsibility towards his companions, to whom he, in turn, entrusted his own safety in the certain knowledge that they, on their part, would not let him down. At all times he took their own limitations into consideration, as well as his own, especially if he was the leader. It was axiomatic that the accepted leader in every group had to be obeyed implicitly, and that the basis of sound climbing was comradeship and co-operation, and not competition. The result has been that accidents have been rare, with no fatal accidents in over 50 years at organised Club meets, a record matched by few mountain clubs in the world.

It was early decided to hold an annual camp in the Drakensberg during July, and in 1920 the first of these was held at Mont-aux-Sources. There followed a series of camps, magnificently organised, superbly run, which soon became the Mecca for mountaineers throughout South Africa, and even from overseas, the only failure being a somewhat disastrous one in 1926, in the Malutis. Here the weather was bitterly cold, the transport broke down, as well as the catering arrangements. Its only memory now is preserved in the well-known camp song, "Oh, Malutis, never again!"

The organisers of these Camps soon developed a set routine. Len Carr, the caterer, added to his laurels year after year with better and better menus, and Dorothy Robbins became the accepted Organiser of the Camps, doing a magnificent job which was justly recognised in 1961 by the award of the coveted Gold Badge. (This is a Badge awarded annually to a mountaineer who has rendered signal service to the cause of mountaineering.) On occasions the various Berg Hotels helped out with the catering, notably the Zunckels at National Park Hotel, Albert van der Riet of Cathedral Peak Hotel and Bill Gray of the Nest Hotel. A fine African staff was recruited, many of whom remained on year after year. On the last night of each camp a presentation would be made to them. With all the climbers gathered round, and the firelight flickering on their faces, and on the dark faces of the African men, Martin Winter would make the presentation. "*Lapha entabeni yoKhahlamba yindawo kaNkulunkulu,*" he would say. "*Thina siphuma edolobheni, lapho kukhona ukuduma okukhulu komsindo wokujaha kakhulu.*" (Here in the Drakensberg Mountains is the place of God. We have come from the towns, where there is the great thunder of hurry.)

At these camps climbers were divided up into small groups of seven to ten, care being taken to see that the various members of a team were suited to each other in age, temperament and skill. Each group was headed by an experienced climber who knew the area and was an expert cragsman. Meals were served in comfort in camp, on long wooden tables in the open air, and rough deal seats. Drums of hot water were kept going for those who rather shied at the icy dip in the Berg streams.

Best of all was the huge camp fire round which everyone gathered after the evening meal. An oval space was always reserved for this, surrounded by a screen of upright tambookie thatching-grass, for the night-winds in the Berg can bite to the bone. Here, in the centre, huge logs of protea and bottle-brush wood were piled, and soon the flames would crackle and leap, lighting up the climbers as they lay around wrapped in their warm blankets, pleasantly relaxed after the day's climb. And soon the songs would start up, traditional songs of the Natal Mountain Club, *Old Climbers, Bold Climbers; As we lie in the camp fire's golden glow; When on the slope you grunt and grope*, and many others, flung out uproariously on the night breeze, as it sighed in the long grass outside. It is then, as the leaping sparks fly upwards, that nostalgic memories of the early days come to the older club members, as they sit round the fire, memories of the special train that used to be provided by the Railways to convey campers from Maritzburg to the railhead at Bergville, memories of the arrival in the early hours of a grey winter's morning on the station platform, of the dash to the Hotel, where a magnificent breakfast of steaming coffee and smoking eggs and bacon awaited them, memories of Otto Zunckel's wagon as it rumbled into the mountains with their baggage and tents. There were no roads and no bridges, but the wagon always seemed to get there. Many walked the whole way from Bergville. The men wore knickerbocker suits and the women long skirts. There followed memories of the unconquered peaks and of forgotten climbs, of delicious home-made farm food, of bright purple Msobo jam, of the eager freshness of winter mornings, when the frosted grass crackled under your feet, and of the warm comradeship of the camp fire after the day's climb.

They must have been halcyon days in those early 1920's. A whole mountain world, unknown and unexplored, lay open to the climbers of yesterday. With bewildered delight they penetrated into untrodden valleys, gazed spell-bound into tremendous gorges and jagged chasms, and gasped in wonderment at the breath-taking view spread out below them from the summits of the peaks they climbed. "Bliss was it in that dawn to be alive."

Soon the knickerbocker suits and the skirts gave way to khaki clothing. The ladies threw away their skirts, and took to shorts. And soon the khaki shirts and shorts were no more, and the bright colours of the modern young man and his girl friend appeared on the scene. The long, heavy roll of grey blankets was bundled into the loft, and out came the light, down sleeping bags – blue, orange and red, and the gaily-coloured anorak. Beale's alpine rope gave way to the

64

light modern nylon rope, and the ox-wagon was replaced by the lorry and the motor-car. The last ox-wagon was used at the 1934 camp in the Mnweni Valley.

If equipment was primitive in those early days, conditions were even more so. There were no dehydrated foods, no well-defined Contour Path giving easy access from one area to another, no maps, no roads into the mountains. In December 1920 Bassett-Smith and Kingdon, after spending a couple of weeks in the Royal Natal National Park area, were unable to get back because both the Tugela and the Singati were in flood. They had to borrow horses from Mr. Williams, who was running the Hostel on *Goodoo* farm, and make a wide detour, riding up Oliviershoek Pass and on to Harrismith, where they caught a train for Natal. But what of all that? The world was young and the mountains called.

The Cape climbers, especially, who started to attend the Natal camps in 1921, found conditions very different from what they had been accustomed to. The country was wilder and much more rugged, the approaches long and difficult. There was often a long trek, two to three days in length, before the climber even reached the base of the mountain he wished to climb, very different from the Cape mountains, which you could reach in a few hours. Sub-camping was necessary. This was an especial hazard on the summit. In the early days it was considered far too dangerous to attempt a night out on the summit in winter. D. Gordon Mills, an experienced climber, said as late as 1930 that it was quite out of the question to sleep out on the summit at any altitude over 7 000 feet. It was not until 1936 that this was first tried. In July of that year Brian Godbold, Mark Frank, H. C. Hoets and Naomi Bokenham broke the taboo by sleeping out on the summit of *Cleft Peak*, (3 282 m). The snow was waist deep on the lower slopes, and the snow-fields stretched for miles around. They pitched their tiny tent on a level patch of stony ground. The stars glittered in a violet sky, and during the night their food and their boots froze, but they were well content.

Memories . . . And soon the fire dies slowly down, the golden moon climbs the sky and floods the valley, and the younger ones, huddled in their blankets, creep off one by one to their tents, for youth is headstrong and tempestuous, and demands long hours of sleep. But the old stagers, the 'abadala' (the old ones), stay on, for sleep comes hardly to the aged. They wrap their blankets more closely around them, and the pipes come out, and the talk turns to the older days, and to the men who were the pioneers in this unknown land and whose voices are now stilled forever. And the firelight flickers and grows dim, and overhead is the beating of wild wings . . .

On a day in 1900 Col. L. C. Amery, the "Times" war correspondent, stood on the summit of the *Amphitheatre* and gazed awestruck into the depths below. He had climbed to the summit by the easy route, allegedly with military despatches, though why he should climb to the summit of the Drakensberg with military despatches is a little difficult to understand. He descended, however, down the sheer wall of the Drakensberg. Twenty years later he claimed that this was a point midway between *Sentinel Peak* and *Eastern Buttress*, but this is even more difficult to accept than the military despatches! It is more likely to have been at a point just south of the *Eastern Buttress*, and this exploit is commemorated to-day by *Mt. Amery*, which is where it is thought he made his descent.

A few months earlier an even better-known climber had visited the same area. Dr. A. C. Stark was a retired medical practitioner, who was visiting South Africa at the time. He was a member of the Mountain Club of South Africa and of the British Alpine Club. A keen ornithologist, he was busy writing a book on South African birds. He had climbed extensively both in the Cape and in the Drakensberg, and often slept out alone in the mountains in pursuit of his hobby. It is fortunate that on the day he stood on the summit of the *Amphitheatre* he did not know the fate that awaited him within a few short weeks. When the Boer War broke out he volunteered for medical service in Ladysmith, and was killed by a Boer shell on 18th November 1899 as he left the front door of the Royal Hotel. The bronze plaque, let into the pavement, at the spot where he fell, is still to be seen. His four-volume work on South African birds was published after his death.

But it was a group of Free State climbers who first started organised climbing in the Drakensberg. In 1908 an eccentric Irishman, Tom Casement, appeared on the scenes. In 1909 he took over Rydal Mount Hotel in the Witzieshoek area. Rydal Mount was the gateway to the Mont-aux-Sources area in those days, and soon Tom Casement and his Basutho boy, Melatu, commenced a series of sensational climbs. Tom was the brother of Sir Roger Casement, who was hanged by the British in 1916 as a traitor, and it is possible that Sir Roger even accompanied Tom on some of his climbs, for he visited Rydal Mount round about 1910 or 1911.

Tom himself was a lovable, great-hearted rascal of a climber, headstrong, impetuous, and with an explosive vocabulary that secretly greatly delighted the ladies, who were always on tenterhooks as to what he would say next! He soon proved himself to be a magnificent climber and soon the *Amphitheatre*, *Sentinel Peak*, *Eastern Buttress*, and even peaks to the south, knew the call of his voice. We tell the story of some of these climbs in a later Chapter.

But then World War I broke out. Tom joined up and served with distinction in the South African forces, attaining the rank of Captain. After the war he lived a roving and restless life. For a time, in 1919, he was associated with Hans Merensky, prospecting for diamonds on the Vaal River, and might have become a wealthy man. But his restless disposition would not permit of his sticking to any job for any length of time. His brother's tragic fate, too, had distressed him greatly, and he placed himself in the hands of General Smuts. It was thought better that he should leave the country. Round about 1921 he returned to Ireland. Early in the 1940's he was drowned, tragically. His body was fished out of the waters of the Liffey early one morning. It was thought probable that, returning to his rooms the previous night, he had taken a short cut across the canal by a narrow plank bridge over the top of the lock gate, missed his footing in the darkness, and fallen in. At the time he was said to be an Inspector of coastal rockets, though what Tom would be doing with rockets is difficult to imagine. He probably didn't know much about them, but that wouldn't worry Tom in the slightest! A roisterous, lovable, swashbuckling fellow of a mountaineer!

From 1912 to 1914 Tom Casement was associated with a very different sort of climber. Father A. D. Kelly was a Father of the Sacred Mission, who had arrived in South Africa in 1902, younger brother of Father Herbert Kelly, the founder of the Mission. At the time Alfred Kelly was Priest Vicar of the Cathedral at Bloemfontein. In his day he had been a semi-blue for tennis at Oxford, and was tennis champion of the Orange Free State. Before coming to South Africa he had done a little climbing in the Lake District. He was almost totally deaf.

He soon started climbing in the Drakensberg with Tom Casement. He and Tom were in the party that first climbed *Cathkin Peak* in 1912. When they arrived at the head of the Monk's Ravine, where the really difficult part commences, Tom and Father Kelly went on ahead impetuously, leaving the rest of the party behind. Soon, however, they found themselves in difficulty, pinned like butterflies on the sheer face of the cliff, and neither able to move, the deaf padre on one end of the rope in a position suggesting earnest prayer, and Tom at the other, purple with fury and letting loose such a string of profanity as those ancient rocks had never heard. It was fortunate that the good padre was deaf! But they managed to extricate themselves, and soon rejoined the others. Father Kelly did most of his climbing in the Mont-aux-Sources area, but there is a tradition, unconfirmed, that he reconnoitred a route up *Monk's Cowl*.

In June 1915 he returned to England, continuing his work in the training of Sacred Missioners at their Headquarters at Kelham Hall, Newark. He still spent most of his holidays climbing in the Lake District. Did he ever, I wonder, while climbing those benign and gracious hills, think back on the terrifying precipices of the Drakensberg mountains which he had helped to scale? He died, after a short illness, on March 19th 1950, at the age of 77, a dedicated priest to the last.

Another noted climber at this time in the Mont-aux-Sources area, from Johannesburg this time, was W. J. Wybergh. He is chiefly remembered for his first successful ascent of *Sentinel Peak*. But when I think of W. J. Wybergh, it is not of that day in 1910 when he stood, the proud conqueror of *Sentinel*, but rather of that night in the winter of 1911, when he failed in his attempt on *Cathkin Peak*. He and Col. J. P. S. Woods, farming at *Heartsease*, had set out to climb the virgin peak via the South Gully. Up Monk's Ravine they went, and so into the Gully. But Woods began to suffer from mountain sickness, and went back, while Wybergh went on alone, with his Zulu guide, Nongale. The rock walls of the Gully began to close in around them, packed with snow and ice. Darkness fell, and they had to sub-camp on a narrow grass ledge. That night, long after Nongale had entered the land of dreams, Wybergh sat alone by the embers of his fire, looking down on the Injasuti Valley far below him in the moonlight, with the shadowy forms of peak and pinnacle around him, and the starlight gleaming frostily on the snow and ice. Recalling those lonely hours in later life, Wybergh said:

> "Nights like these dwell in unfading memory with the mountaineer, and when the day comes that our bones are stiff and our backs are bent, it will be good to know that such things have been, nay, still are, for though mountain and climber vanish away, beauty never dies, nor the love of it."

Truly a great-hearted mountaineer, and one who had reached into, and found, the very heart of things!

The Natal Club held their first July Camp in the Mont-aux-Sources area in 1920. The news soon spread, and the camp the following year, in the same area, was the first to attract climbers from further afield. From then on these camps were visited regularly by a galaxy of climbers from the Cape, whose names are household words in the mountaineering world to this day, and the infant Natal Club was able to learn much from their experience, technique and skill. "Oompie" Liddle; G. T. Amphlett; Stan Field; Ken Howes-Howell; W. C. West; Ken Cameron; G. T. Londt; Jannie Graaff (the first South African to take part in a genuine Himalayan mountaineering expedition); "Grandpa" Eastman; Elsie Esterhuizen, with her passion for botanizing; Colin Inglis; that "Grand Old Man of the Mountains", T. P. Stokoe; Paul White; and the two Berrisford brothers, all took the long trail northwards and landed up at some time or another at the Natal Camps, and helped in the exploration of the Drakensberg.

One of the earliest was G. T. Amphlett and his wife, though they first appeared on the scenes long before the Natal Camps were established. Amphlett was a member of the select Alpine Club, and had climbed extensively in the Cape. He was Secretary of the Standard Bank of South Africa, and later, Acting General Manager. A most lovable man, quiet, modest, unassuming, he had a profound influence on the destinies of the young Mountain Club of South Africa, established in the Cape in 1891. Said one who knew him, "His whole life was a battle for all that is noble, fair and true". He was awarded the coveted Gold Badge of the Club in 1912. He died at the age of 62 in Rhodesia, on 27th February 1914, while waiting for W. C. West for a trip to *Kilimanjaro*. He and his wife made the third ascent of the *Sentinel* in November 1910, and the same month made a reconnaissance of the North-east ridge of *Cathkin*. Two years later he was back, and took part in the successful first ascent of the peak in December 1912. His name is still remembered in the Drakensberg, for the peak next to *Sterkhorn*, north-east of *Cathkin*, has been named after him.

William Croucher West, with whom he often climbed, was another overseas man. He came out to South Africa with the British army during the Boer War, liked it, and decided to stay. He settled in the Cape. As a boy he had met Edward Whymper, of Matterhorn fame, and knew George Mallory, lost on Everest. He was the first British subject to ascend *Kilimanjaro*, climbing solo, and often climbed with General Smuts, who called him "Kilimanjaro" West. He soon became a veteran Cape climber, and was awarded the Gold Badge in 1914. He only visited the Drakensberg once, as far as I have been able to discover, and that was when he climbed *Cathkin* in 1912. He died in 1957, 80 years of age, climbing to the last, "one of Nature's gentlemen and a true mountaineer" as his life-long climbing companion, Ken Cameron, once said of him.

Ken himself climbed extensively in the Drakensberg. He was an insatiable mountaineer. Up to date, he has made 2 600 ascents of Cape peaks in a climbing career that started at the age of seven, in 1894. To-day, at the age of 85, he is still going strong! (Mountaineers appear to be a long-lived breed. The Cape Town Section of the Mountain Club of South Africa alone has 34 members, each of whose membership goes back to 50 years and over.) He has been a member of the Mountain Club of South Africa for 68 years, for at the age of 17, young as he was, the Club had relaxed its rules and admitted him to full membership.

He soon became active in the Drakensberg, and was amongst the first of the Cape climbers to discover the potentialities of the annual Natal camps. He attended the second camp, in 1921, when he made the first ascent of the formidable *Outer Mnweni Needle*. He also made an attempt on the *Inner Needle*, and was only forced back 60 metres from the summit. This camp also saw him on the slopes of *Cathedral Peak*, where he made the second recorded ascent, and during the same month he made a first ascent of the Singati Gully, with Basset-Smith and Kingdon. In the 1927 Camp he made a second ascent of *Mt. Amery*, and also climbed to the summit via the Inner Tower Ravine. Again in 1938 he was back, attending the 1938 Camp in the Ntonjelane.

T. P. Stokoe, the botanist, also climbed in the Drakensberg, attending the 1927 Camp at Mont-aux-Sources. As we have said, mountaineers appear to be a long-lived breed, for Stokoe died at the age of 93, collapsing on his last trip into the mountains, in the Cape. Professor Rycroft, Director of Kirstenbosch, was fortunately with him at the time, and brought him home, where he died peacefully a few days later. Botany was his great passion, and he rediscovered many plants which had been lost, and discovered many new ones. Several species have been named after him.

Ken Howes-Howell was another of those grand old characters to whom mountaineering owes so much. As a youngster he started climbing in the Du Toit's Kloof Mountains, and that was the start of a long climbing career. He did much to foster a love of mountaineering amongst the boys of S.A.C.S. After his death in 1967 the Cape Cine Club, which he had founded in 1941, produced a film on his life, which they called "A Man of Honour". Here in the Drakensberg we were fortunate in having the benefit of his wise guidance and mature wisdom on several occasions, notably at the 1936 Camp in the Umlambonja, when, with Brian Godbold and four others he made the first ascent of the *Pyramid* (2 827 metres), a most sensational climb.

E. Stanley Field was really a Natal man, having been born in this Province, but at an early age he went to the Cape, where he became a leading attorney. He started climbing as a young man immediately after World War I. With his strong, positive personality and his great qualities of wisdom and leadership, he did much for the Mountain Club, both in the Cape and Natal, and for mountaineering generally. He was awarded the Gold Badge in 1938, and was President of the Club from 1962 to 1969. Two days after taking the chair at the Annual General Meeting of the Club on 7th December 1969, he died at the age of 65. He attended many of our Natal camps, and made several first ascents, notably the *Ndedema Dome* and the *Witch* at the 1935 Camp in the Ndedema Valley.

Paul White, one of the most remarkable climbers of his generation, only attended one Natal camp as far as I know, the 1958 Camp in the Mnweni. He will always be remembered for his wonderful baritone voice, rising superbly into the night air round the camp fire, and the haunting notes of his recorder, produced so mysteriously from his ruck-sack on the most unlikely occasions. From 1958 to 1967 he was Natal's representative on the Central Committee. He climbed smoothly, decisively, in a style lovely to watch, but this did not save him, for he fell to his death from near the top of Turret Arête, in Orange Kloof, on 16th July 1967. He was 45 years of age at the time.

Perhaps the most amazing climber ever to visit our Natal Drakensberg was George Londt, the most brilliant climber South Africa has ever produced. He certainly dominated the Cape scene from 1911 to 1927. He was short and wiry, with a magnificent physique, 165 cm of packed, dynamic energy. His only handicap was his size – he was often too short to reach the holds he wanted. Then he would jam the second man into a crack, and climb up and over him. But he made up for his lack of size by his sheer strength and ability and by his stamina.

Londt was a young man on the Accounting Staff of the Southern Life Association. He was somewhat of an individualist, unduly sensitive, and was not an easy man to get on with. He often broke with his climbing companions. But he was essentially an honourable and a modest man. In 1925 he climbed *Kilimanjaro* with only two porters, and slept the night alone in the crater at 5 889 metres. He then did an extraordinary thing. As proof of his exploit he brought back with him the record book kept at the summit. A storm of abuse and indignation broke over him, both overseas and here, where he was heavily attacked in the South African Press. Londt resigned from the Mountain Club, and for a time gave up climbing, but he did arrange for the subsequent return of the book.

In the Cape he reeled off an amazing number of dramatic climbs, perhaps his finest being the Klein Winterhoek Frontal, a climb which has been compared with the North Face of the Eiger. It involves 1 220 metres of sheer, towering rock. Londt climbed this enormous cliff in 9½ hours. Here in the Drakensberg he attended several July camps. He and Ken Cameron were the first two Cape climbers to attend a Natal Camp, the Mont-aux-Sources one in 1921. Londt arrived early at this Camp, before the others, and pushed on south to *Cathkin Peak*. He took with him the minimum of equipment, even leaving his rope behind. He finally pitched up at Carter Robinson's farm, and announced his intention of climbing the peak. Neither Carter Robinson nor his brother was available, but they supplied him with a Zulu, Mesaga, and the two men set off. Before they left Londt cadged 10 metres of knotted riempies from Carter Robinson to use as a rope. On his way up the lower slopes he spotted a peak midway between *Cathkin* and *Mont-aux-Sources* which rather took his fancy. "It was shaped," he said afterwards, "like the upper half of a bottle, with the ridges running up on either side in a remarkably regular manner." This must have been the peak famous in later years as the *Bell*.

They slogged up Monk's Ravine and into the South Gully, and by 4 p.m. had reached 2 450 metres. By this time Mesaga was exhausted, and wanted to make camp, but Londt pushed on through towering walls of basalt. By 5 p.m. they had made another 450 metres, climbing fast, but darkness was now upon them, and they had to make camp on a grass ledge. That night the weather deteriorated. It was bitterly cold, and all through the long hours of darkness the wind howled dismally about the rock pinnacles. "A colder night," said Londt later, "followed by a colder dawn was never spent by me." Mesaga was exhausted and frankly terrified. He spent the night trying to light the grass to warm his toes. I wonder whether either of them thought of the similar night spent in the same spot by W. J. Wybergh, ten years previously almost to the day!

Next morning the chimneys and cracks were coated with ice a foot thick, but Londt set off immediately, up a chimney, using the riempie rope for the first time. It was a grim climb, taxing them both to the uttermost, but at last they stood on the top. It was so bitterly cold that Londt could hardly write his record in the tin left at the top by West, Casement, Amphlett and Kelly 9 years previously, but to Mesaga's ill-concealed delight, they set fire to the grass, and Mesaga was able to toast his toes at last! On the way down they met Robinson Junior, who had come up to join them. They breakfasted together on a small ledge.

Londt died on 13th November 1927. He was ascending the final pitch of Rainbow Crag on Table Mountain. He was almost at the top when he reached up, found his grip, and suddenly released it for no apparent reason, falling to his death. He was 37 years of age.

We still haven't mentioned the most beloved and best known of them all, "Oompie" Liddle, "Oompie", with his charm, his delightful sense of humour, his impish leg-pulls, his cheeriness, his good fellowship, and his inexhaustible store of songs. He did much to introduce other Cape climbers to the Natal camps, and was identified with these camps from the earliest days. It was "Oompie's" greatest pleasure to give pleasure to others. He lived in Kimberley, and thought nothing of driving 1 300 km through the night, over atrocious roads, to spend a long week-end in the Berg. He never kept any record of his climbs – the joy of the climb was all that mattered – but one who knew him said, "There are few peaks between *Garden Castle* and the Malutis on which he has not set foot". He died suddenly in 1934 after a week-end camp in the Bainskloof area.

There is a mountain at the head of the Setene Valley, not far from *Mont-aux-Sources*, which the Zulus call *Ntaba Ndanyazana*, "The-somewhat-high-mountain-where-the-lightning-strikes". Its lines are mild and gracious. It rises proudly from the valley, and gazes down in calm serenity on the plains below. "Oompie" climbed this mountain in 1930, and he loved it. Its name was changed to *Mount Oompie*.

In 1931 the Transvaal Mountain Club was formed, and it was not long before its members were attracted to the Natal Drakensberg and to the joys of the annual Natal camps. Doyle Liebenberg was one of the first. He had attended Natal camps long before 1931, and soon he introduced Harry Barker to them. From then on the Natal climbers, in addition to what the Cape climbers had been able to give them, had the benefit of the experience and the enthusiasm of as fine a band of mountaineers as South Africa has seen. From 1934 onwards there were few Natal camps that were not the better for their presence. Mike and Elizabeth Burton, Hans and Else Wong, Tony Hooper, David Bell, Dick Barry (only once), John Langmore, Tobie Louw, Ted Scholes, Emil Ruhle, Charles Gloster, R. F. Davies, R. Forsyth, Tom Bright, Jackie Botha, and Cyril Nicholls all made notable contributions to the opening up of the Drakensberg.

Doyen of them all was Doyle Liebenberg – genial, solid, with his broad, contagious grin and the twinkle in his eyes, a magnificent climber. Many a young enthusiast has had cause to bless his warm friendliness, his patience, the allowances he made for the frailties of others. If I were in a tight corner I would rather have Doyle at my side than any other man. At the 1934 camp, a young man of 29, he made a first ascent of the *Outer Horn*, with "Doc" Ripley, Botha-Reid, and F. S. Brown, and the following year, on Good Friday, he made the first ascent of the Amphitheatre Wall, a landmark in Natal climbing history. To-day at the age of 67, he is still climbing in the Drakensberg. In 1962 he was awarded the Gold Badge.

Harry Barker has the ideal build for a climber – long, lean and wiry. In the Transvaal he soon established himself as one of the best of their many capable climbers. Led by Dick Barry less than a month before the latter's tragic death in 1938, he opened up the extraordinarily difficult Waterberg climb, Zimbabwe Tower. Harry will be chiefly remembered for his songs, many of which he composed himself, and for his rich baritone voice, rolling out the notes of *When I was a bachelor I lived by myself*, and the haunting notes of what has come to be called the Transvaal Song, *When the moon above the krantzes silvers all the veld below*, and many others. To-day his bones creak a little more than they used to, and he finds the gentler slopes more to his liking than the terrifying precipices he used to scale in his youth, but he has never lost his love of the Drakensberg. He has a holiday home only a couple of kilometres away from my own home, under the shadow of *Cathkin Peak*, from where he and Margot still sally forth into the hills and valleys they love.

Hans and Else Wong, the conquerors of the *Bell*, had their best days in the early 1940's. Year after year they made the long trip down from the Transvaal, and were responsible for opening up a number of new routes in the Drakensberg. It was Hans and a Transvaal party that finally conquered the grim *Monk's Cowl* in 1942. Hans and Else will always be remembered for their magnificent first ascent of the *Bell*, in the Cathedral area, in 1944. This is the peak that George Londt had spotted in 1921. Perfectly symmetrical from all sides, and shaped like a gigantic bell, it towers up 450 metres from its base, and had fascinated mountaineers for many years. Howes-Howell said of it, "It is quite out of the question as a climbing proposition", and Harry Barker was inclined to agree with him. Doyle Liebenberg had a crack at it in the winter of 1943, selecting the south-west face for his attempt. He was beaten by hard-driven snow and heavily-iced rocks. But the Transvaalers were not to be beaten. In May 1941 Hans Wong, Jackie Botha and Tom Bright set out to climb the peak. They, too, were defeated. "Bell, we will toll you yet," they said. And toll it they did, or rather Hans Wong did. Three years later, on 17th January 1944, he was back, with his wife Else this time. They started their climb on the east side, facing *Cathedral Peak*. From there they worked their way on to the south face, and then round to the west side, facing the *Outer Horn*. The climb proved to be a little easier than they had anticipated, but in places it was very exposed and some of the stances were perilously small. It was a glorious summer's day, and the cliff faces were plastered with masses of flowers – red Dieramas, blue Moraeas and Lobelias, purple Vellosias, pink and white Ericas, and great clusters of the scarlet *Gladiolus cruentus*, popularly known as the "Suicide Lily". Finally they reached the top and built their cairn. They decided to call the route they had opened up the "Gladiolus Route".

Ted Scholes, who started climbing in the Magaliesberg in 1948, has at least three remarkable climbs in the Drakensberg to his credit. In August 1950 he and two others conquered *Devil's Tooth*, in the Mont-aux-Sources area, an epic climb, the full story of which we tell elsewhere. During Easter of the same year he pioneered the first frontal route up the face of *Giant's Castle*. Up until then there had been only two recognised routes up the *Giant*, the Giant's Castle Pass and the Eastern Gully. Just beneath the final peak, on the main face, is a slanting chimney, running down from left to right, and it was up this chimney that Ted led the rest of his party, Joan Knox, G. Burrow and R. Forsyth. It proved to be a thrilling and sensational climb, and is still regarded as one of the finest rock climbs in the Drakensberg. To add to their difficulties, it was a drizzly day, and the rocks were wet and slippery. Just below the summit there is a huge overhang, and the party had to traverse out to the left, on to the open face, a spine-tingling manouvre that took it out of them. Eventually, five hours after starting the climb, they scaled the final rock slabs and were on the summit.

In December of the same year Scholes was in the Injasuti area, with Lorna Pierson, R. Forsyth, and Des Watkins. Here the three *Triplets* soar up into the sky, the *Eastern*, the *Western* and the *Middle*. They decided to make the *Eastern Triplet* their target. They first ascended the narrow south-facing gully which leads up to the nek connecting the peak to the main escarpment. Here in the gully they camped for the night, which was wet and drizzly. High above them the grim peak they were to climb towered up into the darkness. At the head of the gully next day they climbed first a spear-like *gendarme*, and this gave access to the south-west face of the giant peak, and a few hours later they were building their cairn on the top.

But undoubtedly the finest climber of them all was Dick Barry, although he only visited the Drakensberg once, and it was the last mountain he ever climbed. Richard Vincent Merriman Barry, the Mallory of the Drakensberg, has caught the imagination of people even outside South Africa, for not only had he made a name for himself amongst overseas mountaineers, but when he tried to climb *Monk's Cowl*, his tragic death on 29th January 1938, was the first fatal climbing accident in the Drakensberg, and Dick was one of those gifted individuals who, because they are beloved of the gods, have to die young. As a climber he was superb. He had unusual physical powers, and tremendous pertinacity, invincible courage, and a gay, happy disposition. His knowledge of climbing techniques was profound. Always safe on rock, he moved with a swiftness, a cool deliberation, a grace and a strength that was a joy to watch.

Dick matriculated with 1st Class Honours at St. Andrew's College, Grahamstown and three years later graduated as gold medallist at Birmingham University, at the head of his year. He trained as a mining engineer. It was while he was overseas that he developed his love of climbing. He made a number of first ascents in England, Scotland, Wales, Switzerland, the Austrian Tyrol and Jugo-Slavia. One of his major achievements was a record-breaking double traverse of *Mont Blanc* from north to south in three days, with guide Armand Charlet. Between March 1934 and April 1935 he did 93 rock climbs in Great Britain, 85 of which he led. Many of these were first ascents. With all his great gifts, he was modest and unassuming.

Back in South Africa in 1937, he was soon recognised as one of the best of the new breed of young climbers. In six short months he opened up 11 new routes. Many of these were "F" and "G" grade climbs. Mountaineering was his passion. His library contained nearly 100 books on the subject.

He fell to his death on *Monk's Cowl* on the evening of 29th January 1938. Like Rupert Brooke on far-off Scyros Island in the blue Aegean, he had given up to the mountains he loved

the years to be
Of work and joy and that unhoped serene
That men call age.

We shall tell the full story of his last climb in a subsequent Chapter.

In the meantime Natal had nothing to fear! The young men of the newly-established Club soon showed their mettle, and built up a team of rock-climbers and mountaineers every bit as good as the best that the other Provinces could show.

Hubert Botha-Reid was the real father of the Club. He and D. W. Bassett-Smith and R. G. Kingdon had been exploring and climbing in the Drakensberg with their wives for some years prior to the formation of the Club. Botha-Reid, or "B-R" as he was affectionately called, was the son-in-law of General Botha. An ex-Springbok of 1906, and Master of the Supreme Court in Pietermaritzburg, he was a man of tremendous strength and immense endurance. He had that rare gift of being able to bring out the best in those with whom he climbed. Friendly, approachable, he inspired others with an abiding love of the mountains. Said Maurice Sweeney who knew him well, "He was the friend of all who loved what he loved". No finer man could have been found to guide the destinies of the infant club.

Kingdon and Basset-Smith were both schoolmasters. R. G. Kingdon (he married a second cousin of mine) hailed from Maritzburg College. He had come out to this country as a young schoolmaster in 1911, and for a time coached College 1st XI Cricket. Both he and his wife were individualists, and kept pretty much to themselves. It was difficult to get to know them. But they were amongst the first to fall in love with the Drakensberg, and the two of them, together with Mr. and Mrs. Bassett-Smith, spent most of their holidays in the mountains. Somewhat of a recluse, Kingdon's second great love was good books, and he collected large numbers of these with discrimination and taste.

D. W. Bassett-Smith was another young schoolmaster, straight out from Oxford, who had found a post at Hilton College in 1914 as the school's first Science Master. He, too, soon discovered the Drakensberg – not only its towering peaks and the joy of climbing them, but also a world of nature, of trees and flowers, of insects and winged creatures, of ferns and grass lands, which gave full scope to his love of all living things. He later became Second Master at the School, and acted as Headmaster on at least four occasions, for six months at a time. In his later years he forsook the mountains for the coast, and eventually retired there, to his pleasant seaside plot at Port Edward. The two men soon began to chalk up a series of first ascents – *Cathedral Peak* in 1917, a new route up Sentinel Gully from the Tugela Gorge in 1919, the first ascent of the wall of the Berg at the head of the Singati in 1920, and the *Outer Mnweni Needle* with Ken Cameron in 1921. He died in 1950.

Bill Marriott was another foundation member of the Club. He was known to all as "Scaly" as he had once been heard telling a young girl in camp that he was "scaly with experience". He was a keen horticulturist, and his work on fruit flies was especially valuable. One of the fruit flies has been named after him. He is another who will always be remembered for his songs around the camp fire, and for his birthday parties in his bell-tent, lasting long into the night, for Bill had his birthday in July. In his later years he grew too old to attend camp, but he never lost his interest in the Club, and the news of his passing, received during the 1965 July Camp, brought back a flood of memories of Old Bill Marriott, and of his songs.

Dr. Archie Park-Ross was one of the early stagers whose memory is now legendary, "P-R", with his endless fund of impossible stories, his tremendous energy, his simple kindliness and quiet helpfulness, his tolerance, and his delightful sense of humour. On the last morning of camp, as home-going parties were setting off, he would mount a near-by rock and, bearskin cap on head, would sing out in his rich Scotch brogue, "Will ye no' come back again!"

"P-R" was a senior officer of the Union Health Service in Natal, and it was quite amazing how, year after year, serious outbreaks of infectious diseases would occur in the area where the Natal camps were being held, each one requiring his immediate, and personal, attention! He was a foundation member of the Club, and for many years its President. He loved the mountains and everything to do with them – the flowers, the wild creatures, the clouds that wove their patterns on the changeless face of the peaks, the winds that companioned the night. He celebrated his 60th birthday by making the second recorded ascent of the Amphitheatre Wall by a new route, on 19 January 1939. Ten years later, to the day, on his 70th birthday, he climbed *Cathedral Peak*. When he grew too old for mountaineering he retired to his home at Hilton Road, and there, with his wife Mary (herself a fine climber), he dreamed his days away in his lovely garden in quiet happiness, until in 1958, at the age of 77, he set his face to the last long climb.

"Doc" Ripley was one of the most delightful of the old characters. Doc had a small, wiry, monkey-like frame (I have never seen a hairier man in the mountains!) and an ancient, battered hat that appeared year after year in camp, and his shirt was always hanging out. He had a fund of amusing wise-cracks and camp fire songs, and a quaint American-Cockney accent ("Pass the Rarck salt!") Doc had an unbroken record of 39 Camps without a break, and when, at the 1960 Camp, he failed to turn up, there was a great emptiness. When he died in May 1967 he was mourned by many. He had a wire-haired terrier, "Micky", who slept at the bottom of his sleeping-bag every night. Tough, agile climber as he was, he had a strange lack of a sense of direction, and was always getting lost. His deep understanding of his fellow men, his enviable sense of humour, and his ability to laugh at himself, endeared him to all who had the privilege of climbing with him.

Doc was born in America, in the State of Connecticut, and trained as an entomologist at the University of Illinois. When he came out to South Africa in 1920 he joined the Staff of the Cedara Agricultural College, an institution to which he gave a lifetime of devoted service, which, incidentally, did not cease with his official retirement in 1955. To-day his son, Dr. Sherman Ripley, of the University of Natal Medical School in Durban, carries on the old tradition of dedicated service, both to his profession and to Natal mountaineering.

Doc will be chiefly remembered for his witty, and sometimes libellous, songs with which he regaled his fellow-climbers round the camp fire. He was the author of the traditional Natal Mountain Club Song, *Old Climbers, Bold Climbers*, in which he mercilessly, but without malice, pilloried his fellow-climbers. He always insisted on leading his own verse himself, in his rich American-Cockney brogue:

> *Old Doc, the blighter, was an expert in the bush,*
> *He never found a route except by chance,*
> *And all along the mountain-tops, in chimney and in crack,*
> *You can still find the remnants of his pants.*

The climbing record of first ascents of Brian Godbold, gaunt, lean and long-legged, reads almost like a Drakensberger's *vade mecum*. He started his climbing career at the Cathkin Camp in 1933, when he climbed the *Turret* for the first time, and opened a new route up *Sterkhorn*, and then followed in quick succession the *Ntonjelane Needle* and the opening of a frontal route up the *Saddle* in 1934; the *Ndedema Dome*, the Ndedema Pass and the *Witch* in 1935; the *Pyramid* and an equally sensational climb up *Outer Horn* in 1936; the *Old Woman Grinding Corn* in 1937; the north-west face of the *Mitre* in 1938; and *Cleft Peak Frontal* in 1946. All these were "firsts". Brian has a *penchant* for night-climbing. I once watched him climb the tremendous precipices of the *Inner Mnweni Pinnacle* from my camp on the other side of the valley, two kilometres away. He started his climb at about 3 p.m., reached the top at about 9 p.m., and then I watched the pin-point of light, his torch, as it slowly crept down the sheer face of the peak, until it reached the nek at midnight. He was one of the first men to risk sub-camping on the summit in winter, when it was thought this meant certain death. But he tells one story against himself. A dear old lady, staying at Cathedral Peak Hotel, was horrified at the ruffianly appearance of "those dreadful men from the Mountain Club Camp". When Mrs. Godbold told her that her husband was one of them, the old lady remarked, "But, my dear, *you* seem quite nice!"

Stan Rose, though not one of the original members of the Club, was one of the dominant figures of the 1930's. He was a most versatile man, the holder for many years of the Western Province Half Mile record, runner-up in the welter-weight boxing championship, and a first-class Hockey player. He was a skilled and dedicated climber – he was credited with knowing no less than 80 different kinds of knots! And, finest of all, thought some, he was a magnificent blower of the bag-pipes! One of his greatest climbs was the first ascent of the *Pyramid* in 1936, with Brian Godbold and Ken Howes-Howell.

Almost the sole remaining members of the climbers of yesterday are Professor G. M. J. Sweeney and his wife "Snib". Maurice Sweeney is not a foundation member of the Club, but very nearly so, for he joined in 1922. "Snib" joined a year earlier. They are the last surviving members of the old brigade, and few have done more than they to explore the Drakensberg. None know it better. "Snib" holds the honour of being the first woman on *Cathkin Peak*. In 1927 Maurice produced the first comprehensive map of the Drakensberg, as we have seen, and this map, and its later editions, is still a treasured item in the ruck-sack of every Natal mountaineer. He was awarded the Gold Badge in 1956. As a young man he took part in the climbing of most of the major peaks. When he and "Snib" married, they spent their honeymoon in the caves of the Drakensberg, and when the first baby arrived, they designed a special type of ruck-sack carrier, so that, with the baby on Maurice's shoulders and "Snib" at his side, they could still wander, carefree as ever, in the hills and valleys they loved. To-day Professor and Mrs. Sweeney have their holiday home in the beautiful Cathkin area, from where they can still gaze on the peaks, for, to use their own expression, they have "an enduring passion for the mountains". "Mountains are to the mountaineer" says Maurice, "an enduring passion, and it does not matter much that heart, lungs and iimbs prove unco-operative. Love begets love, and if a man goes to them humbly and affectlionately, the mountains will lavishly repay his devotion."

And a final salute – and "*Vale*" – to Phyllis Goodwin. Natal is fortunate in having produced a number of lady climbers of distinction. Greatest of all was Phyllis Goodwin. She joined the Natal Mountain Club in 1942, and from then on no July Camp was complete without her cheery presence. She showed early on that she possessed a particularly high standard of mountaineering. She helped to open up a number of new climbs – the South Face of the *Pyramid*, the North Face of *Mt. Oompie*, the Singati Wall, and the Great Arête on the *Eastern Buttress*. In 1946 she undertook a strenuous traverse of the summit, from *Cathedral* to the *Sentinel*. She was the first woman to climb the *Column* – and few *men* have tackled this fantastic climb – and she was the first woman on *Mponjwana*. She had an intimate knowledge of the

Drakensberg, and knew all its secrets – the standard routes on all the major peaks; the caves, the well-known ones and the remote and inaccessible ones known to few; the best camp sites, the paths, the water-points, the birds and the Bushman paintings. Emily Arnold who knew her well and often climbed with her, said of her, "Phyl loved all wild things – the untamed mountains, the rushing Berg streams, the sky, the stars, the birds, the animals and the flowers".

One day in 1967 she started to climb a hill near her home at Blackridge, near Pietermaritzburg, to see if an unrecognised flower which she had found a few days previously had opened. It was her last climb. Near the top she was struck down by an African assailant, and savagely murdered. To those who knew her as friend and fellow-climber she is still remembered with affection and gratitude.

No account of the climbers of the Drakensberg would be complete without a reference to the Zulu and Basutho guides, who accompanied their masters into the high places. Indeed, such fine climbers were many of them that the terms "master" and "servant" fell away, and they became fellow-climbers.

One of the best known was Melatu, Tom Casement's boy. Melatu (the name means a debt) was a Mosutho, tall, gaunt, tough and wiry. Father Kelly said of him that he was the only African boy he knew who climbed and who liked it. He claimed to have accompanied Casement on the latter's ascent of the *Sentinel*, the *Eastern Buttress* and *Cathkin*. He is not quite correct about the first two, though he did climb them shortly afterwards. He certainly accompanied West, Amphlett, Kelly and Casement on their historic *Cathkin* climb in 1912, and he was with Casement when he made the terrifying ascent of Sentinel Gully in 1911. He also accompanied Father Kelly on the latter's climb up the *Inner Tower* in 1913, though it is doubtful whether he reached the top. Melatu was born about 1870, and was still climbing in 1930 at the age of 60.

Charlie also was a guide, a Zulu, whose name is legendary in the Mont-aux-Sources area. His Zulu name was Maqadi Ngcobo. He was born in the shadow of the *Sentinel*, and this has been his home ever since. When Williams was leasing Coventry's farm round about 1917 he engaged Charlie as a herd boy, and later he was employed to fetch visitors to the Hotel by donkey-cart from Bergville. Later still he was promoted to guide. Doyle Libenberg, who knew him well, (he once carried Doyle home on his back after Doyle had broken his leg on the slopes of *Eastern Buttress* in 1932) has described his distinctive character – his very genuine love for, and knowledge of, the mountains, his profound understanding of his fellow men, and his roguish approach to life. He loved to pull the legs of the people whom he led into the mountains. After supper in the Hut on the summit he would tell to a rapt audience the story of how a party of 20 Basutho, returning from the mines, were caught in a snowstorm on the slopes of *Mont-aux-Sources*, and all perished. At the psychological moment, with perfect timing, he would suddenly leap up, fling the door of the Hut open, and bid the ghosts of the 20 Basutho enter! In fact Charlie had a fund of quite impossible stories with which he would regale his audience in the long winter nights. But he was never malicious, always thoughtful and considerate, and in an emergency, magnificent. On one occasion the Acutt family from Durban were caught in a blizzard on the summit. He saved the whole family, leading them down the Chain Ladder, and carrying Miss Acutt, whose feet were frost-bitten, all the way from *Sentinel* to the Hotel, a distance of twenty kilometres.

In 1960 Charlie was still "guiding", well on in years by then, but shortly after that advancing age called the inevitable halt, and Charlie retired to his kraal and to his beer under the shadow of the *Sentinel*, where for many years he still told his impossible stories, not to the tourists this time, but to the ring of wide-eyed and fascinated umfaans,* gathered round him in the sun. He died early in 1964.

What Charlie and Melatu were to *Mont-aux-Sources*, Mtateni Xosa, familiarly known as

* umfaan: a small boy (Zulu).

John, was to *Cathedral Peak*. For 45 years John has been "guiding" in the Cathedral area, and he is still hard at it. Several years ago he gave it up for a short while, and found a job in a Durban garage. The "abelungu" (white men) of to-day, he told me, were not like the "abelungu" of the old days. To-day all they wanted was to sit around and play cards and drink and loaf in the sun round the swimming bath. They never even looked at the mountains these days. John was disgusted, and sought solace in the bright lights of Durban. But the call of the mountains was too strong, and soon he was back, and once again the mountain kloofs rang to John's melodious yodel. For it was John who introduced yodelling into the Drakensberg. Some Austrian tourists taught him the art many years ago. John became quite proficient at it, but the little umfaans who tried to imitate him, did not! To-day, all the way from *Giant's Castle* to *Mont-aux-Sources* you will hear that haunting call murdered in cold blood by the little herdboys on the mountain slopes.

John has a wonderful record of safety, of which he is justly proud. Not once, in all his 45 years of guiding, has he had an accident. Tough as nails, he will climb *Cathedral Peak*, (3 004 metres) every day of the week for six days, except Sundays, when John always insists on his pipe and his beer and a few hours in the warm sunlight. George Thomson once took him with him to the summit of the *Bell*. But the giddy precipices proved almost too much for a man even of John's calibre. When George congratulated him on being the first Zulu to stand on the lofty summit, John replied with a sickly grin, "Yes, baas, and the last!"

CHAPTER VII

GEORGE THOMSON

"Proud to visit the margins of death"
—ERNEST RAYMOND

Once in a while the mountaineering world throws up a climber who, with no training or experience, produces the most sensational climbs from the very start of his climbing career, individualists who break all the rules, and yet who "get there". Of such was Gustav Nefdt of *Toverkop* fame, in the Cape, and of such was George Thomson.*

Thomson was quite the most extraordinary climber ever to visit our Natal Drakensberg. He was a New Zealander who came out to this country in the early 1940's. Fair-haired, wiry, tough, he pitched up one day at Cathedral Peak Hotel and asked for a job. Albert van der Riet was busy at the time building his new Hotel. George was a bricklayer by trade, and the deal was made. The only problem was that he had a bad heart, but he set to work. He was about 40 years of age.

George had never climbed a mountain in his life before, though in New Zealand, where he was a keen fisherman, he used to descend difficult rocks to out-of-the-way fishing spots. In the intervals of building he would look up at the majestic peaks around him, and soon he decided to have a crack at them. He did not know the first thing about mountaineering. He did not know that you should never climb alone. He did not even know that you should always use a rope, especially for the descent, until the fellows of the Natal Mountain Club got hold of him and taught him. But he tackled alone, and without rope, and conquered, peak after peak in the Drakensberg that had never been climbed before.

In spite of his bad heart he had tremendous energy and stamina. I have known him set out from the Hotel at first light with a couple of companions, climb several peaks steadily, and without a break throughout the day, and arrive back just before dark. His companions were exhausted, but George promptly attacked a four-course dinner, and then danced well on into the small hours.

His most remarkable climb was undoubtedly that of the *Column*. Have you ever seen the *Column?* It towers up, a terrifying 500 metres, from the Tseketseke valley, 500 metres of sheer, incredible rock, like a huge, protruding fang. Half-way up the face is protected on all sides by a tremendous overhang. It had never been climbed, and according to every knowledgeable expert, never would be.

One day in December 1945 George decided to have a go at it. He persuaded another young fellow to go with him, and together they made their way to the foot of the peak. Arrived there, his companion took one look at the staggering precipices towering up into the sky above them, and said "Not on your life! You can break your neck if you want to, but not me!"

So George proceeded to climb the peak alone, and without rope. Slowly, inch by inch, he worked his way up the sheer face of the peak, up and over the overhang, across the final slabs with scarcely a toe-hold, while his friend watched, spell-bound, from down below. At last he heaved himself over the final rocks on to the summit, and stood there, the first human being to do so, a tiny speck against the blue of the sky.

If the ascent had been extraordinary, the descent, without rope, must have been terrifying, even for a man of George's iron nerve. Soon after he left the summit on the way down, he lost

*The spelling "Thomsen", used by several writers, is incorrect.

77

his route. He found himself on a narrow ledge, less than a metre wide, with no way down from it and no way of reversing his climb and climbing back. He was alone, on top of a most exposed, detached peak, without a rope, and a sheer drop of 500 metres below him. The only hope was another ledge, about 3½ metres below him, equally narrow. He knew he would have to jump it, and he knew, with cold certainty, that it would be almost impossible to keep his balance once he landed on the ledge. But below that was a small bush, in a chimney, 12 metres down. He calculated that if he went over the ledge he might manage a "controlled fall", with arms and legs pressed against the walls of the chimney, and that with luck he might be able to grab the bush as he fell past it. He has told me himself what happened. "I knew I would have to jump it," he said, "and I didn't like the look of it, but I said to myself, 'George, my boy, the longer you look at it the worse it gets, so – just you jump!' " He jumped, landed on the ledge, grabbed at a tuft of grass, which came away in his hand, and slid right into the chimney. But as he went down he was able to grab at the small bush, and this saved him. He had sustained a nasty gash on the leg, and was badly shaken, but that didn't worry George! Calmly he continued his descent.

His next pitch was an "F" standard grass pitch, 45 metres long, and horribly steep (an "F" standard grass pitch is more dangerous even than "F" standard rock, for rock is at least firm, while a grass slope at that angle offers neither foot nor hand-hold). This was nearly as unpleasant as the chimney down which he had fallen, but he managed it, and then continued steadily on down severe rock until, several hours later, he was down and off the mountain. Two years later Jannie Graaff called the *Column* "In all probability the most difficult peak in the Union". And it had been climbed by a novice, solo, and without rope!

The *Column* taught George a lesson. It was after this that he began to learn the technique of roping, and soon he became an expert.

I shall always remember my first meeting with George. It was in 1946, soon after I had started mapping the Cathedral area. I pitched up late one afternoon at Twins Cave, and had just finished unpacking when a wiry-looking man of about 40, with a tremendous pack, walked into the cave. We greeted each other – he was on his way, he said, to the Rockeries area. I made him a cup of coffee, and after supper we settled down round the camp fire with our pipes. "Done much climbing in this area?" I asked. "Oh, just a bit," he said, "nothing very much." He seemed to be far more interested in what I was doing. Next morning we went on our respective ways, and it was not until a week later, when I returned to the Hotel, that I discovered that my friend of that night had been the famous George Thomson.

George's first climb was round about 1944. He set out for the *Pyramid* one day with Stan Rose who had been in the party which had made the first ascent in 1936. George had just been given six months to live on account of his heart, and Stan was on recuperative leave from the army, so that for both men this was something of a trial day. Stan of course led, but when they arrived at the crux pitch he did not feel quite up to it. George asked if he might take over, and to the astonishment of his companion, he went through to the top like a veteran, first on the rope. After that there was no holding George, and there were few week-ends that did not see him out in the mountains.

But it was not only his rock-hard nerve. It was, also his tremendous stamina that made him the climber he was. Tuesday, September 23, 1947 was a clear sunny day in the great basin of the *Amphitheatre*, in the Mont-aux-Sources area. Sitting on the edge, not far from *Beacon Buttress*, were two young people, admiring the tremendous view stretched out below them, Tom Pinkney and his girl friend. Below them was a drop of more than 500 metres. Suddenly the girl's scarf slipped out of her fingers, Tom Pinkney bent forward to retrieve it, over-balanced, and went over the edge. His body landed on a ledge, 280 metres down.

In order to recover the body the authorities immediately enlisted the help of George. He came over from Cathedral Peak, and he and Peter Pope-Ellis, Warden at the time of the Royal

Natal National Park, attempted to climb up from the bottom, but they failed. The following day, with a third companion, Peter Henning, they went up the bridle path to the summit, and at 2 p.m. they went over the edge at Beacon Buttress Gorge. Two African Forest Guards let them down to the first ledge on a length of rope, and then threw the rope down after them. There was no turning back. By nightfall they were down on a narrow ledge, level with the body, and about 50 metres away from it, but in between was a sheer rock face. Here they camped for the night.

Twenty-four hours of stark terror lay ahead of them. At 8 p.m. the weather changed. It started to rain. By midnight a blizzard had blown up. Weary and frozen, with no blankets or sleeping bags, the three men crouched, shivering, throughout the night on their narrow ledge, taking it in turns to be the middle man. Every now and then the silence was broken as great boulders, loosened by the rain, came tumbling down the mountain side.

Next morning it was still snowing, and the mountain was shrouded in mist. It was impossible to reach the body, and the only escape was to continue the descent down the mountain side, and into the Gorge at the bottom. There followed twelve hours of nightmare climbing. Peter Pope-Ellis admits that they would never have survived had it not been for George's skill, courage and cheerfulness, as they abseiled their way down the Amphitheatre Wall. They were well off the standard route, and soon lost their way on the mist-shrouded face of the cliffs. It was bitterly cold, and their fingers were so broken and frozen that they had to use their teeth to tie knots in the rope. On one section their doubled 75-metre rope was not long enough to reach the bottom of the cliff they were descending, and they were forced to abseil on a single rope. (In abseiling a double rope is used, the top threaded through a loop so that it can be retrieved and used again. When abseiling on a single rope, the top is firmly attached to a rock outcrop, and cannot be used a second time.) But George was equal to the occasion. He came down last, after tying a trick-knot of his own invention. At the bottom all you had to do to recover the rope was to release the tension on it and give it a flick and the rope would come tumbling down! One stands quite horrified at the ingenuity of a man who can trust his life to a thing like this! At midday they came to a tremendous waterfall, part of the huge Tugela waterfall, down which they had to rope, swinging down one at a time in the icy-cold water, the mist hiding from them what lay below. Eventually, on the point of exhaustion, they were down, at about 6 p.m. to find two African Game Rangers waiting for them at the bottom, with food and a roaring fire.

In the meantime the affair had aroused considerable interest, and the Natal Provincial Administration had to close the whole of the summit area to the public, so as to thwart morbid sensation seekers who wished to gaze down on the body. They also placed a ban on all further attempts at recovering the body, not wishing to incur any further loss of life.

A week later I spent the evening of Friday, October 3, at Cathedral Peak Hotel on my way to the summit.* I bumped into George Thomson, and we spent the evening in his room together. He told me he was leaving early next morning with two climbing companions in a final bid to recover the body, in defiance of the Natal Provincial Administration ban. I was away in the mountains for ten days, and on my return I read in the papers how George and his two fellow climbers had managed, after a terrific effort, to reach the body, but it had been impossible to get it down. They had to content themselves with burying it on a near-by grass ledge. What fairer resting place could a man wish for!

George's tremendous stamina was used to good effect on another occasion when he took a party of climbers to the top of the *Cockade*. This is an easy peak on the summit of the escarpment, midway between Organ Pipe's Pass and the Cathedral Range. They reached the summit without mishap, but suddenly a tremendous storm blew up, with driving wind and snow. Soon

---

* This is the trip I have already described in Chapter V. See page 57.

the snow grew heavier, and things looked bad. George ordered an immediate descent, but, with one of the girls in the party tiring rapidly, it soon became obvious that they would never reach the Hotel before dark. George decided to make for Twins Cave, to the immediate west of the *Mitre* in the Cathedral Range, where there was good shelter. But soon after setting out the girl collapsed. In the howling blizzard George heaved her on to his back, and carried her all the way to the cave. Arrived there in sub-zero temperatures, with the rest of the party lying exhausted on the floor of the cave, George bustled about, building a fire, fetching water, sorting out gear, and making the best arrangements he could for the night which lay ahead.

Mponjwana, and its first ascent by George Thomson, is another Berg classic. The story of its conquest is another of the tales that old climbers tell, as they gather round the fire at the end of the day.

Mponjwana, at the head of Rockeries Pass, in the Mnweni area, is one of the mightiest peaks in the Drakensberg. One huge, solid block, soaring up into the clouds, it is separated from the main escarpment by a tremendous chasm, less than 75 metres across, but 450 metres deep. Bassett-Smith had investigated it in 1922. "The peak is perhaps the grandest to be seen anywhere," he said. "It is a huge pillar of smooth rock, rounded on the top, fully 2 000 feet in height, and seemingly inaccessible from all sides. It is too severe a climbing proposition even for baboons."

But baboons or not, George decided early in 1946 to tackle the peak. He was able to team up with Kenneth Snelson, a young Naval officer who was holidaying in South Africa at the time. Snelson was a member of the Cambridge University Mountaineering Club, and had had Alpine experience. He later climbed with Jannie Graaff in the Himalayas.

They left Cathedral Peak Hotel before sunrise on the morning of April 8, 1946, with food for four days, and made their way up the Umlambonja Pass to the summit. It was a long, hard slog, their packs were heavy (30 kg), and near the top, which they reached at 2 p.m., the altitude began to tell, and their progress was slow. They pitched their tent that night beside a small stream near the *Saddle*, in Lesotho. It was bitterly cold, and the stars sparkled, clean and bright in a cloudless sky.

Next morning they were up early, continuing their trek northwards along the summit over ice-encrusted grass, which crunched crisply under their feet. By 10 a.m. they had reached Mponjwana Cave.

This cave is one of the best-known in the Drakensberg. Situated in a small lateral gully, it faces directly across to mighty *Mponjwana*, and is an admirable jumping-off place for an assault on the peak.

After making themselves comfortable in the cave, they went out to the edge of the escarpment to examine the peak, only 75 metres away. At first their hearts failed them. Snelson was frankly appalled. George himself wondered whether the peak would ever be climbed. "Grimly," he said afterwards, "I determined to go through with it, though I never at any time overlooked the fact that the mountain would be a supreme test of human ability." After a preliminary inspection of the mighty face, they descended the 450 metres to the nek between the escarpment and the peak to examine more carefully the quality of the rock. Then, disconsolately, they returned to the cave for a quick meal. They had not found even a vestige of a route on the sheer, appalling face of the giant.

In the afternoon they continued their survey. Snelson went south, in the direction of Rockeries Pass, and George climbed to some higher ground behind the cave. Here, sitting on a rock, he vainly searched the great face in front of him for a starting-point for their climb. Suddenly he saw three wild pigeons flying across four water-worn grooves running up from the base about 450 metres below him. "Concentrating on these grooves," said Thomson later, "I concluded that it might be possible to ascend one of them and make a traverse out to another. At a point where this latter groove looked unclimbable, I saw the possibilities of another traverse on to the sheer face. From then on, for 500 feet or so, the angle seemed fairly easy. That was enough for me. I rushed back to Ken, whom I found waiting at the head of the Pass, half an hour's walk away. 'I have found a route,' I exclaimed enthusiastically. 'How about returning to the cave, having a good night's rest, and tackling the monster tomorrow?' "*

That night, lying in their sleeping bags, they watched the mists playing around the mighty face of *Mponjwana* in the moonlight, and listened to the wind in the crags. They thought of the morrow, and wondered what it would hold for them.

Next morning they were again up early. After a quick breakfast, they left the cave at 8 a.m., climbed down to the nek, and by 8.30 a.m. were ready to start their way up the 550 metres of precipice that towered above them. After climbing up the two water-worn grooves that the pigeons had shown them, they were confronted by several pitches of "E" standard, almost vertical. The last of these led into a chimney, and then followed two more chimneys, one of which was very narrow, and the other with a deadly overhang. They surmounted this, and then came several slabs of sheer rock, necessitating some most difficult traverses. The worst of these was a very steeply-sloping slab, but fortunately they managed to find some small, undercut fingerholds in the overhanging face, at about the level of their knees, and this gave them the necessary support.

By this time they had reached the north-east shoulder of the mountain, and were only 100 metres from the summit. But the most terrifying part of the climb still remained. At this point their way seemed blocked. George attempted a slanting traverse to the left, failed, and returned to where he had left Snelson. The only answer was to go straight up. This was, perhaps, the most hair-raising part of the climb, for the rock was vertical, loose and dangerous, but they surmounted it successfully, and the summit could now be seen, not far off.

Now they were confronted, however, by a terrific chimney, only five metres high, but with a most dangerous overhang at the top. George took it. In order to surmount the overhang, he had first to find a firm hand-grip on the top of the overhang, and then to put his full weight on his arms, his legs dangling uselessly into space. Feeling round for his hand-grip, he dislodged a number of stones, which cascaded down on top of them and nearly put an end to the climb. All he could find was a loose boulder, but it might just hold. If it didn't, there was nothing to stop him hurtling down 500 metres to the bottom. Then, with the boulder firmly in his grip, and his whole weight on his arms, he launched himself desperately on to the upper part of the overhang, and just made it. The boulder had held. Another minute, and Ken had joined him. Now the worst was over and the rest easy – a steep grassy slope and one final rock pitch, and they were on top. It was half past twelve.

They built the traditional cairn, wrote their names on a sheet of paper, with the crest of Ken's ship, *H.M.S. Glasgow*, on it, and placed it in a cigarette tin. This they stowed carefully away in the heart of the cairn. Each man collected a piece of rock crystal as a souvenir, and at one o'clock they commenced the descent. George had by now learnt to abseil, and they abseiled down almost the entire length of the climb. By 5 p.m. they were back in their cave, the billy was boiling, and the soup ready. By the time supper was over, darkness had fallen, and the moon was shining. They packed up, descended Rockeries Pass by moonlight, and camped for the night at the bottom.

Most of Thomson's climbs were in the Cathedral and Mnweni areas. I met him once in the Cathkin area, a year or so after his celebrated climb of *Cathkin Peak*. This was one of his earlier climbs. He set out one December with two companions to climb the peak. At first all went well, but near the top he found an old rope dangling down the cliff face, which had been

---

* This is the correct account of the 'pigeon' story, as given by Thomson himself. Another version, which has found its way into print on several occasions, to the effect that near the top, where they could find no way up, Thomson saw a pigeon flying off what he deduced must be a tiny ledge, and that this opened the way to the summit, is incorrect.

there for many years. Now, of course no experienced climber will trust himself to an old rope, left dangling by a previous climbing party, but George did not know this. He started to shin up the rope. It broke, and George passed rapidly out of sight! He fell more than 30 metres, and finally landed up on a narrow ledge, badly concussed and with a broken ankle.

After recovering, he said to himself, "George, my boy, if you don't climb this something-something mountain, you'll lose your nerve, and you'll never climb another mountain in your life, so – up you go!" He went up, collected his two terrified companions, and took them with him to the summit. And then a hailstorm came down and battered in what little was left of his concussed head. It was one of George's principles never to cry quits, but for once in his life he did. He told his two companions that he didn't think he could reach home with his injured ankle, and asked them to go for help. They set off immediately, leaving him at the top, and eight hours later broke into a very startled Christmas Eve party at Champagne Castle Hotel, with their news. Mr. van Heyningen, the proprietor, set off immediately on horseback with a rescue party and a mountain stretcher. They reached the base of the mountain at dawn – and – there was George! He had managed to climb down the mountain, alone, and at night, with a broken ankle, and was bashing away for home on his hands and knees!

Thomson's last ascent was the *Outer Mnweni Pinnacle*, which he climbed in December 1948 with Charles Gloster. This is one of the really dangerous peaks in the Drakensberg, and their route has never been repeated, though the summit has been reached on other occasions by a different route.

This ended George's climbing exploits. In 1949 he emigrated to Rhodesia, where he worked for a time with a firm of Salisbury builders. Later he established a contracting business on his own in Sinoia. Here he married for a second time, and had two children. His son is at present studying Civil Engineering at Cape Town University, and his daughter is still at school in Sinoia. His son by his first marriage is a Missionary doctor in Papua, and his daughter is married to a Pastor in Switzerland. Late in 1960 he contracted Hepatitis, and on 5th May 1961 he died in a Salisbury hospital.

What are we to say of George as a climber? What of his relations with other climbers? A true climber will not take unjustifiable risks. "Climb if you will," said Edward Whymper, "but remember that courage and strength are naught without prudence." George, I am afraid, lacked this. He was an unorthodox climber, an individualist, often impetuous, sometimes reckless. In his early days the Natal Mountain Club tended to look askance at him, and although various Club members did climb with him, I do not think he ever attended a July Camp. He was too much of an individualist for this. But when all is said and done, one cannot help but admire his matchless courage, his cool nerve, and the sheer zest and joy which he brought to his climbing. He loved to be the first to stand on top of a virgin peak, but he loved far more the effort required to get there, the sweat, the toil, the grim determination, the calls on every last drop of clenched determination he had. These were the things that counted. Certain it is that for years to come the tales of his exploits will be told round many a camp fire.

Why do men climb mountains? Why are they so eager to accept the challenge of the high peaks? When George Mallory, of Everest fame, was asked that question, he replied "Because they are there". This is no evasion of the question. Those who have known the silence of high places, the beauty of snow-girt peaks, good fellowship round the camp fire, night bivouacs under the stars, the long tramp home in the evening light after a day on the hills, will know that there is more in that short answer than mere evasion. It *is* because the mountains are there – steadfast, immutable, holding their pools of blue light between banks of drifting cloud, the air sweet with the scent of flowers. They belong to the world of cloud and wind and open skies. The mountains hold peace, and fulfilment, and healing. When men climb mountains they go in search of themselves. They seek for mastery over self, mastery over their fears, a greater self-knowledge, a deeper sensitivity to the sheer joy of being alive. They seek a beauty that is not of this world. Their motives are essentially personal. The mountaineer finds a challenge there that is both physical, mental and spiritual. And the fact that death is often at his elbow is but a heightened joy, for danger is the salt of life. When you visit the margins of death you are more conscious of life, and life takes on a sharpness, an intensity, a clarity that you will find nowhere else. Yes, men climb mountains because they *are* there.

*　　*　　*　　*

And so the firelight flickers on the shadowed faces, and the logs crackle and fall with a thud, one by one, and the sparks fly up into the star-spangled sky, while the songs of the mountaineers float out hauntingly over the quiet hills. But always, in even the merriest song, there is the bitter-sweet hint of melancholy and regret, for deep down in each man is the sure and certain knowledge that though the hills are eternal, muscle and bone and sinew are not. Always there is the certainty that one day joints will grow stiff and muscles fail, the eye grow dim and sinews soft. Always is the knowledge that this must end, and that high action must give place one day to the easy chair in the garden and the quiet pipe. And after even that ... Afterwards ... ?

Will there be
Bright lights of noon
That leap on running water
And laugh back the sun,
Tall green trees
Drowsy with dreams,
And cool green shade —
Lush green grass too?

Will there be
The lilt of seas
Softly murmurous
Upon white shores;
And mountain spires
Grey-aged with silence,
Sad sunset's afterglow —
White moonlight, too?

Will there be
The sheen of eyes
That smile, and smiling give
Ease and quietude;
And distant stars,
Laughter, and velvet night,
And voices raised in song —
Quiet voices too?

And Afterwards —
Shall I know
The still white wine
Of Beauty's self,
The strong red wine
Of Beauty's love,
And shall I drink of these —
*Afterwards?**

* 'Icarus', in the Mountain Club Journal, 1949.

PART 2

In which the reader surveys the scenery, and watches some of the characters in action.

CHAPTER VIII

GHOST HOTEL

"As we lie in the camp fire's golden glow
We sing of the days of long ago;
We sigh at sorrows long foregone,
At hearts that loved and eyes that shone."
—SONG OF THE TRANSVAAL MOUNTAIN CLUB

It was a crisp, winter's afternoon in 1967. I stood under the ruined verandah of an old building In the Witzieshoek area. The window-panes were all broken, the gutters falling down, one wall leaned drunkenly out, a huge gap between it and the other wall, and the wind sighed drearily through the sagging roof.* It was ringed round with smoke-blue mountains, and over all hung the brooding precipices of *Mount Qua-Qua*, enigmatic and silent.

This tumbled-down ruin was once the Mecca of travellers from all over the world. To it came the climbers of long ago, from far and near, for it was the only means of access to the famed *Mont-aux-Sources*, and to the wonders of the Drakensberg. Its name was Rydal Mount. On that winter's day the only sound in the spacious rooms that once echoed to the laughter of relaxing guests was the sigh of the wind and the muted chatter of the occasional umfaans, who gazed with curious eyes through the broken window-panes. I wandered, fascinated, through the deserted rooms, peopled only by the ghosts of men and women long since dead.

Rydal Mount lies in the Witzieshoek area, due west of Harrismith, in the angle formed by the arm of the Drakensberg running north-east from *Mont-aux-Sources* into the Transvaal, and the Malutis running north-west into Lesotho. "Witzieshoek," wrote J. J. Ross in 1928 (he was the Superintendent of the Witzieshoek Mission Station) "with its proud and lofty mountains, clear water and lovely surroundings, is surely one of the most beautiful places in our land. The climate, though cold in winter . . . is amazingly healthy. When the mountains are covered in snow in winter, one cannot cease from gazing at them; and after the first summer rains, when the mountains and the high hills are clothed in a rich green, and the streams foam and froth over the stones and waterfalls, then, indeed, is a tramp through the mountains healthy, strengthening and inspiring both for soul and for body."

Rydal Mount owes its origin to Herbert Smith, who, with three brothers, arrived in the Witzieshoek area from Pietermaritzburg, round about 1880. Herbert started to farm, and built a rough farmhouse on the gentle slope of a hill, facing *Mount Qua-qua*. But he soon realised the potentialities of the place from a tourist point of view. To the south, heaving up into the blue African sky, was the *Sentinel*, and the *Amphitheatre*,† only eight kilometres away, and easily accessible via the Namahadi Pass. This pass lies roughly at the junction between the main Drakensberg Range and the Malutis, which form the northern boundary of Lesotho. In the early days it was one of the chief highways from the lofty Lesotho plateau down into the plains of the Eastern Free State. It was formerly known as Mopeli's Pass, or Monontsa's Pass, and is about 1½ km west of the present Chain Ladder, near the source of the Eland's River. It was also known at one time as the Gould-Adam's Pass. To the west were the Malutis, haze-blue in summer, snow-capped in winter. While lacking the grandeur of the main Drakensberg, they were very lovely. To the north were the huge red precipices of *Mount Qua-qua*. This was a tremendous sandstone block of a mountain, and it seemed to dominate the whole area. It was

---

* Since these words were written the building has been entirely demolished.
† The reader is referred to the sketch on page 96.

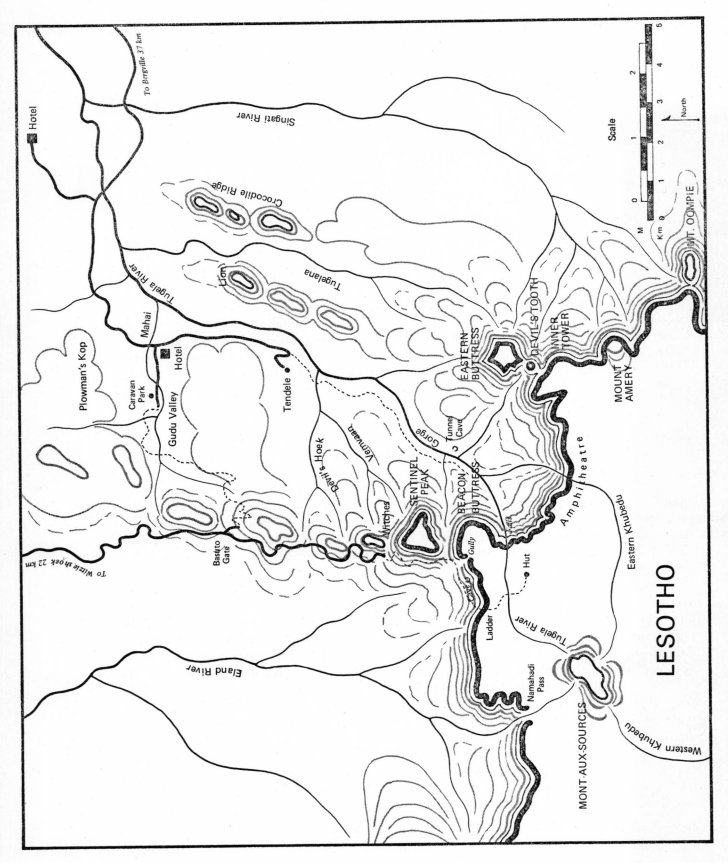

Map of Mont-aux-Sources Area

88

the home of the mountain eagles, and offered closer, and easier, climbs than the *Amphitheatre*. In 1890 Smith started taking in paying guests, and soon the place began to be known for its warm, genial hospitality, and as a starting point for those to whom the mountains called.

In 1909 it was taken over by the eccentric Irishman we have already met, Tom Casement, brother of the notorious Sir Roger Casement. Sir Roger at the time was the British Consul in the Belgian Congo, and actually visited his brother soon after Tom had taken over the place. It was Tom who finally converted the old farm-house into a roomy and comfortable Hotel, with outside rooms, and a dance floor. Soon holiday makers from far and near were descending on the place.

These days under Tom Casement were the best days that the Hotel was ever to know. Rail-head was at Aberfeldy, 35 km away, or through Kestell Road (52 kilometres), and Tom ran a coach service to bring his guests to the Hotel. But the roads were little better than wagon tracks. There were no bridges, and wet weather could mean flooded rivers, and travellers held up for weeks at a time. During holiday seasons, especially at Christmas, Tom's transport was unable to cope with the crowds, and local farmers from all around piled in to help. The roads were choked with American buck-boards, spiders, buggies, dog-carts, wagonettes and traps of every description, as they all took to the roads to bring Tom's guests the 35 kilometres to the Hotel. Great clouds of dust hung above the roads over the Free State plains, as the buggies all converged on the little Inn, with whips cracking and the raucous cries of the drivers. At the end of one Christmas season more than 600 guests had enjoyed Tom's hospitality. Days were spent in riding and hiking through the lovely country of Witzieshoek, where the Eland River flowed, and in the evenings fair ladies in their bustles and moustachioed gentlemen in their stiff Edwardian collars and Norfolk jackets danced long into the night to the fiddles and the castanets.

Most famous of all was the trip to the summit, organised to the last detail by Tom, himself no mean mountaineer. Parties would leave on horseback in the early morning, and ride through the pleasant valleys of the Eland to the foot of the Namahadi Pass. Here they would sleep the night in Suai's Cave. It is to be hoped that the ghosts of past occupants did not haunt the dreams of the tired riders, for blood had been shed years ago in this cave at the foot of the quiet mountains. A party of raiding Bushmen had caught two of the herd boys of Moshoeshoe, and had gouged out their eyes. It was a time of blood, and blood could only be answered by blood. The spearmen of Moshoeshoe gathered one night to avenge the deed. They surrounded Suai's Cave, where the Bushmen were sleeping. At three in the morning they leapt in to the attack, and all, old men, women and children, were hacked to death, all except the young girls, who were more useful alive than dead. Such is the story of Suai's Cave.

Next morning the riders would ascend the Pass, up Jacob's Ladder, reach the summit, and gasp as they gazed at the fairest view in all Africa, *Mont-aux-Sources*, the 3 000 metre precipices of the *Amphitheatre*, and the vast plains of Natal spread out far below. Here too were the Tugela Falls, the water pouring over a 1 200 metre drop into the gorge below, except in winter, when it was all iced over. Then back home, unless they planned a longer stay, in which case they slept in Crow's Nest Cave, near the site of the present Mountain Club Hut. And everything, supplies, equipment, horses, guide, for only R2 a day.

Those must have been wonderful days in the high Drakensberg, with Tom and Father Kelly and Melatu, and an occasional visit from the Amphlett's, who lived in Cape Town – first ascents, lonely valleys, virgin peaks, all to be explored and sampled. *Sentinel* was the first to be climbed. In 1909 W. J. Wybergh from Johannesburg reconnoitred the peak, but he had no companion with him, and could not tackle the climb alone. Next year, however, he persuaded Lieut. N. M. McLeod, of the Royal Field Artillery, stationed at Harrismith, to accompany him, and together the two men made their way to Suai's Cave, where they spent the night.

Next morning they set off for the peak. According to Wybergh's subsequent account it would appear that they decided to go straight for the peak, up the lower slopes, rather than up Namahadi Pass, along the summit and down the gully. It was 5th October 1910, and the day dawned misty, with the promise of rain.

The northern and eastern faces of *Sentinel Peak* are almost sheer rock (the eastern face has never been climbed), but the southern and western faces are more broken. It is the western face that is usually climbed to-day, but Wybergh and McLeod elected to make their attempt on the southern face. As they climbed up the lower shoulder of the mountain the mist closed in around them, and the wind blew bitter and cold. It was only with considerable difficulty that they managed to find their way on to the south face. Soon after reaching the climb proper, the mist suddenly cleared, and they saw in front of them a long diagonally-sloping crack, which looked promising. Roping up, they tackled it, and soon emerged from the crack on to a good, large platform. This however led them to a huge perpendicular cliff, with no friendly crack this time. Traversing to the right, they found a narrow, saw-toothed ridge, almost overhanging the vertical cliffs of a profound gulf on the Natal side, with the Tugela River far below. By now the mists had closed in again, and the dislodging of a boulder, followed by a long interval of silence, spoke eloquently to them of the depths below. The only way was up this saw-toothed ridge.

But they were lucky. The ridge broadened out, and soon they were on steep slopes of alternating rock and heather, and they made good time. Soon however another vertical cliff loomed up above them in the mist, and they called a halt to consider the position. Fortunately the wind had dropped, and then, to their left, they saw dimly through the mist another steep and narrow ridge, stretching up into the swirling dimness above. It offered the only hope. "A fine bit of climbing it was, too," says Wybergh, "with firm rocks and good holds, and therefore perfectly safe for the climber, but also with abysses on both sides of a character to satisfy the most exacting lover of the sport." It got steeper and steeper, but just when the difficulties seemed insurmountable, a narrow ledge appeared on the left, which took them on to the western face, and enabled them to circumvent the difficult bit.

This proved the crux of the climb. "A short scramble," says Wybergh, "and then suddenly the slope eased off; we looked in vain for further cliffs above us and then realised that the peak was conquered."

They lingered on the summit for a brief while in the hopes that the weather would clear; every now and then a gleam of pale sunshine appeared in the rifts of scudding mist, but it was not to be, and they had to start the descent. Two hours later they were down at the base of the peak, but it was still only midday, and they decided to have another crack at the summit. McLeod had noticed a rather intriguing chimney which he thought might offer an alternative route. Wedging themselves into the cleft, and worming their way up with feet and back, they made it, and for the second time that day stood on the summit. Once again, however, the mists denied them the view they had so eagerly anticipated, and, regretfully, they had to climb down again.

It was 5th October 1910, a date to be remembered, for it was the first page in the first chapter of the long story of man's conquest of the peaks of Quathlamba. The climbs of the Stocker brothers in 1888 had been merely the prologue. On 5th October 1910 the curtain finally went up on the drama. On this day man first set his face to the high peaks, and accepted their immutable challenge. Down the years his vision has never dimmed. And to-day the challenge is still there, for always there are unclimbed routes to be explored and new heights to conquer. All this, of course, was but one small facet in man's eternal search for the unattainable, in his inward drive down the ages to struggle always from the lowlands to the heights, but remember that the sparkle of the gem comes from a hundred small facets, and that each facet is important in itself. The response of the climber when he sees for the first time the virgin peak enwreathed in cloud is symbolic of man's impulsive urge to march onwards, always, into the unknown,

"to strive, to seek, to find, and not to yield".

It was the first page. The other pages followed swiftly. Back at Rydal Mount, Wybergh was so thrilled with his climb that he persuaded Tom Casement to come up with him immediately on a repeat performance, and a few days later the two men were back on the peak. This time fortune smiled on them, the weather was perfect, and they were rewarded with what must surely be one of the finest views in all Africa. Not content with that, the indefatigable Wybergh was back again a month later, this time with a large party, consisting of his wife and his twelve-year old daughter Betty; Mr. and Mrs. Amphlett; Miss Jagger; Tom Casement; G. J. Miller, a Bloemfontein journalist; Miss Gordon-Smith, and the faithful Melatu. Only Miller and Miss Gordon-Smith failed to make the top. The party assembled at Rydal Mount and this time proceeded up Namahadi Pass to the summit, and down the gully to the base of the peak. Again the weather was bad, and they climbed in mist, rain and thunderstorms, but eight of the party reached the summit. The first lady there was Mrs. Wybergh, while little Betty not only climbed well and reached the top, but later was to develop into a very fine mountaineer herself.

This was the start of Tom Casement's climbing career. He teamed up with Father Kelly and G. J. Miller after that, and, with Tom's Basutho servant Melatu, the four men made a number of sensational ascents in the area.

Six months later, in May 1911, Tom and Melatu made their way over Basuto Gate Pass and down into the gorge of the Tugela River. From there they climbed Sentinel Gully. This is the gully which runs up from the Tugela Gorge to the nek separating *Sentinel Peak* from the main escarpment. Even Tom, who had nerves of iron, described the climb later as "terrifying". The gully was packed with huge, loose boulders, heavily iced up, and the cold was intense. Three large and difficult waterfalls blocked their way, and had to be circumvented. They only just managed to reach the top.

On 13th June 1913 Father Kelly and Miller accomplished a first ascent of *Inner Tower*. The *Inner Tower* consists of three summits separated by narrow clefts about 20 metres in depth. From the top of the *Amphitheatre* wall the two men descended into the nek separating the *Tower* from the main escarpment, and from there contoured along the south face of the *Tower* and into the first of the two smaller clefts. From this cleft they climbed the left-hand, western, wall, and so reached the highest of the three summits, the one nearest the escarpment edge.

The next dramatic event took place on Friday, July 10, 1914. That night Melatu came running in to Tom Casement, who was entertaining his guests at Rydal Mount. "Baas," he cried out excitedly, "there is a fire on top of *Outer Tower!*" The peak had been climbed at last. Melatu set out hot-foot to greet the victors.

The victors were the same two men who had climbed *Inner Tower* a year previously, Father Kelly, the climbing priest from Bloemfontein, and G. J. Miller, the journalist. They had left Rydal Mount the previous day, made their way over Basuto Gate Pass, and so into Tugela Gorge, where they camped for the night.

Next morning, just as it was getting light, they left camp at 6.45 a.m. and made their way up the stream running up to *Devil's Tooth*. By 1.30 p.m. they had reached the nek between *Devil's Tooth* and *Eastern Buttress*, called in those days *Outer Tower*, and from there they made their way on to the northern face of the peak, facing the Tugela Valley. Here they found a narrow and very steep gully, up which they climbed, and by 3 p.m. they were on the summit, perilously late for that time of the year. By now, they were tired. They decided to spend a couple of hours resting, and at 5 p.m., after firing the grass, and with only half an hour's daylight left, they commenced the descent. By the time they had reached the nek at the base of *Devil's Tooth*, it was dark.

They managed to climb a little way down the gully in the dark, and then found a small ledge, with sharp pitches above and below, where they spent the night. Nearby was a narrow crack, and by squeezing into this they managed to catch a little water as it fell, drop by drop. Better still, they also found some dead trees in the gully, and managed to keep a fire going for most of the night. They had no blankets, and for food only 57 grams (two ozs.) of chocolate. It was too cold to sleep, and through the long hours of the winter night they sat and dozed around their fire. Next morning, 27 hours after leaving it the previous day, they reached their camp down in the Gorge, and there, to their surprise, they met Melatu, uttering howls of delight and waving a big bag of food. "He who does not know the joy of climbing," said the good Father after this climb, "does not know what joy is, and this reaches its acme when it is crowned by the achievement of a first ascent."

Four weeks later, not to be out-done, Tom Casement made a second ascent of the peak, taking Melatu with him to the summit.

After Casement left Rydal Mount for the East African Campaign in 1915, it was again taken over by Herbert Smith, until he died about 1918. But its best days were over, and from the time Casement left, a steady decline set in. Water was always a difficulty. In the early days it used to be carted up from the river in drums by ox-wagon, but it was scarce, and exasperated guests, coming in hot and tired after a day's climb, were told "Sorry, no water!" Being outside of a municipality no liquor licence was available, and in 1919 Mr. Coventry, first lessee of the new Hotel on the Natal side, started to cut a series of paths to the summit, making for much easier access from the Natal side than the one up the Namahadi Pass. Worse still, it fell into inexperienced hands. From about 1919 to 1922 a Mrs. Enslin had it, and she ran it like a Girls' Boarding School, with all sorts of irksome restrictions. It must have been about this time that a ribald song used to be sung in the neighbouring farm-houses to the tune of *There is a Happy Land, Far, Far Away*:

> *There is a boarding-house*
> *Not far away,*
> *Where the guests get rotten eggs*
> *Three times a day.*

It revived for a time under Dr. Andries Cronje round about 1925. Dr. Cronje added rondavels, an ablution block, and a polished stone floor in the Lounge, still to be seen in 1967. He put in a pump and engine, and built a swimming bath. Then a younger brother of Cronje took over and it finally fell into the hands of another Irishman, by the name of Ostack. But competition with the Natal side was too keen. The new Hostel at what is now the Royal Natal National Park, had recently been taken over by Otto Zunckel and his son Walter, and was flourishing, attracting guests from far and near. Rydal Mount finally closed down in the early thirties. The land and the buildings on it were purchased by the Government, and added to the neighbouring Witzieshoek Bantu Reserve, and the buildings were demolished in 1969.

On the day I visited it in 1967, an air of sadness hung over the forgotten buildings. Two ancient oak trees still stood guard over the front entrance, but the grass had grown right up to the very doors and into the cracks of the stone walls. To the right of the steps, almost hidden in the long grass, a rose tree, planted no doubt in the early days, still struggled bravely above the choking grass, but for the rest the gardens and the terraced lawns were no more. The rooms which once echoed to the sounds of gay laughter and the soft swish of skirts, were deserted and empty. Toilet appliances had been stripped off the walls, wash basins hung drunkenly from their fittings. The swimming bath was cracked and full of weeds and stagnant water. The laughter and the bright lights were no more, the whiskered gentlemen and the ladies with the sigh and the lowered eyelash, all had gone. Only the whisper of the wind in the long grass was the same as it was in those days of long ago.

And over it all broods *Mount Qua-qua*, serene, aloof, unsmiling, ageless. For what are the brief antics of puny man in the face of its hundred million years!

Witzieshoek itself, of course, has a history much older than that of Rydal Mount. The first inhabitants, as far as we know, were the Bushmen. Then round about 1700 A.D. the Amatheza, as we have already seen, crossed over the Drakensberg at Gordon's Pass, the present Basuto

Gate. They settled for a while in the valley, then moved on into the valley of the Caledon. They were followed by the Bahalanga, and the Wars of the Mfecane, when the pleasant valley was drenched in blood. When the Voortrekkers passed through the area on their way down into Natal in 1837, they found the Makholokoes living there, under their Chief Oetse. Oetse was a bit of a rogue and a scoundrel. He was a famous witch-doctor and rain-maker, consulted from far and near, even from as far away as the Natal coast. The Boers, exasperated at last with him, drove him out in 1856. His last refuge was a huge cave on the eastern slopes of a hill above Monontsa, the royal kraal of Paulus Mopeli, brother of Moshoeshoe. It was 140 metres long, 50 metres deep, and 30 metres high. Here he took refuge. It was found impossible to drive him out, and the only hope was to starve him into submission. The Boers surrounded the cave, sat down, and prepared to wait. But one night Oetse and a few of his men crept out and fled into Lesotho. (Another story is that he trekked down into Natal, and from there into Pondoland, where he died, but the former account is more likely to be correct.) The rest of his followers surrendered, but Oetse lived on and gave his name to the area, Oetse becoming corrupted into Witzie.

The tribe now inhabiting Witzieshoek is a branch of the Basutho. They originally came from the area between Clocolan and Ladybrand. Their Chief was Paulus Mopeli. He became involved in the war of 1866 between the Boers and the Basutho. Mopeli eventually made peace with President Brand, and in 1868 was given the Witzieshoek area in which to live. Soon after settling there, Paulus Mopeli appealed to President Brand for a Mission Station to be established in the area, and this was done in 1873. Such was the origin of the well-known Mission Station at Witzieshoek. Mopeli, obviously a very enlightened man, died shortly before the Anglo-Boer War of 1899-1902, deeply mourned by his people.

A few years prior to 1928, the Free State built a road into and through Witzieshoek, with the idea that eventually the Lesotho Government might carry it on from there into Lesotho, up the Namahadi Pass. This was never done. A few years ago, however, the Free State Provincial Administration began extending this road on their own account up the spurs of the Drakensberg, to Basuto Gate, the old Gordon's Pass. From here it joined the original bridle path, cut by Walter Coventry in 1919, and known to thousands of mountaineers who have followed its winding course to the summit. This path has now been converted into a wide, modern motor road, which leads right up under the *Witches*, and almost to the final precipices of the *Sentinel*. I have no doubt that some day it will continue on into Lesotho possibly through a tunnel to the summit. Namahadi, by the way, is the Basutho name for the Eland River. It means "much meat". In its lower reaches the river enters a series of gorges, into which the game would be driven and killed. Hence there was much meat.

Yes, *Mount Qua-qua* had much of interest to gaze down upon in its hundred million years. But strangest happening of all was surely the story of the boat that was "launched" at Witzieshoek, "sailed" down to Durban, and from there over to Europe.

In July 1883, 246 Norwegians had been settled at Port Shepstone on the Natal coast to help the infant fishing industry. The following year, however, was the worst year of the depression which hit Natal about that time. Many of the Norwegians failed, and many gave up. Three of them, Zefanias Olsen, and two brothers, Ingvald and Bernhard Nilsen, arrived one day in 1885 at Witzieshoek. Here, strangers in a strange land, far from the sea, their natural home, their hearts ached for the singing of the wind in the sails, and for the fiords and rivers of their native land. They decided to build a boat, sail the ocean seas, and return home!

They cut timber in the forests (in those days Witzieshoek was far more densely forested than it is to-day), and set to work, planning a $4\frac{3}{4}$ ton boat. It was 6 metres long, 2,1 metres broad, 1 metre deep, and 45 cm above the water-line. The rigging consisted of one mast, a top-mast, a main sail, a gaff and top-sail, a foresail, and a studding sail with yard. They named it *The Homeward Bound*.

By March 1886 it was ready, and "launched" on its long journey. It was loaded on to an ox-wagon, and proudly "sailed" down the long white ribbon of road, through Natal, to Durban, a "voyage" of some 465 kilometres. Arrived there, it was launched, and on 2nd May 1886 it crossed the bar and headed for the open sea.

They reached Cape Town without mishap, and received a tumultuous welcome there. In one of the local papers appeared the following verse:

> *Welcome, tiny craft, to Table Bay,*
> *We have looked to you for many a day.*
> *Now you have come, we say all round,*
> *May God watch over the "Homeward Bound".*

On her voyage from Cape Town she called at St. Helena and Ponta Delgada in the Azores, arriving at Dover on 28th March 1887, exactly a year since its "launching" at Witzieshoek. Here they were feted and the boat was exhibited at the Crystal Palace. But it never reached Norway. Zefanias Olsen fell in love, married, and settled down in England, while the two Nilsen brothers continued on to Norway in another boat. They were pioneers of a very special order, for this was the first boat to be built in South Africa that sailed to England, and surely the only boat ever to be built in the Drakensberg!

Yes, there was much to see, and only the eagle in his rocky eyrie knows what *Mount Qua-qua* thinks of it all, dreaming his long sleep in the caverned clouds.

CHAPTER IX

MONT-AUX-SOURCES AND THE ROYAL NATAL NATIONAL PARK

> *"They leap the sky,*
> *They tear at the clouds,*
> *Foam drips from their steep jaws."*
> —LEONORA SPEYER

For sheer magnificence of mountain scenery it would be difficult to find anything more awe-inspiring than the Mont-aux-Sources area of the Natal Drakensberg. Its very symmetry captures the imagination – the huge curved wall of the *Amphitheatre*, flanked at each end by two mighty peaks, the *Sentinel* and the *Eastern Buttress*, with the Tugela River pouring over this majestic wall, one of the highest waterfalls in the world, down into the Gorge below. Against these mighty bastions the clouds break in glorious spray and the winds roar their sonorous song. But when they sleep, as sleep they will, you will find here the stillness of eternity, with only a solitary eagle, a speck in the blue immensity, patrolling the skyways. Colonel Amery, who visited the area in 1900, maintained that there was nothing in the whole of the Canadian Rockies to touch it, and it is questionable whether there is anything in Europe or America comparable to the seven kilometres of canyon below the Falls.

It was one of the first areas in the Drakensberg to be opened up. As far back as the 1850's guide books of the period mention the *Amphitheatre*, the Falls and the Tugela Gorge. In those early days the *Amphitheatre* was called the *Saddleback*, the name appearing even as far back as 1836, a whole year before the Voortrekkers came to the area. Later it was changed to the *Horse-shoe*. The name *Amphitheatre* seems to date from the early 1900's. In 1884 the whole area was surveyed, and farms, State land and Bantu Reserve boundaries were demarcated. In those early days woodcutters were active, and several wood-cutting concessions were granted. Dooley, well-known to to-day's tourists, was named after an Irish woodcutter who lived there in the 1880's.

But long before the harsh ring of the wood-cutter's axe was heard in those quiet valleys, man had ventured there. Hunting parties would make their way up the Valley of the Tugela, and gaze in awe at the tremendous Gorge through which the Tugela River rumbles and roars, and at the mighty basalt cliffs that closed in and soared up around them into the sky.

Even the odd tourist came. In 1878 Edith Pickering married Fred Kelly. She was a young girl of 19 years of age, with plenty of spirit, who had run away from home in England and come to Natal in search of adventure. But she carried with her a letter of introduction from Bishop Colenso, and this paved the way for her entrance into the best society in Pietermaritzburg. After a couple of years as a governess she came up to the Northern Districts of Natal, and here she met Fred, who was farming at *Lytton*, between Ladysmith and Oliviershoek. Soon they were engaged, and then married. Captain Allison, the Border Agent at Oliviershoek, was one of the sponsors at her wedding.

When Fred asked her where she would like to go for her honeymoon, she said, "I have seen the Drakensberg Mountains, and fallen in love with them. I have been in love with them ever since, and I shall remain in love with them till I die. Fred, I would like to go to the Drakensberg in an ox-wagon." And to the Drakensberg they went. Fred took his young bride to the Mont-aux-Sources area, and they camped in their wagon in the Tugela Valley, not far from the Gorge.

It was one of the wildest spots they could have chosen. Their piccanin had come from a tribe of one-time cannibals. During the days they explored the Gorge and the huge rock chasms,

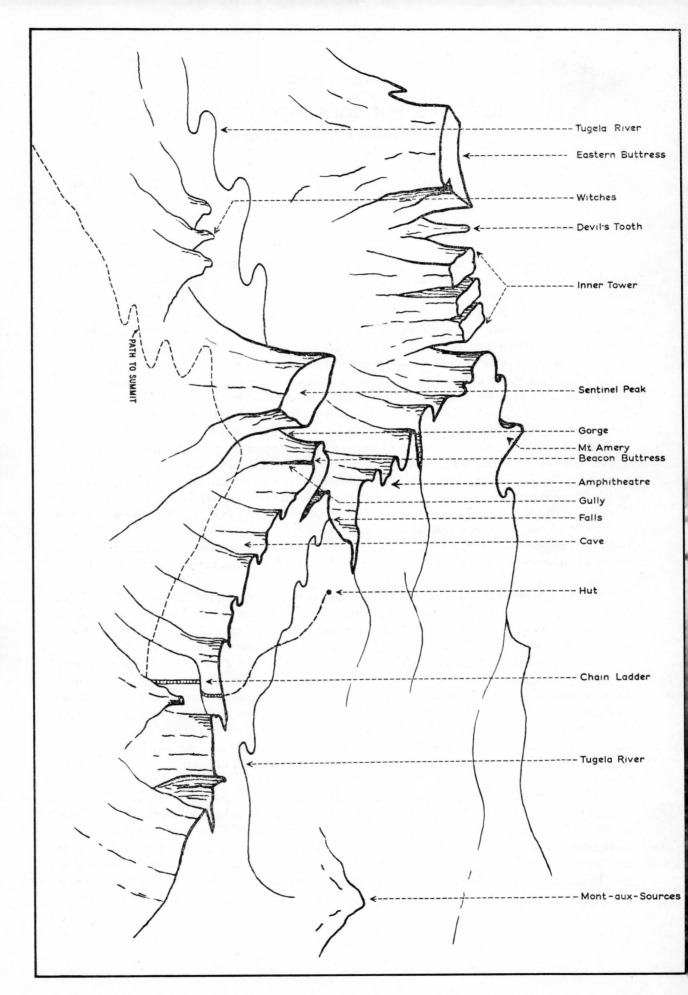

SKETCH OF MONT-AUX-SOURCES
FROM IMAGINARY HIGH POINT, LOOKING SOUTH

PATH TO SUMMIT

Tugela River
Eastern Buttress
Witches
Devil's Tooth
Inner Tower
Sentinel Peak
Gorge
Mt. Amery
Beacon Buttress
Amphitheatre
Gully
Falls
Cave
Hut
Chain Ladder
Tugela River
Mont-aux-Sources

and gathered flowers on the grassy slopes of the hills. At night they heard the strange cries of leopards. They even came across a party of Bushmen, "weird-looking creatures, hardly bigger than a child of ten," Edith used to tell her grandchildren in later years. These must have been amongst the last remaining Bushmen in the Drakensberg, though it is possible they might have trekked down temporarily from Lesotho.

Edith never forgot her honeymoon in the Drakensberg. In her old age, living peacefully at Henley-on-Klip, she used to tell her grandchildren, "I would like every South African to see the Drakensberg Mountains, to know them as I know them, and to love them as I love them."

Eight years before Edith Pickering's honeymoon, in 1870, Dr. J. W. Matthews, who later became the Vice-President of the Legislative Council of the Cape, had also visited the area. He has left us a vivid account of this visit, and of his climb to the summit. He stayed with Captain Allison, the Border Agent, who had his post just over eleven kilometres from the Tugela Falls. This must have been somewhere near the site of the present National Park Hotel. After visiting the Cannibal Caves of Chief Sidinane, he left for a two or three day trip to the summit, accompanied only by three African guides. They climbed over what they called a spur of the Drakensberg, and so down into the Orange Free State. This was almost certainly over the Pass which we know to-day as Basuto Gate. Here they entered a lovely valley, a tributary of the Eland River, boulder-hopped up it, and then, after exploring a cave with Bushman paintings, proceeded up the Namahadi Pass. Arrived at the top, they stood spell-bound at the magnificence of the scene. The summit was covered with scarlet and purple heather, but it was the mighty drop into the Tugela Gorge below that fascinated them. "Stupendous magnificence" and "savage grandeur" are phrases that drop readily from the pen of Dr. Matthews.

He celebrated his climb with a bottle of champagne, and left the empty bottle in a cairn of stones with a note inside describing his trip. Then they collected some small twigs for a fire, heaped up some heather for a bed, and slept soundly throughout the night.

Next morning, after a magnificent sunrise, Matthews was again on the edge of the escarpment. Lying on his stomach, he crept to the very edge, while the guides held his ankles, and peered over. He hurled a rock down the sheer drop, timing it with a stop-watch. It took twelve seconds to reach the first ledge. How many hundreds of tourists have not done exactly the same thing in the years that followed! After hunting around without success for dinosaur remains, they set out for "Umbundi's Pass", by which route they hoped to return home to Allison's.

From here on the account of his trip becomes a little difficult to follow. "Umbundi's Pass" was supposed to lead to the "Ulandi Valley". Neither of these names is known to-day. Matthews says they travelled south for two or three miles to the head of the Pass. There is an Mbundini Pass, south-east of *Mont-aux-Sources*, which leads down from the summit to Natal, but this is ten miles (16 km) away, and not two or three, and very different from the Pass which Matthews described. It is possible to descend via a very steep ravine between *Inner Tower* and the main escarpment, and this is certainly two or three miles south of *Mont-aux-Sources*, but to-day this necessitates the use of rope. Nevertheless, I think this must have been the "Pass" to which Matthews refers. It is not a route normally taken by to-day's tourists.

According to Matthews, they reached the head of the pass and commenced the descent at about 10 a.m. It was a narrow and dangerous gorge. They climbed down for two hours, but were suddenly brought to a stop by a steep, smoothly-worn chasm in the rock, a huge waterfall, and a large, deep pool of water, clear as crystal, at its bottom. They had to turn back for some 90 metres to circumvent the pool, and creep along a narrow ledge, and so down into the valley, which they followed home.

And so the years rolled by, until, in 1903, Walter Coventry bought the farm *Goodoo*. Walter was a grandson of John Coventry, farming at *Acton Homes*. In 1903 he was a young man of

27 years of age. He had first visited the area in 1898, with his two brothers, liked it, and decided eventually to build there. The first room of the house which was eventually to grow into the Royal Natal National Park Hotel was built in 1903. So began an association that was to last for 23 years. In 1926 he and his wife left for another farm a few kilometres away, which eventually became the present Caverns Guest Farm. He died in 1965, at the age of 89.

Few men have done more for the National Park area than Walter Coventry. His fame spread, and he soon became known as "The Man of the Mountains". He loved the simple things of life – growing things, the shy creatures of the forests and the mountain slopes, the sounds of dawn and sunset. With his rare sense of humour, his genuine kindliness and readiness to help, his warm friendliness, he won the hearts of all who had the privilege of sharing his home in those early days. His daughter Doreen married William Chalmers, the man who carved a gigantic statue in the Mont-aux-Sources area, from a 9 100 kg rock, 6 metres long by 2½ metres high. It depicts a reclining angel, and is called "The Spirit of the Woods". It is still there, and always will be, for to move it would cost R20 000!

Goodoo, the farm Walter Coventry bought, means "Smoking Horn". He bought it for £1 an acre from a Mr. van Rooyen, a butcher from Bergville. He had a vague idea of attracting holiday-makers to the area. He put in a Mr. W. G. Brighton as tenant.

It was a lonely and isolated spot. The nearest railhead was Ladysmith, 93 kilometres away. The nearest village was a small outpost, called Upper Tugela, on the farm *Klein Waterval*, 45 kilometres away. In the year that Coventry bought *Goodoo* it was renamed Bergville. The only connection between *Goodoo* and Bergville was a rough native sledge-track. But this did not deter the eager holiday-maker, and soon *Goodoo* began to receive a thin stream of guests. Brighton used to meet them at Ladysmith with his ox-wagon, convey them to Bergville, and then from Bergville to *Goodoo* by sledge.

The area in those days consisted partly of Bantu Reserve, partly of farms which had been surveyed and bought, and partly of unoccupied farms that belonged to the State. In 1906 the Hon. W. F. Clayton, Minister of Agriculture and Lands in the Natal Government, took the first step in the establishment of a National Park. In that year he proclaimed the unoccupied areas a National Park. Clayton also arranged for the Natal Government Railways to send a photographic team into the area, consisting of Messrs. Tatlow, Watkinson and Allerston, to publicise it, and this resulted in a fine set of photographs which for many years adorned the railway carriages of the Natal Government Railways.

In 1908 the territory was explored by Senator Frank Churchill, Col. (later General) J. S. Wylie, and Col. Dick, under the guidance of Walter Coventry, and they decided to go ahead, expand the area, and develop the Park to its full potential.

But times were bad, and shortly before Union the Natal Government decided, because of lack of funds, to abandon the scheme, and sell the land. It was bought by General Wylie, and after Union this public-spirited gentleman sold it back to the Government at cost price on condition that it remained for all time a National Park for the people of South Africa. A new start had been made.

At first accommodation was primitive in the extreme, but in 1913 Mr. F. C. Williams, who was leasing Coventry's farm *Goodoo* at the time, built a small Hostel on the site of the present Hotel, and more and more people began to come to the area.

In 1916 the Secretary of Lands authorised the reservation of five extra farms and a certain portion of Crown Lands, totalling approximately 3 300 hectares. The Natal Provincial Executive Committee then formally took over the Park, and on 16 September 1916 an Advisory Committee was appointed to control the Park. In 1919, the farms *Goodoo* (486 ha), *Dooley* (283 ha) were bought from Mr. Coventry, together with *Basuto Pass, Devil's Hoek, Vemvaan, The Pastures* and *Diamond*. In addition, 1 109 ha of Upper Tugela Trust Land were taken over without alienation from the Native Trust, and this brought the total area of the Park to 6 313 ha. Williams' small Hostel was enlarged, becoming the first National Park Hostel, and Walter Coventry was installed as the first lessee. The Hostel could now take 12 guests.

Coventry immediately set to work to establish the Park on a sound basis. The first paths were laid out. Prior to 1919 the route to the summit was still the route taken by Dr. Matthews in 1870 – up Goodoo Pass, over the nek at Basuto Gate, down into the Free State, and then up the Eland's River to Namahadi Pass and so to the top. One of the first things Coventry did was to engineer a shorter route. From Basuto Gate he struck off left, straight for the *Sentinel*, instead of going down into the Free State, building the path so well-known since then to thousands of tourists. It was ready for use in 1924. In those days the final 150 metres to the summit were negotiated via what became known as the Gully, with a spacious cave near the foot in which climbers spent the night. In 1930 the Natal Provincial Administration installed two sensational Chain Ladders (100 rungs) to surmount the final rock wall, so as to by-pass the Gully. This Gully was often rendered impassable in winter through being choked with snow and ice.

August of 1924 also saw Walter Coventry taking over the newly-created post of Park Superintendent, at the princely salary of R10 per month. Two and a half years later, in November 1926, he resigned his post, after firmly establishing the infant Park as one of South Africa's premier tourist attractions.

Those were great days immediately after World War I and in the early 1920's. Walter and his wife gave to the Hostel a homely, cheerful air, and did all they could to ease the way of the climber who wished to explore this as yet largely unknown area. If you went off for the day, you were not just given a packet of sandwiches and a flask of cold tea. Always there was a party of guides ahead of you, and you would turn a corner of the path in a forest to find a white table-cloth laid out on the ground, gleaming cutlery, and a pot of steaming porridge, smoking bacon and eggs, and a can of boiling coffee awaiting you for breakfast. It was the same for lunch with cold meat and salads tastefully arranged, again on a white table-cloth. By dusk you were back at the Hostel to a roaring fire, and sitting round the huge table with Mr. Coventry at one end and Mrs. Coventry at the other. Mrs. Coventry was rigorously opposed to any form of liquor, and I am afraid there was a good deal of surreptitious drinking in the barn! If you reported ill, Mrs. Coventry would march into your rondavel with a huge medical book under her arm. She would sit down in the chair, give you a searching look, and then proceed to read out a long string of symptoms of the most alarming nature, while the patient's hair literally stood on end. But the treatment was always the same: "Open your mouth – wide!" And down would go a big dollop of castor-oil! And everyone, even if it were Lady May Cambridge or Princess Alice, would have to take their turn in the queue for the one and only early morning bath.

I shall always remember the Coventry guest-house in those days in the early 1920's, for it was during Easter of 1924 that I spent six happy days there, and knew for the first time the lure of those beautiful mountains.

When Mr. Coventry resigned in 1926 the Hostel was taken over by Otto Zunckel and his son Walter. Otto, with his wonderful personality and understanding of people, made a perfect host, and he gave to his Hostel a unique spirit of warm geniality, camaraderie and friendship, while the cooking of his charming wife Mathilda was a thing you dreamed about long into the night, after you had left their hospitable roof.

On 1st March 1939 Otto and Mathilda retired to their new home at the summit of Oliviershoek Pass, and the Hostel was left in the capable hands of their son Walter. But tragedy struck on the night of December 10, 1941, for on that night the Hostel was burnt down. Walter set to with redoubled vigour, and re-built it on larger and more spacious lines, and in 1947 it housed for a brief while the Royal family during their tour of South Africa, thus giving to the Park the right to the title "Royal Natal National Park".

In the meantime the Advisory Committee, which had been established in 1916, had been abolished in January 1942. For six years the Park was administered by the Executive Committee of the Natal Provincial Council, until the formation of the Natal Parks, Game and Fish Preservation Board in December 1947. In August 1946 Mr. Peter Pope Ellis, the well-known cricketer, was appointed the first full-time Warden of the Park. Periodically, too, over the years, the boundaries of the Park were enlarged. In 1950 two farms, *Rugged Glen* and *Ungiyeza*, were purchased, bringing the area up to its present figure of 8 094 hectares.

To-day the Park, with its fine modern Hotel, still on the old site at *Goodoo*, its Hutted Camp at Tendele, its caravan park, its Fish Hatchery (the largest in Natal), and its well-posted bridle paths, is one of the finest holiday resorts in South Africa. The valleys are richly wooded with yellow-woods, Cape Chestnuts and Black Ironwoods; countless streams and waterfalls pour down the mountain-sides, and flash in the sun; while the wild flowers make of these lovely valleys and green slopes a botanist's paradise. The bush-buck, the white-tailed gnu, the grey rhebuck, the baboons and the rock-rabbits live here in peace, and the Black Eagle and the mighty Lammergeyer circle the skies in lordly indifference.

Over it all are the great peaks.

The *Amphitheatre* is easily the most spectacular of them. This is a huge mountain wall, slightly curved, four kilometres in length, and 1 500 metres high, its precipitous sides sculptured into a fantastic maze of towers, minarets and spires, and deeply-etched chasms and gorges.

Here is the birth-place of the Tugela River, one of the great rivers of South Africa. Its very name, which in Zulu means "startling", has been woven into the warp and woof of our history. Known to shipwrecked Portuguese sailors, closely connected with the rise and fall of the Zulu nation, discovered by French explorers, forded by the hardy Voortrekkers, harnessed by colonising Englishmen, king-pin to-day of the mighty Tugela Basin Development Scheme, and with battle-honours dating from the Anglo-Boer War, it rises on the summit of *Mont-aux-Sources* itself, some two or three kilometres inland from the edge of the escarpment. For a short distance it ripples over the great plain, and then suddenly, it plunges over the mighty wall of the *Amphitheatre*. In summer, after a Drakensberg storm, the roar of its thunder can be heard from away down the valley, but in winter its voice is stilled, for the bitter cold of the heights seizes and holds it, and it freezes solid. The height of the Falls is a matter of considerable controversy. Estimates vary from 620 metres to 950 metres. The latest figure is 855 metres.

After its dizzy plunge, it gathers momentum, thunders its way through the Gorge at the bottom, until it breaks out into the open plains, and starts on its long journey to the distant sea.

The summit of the *Amphitheatre* is easily reached from the western, Lesotho, side via the well-known bridle-path (now a motor road) and the Chain Ladder. The frontal face is another matter – a sheer mountain wall. Many attempts were made over the years to scale its terrifying precipices. George Londt and Frank Berrisford attempted to climb it in July 1922, but were forced back. The precipices were too heavily iced up. It was not until April 1935 that it was finally climbed. On Good Friday, 19th April, Doyle Liebenberg led a strong party consisting of Mark Frank, Aimée Netter and Mary Lear to the summit. Four years passed before the second ascent was made. On 19 January 1939, Dr. A. H. Park-Ross, Walter Zunckel and Mungo Park-Ross, scaled the wall for the second time. It was "P.R.'s" 60th birthday.

This summit is a vast plateau, called by the Basutho *Pofung (Empofeni)* or the Place of the Eland. Three kilometres inland from the edge of the escarpment is *Mont-aux-Sources* itself, 3 282 metres high, where Arbousset and Daumas had stood in 1836, and where the four rivers, the Eland, the Tugela, the Western Khubedu and the Eastern Khubedu, rise. A remarkable example of river capture is to be seen here. Originally the Eastern Khubedu flowed in a wide curve from *Mont-aux-Sources* down into Lesotho, but with the gradual eastward retreat of the escarpment, this curve was cut, resulting in the river flowing down the escarpment and into Natal, instead of through Lesotho.

Here, too, on the summit, is the Natal Mountain Club Hut, a haven of refuge in the early days for climbers from all over the country. It was built by Otto Zunckel and his son, Walter. All the material, other than the stone, had to be carried up over 21 km of mountain paths and a vertical distance of 1 850 metres.

It was officially opened during Easter of 1930. Climbers came from far and near for the ceremony. Of course "Oompie" Liddle was there, motoring all the way from Kimberley. Mrs. Botha-Reid was asked to open the Hut, a gracious tribute to the wife of the "father" of the Natal Mountain Club. That night they held a magnificent party in the Hut, and next day they "christened" *Mount Amery*, 4¼ km away. Mr. Botha-Reid performed the ceremony this time, using a bottle of petrol, as all the champagne had disappeared at the party the night before! The subsequent history of the Hut is a sad one. Originally it was beautifully equipped with wooden tables, bunks, comfortable mattresses, blankets and primus stoves. To-day it is no more than an empty shell, without even windows or doors. It became virtually impossible to prevent its contents being plundered by the Basutho, and a subsequent dispute over the ownership of the land on which it stood led eventually to its total neglect.

Before the construction of the new Mountain Road from Witzieshoek to the base of the *Sentinel* there were few lonelier spots on earth than the Plains of the Pofung. But in 1866 they were invaded, quite literally, by an army. During the Basuto War of that year Commandant Visser, with 546 burghers and 61 native scouts, ascended to the plateau and camped there for a brief while. In 1917 a Police Post was established not far from the eventual site of the Mountain Club Hut, and manned by a detachment of the Basutoland Mounted Police. But it was so isolated and lonely, and the altitude so great (it was the highest inhabited spot in South Africa, probably in the whole of Africa) that eventually it had to be abandoned.

Such, then, is Pofung, the Place of the Eland. "Here", said one who visited it in the early 1890's, "the air is filled with all the mystery, the loneliness, and the beauty of Africa".

Immediately to the south of the *Amphitheatre* is *Mount Amery*, and here the wall of the Drakensberg is a little easier. It drops down into the valley of the Singati, which means "Dancing Water", and this section is sometimes called the Singati Wall. It was this wall that Captain Amery descended in 1900. His claim, in later years, to have descended the Amphitheatre Wall can hardly be substantiated, for this can only be done by expert mountaineers equipped with rope. The Singati Wall was climbed for the first time by D. W. Bassett-Smith and probably R. G. Kingdon, round about 1920. *Mt. Amery* frontal (a new route) was first climbed in September 1955 by Robert and Malcolm Moor and Martin Winter. I had had the pleasure of introducing the two former young men to Drakensberg climbing a few years previously while they were still schoolboys.

To the north of the Tugela Falls, but still part of the escarpment, is *Beacon Buttress*. It derives its name from the beacon on its summit, where Natal, the Free State and Lesotho all meet. From this point on a clear day portions of three Provinces of the Republic – Natal, the Transvaal, the Orange Free State can be seen together with Lesotho. T. V. Bulpin claims that even portions of the Cape Province are visible.

North-east of *Beacon Buttress* is the *Sentinel*, one of the grandest of all Drakensberg peaks, and the first major peak to be climbed. When, and why, and by whom it was first called *Sentinel* is not known. In 1905 it had not been named at all. In 1910 it was called by the two names, *North-east Tower* and *Sentinel Peak*. As late as 1914 it was still being called *North-east Tower*. Its Zulu name is *Ntabamnyama*, the Black One. The previous Chapter has described how it was first climbed by W. J. Wybergh and Lieut. N. M. McLeod in October 1910.

The western face of the mountain, which faces the Chain Ladder, is fairly easily climbed, there being only two pitches requiring rope. Several other routes, however, of a much higher standard, have been opened up since the first ascents were made. The last of these was in 1959. On February 17 of that year Pam and Peter Angus-Leppan pioneered a route up the north face. As one fronts the peak from the bridle path below the *Witches*, one notices a long crack, slightly to the right of the highest point, running diagonally down from right to left. At the commencement of the crack is a small *gendarme*. It was up this crack that Pam and her husband made their climb.

Next to the *Sentinel*, and high above the bridle path, are the *Witches*. Prior to 1917 they were called *The Three Fingers*.

The southern bastion of the *Amphitheatre* is a little more complicated than the northern. Working from the outside in, towards the main escarpment, we have, first, the *Eastern Buttress*, sometimes called the *Outer Tower*. It was originally called *South-west Tower*. Then comes the fearful-looking *Devil's Tooth*, a thin, narrow spire about 50 metres lower than *Eastern Buttress*, but with 200 metres of sheer and apparently unclimbable sides. Beyond *Devil's Tooth* and next to the escarpment, is *Inner Tower*. At one time it was thought that there were two of these Towers, and they were called the *Middle* and the *Inner Towers*. In 1945, however, Stan Rose, Elizabeth Burton, and Hans Wong proved definitely that there is no *Middle Tower*, but only one block of basalt, with three summit plateaux separated from each other by narrow gaps about 15 to 20 metres in depth. They ascended all three summits. The term *Middle Tower* has now been abandoned, and this huge block of solid basalt is called *Inner Tower*. We have already told, in the previous Chapter, the story of the first ascents of *Eastern Buttress* and *Inner Tower*.

The story of the conquest of *Devil's Tooth* is as dramatic as any in the climbing history of the Drakensberg. From the very earliest days it had captured the imagination of veteran climbers, but so stupendous were its towering cliffs, and so smooth, that few thought it would ever be climbed.

It was given the name it bears to-day round about 1920, but by whom is not known. Prior to this it was called *Cleopatra's Needle*. Tom Casement, Father Kelly and G. J. Miller all had a look at it, and pronounced it quite unclimbable. They did not even attempt it.

By 1947 it had still not been climbed. Starkly it stood there, soaring up into the clouds, the last major unclimbed peak in the Drakensberg, possibly in the whole of South Africa. *Monk's Cowl*, *Column*, the *Bell*, the *Western Injasuti Triplet*, all had fallen. *Devil's Tooth* still stood there, proud and inviolate. It was a challenge few mountaineers could resist.

The first serious attempt on it was made in 1947. In that year Tobie Louw and Bill Curle set out, determined to be the first to breach its lonely summit. They had to turn back almost at the very foot of the peak. So sheer and smooth were the rock faces that it was almost impossible even to get on to the peak.

A month later Jannie Graaff and Tom Bright tackled it. It took them three hours and several pitons to make a traverse of 25 metres. This only brought them to the base of the pinnacle. They returned the following day, but again had to admit defeat. It was after this attempt that Graaff gave it as his opinion that only a team of dental mechanics would ever be able to extract the Tooth!

Three more unsuccessful attempts followed, and then, in August 1950, one of the strongest teams ever to be assembled in the Drakensberg gathered at the Hotel. It consisted of Des Watkins and his wife Jean, Charles Gloster, Barry Anderson, Ted Scholes, David Bell, Peter Campbell and Willie Politzer, all expert cragsmen. Half of these were Natal climbers and half from the Transvaal.

They set off from the National Park Hotel at 10 a.m. on Saturday, 5th August 1950, making their way up the Tugela River, into Tugela Gorge, and then striking left up Devil's Tooth Gully. There can surely be no peak in the whole of South Africa with a finer approach than *Devil's Tooth*. As they penetrated closer in to the Amphitheatre Wall, spire after spire, minaret upon minaret closed in around them, a maze of turrets and towers ending in the tremendous wall of the *Amphitheatre* itself. The climb up the Gully from the Gorge, to the base of the peak, is close on 1 200 metres, and as they climbed higher and higher the whole vast panorama of the *Amphitheatre*, from *Sentinel Peak* to *Eastern Buttress*, opened out before them.

Several years prior to this, during one of the abortive attempts on the peak, Bob Davies had discovered a cave underneath the *Tooth*, dry, well sheltered, and capable of accommodating eight to ten people. It is about 250 metres below the nek connecting the *Tooth* to the *Eastern Buttress*, 30 metres above the point where Devil's Tooth Gully divides on either side of the *Tooth*, on the *Eastern Buttress* slopes. They decided to use this cave as their base.

By late afternoon they had reached it, and were soon settled in. Before having their supper they sat at the entrance of their cave, looking straight across to the magnificent pinnacle towering above them, which they hoped to conquer, outlined starkly against a deep blue sky. The sun was just setting, and the peak glowed richly against the intense blue of the sky, "godlike in its appalling sheerness and utter impossibility", as one of them wrote afterwards. They wondered what the morrow held for them.

Next morning they were early astir. A stiff scramble up the left-hand gully, involving two short "D" pitches, and a grass traverse clock-wise round the back of the *Tooth*, and to the front again, brought them out on to the west face, where it abutted on the *Inner Tower*. From this point climbing was to commence. It was 9.30 a.m.

Previous attempts on the peak had established the fact that the only feasible route was on the side facing the Tugela, starting in the nek between the *Tooth* and *Inner Tower*, and veering left towards the north-eastern face. The whole base was surrounded by a 30 metre high barrier of overhanging rock with only one break in it, a rotten, bulging face leading up to an even more difficult recess. It was this face which had beaten all previous climbing parties.

It was decided that David Bell, Peter Campbell and Ted Scholes would do the actual climb. The rest of the party remained below as a support group, to be brought up later: three men climb much more **quickly** than eight.

David Bell led, and two pitches of "E" and "F" standard brought them to the foot of the bulging face which led to the recess. Here Ted Scholes took over, and belayed by two ropes he worked his way up until he was baffled by an unclimbable overhang just below the recess. Standing in a most precarious position, he made a supreme effort, and managed to hammer in a piton on the face above the overhang. To this he clipped a karabiner and one rope, and retired, exhausted. The manouvre had taken it out of him more than he cared to admit, and the other two insisted that he take a long rest. He was "out" of the climb for the next hour.

Now David Bell took over again. He climbed as far as the piton, but even with the help of this piton he found it quite impossible to surmount the bulge. It was two metres high, absolutely smooth, and it had to be surmounted if the recess, the only way through the overhangs to the summit, was to be reached.

David first of all managed to hammer in another piton, 30 cm below the previous one, through which he passed a short sling. Now came a piece of really tricky climbing. The sling was hanging down from the lip of the overhang, and about 30 cm from the rock face. Standing precariously on nothing more than a small friction hold with his left foot, David was able to lift his right foot almost shoulder high, and to place it in the sling, and then, with a terrific effort, hoist himself up. His free left foot found a small bump on the smooth upper face of the bulge, and then, a grab at a small grass tuft, a mighty push-off with his right foot from the sling, and a slight friction hold with his right hand, and he was up and over. It was a manouvre that would have taxed the strength and skill of the most expert gymnast. Once into the base of the recess, David made a piton belay, and brought up Peter Campbell.

But the recess itself was horribly smooth and sheer. High above were more overhangs. Peter now took over. Standing on David's shoulders he managed to get started up the recess. He reached a crack, into which he hammered a piton for a running belay, and attempted to climb on, but he failed. He had to return after accomplishing nothing more than the piton.

David now took the lead again, to give Peter a chance to recover his strength. He reached the piton, and using this as a handhold, he swung left across and into the recess. Here he found a handhold, and drove in another piton. "Holding on at this point," he says, "was not funny, but I managed to get about four feet up the crack, and knocked in a rather insecure piton." Belaying himself from this, he went down and rejoined Peter. Ted Scholes was still recovering his strength, far below them.

Peter, now rested, went up. He reached the last piton, and with a tremendous effort, surmounted an awkward projecting block, and reached the top of the recess.

And now a cheer went up from the support party far below, who had been breathlessly watching the three men climb. They had spent the last two or three hours sending up, at intervals, relays of tea and dried fruit by a light line to the well-nigh exhausted men above.

Peter now brought David and Ted up. Ted was now well rested after his heroic effort at the bulge. All three were now at the top of the recess. It was 3 p.m. They had taken five hours to climb 50 metres. Above them still loomed a further 100 metres of unknown and frightening rock. The possibility of being benighted on the *Tooth* was too dreadful to contemplate, so it was decided that the three men would press on alone, as fast as possible, in an attempt to reach the summit and descend before sunset, which would be at about 5.30 p.m. They dared not wait to be joined by the remainder of the party, still waiting below at the foot of the rock.

By now the exposure was appalling, and they were tired. Stupendous precipices still towered menacingly above them. Ted started off to explore the next pitch. He climbed swiftly. A very exposed "E" pitch brought him to the foot of a chimney. He quickly surmounted this, and then, to his indescribable relief, he found the upper defences had been penetrated. The last pitch was surprisingly easy after their grim battles lower down, and by 4 p.m. all three were at the top.

They built the usual cairn of stones. The summit was a bare three metres square, just room for the three men to stand on. They decorated the cairn with the tattered remains of Peter's pyjamas, which he had insisted on wearing underneath his shorts for additional warmth. Then they abseiled down, reaching the bottom about sun-set.

Drakensberg rock is very different from the rock of the Cape Mountains. It is friable, and breaks away easily. It is dangerous. I knew a well-known climber once who had climbed in the Himalayas. He refused to climb in the Drakensberg. He had too much respect for his neck, he said! It is surprising, therefore, that there have been so few accidents in our Drakensberg mountains. In fact, the only one I know of in the Mont-aux-Sources area, due to a rock breaking away, was the tragic death of Ross Osborn in 1953.

Ross was a second-year law student at Natal University in Durban. He was a fine student, keen athlete, and a member of the S.R.C., of which he had been Secretary the previous year, a potential Rhodes Scholar. He and a friend, Mr. S. Ferguson, also of Durban, set out to climb the *Amphitheatre* on Wednesday, 25 November 1953. They reached the Hut about noon, and then decided to come down via the Inner Tower Ravine, the route almost certainly taken by Dr. Matthews in 1870. Half way down they encountered a high waterfall, with steep rock faces on each side. This could easily have been the same waterfall that Dr. Matthews had encountered. After several attempts at circumventing this, they gave up, and decided to climb back up the Ravine, Ferguson leading. Ferguson reached the top, turned round, and was horrified to see the rock which Ross had grasped, breaking away, and Ross falling backwards into space.

It was impossible for Ferguson to reach the body – he could see it wedged amongst some rocks far below – but Ross was obviously dead and there was nothing he could do. He raced back to the Hut, where he found two married couples. One of them, a Mr. de Wit of Pretoria, offered to go for help. It was now dusk, but he set off immediately, heading for the Chain Ladder. Throughout the early hours of the night he made his way down the mountain side, arriving at the Hotel at 11.15 p.m. The alarm was raised. Mr. G. L. Harkins, Manager of the

Hotel, organised a rescue party of ten Europeans, including Bill Barnes, Peter Pope-Ellis, Pip Adelson, Nick Kaltenbrun and Arthur Cross, while a priority telephone call was put through to Martin Winter at Frere, asking him to come over and head the rescue operation. Martin set out at midnight, and arrived in time to join the rescue party which set off on horseback at 4 a.m.

They climbed up Goodoo Valley to Basuto Gate, and then up the bridle path to the Chain Ladder. Here they left their horses and made their way on foot up the ladder and along the plateau to the Hut, which they reached at 8.30 a.m. Ferguson was waiting for them and together they went on another three kilometres to the head of Inner Tower Ravine. After a short search they sighted the body about half way down. Led by Martin Winter, three of the men, Martin himself, Bill Barnes and Pip Adelson, then commenced the descent. Almost from the start they had to use rope. About midday they reached the body, and then the really difficult part of the operation commenced. Using their rope they had to lower the body down precipitous rock faces, abseiling down themselves afterwards. It was a perilous and exhausting job, and even at the bottom of the Ravine their troubles were not over, for they still had to make their way down to the Tugela Gorge through some of the roughest country in the Drakensberg. Here, however, they met a party of African Game Rangers who had been sent up the Tugela Valley from the Hotel as a support group. Almost at the end of their tether (they had not slept at all the previous night) they stumbled and fought their way down the precipitous slopes, choked with bush and scrub, until, just as dusk was setting in, they reached Tunnel Cave.

In the meantime a new force of helpers had arrived, and this group was able to get Ross Osborn's body down to the Hotel late that night. The three men who had recovered the body spent the night in the cave, and only reached the Hotel the following day.

Perhaps the worst tragedy, and the most complex rescue operation ever to be mounted in the Drakensberg, was that of April 29 to May 4, 1959.

On Wednesday, April 29th, a party of fifteen University students from Johannesburg left the Hotel for a light-hearted trip to the summit of the *Amphitheatre*. It was a clear morning, but the Warden of the Park, Joe Stanton, warned them that the Weather Bureau had forecast a cold front moving up from the Cape, and that heavy snow could be expected on the Drakensberg that night. He advised them not to go, or at the very least to take plenty of warm clothing with them. They ignored the warning. They proceeded up the usual bridle path to Basuto Gate in high spirits, and then up the long haul to the *Witches* and *Sentinel Peak*. In the late afternoon, however, the sudden change in the weather, which had been foretold, occurred. Black and ominous clouds began to sweep over the peaks, thunder growled, and the wind howled eerily amongst the crags. Soon it began to rain, and the temperature plummeted almost to zero.

By this time the party was strung out along the bridle path between *Sentinel Peak* and the Chain Ladder, a distance of about $1\frac{1}{2}$ km. Those in front made a dash for the Chain Ladder, which led to the summit plateau. But before they reached it, a blizzard swept down on them and heavy snow began to fall. Most of them managed to surmount the ladder, and, once on top, made a dash for the Mountain Club Hut. This is a trek of $2\frac{1}{2}$ kilometres. When they reached it they were at the end of their tether.

But darkness had now fallen, and a small group of students, including Keith Erasmus and two girls, Cynthia Bennett and Joy Jansen, both 19 years of age, were unable to reach the ladder in time. They found themselves left behind, in pitch darkness, in sub-zero temperatures and a howling blizzard.

In the meantime another party was approaching the Hut from the opposite direction. Mr. Arthur Bowland, well-known *Natal Mercury* photographer, Miss Dorothy Rees, and another reporter had been spending a few days at Oxbow, 35 km away in Lesotho, with Mr. Dick Reed, the Basutoland Government's Meteorological Officer at Oxbow. Together with Mr. Reed, they had ridden over to the Mountain Club Hut on this same day. They arrived just after the first batch of students.

As soon as Mr. Reed heard that a small group had been left behind, below the Chain Ladder, he immediately took command of the situation. He set off with three of the men, Brian Kerr, Peter Christensen and John Edgerton, in thick mist, carrying food and warm clothing for the party stranded below. They reached the Chain Ladder, and, whipped by driving rain and snow, managed to reach the bottom. Here they found the two girls, Cynthia Bennett and Joy Jansen, in a state of collapse. Reed said afterwards that they could not have survived another hour.

They managed to get the two girls into the cave, not far from the Gully, which used to be the old route to the top before the Chain Ladder was built. But the girls were now in a coma, and the situation was desperate, for, in addition to their other troubles, Keith Erasmus was still missing. Reed decided to go back for further help, leaving Kerr, Christensen and Edgerton to care for the girls.

By now the ladder had begun to ice up. In a fierce gale and driving snow Reed made a nightmare ascent of the ladder. Near the top he missed his footing on the slippery ice. Telling the story later, Reed described how, by a sheer miracle, his boot had caught in a rung of the ladder, and this had saved him from plunging to the bottom. For a moment he hung upside down, and then, with a tremendous effort he managed to seize another rung, regained the ladder, and reached the top. Arrived there he raced for the Hut, but in the mist and driving snow he lost his way, and it was some time before he reached the others in the only shelter on that icy, storm-driven plateau.

Meantime, what had happened to Keith Erasmus? He had been almost the last of the long string of climbers on the bridle path, and was badly affected by the altitude and the cold. By the time he had reached the base of the *Sentinel*, the blizzard was upon him, darkness had fallen, and he was in a state of complete mental and physical collapse. One of the girls in the party remained behind with him on the path until he was incapable of moving any further, and then she went for help. She had nothing to cover him with. Exhausted herself, and clothed only in thin silk shirt and shorts, she set off as fast as she could for the Chain Ladder.

Away up in the cave, 30 metres above the path, the girls had now been made as comfortable as possible, and Peter Christensen decided to go and look for Keith Erasmus. Back along the path he went, and then, huddled up against a rock and unconscious, he found Keith. Near-by was his ruck-sack and ice-axe, both coated with ice. His clothing was stiff with ice. Covering him in his own lumberjacket, he sped back to the cave. Here he told Brian Kerr and Edgerton that he had found Erasmus, and was going on up the Chain Ladder for help. The two men accompanied him to the foot of the ladder and saw him up the first few rungs, from where he disappeared into the mist above. He was never seen alive again.

Reed was now back at the Hut, and soon the girl who had remained behind with Keith Erasmus staggered in with the news of Keith's serious plight. Again a rescue party set out, a strong one this time, consisting of Reed, Arthur Bowland, the reporter, Tom Edgerton, Neville Davis, Mike Brown and George Tempest. But they never even made the Chain Ladder. On that bitter, mist-enshrouded, windswept plateau, lashed by driving rain and whirling snow they completely lost their way.* They wandered helplessly around for several hours, crossing iced-up streams and plunging into deep snow-drifts, before finding their way back to the Hut. Several times they heard faint cries in the night, but could not locate the direction of the sound. They must have come from Peter Christensen.

By next morning, Thursday, it was still snowing. What had seemed at first to be merely a local storm was obviously something much bigger and more widespread, almost certainly a cyclone from the South Pole. But they were able to take stock of their position. The party was

* After this tragedy the authorities erected a single strand of wire leading from the Chain Ladder to the Hut, to guide people along the summit in bad weather. If it had been in place before this tragedy, Christensen would not have lost his life.

now intact, except for Keith Erasmus and Peter Christensen, and the two men and the two girls in the cave down below. Keith had been left on the path between *Sentinel Peak* and the Chain Ladder. Peter was assumed to be still in the cave with the others. It was doubtful whether Keith could have survived the sub-zero temperatures of the previous night in the thin clothes he was wearing. An urgent message was sent down to the Warden of the Park, Mr. Joe Stanton. Then it was discovered that Peter Christensen was also missing. Rescue operations swung swiftly into action.

For the first time in Drakensberg climbing history walkie-talkies were used, and also a helicopter, piloted by Captain Scott of Johannesburg. Martin Winter was again alerted, and asked to take charge of the rescue operations. Crack climbers from Durban, Maritzburg and Estcourt converged on the site, together with Natal Parks Board officials, African Game Rangers, a doctor, and Police from both Natal and Witzieshoek. Even Basutho chiefs from adjoining areas in Lesotho offered help, and sent contingents of their men. By Thursday evening 29 experienced mountaineers had gathered at the Hotel or were on their way up. They were equipped with ropes, climbing gear and walkie-talkie radio sets. A complicated organisation for supplying them with food was set up.

While the search for the two missing men went on, the party of students was being evacuated to the base, a long and wearisome process, for by now the Chain Ladder was completely iced up and considered far too dangerous, and they had to use the much longer and time-consuming Gully. (This Gully dips off the summit from a point almost at the top of *Beacon Buttress*. It is a long walk, and a stiff climb, from the Hut to the lip of the Gully.) Then the rescue and search parties took over the Hut.

It continued to snow throughout the Thursday, and conditions on the summit grew steadily worse. The Tugela River was completely frozen over and heavy snow and mist blanketed the area. Though any chance of the two missing men being found alive was by now almost nil, the rescue teams continued their search throughout the day. That night the weather cleared, and Friday dawned with the sun shining on the vast snowfields. It was not long before the body of Keith Erasmus was found. He had fallen over a 20 metre cliff, not far from his abandoned ruck-sack and ice-axe. But of Peter Christensen there was no sign. He had simply disappeared into that frozen night. He might have fallen over, or been blown over, the edge of the escarpment, and his body become wedged in some impossible chasm, in which case it would never be found. He might have wandered off into Lesotho. He might have simply died of exposure on that terrible night. Or he might, miraculously, have survived under some sheltering rocks, though few thought this was possible. Throughout Friday and Saturday the search went on. Both those days were clear, and the helicopter was used to good purpose, crossing and criss-crossing the bewildering maze of jagged spires and ice-encrusted chasms.

But Sunday experienced another heavy fall of snow, and on Monday it was again snowing hard. All hope of finding Christensen alive had now faded, and it was decided to abandon the search for the time being.

The winter of 1959 was a hard one. For many months the snow lay thick on the ground, choking up the gullies and filling the deep clefts in the rock faces. It was not until four or five months later, when the snows finally began to melt, that Christensen's body was found.* A Basutho herd-boy, herding his cattle, stumbled upon it by accident, and raised the alarm. The body was discovered not far from the edge of the escarpment, but well beyond the Hut. It was

---

* This tragic episode emphasises the prime importance, indeed the absolute necessity, of always keeping the party together when out climbing in the Drakensberg. Speed must be governed by the ability of the *slowest* member of the party. The leader should never allow the party to scatter. He should place the next strongest and most experienced man he has *in the rear*, and he should keep in constant contact with him, by calling to him periodically if necessary. This is not the only fatal accident that has been caused in the Drakensberg through stragglers getting left behind in the dark and then becoming lost.

obvious that he had climbed the Chain Ladder on that fatal night, and, in trying to find the Hut in the mist and darkness, had passed it, become lost, and wandered on helplessly until death had claimed him.

He had given his life for his friend. On that grim night so many months before, thinking not of himself, he had covered Keith Erasmus with his own lumber-jacket, and had thereby surrendered his one hope of survival.

To-day, on the spot where his body was found, is a simple slab let into a block of Drakensberg basalt. The inscription reads:

"In loving memory of Waldemar Peter
Christensen, who fell asleep here,
29th April, 1959, aged 23 years."

CHAPTER X

THE LOVELY MNWENI

"Red road winding, winding up the valley,
Blue hills calling in the cool of eventide."
—ANON.

As one travels along the road from Bergville, leading to the Royal Natal National Park, one passes through the African settlement of Rookdale, a few kilometres after leaving Bergville. On your left is a broad valley, and beyond, the towering peaks of the Drakensberg. Opposite the Rookdale Mission Station is an insignificant little road, leading into this valley. You can easily miss it. For a short while it meanders through dusty mealie fields, and then it dips down into the Mnweni where it crosses the river. From there it heads up into one of the fairest valleys that I know of in the whole length of the Drakensberg.

This beautiful valley, the Valley of the Mnweni, is all Bantu Reserve. Here you will find no Hotels, no Caravan Parks, no tarred roads, in fact no roads at all, once you reach the end of the winding red road leading into it. Down in the valleys live the remnants of the Amazizi and the Amangwane, pathetic survivals of the wars of Shaka, but in the upper reaches, and underneath the great peaks, there is no-one. You can march for days on end and never meet another human soul. You have to be entirely self-contained in the matter of food and bedding, and the only sounds are the cry of the Black Eagle, and the rippling of the mountain streams.

For this is a land of rivers – the great Mnweni itself, rising in the Mnweni Cut-back behind *Mponjwana;* the Setene, flowing out from under *Mount Oompie;* the Ifidi, remote yet beckoning; the Amanzana; and the two Ntonjelanes, Ntonjelan' ephumalanga and Ntonjelan' eshonalanga. The very name *Ntonjelane* means "oozing of water". Never are you out of the sound of their cool waters.

Here too you will find some of the grandest peaks in the whole of the Drakensberg. *Mponjwana,* mightiest of them all, dominates the area. This is the peak climbed by George Thomson and Kenneth Snelson in 1946. Behind it is Mponjwana Cave, known to hundreds of mountaineers down the years, and close by is *Rockeries Peak.* In front are the *Inner* and *Outer Mnweni Needles,* and the *Organ Pipes* (not to be confused with a similar line of fluted columns in the Cathedral area.) To north and south stretches a long line of lesser peaks, to the north *Mt. Oompie* (2 871 m), the *Ifidi Buttress* (3 219 m), the two *Ifidi Pinnacles,* the *Abbey* (3 089 m), the two *Mnweni Pinnacles,* and to the south the noble *Saddle,* with its two flanking peaks, *North Saddle* (3 153 m) and *South Saddle* (3 109 m), and the long horizon of the Cathedral Range. And here, too, you will find those shy and secret valleys, far from the haunts of man, the valleys of the Setene, the Mbundini, the Icidi, and of the two Ntonjelanes.

The Rockeries area itself (the name goes back to at least 1905) consists of *Mponjwana,* the two *Mnweni Needles,* and the mountain mass immediately to the south of *Mponjwana.* The Zulu name for it is *Ntabamabutho,* meaning the "Mountain of the Warriors". During the troubled times of Shaka, an Amangwane impi camped in its shadow, hence the name. It was known to Europeans in the very early days. We have already seen how the Stocker brothers climbed here in 1888. The areas to the immediate north and south, however, remained largely unexplored until the early 1930's. High up in a lateral stream of Ntonjelan' ephumalanga, beneath the soaring precipices of *South Saddle,* is one of the most beautiful of Drakensberg caves. This is the cave I had used in 1947, as described in Chapter V. Prior to 1930 it had only been used twice

Map of Mnweni Area

Tugela River

Rivulette

Hoffenthal M.S.

X
Scene of massacre

To Rooddale 2 km

Mhlwazini R.

To Winterton 45 km

Umlambonja River

Ganapu Ridge

Cathedral Peak Hotel

Ntabakunetha

Mnweni River

Police Post

Nxaye

Puddings

Cathedral Peak

Ball

Outer Horn

Inner Horn

Mngoni

Isandhlwana

Scramble

Ntonjelan' ephumalanga

Chessman

Mitre

Cave C

SOUTH SADDLE

Twins

Cave C

Amanzana

Ophondweni

Ntonjelan' eshonalanga

NORTH SADDLE

Ntonjelane Pass

Mnweni River

OUTER NEEDLE

INNER NEEDLE

Organ-Pipes

MPONJWANA

SADDLE

Singati River

Devil's Tooth

Inner Tower

Mt COMPIE

Ifidi Pinnacles

Setene R.

Ifidi R.

Tcidi R.

Cave C

Rockeries Pass

Mnweni Pass

Eastern Buttress

IFIDI BUTTRESS

Mbundini R.

Cikicane

MBUNDINI BUTTRESS

ABBEY

Pass

Fangs

MNWENI PINNACLES

Scale

Miles

Kilometres

North

0   1   2   3   4   5   6

0   6   8   10   12

0   1   2   3   4   5   6

by small climbing parties, while up to 1930 the Ntonjelane Pass, just beyond the cave, had never been traversed by a white man, as far as is known, apart from the Stockers in 1888.

Of the area to the north, between *Rockeries* and *Mount Amery*, William Anderson, of the Surveyor-General's Department, said in 1907 that it was "practically unknown and inaccessible . . . an inhospitable region". He said further that there was no known Pass between *Goodoo* in the Natal National Park and Bushman's Pass, south of *Champagne Castle*. Actually there are at least five, well-known to-day. A map in Henry Brook's *Natal*, published in 1876, shows the Mnweni rising near *Ntabamhlope*, south of the Little Tugela, 65 kilometres away from its correct position!

The *Mnweni Needles* (not to be confused with the *Mnweni Pinnacles*) are the two pyramid-like peaks which jut out from *Mponjwana*. The *Outer Needle* (2 890 m) was the first to be climbed. In July of 1921 Ken Cameron, Bassett-Smith, R. G. Kingdon and Mrs. Bassett-Smith set up their camp at the confluence of Saddle Stream, which rises at the *Saddle*, and Ntonjelan' eshonalanga. The next day, July 22, they set out to climb the peak, making for the south-east ridge. It was a long, hard climb, and by eleven o'clock Mrs. Bassett-Smith and Kingdon had had enough. They dropped out and rested on a ledge, while Cameron and Bassett-Smith battled on alone. After 5½ hours, at 1.30 p.m., the two men finally reached the top.

A few days later Cameron and Bassett-Smith made an attempt on the *Inner Needle* (2 905 m). It proved to be a far more severe climb than the *Outer Needle*. They managed to climb to within 60 metres of the summit, but the prize was not to be theirs, and they had to give up. For 22 years the peak remained inviolate, and it was not until 1943 that its summit was finally reached. In May of that year A. S. Hooper, P. B. Fenger and Elizabeth Burton, climbing in a high wind, were the first to conquer it.

The two *Mnweni Pinnacles* are shy peaks. Rarely do they reveal their spear-like summits to the eye of man, for they are hidden away in the Mnweni Cut-back. The *Inner Pinnacle* (3 100 m) appears the more formidable of the two, with its slender pointed profile. The *Outer Pinnacle* (3 096 m) has a broader base, and appears the easier, but this is not so. The *Outer Pinnacle* still ranks as one of the most difficult climbs in the Drakensberg. In spite of this, it was the *Outer Pinnacle* that was the first to be climbed. On 20th December 1948, George Thomson, Charles Gloster, Des Watkins and Barry Anderson climbed down an easy gully from the top of the escarpment to the base of the *Inner Pinnacle*. From there they made their way into the nek between the two *Pinnacles*, and so on to the face of the peak. Half-way up Watkins and Anderson found the going too severe, and had to fall out, but Thomson and Gloster went on alone to conquer the peak.

Seven months later the *Inner Pinnacle* was climbed for the first time, the honour going to Jannie Graaff, Phyl Goodwin, Bob de Carle and Roy Buckland. The date was 16th July 1949.

Saddle (2 972 m) is one of the most prominent peaks in the Drakensberg. The Stockers called it *Segwana Cirque*, though where they got the name *Segwana* from I have not been able to discover. The Zulu name is *Ntaba Busuku*, "The Mountain of the Night", because, they say, the night clings to the face of the mountain, the southern buttress sheltering it in the morning, and the northern buttress in the afternoon, casting long purple shadows across its mighty basalt face. It consists of a sheer, slightly-curved wall, with two flanking peaks, *North Saddle* and *South Saddle*. Both these peaks are separated from the main wall of the escarpment, *North Saddle* by a steep and narrow cleft, which can only be negotiated by a crack climber. The central wall of *Saddle* is easily climbed from the summit of the escarpment, while a frontal assault, via a wide crack, is not difficult. This route was opened up in July 1934 by Brian Godbold and F. E. Ellis.

South Saddle is not a very difficult peak to climb, certainly from the escarpment summit. The first man to reach the top was Jannie Graaff, in 1947. Climbing solo, he descended into the 60 metre gap which separates the peak from the main escarpment, and so on to the face and up to the summit.

North Saddle is a very different proposition. The Stockers first had a look at it in 1888, but they did not even attempt it. Bassett-Smith explored it, and made an abortive attempt to climb it in July 1921. He did, however, manage a first ascent with O. K. Williamson via the Western Buttress Gully. In September 1968 the main face was climbed by Roger Fuggle, Tony Dick, Carl Fatti and B. Manicom, from the Ntonjelane Valley.

Rockeries Peak was the last great peak in the Drakensberg to be conquered, though it still does not rank with the peers, like *Column* and *Devil's Tooth*. It proved to be a long and exhausting climb for R. F. Davies, J. Slinger, J. de V. Graaff and D. Williamson. They camped in the valley below on a day in 1953, and set off for their climb in the early morning, but it was not until 21 hours later that they were back in camp after conquering the peak. *Rockeries Peak*, not to be confused with *Rockeries Tower* (*Mponjwana*), is the last of the serrated peaks which stretch out in a south-easterly direction from the main Rockeries *massif*. It is known to the experts as "Pinnacle D".

There are many other first-class climbs in this little-known area, of which we need notice only the two *Ifidi Pinnacles* and the *Ntonjelane Needle*. The *South Ifidi Pinnacle* was first climbed by Gillian Bettle and Martin Winter in 1952, while the *North Pinnacle* fell to Martin Winter and Malcolm Moor in 1959. The *Ntonjelane Needle* was first climbed by Brian Godbold in 1934. This slender spire is the last of the *Chessmen*, nearest the *Mitre*, and the word *Needle* is very appropriate, for it has a small hole in the tip, like the eye of a machine needle.

I first came to the Eastern Ntonjelane (Ntonjelan 'ephumalanga) in October 1947 while I was mapping the Cathedral area, when I dipped down from Twins Cave and spent those never-to-be-forgotten days in the cave beneath the towering precipices of *South Saddle*, which I have already described. I loved it then, and I have loved it ever since. Four and a half years later I was back, with my son Malcolm this time, still a schoolboy. We traversed the whole of the valley during Easter of 1952, entering from the Cathedral area by way of Ganapu Ridge and the *Three Puddings*, spending three days in the cave below *South Saddle*, and then trekking across into the Mnweni. Here we discovered a series of magnificent rock pools, each the size of a small swimming bath, into which the Mnweni River roared and foamed. We spent a day here, and then went over *Mole Hill* and across the Ifidi River. At the top of *Mole Hill*, which we climbed, we had lunch and left a couple of empty Oxo tins there. Years later I read an account in the Mountain Club Journal of 1958 of another ascent of *Mole Hill*. The party that climbed it were hoping to make a first ascent, but to their surprise, and chagrin, found at the top an ancient Oxo tin! We were now in the lovely valley of the Setene, and here we lazed away four days on warm, sunlit grass, before crossing over the Mt. Oompie Ridge into the Singati Valley, and so into the Tugela and the Royal Natal National Park. We have been back many times since.

On most of these trips we established the most cordial relations with the Amazizi and the Amangwane, hoeing in their fields as we passed by. Always it was "Phumaphi?" "Uyaphi?" ("Where do you come from," and "where are you going?") the handing over of the inevitable handfuls of "ugwayi" (tobacco), and the final cheery "Hambani kahle, banumzane" ("Go well, sirs") from them, and from us "Hlala kahle" ("Stay well"), as we went on our way.

But once it was not so.

We had entered the Valley this time by the lovely red winding road which branches off from Rookdale Mission. It was December 1955, midsummer, and we marched all day in the blinding heat, but always with the beckoning mountains before us. Towards dusk we reached the Mnweni River, which we would have to ford. In the mealie fields were a group of Amangwane still busy with their hoes. But there were no cheery greetings this time. We were met with silence and averted eyes. The river was in flood, the crossing would be difficult. We were tired. Under normal circumstances I would have suggested camping for the night on the nearer bank, and tackling the crossing in the morning. But I was filled with a vague sense of uneasiness. Malcolm was still only a young lad, and I did not wish to alarm him. I said nothing, except

112

"Let's cross now". That night, sitting round our camp fire, he said to me, "You know, Dad, I'm glad we decided to cross first, before we camped for the night. I didn't like the look of those Amangwane."

Two months later, almost to the day, the news broke: "Policemen hacked to death. Grim scenes of massacre in Drakensberg foothills." The scene of the massacre was only a short distance below where we had crossed the river two months previously.

On Tuesday morning, February 21, 1956, a large party of seven European policemen and 15 African constables had set out from Ladysmith on a dagga raid into the Mnweni Valley. In command was Sgt. S. J. D. de Lange, of the Ladysmith Police, 46 years old, a married man with five children. He was due to go on pension in three years' time. He was an extremely popular police officer, not only with his comrades in the police, but with the Africans of the whole district. He knew them and their ways, and he was always scrupulously fair in his handling of them. They knew him as "Sergeant Shorty".

These dagga raids are made periodically into the Bantu Reserves of the Drakensberg, which are notorious for the large fields of dagga cultivated there. On these raids quantities of dagga are destroyed, and any Africans found in possession of the weed arrested.

On that first day quantities of dagga were found and a number of arrests made. That evening some of the police returned to Bergville, but a large party camped at *Rivulette*, the farm of Mr. Carl Zunckel.

Next morning the police split up into several smaller "sorties", with about eight men in each party. On the previous day they had been armed with Sten guns and revolvers. On this particular day they left their Sten guns in camp, and were armed only with revolvers. The weather was wet, drizzly and cold.

Sgt. de Lange's party consisted of himself; Lance-Sgt. J. Koorts, 33 years of age, and only recently married; Constable T. Kruger, a young man of 22 years of age, who had just been transferred to Ladysmith from Witzieshoek; an African Sergeant, Sgt. Langa; and four African constables, Gabela, Xaba, Sitole and Mbendse. They made good progress, and again quantities of dagga were found. In one small area over 50 dagga fields were discovered, one of them nearly $2\frac{1}{2}$ ha in extent. Soon they made their way up the Mnweni River, to a point only a couple of kilometres below where we had crossed two months previously. Here they confiscated another big haul of dagga. This they left at Zondo's kraal, and Constables Xaba and Sitole were assigned to guard it. The rest of Sgt. de Lange's party then proceeded on to the further side of a small stream.

Up on the hillside, however, above Zondo's kraal, trouble seemed to be brewing. A large group of Amangwane tribesmen appeared to be gathering, and from behind them, on the higher slopes, came the high-pitched, throbbing "hihiza-ing" of the women, as they egged their men on.

Suddenly the impi armed with sticks, knobkerries and assegais, began to move down the hillside in the direction of Zondo's kraal. Constables Xaba and Sitole, left on guard there, saw them coming. For a few moments they held their ground. Then they began to move slowly away, in the direction of the rest of the party. Suddenly, the "hihiza-ing" of the women swelled to a mad frenzy, Xaba and Sitole ran for it, and the impi swept down upon them.

Sitole was the first to fall. A knobkerrie from the pursuing impi arched across the sky, struck him on the head, and he fell dead. Xaba managed to cross the stream and reach Sgt. de Lange, and the seven men closed ranks into a tight knot.

Meanwhile on the other side of the stream the impi had reached the body of Sitole. Here they halted. Suddenly Constable Kruger drew his revolver and fired a single shot.

Galvanised into action as the echoes of the shot died away, Sgt. de Lange sprang forward. He first of all remonstrated with Kruger for firing his gun, and he raised his hand and called on the impi to desist and to talk matters over with him. The impi hesitated, and for a moment it looked as if de Lange's tactics would be successful, but one man continued to urge them on. The "hihiza-ing" up on the hillside rose to a wild scream, a single cry of "Bulaleni abelungu" ("Kill the white men") rang out, and the impi moved swiftly in to the attack.

Thirty seconds later it was all over. Constable Mbendse managed to fight his way clear. As de Lange saw him breaking free he called to him to go to Zunckel's for help, but a moment later de Lange himself was down before he could even draw his revolver. Sgt. Langa, ringed with a dozen assegais, fell down the bank into the stream, struggled up, and managed to get away in the direction of Zunckel's farm. Constable Kruger, with a blow on his head, also fell into the stream, but not before he had managed to fire another shot, killing his man. The other three men, like de Lange, went down under the plunging assegais and the savage knobkerries of the Amangwane. And then there was silence. So sudden had been the attack on the police patrol that only Constable Kruger had had time to draw his revolver.

Fifteen minutes later (it was now 3 p.m.) an exhausted Mbendse raced up to Carl Zunckel's farm and gasped out de Lange's message: "Ek is in moeilikheid!" ("I am in trouble"). Four European policemen who were at the farm set off immediately, in the direction de Lange's party had taken. In the long grass, on the banks of the stream, next to a huge patch of dagga, they came upon the grim scene, the bodies of Sgt. de Lange, Lance-Sgt. Koorts, Constables Gabela, Xaba and Sitole, hacked to death. They had been so badly mutilated that they were hardly recognisable. Sgt. de Lange had 23 wounds in his body. Beside them lay one of their attackers dead. Constable Kruger and Sgt. Langa were missing, and it was thought they had been taken hostage by the fleeing Amangwane tribesmen, who by that time had all disappeared into the fastnesses of the Drakensberg.

The police reacted swiftly and immediately. From all sides they swooped on the area. Bergville rushed in an emergency squad of police that night, and during the rest of the night reinforcements began to come in from Ladysmith, Colenso, Dundee, Bergville, Winterton, and Estcourt, every available man being put on the job. A detachment of 30 armed police was sent up from Divisional Headquarters in Pietermaritzburg. Local farmers offered their help. The Hotel at Bergville was turned into a temporary barracks. Captain Patrick Dillon, Ladysmith's District Commandant, moved in to take personal command of the men in the field.

Early on the Thursday Col. R. de Wet van Heerden, Deputy Commissioner of Police for Natal, and Col. W. A. E. Ayres, Chief of the C.I.D., went up from Pietermaritzburg to take over-all charge of the vast police operations that were planned in the area. Harvard aircraft of the S.A.A.F., under Major R. A. Gerneke, were flown in to guide the searching patrols. They were fully armed with machine guns, and the pilots carried pistols. Brig. C. J. Els, Assistant Commissioner of the South African Police, flew down from Pretoria. By Thursday night 85 European and African Police were camped on Mr. Carl Zunckel's farm. All were thrown into the hunt.

At the actual scene of the attack a radio station was set up, and with this the police kept constant contact with the patrolling Harvards and with Police Headquarters in Pretoria.

On the first day, two Amangwane tribesmen were shot dead, two were wounded, and 19 arrested. Day after day the hunt went on for the killers. Chief Ndungunye Hlongwane, Chief of the Amangwane tribe, gave his full support, and arrested several of the killers himself. Preparations were even made to bomb the fleeing tribesmen, should they attempt to escape over the passes into Lesotho.

In the meantime, Constable Kruger and Sgt. Langa had turned up. When the attack started, Kruger alone, as we have seen, had managed to draw his revolver, and had shot one of the killers. Then, in the confusion, he escaped, making his way up the valley. Here, in a cave under a waterfall, he found refuge, and hid from the searching Amangwane. He stayed hidden until nightfall, listening to the sounds of the tribesmen as they looked for him and tried to ferret him out. Night fell, and then he saw the lights of the truck which had come to remove the bodies of his comrades. Dazed and shaken, he stumbled along a shallow river, and then followed the lights of the truck back to Carl Zunckel's farmhouse, into which he staggered in the early hours of the morning. He was immediately rushed off to hospital.

Ladysmith, in the meanwhile, shocked at the tragedy, was a place of mourning. Flags at the Town Hall, the Municipal Offices and the Police Station were flown at half-mast. The families of the dead men received messages of sympathy from Mr. C. R. Swart, Minister of Justice, who announced the news of the tragedy to a hushed House of Assembly.

Day after day the hunt went on, and the Harvards droned in the clear sky above the high peaks. Day after day it went on, until the last of the killers were rounded up, to stand trial at the Native High Court in Pietermaritzburg, and peace came again to the remote Valley of the Mnweni.

Months later the Supreme Court in Pietermaritzburg opened with Mr. Justice A. A. Kennedy on the Bench, supported by two assessors. The dock was crowded with 26 Amangwane tribesmen. When, at last, on 9 August 1956 judgment was delivered, it was a scene believed to have had no parallel in South African criminal history, indeed in the whole of the British Empire – 23 men sentenced to death together (one was subsequently reprieved, 24 hours before the execution). The nearest approach to it had been four years previously when eleven Basutho, including a chief and a chieftainess, had been executed in Maseru for a ritual murder.

And so, at last, the police were able to close their file. But still to this day, the tribesmen of the Amangwane tell of the day when the great birds came to their mountain home, and smelt out the killers of the white men.

High up on the summit, behind *Mponjwana*, or *Rockeries Tower*, as it is sometimes called, is the cave we have already referred to, Mponjwana Cave. It was here that we nursed Godfrey Symons, on that day back in 1958, when a billy-can of boiling water spilt over his foot. It was Godfrey's first trip into the Drakensberg, and it was indeed a baptism of fire for him. Three days after it happened he marched all day, with a heavy pack, all down Rockeries Pass and through the foothills, back to our car, refusing all offers of help. If he had accepted our offer to go for a horse, he might have escaped the long weeks in hospital that awaited his return to civilization. But it is not in Godfrey's nature to cry quits. And it was here that Malcolm and I spent that memorable Christmas of 1956, when morning after morning the sunrises blazed in a splendour of bronze and gold over the distant Cathedral Range, and in the afternoons the peaks played hide and seek in the mist.

But to Martin Winter, veteran Drakensberg climber, Mponjwana Cave will always be associated with the memory of Derek Schaeffer.

Early in 1952 three young people teamed up as a climbing team, Martin Winter, farming near Frere, member of one of the oldest of Natal families (Winterton is named after his grandfather); Gillian Bettle, a young school teacher; and Derek Schaeffer, a promising Durban musician. To be a good team, there must be complete "sympathy" what the French call *rapport*, between the various members of the team. There was exactly this understanding between Martin, Gillian and Derek. They climbed many peaks together, and they climbed well, notably the south-east arête of the *Outer Tower* in the Royal Natal National Park, the northeast buttress of *Cathkin*, and the *South Ifidi Pinnacle*. They were ideally suited to each other.

On Friday, 3rd April 1953, they set off from Cathedral Peak Hotel at 1 p.m. for an Easter week-end attempt on the *Rockeries*. They headed up the Umlambonja, with the intention of a first-night stop at Twins Cave, the cave I had used in 1947 when I had mapped the summit escarpment. But darkness overtook them before they reached the cave. A wet, drizzly mist came down, their packs were heavy, and in the intense cold, wet through, they had a pretty miserable last hour and a half before they reached the cave. Derek, especially, was making heavy going. He thought he was in for a bout of 'flu.

They slept well, however, and were up at dawn next day, following the usual route to the

Rockeries along the edge of the escarpment, past Ntonjelane Pass, the *Saddle*, and so on to Rockeries Pass and Mponjwana Cave. Unfortunately, the mist again came down, and it was bitterly cold. They arrived at the cave just before dusk, tired out. Derek was in good spirits, although again, during the day, he had gone poorly. That night it was bitterly cold.

Sunday dawned clear, but soon the mists began to swirl about the ice-clad peaks, and a bitter north gale blew up. The rock was wet and slippery. Derek decided to rest that day, while Martin and Gillian made a preliminary reconnaissance of the peak they were to attempt to climb the following day. Derek went with them as far as the gap between *Rockeries Tower* and the escarpment edge, and then returned to the cave. Martin and Gillian were back about 1 p.m. Derek was asleep. He slept most of the day, saying he felt terrible, although towards evening he seemed to revive a bit, and joined eagerly in their conversation.

Next morning, Monday, again dawned clear, with a magnificent sunrise. While watching it, the other two suddenly noticed that Derek was rambling in his talk. They examined him, and found him very weak and almost completely helpless. Thoroughly alarmed now at his sudden deterioration, they decided it was essential to get immediate help. Martin set off right away, leaving Gillian behind to care for the sick man.

All along the escarpment edge, past *North Saddle* and *South Saddle*, and down the Umlambonja, Martin raced. In 3¾ hours he covered what it had taken them a day and a half to cover on the way up, a most remarkable feat which must rank high in the annals of Drakensberg mountaineering. Then he burst into Cathedral Peak Hotel, and gasped out his story.

Albert van der Riet, the proprietor, known to so many mountaineers for his kindness and ready helpfulness, immediately swung into action. He summoned Fred Zunckel and his plane by telephone, obtained the best telephonic medical advice that he could (the trouble was diagnosed as pneumonia), collected medical supplies, especially penicillin, and then cared for Martin, who by then must have been on the point of exhaustion. At 2.30 p.m. he drove Martin down to the air-strip, and at 3 p.m. Martin and Fred Zunckel took off, flying back to the *Rockeries* to make an attempt at landing. Behind the cave was a fairly level piece of ground, but it was found to be strewn with rocks, and after several attempts Fred had to give up. A landing would have been sheer suicide. As they flew off, Gillian's tiny figure could be seen at the entrance of the cave, waving hopefully.

Fred now flew down the Orange River in the direction of Mokhotlong, 43 kilometres away. Here he dropped Martin at the air-strip, and then flew back to Cathedral to organise a stretcher-party which was to set out at first light the following day. Martin's plan was to ride back himself that night to the cave with the penicillin.

By 8 p.m. Martin and his party were ready and mounted and on their way. They had with them the Resident Medical Officer, and several Mounted Basutho Policemen. In the darkness progress was painfully slow and dangerous. Several times they had to cross the Orange, the water coming up to their feet. In places it was so steep that they had to dismount and lead their horses, and even then they were in great danger of crashing down into the depths below. They rode all through the night. Dawn broke. There was no sign of the escarpment, and they rode on.

At last, at 10 a.m. on Tuesday, after 14 hours in the saddle, they came out at the Ntonjelane Pass, instead of at the Mnweni, eight kilometres south of where they should have been, but at that very moment they could see the stretcher party coming up over from the *Twins* – five Africans, and Mike Barrett, Bill Brockbank and Eddie Malan.

By this time the horses were exhausted, so, abandoning his mount, Martin made for the stretcher party on foot, joined it, and together they raced on to the cave.

Gillian, of course, was delighted to see them. Alone, she had cared for Derek all the previous day and night, with no sleep at all, had fed him, kept him warm, and changed his clothes when wet. She had seen the plane, but could not know what was happening. She had done a wonder-

116

ful job. Derek was unconscious, but Martin injected the penicillin immediately, and then began to make preparations for the return home.

By that time the Medical Officer had arrived, but he could do nothing more, as he had no penicillin. During the morning a plane had flown over and dropped something, which they later discovered had been a package of penicillin, but in spite of a search they had been unable to find it.

After a hurried lunch they set off at 3 p.m., down Rockeries Pass. Anyone who knows this Pass will realise what a nightmare journey they must have had. It is nothing but a wild jumble of rock and stone, and in places very steep. In fact, to-day it has been practically abandoned. Fortunately by this time three more Africans had joined them, but even so, with relays of bearers, the going was painfully slow and difficult.

And all the time the plane circled slowly in the sky above them, unable to help, but keeping ceaseless watch. Periodically they signalled to it – a white flag which was to signify "life". The black was to signify "death".

By nightfall they were down 460 metres, and here, under some huge overhanging boulders, they made camp. Derek was made as comfortable as possible, in a sheltered place, and then they gathered round a fire for what little food they could muster – their supplies were running out. No-one had any sleeping kit, so they slept round the fire. Fortunately the weather was settled, and it was not too cold. Derek had responded a little to the injection, and his breathing seemed easier and more regular.

Next day, Wednesday, the 8th, they were off at first light, and made good progress on the easier ground. At midday, down in the foothills, they reached a sledge drawn by a team of eight oxen, which was waiting for them. Again, they were able to speed up with the help of the sledge, for this proved to be a fast and relatively comfortable means of transport.

But their food had by now given out, and their strength, especially that of Martin, was beginning to fail. Martin had already had two days and a night of non-stop physical effort, with little food, and only an hour or so of troubled sleep on the second night. At Makwela's kraal they were fed with dokwe* and boiled mealies, and then they hurried on.

Soon they reached the Ntonjelane. The river was full. They had to carry Derek across.

With night drawing on, they neared the Mnweni. Before they crossed it, Dr. van Heerden, the District Surgeon, came over and gave Derek another two injections of penicillin, and sounded his heart. It was still fair, but his lungs were in a poor state, and from his shallow breathing it seemed clear to the watchers that the end must be near.

Then they commenced the crossing. The river had come down in full flood, the water was waist deep, and flowing like a mill-race. In the fading light they carried Derek shoulder high, stumbling and floundering in the icy water. The bearers were told to let go their grip if they missed their footing. One last uphill grind, and they were at the waiting ambulance.

And not only the ambulance. There was food and drink, and a crowd of waiting journalists and jostling photographers, with cameras and popping flash-bulbs. They brushed them off, and hurried on to Bergville, where Derek was given oxygen, and then on to the Provincial Hospital at Ladysmith. He survived the journey, but, as he was being placed in his bed, he died. Gillian and Martin had lost a stout-hearted friend, and the wonderful climbing combination they had built up over the years was at an end.

*   *   *   *

Three months later Martin was back at Mponjwana Cave, and I close this Chapter with a brief excerpt from his Log Book:

* Dokwe: Mabele porridge allowed to go sour by non-alcoholic fermentation (Zulu).

"At sunset on 10th July we held a ceremony on the point opposite *Mponjwana*, where I scattered Derek's ashes. The casket lay on this lonely hill-top, and on it was laid a sprig of Berg heather, with a few yellow daisies. Near-by was an ice-axe, standing erect. Present were Francis, Terry, Archie, John, Tony and myself. While we prayed I scattered the ashes over the edge of the escarpment, and then buried the casket near the summit."

CHAPTER XI

CATHEDRAL OF THE SKIES

"Here they heard a subtler music and saw wider visions."
—GENERAL SMUTS, AT THE UNVEILING OF
THE MOUNTAIN CLUB WAR MEMORIAL AT
MACLEAR'S BEACON, TABLE MOUNTAIN,
25TH FEBRUARY 1923.

It had been an unusually hard month at the school of which I was Headmaster. Perennial Staff shortages, together with the August winds which are the curse of our Natal spring months, coupled with a whole series of intractable problems, had set my nerves on edge. We were fortunate in having at the school one of the finest sets of youngsters one could wish to have. Secretly I was more than a little proud of them, but even the best of youngsters can, at times, raise your blood pressure, and when the bell rang at three o'clock on that Friday afternoon, I could quite cheerfully have wrung the necks of the whole lot of them!

Suddenly I thought of *Cathedral Peak*, and the broad valleys of the Umlambonja and the Umhlonhlo, the country I had grown to love when I had mapped it for Albert van der Riet, during 1947 and 1948. The bottle-brushes with their scarlet flames would still be out, the sky would be blue, and the trees of the forest would be standing, tall and proud, in their deep kloofs.

And why not? Monday was a holiday. Six hours would take me to the top of Organ Pipes Pass and to the high cave in the summit rocks of *Indumeni Dome*, overlooking the Pass. Three days were mine, and mine alone. I could leave for home again by midday on the Monday, and still be back in time for school on the Tuesday. Why not? It took me only half an hour to get my sleeping bag out and to pack my ruck-sack.

I camped that night in the valley of the Umhlonhlo. Next morning rabbit tracks laced the dew-laden grass, and the world was young. By midday, in clear sunlight, I was sitting at the entrance of my cave, and the billy was about to boil. Far below me the cloud shadows drifted across blue and distant hills. Everywhere was a great stillness. Always down in the Little Berg, is some sound, the rustle of leaves in the wind, the hum of insects, the tiny splash of water. On the summit there is utter silence. Even the rustle of the wind in the grass is muted or stilled altogether.

But not quite. Away to my right, across a maze of shadowed valleys, was *Cathedral Peak* and the *Bell*. And, surely, was that not the *Bell* tolling! I could have sworn I heard its plangent notes, faint and clear over miles of empty space, calling to worship. And I certainly heard the throbbing thunder of the Organ Pipes, far below, a sonorous thunder that swelled up into the vast dome of the arching sky, as the winds stirred and woke from their long sleep.

The view from the summit of the Drakensberg is always breathtaking. Never is it more so than in that short stretch of mountain splendour between *Indumeni Dome* and the *Umlambonja Buttress*. Here is a vast panorama of toppling crags, battlemented spires, ruined towers and impregnable fortresses. Dark clefts fall sheer into the valleys a thousand metres below. Peak on peak stands clearly etched against blue horizons. And everywhere are the clouds. Sometimes they sail in solemn splendour, slowly and ponderously, across the sky. Sometimes they lift and curl and boil around the indifferent peaks, opening up to reveal brief, tantalising glimpses of yawning, black abysses and shadowed gorges, only to close in again with their clinging white

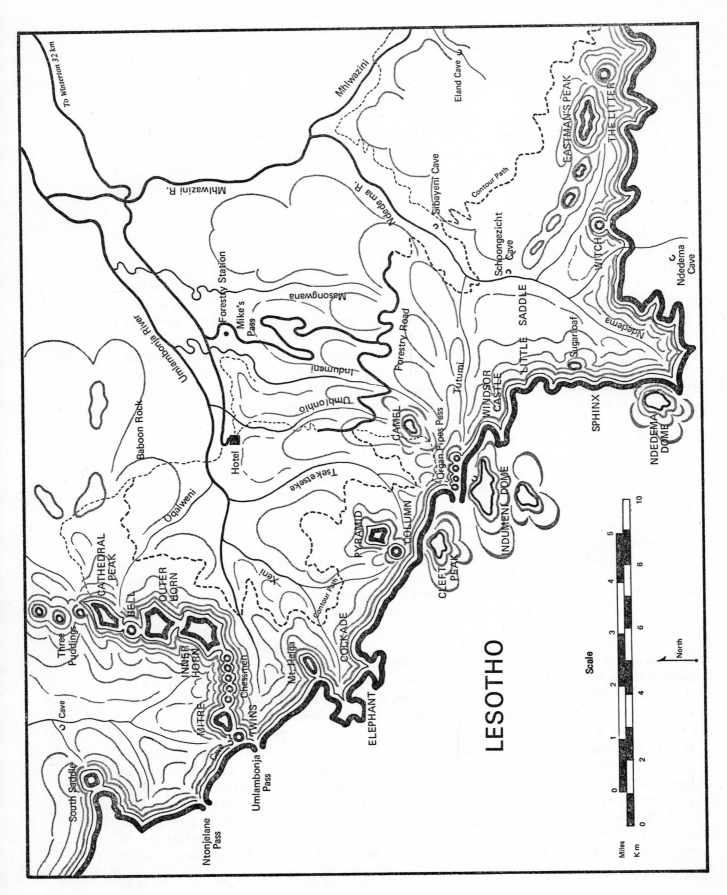

Map of Cathedral Area

LESOTHO

Scale

North

120

From the lip of the Tugela Falls.

A winter's morning.

Sunrise from the summit of Gray's Pass.

"Barrier of Spears"

From the summit of Cleft Peak

Column and the Pyramid in the middle distance.

veils. And sometimes their anger boils over in a black fury of storm and tempest, and the earth trembles.

A glance at the map will show that the Cathedral Peak area owes its grandeur largely to the fact that it is made up of two mountain ranges. There is, first of all, the main escarpment of the Drakensberg, running roughly north and south, and stretching from the *Umlambonja Buttress* to the *Ndedema Dome*, and secondly a most spectacular spur, 3½ km long, jutting out at right-angles to the main Drakensberg, and culminating in *Cathedral Peak* (3 004 m) itself. The peaks of this spur are all the more majestic because, unlike most of the main Drakensberg peaks, they are free-standing. The Umlambonja River rises in the angle formed between this spur and the main Drakensberg, and into it flow such lovely streams as the Oqalweni, the Umhlonhlo, the Tseketseke and the Masongwana.

The whole of this mountain playground was known, and developed, much later than the other Drakensberg areas. Access to it was difficult, as it lies somewhat off the beaten track, and for many years there was no proper road leading into it. As late as 1907 the Third and Final Report of the Geological Survey of Natal and Zululand could say of the area between *Mont-aux-Sources* and *Champagne Castle* that it was practically unknown and inaccessible. According to some of the older Africans living there, the first Europeans to come to the area arrived about 1910. As in other parts of the Drakensberg, these were wood-cutters and hunting parties, followed by farmers who bought grazing farms, and not necessarily occupying them. The name *Cathedral*, however, goes back to at least 1905, though, as we shall shortly indicate, this may not have been the peak we know as *Cathedral* to-day.

By 1918 eight farms had been established in the area, *Solar Cliffs, Brotherton, Gewaagd, Tryme, Inhoek, Schaapkraal, Hopeton* and *Leafmore*. These all belonged to I. J. M. Buys ("Ryk Isak Buys", not to be confused with Groot Isak Buys, his cousin, another prominent character of the period). Ryk Isak farmed at Kransfontein, in the Free State, and in 1918 he sent his foreman, Sybrand Vermeulen, down to live at *Tryme* to look after his eight farms. Sybrand must have been one of the earliest permanent residents in the area. He prospered, and later he bought *Tryme* from Buys. In 1924 Ryk Isak sent another of his foremen down, to live at *Leafmore* and look after his sheep there. He was Willem J. Oosthuizen. *Leafmore* and *Hopeton* are on the left bank of the Umlambonja, just below the present Hotel. He lived in a little plat-dak house on the boundary of *Leafmore* and *Hopeton*. Its ruins can still be seen to-day, but even in Oosthuizen's time it was an old house. During the 1914 Rebellion, horses in the Free State were being commandeered by the military, and Ryk Isak sent all his horses down to *Leafmore* and hid them there, even quartering some of them in the bedroom, it is said! Then Oosthuizen, the foreman, in his turn bought *Leafmore* and *Hopeton*, and it was probably he who built the present *Leafmore* homestead.

By now Ryk Isak was tired of his Berg farms, and one after another they were sold, *Solar Cliffs* to Mr. Anton Lombard; *Brotherton* to Stoffel van Rooyen, another of Isak's foremen; and *Gewaagd* to Jan P. Roux who married one of Isak's daughters. Finally, in 1937, Philip van der Riet, farming at *Olivia*, near the present Olivier's Hoek Police Post and store, bought *Inhoek* and *Schaapkraal* from Isak, with the idea of building an Hotel there.

But it was Albert, his son, who was the moving spirit in the venture. Albert knew the area well. As a boy he had hunted in the valleys of the Umlambonja, the Umhlonhlo and the Mhlwazini. In 1934 he had stocked the Umlambonja with brown trout from the Mooi and the Bushman Rivers. In 1938 he selected the site of the present Hotel. It had one great asset – it was nearer the mountains than any other Drakensberg Hotel.

And so the Cathedral Peak Hotel, known to thousands of South Africans for its gracious hospitality and its magnificent scenery, was born. Like Otto Zunckel and his sons, Albert was a born hotelier. He and his charming wife, Doreen, brought to their Hotel that personal touch, that genial friendliness and that gracious charm which has made the Cathedral Peak Hotel one of the best-known and best-loved holiday resorts in South Africa.

In 1938 they started to build. Their nearest railhead was Winterton, a tiny village 45 km away. Established in 1905, it was first called Springfield, and five years later was re-named Winterton, after Mr. H. D. Winter, Secretary for Agriculture in the Natal Government. Between Winterton and the proposed Hotel was a road which in places was little more than a sledge track, but undaunted Philip and his two sons laid the first bricks. They welcomed their first guests in time for Christmas 1939.

To-day Albert van der Riet is the leading Drakensberg hotelier, undisputed king of the beautiful Cathedral area where his Hotel is situated, and a great and genuine lover of the mountains. But I do not know which he loves more, the mountains or the sea, for Albert has an even bigger claim on fame: at 70 years of age he is one of the world's greatest big-game fishermen.

His records are fantastic. He is one of the only two men in the world to have bagged the three greatest big-game fish – marlin, blue fin tuna and broadbill swordfish – of more than 363 kg (800 lbs.) The other man is an American, Kip Farrington. He also holds the world record for the biggest catch of blue fin tuna in one day, eight tuna caught in the Bahamas during the Big Game Fishing International in 1962. The next day he landed seven more!

For many years he skippered the South African team in the Bahamas International, and led his team to victory three times in nine years, South Africa being the only country in the world to do this. Twice in those nine years he was the individual winner.

Altogether he has caught 59 giant marlin, 79 tuna, and several broadbill swordfish, including a record one of 374 kg (824 lbs.) This latter fish is the greatest of them all, the dream of every big-game fisherman. Such a magnificent fight does it put up that few are ever landed.

Through it all Albert has won the respect and the deep affection of the world's top fishermen. His warm camaraderie is still to-day a by-word amongst them all. In every competition he made a practice of sending each rival competitor a case of South African wines at his own expense. In 1969 South Africa was barred from the Bahamas International because of political pressure. To a man, the other competing teams immediately withdrew, in sympathy with the South African team, but particularly because of their high regard for Albert van der Riet. What a tribute to a simple, unassuming man!

Albert has many trophies. Perhaps the two that he values most are for sportsmanship. Both were awarded because, alone, he protested, successfully, against what he considered unjust penalties imposed on rival competitors.

In the area, *Cathedral Peak* itself, at the end of the subsidiary chain, is easily the most dominant peak of all. Its name is something of a mystery, for anything less like a cathedral is difficult to imagine. Many years ago it was called *Zikhali's Horn*.

Zikhali was the son of our old friend Matiwane. When Matiwane was killed by Dingane, Zikhali's life was spared. But when Dingane was assassinated, Zikhali fled to Swaziland, and took refuge with King Sobuza. There he fell in love with Sobuza's daughter, Nomlalazi. The king, however, had heard too many stories of Matiwane. He did not want his royal house allied with anyone even distantly related to this old scoundrel, certainly not his son. There was only one way out of the difficulty, Zikhali must go the way of his father. A plot was duly hatched, and it was arranged that Zikhali would be set upon one night in his hut, and murdered. But the young lady came to hear of the plot, and warned her lover in time. Zikhali got out as fast as he could, and headed for the pleasant hills and valleys of the Drakensberg, where he had spent his boyhood. Here he was given permission to settle. He gathered together the scattered remnants of the Amangwane tribe that had been left behind when Matiwane fled to the Free State, and there, in due course, Nomlalazi joined him. They married, and to this day the Chief of the Amangwane tribe, in the Upper Tugela Location, is a descendant of his – Tshani, though as he is still under age a relation of his, Mbeka, is acting for him. The Amangwane royal house is thus partly Swazi. Zikhali and his young wife established their kraal under the shadow of the peak which for many years was known as *Zikhali's Horn*.

Bishop Colenso visited him in 1854, and was not impressed. He describes him as "not of very prepossessing appearance. He looks dissipated, and is very haughty and over-bearing in his manners." D. C. F. Moodie, however, the author, described him as "truly a magnificent savage, tall, fine features, commanding appearance, and polite and dignified in manner". He died in 1863, having fathered 28 sons, one of whom was involved in the murder of Moncrieff.

How, and when, the name was changed to *Cathedral Peak* is not known. The name *Cathedral* first appears round about 1905. I have long had a suspicion that there has been a transposition of names here. 11 km to the north-west of *Cathedral* is the mountain which we have already dealt with, the *Rockeries*. This mountain *does* look exactly like a cathedral. From the plains of Natal it appears a solid, rectangular block, with a cathedral-like spire at one end, *Rockeries Tower*, or *Mponjwana*. I had wondered whether this mountain mass had not originally been given the name *Cathedral*, and whether popular usage had not later transferred the name to the much better-known *Zikhali's Horn*. This is rendered more feasible when one remembers that *Organ Pipes Pass* and the *Bell* were names already known in the area. A year ago I was able to establish the correctness of this theory. I discovered in the Natal Archives an old map of Natal by Masson, published in 1904, which clearly named the *Rockeries* "The Cathedral", and at least two Government maps have perpetuated this. The 1 : 250 000 Topocadastral Map, published in 1936, and the 1 : 250 000 Topographical Map, published in 1948, both call Rockeries Pass *Cathedral Pass*.*

When it was that the name was transferred from the *Rockeries* to the present *Cathedral Peak* I have not been able to discover. By 1916 the present nomenclature had been clearly established.

Personally, I regret that the original Zulu names have not been used in the naming of our Drakensberg peaks. *Cathedral Peak* should have been called either *Zikhali's Horn* or, an even earlier name, *Mponjwana*, which means the Little Horn; and *Rockeries* (I cannot imagine a worse name for a mountain!) should have retained its Zulu name of *Ntabamabutho*, the Mountain of the Warriors. To call it *Mponjwana* is quite incorrect, for this is the original name for *Cathedral Peak*.

Whatever its correct name, *Cathedral Peak*, *Zikhali's Horn*, or *Mponjwana*, it is a noble peak and a landmark for miles around. It is easily climbed in a day from the Hotel, no rope being required. Tony Hooper holds the record: from Hotel to summit and back in six hours twenty-five minutes! The first ascent was made by D. W. Bassett-Smith and R. G. Kingdon in July 1917.

Working now inwards towards the main escarpment, the next peak is the *Bell* (2 930 m). The various attempts to climb this peak have been dealt with in Chapter VI. Next to the *Bell* are the two Horns, the *Inner Horn* (3 005 m), and the *Outer Horn* (3 006 m). They were named about 1923, the names obviously being derived from the Zulu name for *Cathedral Peak*, *Mponjwana*, The Little Horn.

The first to be climbed was the *Inner Horn*. In 1925 a party led by H. G. Botha-Reid was the first to reach the summit. The area was still largely unknown. Only four peaks in the area had so far been named – *Cathedral*, the *Bell* and the two *Horns*. In 1940 Mike and Elizabeth Burton opened up a new route on the *Inner Horn*. Mike was a prominent Transvaal climber. His death a few years later in World War II brought to an end a most promising climbing career.

It was not until 1934 that the *Outer Horn* was climbed. The honour went to Doyle Liebenberg, Doc Ripley, H. G. Botha-Reid and F. S. Brown. On this first occasion they climbed the Western Buttress face. This peak actually offers several climbs of moderately difficult standard.

* The Military Map compiled for General Sir Redvers Buller in 1900 also calls the *Rockeries* 'Cathedral'. See page 279.

A party led by Brian Godbold made a sensational ascent in 1936, while in 1940 Doyle Liebenberg's party discovered a new route up the east face. This was a fairly easy route of "C" standard, which had been missed by previous climbing parties.

Next to the two *Horns*, and still moving westwards, are the *Chessmen*. These consist of a whole series of small, jagged spires, at about the 3 000 metre level, and extending for about 800 metres. They look formidable from below, but are quite easy to climb, most of them being "B", "C" or "D" standard. The Zulu name for them is *Ibotwana*, meaning "The Children". In the early 1930's they were called *Saw-tooth Ridge*, while the Stockers called them the *Needles*, but in 1931 Professor Sweeney gave them their present name and entered it on his map. By 1936 the new name was in general use. A traverse from one end of the *Chessmen* to the other offers a most spectacular, and not too difficult, climb.

Next to the *Chessmen* stands another prominent peak, the *Mitre*, (3 023 m), also named by Professor Sweeney in 1931. The first ascent was made during the July camp of 1938, by a party led by Brian Godbold. They approached the peak from the Ntonjelane Valley, and climbed its northern face. The second ascent was made in May 1941 by Tony Hooper and three ladies, Margery Robinson, Mary Lear and Else Wong. This was a new route, up the north-east face.

Between the *Mitre* and the escarpment lie the *Twins*. Actually there are three summits, and the peak should more correctly be called the Triplets, but from down below one of the three summits is hidden behind the others, and there appear to be only two summits. It is better to retain the name *Twins*, to avoid confusion with the *Injasuti Triplets* further south. Here too, in the north face, is the well-known Twins Cave. The three summits were reached for the first time during the 1931 July Camp in the Ntonjelane Valley, by a party led by Professor Sweeney.

The peaks along the main Drakensberg, stretching from the *Twins* southwards for 15 km, are all on the escarpment, except for two free-standing peaks, *Column* (2 929 m) and *Pyramid* (2 926 m). Working from north-west to south-east they are the *Umlambonja Buttress*, *Elephant* (3 139 m), *Cockade* (3 112 m), *Cleft Peak* (3 281 m), *Castle Buttress*, *Indumeni Dome* (3 255 m), *Windsor Castle* (3 065 m). Behind them stretch the rolling hills and valleys of Lesotho, that fascinating land of sunshine, cloud, horsemen, blankets and trout streams. South-west of *Windsor Castle* lies the Ndedema Cutback, with *Little Saddle* (3 075 m), the *Sphinx*, the *Sugar-loaf* and *Ndedema Dome* (3 063 m) as the main peaks.

This whole area had been visited briefly in 1925 by members of the Natal Mountain Club. Organ Pipes Pass was opened in that year by Professor Sweeney and Reg Holden, and *Indumeni Dome* named. In 1936 the Natal Mountain Club held their July camp in the Umlambonja Valley, and a much more thorough exploration of all the peaks from the *Twins* to *Castle Buttress* and beyond was made. Many of the names of these peaks date from this occasion. The peaks between *Castle Buttress* and *Ndedema Dome* had been explored the previous year during the Camp in the Ndedema Valley. They are all easily climbed from the western, Lesotho, side, in other words from the summit of the escarpment. The escarpment is reached without difficulty via Organ Pipes Pass.

This pass lies immediately south of *Castle Buttress*, beneath the massive bulk of *Indumeni Dome*, and has been known since the earliest days. It was the pass used by the emissaries of Moshoeshoe in 1823, when he sought help of Shaka. At the top is a line of huge fluted columns from which the name Organ Pipes is derived. But in the early days it was known by many other names. At one time it was called Old Bushman's Pass, and also Qolo-la-masoja, the Soldiers' Ridge, and one old map calls it "Soldaten pas". I am not sure whether this name derives from the fluted columns, which might be regarded as a regiment of soldiers standing at attention, or from the fact that tradition associates it with military action. Old cartridge shells of the soft Martini-Henry type have been found in the Pass, and there is a tradition that the Carbineers hunted Bushmen there in the 1860's.

A rain-swept, windy night in March 1947 saw a feat of epic courage and endurance enacted in this mountain pass. Five months earlier, on the night of October 26th, 1946, a Mr. and Mrs. Louw, an elderly couple living at Chieveley, had been murdered in their beds. Three natives were arrested by the police and lodged in the Estcourt jail, but on the night of December 16 they slit the throat of one of their guards and escaped. Two of them were re-arrested almost immediately, but the third, Xungu Ntshaba, vanished completely. Sgt. Boshoff, of the Estcourt Police, was put in charge of the case. I knew him well. For a long time he would not talk of what happened but eventually I managed to get the story out of him. Week after week, relentlessly, he followed the trail. Several times he nearly caught up with his man, only to be disappointed at the last minute. Three months went by, and then Boshoff heard that the wanted man was in the Cathedral area, and was about to escape into Lesotho via the Organ Pipes Pass. Hot-foot, Boshoff set out. He arrived at the Hotel at 4 p.m., and immediately left for the Pass. It was a cold, wet, rainy night, and all through the hours of darkness he climbed, higher and higher, with no equipment or warm clothing.

At dawn he came out on the summit, and at a quarter to seven he was approaching a Basutho kraal on the hillside. The dogs started to bark, and a man ran out from one of the huts and made off up the mountain side. Boshoff brought him down with his second shot, through the thigh, and then began the long march back home into Natal with his prisoner. The rain turned to snow. It got darker and darker. With the wounded man handcuffed to him, weary and exhausted, Boshoff stumbled down the Pass and back to the Hotel. It took him thirteen hours (the normal time would be about two and a half to three hours), and darkness had already fallen again before he reached the Hotel. His boots were in tatters, his feet raw, eyes red and swollen from snow-blindness, but he had got his man!

The highest of these peaks on the main escarpment is *Cleft Peak*. This is one of the highest points in the whole Drakensberg, and the view from this summit is truly magnificent. The whole range, from *Champagne Castle* to *Mont-aux-Sources* is seen stretching north and south, together with the peaks of the Cathedral Range, and *Pyramid* and *Column* in the foreground. It was first explored in 1936 by Doyle Liebenberg and Doc Ripley. They made their way up Organ Pipes Pass, and then turned north and ascended the south face, an easy but rather exhausting climb. It is the route taken to-day by the average tourist.

A much more sensational ascent of the peak, however, was made in 1946. *Cleft Peak* gets its name from a huge vertical gash in the mountain side, running down slightly from right to left as one faces the peak from the Natal side. It was up this narrow and nearly vertical cleft that the ascent was made by a party of three climbers, consisting of Brian Godbold, A. Millard and Mrs. Millard.

They left the main camp down in the Umlambonja, and sub-camped at the base of the mountain. Next morning, 17th July 1946, they set out at 5 a.m., a full hour before it was light, and after some stiff climbing, managed to get into the cleft. There followed "some of the most strenuous and sustained chimney work ever experienced by any member of the party". (I am quoting Brian Godbold himself.) The cleft was very narrow, and choc-stones abounded. They climbed in light clothing and takkies. So narrow was the cleft that they were unable to carry their packs on their backs. These had to be hauled up one by one by rope. It was back-breaking work. Hour after hour they battled their way upwards. By 5 p.m. they were very near the top, but night came on before they could reach the summit. The cold was intense in this narrow cleft into which the sun never shone. They climbed in the light of torches dangling from their necks, their fingers frozen and groping desperately for the tiny finger-holds. The final chimney was quite impossible, and they had to traverse out in the inky darkness on to the sheer right wall, and thence up a gully. This was the most dangerous and spine-chilling part of the whole climb. Double roping was necessary.

Finally, at 8.30 p.m., they were out and on top, in a bitter wind and clad in the thinnest of clothing. And they were still six hours away from home and shelter! Wearily they made their way down the south face of the mountain to the escarpment plateau, and then commenced the long march home, down Organ Pipes Pass, skirting the *Camel*, from there into the Valley of the Umhlonhlo, and so home to base camp in the Umlambonja. Dead-beat, they stumbled into camp at 2.15 a.m., after nearly 24 hours of non-stop climbing. This must surely rank as one of the greatest climbing feats in the Drakensberg.

It was on this wind-swept plateau above Organ Pipes Pass that I once experienced one of the most terrible storms I have ever known. Natal storms are often tremendous. Nowhere are they more impressive and more frightening than in the Drakensberg. Here is the birth-place of our Natal storms. Here the clouds gather and build up, and then sweep down over the land, travelling for hundreds of kilometres. But sometimes they seem loath to leave the place of their birth, and for hours on end they pound and hammer the mighty crags. That is what happened on that summer's day in 1948 when, late in the afternoon, all hell broke loose on that lonely plateau.

I had been mapping the area around *Windsor Castle* and *Little Saddle*, and was returning to my cave behind the fluted columns of the Organ Pipes. It had been a long, hard day, and I was tired, but I was not too tired to notice a subtle change in the atmosphere. As I began to round the shoulder of *Indumeni Dome* (by a strange coincidence the very name, in Zulu, means "The Mountain of Thunderstorms") I became vaguely conscious of a stillness in the air. The bright beauty of midday had gone, and in the dead, windless atmosphere there was a hint of menace. Then I noticed that heavy, dark clouds were gathering over *Cleft Peak* and the *Pyramid*, and from the north came the distant mutter of thunder, but it was still a long way off, and I was not unduly concerned.

Suddenly, with one mighty roar, the world exploded – one single, terrifying crash. So close was it that I could hear the thin, sharp crackle of the lightning a split second before the roar came, and smell the sharp, pungent smell of sulphur. Then silence, utter and complete, in some ways even worse than the actual thunder-clap. In times of danger it is a great thing to have another human being beside you. Though he can do nothing to help, his very presence warms the heart and helps to cut the gathering web of terror. That is what makes mountain-climbing in the company of stout comrades the heartwarming thing it is. But I was alone, on an empty plain, and even in the short time it had taken me to realise the predicament I was in, there came a second ear-splitting crash, followed, as before, by utter stillness. Not a blade of grass moved. Not a sound. I was very conscious of the fact that in a thunderstorm one should on no account run (this builds up static electricity and attracts lightning) but I moved as fast as I dared. The only shelter was the escarpment edge, a kilometre away, and I made for this.

But long before I reached that haven of refuge the fury of the storm was upon me. Suddenly it was so dark that I could hardly see where I was going. And now, one after another, with terrifying regularity, came those thunder-crashes, the noise at last merging into one long, continuous roar. Then the rain came in solid sheets, and the wind, and lashing hail. It beat into my face and tore at my clothing as I struggled on.

How I reached the edge and stumbled over I do not know – a short, steep slope before the final 300 metre drop, and with a line of over-hanging rock half way down. Within seconds I was there and flinging myself under the sheltering overhang.

From there I watched the storm. The wind leapt the crags, roared down into the depths below and slammed the rain in savage gusts against the streaming precipices. The day was drowned in darkness, except when it was lit by the angry flame of the lightning, which by now was almost continuous. The noise was simply appalling – the maddened howl of the wind, the thunder, the hail, and the torrents of falling rain, all blended in one wild, roaring tumult of sound. I watched the lightning striking the pinnacles of *Castle Buttress*, and probing into the cauldron of boiling clouds below. It almost seemed a thing alive, streaming like molten iron.

126

Were you safe under sheltering rocks? Did lightning strike there? I could not remember, and I did not even try to, for my mind was numb under the shattering blows of the thunder-crashes.

And then came the noise of the water, even above the roar of the storm. The sound came from behind, a new sound to be added to the cacophony of sound around me, menacing, all the worse because of the threat of the unknown. At first I could not make out what it was. It sounded like an express train at the far end of a tunnel. And then over the edge it came, a roaring flood of hurrying water. Fortunately the line of rock above me broke its course, and it thundered past on both sides, pouring down the slope and into the depths below. And still the thunder roared, as if imprisoned within the mighty battlements of the peaks.

The storm lasted for well over an hour. Every now and then it would slacken off, and the worst seemed to be over, but back it came with re-doubled fury. But at last it rolled away, down into the valleys and away over the plains of Natal. Intervals began to appear between the flashes of lightning and the crash of the thunder. Slowly the peaks separated themselves from the clouds, and began to stand out against a rain-washed sky. Up from below came the sound of innumerable waterfalls, drowned hitherto in the roar of the storm, and wraiths of white mist began to drift slowly across the face of the peaks. And then, away to the north-west, the sky slowly gleamed a pale lemon-green as the night crept up from the valleys below. The daylight died, and soon it was quite dark.

I shouldered my ruck-sack and my survey instruments and made my way down by torch-light over the sodden ground to my cave behind the Organ Pipes.

Lightning is always a hazard in the Drakensberg, and fatalities are not unknown. Several years ago three young men, riding back from *Mont-aux-Sources*, were all struck dead. The coins in the purse of one of them were all melted into one solid mass. What should one do if one is caught out in the open in a storm such as the one I have described?

Remember that the safest place is a car or a brick building. Make for either of these if you can. African huts are death-traps, and there is never a summer in Natal without at least half a dozen going up in flames after being struck by lightning. This is because they get wet and their insulation is poor. One should keep away from trees. A clump of trees is safer than a single tree, but even clumps of trees should be avoided. Keep away also from iron fences and from cattle. If one is on horseback, one should dismount, and move away from one's mount. Keep away also from rock out-crops, and it is unwise to try and shelter under an overhang. (I was quite wrong in attempting to do this in the storm I have described above.) The experts say one should keep off high points, and there certainly is something in this, though I have often been high on the slope of a mountain and watched the lightning striking below me. The safest thing to do if one is caught out in the open in a bad storm is to sit (not lie) down, in the wide open veld with one's knees hunched up and one's arms around them, and if possible wearing a waterproof cape, and simply sit the storm out. Above all, don't panic. I know that in the middle of a bad electric storm one feels so alone and exposed, like a butterfly pinned to a blank wall, and the lightning seems to be malevolently trying to seek you out, but remember that the world is a big place, and you are only a tiny speck, and that the chances of your being hit, providing you heed the precautions listed above, are extremely small.

There are still two free-standing peaks in the Cathedral area that we have not dealt with yet, the *Column* (2 929 m) and *Pyramid* (2 926 m). These two peaks stand just below *Cleft Peak*, to the right as one is climbing Organ Pipes Pass. We have already described the climbing of the *Column* by George Thomson in Chapter VII. Ten months after his historic climb he was back on the peak, climbing it this time with Tobie Louw and Bill Curle on 31st October 1946. The first woman to climb the *Column* was Phyllis Goodwin, in 1946.

The peak was named in 1930 by that inveterate map-maker and namer of peaks, Professor Sweeney.

Pyramid, standing next to it, though easier to climb than *Column*, still ranks as a difficult climb, and only the most expert mountaineers will tackle it. It was given its name in 1930, again by Professor Sweeney, while the first ascent was made six years later, in a most sensational climb. The party to achieve this "first" was a strong one. It consisted of Ken Howes-Howell from the Cape, Brian Godbold, Stan Rose, Charles Axelson, H. C. Hoets and Naomi Bokenham. They started their climb on the eastern ridge, traversed on to the north face, and reached the top at 1.25 p.m. Here they lit a fire to announce their success to the rest of the Natal Camp, gathered far below in the Umlambonja Valley, and built the usual cairn of stones in which they left a record of their climb. When Doyle Liebenberg and his party climbed it for the second time in May 1941, they found that lightning had destroyed the record of this first ascent. The only sign left of the first climb was a fused aluminium container.

It was on the slopes of the *Pyramid* that young Michael Stephens, gifted son of Mr. H. B. Stephens, Conservator of Forests for Natal, met his tragic death on December 29th, 1950. The party had already climbed the peak and were on their way down, when Michael slipped and fell 40 metres, to be killed instantly.

He was not the first young man to meet his death in the mountains of the Cathedral Peak area. On July 13th, 1942, a young man from the Belgian Congo, Auguste Hellemans, fell to his death from the summit of the *Inner Horn*. He was standing near the edge, after having climbed the peak, and, not realising how close to the edge he was, stepped back and went over.

On October 21st, 1947, Hans Otto Marcus fell from Baboon Rock. Baboon Rock is the large block of sandstone at the summit of Ganapu Ridge, immediately opposite the Hotel. Climbing alone, he lost his way in the mist. The search party found him at the foot of the Rock with a broken back. Both men are buried in a small plot behind the Hotel.

Then there was the accident that should never have happened. The Blue Pool is a favourite picnic spot up the Umlambonja Valley, only a couple of kilometres from the Hotel. The walk there is a pleasant one, and involves no climbing whatever. On December 1st, 1953, Mr. Ralph Bollen, Headmaster of Kensington South School, was walking along the path with his wife and a woman friend. He tripped over some object in the path, fell five metres down a rocky decline, and died almost immediately.

On October 13th, 1959 it was the turn of the *Outer Horn* to claim its victim. On the previous Saturday night, October 10th, two young girls had arrived at Cathedral Peak, Flelette van Zyl, a 19-year-old Public Service Department employee at Onderstepoort, and her friend Madge Rorke. That night they camped beside the river below the Hotel, and on Sunday morning they set out for the *Outer Horn*. Taking it easy, they camped that night in the foothills below the peak. Monday they spent exploring, and on the Tuesday morning the two girls set off to climb the peak. By midday both of them were pretty tired, but Flelette was anxious to push on. She told Madge that she would go on ahead, but that she would return about 2 p.m. When she failed to turn up, Madge went on to look for her, but could not find her. Panic-stricken, she decided to go down immediately to the Hotel for assistance. By now it was late, however, and she could not reach the Hotel before dark. She slept out alone that night on the mountain side, and arrived at the Hotel, on the Wednesday morning.

Mr. van der Riet immediately alerted the Bergville police, and two parties of police came out. Fortunately Stan Rose, an experienced mountaineer, who had been in Ken Howes-Howell's party on the *Pyramid* in 1936, was holidaying at Cathedral Peak, and he led a third party into the mountains to search for the missing girl. The three parties searched all day Wednesday, without success, but at 10 a.m. on the Thursday morning Stan Rose's party found Flelette. She had fallen 100 metres down the north-eastern face of the mountain, and had been killed instantly. A stretcher-party was waiting on stand-by duty, and they managed to bring the body down to within 6½ kilometres of the Hotel, but now darkness was falling and the stretcher-bearers, who had been all day without food or water, were too exhausted to continue any longer. The body had to be left out on the mountain-side in the care of two police guards, and the journey back to the Hotel completed the following day.

The last tragedy occurred in September 1970, and the scene this time was the *Bell*. Three Natal University students, Ian William Dawson, Charles Barber and Carlos Freer, set out to climb the peak. Ian and Charles were roped together, but Carlos was not. Near the top of the climb, the two men who were roped together fell 60 metres to their deaths.

The Natal Mountain Club Rescue Team, under Dr. Sherman Ripley, was alerted on the Sunday morning, and they swung immediately into action. They were assisted by officials of the Natal Parks Board, the Police, and an Air Force helicopter. The rescue team consisted altogether of 20 men, and between them they brought the bodies down within 24 hours of the accident happening.

It is a tragic tale of young lives lost, but it will be a sad day for South Africa when its sons and its daughters, its young men and women, fail to respond to the challenge of danger. It is part of the price we pay in the making of men. And let it not be thought that any part of the Drakensberg, let alone Cathedral Peak, is dangerous for the careful holiday-maker. Every one of the accidents we have recounted above, with the possible exception of young Michael Stephens, was due to carelessness, foolhardiness or inexperience. Follow two golden rules: never go out alone (I admit I have not always followed this advice myself!) and always have with you someone who is experienced and who knows the area. The old club rule of the Natal Mountain Club prohibited parties of less than three. If one was injured there was always another to stay with him, while the third sought help. If you follow these simple rules no harm will befall you, and for long years to come you will be able to enjoy the beauty of this lovely land.

The foothills of the Cathedral area are perhaps not as spectacular as the high peaks, but they are amongst the most beautiful in the whole Drakensberg. Here you will find a land of clear mountain streams and age-old forests, of frothing cascades tumbling into pools of laughing water, of green mountain slopes and secret kloofs, of wild flowers and singing birds. The main river is the Umlambonja, rising in the angle formed by the Cathedral Range and the main Drakensberg. Umlambonja means the hungry dog. Thirty-two kilometres to the south, in the Giant's Castle Game Reserve, is a river called the Injasuti. This means the well-fed dog. According to the Zulus, the game in the early days was plentiful in the Giant's Castle area, and the dogs were well fed. In the Cathedral area the game was scarce, and the dogs went hungry!

Beauty spots and picnic spots abound. One of the most beautiful is Rainbow Gorge. It is only about an hour's walk from the Hotel. At 4½ km the path enters a magnificent forest, and about ¾ km further one of the loveliest pools in the district is encountered, fed by two waterfalls. Continue on, and about one km further on you will enter a tremendous gorge, through which the river tumbles and roars. High up on the enclosing walls two gigantic choc-stones have become wedged, stones that fell into the gorge a million years ago, and have remained there for all time. Higher up still are some little-known Bushman paintings, including a unique one depicting a rope ladder stretched across what must be the walls of the gorge.

Over the years I have grown to love the Cathedral area. It has meant more to me than merely the grandeur of the soaring peaks, the beauty of quiet valleys, and the green solitudes of age-old trees. To me these green solitudes and these forests are the hushed aisles of a great cathedral, and *Cathedral Peak* itself is the high altar from which the sounding winds deliver their message, the sermon that General Smuts once called the Religion of the Mountain. Speaking at Maclear's Beacon on *Table Mountain* on 25th February 1923, when he dedicated the memorial to the mountaineers who had fallen in the Great War, he spoke these noble words—

"The sons of the cities are remembered and recorded in the streets and squares of their cities, and by memorials placed in their churches and cathedrals. But the mountaineers deserve a loftier pedestal and a more appropriate memorial. To them the true church where they worshipped was Table Mountain. Table Mountain was their cathedral where they heard a subtler music and saw wider visions and were inspired with a loftier spirit. Here in life they breathed the great air; here in death their memory will fill the upper spaces.

"We may truly say that the highest religion is the Religion of the Mountain . . . the religion of joy, of the release of the soul from the things that weigh it down and fill it with a sense of weariness, sorrow and defeat . . .

"The mountains uphold us, and the stars beckon to us. The mountains of our lovely land will make a constant appeal to us to live the higher life of joy and freedom."

I wish someone had said something like this of our own Drakensberg Mountains!

CHAPTER XII

CATHKIN

"Champagne shall be my Castle gay,
Cathkin shall be my bed;
The Sentinel shall be my watch
And the Monk's Cowl clothe my head."
—SONG OF THE S.A. MOUNTAIN CLUB

If you take the footpath from the Cathedral Peak Hotel that leads up the Valley of the Umhlonhlo towards Organ Pipes Pass, you will meet at about the 2 000 metre contour level the Forestry road running for about 12 km roughly east and west. This road used to be a section of the well-known Contour Path, built in 1937 by Mr. J. van Heyningen, the Forester in charge of the Monk's Cowl Forest Station, to link up the Cathkin and Cathedral Peak forest areas. It kept roughly to the 2 000 metre contour throughout its course, curving in and out of the great valleys that cut into the mighty escarpment of the Drakensberg. Since van Heyningen's day it has been extended southward from *Cathkin Peak*, where it started, down into the Injasuti area, and northward to a point under *Cathedral Peak*. The Natal Parks Board, on its part, started some years ago to build a similar path on the northern slopes of *Giant's Castle*, driving northwards. When these two paths meet there will be something like 200 kilometres of well-graded pathway, stretching from *Giant's Castle* to *Cathedral Peak*, giving easy access to all the peaks that lie between these two points. (See maps on pages 120, 132 and 148).

Turn left along this Forestry road, and head east. You will enter, first of all, the cool green shadows of the Forestry Department's plantations. Out into the open again, you will walk along pleasant slopes, until, 12½ kilometres after you enter the road, you will come out at the top of the Ndedema Gorge and Valley, the road ends, and you are on the old Contour Path.

This is one of the finest of all the Drakensberg valleys, and from here the view is breathtaking. From far below, 400 metres down, comes the restless thunder* of the Ndedema River as it enters the spectacular Gorge. The steep grass slopes are studded with wild flowers, and with enormous rocks, while away to your left is the green expanse of the Ndedema Forest, stretching right down to the hurrying waters of the river. To your right is the deep cut-back the river has made into the tremendous wall of the Drakensberg, with *Ndedema Dome* (3 063 metres) at its head. This spectacular Gorge is almost certainly one of the last refuges of the Bushmen in the Drakensberg. It provides excellent cover, and is one of the remotest valleys in the whole area, far from human habitation. It is quite close to Eland Cave, which we shall refer to shortly. A large number of caves and paintings have been discovered in this valley, particularly by Mr. Harald Pager, who has made a special study of the Gorge.

Around it are the ageless peaks – the *Witch* (3 062 m), the *Sphinx*, *Little Saddle* and *Sugarloaf*. At the head of the Ndedema River, beneath the *Dome*, is a magnificent amphitheatre of rock walls, which narrow, underneath the *Dome*, into a vast crack, only a few metres wide. Below you, not far from where the path crosses the Ndedema, are two well-known Drakensberg caves, Sibayeni and Schoongezicht.

Continue down the path for 5½ km into this tremendous valley. As you cross the river at the bottom, you will see the lovely Tutumi Valley on your right, sweeping up to the *Organ Pipes*. Looking down upon you, serene and aloof, is *Little Saddle*.

Now you have before you a long, long pull as you climb up out of the valley on the other

* The word 'Ndedema' means, in Zulu, 'the reverberating one'.

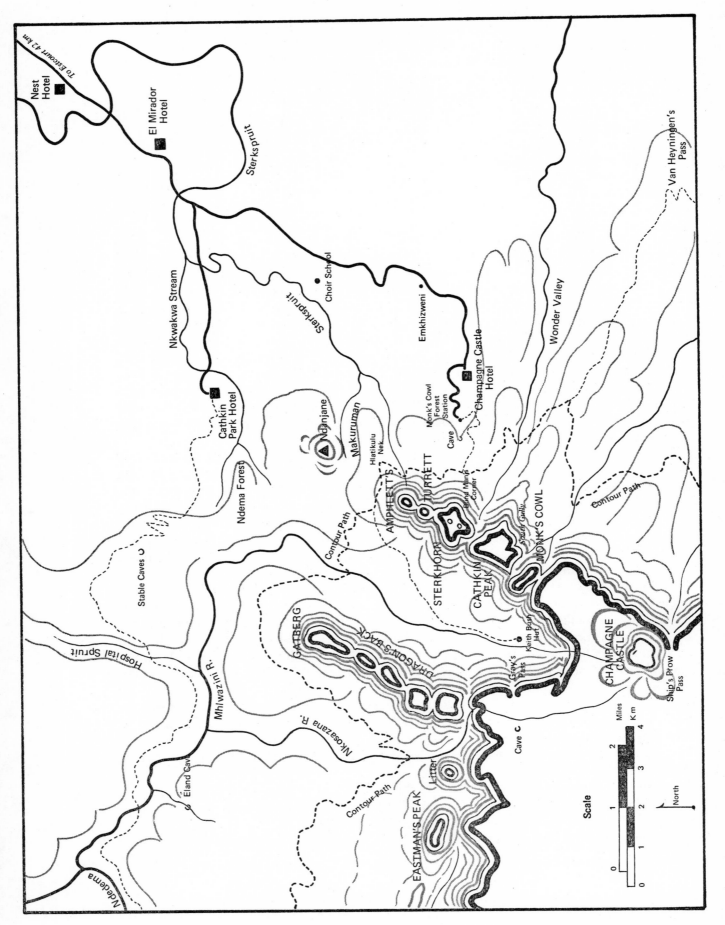

Map of Cathkin Area

side. For eight kilometres the path climbs up, getting higher and higher, until it comes out on the broad uplands underneath *Eastman's Peak*. This peak was named after H. A. ("Grandpa") Eastman, who was the first to reach the summit during the 1935 Natal Mountain Club Camp. "Grandpa" Eastman was a Cape climber. For many years he was Cape Town's Borough Electrical Engineer. To-day he lives in retirement under the mountains of Somerset West.

The Africans in their kraals, in the Cathkin area, still tell the story of the grim battle that was fought on the slopes of this mountain many years ago, between a regiment of Zulus and a tribe of Bushmen who had been raiding their cattle. The little yellow men were cornered on the slopes of the mountain. Their only retreat was upwards, and gradually they were forced back until they reached the summit. Here they made their stand. The Bushmen lay flat on their backs, and by putting their big toes through a riempie (thong) tied to the centre of the bow-stave, they were able to use both hands and discharge their arrows at great speed, high into the air, the arrows falling vertically on their attackers. The Zulus, terrified of the effects of these poisoned barbs, fled in terror, and the little yellow hunters were able to escape under cover of darkness into Lesotho.

An even more interesting story, with a touch of mystery, attaches to a cave in a small valley at the base of *Eastman's Peak*. Towards the end of June 1926 Dr. Ernest Warren, Director of the Natal Museum in Pietermaritzburg, received this quaint letter from Mr. J. S. Lombard, brother to Anton Lombard, farming at *Solar Cliffs* in the Lower Mhlwazini Valley:—

> "Dear Sir,
> A few days ago I find a whole Bushman outfitting Bow holster with a bow in it – and a long wooden box with a lot of airos in it also a leather poison bag and two knives this things still in order it is very wonderful to see such old things – I find it in a cave on top of the Small Drakensberg Cathkin Peak as I want to sell it perhaps you will make me an offer for it or anybody else thats why I writing to you – hope you will please let me now by letter whats your opinion – I had a few offers already but it is worth that."

Dr. Warren duly replied that the Natal Museum would be pleased to acquire the Bushmen articles found. He asked for further details, and also asked Lombard to state his price. Lombard replied that he had already had offers of up to £10 from several Museums as well as private persons, "but I like that these things go Direct to the Museum in the province where it is find. You can have it for the sum of £6 10s. Free on Rail."

And so the deal was concluded, and the £6 10s. duly handed over. On receipt of the articles Dr. Warren wrote again asking whether there were any paintings in the cave, and whether any search had been made for pieces of pottery, bone or metal ornaments. Lombard duly acknowledged receipt of the letter "about old bones and potterys and so on", and said that he had in fact located "a few bones and something else", which he would forward if Dr. Warren wanted them. The "something else" turned out to be a portion of a bone arm-ring.

> "I am sorry when I dick those things out I break it," said Lombard, in a third letter. "I wonder if you could tell me what is this bengal of made Ivory or what? This cave have many nice paintings you can see they stayed a very long time in there. I couldn't find any whole potterys only broken pieces."

The complete find, as handed over to the Museum, consisted of a bow, together with bow-case and quiver, 20 arrows, a curved metal blade inside a leather thong, a small leather bag, and a wooden spatula for applying poison to the arrows.

And then the whole story came out. Lombard, hunting in the area, had discovered the cave in a small lateral tributary of the Mhlwazini, on the lower slopes of *Eastman's Peak*. It was about 90 metres long, 6 metres deep, and contained over 1 000 individual paintings, of the most exquisite artistry. Amongst them was a picture of an eland nearly a metre in length. Hunting around in the cave, Lombard had climbed up to a ledge of rock, about 1,2 metres wide and about 6 metres above the level of the floor. Here he had found the Bushman hunting kit, all in a perfect state of preservation.

But it was the angle on the find supplied by Mr. W. Carter Robinson that lifted it into the realm of mystery. Robinson was farming at the time in the Sterkspruit valley, at *Deelpunt*, and he visited the cave a few days after Lombard had discovered it. Climbing up to the ledge, Robinson noticed that it was a Bushman's sleeping quarters. In front was a low wall of piled-up stones and inside was a layer of grass, which looked as if it had been cut only four to six months previously! Who had built that tiny shelter in one of the remotest caves of the Drakensberg? Who had cut that grass? And to whom did those bows and arrows belong? Is it possible that even as late as 1926 a few isolated Bushmen still remained in the Drakensberg? It seems hardly credible, but how otherwise can you explain those well-preserved bows and arrows, and that recently-used sleeping place? Harald Pager, who has made a special study of the Ndedema Gorge and of this particular cave, says that it is not impossible. He points out that even now one can still walk for days in these parts without seeing another soul, and that if one wanted to avoid people, it would not be difficult to do so, for weeks or months, perhaps even for years.

To-day these relics of an ancient past, which may have lived on into the twentieth century, are preserved in the Natal Museum in Pietermaritzburg, and the cave is known variously as Makambi Cave, Eland's Cave, or Lombard's Cave.

Back along the path, it still proceeds southwards, one of the loneliest stretches in the Drakensberg. Then, suddenly, you come out high above the Valley of the Nkosazana, another of the great valleys of the Drakensberg. Far below you, as with the Ndedema, the river croons its ancient song as it hurries through the valleys of the Little Berg. On the other side the path clings to the slopes of *Gatberg*. If you could walk across in a straight line you would do it in 15 minutes, but before you have traversed the downward slope, crossed the river at the bottom, and climbed the far slope, two long hours will have sped by.

It was in the upper reaches of the Nkosazana, near to where the path crosses the river, that cinnabar was "discovered" in the early 1920's. Cinnabar is a red mercuric sulphide, and is the common ore from which mercury, or quicksilver, is derived. It is usually found in an earthy form of bright red colour. And here, certainly, were the red earths, perhaps of a slightly purplish tinge, but undoubtedly red. And the assessors had been handed small quantities of what was undoubtedly quicksilver. Soon the wildest stories were being told in the pubs of Winterton, Bergville and Estcourt. One enthusiastic farmer even claimed that he could hear the mercury dripping on to the ground inside a crevice he had discovered! Prospectors from Estcourt, Bergville and Winterton, and even further afield, moved in to stake their claims and to make their fortunes. For months they lived and toiled in the mountains. Supplies were brought in by donkey, up the slopes of the Little Berg, and across the plateau to the Nkosazana. The remains of the tracks, in the Cathkin area, and up the *Brotherton* headland in the Cathedral area, are still to be seen, and you can still see the holes that the prospectors dug. But alas! I am afraid the original "finds" had been salted, and the red earth was nothing more than outcrops from the Red Beds, and the prospectors soon departed, angry and disillusioned. Those who took part in the "rush" are reluctant to-day to divulge the name of the suspect. A veil of secrecy has been drawn over the whole affair, for the suspect's family still lives in the district, and men just aren't talking!

Gatberg (2 408 m) is the mountain with a hole bored right through it, near the summit. From below it looks quite small, only a few metres across, but I have stood inside that hole, and I can tell you that you would easily get a two-story building inside it. Its Zulu name is *Ntunja*, meaning the eye of a needle. There is another mountain in Natal with a hole right through it. This is the well-known *Kranskop*, near Greytown. Actually at one time there were two holes –

one has since fallen in – and the Zulu name for this peak is *Ntunjambili*, the mountain with two holes.

In the tally of Drakensberg accidents perhaps the strangest of all can be claimed by *Gatberg*. On Monday, 13th September 1937 Mr. R. Stuart Armstrong and Mr. T. H. Archbell left Kroonstad in a Hornet Moth light plane to fly to Durban. Armstrong was the owner of Armstrong's Garage on Durban Beach. Archbell, 21 years of age, who was piloting the plane, was a member of one of Natal's oldest families, a great-grandson of the missionary James Archbell. Both men were keen and fully-qualified pilots.

They set off at 6.40 a.m., but over the Drakensberg they ran into heavy mist, lost their way, and at 8.15 a.m. crash-landed on the slopes of *Gatberg*. As young Archbell saw the ground looming up through the mist, a couple of metres below him, he had the presence of mind to put the left rudder full over, tipping the plane so that the right wing would take the impact and not the front of the machine. This saved them from serious injury. Armstrong was thrown clear and sustained a gash across the forehead and eye. Archbell was uninjured. The plane, however, was badly smashed up. Surrounded by heavy mist, they had not the faintest idea where they were, except that their altimeter, which read 7 000 feet (2 134 m) indicated that they must be somewhere in the Drakensberg. They spent the remainder of the day and the following night in the plane. Next day, with no signs of life around them, they climbed the slopes of *Gatberg*, and with the mist beginning to clear, they spotted, 10 km to the north, far down the valley of the Mhlwazini, and on its right bank, a small plantation of gum trees, which indicated a homestead.* They decided to head for this, and at 9.30 a.m. began the long descent into the valley of the Mhlwazini.

Meanwhile an extensive air search for the missing plane had been mounted. Nothing could be done on the Monday, owing to the heavy mist, but on the Tuesday a number of planes took off from Durban. Amongst them was a Hornet Moth piloted by Captain Noel J. O. Carbutt, head of Natal Aviation, with a *Mercury* reporter on board as a passenger. They could not see *Cathkin Peak*, still shrouded in mist and rain, as they flew past, so decided to fly on to Ladysmith. Here they had lunch, but during lunch the weather cleared, and at 3 p.m. they set off again, planning to search the area between *Cathedral Peak* and *Cathkin*.

It was the *Mercury* reporter who first spotted the plane. Far down, on the slopes of *Gatberg*, he caught a gleam of something which he at first took to be an iron shed. Closer inspection, however, revealed a crimson line between the two crossed greyish-silver arms. "It's the plane!" yelled the reporter above the roar of the engine. And the plane it was, though there was no sign of life around it. They headed straight back for Stamford Hill, from where they immediately telephoned Cathkin Park Hotel with the news. It was now 5.30 p.m.

At the Hotel Otto Zunckel, his two sons and a number of other men were busy making plans for an extensive ground search for the following day. At almost the same moment that the telephone message came through, Madolawana, an African guide, came galloping up to the Hotel on horseback. "Ngilitholile ibanoyi ngale kweNtunja!" he shouted (" I have found the aeroplane behind Gatberg!"). Then breathlessly he told his story. He had ridden up to within ten metres of the wreck, and shouted. There was no reply, and, afraid to approach closer to where there might be dead men, alone in the middle of the mountains, he had galloped on to Cathkin Hotel to tell the baas there what he had seen.

"Almost certainly dead," said Otto Zunckel. "Still, there's just a chance we may be able to save life. We must leave immediately."

They set off just after dark, 11 Europeans and 14 Africans, with Otto Zunckel in the lead. Up the long and steep Jacob's Ladder they went, in single file, with the moon trying to shine

* This homestead, on the farm *The Climb*, belonged to the Vermeulens, and is immediately opposite Lombard's homestead on the farm *Solar Cliffs*, in the Mhlwazini Valley, 4 km above the junction of the Mhlwazini and the Umlambonja.

through the clinging mist, up to the summit of the Little Berg, down steep slopes into the Mhlwazini, and up the other side, stumbling, falling and cursing in the darkness. One African fell down a krantz and gashed his head severely.

At last, close to midnight, they found the red and silver wreck on the lower slopes of *Gatberg*. Some of the men, fearing the worst, approached it with raised hats. The starboard wing was smashed, the engine had been ripped from the frame, and was lying some little distance away, the under-carriage was crushed, but the cabin itself was intact. And there was no sign of the men! Nor was there any blood, apart from a small smear on a pair of overalls. An examination of the interior revealed how the airmen had adopted every possible means to protect themselves from the bitter cold of their 2 134 metre altitude by stuffing every crevice and gap in the cabin with socks, paper, gauntlets and odds and ends. To cover the front of the cabin, where the engine had broken away, they had torn the fabric from one of the wings and tied it securely inside the cabin. There were also the remains of a meal. The men were obviously alive, but where were they?

Actually, at that moment they were safe and sound in their beds at a lonely farmhouse, 10 km away.

After leaving the plane on the Tuesday morning, they first of all had the surprise of their lives when they ran into an African Forest Guard, and were promptly arrested for being in the Forest Reserve without a permit! This seemed a heaven-sent opportunity of reaching civilisation, even if it did mean being in the clutches of the law, but when Mantish, the Guard, heard their story, he agreed to let them go, as the farm, towards which they were heading (which he told them belonged to a Mrs. Vermeulen) was much nearer than the Monk's Cowl Forest Station, to which he had intended taking them.

The men then continued down the Mhlwazini Valley, past the junction of the Ndedema, and arrived at Mrs. Vermeulen's farm at 2 p.m. Mrs. Vermeulen and her daughter, terrified at first at the sight of two grim-looking strangers with their clothes covered in oil,* soon realised the plight they were in, and took them in for the night. Next morning the two men continued on down the valley to a point where the present Cathedral road crosses the Mhlwazini. Here they met a mule-cart, which Mrs. Vermeulen had arranged for them, and from there they proceeded to Bergville.

Later Gert Maartens, brother of Hendrik Maartens who started the Champagne Castle Hotel, was given the contract to bring down the wreckage of the plane. He brought down the engine and other parts of value on the back of a donkey, but for many years parts of the frame still lay on the mountain side, below and quite near to the present Contour Path.

Now you climb up round the shoulder of *Gatberg*, and then you look down into yet another magnificent valley, the Valley of the Mhlwazini. High on the opposite slope is Hlatikulu Nek, the gateway to the Valley of the Sterkspruit, to *Cathkin Peak*, and to *Champagne Castle*.

Champagne Castle itself (3 377 m) is a rounded dome, set very slightly inland, and the second highest point on the escarpment. It is not particularly impressive, but it is ringed by mighty cliffs on two sides. At only one point are these cliffs breached, by a gully known as Gray's Pass, slightly to the north-west of the source of the Mhlwazini.

The most feasible way of climbing *Champagne Castle* is to proceed over Hlatikulu Nek (if one sets off from any of the Berg Hotels in the area), turn left up the Valley of the Mhlwazini to Base Camp, immediately under the final wall of the Drakensberg, and then climb up the steep slopes in front of you, and so into Gray's Pass and up to the summit. It is a climb that can be done by the veriest tyro, so long as he has two strong legs and plenty of stamina. No rock work at all is involved, apart from the very easy rock in the Pass itself. *Champagne Castle* was first

---

* The Vermeulens were recluses. Whenever visitors came to the valley the whole family would run off and hide.

Monk's Cowl, with Cathkin Peak to the left and the cliffs of Champagne Castle to the right.

Winter idyll.   *The summit of the Amphitheatre.*

The Mountain Club Hut, Summit of the Amphitheatre.

SKETCH OF CATHKIN AREA

FROM IMAGINARY HIGH POINT, LOOKING NORTH-WEST

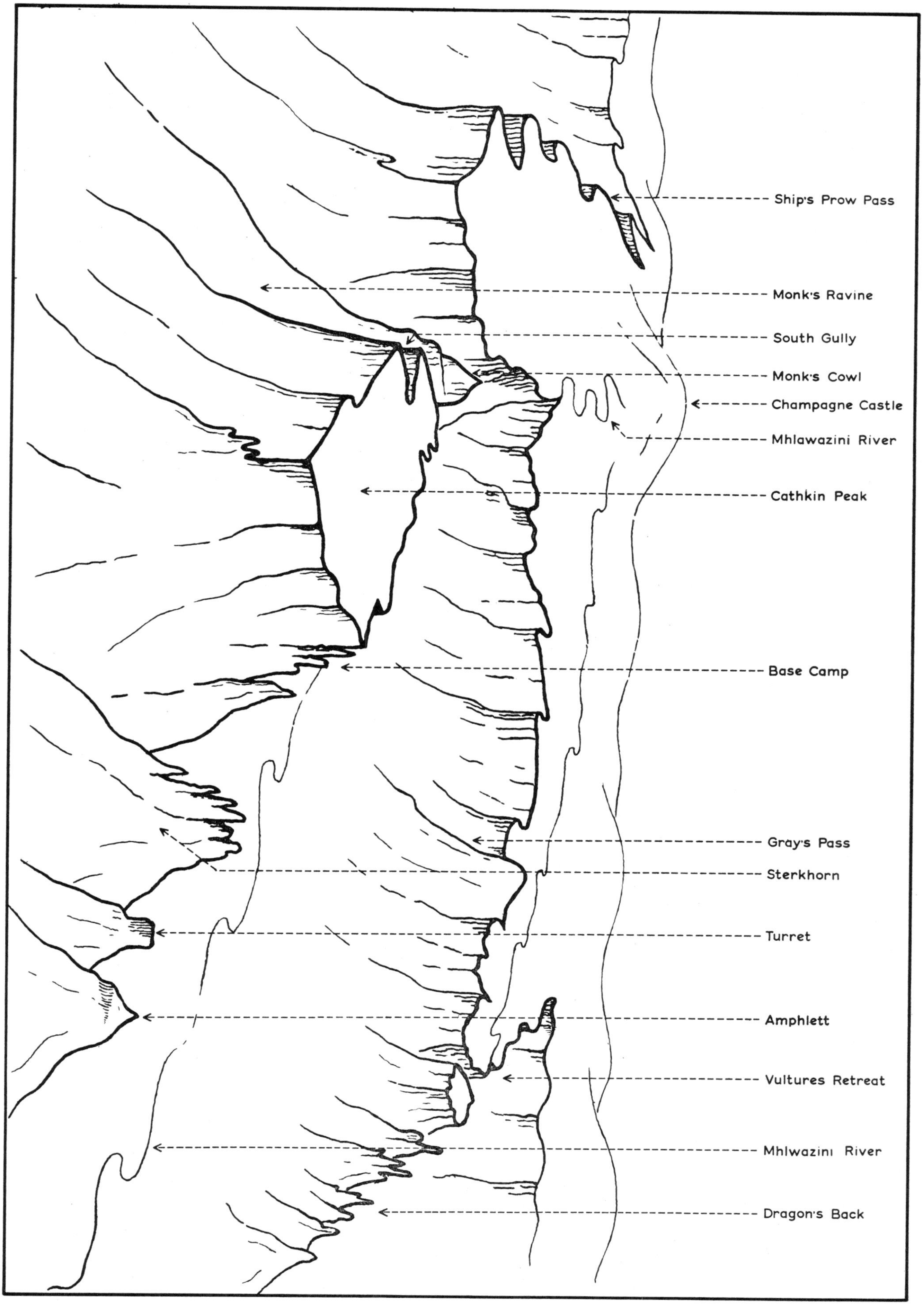

--------- Ship's Prow Pass

--------- Monk's Ravine

--------- South Gully

--------- Monk's Cowl

--------- Champagne Castle

--------- Mhlawazini River

--------- Cathkin Peak

--------- Base Camp

--------- Gray's Pass

--------- Sterkhorn

--------- Turret

--------- Amphlett

--------- Vultures Retreat

--------- Mhlwazini River

--------- Dragon's Back

climbed, traditionally, by Major Grantham in 1861, while the first authenticated and recorded climb went to the Stocker brothers in 1888.

Cathkin Peak (3 149 m) is a very different proposition. It is a huge, free-standing block of a mountain, and is one of the most prominent landmarks in the whole of the Drakensberg. Stupendous cliffs ring all four sides of the mountain, but on the south face there is a fairly broad gully, which makes a deep indent into the symmetrical face of the giant. It is filled in with rock ledges and slopes of debris on its right side, and with steep rock faces on its left side. This offers the only feasible route to the summit. Even so, it is a climb that can only be undertaken by a team of experienced mountaineers. For nearly fifty years it drew climbers eager to be the first to breach its virgin inviolability. We have already referred to several isolated episodes in these attempts. The time has now come to tell the full story.

First to set foot on the upper slopes of the peak were the Stocker brothers, although it is possible that earlier, unrecorded, attempts had been made, for the South Gully was already known in 1888 when the Stockers made their attempt.

On 12th August 1888 they moved into the South Gully and commenced climbing. They finally reached an altitude of 2 995 metres* with 154 metres still to go, but here they were confronted by what appeared to be an unclimbable wall, and as their time was running out, they decided to retreat. Three months later they were back for a second attempt, but bad weather and trouble with their transport defeated them, and this time they did not even reach the South Gully.

In November 1909 Mr. and Mrs. Amphlett made a reconnaissance of the peak. They attempted to climb the north-east ridge, but the weather turned against them and they had to give up the attempt.

Between 1888 and 1911 there must have been a number of attempts at climbing the peak, of which we know nothing. W. C. West, who was one of the six men who finally climbed it in 1912, said that the officers of various regiments stationed in the vicinity often tried to scale the peak. As we shall see, an attempt was definitely made in 1907 or 1909, by two Cape Town climbers and a Durban man, but we know nothing of the details of this effort.

The next attempt of which we have a definite record was made by Wybergh in 1911, when he spent the night high up in the South Gully, a night bivouac we have already described in Chapter VI. The party consisted of Mr. and Mrs. Wybergh and Col. J. P. S. Woods. They approached the mountain from the south. Wybergh and Woods first ascended the slopes of *Champagne Castle* to the left of Monk's Ravine. (Monk's Ravine is the deeply-incised southern gully that runs up to the base of *Monk's Cowl*, between *Champagne Castle* and *Cathkin Peak*.) From here they could look into the South Gully, but were rather doubtful of it, so they climbed up the Ravine to the base of *Monk's Cowl*, went down the other side into the Mhlwazini, and explored the north-west face, without any success, however.

Next day Woods was suffering from mountain sickness, so Wybergh made an attempt on the South Gully, accompanied only by his Zulu guide, Nongale. High on the slopes of *Cathkin* they found a cairn of stones, inside which was a tin containing a card inscribed with the following words:–

> August 1, 1907
> D. O. Reynish, Mountain Club, Cape Town
> John S. Mann of Durban
> A. Beevers, Cape Town

The date was indistinct, and might have been 1909. Of this attempt on the peak we know nothing beyond these names and the date. As we have seen, Wybergh, like the Stockers before

---

* This height has been adjusted. Their altimeter actually read 10 120 ft. (3 085 metres), but it was about 90 metres out.

him, after climbing well up the South Gully, failed at the final pitch, this time owing to the Gully being iced up. Unlike the Stockers however, he spent the night in the Gully.

Finally in 1912 a very determined attempt was made to climb the peak. A strong team of climbers assembled at Col. Wood's farm *Heartsease*. They consisted of W. C. West and G. T. Amphlett from Cape Town, together with Amphlett's coloured servant, Tobias. Father Kelly came from Bloemfontein. He and Tom Casement rode down from Rydal Mount with the faithful Melatu, over 160 km in two days. They left Col. Woods' farm on the morning of 10th September, camped for the night at the foot of the mountain, and reached Monk's Ravine at 11.30 a.m. on the following day. Here, although the account is not very clear, they must have spent the night.

Next day, 12th September, they climbed the Ravine, where they saw the cairn and card that Wybergh had discovered a year previously. A little further up they found another bottle, with a note inside, which read: "Take the ice-slope to the right. Then up the Gorge, and away to the left and up the Peak. You will have a jolly good view, even if you have to go home without climbing *Cathkin Peak*. George Scott, Colin S. Nunn, August 1st, 1912."

Then they entered the Gully and climbed steadily for several hours. When they came to the last difficult pitches, which had defeated the Stockers and Wybergh, they at first decided to leave Melatu and Tobias behind, but they were both good climbers, and were so obviously disappointed at being left behind, that eventually they decided to take the two boys up with them. Climbing slowly now, and with infinite care, the six men made their way steadily up the final precipices, and reached the top at 2.20 p.m.

It had previously been considered that *Cathkin Peak* was higher than *Champagne Castle*, but when they reached the summit it was obvious that both *Champagne Castle* and *Monk's Cowl* were higher than *Cathkin Peak*. Their aneroid gave a height of 3 200 metres. The actual height is 3 149 metres.

We have already told the story of the second ascent, made by Londt in July 1921. Up to 1955 the only accepted route up *Cathkin* had been the South Gully, but on September 20, 1955 A. Leeb du Toit, Keith Frank Holderness Bush and N. D. Harte climbed the north face for the first time. It taxed their powers to the utmost, the climb terminating in a 100-metre chimney, very wet, slippery and dangerous in the rainy months, but quite feasible in the drier months. But the climb ended in tragedy. While abseiling down the sheer cliff face the sling attached to the rope holding Keith Bush broke, and he hurtled hundreds of metres to his death. Keith was a most promising Natal University student, son of Professor Frank Bush, also of the University. Amongst the many letters received by his parents at the time of the accident, was this moving tribute from one who knew Keith well:—

> "At the hour of his tragic death Keith had no idea of impending disaster. He was with friends and fellow-students in the mountains he so loved, and with them he had just achieved a difficult and hazardous climb. He had done something worthwhile and he must have been filled with a sense of accomplishment for the brief time he and his comrades remained on the top of the conquered peak (*Cathkin*) and surveyed the scene spread out before and below them. Must not that have been a glorious moment! And in that moment, with no sense of pain or danger, he passed on."

His memory is enshrined to-day in the Keith Bush Hut, in the upper reaches of the Mhlwazini Valley, just below the spot where he met his death.

Cathkin Peak was named after David Gray's farm *Cathkin*, a name he had obtained from Cathkin Braes, near Glasgow, David Gray's home city. David Gray, it will be remembered, had settled in the area in 1858. The full story of the naming of *Cathkin Peak* and *Champagne*

Castle, has been told in Chapter IV. The Zulu name for *Cathkin* is *Mdedelelo*, meaning "make room for him". It is usually applied to a bully who pushes everyone else out of his way.*

Between *Cathkin* and *Champagne Castle* is *Monk's Cowl* (3 234 m) a peak which has caught the imagination of people to a greater extent, possibly, than any other Drakensberg peak. This is possibly due to its inaccessibility (tucked away behind *Cathkin* it is seldom seen by the ordinary tourist), to the fact that for many years it was listed as unclimbable, and also because it was the scene of the first fatal climbing accident in the Drakensberg. *Cathkin* is a huge, solid block of a mountain: *Champagne* is a rounded dome: *Monk's Cowl* is sharp and pointed, like an up-thrust fang, and there is something almost sinister and menacing about its lowering precipices. Hans Wong, who finally conquered it in 1942, spoke of its "cold, fascinating beauty". It was a challenge that few mountaineers could resist.

Who named it is not known. The name goes back as far as 1912 at least, so it was not one of the peaks named by the Natal Mountain Club. The Stockers knew it in 1888, but not as *Monk's Cowl*. They knew it as *Inkosana*, meaning a petty chief, obviously the Zulu name for it.

There is a tradition, unconfirmed, that Father Kelly had attempted to climb the north-east face, round about 1914. Many others must at least have taken a look at it, only to be repelled by those towering black precipices. George Londt made a brief reconnaissance of it in 1921. Londt seldom believed a route impossible, but after this visit he said he doubted very much whether the peak would ever be climbed. Few mountaineers could resist its lure, however, and the story of the various attempts to climb it make up one of the finest epics of Natal mountaineering. Only two of the six attempts I shall describe succeeded, but what of that! It was the unending effort, the cool courage, the refusal to accept defeat, the iron nerve of the men who made these attempts that counted, and in that respect not one was a failure.

In January 1938 the first serious attempt at climbing the peak, since Father Kelly'spossible attempt in 1914, was made by Dick Barry and Colin Gebhardt. We have already referred to Barry's magnificent record, in Chapter VI. I shall tell the story of their attempt in Gebhardt's own words:—

"We arrived at Cathkin Hostel on the 28th January 1938, obtained permission from the forestry ranger to camp out in the mountains, and left the same day, arriving at the foot of Cathkin Gully that afternoon." (Note: Cathkin Gully is the Gully running up from the Mhlwazini to *Monk's Cowl*, and is the counterpart of Monk's Ravine on the other side of the mountain. The men were approaching the nek between *Cathkin* and *Monk's Cowl* from the north: the Cathkin attempts of 1911 and 1912 had been made from the south of this nek.) "We pitched our camp, and decided to start our climb early next morning.

"At about 6 o'clock next morning, the 29th, when we woke up, the weather was unsuitable, with heavy mist and light rain. However, at half past seven it cleared up and seemed to be a lovely day, so we decided after all to give it a trial. We left at about 8 o'clock from our base camp, each carrying a ruck-sack, with a few provisions, a spare rope or two and a few pitons. It must have been just after nine by the time we had slogged up to the top of the gully between *Monk's Cowl* and *Cathkin*. Again it started raining. Dick had a type of portable oilskin tent with him. The two of us managed to get under this and thus kept comparatively dry. We must have sat there for quite an hour. Anyway, as soon as it cleared up we pushed on again, making a fairly long traverse to the right.

"Then started our first rock work, about 'D' standard This we did withou much bother. Then we started the real rock work. We did the first pitch, about fifty feet of 'E' standard, then a fairly long grassy stretch and two or three more rock pitches with these grassy slopes between.

"Then came the final rock assault. This we judged, if I remember correctly, to be about four hundred feet. I remember Dick remarking that if we managed that, then there would be

* Mr. S. Bourquin suggests that the more likely meaning is 'He who wears out with fatigue': *dedelele*, referring to mental or physical fatigue.

only about a hundred feet or so of scrambling to the top. Dick went on ahead. He was in good climbing form, not that I had ever seen him otherwise. He went up about sixty feet to where he found the first stance. Unfortunately there was no form of belay he could use other than a shoulder, or hip belay. He pulled up the two ruck-sacks, one at a time. Then he threw the rope to me. I started climbing. It was very difficult work, more difficult than I had judged from the ease with which Dick did it, and it was extremely sensational. There was about a thousand-foot drop just to the left of us. I judged this pitch to be about double star 'E' standard, similar to the 'Red Corner' climb that Dick and I opened up at *Tonquani*. Up on my way I went and I completed the climb to within two feet of Dick. I still remember his smile and his saying 'Good climbing, Gebby'. I remember putting my right hand out, taking hold of a handhold so as to keep my balance and wanting to take a step up next to Dick so that he could carry on with the next pitch. As I took the step, my handhold came out, a rock weighing about 6 lbs. I lost my balance and down I went.

"Dick, being quite unprepared for anything like that, couldn't hold me, so of course after I had fallen the length of the rope, I jerked him off the stance. Down we went, dropped this first pitch of about sixty feet, rolled down a slope, dropped down about another twenty feet, rolled another slope, dropped another pitch of about thirty feet, and came to rest close to the edge of another fifty-foot pitch. We weren't very badly hurt then, though Dick was unconscious. The time must have been about 3 o'clock. My leg was badly bruised and one finger hurt. Dick had a cut on his head. I happened to have a bandage in my pocket, so I bandaged his head and did the best I could for him until he regained consciousness, about two hours later. He was then quite cheerful, complained a bit about a headache, and was in fact more concerned about me than about himself. We knew then that our attempt had failed, so we decided to start the descent. We only had one difficult pitch to overcome; then the rest of the descent would have been comparatively easy."

They were now, however, in a dreadful predicament. They had no spare rope, their ruck-sacks, pitons and other climbing gear had been left behind at the point from where they had fallen, they were alone and badly shaken on the precipices of a hitherto unclimbed mountain, and night was coming on. It was a situation enough to shake the nerve of the stoutest climber. Colin Gebhardt continues his account:—

"I was then in a better condition than Dick, so I was to act as leader and belay Dick down this fifty-foot pitch. He tried, and tried – had about five attempts to get down – but I suppose owing to his condition then, he couldn't make it. Then he decided that I should go down. He would watch how I did it, then he would be able to follow me. I managed to get down. He tried again and again and again, but couldn't get himself to do it. Then he decided that he would look around and see if he couldn't find an easier way down. I called him and besought him to come back, because I knew there was no other way down.

"Well, he went. Away over to my left I lost sight of him, but could hear him answering my calls every now and then. Then suddenly no more answers. I knew immediately Dick was dead. God knows how I did, but I knew. If he had fallen I knew just about where I would find him. I started on my way down and around that way. My leg was painful and the going slow. Then it got too dark to go on. I went into a little cave we saw on our way up. There I waited for daylight to come. As soons as it was light enough I continued on. I found Dick's body just about where I had expected. He was dead. I tried to carry him, but was too exhausted to lift him, so I had to leave him and go for help . . ."

Gebhardt's dash down the mountain side for help is an epic in itself. Bruised, dazed, maimed and drenched, after a night alone high up on those staggering precipices, and with the knowledge that his friend was dead, he managed to get down off the mountain and into the Valley of the Mhlwazini. He had been without food for twenty four hours, his boots were gone, for they had climbed in stockinged feet, and all his warm clothing had been left behind. For twenty kilometres he staggered on, over rough mountain tracks and down the boulder-strewn course of the Mhlwazini River, until, on the point of collapse, late on the Sunday morning, he stumbled into Cathkin Park Hotel with the news of the tragedy.

Again it was Otto Zunckel and his two sons, Udo and Gerald, who took charge of the rescue party. Within half an hour of Gebhardt's arrival they were off on the long climb up the Little Berg, into the Valley of the Mhlwazini, and up to Base Camp. They arrived at the foot of *Monk's Cowl* late on Sunday evening, but that night heavy rain came down, and it rained steadily all the next day as well.

Conditions in the relief camp were indeed grim, that Sunday night and Monday. Torrents of rain fell, and it was bitterly cold. They had no blankets, and their food ran out. So bitter was the weather that the 11 Africans whom they had brought up with them were invited into the white men's tent. Tuesday the weather was equally bad, but on the Wednesday an attempt could be made to reach the body. It was Udo Zunckel who found it, wedged face upwards between two huge rocks. The eyes were open, facing the peak. Almost every bone in the body was broken. It was placed in a sack, lowered by rope down two steep cliffs, and so on to a grassy slope. Here it was placed on a stretcher, and the march home began with relays of bearers.

On the Thursday morning, at 10 a.m. a simple burial service, taken by Canon Harker of Estcourt, was held on the slopes of the Little Berg near Cathkin Park Hotel, at the only point where the tip of *Monk's Cowl* can be seen. The headstone was a block of Drakensberg sandstone, and the grave faced *Monk's Cowl*. The inscription reads:—

Richard Vincent Meriman
BARRY
who gave his life to the
mountains he loved
MONK'S COWL
Jan. 29th, 1938
Aged 22 years
I will lift up mine eyes unto the
hills from whence cometh my help.

Harry Barker, his friend and climbing companion, who had come down from Johannesburg to help in the recovery of the body, said of him afterwards: "His death was a tragedy in the noblest sense, for it was his very virtue – his courage – which was the cause of it. But not in vain did he live and die, for his spirit lives among his friends, and his memory will inspire them."

Barry and Colin Gebhardt had attacked the north-west face of the peak. Nearly 15 years later, in May 1952, two other young climbers also found themselves on the same north-west face of the peak, right on Barry's route, though they did not know it. Des Watkins, well-known Natal climber, and Gillian Bettle, were attempting a new route on the inscrutable peak, which, as we shall shortly recount, had already been conquered ten years previously. After climbing a ledge at about the 3 000 metre mark, they turned a corner and suddenly came across a rucksack tucked into a crevice. It was Barry's, and after getting over the shock of finding someone else's rucksack hidden so high up in the clouds, they suddenly realised that they were on Barry's route, and that this was as far as he had got.

It was at this point that Watkins himself slipped and fell, at almost the same spot that Barry had fallen. He fell about 15 metres and cracked several ribs, so the two had to give up. Five months later, however, Watkins was back, determined to reach the ruck-sack and clear up its mystery. This time he had with him G. Cairns and T. Norcott. Climbing steadily, they reached the same spot. The rucksack was still there. After nearly fifteen years it was in bad condition, but its contents had been well-preserved in that high, dry spot, so inaccessible that even the baboons had been unable to reach it. Inside the rucksack they found some butter in a plastic jar. Though rancid, it was still edible. A pair of trousers were quite wearable, and a camera was in good condition. There was also a pair of climbing boots, a coil of rope, rubber tennis shoes, and a piton, all in nearly as good condition as when last used. Most pathetic of the contents was a small tin with a note inside, signed by Barry and Gebhardt. So confident had they been of reaching the top, that they had prepared the note beforehand, intending to leave it inside the cairn they would have built on the summit, and which was never to be theirs. The three men brought the gear down safely, and the film in the camera was sent off to be developed.*

This north-west face, which Barry and Des Watkins had both found impossible, was finally conquered in 1962 in a dramatic climb by Martin Winter, Malcolm Moor and M. Makowski. It included a pitch of 3½ metres which took 3½ hours to climb, and a spine-tingling hand-traverse, with legs dangling over an overhang.

But to go back. The tragic death of Dick Barry added yet another facet to the challenge of the peak. Men were even more determined to climb it.

In 1939 John Langmore, who had often climbed with Barry, led a most determined and carefully prepared assault on the west face. No-one could have led the climb with greater skill and courage than John Langmore, but this assault also failed. This was largely due to the weather. Heavy snow fell, and thick mist came down. The pitches and the chimneys were all iced up, and the cold was bitter. There was only one thing for it – retreat.

All the attempts so far had shown the near impossibility of the northern and north-western faces. In 1942 Hans Wong decided to have a go at the southern face. He persuaded three other Transvaal men to go with him, Jack Botha, Emil Ruhle and Tony Hooper. As they approached Champagne Castle Hotel in their car, a devastating storm broke over them. Trees were up-rooted, the front of the car was lifted bodily into the air by a tremendous gust of wind. A near-by house collapsed like a pack of cards. It was almost as if the guardian spirits of Quathlamba were making a last desperate effort to protect the inviolability of the virgin peak.

Next morning, Sunday, 10th May 1942, they left the Hotel and headed for the Mhlwazini Valley and Base Camp. Arrived there, they climbed the treacherous gully between *Cathkin* and *Monk's Cowl*, reaching the nek, and the base of the mountain, at midday. From there they traversed round the base of the mountain on to the nek between the *Monk* and *Champagne Castle*. They slept that night in a small cave in the nek, in sub-zero temperatures, with great chunks of ice all round them. They had to pile on every stitch of clothing they had.

Next morning dawned a perfect winter's morning – bitterly cold but bracing. They started to climb at 7.30 a.m., building, first, a beacon to show the start of the route. It was so cold that they had to climb with all the clothing they had. Three difficult pitches ended in a long traverse to the left over sloping slabs. The fourth pitch was easy "D" standard, but the 5th pitch was tricky, 10 metres of badly-sloping rock. Then followed several quite easy pitches, leading to a really difficult one, 20 metres of tough "E" star. But now the summit was not far off. One final krantz, and they were on top. It was 10.30 a.m. They built a tremendous beacon, abseiled down, and the climb was over – the peak at long last had been conquered.

Back at the Hotel, Oom Hendrik Maartens, the proprietor, flatly refused to believe the great news, claiming that the climb was impossible. Next day he secretly sent his young nephew up *Champagne Castle* to confirm the beacon. It was only when the young man returned with the news that there was indeed a beacon on the summit of the peak, that old Oom Hendrik would believe the news.

To return to Dick Barry, how was it that, expert climber as he was, experienced, with an impressive series of first ascents to his credit, he had allowed himself to get into a position on the *Cowl* which led to his death? I put the question to Harry Barker, who knew Dick well and had

* The film, when developed, revealed nothing of interest.

often climbed with him. Dick, said Barker, was impetuous. He liked to climb fast. He hated the long waits while other climbers in a team were being brought up. Dick always climbed, therefore, with a minimum of companions. On the day he died he climbed with only one. Supremely confident in himself, he did not worry to anchor himself properly to the rock when he was belaying Gebhardt. The result was that when Gebhardt fell, Barry, alone, could not hold him, and was jerked off his stance. Both men fell, Barry sustaining grave injuries. Dazed and shaken by the fall, even his iron nerve and superb skill failed him, and he fell to his death.

Whatever the reason, we can but salute a very fine, and a very gallant, climber.

Next to Cathkin stands the pyramid-shaped *Sterkhorn* (2 973 m). *Sterkhorn* has two summits *Sterkhorn North* and *Sterkhorn South*. *Sterkhorn North* is slightly lower than *Sterkhorn South*, and is very easily climbed. *Sterkhorn South* is a much more difficult proposition. It was first climbed, as we have seen, by the Stocker brothers in 1888, after two unsuccessful attempts. In 1947 *Sterkhorn* was adopted by the Moth organisation as a National War Memorial, a cross erected on the summit of the North peak, (it shines when the sun is at a particular angle on it), and the mountain renamed *Mount Memory*. The name has not caught on, however.

The next peak on this miniature range is the *Turret*, much lower than *Sterkhorn*. It is a small, rectangular block, with vertical sides, but not too difficult to negotiate. It was first climbed during the 1933 July Camp by F. E. (Tom) Ellis and Brian Godbold, and named *Tamma's Tower*, the Tamma being a corruption of Tom. The name however faded, and Sweeney's alternative suggestion at the time, that it be called the *Turret*, has survived, though it is still occasionally called *The Tower*.

And, finally, *Amphlett's*, the sharp-pointed peak to the right of the *Turret*, named after G. T. Amphlett, who was one of the six men who made the first ascent of *Cathkin*. It is easily climbed by a north-facing gully.

Underneath the brooding precipices of *Cathkin Peak* lies the smiling valley of the Sterk-spruit, one of the first areas in the Drakensberg to know the advent of man. First came the Bushmen, and then the Amazizi. Several of their burial places have been discovered in the valley. Then, from his lofty throne high in the heavens, the giant peak watched the coming of the white man, and gazed down upon his antics in the valley, far below. First came the Voortrekkers, pushing up from their encampments on the banks of the Great Tugela and the Little Tugela, and staking out their farms – *Opperman's Kraal*, *Buffelshoogte*, and many others. Then, in the 1840's large numbers of the Dutch farmers moved out, and the Englishmen moved in, one of the first being David Gray, in 1855.

Then came the woodcutters, sawing timber for the developing villages and towns of the Midlands. Sawyer Nelson was busy in the Cathkin forests in the early 1890's, and Van Gruening in the Injasuti. To this day you can still see some old graves where his homestead used to be. In the Makuruman, only a couple of kilometres from my home, a Mr. Kruger dug his saw-pits and built his home. The foundations are still there to-day, and so are the saw-pits. For many years the Makuruman was called Krugerbos.

Then, over the years, came men and women who shunned the towns and the cities, and found a habitation in the wilderness, and a home – eccentrics, some of them, each playing his brief part, until each in turn "crept silently away to rest", while *Cathkin*, in quiet understanding, looked down and approved.

Hodgson was one of them. "Old Man of the Berg" they used to call him. He lived alone with his dogs in a mud hut under the shadow of *Cathkin* in the Injasuti Valley. He was well-spoken – had been an officer in the British Army. He painted pictures, and wrote for the papers, but was chiefly known for the Zulu busts he used to model in clay and sell to the visitors at Champagne Castle Hotel. Who was he? What was his story? Why had he buried himself in one of the loneliest valleys of the Drakensberg? No-one knows. In 1935 his body was found in a pool of water not far from his mud hut. He had been murdered.

*Ice-pinnacles
below Mponjwana.*

*Light floods into the great
Ntonjelane valley as the sun
begins to rise.*

Tranquillity. Cathkin Peak and Sterkhorn.

*The Cathedral Range
reflected in a mountain vlei.*

*A strange rock pinnacle in
Organ Pipes Pass.*

Another was Robert Hope Moncrieff, also living in a mud hut in the early 1860's. Moncrieff, as we have seen, was a brother of the Colonel Moncrieff of the British Army, who had invented the Moncrieff gun, used in the Crimean War. Robert Hope Moncrieff's servant at his isolated farm under the Little Berg, near the Maze, had been regimental servant to Colonel Moncrieff. Robert Hope Moncrieff had come of a noble family. What strange circumstances had driven him, also, to this lonely spot, thousands of kilometres from his ancestral home in Scotland? He, too, was murdered, and we tell his story in Chapter IV.

There were many others. In 1912 W. Carter Robinson found the grave of a European far off the beaten track, on the slopes of *Sterkhorn*, overlooking the Mhlwazini River. The stones were neatly packed around it. Though old, it had obviously been well-prepared. Whose was it? Again, no-one knows.

In 1942 a lonely skeleton was found on the slopes of *Cathkin Peak*, with 40 golden sovereigns in what remained of the pocket. At first it was thought the skeleton belonged to a Dr. Haviland, an entomologist who had set out from Couch and de Barth's store near *Ntabamhlope* (the present White Mountain Inn) on his bicycle in 1907. He had disappeared into the Drakensberg and was never seen again, though his bicycle was found some time later in a mountain cave, 10 or 11 kilometres away. But this supposition was later discounted, and the mystery remains.

Incidentally de Barth himself was a remittance man, an illegitimate son of King Edward VII and the Duchess de Barth. He, too, could have told a fascinating story, had he wished.

Then there was the inevitable Irishman. He was Pat McCormick, a Sinn Feiner who had been kicked out of Ireland. He, too, found a home in this lovely valley. He and his brother became bushrangers and cattle rustlers, and lived in a cave in the Nkwakwa stream, at the top of the Ndema forest, just above the present Cathkin Park Hotel. On one occasion, in 1906, Pat shot 40 oxen he had stolen and pushed them over a cliff, rather than let them fall into the hands of their rightful owners!

To-day the cattle rustlers and the bushrangers and the throw-outs from society have gone, and the Sterkspruit Valley offers a home to the retired engineer, the pensioned schoolmaster, and the leisured archaeologist who seeks quiet to pursue his studies.

Four Hotels serve the area. First to be established was Cathkin Park Hotel, started in 1929 by W. Carter Robinson. Carter Robinson, who died only recently, was a fine old man who lived practically the whole of his long life in the Cathkin area. None knew it better. Born in Pietermaritzburg in 1889, he came to Cathkin as a young farmer in 1910, and promptly announced his arrival by being the first man to climb *Gatberg*. From January 1924 to October 1934, as we shall see in a later Chapter, he was first Honorary Forester and then Stipendiary Part-time Forester, and it was largely due to his efforts that the present Forest Reserve was proclaimed in 1922. In 1925 and 1926 he had the enterprise to stock the upper reaches of the Mhlwazini, the Injasuti and the Sterkspruit with brown and rainbow trout from Jonkershoek in the Cape. In 1929 he opened the first Drakensberg Hotel in the area, and called it Cathkin Park Hotel. In 1935 he sold it to Otto Zunckel, and Otto put his two sons, Udo and Gerald in to run it. For many years Udo and Gerald ran the Hotel in the well-known Zunckel tradition, and built it up to its present status as one of the premier Drakensberg Hotels.

Cathkin Park Hotel was quickly followed by Champagne Castle Hotel. Hendrik Maartens, familiarly known as Oom Hendrik, had catered for several of the Natal Mountain Club July Camps, particularly the 1928 one, and had become impressed with the potentialities of the tourist trade. Round about 1930 he bought the farm *Wostyn*, and erected the first buildings which were eventually to grow into the Champagne Castle Hotel that we know to-day. In 1943 he sold it to Mr. J. van Heyningen, the local Forestry official, for £6 000. Three years later van Heyningen sold it for £23 000.

In 1940 Captain H. C. Whelan, an ex-Indian Army officer, came to the area, and decided to start an Hotel of his own. He bought part of the farm *Heartsease* on the left bank of the

Sterkspruit, and there built the well-known El Mirador Hotel, the Hotel with the friendly atmosphere.

And finally, in 1943 David Gray, grandson of the original David Gray, built an Hotel on his farm *The Nest*, not far from old David Gray's original homestead, and so the Nest Hotel, known to thousands of bowlers from far and wide, came into being.

In 1954 Mr. R. W. Tungay, News Editor of the *Natal Daily News*, bought the beautiful farm *Dragon Peaks* in this same Sterkspruit Valley. It was to be the birthplace of a dream, and it was to his son John Tungay that the dream came. The year was 1966.

The Little Berg, where *Dragon Peaks* is situated, is a land of singing streams and whispering forests, a land where liquid bird calls greet the dawn, and where the yelping cry of the Jackal Buzzard breaks the noonday silence, where the diapason organ notes of the thunder roll amongst the crags, and where the winds sing their immemorial song amongst the tall trees of the forest. To John Tungay came the dream that the songs of this lovely land should blend with the clear, sweet voices of boyhood, and that together they should make music in the hills and valleys of the Drakensberg.

And so it was that on 23rd January 1967, the Drakensberg Boys Choir School was opened, and the pleasant valleys of the Little Berg awoke to a new and a strange sound, the laughter of boys and their clear voices lifted in song. From the towns, villages and farms of South Africa they came, each boy carefully selected, and each with outstanding singing potential. Half were English speaking and half Afrikaans speaking, and the initial enrolment was 25. A Board of Governors was appointed, on which I was asked to act as Chairman (the School is only a couple of kilometres away from my home), a dedicated Staff engaged, and the School was away to a good start.

Set in the heart of the Drakensberg mountains, with a scenic backdrop of towering mountain peaks, with the ice-cold crystal waters of the Sterkspruit running past its playing fields, no school could have had a finer setting. The surrounding country, with its virgin forests and mountain gorges, holds for the impressionable mind of a boy all the thrill of adventure and exploration, while the gentler slopes with their wild flowers and tumbling streams cannot do otherwise than instil in him an enduring love of beauty. The singing of the boys has brought joy and pleasure to tens of thousands of people throughout South Africa, and overseas as well.

Perhaps most important of all, and tying up with the training of character, was the determination that the School would turn out, not a crowd of cloistered choristers with pale, angelic faces, but young men who were tough and physically active, with strength of character and initiative. "Too many people," says John Tungay, "think of choir boys as insipid little angels. What's wrong with a choir boy being tough? Surely a boy can lead a healthy, normal life, and still enjoy singing for the sheer love of it." If you doubt this, you should see the little chaps in the rough and tumble of the boxing ring of an evening, after their Prep. has been done! A Durban newspaper recently carried an article on the School under the heading "Angels in Boots".

A leading music critic on one of our major newspapers wrote after one of their concerts: "The pure sound and immaculate harmonising were of a quality as rare and refreshing as the exhilarating air of the upper slopes of the Drakensberg, and as effortless as the flight of an eagle."

The dream had come true!

CHAPTER XIII

THE GIANT'S CASTLE GAME RESERVE

"They shall dwell safely in the wilderness and sleep in the woods, and none shall make them afraid."

— BOOK OF THE PROPHET EZEKIAL

The Giant's Castle Game Reserve was proclaimed in 1903.

Prior to this time the area was very little known. From as early as the 1850's we hear of commandos setting out in pursuit of raiding Bushmen and visiting the area of Giant's Castle, but their activities centred round the country to the south of the peak, in the valleys of the Loteni and the Umkomaas, rather than to the north, the area of the present Reserve. Early maps show a number of bridle paths south of *Giant's Castle*. There are none to the north. No doubt hunting parties often visited these mountain slopes, but they left no written record behind them. Major Grantham must have spent some time here in 1860 when he was drawing up his military map. But there was little else.

In February 1864 a small survey party left the Dargle for the Drakensberg. It consisted of Bob Speirs, Augustus Bovill, (a surveyor) and the three Bucknall brothers, Henry, Edgar* and Fred. They discovered a new pass at the head of the Bushman's River, which is almost certainly the pass we know to-day as the Giant's Castle Pass, and they climbed the *Giant*, again almost certainly by this pass. They took two hours to reach the top, where a tremendous thunderstorm swept down on them, and then they walked south along the top of the escarpment, discovering yet another, and better, pass at the head of the Loteni. I believe this to be the Hlatimba Pass, which figures in the Langalibalele Rebellion. (See Appendix 1.)

The party were out ten days altogether, returning on February 9th, covered in mud (it had rained most of the time) and ravenously hungry. "My word," says John Shedden Dobie in his *Journal*, "How they did pitch into the tucker, before dinner (more cooking had to be done!) as well as after! Ditto, ditto at supper, and spasmodically at all times during the evening! I think I heard some of them at it during the night!" Dobie seemed to know the area fairly well. He has several references to *Giant's Castle* in his *Journal*. There is no record, however, of his having climbed the mountain, though he was nearly included in the survey party we have described above.

The end of 1873 and the first six months of 1874 saw considerable activity around *Giant's Castle* and it became internationally known, for this was the time of the Langalibalele Rebellion. For some months a detachment of the 75th Regiment was encamped at the junction of the Bushman's River and the stream which rises in the Langalibalele Pass, just below the Main Caves. Their cook carved the figures 75 on a large rock just outside their camp. During the first six months of 1874 John Eustace Fannin, as we have seen, was commissioned by the Government to survey the passes in the area, and Colonel Durnford was ordered to blow up these passes. Both men spent about six months in the area.

For 29 years nothing more was heard of *Giant's Castle*, and then, in 1903, the Natal Government proclaimed it as a Game Reserve. On November 9th of that year, the first Game Warden, Sydney Barnes, pushed his way up Bushman's River Valley to take charge of his new domain. It was a wild and beautiful stretch of country, twenty-five kilometres of towering peaks, of

---

* A little over a year later, in May 1865, Edgar Bucknall was savagely murdered by some Africans on the Natal-Transkei border. His body was never found.

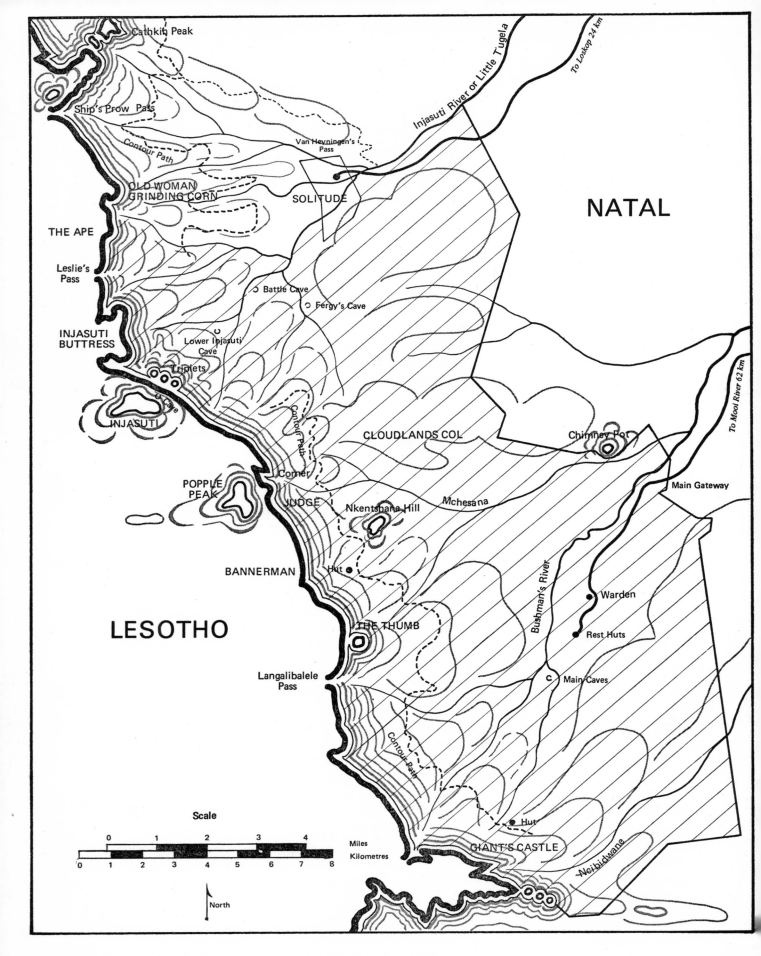

Map of Giant's Castle Game Reserve

remote and lonely valleys, where the only sound was the singing of the mountain streams. The winds blew fresh and sharp, the air was like the clean bite of dry wine, and the dawn came quietly over far horizons.

The original idea of the Reserve was to protect the fast disappearing herds of eland that roamed the mountain slopes. From an estimated three to four thousand, they were now down to about 200, and would soon disappear completely unless something were done for their protection. Originally 12 140 hectares were set aside, but from time to time this was added to, and to-day the Reserve stands at over 40 000 hectares. It stretches from *Giant's Castle* in the south to the *Old Woman Grinding Corn* in the north.

And so it was that on a summer's morning, towards the end of 1903, Ranger Sydney Barnes stood on a small eminence and surveyed his new domain. Behind him towered the sandstone cliffs of the Little Berg, red, and yellow, and brown, streaked with grey and black. To his left, heaving its massive bulk up into the very sky, was *Giant's Castle* itself, 3 316 metres high. Two hundred metres below him, flowing strongly and steadily, was the Bushman's River. Its faint murmur reached him in the silence of the early morning, the only other sound the sigh of the wind in the sugar bushes. And beyond, a wild glory of tumbled mountain peaks and mysterious, untrodden valleys.

He had managed to get his wagon up as far as Witberg, the present entrance gates to the Reserve. From there it had been a case of African porters and hard foot-slogging, twelve kilometres of wild and broken country, the valley of the Bushman's, without even a native footpath to guide their way.

No man could have lived a lonelier or more isolated life. For months he lived in a mountain cave. The nearest white man was a two-day trek away, the nearest store the one at *Ntabamhlope*, under Couch and de Barth, and when the bitter snows of winter swept down from the heights and choked the valleys, he was snowed in for months at a time.

From the day he arrived he kept a diary, jealously guarded by subsequent Wardens of the Reserve. I have seen this diary. Absorbed, I have read its faded pages. The years have rolled back, and I have shared with Sydney Barnes his lonely life. I have sat beside him in his mountain cave as, wearied after a long trek into the mountains, he brewed his coffee before turning in, while the sunset faded on the peaks. I fought with him the mountain fires, and I watched him as, tireless and relentless, he went on the trail of the occasional poacher.

There were leopards, and later on jackals, to be fought, game counts to be made, and boundaries to be inspected. I was with him when he explored the far Injasuti for the first time, and I watched his house slowly rising on the site of Bill Barnes' present lovely mountain home. And I was with him, too, on that grey, wet morning of February 1, 1906, a day of mounting fear, as Barnes and his African Rangers went out in search of a lost man.

On January 12, 1906 a young junior cleric of St. Peter's, in Pietermaritzburg, the Rev. C. C. Bates, had arrived to spend a few weeks with Barnes. On the morning of January 31 he went out for a stroll after breakfast, and he never returned. By lunch time Barnes was beginning to wonder what had happened to him. As the afternoon wore on he became vaguely uneasy, especially when a tremendous thunderstorm swept down on them. At dusk it was still raining, and there was no sign of the young man. By now genuinely alarmed, Barnes stood in the porch of his new home, peering out into the gathering dusk, but nothing moved save the swaying of the trees against the night sky, and the only sound was the ceaseless roar of the rain. All through the night it came down, and as the first light of day filtered through the wet and clinging mist, Barnes raised the alarm. Collecting together as many of his African Rangers as he could, he set out, up into the mountains. All through the day they groped about in the wet valleys, and on the mist-shrouded slopes of the hills, calling, and listening. They managed to follow Bates' spoor almost to *Giant's Castle* itself, and then lost it. As dusk fell, weary and exhausted, they stumbled back home. It was still raining, and it rained all that night, but early the next morning they were off again, taking a different route this time. Again they drew blank, and again, for the third night in succession, they listened to the rain pelting down.

Early the next morning, as they were preparing a hasty breakfast before setting out for the third time, they were startled by a sudden whine at the back door, and Bates' fox terrier, who had accompanied his master on his walk, came cringing through the kitchen door, starved and half frozen. This time they followed Nip's spoor, until once again the driving rain washed it out, and there was only the wet grass, and the silence, and the mist.

Bates was never found. They continued the search for many days, and even for years afterwards, at long intervals, but all to no purpose. The inviolable hills kept their secret. What happened to him? No-one will ever know. There is one final post-script in the Diary. In September 1906 Ranger Roden Symons took over from Sydney Barnes. Towards the end of his stay, in 1915, he made the following entry in the Diary which he had taken over from Sydney Barnes:—

"The search for Mr. Bates failed. Nothing was ever found of his body. During the nine years I was in charge here I found several skeletons, but they were most probably those of rebels killed in the Langalibalele Rebellion. I personally think that Mr. Bates was benighted at the foot of the mountain, and taking refuge in one of the numerous dry water-courses, died of exposure, and the body washed away by the floods on February 2nd."

But there is yet another postscript. Although it throws no light on the mystery, it is a very strange coincidence. Only a few years prior to young Bates' visit to *Giant's Castle*, round about 1898, another young man, also by the names of Bates, and also on a visit, but to Cape Town this time, went for a walk up *Table Mountain*, also after breakfast. He, too, never returned. The police, and members of the Cape Town Mountain Club, organised search after search, all to no avail, and eventually the whole thing was called off. But here the two stories differ. Years later, two young men, climbing on Kloof Corner Ridge on *Table Mountain*, found a skeleton on a narrow ledge. Among the remains of the skeleton was a badly tarnished watch, though still in working order, and a wallet, which clearly established the identity of the body as that of Bates. To-day among the other relics in the Club Room of the Cape Town Mountain Club one can still see that old and badly tarnished watch.

To return to Giant's Castle. Sydney Barnes spent three lonely years at the Reserve, and in September 1906 he handed over to Ranger Roden Symons.

When Symons took over, the Reserve was pretty much as Barnes had found it. A house of sorts had been built, but the nearest neighbour was still 30 kilometres away, there were still no roads, and of course cars were unknown. His only companions were the wind in the long grass and the bark of the mountain baboon.

With time on his hands, and with an active mind and still more active body, Roden Symons decided to take up Oology (egg-collecting) as a hobby, a hobby which he has passed on to his second cousin, Godfrey Symons, a good friend with whom I have often climbed in the Drakensberg. To-day Godfrey has one of the finest egg-collections in the country, and a knowledge of birds and their nesting-habits second to none, while Roden Symons is an old man living with his memories at Sweetwaters, just outside Pietermaritzburg.* I recently spent a very happy morning with him, as he yarned away of those days more than half a century ago. He soon found that bird-nesting in the Drakensberg was no picnic. The precipices were terrifyingly steep, and the forest trees often unclimbable. Day after day he went out, pin-pointing the nests of the Black Eagles, the Jackal Buzzards, the Martial Eagles, and the occasional Lammergeyer. On one occasion he went over the edge of a cliff on a length of rope, but the rope jammed in a crack, and his African Game Guards were unable to haul him back. Above him was an overhang, and though he tried desperately, he was unable to climb it and free the rope. For some

*He died on 28 September 1972.

150

time he hung there suspended. Eventually, by shouting up, he managed to persuade one of the Guards to climb down and free the rope.

The yellow-woods offered a different problem. Their boles towered up, smooth and sheer, for 10 to 15 metres, but at the top was the coveted nest of a Martial Eagle or a Yellow-billed Kite. Here he worked out a system of iron spikes which he would drive into the smooth trunk, and up which he would climb. In the Reserve itself he continued the lonely work of his predecessor, and watched it growing in strength and stature.

For three years he worked alone, but in December 1909 he was joined by his younger brother, Bryan. Bryan spent two years in the Reserve as Assistant Ranger, and when he left in 1911 his place was taken by a young man of the name of Philip Barnes. Philip was no relation of the original Sydney Barnes. He had been in the employ of the Natal Government Railways, in Durban, but, disliking the job, he gave it up in 1911 and took over the vacant post of Assistant Ranger in the Giant's Castle Reserve.

Roden Symons spent nine years in the Reserve, and in 1915 was asked to take over the infant Hluhluwe Reserve, in Zululand. He had done a magnificent job. By the time he left there was even a road of sorts, and before he said good-bye to the Reserve he had the proud distinction of being the first man to drive a battered Ford motor car over its bumpy surface and into the silence of the great peaks. Philip Barnes, his Assistant, had recently married, and when Roden Symons left in 1915, he was the obvious choice to take over as Warden.

I often wonder what his young wife Rosie must have felt when he led her into his mountain home. There certainly was a house of sorts, but she often had to cook under an umbrella, because it leaked so badly. There certainly was a road, but it was often blocked by landslides and snow for weeks at a time. There certainly was a doctor, but he was 50 kilometres away at the other end of this road, and she had a growing family of children to bear and to care for. But they all managed to survive. Amongst the children was a little chap named Philip after his father, but he was soon dubbed "Bill", and as Bill he has remained. To-day Bill Barnes still lives in the same house, greatly enlarged, and after being Warden of the Reserve for 15 years, is now Regional Warden of the whole Drakensberg.

Philip however is the real father of the Reserve. His two predecessors, Sydney Barnes and Roden Symons, had of course laid the foundations well and truly. But it was Philip and Rosie who, in a life-time of dedicated service, built the Reserve up into the magnificent place it is to-day. They were both well fitted for the job. They seemed to thrive on the isolation and the loneliness. They even built a little hut, deeper still into the mountains, in one of the forests of the Injasuti, 15 km away, to which they would periodically retire, "to get away from it all"! Its ruins are still to be seen to-day.

One of the early problems was the wild dogs. These great ferocious animals would come in from Lesotho, raiding the game in the valleys of the Little Berg, and killing for the sheer love of it. Over a period of two years Philip Barnes and his Rangers found the remains of 50 eland and 250 smaller game. All attempts at eradication failed, but one morning in 1918, W. Carter Robinson and his brother, M. E. Robinson, came over from the Cathkin area, and a last determined effort was made to eradicate the menace. On the slopes of the main Drakensberg, in the headwaters of the Bushman's River, 17 wild dogs and one hyena were killed. The whole pack was finished off, and they have never been seen since in the Reserve. To-day *Nkentshane Hill*, a lesser peak in the Reserve, commemorates the episode (iNkentshane is the Zulu name for a wild dog.)

But still there were the jackals to hunt (Philip killed 600 of them in his 32 years in the Reserve), the roaring grass fires to control (in 1942 Philip's outhouses were burnt down, and he himself nearly lost his life), and poachers to eliminate (in 1941 Mzania, one of Philip's Game Guards, was almost stabbed to death by an infuriated poacher.)

At last, in December 1947, the Reserve said good-bye to the man who had done more to establish it than any other, and Edward Thrash took over, with Bill, Philip's son, as his Assistant. Philip and Rosie retired after 32 years of dedicated service to the Reserve they loved, to spend the evening of their lives in Estcourt, where Philip died in 1951 and Rosie 16 years later.

At the Reserve itself the work went steadily on. Edward Thrash remained at the helm until 1956, when Bill Barnes, who in the meantime had spent five years at the Royal Natal National Park, took over with his wife, Leila, and the two names, *Giant's Castle* and Bill Barnes, became synonymous. In 1971 Bill was promoted to the newly-created post of Regional Warden of the Drakensberg, and Keith Meiklejohn, his Assistant, took over as Warden of the Reserve.

Focal point of the Reserve is the great bastion of *Giant's Castle* itself, at its southern end. This huge mass, connected to the main escarpment by a narrow nek, is one of the cornerstones of the Drakensberg, swinging the range from north-east to south-west. At 3 316 metres it is also one of the highest points in the whole Drakensberg. The name *Giant's Castle* was originally given to the present *Garden Castle*, 53 kms to the south, by Captain Allen Gardiner in 1835, as we have seen. Dr. P. C. Sutherland, Surveyor-General of Natal, is usually credited with transferring the name to its present *locale* in May 1865, but he was merely giving official recognition to an already long-established custom. As early as the 1850's Government reports of Bushman raids were calling the peak by its present name. In March 1856, for instance, Captain Allen pursued a gang of Bushman raiders into the upper waters of the Loteni, and he uses the name *Giant's Castle* for the mountain immediately to the north of the Loteni. In 1859 Dr. R. J. Mann, Superintendent of Education, published a guide book to the Colony of Natal, and he, too, gives *Giant's Castle* its present, correct position, though he errs in referring to it as having been named by Captain Allen Gardiner.

Its Zulu name is *Bhulihawu*, the place of the shield thrasher, or *Phosihawu*, the shield flinger. Mr. H. C. Lugg thinks the name may refer to an actual individual who lived in the shadow of the mountain. I prefer to think that this is yet another example of the rich poetical imagery that is so typical of the Zulus. *Giant's Castle* is, indeed, the birthplace of storms. Round these tremendous precipices the clouds gather and the thunder roars, like the thrashing of a mighty shield. But suddenly the great storm-clouds are flung out across the waiting land as one flings a shield, the storm begins to move out over the plains of Natal, and so we have *Phosihawu*, the shield-flinger.

It was first climbed, as we have seen, in 1864, and this was almost certainly up the wide gulley that runs up to the nek joining the peak to the main escarpment, on the northern side. This is the route normally taken to-day, and it is quite easy. It is known as Giant's Castle Pass. A more difficult route is up the Eastern Gully. The eastern face of the mountain is split by a tremendous chasm, running right away up to the summit, and, provided it is not iced up in winter, it can be climbed fairly easily without rope.

In 1954 Martin Winter ascended the South Peak via the south-east Ridge, and in 1960, after several attempts, Des Watkins conquered the South Face via the Elandshoek Ridge. We have already told the story of Ted Scholes' climb up the North Face.

From the summit of this mighty peak the climber looks down on the whole of this vast Reserve. Immediately below is the lovely valley of the Bushman's River, with the hutted camp run by the Natal Parks Board, and the Warden's house. Set amongst the rocks and natural bush of the Little Berg, in the middle of a wild flower garden, this hutted camp will be one of your pleasant memories if you ever visit the Reserve. The cottages are all thatched, built of natural stone, and blend in with the surroundings. Most of them are four-bedded, and provided with bedding, linen, crockery and cutlery. All you bring is your food. An African servant is provided to cook your food and service your cottage. Altogether there is accommodation for 40 guests. The delightful wild flower garden is a tribute to the devoted work of Mr. and Mrs. K. B. Tinley, Camp Superintendents for 15 years.

The policy of the Parks Board has been to retain the area in its natural state as far as

The Northern Ifidi Pinnacle.

The fury of the storm.

Giant's Castle.

The soaring pinnacle of the
Western Injasuti Triplet.

possible. There are no roads in the Reserve, apart from the access road which leads to it, though jeep trips over rough tracks are provided by the Warden and his Rangers for those who wish to go farther afield. For those who are more adventurous still, and who are prepared to shoulder a ruck-sack and strike into the heart of the mountains, a series of mountain huts, simply equipped and provided with gas, is being built. Already two are in use, one under the North Face of the *Giant*, and one at *Bannerman*

From the pleasant settlement at the foot of *Giant's Castle* the eye wanders to the ridge on the left bank of the Bushman's River, over this to the valley of the Mchesana, and from there up to Cloudland's Col, a high ridge of the Little Berg, running out from the *Corner* and stretching finally to the high country around *Ntabamhlope*.

On the other side of this ridge lies the Injasuti, surely one of the most beautiful areas in the whole Drakensberg. The Injasuti River, or the Little Tugela as it is known in its lower reaches, rises in the maze of valleys that lie beneath the *Great Injasuti Buttress*. From here it broadens out into a magnificent, deep-cut valley, a valley of tumbled rocks, of red sandstone cliffs, and of dark, lush forests alive with the timeless hum of insects and the sound of rippling waters. Here is Battle Cave, with its magnificent Bushman paintings, one whole panel depicting an attack on the cave in bygone days, and the Lower Injasuti Cave, one of the loveliest caves I know of. Here, too, is Fergy's Cave. Sgt. I. Ferguson was a policeman of the middle 1940's, who had been given the job of safeguarding the Reserve against poachers. He preferred to live out in the wilds, and for many years made this cave his headquarters.

I shall always associate this remote valley with the golden days of autumn, for twice in years gone by, when my work had pressed heavily upon me, I came to this quiet valley and to the Lower Injasuti Cave in the autumn time, and found peace here. On both occasions the whole valley blazed in a riot of red, gold and yellow, and the trees were leaping flames of scarlet and bronze. In memory I still return to those golden April days and those velvet nights, to the sparkle and freshness of dawn, to the pungent smell of the camp fire at dusk, and, always, to the flaunting banners of those marching trees.

Of the higher peaks in this area there are the *Great Injasuti Buttress* (3 207 m), the *Old Woman Grinding Corn* (2 986 m), and the three *Triplets*. The *Old Woman, kwa Mfasizwa ugay' amabele*, is a remarkable peak, connected, like *Giant's Castle*, to the main escarpment by a narrow nek. The appropriateness of the name can be realised if one looks at it from the north. From here the outline is exactly that of an old woman crouched over her grinding stone, and bending slightly forward. It was first climbed by Brian Godbold, Charles Axelson and Norman Hodson on 25th July 1937. They climbed the gully immediately south of the nek, up on to the nek, and from there traversed out on to the north face, a route which finally took them to the top.

South of the *Buttress* and the *Old Woman* are three free-standing remarkable peaks known as the *Triplets*. All three are very close to the escarpment edge, but completely separated from it. The *Eastern Triplet* (3 170 m) is a huge, massive block of basalt, towering up into the clouds. Next to it, like a thin flange, is the *Middle Triplet* (3 155 m). The north-eastern face of this peak, facing out into Natal, is smooth and sheer, and so close is it to the escarpment edge that from a little distance away it seems to blend in with it, and is seldom seen as a separate peak. In fact, for many years it was not even known to exist, and early accounts refer merely to *The Twins*.

The *Western Triplet* (3 187 m) is one of the most terrifying peaks in the Drakensberg. It towers up like a menacing spear, and ranks in difficulty with *Devil's Tooth* in the Royal Natal National Park and the *Column* in the Cathedral area. To add to its difficulty, the rock is crumbly and dangerous. It was first climbed by David Bell and R. F. Davies on 3rd July 1951. They climbed down from the edge of the escarpment on to a thin knife-edge which connected the peak to the main escarpment. From this knife-edge they reached the south-east ridge and then climbed its south-eastern face.

The *Eastern* and the *Middle Triplets* were conquered in December 1950. The *Eastern Triplet* was climbed by a party led by Ted Scholes, consisting of Lorna Pierson, R. Forsyth and Des Watkins. This climb has been described in Chapter VI. The *Middle Triplet* fell, a few days later, to Lorna Pierson, Gillian Bettle and Des Watkins.

Although the lower reaches of the Injasuti were probably amongst the first to be visited by Europeans (these valleys were only about 25 km away from Gert Maritz's laager of 1838 on the banks of the Little Tugela), the upper reaches and the region of the great peaks were amongst the last to be explored. In 1937 the Natal Mountain Club held their annual July camp in the area for the first time, and made a thorough exploration of its possibilities. The *Great Injasuti Buttress, Scaley Peak*, the *Lion*, the *Injasuti "Twins"*, (the name was later changed to "Triplets") Leslie's Pass (named after Roden Symons' son, Leslie), and Marble Baths Stream, were all named. *Kwa Mfasizwa ugay' amabele*, an already-existing Zulu name, with its English equivalent, *The Old Woman Grinding Corn*, was adopted as the name for this peak.

Mr. P. R. (Bill) Barnes, stocky, tough, bronzed, and one of the finest climbing companions any man could wish for, has been the moving spirit in the development of this mountain sanctuary for the last 15 years. He believes that the mountains are the heritage of all, but he is not prepared to throw them open to the hordes of trippers who would destroy and desecrate. For the genuine lover of the mountains he will do anything, and he believes passionately that young people especially should be taught the lure of the wilderness. Many a party of schoolboys and schoolgirls, who have spent a few days in the Reserve, have learnt to bless the name of Bill Barnes. He believes that any attempts that are made to make the Drakensberg more accessible to the general public must ensure that its natural beauty remains untouched. Tarred roads are "out" as far as he is concerned. Tarred roads bring fast motor cars, and beer cans, and erosion. Tarred roads bring filling stations, and speed, and pollution. He will have none of these. He would like to see rather a series of bridle-paths, with every now and then an isolated cabin, fitted up with gas and bunks, to give a night's shelter to hikers and mountaineers who are out for several days.

He has already converted the Main Caves, about 1½ kilometres from the hutted camp, into a natural Museum. Here a set of life-size Bushman figures is grouped around an open hearth. One of them, the Old Man of the cave, is busy painting an eland on one of the walls. Many of the items used were actually found in the area. Others are exact replicas of items found elsewhere, such as bows and arrows. It is all uncannily real, and as you sit on a nearby rock and take in the scene, time loses its meaning, the years roll back, and the ancient past lives again. But suddenly you are reminded that you are still in the 20th Century, for round your shoulder is a small portable Tape Recorder, and, to a background of Bushman music, the commentator is telling you of the Bushmen of long ago, of their way of life, and the meaning of the various articles in the cave.

Other ideas that Bill has put into practice are the Wilderness Trails, when you go out for two to five days, on horseback, accompanied by the Trails Officer, sleeping out in the open, or in mountain caves. Then there are the jeep rides, when the jeep carries you up and down impossible slopes. Your heart is in your mouth most of the time, but you penetrate into the very heart of the Reserve, and are able to watch the game at close quarters.

There is fishing, also. These clear, frothing mountain streams have all been stocked with brown trout, and to-day there are 25 km of fishable water in the Reserve. If you want a fore-taste of heaven, get up early one sparkling morning, catch your trout while the dew is still on the grass, and then savour the smell as he sizzles on an open fire before you start your climb. Bill himself is a great fisherman – and not only for the sport of it. I have known him go off into the mountains for several days with only a fishing rod over one shoulder, and a mysterious small black bag on the other. "You can live for days," he says with a speculative twinkle in his eye, "on nothing but whisky and trout!"

But the richness of the Reserve has to be seen to be believed. Altogether 70 sites of Bushman paintings have been discovered so far. The scenery, of course, is magnificent. In the clear air, under the sun of summer, the hills are a carpet of green, and in the autumn their gold sweeps tranquilly up to the blue of distant peaks. There are literally hundreds of species of wild flowers, trees and ferns. The bird life is fantastic: 148 separate species of birds have already been identified in the Reserve. And on these rolling hills roam the eland, the oribi, the rooi and the vaalrhebuck, the blesbok, the hartebeest, the wildebeest, and on the high ledges of the mountains the shy little klipspringer browses.

When the Reserve was first proclaimed in 1903, its main object was to provide a sanctuary for the fast-disappearing eland, one of the noblest, and certainly the largest, of South Africa's antelopes. At one time it was the commonest antelope in the Drakensberg. We know this from accounts of early hunters, and also from the Bushman paintings that adorn the cave walls in the sandstone cliffs of the Little Berg where the eland is the commonest animal depicted. But by the turn of the century the countless thousands that roamed these mountain solitudes in peace and security were down to a meagre 200. W. Carter Robinson considered that in 1900 there were only 20 left in the area of the present Reserve.

The eland, *Taurotragus oryx* (the Zulu name is *Impofu*) has a height of 150 cm to 180 cm, about the size of a large ox, and a weight of up to 820 kg. He is buff-coloured, turning to grey as he grows older. He has a very distinct black vertical stripe from his horns to the root of his tail, and long, hanging dewlaps. Both sexes have fairly long, spiralled horns. The eland is both a grazer and a browser, and is particularly partial to *Buddleia salvifolia* and *Halleria lucida*. In his wild state he is nervous and wary. If a herd of eland spots you – they have excellent eyesight – they will stand still for a few moments and then make off at a brisk trot, either up a slope or round the shoulder of a hill, seldom down-hill. Their call is a low, barking note. Although a large animal, the eland is not aggressive. He has amazing powers of jumping, and will easily clear a two-metre fence.

The Drakensberg eland are of especial importance, because they are the only ones in South Africa (excluding South-West Africa and Botswana) which are directly descended from the original eland of that particular district. In the Sudan there is a giant species *Taurotragus derbianus gigas*, which goes up to 1 000 kg in weight.

To-day, in Natal, they are confined to the Giant's Castle Game Reserve, and also to the Kamberg and Loteni Reserves, south of *Giant's Castle*. Their numbers are estimated at 1 500 altogether, with 800 of them in the Giant's Castle Reserve. Under natural conditions it is almost certain that they used to winter in the Thornveld, spending only their summers in the Drakensberg, but due to increased hunting and to the opening up of the Midlands of Natal to the early settlers, they sought permanent refuge in the Drakensberg. They are still, however, great wanderers, and the Natal Parks Board have found it necessary to erect a strong 220 cm 10-strand eland fence around the Reserve. In 1958 two were killed in the Upper Tugela Location, between Cathedral Peak and the Royal Natal National Park. They were probably following their old instinct of migrating to the Thornveld. This concentration in the Drakensberg throughout the year is already causing problems due to overstocking and over-grazing.

The eland is a docile animal. Even bulls in captivity rarely become vicious. About 1745 a young eland bull was sent to William of Orange from the Cape. It was tamed, and was taught to pull a trap. The meat is tender and most palatable. As far back as 1848 Methuen proposed that the eland should be domesticated. In 1914 Theodore Roosevelt wrote: "We have rounded up a herd of eland quite as easily as we could round up old-style Texan cattle. Eland are easily tamed, and although so big, are less pugnacious than any other big antelope. The American Government should make a business of importing, taming and training them."

Actually there have been several attempts at domesticating the eland. A notable one was made at Askanya Nova, in Southern Russia, in 1895, where a good deal of useful information was collected. In 1954 a small herd was established in Zezani, in the heart of the Rhodesian

Mopani country, 120 km from Beit Bridge. It was soon found that eland would flourish in an area quite unsuitable to cattle, and Mr. John Posselt, in charge of the experiment, formed the opinion that eland meat was equal, if not superior, to beef. Unfortunately Mr. Posselt was transferred in 1961, and the experiment came to an end.

Here in the Drakensberg the first attempts to domesticate the eland were made as far back as 1907. In that year Roden Symons caught a number of calves and sent them to Cedara. Nothing came from this attempt, but a year or so later calves were supplied to several farmers in the Midlands, notably to Andrew Sclanders and the Moe brothers at New Hanover. The Moe's were the most successful in achieving results, and one of the brothers actually rode an eland round the show ring at the Royal Agricultural Show in Pietermaritzburg. Amongst others General Smuts obtained a pair from the Reserve, and Roden Symons took them up personally to Irene and had the privilege of lunching with the General.

But the most ambitious experiment so far is undoubtedly that being carried out by the Natal Parks Board at Loteni, on the southern slope of *Giant's Castle*. Here an Eland Domestication Unit has been established, and Professor C. W. ("Clem") Abbott, Head of the Department of Dairy Industry at the University of Natal, recently spent a year's sabbatical leave here, studying the eland. This herd has now reached about 40 head, and invaluable information has been obtained concerning the growth and handling of the domesticated animal.

Prospects of increasing the world's steadily decreasing supply of protein foods in this way are good. It has already been proved that the eland can be domesticated, that the meat is excellent, and that eland farming can be carried on successfully in areas too dry for conventional cattle farming. But the work is only in its infancy, and much has still to be done. The Russian experiment showed that small, selected herds soon deteriorated through inbreeding, and the present small numbers of eland (a couple of thousand at most, compared with the millions of beef animals) preclude the possibility of larger domesticated herds at present. Eland milk is different from cows' milk, but is very nutritious. Again there are possibilities, but years of selective breeding will be required before a good milking strain can be developed.

To-day, in the Giant's Castle Game Reserve, and in the area south of *Giant's Castle*, the eland is flourishing. From being on the danger list, numbers have now increased to a figure which makes the future of the eland assured.

Not content with preserving the existing herds of eland, the Natal Parks Board are busy re-introducing three species of antelopes which used to roam these mountain slopes in the past, but which fell to the hunter's gun and disappeared. These are the Red Hartebeest, the Black Wildebeest and the Blesbok.

By 1960 the Red Hartebeest, *Ancephalus buselaphus cacama*, had completely disappeared from Natal and Zululand, although at one time they were fairly common, especially in the Drakensberg. It was in the early 1960's that an effort was made to re-introduce them into the Giant's Castle Game Reserve. Animals were imported from the Kimberley district and from South-West Africa. In 1962 two were released in the Reserve. By October 1968 a nucleus herd of 30 had been built up, but so far they have not settled down very well. At the moment their numbers stand at 17.

The Red Hartebeest is not a handsome animal. He is too short in the body, too long-legged, and rather high in the shoulder. The face is long and narrow, and the horns, present in both sexes, take a right-angled curve backwards about two-thirds of the way up. The coat, as the name indicates, is reddish-brown, with a purplish sheen on the back. Their gallop, too, is ungainly. They seem to bounce along on stiff, jointed legs, though they have a considerable turn of speed.

The call is difficult to describe. Mr. P. R. Barnes describes it as like air being expelled through lips that flap loosely to the accompaniment of a low, base note.

The Black Wildebeest, *Connochaetes gnu*, sometimes known as the White-tailed Gnu, is an even more ungainly animal. Sometimes, it would seem, the Creator, in a mood of impish satire, seizes the tools of the satirist and creates something almost out of a nightmare. Some of the lizards and geckoes are like this. And He must have been in a particularly impish mood when He created the Black Wildebeest. With his shaggy coat, his drooping head and neck, his thin, ungainly, spindly legs, his bleary eyes, his scruffy beard standing out in every direction, and his hang-dog, half-witted expression he is, indeed, the hippie of the animal world!

He nearly became extinct. Early travellers tell of vast herds of Black Wildebeest on the plains of the Transvaal, the Orange Free State and Natal. He certainly roamed the slopes of the Drakensberg. But his numbers soon began to tail off. It was found that his skin could easily be converted into leather of a fine quality, and a big trade developed in these skins, many being exported overseas. The last one was shot in Natal in 1916. By 1946 the total population, including specimens in zoos throughout the world, was down to 1 100. But in 1954 the Natal Parks Board began to re-introduce them into the Province. Specimens were obtained from the De Beers farms, near Kimberley, and sent to the Giant's Castle Game Reserve and to the Royal Natal National Park. They have done extremely well. By 1960 the Giant's Castle Reserve had 32. The Black Wildebeest is well-known as the galloping beast on the Natal Coat of Arms, and he also appears on the reverse side of our present 2c coins.

There is no doubt whatever that the Natal Parks Board have done magnificent work, not only in the establishment and running of its Game Reserves (there are no less than 26 of them in Natal) but in its control of wild life generally, and in the re-stocking of the Reserves with species that had died out.

But there are big dangers ahead.

There are some who hold that prior to the European settlement of the country, the game was largely migratory in character. Animals rarely wintered in the Drakensberg, preferring the sweeter grass and warmer valleys of the Thornveld. To-day, with our fences, our railroads, our ploughed lands, our developing towns and cities, this is impossible, and the game is confined to one area all the year round. This leads to damage through over-grazing. Once man interferes, in any way whatever, with the delicate balance of nature, he is in trouble. Chain reactions set in, with incalculable results. Damage to over-grazing could lead inevitably to eventual paddocking and artificial feeding, and your Game Reserve is reduced in status to that of a glorified zoo. If this happens it would have been a direct consequence of the tourist's desire to see game, for the species which are being introduced are in little danger of dying out. In other words it is apparently the profit-motive which is dominant, and the results would be that fauna would be protected at the expense of flora. This is the view of Professor H. P. van der Schijff, Professor of Botany at Pretoria University, and Mr. U. W. Nänni, formerly Forest Hydrologist in the Department of Forestry, agrees with him.

This clash of interests between the demands of the tourist industry and the demands of the nature conservationist is an ever-present one. When our Game Reserves were first proclaimed, they were designed purely for the protection and conservation of game. It was only later that the tourist came along and wanted to see the game. In America this tendency has reached alarming proportions. The Yosemite National Park in California is never free of thousands of tourists per day. One can never get away from *people*, and their noise drowns the thunder of the famed Yosemite Falls. The Kruger National Park, with its huge camps, its stores and its restaurants, its tarred roads and its filling-stations, is in danger of going the same way. So far, I am glad to say, the Natal Parks Board has resisted this pressure. I hope they long continue this policy. There should be no roads in the Reserves, apart from the access road. There should be little, if any, extension of the present hutted-camp facilities. Bill Barnes' idea of a series of mountain huts, at 15 km distances, fitted with bunks and supplied with gas, is excellent. They would be designed for the man who was prepared to go out on the two legs God gave him, carrying his food on his back, and glad to make the effort needed to enjoy what nature has to offer.

Should we not make a distinction between Reserves and recreational areas? Nature Reserves, certainly, should be primarily for wild life conservation. They can be used for outdoor recreation within reason, but they should be kept primarily for the genuine lover of nature. Even our Drakensberg Hotel resorts are losing their original purpose. I have seen these resorts invaded by a motley crowd who cared for nothing more than their bowls and their tennis and their golf, their cards and their sundowners. They never once lift their eyes to the mountains, they never once venture into them, and never once do they feel their hearts stir with wonder and delight at the wild life around them. Tennis and bowls and golf are legitimate and very worth-while recreations, but are they wanted in the mountains?

In his Annual Report for 1967/68 Dr. D. Hey, Director of Nature Conservation for the Cape, said: "It is most important to reduce the public pressure on nature reserves and national parks by providing recreational facilities elsewhere for those who are not particularly interested in wild life, but merely wish to relax out-of-doors. It is quite possible for a Nature Reserve to be destroyed by an excessive number of visitors." He could not have put it more clearly. Let us at least keep our Drakensberg Reserves inviolable from this sort of thing.

Man has got to do a lot of re-thinking if he is to survive. In the past he has adopted the arrogant assumption that he is apart from the animal kingdom, sole owner of the world in which he lives, that he is the Lord of Creation and could do what he liked with his environment. And what has been the result? Since 1600 A.D. the world has lost 162 species of birds, and 106 mammalian species, 38 of the latter within the last 50 years. And year after year he spews out, at an increasing rate, his polluting gases into the atmosphere and his filth into the oceans.

Man is not a distinct entity. He is an inseparable part of the whole world of nature, and you, and I, and all the creatures of the wild, are fellow-travellers, with a common goal, a common destiny, and a common fate on a small and very vulnerable planet travelling through the depths of space.

CHAPTER XIV

THE SILENT SNOW

The silent snow possessed the earth
— TENNYSON: IN MEMORIAM

I shall never forget that evening late in June 1969, when the telephone rang with a message from the Cathedral Peak Hotel to the effect that my son, Malcolm, was missing on the summit of the Drakensberg in a snow-blizzard. For twenty-five years, in storm and sunshine, we had climbed the Drakensberg together, since that day many years ago when I had taken him, a little lad of ten years of age, on his first trip into the mountains. (Even in those days I used to make him carry his own pack – a little canvas bag made by his mother, 40 cm square and weighing 4 to 5 kilograms. To-day he carries his own full-size 35 kg pack, plus his father's as well!) Never once had we ever run into any serious trouble. Now he was missing, in a blizzard that had already lasted two days. Ten days previously I had dropped him off at the end of the new mountain road underneath *Sentinel Peak*, with two other young men, Mally Black and Robert Wood. They were setting off on a summit traverse from Mont-aux-Sources to Champagne Castle. Neither Mally nor Robert had ever climbed in the Drakensberg before; this was their first trip. It was Robert's voice I had heard telling me that evening that Malcolm and Mally were missing. But what had happened? How had they got separated? Why was Robert at Cathedral Peak Hotel, when they had never intended going anywhere near the place? And where were the other two?

There was nothing I could do that night. I knew Malcolm was fully capable of looking after himself in the mountains, and he was not alone. He had set off with food for at least ten days. I told Robert to put up for the night at the Hotel, and I would be out first thing next morning to look into things. I left at the crack of dawn, and arrived at the Hotel at about 8 o'clock. I shall tell the story of what had happened in Malcolm's own words:

"When we got to the summit of the escarpment on that first day we found, as we had expected, that the whole area was blanketed in heavy snow. The Tugela River was frozen over completely. We did not worry at all, however. We had plenty of warm clothing and food, a small Alpine tent, and, though it was bitterly cold, the sun shone in a cloudless sky. We set off in high spirits on our long trek south.

"The first thing that went wrong was Robert. We found that he just couldn't take it. Apparently he was suffering from what is commonly known as Mountain Sickness. As you know, he is a keen sportsman, and loves the open-air life, but the altitude was just too much for him. Some people are like that. He kept lagging behind, and seemed to have no energy at all. The snow, too, was very deep in places. With our heavy 35 kg packs we kept breaking through the thin crust and sinking in, often up to our waists, and the going was painfully slow. By the afternoon of the sixth day we had only reached the *Abbey* and the Mbundini Pass.

"But it was unbelievably beautiful. Usually the summit, at this time of the year, is cold, bleak and desolate beyond description. Now vast snowfields stretched away to the distant horizons under a sky more intensely blue than any I have ever seen. The sun shone crisply, and black rocks, jutting out from the all-encircling snow, were sheathed in gleaming ice. Gigantic icicles hung from the rock faces, like giant teeth, hungrily bared. Over all brooded that intense silence which you always get on the summit after a snow-storm.

"We camped that night, our sixth night, on the edge of the escarpment, overlooking the

159

Abbey. Next morning we were up early. The weather was still fine. But it was from this point that things went really wrong.

"From the Mnweni Cut-back you can clearly see the line of the Berg, past the *Mnweni Pinnacles*, to the head of the Mnweni Pass, and then sweeping round to *Mponjwana*, the high ground round the *Rockeries*, and Mponjwana Cave. In actual distance the day's march would be short, for we had decided to sleep in Mponjwana Cave that night, but this particular stretch of the Drakensberg is a photographic paradise, and Mally and I were anxious to spend some time photographing those fantastic spires that make this particular stretch so memorable. As we were packing up after breakfast Robert suggested that he might follow a Basutho trail that headed, quite clearly, for the Mnweni Pass, and wait for us there, so as not to hold us back with his slower pace. I did not quite like it, for I know that one should never separate in the Drakensberg, but there seemed to be no danger in it: the head of the Pass was clearly visible from where we were, nothing could possibly go wrong so long as he kept to the path. Eventually I agreed.

"Mally and I spent a useful morning with our cameras, amongst other things, incidentally, exploring a huge ice grotto we came across, with icicles at least ten metres high. At two o'clock we set off for the Pass, about two and a half hour's walk away. Robert's footprints were clearly visible in the snow.

"But when we reached the Pass he was nowhere to be seen, nor was there any sign of his ruck-sack. What was more, the snow in the vicinity of the Pass had melted, and we could no longer trace his footsteps. We weren't unduly worried, however, as it seemed likely that he might have strolled off to see the view, and would return before dark. We sat down to wait.

"Gradually the shadows deepened, and the sky turned a dull, angry red. Suddenly it was dark, and the stars were shining in a jet-black sky.

"We still weren't worried. We argued that Robert had probably gone on to Mponjwana Cave, and was getting everything ready for the night. Perhaps he had already cooked the evening meal. With enormous appetites we set off up the slope to the cave.

"Though we were hungry and a little tired we enjoyed that walk in the moonlight, for by now the moon had risen. The slope is a north-facing one, and much of the snow had melted. Perfect silence reigned. The air was fresh and still. The only sound was the occasional crunch of snow at our feet, as if we were walking over a floor of fragile glass, as we climbed steadily towards *Mponjwana*.

"We reached the summit of the ridge at about nine o'clock. The cave was now only 50 metres away. We gave a long, drawn-out call, and then another. But there was no reply! Blankly, in stunned silence, we stared at each other. Robert was missing!

"To be out alone at night in the middle of the Drakensberg, in country to which you are a stranger; to realise that you are lost in one of the most desolate and inaccessible regions in South Africa, in a wilderness of snow and ice, without map or compass, would indeed be a frightening experience. We decided that we must make every effort to find Robert that night.

"We dumped our packs in the cave, and climbed to a high point immediately above the cave. From here we spent the next hour flashing our torches in every direction, and calling at the top of our voices. We were met by complete silence.

"Back at the cave we lit a candle and took stock of our position. There was nothing more we could do for Robert that night. A thorough search would have to wait for the morning. The next most urgent thing was a meal. We had been without food for nearly twelve hours.

"And then, suddenly, the full horror of our position dawned on us: we were without food, or nearly so! Owing to Robert's condition it had been arranged that he should carry the lighter items, such as the food, while Mally and I shared between us the heavier items – the tent, the medical supplies, the snake-bite outfit and the photographic equipment. We emptied our ruck-sacks and pooled the contents – two small portions of cheese, a quarter-slab of chocolate, some sugar, a few packets of Kool-aid, and a handful of biscuits! Common-sense demanded

160

that we head immediately for civilisation, where fresh supplies could be obtained. Even this would take one, possibly two, days, and we had barely food for even this. But how could we leave Robert, alone and lost in those snow-covered wastes? We decided to devote one whole day to a thorough search for him, and then, if we failed to find him, to head for home as fast as we could and raise the alarm.

"The first thing we noticed next morning was half a dozen vultures circling over Rockeries Pass! Had Robert fallen to his death during the night? We headed straight for the spot, a kilometre away along the summit, in the direction of *Cathedral Peak*. For a full hour we searched, examining every crag and fissure, all to no avail. There was nothing.

"We then decided that I should return along our previous day's route to the place where we had camped in the Mnweni Cut-back. It was just possible that Robert had turned back to look for us on the previous day, and that we had missed each other. Mally would continue the search round Rockeries Pass and beyond.

"It was a long slog back to our camping spot of two nights before. Longer still seemed my search. By 2 p.m. I realised it was hopeless, and I set out to return to the cave.

"But now it was obvious that a change in the weather was coming. All day the air had been strangely motionless and warm. Now, suddenly, a cold wind sprang up from the south. Within seconds it became a wild, ripping, icy gale that knifed through every stitch of clothing I had. Then the storm gathered with amazing rapidity. It swept swiftly across the plains of Lesotho and broke with a roar over the waiting peaks. I raced for the cave.

"Mally was there to greet me. He too had had no success, but he had managed to gather a little firewood. Crouched over our tiny fire that night, with the fiendish howl of the wind outside, we again took stock of our position. We could do nothing more for Robert. With a blizzard that might last for days upon us, and with no food, our own position was now perilous in the extreme. There was nothing for it but to head for home as rapidly as possible, raise the alarm, and see that a full-scale search was organised as quickly as possible. We hoped our food would last out long enough to permit of our doing this.

"Next morning it was snowing hard. We packed up, put on all the warm clothing we had, and with snow-anoraks pulled tightly around us, stepped out into the storm. We had decided to head south, for Cathedral Peak Hotel, the nearest point where help was available. We would trek along the escarpment edge, past *Saddle*, and so down the Umlambonja Pass, a trip that could be done in less than a day if necessary, but which, in our exhausted state, and with the storm still raging, might take up to three days.

"I do not like to think about that trek. Our faces were soon crusted with ice, our beards stiff with icicles. Throughout the day it snowed, and every now and then the hail came down, savagely, wind-whipped. At times the mist was so dense that we could see no more than a metre or so ahead of us. We knew that if we were ever to find the Umlambonja Pass the weather would have to clear considerably, for the Umlambonja is one of the most difficult passes in the Drakensberg to find. It is narrow, and dips down from the summit at a high point along a ridge. Many an experienced mountaineer has failed to locate it in mist. To find it in a snow-storm such as this would be virtually impossible.

"We staggered on throughout the long morning, and into the afternoon. The weather worsened steadily. Soon the snow was swirling down more heavily than ever. Visibility was reduced to nil. The wind changed continually, confusing our sense of direction. At one stage we found that we had wandered far into Lesotho, and had to spend two hours retracing our steps. By 4 p.m. our strength was almost gone. We had been more than two days with little, if any, food. We were reaching the end. Exhausted, we tumbled down under some sheltering rocks, and once again summed up the position.

"Our plight was now desperate. We were lost in a blizzard with only the shelter of a tiny tent. Our food supplies now consisted of a little Kool-aid and four biscuits. To make matters worse, while Mally had been crossing a frozen stream, the ice had broken in under him, and he had fallen through, up to his waist in icy water. He was wet through, and I was little better. Even our sleeping bags were wet. It was now 4 p.m., and already we could feel the temperature dropping. Soon the deep freeze of night would claim the summit. We could hardly expect to survive that night.

"We decided there was only one thing to do: get down off those icy heights as quickly as possible, get down before night, head straight for the escarpment edge and take the first route, no matter how precarious, to the lower levels. Forget about trying to find the Umlambonja Pass. That could wait. We staggered to our feet and shouldered our packs.

"And then, suddenly, the most dramatic change I have ever known took place. Suddenly, the clouds parted, patches of blue sky began to appear. A warm wave of pale sunlight spread across the snow. Moments later the mist was breaking everywhere, and the peaks, wreathed in drifting trails of mist, wet and sunlit, were standing out against a rain-washed sky. And, best of all, there was *South Saddle* behind us, the *Mitre* in front, and Umlambonja Pass only a kilometre away!

"It is amazing how quickly one's spirits, even one's strength, can revive. I believe that we could have climbed Mount Everest at that moment!

"Half an hour later we stood at the head of the Pass, knowing that food and warmth and safety were now only five hours away. With luck we might even reach the Hotel before midnight.

"After a short rest we began the difficult descent. The head of the Pass was choked with ice and snow, and we had to move with extreme caution. Three quarters of an hour later, just below the snow-line, we heard for the first time in ten days the sound of running water. There is no more lovely sound than a little trickle of water tumbling down a gully when the voices of nature have been silent for so long. It called for a celebration, so we treated ourselves to a drink of Kool-aid!

"But our new-found strength was short-lived. As night came on our spirits began to ebb, the clouds closed in once more, and soon it was raining. On the summit, of course, it would be snowing. With the help of one small pen-light torch we made our way very slowly down the slippery gully. It was the blackest night I have ever known. We tripped, and stumbled, and fell, grazing our shins on the rocks and tearing our hands on thorn-bushes and briars. Lightning flickered on the far peaks.

"At about nine o'clock we entered a thickly-wooded gully. The rain was still teeming down and we had been on the go now for nearly sixteen hours. Reluctantly we had to face the truth that we could not reach the Hotel that night. We were too tired even to pitch the tent. We simply spread our sleeping bags out on the wet ground, pulled the tent over us, and fell asleep.

"There is not much else to tell. If Robert were to be saved, speed was now the all-important thing. We were up before it was light, and with what strength we could muster we sped down the valley. As we passed the junction of the Oqalweni two hours later we heard, faint and clear on the still morning air, the breakfast bell ringing from the Hotel, two and a half kilometres away.

"And there, to our amazement, was Robert! You can imagine with what indescribable relief we saw his red beret and green jersey, just outside the Reception Office. He had got in late the previous afternoon."

After the two men had polished off three plates of porridge and two helpings of bacon and eggs, to say nothing of the heaped plates of toast and marmalade, we all piled into the car and headed for *Emkhizweni*. During the drive over we heard the full story of what had happened to Robert.

On the day Malcolm and Mally had spent photographing in the Mnweni Cut-back, Robert had followed the Basutho trail round to the Mnweni Pass, as arranged, only he didn't realise that he had reached the Pass. Thinking that it was still further on, he crossed the plateau below *Mponjwana*, and then came out at the head of Rockeries Pass, thinking that this was the Mnweni Pass. Here he waited several hours.

As darkness came on and there was still no sign of the other two he began to worry. All he could think was that they had missed each other along the way, that the other two had overtaken him and passed him, and were by then far ahead along the escarpment, looking for him. He hurried on in the moonlight, hoping to catch up with them. At 11 p.m. he found a rock overhang, and slept there.

Next morning, now thoroughly alarmed, in unfamiliar surroundings and completely lost, he nearly panicked. He did not know whether his companions were in front of him or behind. He decided that his best plan was to try and find his way down to the Cathedral Peak Hotel. He walked all that day. Towards late afternoon the clouds started to build up, and by evening it was snowing hard. That night, exhausted, he crept under some rocks and fell asleep. Next morning it was still snowing.

By now he was thoroughly frightened. He might be anywhere. He did not know the area, nor did he understand Drakensberg weather. He had no means of telling how long the storm would last. He was fairly comfortable and dry where he was, so he decided to lie up there until the weather cleared. After all, he had plenty of food.

Suddenly, at about 11 a.m., he was startled by the strange sound of a dog barking nearby. The sound seemed to come from somewhere down below, in the mist immediately in front of him. Then suddenly a mangy Basutho puppy leapt up out of the mist at his feet, and scampered off with a frightened yelp when it saw him. He suddenly realised that where a dog could get up he could get down, and within fifteen minutes his ruck-sack was packed, and he was on his way down, cautiously feeling his way through the drifting snow, which was still falling. By an amazing coincidence, one chance in a million, he had sought shelter on the very lip of the Umlambonja Pass, the only safe way of getting off the escarpment in a stretch of 12 kilometres. By late afternoon he had found the Hotel, and he immediately put through a call to me.

This incident, which fortunately ended so happily, shows how even the best-equipped party can come to grief on the summit in snow conditions. The careful mountaineer always treats these conditions with the greatest respect. If one is caught out on the summit in winter with a change of weather, the wisest course is to get down as fast as one can. This is because the passes, the only way of descending the mighty wall of the Drakensberg, are few and far between, and it is often extremely difficult to find them in mist or in a snow-storm. These storms can last for days, and if your food gives out, you could be in for trouble. There have been many cases where climbers, through being caught out on the summit in snow, have come within an ace of death, and have been rescued only in the nick of time. We have already referred to the Christensen tragedy in Chapter IX. But Christensen and his fellow students were not the only ones out in the snow on that bitter night of April 29th, 1959. Two other young men had set out at the same time to walk from Cathedral Peak to Mont-aux-Sources. They were caught in the same storm. They staggered on, lost their way in the swirling snow, their food gave out, until eventually they stumbled into the Hut at Mont-aux-Sources, more dead than alive. Fortunately the search party looking for Christensen had just taken over occupation of the Hut, and they were able to give them shelter and food.

A few suggestions might be useful here for those who plan to visit the high peaks in winter. First of all, make sure you are carrying plenty of warm clothing and plenty of food. If you plan a ten-day trip, take reserve food for another five days. This need not be anything elaborate – a few kilograms of highly concentrated, light-weight balanced food, like Pro-nutro, which doesn't have to be cooked, or a few extra slabs of chocolate – enough to keep body and soul together in an emergency. A small benzine primus stove, or a miniature gas stove, is invaluable, for in heavy snow fuel is next to impossible to find. Excellent stoves, small and light in weight, are available for high-altitude work. Don't take a ground sheet. A foam rubber mattress is much more comfortable and much lighter, and will serve the purpose just as well. It is wise to carry two sleeping bags, an inner and an outer. Modern sleeping-bags are so light that this is easily done. Even if you leave your base camp for a day, and intend returning to it that night, slip a sleeping-bag into your ruck-sack. If you rick your ankle you can't ring up a taxi to take you home on the summit of the Drakensberg! And remember what we have already said: at all costs, keep your party together. Never separate, even for a short while.

Remember too that the great killer on the summit is not cold, but *cold plus wind*. Your body can withstand tremendous degrees of cold, but if the cold is accompanied by wind, you will quickly succumb without adequate protection. Make sure you have wind-proof outer clothing with you. If you have to sleep out in the snow, choose a position sheltered from the wind. On a number of occasions I have survived with ease a night out in the snow, with no tent to cover me, simply by building a snow-wall round my sleeping place. If you have no foam rubber mattress, an excellent idea is to lay down a carpet of the twiggy bush that grows so luxuriantly on the summit, *Helichrysum trilineatum*. It is easily gathered, provides a soft, springy bed and excellent insulation from the cold ground. (It is this bush which is your only source of fuel on the summit.) Get into your double sleeping bags, and you will sleep like a king for twelve solid hours. If the weather is fine you will need no roof over your head. In a snow-storm, your best hope, if you have no tent, is either a cave or a rock overhang. Caves on the summit, unlike the Little Berg, are few and far between (it is wise to pin-point these, incidentally, on a good map before you start your trip) but overhangs can usually be found. Try somewhere along the escarpment edge for these. They are more numerous there.

Remember that everything will freeze during the night. Boots and socks are the main problem, for they are sure to get wet during your day's march through the snow, and in the morning will be stiff with ice, delaying your departure for anything up to a couple of hours, if you do nothing to protect them. If you are landed with frozen boots and socks in the morning, try pounding them with a stone. The better plan, though, is to protect them during the night. Slip them inside your sleeping-bag when you turn in, together with anything else you are likely to need in the morning, such as essential medicines.

If you observe these few simple precautions you need never fear anything the summit can do to you in winter – and you will have the time of your life! It is the man who goes up to the top inadequately equipped, with no reserves of food or warm clothing, who lands in trouble.

I have always been interested in extreme cold, and its effects on the human body. I have found that not only are one's physical responses slowed, but one's mental processes also become dulled. I once slept out near the summit of *Champagne Castle*, at an altitude of 3 355 metres, in the middle of winter, with two companions. We built a snow wall round our sleeping spot, and we all slept well. But next morning we tried to pack in a howling gale, blowing straight off the snow. I have never known such cold in all my life. Someone suggested a mug of hot coffee. It seemed an excellent idea, and after a tremendous battle we managed to get a fire going, and after a lot of coaxing the billy was boiling. Each man was given a mugful of steaming hot coffee, but it was too hot to drink immediately, so we placed the mugs on a rock to cool off a bit. And all three of us clean forgot to drink our coffee until it was too late and the mugs had frozen over!

Adjustment to cold is a highly individual matter. There have been many cases of climbers exposed all night on mountain sides in sub-zero temperatures. Some die, while others, in the same party, survive with little or no adverse effects. During the Korean War thousands of soldiers suffered cold injuries, while others, exposed to the same conditions, suffered no ill effects. Some years ago it was noted that Australian aborigines could sleep naked all night in temperatures close to freezing, while Europeans, even covered with a couple of blankets, could not sleep at all. It is also known that one can condition oneself to cold. I am quite sure that cold baths throughout the year are a tremendous help in this direction. It is well-known that one always feels the cold more at the beginning of winter, before the body has become adjusted to the lower temperatures.

But cold, or rather hypothermia, which means a lowering of the temperature of the body's inner core, can be a subtle and diabolical killer. One should never underestimate it. To beat it, one should know a little about those bodily processes which are set in motion when extreme cold strikes.

When one is exposed to extreme cold* the body responds, first of all, by constricting the blood vessels of the outer skin, with the result that less blood flows to the surface to be chilled. This warmer blood is then concentrated in those vital internal organs, which are thus protected from harm. Frost-bite, in its early stages at least, is therefore one of those protective devices of nature.

The body, having done all that it can to conserve its heat, now sets about producing heat at a greater rate, so as to replace any heat that is lost. The heart beats faster, additional adrenalin is pumped into the blood, and the metabolic rate rises. All these result in greater heat. We feel stimulated. The cold is "bracing", we say.

Then, as the temperature continues to drop, other mechanisms are brought into play. The muscles begin to contract spasmodically, and we "shiver". Again the result is the production of heat. But shivering also consumes a great deal of energy. If the shivering is intense and prolonged, it can result in exhaustion.

So far the temperature of the body's inner core has not been affected. But if heat loss continues, these organs will begin to be affected, and the temperature of the body will soon drop below 99 deg. F. until it reaches about 78 degrees, when death supervenes.

One of the interesting effects of extreme cold is the effect on the emotions. Moderate cold is exhilarating: extreme cold is exhausting. Fits of depression are common, one becomes irritable, there is a loss of judgment, and also, as we have seen, of memory. Members of a climbing team should be aware of these dangers. If they are all aware of them, and take them into account, it is easier to maintain amicable relations.

What causes hypothermia? It is not cold alone, as we have seen. Many a man has survived extreme cold with no ill effects, while others have succumbed when the temperature was well above zero. According to Dr. Lathrop it is caused by a combination of four factors. None of these alone, with the possible exception of the first, will prove fatal. In combination they can be lethal. These four factors are:

> Cold (not necessarily extreme)
> Wetness
> Wind
> Personal pre-conditions, e.g. being particularly
>   susceptible to cold, or in an exhausted
>   condition.

Wind, combined with cold, is certainly one of the biggest contributing factors in cases of hypothermia. "If there were no breeze at all," says Dr. Lathrop, "we could remain lightly clad and quite comfortable at zero degrees Fahrenheit for long periods of time. But let the air stir even slightly, and those calories will go, go, go."

Worst of all, and a real killer, is a combination of cold, wind and wetness. More fatalities are ascribed to this cause than to any other.

To survive on the summit, therefore, in a blizzard becomes a problem of avoiding these combinations.

* Much of my information on Hypothermia in this Chapter comes from an excellent article on the subject by Dr. Theodore G. Lathrop, in the 1968 Mountain Club Journal.

Taking the question of cold, first of all, every effort should be made not only to conserve what bodily heat we have, but to build up reserve supplies of heat, or rather, to replace those supplies of heat that have been lost. Some loss of heat, of course, is inevitable. It is when heat is being conducted away more rapidly than it is being produced, that trouble arises.

Clothing, first of all, must be adequate. Wool is excellent, but this must be supplemented by wind- and rain-proof outer clothing. Remember that the head is the greatest source of loss of heat from radiation. It is an old climbers' maxim: "If your feet are cold, put on your hat." Always cover your head in extreme cold, preferably with a balaclava cap. Most anoraks have attached hoods, which are excellent. Inner clothing must not be too tight. Make it wool if you can, and remember that the main idea is to establish an insulating layer of warm air around your body.

Body heat is derived from two sources – food and muscular activity. Keep nibbling. Sweets, especially chocolate (the hard black variety) are excellent. Intake of hot liquids will also help considerably.

Exercise is essential. Even moderate exercise, such as hiking with a light pack, can increase heat production as much as six times. If you are holed up in a cave or tent during a blizzard, keep flexing your muscles. In 1953 Hermann Buhl, the conqueror of *Nanga Parbat*, one of the highest peaks in the Himalayas, spent the night of 3rd July alone, on the summit of the peak, clothed only in a pair of trousers, a shirt and a thin pullover. He kept himself alive throughout the long night by tramping up and down on his lofty perch.

Wind is your worst enemy. It is amazing how quickly even a moderate breeze in cold weather can lower your body temperature. Always keep a supply of wind-proof clothing with you on the summit. If possible never walk with the wind in your face. Make sure you camp down at night out of the wind. It has been found that merely to wear wind-proof garments over wet clothing raises one's chance of survival, in cold-wet-windy conditions, five times.

But the wind is made infinitely worse if your clothing is wet. Even clothing dampened with your perspiration can lower your chances. Always wear clothing next to your skin that "breathes". The thermal conductivity of water is 240 times that of still air. This means that wet clothing can extract heat from your body up to 240 times as fast as dry clothing, even if the air is still. If it is moving, you can multiply this figure several times. When clothing gets wet it no longer provides that insulating layer of warm air next to the skin that is so essential, and heat is rapidly conducted away from the body. Here wool is your best friend. It has the peculiar power of drying from within, and is the only fabric that can provide warmth even when wet.

One or two further safeguards might be mentioned, before we discuss the treatment of hypothermia. First of all, don't wait to feel cold before putting on protective clothing. Warm clothing will not produce heat: it merely conserves already existing heat.

Secondly, check periodically fingers and nose, for frostbite, both your own and those of your companions. The symptoms are lack of feeling and white patches.

And lastly, if you are in heavy snow, don't put off your night's bivouac until you are exhausted. Camp down in plenty of time, while you still have all your faculties about you.

In the treatment of hypothermia, remember, first of all, never to attempt the time-worn remedy of rubbing frost-bitten areas with snow. This remedy is quite fallacious. You will do far more harm than good thereby, and will add to the likelihood of permanent injury. The best treatment is to re-warm the frost-bitten area rapidly in warm water at 40 deg. C. Failing this, use body heat to save the injured area – put your fingers under your arm-pits, cover your nose with your hand, and so on.

After that, treatment falls under two headings. First, prevent any further loss of heat, and secondly, add heat to re-warm the victim's body. Make your patient as warm as possible. Place him out of the wind, and replace wet clothing with warm, dry clothing. Then put him into a sleeping-bag – but not a cold one. Try and heat the bag as much as you can beforehand. One good way is to put another member of the party into the bag beforehand. This person should strip down to his underclothing so as to transfer as much of his own body heat to the bag as possible. Another good way is to put another person into the bag with the victim. If there is no sleeping-bag available, get two people, one on each side, to huddle up against him. Give him warm fluids to drink, and sweetened foods. Remember that carbohydrates are the foods that are most quickly transformed into heat and energy. Don't give alcohol. Despite the legendary St. Bernard's dog with his keg of whisky, this can cause complications. Alcohol is sometimes administered in the mistaken idea that it will warm up the body. This is quite wrong. What it does is to cause a sudden release of cold blood from the surface vessels to the body's core, which is thus chilled. As we have seen, however, one of the essential things is to ensure that these internal organs remain warm. Also, alcohol thins the blood, and this, too, results in heat loss.

With these few simple precautions you should be 100% safe on the summit of the Drakensberg. Even so, always remember that the unpredictable *can* happen, and be ready for it when it comes. I have already given one instance of this. Here is another which occurred in the early summer of 1970, when two journalists, Terry Baron and Rob Linden, set out to hike from Mont-aux-Sources to Cathedral Peak. For seven days they were held up in a freak blizzard, and nearly lost their lives.

They set out from the Mountain Club Hut at Mont-aux-Sources in high spirits, with food for about six days. At the Mnweni Cut-back, however, their troubles started. (It is strange that from this point their story has many similarities with Malcolm's own adventure.) Here the sky suddenly darkened with heavy clouds, and the air became eerily still, with a sultry, malevolent warmth. With a prickly feeling of fear the two men realised, almost unconsciously, that they were heading for real danger. They decided to make for the escarpment edge, and to try and get down into the Little Berg, but it was too late. Before they reached the edge snow started to fall.

It fell slowly at first, but it was soon swirling down, thick and fast, and the temperature plummeted. Then the wind began to howl and knife through their clothing, and they realised, with visibility down to a few metres, that they would never reach the escarpment, and that their only hope was to pitch camp. With the banshee howl of the wind around them, tearing at their clothing, they managed to get the tent up.

For five days they were held up in the storm, unable to move. Periodically they had to go outside to shovel the fallen snow off their tiny tent, but so bitter was the cold that they could only remain outside for a few minutes. They lost track of time. They were wet through and their tent leaked. Their benzine came to an end, and their food gave out. They rationed themselves to a mouthful of dried meat and a teaspoon of sugar a day, until at last even this petered out, and they were reduced to a tot of whisky and a teaspoon of sugar every 24 hours. And always the demon howl of the wind and the tent shuddering under the hammer-blows of the storm.

At last there came a lull, and the wind dropped. They woke up on the sixth day to find scudding clouds above them, a pale sun trying to break through, and around them the utter silence of vast snowfields.

They were able at last to break camp and to start their hunt for the escarpment edge and a pass. But their troubles were not over. In the heavy snow-drifts the going was painfully slow and exhausting. Terry Baron was hit by snow-blindness, and had to cling on to a strap of Rob's ruck-sack, following blindly. Then the mist came down again, and they gave up hope. By the middle of the afternoon they were finished and had to pitch camp. Next day it was raining, but they still battled on, getting weaker and weaker. At last, unknown to themselves, they struck the very head of the Ntonjelane Pass, just north of the Cathedral Range, and started down. Suddenly two bearded figures in heavy anoraks and balaclavas loomed up out of the mist in front of them. "Are you the two missing journalists?" said one of the two figures, and their troubles were over.

Their rescuers were two members of the Natal Mountain Club Rescue Team, who had been alerted when the two men had been reported overdue.

I know of no more lovely time in the Drakensberg than when the snow comes and possesses the earth. In summer the peaks have a hard bright beauty, stencilled starkly against a turquoise sky, with the clouds breaking around them in a splendour of white foam. In autumn they have a softer, more dream-like quality, as they gaze down timelessly into the sun-drenched valleys of the Little Berg. But when the snows come that whole vast expanse of mountain splendour is sheathed in purest white, glistening in the clean sunlight, the snowfields stretch to the far horizon, and the peaks stand tranquil and proud over it all.

Snow can come to the Drakensberg at any month of the year. Many years ago they had a white Christmas at Cathedral Peak Hotel. While the Boer wagons were still descending the Drakensberg, in early January 1838, the Voortrekkers reported that the whole range was covered in "silver-white" snow. But this is rare. Usually it is when April begins to give way to May that one can expect the first snows to fall, and they will last until well into September, and even October.

It is a strange new world that you will enter as you step out into the snow, and you must learn to adjust yourself to it. The first thing that you will notice is the silence. I know of no silence like it. So hushed is the air that even the sound of your boot scraping on a hidden rock, or the tinkle of an ice-pinnacle as it melts in the sun, is an intrusion and a desecration. If you are lucky, and the bitter cold of night has frozen the surface of the snow, you will be able to walk for long kilometres on the smooth, creamed surface in an elation of spirit you have never known before. But if the snow is only partly frozen, and deep, then the crust will break under your weight every few steps, and you will fall in, and flounder, and lose your balance, and your carefully worked out schedule for the day will go by the board. I once timed myself on the slopes below *Cleft Peak*. It took me an hour to cover 100 metres, and after that I gave up!

When the sun shines, it is still cold, of course, but the air is crisp, and the sunlight a warm benediction, and you can go all day in shorts and bare legs, but once the sun goes you will pile on every stitch of clothing you have. At night there is only one thing to do – climb right into your double sleeping-bags and remain there for sixteen hours, for there is hardly any fuel on the summit, only the twiggy *Helichrysum trilineatum*, and fires are out of the question.

Another of your problems is water. There is plenty of it around, but it is all frozen! Even the larger streams are solid ice, and they will remain so for months on end. You will have to obtain your water by melting the snow, but this is not easy, for, as we have said, fuel is scarce and every twig precious. To obtain one billy-can of water you will have to collect from ten to twelve billy-cans of snow, and it takes a long time to melt this amount of snow. The weather experts will tell you that 12 inches of snow is the equal of 1 inch of rain.

Always there is the problem that anything liquid will freeze solid during the night, even if it is kept in your tent. Eggs, milk, butter, medicines will all be unusable in the morning. Damp clothing will be turned into sheets of crackling armour, boots and stockings will be iron blocks. And don't expect the sun to melt them in the morning. There is no heat in the sun until at least ten o'clock.

But in spite of the bitter cold, perhaps because of it, some of my most treasured memories are of the summit under snow, memories of that day we found a gigantic frozen waterfall on the southern slopes of *Champagne Castle*, at least 15 metres high; memories of the ice-grotto we explored below *Mount Amery*, and of that long, exhilarating march over frozen snow, from the Upper Injasuti Cave to the Langalibalele Pass, after the great snow-storm of 1953. And memories, too, of that never-to-be-forgotten trip to the summit in July of 1957, with my daughter Joan, just out of Training College. The early days of that month had seen one of the heaviest falls of snow ever to be recorded in the Drakensberg, and the authorities had had to close the whole of the summit area in the Royal Natal National Park to the public. We were the

The mighty face of the Amphitheatre Wall and the Tugela Falls.

The Silent Snow.

Winter sparkle.

Snow cameo in the Mnweni area.

After the blizzard.

From the Upper Injasuti Cave.

first to be allowed up after conditions had returned to normal, but we were warned to be careful. Joan and I set off with a young African to carry her pack, for she was new to the game, but he collapsed at Basuto Gate and had to be sent home, and I had to shoulder his pack as well as my own. The Chain Ladder was still iced up, and we only just made the Hut before darkness fell, the whole summit area a white wilderness of untrodden snow. In the early hours of the morning three young men stumbled into the Hut after a nightmare climb through the icy night, having lost half their kit in the snow-drifts, and that was my first meeting with "Tiny" Harries, the man who, eight years later, was to build *Emkhizweni* for us when we came to live out in the Drakensberg. We teamed up with "Tiny" (over two metres tall!) and his half-section, Tim (the third man just couldn't take it, and vanished immediately after breakfast that first morning!) and the four of us spent two magnificent days tobogganing down those glorious snow slopes in brilliant sunlight, and ending up by deciding, at 2 p.m. of our last day, to climb *Sentinel Peak*, and getting back to the Caravan Park well after midnight, nearly famished, with Joan, weary as she must have been, setting to and rustling up a magnificent steaming meal of poached eggs, bacon and coffee for the four of us, at 2 a.m.

It is memories such as these that bring a glow to the heart in the days when, as the Preacher said, the years draw nigh, and the strong men bow themselves, and desire fails, because man goeth to his long home.

PART 3

Tells of peace and of war, and of the folly of man,
whereby he stands in peril of losing his heritage

CHAPTER XV

"THE GEOGRAPHY OF HOPE" – 1

"God made wild animals, and He saw that it was good."
— BOOK OF GENESIS (NEW ENGLISH BIBLE)

The Drakensberg is, above all else, a place of peace. But if I were an artist, and had been given the task of painting a picture to be called "Peace, perfect peace", I would not paint that mountain vlei I came across early one morning, high up in the Setene Valley, with the peaks mirrored in glass-like perfection on its tranquil, unbroken surface, nor would I paint the stillness and the silence of the great snow fields. Rather would I paint the green slopes of a sheltered valley in the Giant's Castle Game Reserve, with the grass undulating softly in the morning breeze, and the clouds beginning their long march across the skies, and in a quiet corner a party of graceful oribi feeding on the rich grass, "studying to be quiet, and doing their own business". For you will not find true peace in engraven stillness, nor in your ivory tower. True peace is to be found only in the heart of teeming life.

And I believe you would have to go a long way to find a more perfect home of peace and serenity than you would find in the hills and valleys of the Drakensberg, where the creatures of the wild have found a refuge, and where they go about their own business in quiet contentment.

Admittedly the game is not as numerous as it used to be. When the first white men moved up into the heart of the Drakensberg the mountains were alive with game. Here they found a land of deep, well-watered soil, of mountain flowers, of sheltered valleys where the grass stood tall and strong, and where ice-cold streams watered the earth. To-day this part of it is much the same. The grass is not quite so tall, but the valleys still dream in the sunlight, the clean winds still blow over the high places, and the peaks still dominate the sky, proud and aloof in their invulnerable kingdom. I doubt whether a single flower species has disappeared with the march of time.

But one thing certainly *has* changed. No longer will you find the mountain slopes alive with game. The cheetah and the leopard, the lion and the rhinoceros, the elephant and the buffalo, all have gone their way down the corridors of the unremembered past. Perhaps that is why, when you *do* come across some of the few remaining wild animals in these mountain solitudes, the sight catches you by the throat, and your heart beats with a strange delight, and you feel a kinship with the great world of nature that is deeper even than your kinship with your fellow-men.

Writer after writer, in the middle 1800's, refers to the vast herds of game that were to be found in the midlands of Natal and along the slopes of the Drakensberg. Charles Barter, writing in 1852 of the area between Harrismith and the Drakensberg, refers to "game in thousands, aye, and tens of thousands, spread over the plains or marching in almost endless line across its surface". The traveller James Chapman, skirting the "lofty range of the Drakensberg" in 1849 says: "at certain times of the day the plains for miles around had somewhat the appearance of a living ocean, the tumultuous waves being formed by the various herds crossing and re-crossing each other in every direction." The Springbok Treks, when countless thousands of springbok trekked over the vast plains of the Free State, were well-known and well-documented. Davie and Gibbons, writing of the area around Prieska in 1888, estimated that 10 000 springbok could stand on one acre, and that ten thousand acres were covered by the moving mass of "trek bokke" as far as the eye could see on all sides. There must have been one hundred million animals. Quagga, wildebeest, zebra, lion, elephants, buffaloes, leopards, hippopotami, and countless herds of antelopes are all mentioned. An old farmer once told Carter Robinson that the game used to come down into Natal from the Orange Free State in thousands in the 1860's during April and May, trekking into the warmer Thornveld. They would take all day to pass one single point. In September they returned.

By the late 1860's all this had begun to change. The game was shot out, first in the areas around the developing towns, and then in the outlying parts, until eventually the remote fastnesses of the Drakensberg were invaded by the hunter and his gun. Men hunted for the sheer lust of killing. The genuine hunter hunted only for the pot; the trophy-hunter hunted selectively for better and better trophies; the butchers, and I am afraid there were hundreds of them, hunted mercilessly, and only to kill . . . and to kill . . . and to kill again.

The *Grahamstown Journal* of 11 September 1860 gives a graphic description of one of these hunts, a hunt arranged in honour of the visit of Prince Alfred, second son of Queen Victoria, to South Africa. This took place in the vicinity of Bainsvlei, near Bloemfontein. "The hunt resembled more the end of a battle than a hunt", said the account. "There, advancing rapidly in line were the huntsmen (how many we could not tell but all possessing guns) and farther on were the unarmed enemy falling thick, and gradually edging away in the direction of the living hedge of Kaffirs, who again forced them back. The slaughter was tremendous, considering that it did not endure beyond an hour. How many fell on the spot or died afterwards of their wounds, or were caught by the Kaffirs, it would be difficult to tell." The writer estimates that some 5 000 head of game were killed, and that no hunt of such proportions was known in the civilised world in that century. To his eternal honour he records that the Prince and his retinue were nauseated by the butchery.

The last elephant was shot in Durban in July 1850, but they survived in the Pinetown district until 1867, when the last one fell to the gun of John Coote Field (after whom Field's Hill is named). He and Captain Spencer Drake shot the last lion in the same district in 1855. By 1856 the last lion had been shot in the Karkloof district, but they still survived in the remoter areas. The traveller John Shedden Dobie saw lion spoor "immediately under the perpendicular cliffs of *Champagne Castle*" (he probably meant *Cathkin Peak*) in 1863, and says that three lions had been seen in the Cathkin area a few days previously. Elephants seem to have survived longer. It is said that the last elephant in Natal was shot by Thys Marais on the site of the present Wagendrift Dam, near Estcourt, in 1875, though Henry Brooks, writing in 1876, said that elephants were still to be found in the Tugela valley. By 1880 all the larger mammals had gone, and with them went the quaggas and the zebras, the oribi and the wildebeest. The quagga to-day is completely extinct. Only the lonely figure of the Black Wildebeest on the Natal coat of arms remained to remind the people of Natal of their former glory.

It is just possible, though, that a few leopards still remain in the Drakensberg. In 1931 a party of climbers from the Natal Mountain Club camp in the Ntonjelane Valley saw a leopard. Mr. P. R. (Bill) Barnes' native Rangers, in the Giant's Castle Game Reserve, recently came across leopard spoor in a remote side valley of the Mchesana River, and there are persistent rumours that a leopard has his lair in the gorge of the Sterkspruit Valley, less than five kilometres from my home. Hendrik Maartens, in the early 1940's, quite definitely heard its grunts and roars. Mr. Carter Robinson, up to the time of his death in 1970, was convinced there were leopards in the Drakensberg. A few years ago my friend Harry Barker spent a night in Cat Cave, in the upper reaches of the Mhlwazini River. During the night he heard a heavy body crashing through the undergrowth, and the unmistakable grunts and coughs of a leopard.

But although the big game has disappeared, the Drakensberg still offers a home to many of the lesser creatures, and to those who love the wild things of nature these mountain solitudes are a perpetual source of wonder and delight. These creatures range from the trap-door

174

spider to the noble eland, from the tiny sugar-bird to the lordly lammergeyer, and all you need to enjoy them are eyes to see and the spirit of wonder.

Perhaps the most delightful of all the wild animals to be found in the Drakensberg are the various species of antelope. There are twelve of these altogether and you will be unlucky if you go for even a short walk in one of the Game Reserves without encountering at least one pair of these lovely animals.

Sometimes, as you set off on your hike, especially in the early morning, you will hear a short cough or grunt. Look carefully, and on the opposite slope you will see a group of animals of a grey to greyish-brown colour, with long, slender necks, long pointed ears, and straight, sharp horns. They are a little larger than a goat. These almost certainly are Grey Rhebuck, *Pelea capreolus*, or Vaalribbok, to give them their Afrikaans name. They will soon be off, loping up the mountain side with their peculiar rocking-horse gait, with the hind-quarters thrown up into the air at each stride. You will notice that their tails are held erect, showing the underlying white "powder-puff". These powder-puffs when they are on the run, the grey colour, and the straight horns make identification of the species easy. They are grazing animals, and they love the higher mountainous regions, being usually found in parties of from two to ten. Their hearing, eyesight and sense of smell are all acute, and they will spot you long before you spot them. The first indication you will have of their presence is the short alarm cough, and when they are on the run they move fast. Only the male carries horns, and these are 20 cm to 25 cm long. The Grey Rhebuck is a direct descendant of one of the earliest races of antelope, and has inhabited the Drakensberg for as long as we know.

Very similar to the Grey Rhebuck is his cousin, the Rooiribbok, or Mountain Reedbuck, *Redunca fulvorufula*. Though they are only distantly related, the two are, superficially, very similar. Look closely, however, and you will see the difference. They are about the same size, but the Rooiribbok, as the name implies, has a reddish-grey coat, with white on the chest, throat and abdomen, and under the tail, while the Grey Rhebuck is greyish-brown. The black horns of the Reedbuck are lyre-shaped and curve forward instead of being straight. Unlike the Grey Rhebuck, the Reedbuck does not like the bleak summits of the Little Berg. He prefers the warm, sunny slopes and the sheltered gullies. You will often find him amongst the scattered proteas and bottle-brushes, on the warm, northern slopes of the Little Berg, in pairs or in small parties of five or six to a dozen. Again, unlike the Grey Rhebuck, he is more approachable. If he thinks he has not been seen, the Reedbuck will remain lying down in the long grass. The Grey Rhebuck likes to run up a slope; the Reedbuck will run either round or obliquely down a hill. The action of the two species in running is very similar, but the tail of the Reedbuck is always fan-spread, and kept tucked in, though occasionally it is "flashed", in which case it appears large and white. The alarm note is a short, sharp whistle rather than a grunt, and it carries over long distances. The Zulu name for this antelope is *Inxala*.

I once caught a magnificent glimpse of a Reedbuck. Leaving my camp early one morning I turned the shoulder of a hill, and surprised a large, fully-grown ram. He bounded off down the slope, head erect, with pounding hooves, and at every leap he let out his sharp, alarmed whistling cry, scattering the morning dew in the early sunlight. I shall never forget it.

The Mountain Reedbuck is closely related to the Common Reedbuck, *Redunca arundinum*, our third species. In fact the young ewes of the two species are almost indistinguishable. The Common Reedbuck is a little larger than his Mountain cousin, growing to a height of 90 cm to 100 cm. His Zulu name is *Intlangu*. He is seen in a variety of habitats, sometimes in open marshy country, but he also likes fairly well-wooded areas, generally near water. He has a somewhat arrogant tilt to his head, and his horns are wide and U-shaped, curving back and then forward. The colour is tawny to reddish-buff, and the under-sides, including the tail, are white. These lovely animals have little of the herd instinct of other antelopes. They are usually found singly or in pairs, and even if several individuals do come together, they will scatter in different directions if disturbed. They, too, run with a rocking-horse gait, with the tails held erect, showing the white under-sides. Once they reach the cover of trees, they will often stand stock-still and watch for several minutes before bolting off again. They are not often seen, as they are night-feeders, and in the daytime are adept at hiding themselves in reeds and long grasses. They will often lie hidden in this way until almost trodden on, before jumping up and making off. They are a smooth grey in appearance, with black or dark-brown stripes on the lower part of the fore-limbs. Similar stripes, but less well-marked, are found on the lower hind-limbs. The tail is thick and bushy, and the ears long and sharply pointed. Like their Mountain cousins, their alarm call is a shrill whistle.

In the higher mountain regions you will, if you are very lucky, catch a glimpse of the Klipspringer, *Oreotragus oreotragus*. His Zulu name is *Igogo*, and he is extremely rare. This dainty little antelope is sometimes mistaken for the Grey Rhebuck, but is actually quite distinct from him. He is much smaller, only growing to a height of about 60 cm. He is a true mountaineer, and loves the rocks and the high mountain slopes. He has even been found on the summits of *Mt. Karisimbi* (4 400 m) and *Mt. Mikeno* (4 300 m) in the Congo. The hooves are highly specialized, and ideally suited for rock-climbing. They are small and blunt, and this enables the little chap to run with amazing sure-footedness over steep rock places. He walks on the tips of these hooves, giving the impression of walking on stilts. The horns, rather wide apart and curving slightly forward at the tips, are short. His coat is a yellowish-olive in colour and blends perfectly with the rocks amongst which he lives. The ears are large, and the head is triangular and pointed. He has only the vestige of a tail. Like the Common Reedbuck, his call is a shrill whistle, and when alarmed he will emit this before bounding up the rocks. Once he thinks he is safe, however, he will pause on the skyline to look back on his pursuer.

The Klipspringer is easily distinguished from other antelopes by its small size, its bristle-like hair, the vestigial tail, and the small vertical hooves. In fact he is very like the European chamois. Another point which makes it very easy to identify Klipspringers is the fact that they are confined to the basalt layers of the main Drakensberg. They are never seen in the Little Berg.

On the front of his face the Klipspringer has face-glands which emit a secretion, and some observers have noted that the animal often rubs this secretion off on to plants of a suitable height. Although the function of this secretion is not fully understood, it has been suggested that this rubbing off on to plants may be a means whereby the males define their territories.

To-day the Klipspringer is one of the rarest antelopes in the Drakensberg. Once they were very common, but unfortunately the early settlers soon discovered that the animal's short, bristly hair was ideal for stuffing saddles, and they were soon shot out. Not only so, but the venison is sweet and tender, and their habit of standing stock-still against the sky-line on top of a mountain crag makes them an easy target for the hunter's gun. They seem to lack the wariness of other antelopes, believing that once they have gained height above their pursuers, they are safe.

Amongst the wild creatures of the mountain slopes there is one who is a particular friend of mine, for he visits us every night in the winter. His name is *Sylvicapra grimmia*, otherwise the Grey Duiker. During the summer months he gives our garden a wide berth, but in winter, when the grass is brown and there is little to eat in the veld, he visits us regularly every night. In the morning we find his little hoof-marks in our flower-beds, and we survey ruefully the wreck he has made of the violas and the pansies and the rose-bushes. He is particularly partial to the young rose-shoots in early spring.

The Duiker is a tough little fellow, and has shown a tremendous capacity to survive in fairly densely populated areas. In the Mnweni area of the Drakensberg, which is all Bantu Reserve, he is one of the few antelopes to have survived.

He is a night-browser, and is seldom seen, though I have often picked him up in the head-lamps of our car, when returning to our home late at night. He is uniformly grey in colour, and grows to a height of about 65 cm. The horns are straight and spike-like, only about 15 cm long and are set well back on the head. Between the horns of the male there is a characteristic tuft of hair. On the female, which seldom has horns, this gives a sort of "unicorn" appearance. Duikers are mainly browsers, and feed on leaves, twigs, berries and wild fruits. The name *duiker* comes from the Afrikaans, and means diver, referring to the plunging, leaping run of the Duiker as he flees. He has two cousins, the Blue Duiker and the Red Duiker, neither of which is found in the Drakensberg. Duikers are usually met with singly, though occasionally they may be found in pairs.

If you penetrate into any of the forests of the Drakensberg, you will sometimes hear a short, sharp bark, followed by a few crashes, and then silence. This is sure to be a Bushbuck, *Tragelaphus scriptus*. Be on your guard. If wounded he can be dangerous. Together with the Common Reedbuck, he is the largest of the antelopes we have considered so far, apart from the eland. The males, growing to a height of 100 cm, are dark brown in colour, with a white bar across the throat. The ram carries a large pair of horns, spirally twisted. Females carry no horns, and are more reddish in colour than the males. They are solitary animals, although couples may sometimes be seen together. They can be dangerous, especially in the mating season, and have been known to kill dogs, leopards, and even man. The male, especially, will defend himself vigorously, and a wounded animal can be especially dangerous. They are only to be found in bush country, and are largely nocturnal in habit, though they are sometimes seen in the early morning and the late afternoon. They are very difficult to approach.

With his bright reddish colour, white markings on neck, abdomen, chest, legs and round the eyes, pointed ears, slender neck and erect head, the Oribi, *Ourebia ourebi*, is a strikingly handsome animal. He has a short, black-tipped tail, and when standing his back is always perfectly horizontal. They are usually to be found in pairs or small family groups, often in long grass. Here the Oribi will often lie concealed, watching you approach, waiting until the last moment, when he will suddenly jump up and make off at tremendous speed, leaping high in the air every now and then, and always landing on his hind legs. He will not run far, however. After 100 metres or so he will stop, turn round, and face the area behind him. His alarm call is a soft, wheezy whistle.

The Oribi is very similar to the Steenbok (not found in the Drakensberg), and is often mistaken for it. One strange difference between the two animals is that the Steenbok digs a hole to urinate in, and then covers it up, whereas the Oribi does not. Oribi were once common throughout the Berg areas, but to-day are rare. Fortunately they are preserved in the Giant's Castle Game Reserve, the Kamberg and Loteni Nature Reserves, and in State Forest areas.

It is the Oribi's habit of leaping high in the air that distinguishes this little antelope from all the others. In fact, he seems to delight in it out of sheer fun, and not only when he is running away. I once came across a couple of Oribis unexpectedly, in a shallow depression of the hills. They were leaping up and down in sheer exuberance of spirit, kicking their heels high in the air and having a wonderful time. Luckily they did not spot me, and I was able to watch them for some time. Eventually they galloped away along the banks of a small stream, still oblivious of my presence.

Oribis are incurably curious. If you are lying down well concealed, with just your head or hat showing, and the wind in the right direction, an Oribi will come forward cautiously, a metre or so at a time, to inspect the strange object. He will stare hard for a moment, utter a squeak and jump back, and then cautiously advance another pace or two. Make the slightest movement, however, and he will be off, heels high in the air.

These seven, the Grey Rhebuck, the Mountain Reedbuck, the Common Reedbuck, the Klipspringer, the Grey Duiker, the Bushbuck and the Oribi are the main antelope species which you are likely to see in the Drakensberg, apart from the three re-introduced species in the Giant's Castle Game Reserve, the Red Hartebeest, the Black Wildebeest and the Blesbok. But there is one other possible species. This is the Grysbok. There is no certainty, however, that this species inhabits the Drakensberg. We do know that there is a small red antelope inhabiting a few of the deep valleys of the Drakensberg, which has been seen only rarely, and the remains of a carcass found some years ago seemed to indicate that it might be a Grysbok. But there is no certainty. The animal is very rare, and little is known of its habits. Like the Bushbuck, the Grysbok inhabits bush country. He is small and speckled grey in appearance. The ram has short straight horns.

These are some of the larger animals that you will see in the Drakensberg areas. But there are hundreds of smaller ones that you will rarely, if ever, see, creatures of the wild who have found a home in these remote valleys and mountain slopes. A very wise man who often took me out with him when I was still a boy on his rambles into the countryside around Ladysmith, and to whom I owe most of my love of the wide open spaces and of the animals who live there, used to tell me that when we went wandering out into the countryside, we might not see a single living creature, but hundreds of eyes were watching us all the time. And he was right. The Drakensberg is a naturalist's paradise, but so often we have eyes that see not, and ears that hear not, and only the trained observer will know where to look and what to look for. Of these are the various species of snakes, which we shall deal with in the next Chapter; the otter, roaming the streams at night; the ice-rat, *Myotomis sloggettii*, (the summit is riddled with his burrows); the vlei-rat, *Otomys irroratus;* the Natal mole-rat, *Cryptomys natalensis;* the Jacot-Guillarmod's Golden Mole, *Chlorotalpa guillarmodii;* the porcupine, *Hystrix africae-australis;* the lizard – the Striped Skink, the Drakensberg Girdled Lizard, and the rare Yellow-throated Plated Lizard; the various species of rabbits and hares, and, of course, the Rock Dassie, *Procavia capensis*. Rock Rabbit, as it is sometimes called, is a very bad name for this little chap, for he is a rabbit neither in looks nor habit.

He is a delightful little creature, about the size of a large guinea-pig, with no visible tail. He is greyish-brown above, sometimes with white underparts, and there is a patch of dark hair in the middle of his back. Dassies live in colonies amongst the rocks, and love to sun themselves on a rocky outcrop, especially in the early morning. They are shy little creatures, however, and will dive for cover at the first sign of danger.

Dassies are a paradox. Strangely enough, they are closely related to the elephant and the rhinoceros. The large incisor teeth are regarded as small elephant tusks, and there are a number of other similarities.

This little fellow was well-known in ancient times as the coney. "The rocks are a refuge for the conies," sang the Psalmist. At one time they lived in trees (there is still one species of Tree Dassie in Natal), but they have gradually adapted themselves to living amongst the rocks. Attempts have been made to commercialise their pelts, but with little success, for the fur is interspersed with long protruding bristles, which spoil it. Their flesh, however, is much prized by the Bantu, and of course the strange substance known as hyracium, which comes from the Dassie, is still used medicinally. This is a black, pitch-like substance found in dassie haunts. Dassies seldom drink water, with the result that their urine is not thin and limpid, but thick and glutinous. This urine is always deposited in the same spot, thickens, and manufacturing chemists buy it as hyracium.

The Dassie is one of the finest climbers in the world. This is due to the semi-elastic rubber-like pads on the soles of his feet. These enable him to cling to vertical cliff faces. He has four toes on each front foot and three on each hind foot, and the hind foot has, in addition, a strong, elongated nail used for scratching and burrowing. He is also able to withstand drops from a great height. In fact, Dassies are extremely difficult to destroy. Their eyesight is excellent, and so too is their hearing, and their sense of smell is keen. I have tried for years to obtain a photograph of a Dassie without success. You can remain hidden for hours at their burrows, with camera at the ready, but they seem to sense that you are there, and will not come out from their rock crevices. Incidentally, it is almost impossible to get them out of these crevices. They inflate their bodies and cling on to the rock face with their suction-pads. They also seem able to elongate their bodies, enabling them to creep through the tiniest of rock crevices. They have been known to negotiate gaps in the face of a precipice of up to 240 centimetres by flinging themselves across the gap and clinging to the opposite face with their foot-pads.

Dr. J. du P. Bothma, of the Department of Zoology, University of Pretoria, is of the opinion that the Rock Dassie has three distinct calls: the short, sharp metallic bark of the sentry, the alarm call; a peculiar, high-pitched staccato squeal, uttered by youngsters; and thirdly a low-pitched, sweet-sounding, whistle-like call, used, apparently, when the Dassie has been disturbed, but is not quite sure what the disturbance is, or whether it means danger.

He is a delightful, amusing little chap, and if you are skilful enough in hiding yourself, and do not approach too near, and have the patience of Job, you will have many happy hours watching his antics on the sun-warmed rocks of his mountain home.

For myself, I shall always remember James. When Malcolm, my son, was still a schoolboy we camped one Easter in the Ntonjelane Valley, making use of the cave under the shadow of *South Saddle*, at the foot of the Ntonjelane Pass. Each evening, after supper, we would relax on a grassy bank just outside the cave, before turning in for the night, I with my pipe. On the krantzes opposite was a family of Rock Dassies. Every evening, exactly ten minutes before the sun set, a single Dassie would pop up and sit perched on the highest rock, outlined against the sky, watching the sunset. He never missed once during the eight days we were there. For some reason I have forgotten we called him James, and we watched for him every evening, and not once did he fail to appear. Three years later we were back at the same cave. As we brought our mugs of coffee out on to the grassy slope that first evening, Malcolm said, "Do you remember James, Dad? I wonder what has happened to him." We looked up, and I'm blest if James wasn't there, on top of the same rock, sniffing the evening air with his little wrinkled nose, and it was exactly ten minutes to sunset!

The Jackal you are not likely to see, as he hunts by night. The Drakensberg Jackal is known as the Black-backed Jackal, *Canis mesomelas*. He is the most persecuted of all wild animals, because of the alleged damage he does to the sheep industry. He stands about 50 cm high. His coat is long and yellow-brown in colour, with a silver and black patch on the top of his back. Lips, throat and underparts are white. The tail is long and bushy.

Jackals usually go about singly or in pairs, but occasionally they hunt in packs. Their call is a long, wailing howl, followed by a number of yapping barks in quick succession. I know of no more spine-tingling, eerie sound in the silence of the night, when you are camping alone, and the call comes floating to you from across the moonlit valley. He has a considerable turn of speed. Travelling in a jeep in the Giant's Castle Game Reserve some years ago we put up a Jackal just as dusk was falling. Although our speed was at least 45 km/h, he managed to keep successfully ahead of us for a considerable distance.

During the day he will lie up in long grass or scrub, or preferably in a burrow or under rocks. The pups are brought forth in burrows or caves. Each litter consists of three to four pups, though larger litters have been recorded. When the pups are no longer suckled, the parents bring in food to them, either carried in the mouth or regurgitated. This power of easy vomiting makes it extremely difficult to kill Jackals by poisoning. In addition to this, the Jackal has the uncanny ability of detecting poison in meat – and this is not from human scent from the handling of the meat. Jackal cubs, kept as pets, and accustomed to being fed by hand, will usually reject poisoned meat.

Their depredations are alleged to be wide-spread and serious. In 1967 the Natal Agricultural Union published figures which, they claimed, showed that more than 28 000 sheep were killed in the province each year by marauding dogs and jackals. For the whole of South Africa it has been estimated that 200 000 sheep per annum are killed by jackals alone. Popular opinion makes him a vicious killer. Not only does he kill, but he will maim the rest of the flock, noses and lips being bitten off.

Extensive efforts have been made to exterminate the Jackal in sheep-farming districts, but without success. In fact, some authorities believe that his numbers are increasing, in spite of the advance of civilisation and the Government's attempts at eradication. The difficulty of poisoning him has already been mentioned. If he goes to earth he is extremely difficult to get out, even when dynamite is used. He is an adept at obliterating his scent, running downstream for many kilometres to put the dogs off his track, and he will feign death with great realism. Even so, in 1950 the Cape Province paid out bounties for 21 302 Black-backed Jackals – without appreciably lessening the menace.

To control Jackals in the sheep farms along the foothills of the Drakensberg the Natal Parks Board have established a pack of hunting dogs and a team of professional jackal hunters. The pack is based in the Kamberg Nature Reserve, just south of *Giant's Castle*. It consists of about 100 hunting dogs, and the hunting season lasts from October to May. During that period they bay up to 50 marauding Jackals. In the off-season, in winter, the dogs are kept in trim by a daily walk of two to three hours, with a more strenuous outing of five hours twice a week. On these five-hour trips they cover anything up to 50 kilometres. They are rarely given meat as this makes them sluggish. Their basic diet is mealie-meal mixed with fish-meal, laced with a vitamin oil. On rare occasions they get a little meat soup.

Four types of dog are used. The majority are pure-bred fox-hounds from imported stock. These dogs hunt by smell, and lead the way to pick up the scent. Behind them come the "lurchers", a type of English wolf-hound mastiff cross-breed. They hunt by sight, and once the quarry is spotted they are off hell-for-leather, leaving the other hounds far behind, still sniffing at the trail. Then there are a few pure-bred fox terriers and cross-bred terrier-corgis. These are fearless, aggressive little dogs, and their job is to follow the quarry when he goes to earth.

When the hunt is on the dogs usually set out in the early hours of the morning, round about 2.30 a.m., and they reckon to finish the job by 7 a.m. or 8 a.m. It is hard and dangerous work, for the foothills of the Drakensberg, even in daylight, are difficult and tough country, and at night, of course, doubly so.

Elsewhere the record of these Jackal Hunt Clubs is not impressive. Lawrence Green tells how years ago all the farmers in a jackal-infested area banded together to rid themselves of the pest once and for all. It was planned like a military operation – a commando of 600 men on horseback, with rifles, shot-gun, dynamite and an army of dogs. They were out two days and a night, sleeping in the veld. They returned with a total bag of nine jackals and one farmer wounded in the rear with a charge of buck-shot!

Strangely enough, some old-timers assert that Jackals have only been known in the Drakensberg in comparatively recent times. Mr. Carter Robinson, who spent a life-time in the Drakensberg, never remembers them in his early days, and Hendrik Maartens, founder of the Champagne Castle Hotel, was quite certain that up to 1925 there were no jackals in the Drakensberg.

Although the leopard has almost completely disappeared from these mountain regions, there are still a few wild cats to be found there. It is not likely, however, that you will ever see one, for they hunt at night and lie up during the day. In all my years in the Drakensberg I have only seen one, probably a Serval which strolled past my camp at the foot of the Mnweni Pass, as the dusk was coming on. The Serval, *Felis serval*, is the largest of these cats. This fine animal has a golden-yellow coat with large black spots, converging on the back and forming bars around the chest. One outstanding feature of the Serval is his large, oval ears. He is about 50 centimetres high, and weighs about 15 kg, and is usually to be found in the thick undergrowth bordering streams. He has a high-pitched, ringing call, and it is this call which usually proclaims his presence, as he is only rarely seen. He preys on the larger game birds, small buck and rodents. His Zulu name is *Ndlozi*.

Another of the cat family to be found in the Drakensberg is the Caracal, a beautiful animal, graceful and slender but powerfully built. His long, tufted ears differentiate him from the Serval, with his oval ears, but he is about the same size as the Serval. The colour of his coat is a bright reddish-brown.

The Caracal can be savage and dangerous, especially if cornered. Like the Serval, he preys on smaller buck, game birds, hares and rodents.

Much smaller than the Serval and the Caracal is the Genet. Genets are about the size of our domesticated cat, and there are three species in South Africa. Only one of these, the Large-spotted Genet, *Genetta tigrina*, is found in the Drakensberg. Genets are blood-thirsty, tigerish little animals, with narrow, pointed faces and large conical ears. The body is elongated and lithe, and the tail fairly bushy.

The Genet is a real killer, and will play havoc in your poultry run if ever he gets in, dealing out death on all sides. He is an adept at squeezing through the narrowest hole in your fence. He will kill a fowl and eat only the head and fleshy portion of the breast, leaving the rest. Although he is a fierce little chap, however, he will make an attractive and affectionate pet if captured young, and he is extremely intelligent. The ancient Egyptians are said to have domesticated Genets and used them extensively as household pets.

One of the most delightful creatures of the wild, and a never-ending source of amusement to visitors, is the Vervet monkey, *Cercopithecus aethiops*. Vervet monkeys are well-known in most parts of South Africa where natural bush gives them the shelter they like. They are especially common in the bush around Durban and in Durban Parks. These fascinating little creatures are fairly common throughout the Drakensberg, especially in the Cathkin area, but less so in the Cathedral area. They are usually to be found in troops, ranging from small family parties of six to a dozen up to 40 or 50.

He is a handsome little chap, with his attractive light-grey coat, long, black-tipped tail and puckish black face. He lives usually on fruits, berries and bulbs, but will sometimes take young birds, eggs and insects. His chief enemy is the great Crowned Eagle, of which he lives in mortal dread.

Large troops appear to consist of a number of harems, each under the leadership of its own adult male. Although the members of a troop usually live amicably together, fights occasionally break out between the males, when the leader is often forced out to make way for a younger member of the troop. They are very agile in trees, leaping from branch to branch when pursued, and they are adepts at hiding themselves in the foliage. When danger threatens, the mother will take her baby into her protective arms like any human mother. In fact there is a particularly strong maternal bond between mother and child. Cases have been known where a newly-born baby has died, and the mother has carried the body around for days, crooning and mourning over it, trying to coax it back to life, until natural putrefaction forced her to abandon the body.

They are delightful creatures to watch, and soon lose their fear of man, although they are unpredictable, highly-strung and excitable. An adult male Vervet, in good condition, especially if he is leader of one of the harems, is, indeed, a fine gentleman, strolling about aloofly in quiet dignity, and beautifully groomed, to the ill-concealed admiration of the ladies in the troop! The youngsters, however, are quite different. They are noisy, obstreperous, full of boundless energy and fun, playing tricks on each other, generally enjoying life and making nuisances of themselves, until suddenly *paterfamilias* has had enough, and Junior gets a well-merited clout which sends him squealing to his mother.

Actually, it is quite amazing how many animals do whack their young, often placing them over the parental knee so as to give them "six of the best". The creatures of the wild, in their wisdom, know that an undisciplined community has little chance of survival in the battle of life, and stern discipline is exercised at all times, particularly by parents over their offspring, and by the leader over the troop as a whole. And it's no use Junior moaning that Dad is a "square". Dad knows just how to deal with that one! Our modern parents, in the permissive society of to-day, surely have much to learn from their humbler brethren!

These, then, are some of the creatures of the wild you are likely to encounter in the Drakensberg. Actually we have only been able to touch the fringe of a vast subject. From the tiny little "whirligigs", the black beetles known as *Gyrinidae*, swimming endlessly around on the surface of their rocky pools, to the lordly Lammergeyer, soaring in proud majesty across the faces of the mountain peaks, the lizards, the scorpions, the beetles, the brilliant coloured dragon-flies, the gay butterflies, the trap-door spider, the chameleon, the damsel flies, the creatures of the night – the otters, the porcupines – they are all there, "complete", as the New English Bible puts it, "with all their mighty throng", ready to delight the heart of the naturalist.

And still we have not touched on the birds. There are hundreds of them.

Sometimes the enthusiastic bird-watcher may find the Drakensberg disappointing in this respect, and bird-life may seem less prolific than in the coastal and lowveld areas. This is partly due to the vast scale of the country, where tiny birds often seem lost against the background of the mighty peaks. But they are still to be found, from the great birds of prey circling high in the lonely skies – the lordly Lammergeyer, the Jackal Buzzard with his yelping cry, the Black Eagle, the Martial Eagle, the Lanner Falcon, the kites and the kestrels, to the lesser birds of the streams and the valleys, the Red-winged Starling, the Cape Robin and the Chorister Robin, the weaver birds, the warblers, the Golden Bishop bird, the Cape Rock Thrush, the wood-peckers, the Yellow Fly-catcher, the crows and the ravens, the kingfishers and the sun-birds, and the Hadedah with his lonely cry. It is a subject for a whole book on itself. I hope some day someone more knowledgeable than myself will write it.

In its peacefulness, its calm serenity, and its quiet purposefulness, this world of the beautiful children of the wilds is a world becoming more and more alien to the one that you and I know, the world that man is busy creating with his technological skill – man, with his sky-scrapers, the clanging roar of his factories, and the mad swirl of his traffic. It is a vanishing world, for it is fighting a losing battle, and if we go on as we are doing, it will one day be but a memory. That day, if ever it dawns, will be one of the saddest days in man's long story, for I believe that this vanishing world has something to say to us, without which we shall be forever immeasurably poorer. We live to-day in a mad, sick society, in a world where the erosion of the soil and the pollution of the atmosphere goes on apace, but where these things are of lesser import than the erosion of man's spirit and the pollution of his mind. I believe that if we are ever to regain our sanity, if ever dignity, quietude, and integrity are to return to this earth of ours, we will have to realise once again our kinship, nay, our oneness, with the creatures of the wild. Here where they live is the good red earth; here the winds blow clean and strong from the mountains; here the clouds march endlessly over wind-swept skies, and here life, the true life of nature, goes on its way untroubled. These things spell healing. In the noble words of Wallace Stegner, Professor of English at Stanford University:

"Something will have gone out of us as a people if we ever let the remaining wilderness be destroyed, if we permit the last virgin forests to be turned into comic books and plastic cigarette-cases: if we drive the few remaining members of the wild species into zoos or to extinction; if we pollute the last clean air and dirty the last clean streams and push our paved roads to the last of the silence, so that never again will people be free in their own country from the noise, the exhausts, the stinks of human and automotive waste, and so that never again can we have the chance to see ourselves single, separate, vertical and individual in the world, part of the environment of trees and rocks and soil, brother to the other animals, part of the natural world and competent to belong in it. We simply need that wild country available to us, even if we never do more than drive to its edge and look in, for it can be a means of reassuring ourselves of our sanity, as creatures, as part of the geography of hope . . ."

CHAPTER XVI

"THE GEOGRAPHY OF HOPE" – 2

"I have loved them and suffered with them my whole life. All that is best in me I have given to them, and I mean to stand by them to the last."
—AXEL MUNTHE, IN "THE STORY OF SAN MICHELE,"
SPEAKING OF HIS LOVE FOR ANIMALS.

I think that of all the wild animals of the Drakensberg, the most fascinating is our old friend *Papio ursinus*, the Chacma Baboon. Gregarious, noisy, almost human in his antics, he is a never-failing source of interest to those who visit the Drakensberg.

Baboons usually go about in troops of between twenty and thirty, wandering over a wide area, turning over stones in search of lizards and scorpions, and scampering with amazing agility over the broken ground of the Little Berg. The troop consists of baboons of all ages. When on the move the full-grown males take up positions on the outside and in the rear. When alarmed or disturbed mothers will make off with their babies clinging to the undersides of their fur. Older children will ride like jockeys on the backs of their fathers. While they are feeding a sentry will be posted on a high point, and it is his job to warn the troop of the approach of danger. He is always easy to pick out: his tail is bent in a sort of loop, a sign of alertness.

Baboons have a poor sense of smell, but their eyesight is amazingly acute, the most acute of any South African animal. When he spots you (long before you can see him) he emits the loud, characteristic baboon bark, and the troop is off as hard as it can go. One rather strange fact is that baboons will always run *away* from danger, even though they may be in a hollow and cannot see from where the danger is coming. I have often wondered whether the sentry is able, in his bark, to indicate where the danger lies and which is the safest line of retreat.

The baboon is a powerful creature with a possible life-span of about 45 years. He will eat almost anything – leaves, bulbs, wild fruits, eggs, small mammals, insects, caterpillars, prickly pears, lizards and scorpions. He has learnt how to snip off the tail of the scorpion so as to avoid the burning sting. Like the Vervet monkey, he has two large cheek-pouches into which he will stuff food to be eaten at leisure afterwards.

He is particularly partial to honey, and if you want a good laugh, watch a troop of baboons as they raid a bees' nest. The troop first of all gathers round the hive, but at a safe distance away, jabbering incessantly, and obviously working out the plan of operations. At last a leader is elected. Watched, fascinated, by the others, he summons up his courage, dashes in, puts a paw into the nest, grabs a piece of honey-comb, and then is off on three legs, holding the honey-comb in his fourth paw. But by now the bees are after him, and they seem to know just where his bare spots are. The baboon barks and shrieks and leaps high in the air as the stings ram home, but he clings on to his booty, reaches the safety of a bush, some distance away, squats behind it, and starts to tuck in, his paws and mouth soon a sticky mess. Then a second baboon darts in, and the act is repeated, to the huge delight of the rest of the troop. But by now the bees are alerted to the fact that this is not just a minor raid on the part of one baboon, but a major assault, and they sally out in force to protect their home. Now it is a free-for-all. Everyone dashes in to get his share of the booty, even mothers with babies clinging to their fur. The babies, being largely hairless, suffer badly, and their squeals add to the din. The noise is appalling – shrieks, yells, grunts, barks mingled with the menacing hum of the angry bees, as the nest is rifled and eventually completely broken down.

Baboons are highly socialized, and have a close-knit family life. It is thought by many that

184

they mate for life, and it has often been known for an erring wife to be severely chastised by an enraged husband. It is certain, also, that the baboon family is a very close-knit unit. Baby baboons stay with their parents for many years, and Mama baboon is a good mother. She may often be seen washing her baby in a mountain pool. She definitely disciplines her child. Spankings are common, and some even say that she takes a stick to them! This is in keeping, as we have seen, with so many of these creatures of the wild. When danger threatens, and the young have to be carried to safety, father baboon always grabs for his own child, not just anybody's. When a new baby arrives it is always attended exclusively by its own mother and father. No-one else touches it, except, perhaps, an older brother or sister. The new baby is closely inspected by the rest of the family, with very obvious cries of delight. It is well-known that older baboons will often sacrifice their lives in defence of their young.

Even the birth of Baby Baboon is strangely human-like. When her time comes, the mother seeks out a quiet place under a bush, her privacy respected by the rest of the troop, except for father, who paces agitatedly up and down in the near vicinity, like any human father.

The babies delight in playing games, games like follow-my-leader, creeping up behind and pushing a playmate off a stone into the water, swinging on monkey-ropes. They tease their parents, until sometimes, going a little too far, Junior receives a well-merited cuff from father. They quickly learn to ride on dogs and pigs, and when grown up they certainly show unmistakeable signs of grief and sorrow on the death of a mate or child.

Have you ever seen a baboon skeleton out in the wilds? I haven't, and I doubt whether you have. What happens to dead baboons is a mystery. Do they, perhaps, bury their dead? No-one knows. It is all too reminiscent of the legendary story of the graveyard of the elephants.

Although there is this strong family bond, again, as in any human family, quarrels do break out. And when a baboon family quarrel breaks out, all the world knows about it! The jabbering, squeals, grunts, angry barks and yells have to be heard to be believed. The language they use must be dreadful! I sometimes hear them, up in the sandstone cliffs of *Wostyn* above our home, a kilometre or so away. I was once climbing in the Cathedral area, many years ago, when I heard a tremendous row coming from the cliffs above me. Suddenly two baboons, locked together in a tight ball, came rolling down the slope towards me. They passed only a couple of metres from where I was sitting, viciously biting and tearing great chunks of hair out of each other, completely oblivious of my presence and of the danger of going over a precipice, intent only on settling scores with each other. They bounced and rolled out of sight, still locked together, into the depths below.

Actually, the baboon is a vicious fighter. Old farmers will tell you of terrible fights to the death between dogs and baboons. The baboon has a fearsome weapon, two large, razor-sharp incisor teeth. When the dog attacks, he will fly at the throat of the baboon. But the baboon enfolds the dog in his powerful arms, crushes him, and then starts in with his terrible teeth, ripping and slashing. Then, with his sharp fangs embedded in the dog's flesh, he will thrust the body away, tearing flesh and ripping bones apart, until, with one last convulsive heave, the body is hurled over a precipice.

There are few more destructive animals in the world than a baboon. When they raid a mealie-field, everything goes within half an hour – mealies, pumpkins, melons, the lot, with fences ripped down and fields of wheat and lucerne trampled to give good measure. When a fowl-run is raided, not a fowl is left alive after ten minutes. They will gouge out the eyes of lambs, and tear lambs and kids open to secure the curdled milk in the stomach. Lawrence Green tells of a Nurses' Home in a remote settlement which was raided by baboons. When the nurses returned to their quarters they found the place in a shambles, vases smashed, chairs overturned, and the radio set wrecked. I can testify to the thoroughness of this wrecking procedure, when the cave I was sleeping in was wrecked in October 1947, as I have already told, while I was mapping the summit in the Cathedral area, and I lost most of my food.

They are clever enough to be able to distinguish between a man and a woman. For a woman they have nothing but contempt. Cases have been known of baboons raiding lonely farm houses when the farmer was away, taking over possession of the verandah, and peering through the windows at the farmer's wife. But at the first sight of the farmer returning, they are off. Stranger still, if a man dresses in a woman's clothes in order to approach them, they will spot it immediately, and again are off. But if a woman, dressed in riding breeches, boots and jacket approaches, she will be completely ignored. A small boy will scare them, but not a grown-up woman.

Baboons have two deadly enemies, leopards and pythons. The leopard is stealthy and cunning. He attacks just before sunset, as the baboons are going to their sleeping places. He singles out one lone baboon, and ambushes it. Without a sound, he leaps on his prey, and bites it in one of two places, either in the neck, or in the spine on the small of the back. If he bites in the neck, death follows immediately. If it is the spine, the hind-quarters are paralysed. But in either case, the leopard immediately flees to a place of safety, for he knows that the troop will counter-attack. High on an inaccessible ledge, he looks down, snarling viciously, and below the baboons gather, and jabber, and roar defiance, until darkness sets in, and the baboons retreat, for they fear the dark. Then the leopard descends, and advances silently on his paralysed prey. One terrifying roar, a single leap in the dark, and it is all over. He knows that the baboons will not attack in the night.

But sometimes the baboons manage to reach the leopard on his lofty ledge, and then ensues a terrific battle such as the wild seldom sees. The baboons leap in, fighting with their great incisor teeth, ripping and tearing. The leopard fights back with his claws, front and back, all four of them, trying to rip the belly open. And only red death, on one side or the other, ends the fight.

Do baboons attack human beings? It is often said that no case has ever been known of an unprovoked attack on a human being by a baboon, and I would agree with this, although something very strange happened in Heidelberg Kloof on a Sunday afternoon one day in December 1967. A little two-year old girl wandered away from her parents who were picnicking in the Kloof, and did not return. A massive search was mounted by the police and farmers in the area, without success, but twenty-four hours later her body was found three kilometres away, on top of a small hill, amongst some rocks. She was dead. The police were convinced it was the work of baboons, who were known to be in the area, but there was never any final proof.

Captive baboons, however, the baboons kept as pets, will sometimes go berserk, with alarming results. A grim story is told of a Harrismith farmer who kept a pet baboon. He went for a walk with the animal one day. Suddenly, as they were approaching the edge of a cliff, the baboon flung his arms round the farmer, pinioned him, and started dragging him towards the edge of the cliff. The farmer fought desperately for his life, using his feet, while the baboon fought back, with his teeth. Mercilessly, the farmer was being carried to the edge of the cliff, and his strength was failing, but at the last moment, as he was about to be hurled over, the man managed to get in a smashing blow to the jaw, and the fight was over. Needless to say, the baboon was shot immediately afterwards.

You will sometimes hear climbers in the Drakensberg say that baboons have rolled stones down on them from the cliffs above. I doubt that this has ever been done with any aggressive intent. Baboons have a well-known habit of turning stones over in their search for scorpions, and if this happens at the edge of a precipice, some are sure to roll over. I can confirm this. Some years ago I was climbing the slopes of *Champagne Castle*, heading for Gray's Pass. Just before one enters the Pass proper, one has to skirt the foot of some high cliffs on the left. On top of these cliffs was a troop of baboons, and as I made my way along the base, several stones came rolling down, one narrowly missing me. When I arrived at the top of the Pass, I circled back to the top of the cliffs, and it was quite obvious what had happened. The baboons had been feeding. Stones were overturned, bulbs up-rooted, and the grass trampled.

Have baboons a sense of humour? I am quite sure they have. I once set out alone from Champagne Castle Hotel, before it was light, to climb *Gatberg*. I left so early that I had to forego my usual early morning plunge. But half way up the Little Berg I passed a waterfall with a delightful pool at the bottom. It did not take a moment to strip and plunge in. But I had no towel, and could not dry myself. At that early hour there was sure to be no-one else about, so what simpler? With nothing else on but a pair of stout boots on one end of me, and a battered pith helmet on the other, I strode out along the path carrying my clothes. I admit I must have looked a cross between David Livingstone and a strip-tease artist, but I still wasn't quite prepared for what happened. Rounding the corner of the Sphinx, a huge sandstone block, I was confronted by a troop of baboons on the rocks up on my left. If ever an animal laughed, those baboons did! The row was dreadful. They clung to each other in helpless mirth, and I swear the lady baboons laughed more uproariously than their husbands!

Baboons have one fear above all others. They are terrified of snakes. They will go mad with terror at the mere sight of a snake. Even a dead snake will provoke paroxysms of fear. When he raises a stone in search of scorpions, the wise baboon always stands behind the stone, reaches forward, and then lifts the stone towards him. He then peers over the top of the stone. If there is a snake there, he promptly drops the stone and clears off with a piercing scream. So great is their horror of snakes, that if a comrade is caught in the coils of a python, they will make little attempt to rescue him, whereas if it is a leopard, they will leap in and fight to the death.

Actually, it is doubtful whether the python, *Python sebae*, exists any longer in the Drakensberg, though he used to be common. Mr. Carter Robinson remembers them. Johannes Lombard shot a large one round about 1925 just above his homestead on the farm *Solar Cliffs*, three or four kilometres above the junction of the Umlambonja and the Mhlwazini Rivers. Another one was killed at Buys' Cave, in the Cathkin area. Though non-poisonous, the python could be a nasty brute, and there are several records of men having been killed by them. The python kills, not by crushing his victim's bones, as many think, but by suffocation. Every time the victim exhales, the snake wraps his coils tighter and tighter, until breathing is impossible.

But the Drakensberg is still the home of many other snakes, both poisonous and non-poisonous. The attitude of most people to snakes is the same as that of the baboon, unreasoning horror and terror, but actually the snake is a most interesting and highly-developed creature. Our terror of snakes is quite unnecessary. There are some 140 species of snakes in South Africa, and only 27 are poisonous. And remember that snakes are far more frightened of you than you are of them. They will move out of your way if they possibly can. Even if one is bitten, the chances that death will result are very remote, because the majority of snakes are non-poisonous, and in the case of the poisonous snakes, modern snake-bite serum is so very effective. At most, not more than 20 people in South Africa die each year from snakebite, and in most years the figure is considerably lower than this. Most fatalities occur amongst Africans in the outlying areas, who rely on African remedies, and who, possibly, cannot reach medical help in time.

There are more old-wives' tales told about snakes than about any other wild creature. The puff-adder cannot strike backwards, as is commonly believed; the young of the puff-adder do not eat their way out of their mother's body; the mamba will not pursue you, especially at the speed of a galloping horse, though he may be aggressive if he is cornered; there is no snake that crows like a fowl; and they do not suck milk from the teats of a cow. A snake has no sucking powers, and the fangs are so placed to make this impossible. And whatever you do, don't believe the story that young children can safely play with snakes and come to no harm. Children have no more immunity from attack than have you or I.

Few people have any knowledge of the physiology of a snake. The snake has no external cars or ear-drums, and cannot hear in the usual sense of the word. When the snake-charmer plays his snake-music on his flute, the snake cannot hear a thing. It is the rhythmic *swaying* of the snake-charmer, and not his music, that fascinates the snake. But he does have a rudimentary type of inner ear, which picks up ground vibrations, and transmits them to the brain by way of the auditory nerve. That is why you so seldom see snakes when you are out walking on the veld or on the mountain slopes. The snake has "heard" you by means of ground vibrations, long before you reached him, and has slithered out of your way. If you are out walking in long, thick grass, take a heavy stick with you. Thump the ground ahead as you proceed and you are practically 100% safe.

Snakes also have very poor eyesight, especially for distant vision. Some can only distinguish between light and darkness. One interesting point is that, like the equipment of the modern photographer, the eyes of many snakes are equipped with yellow-tinted lenses. This filters out excess ultra-violet light rays, and so assists vision. What snakes do detect is movement. If the prey they are hunting remains stock-still for some time, the snake will invariably move off in search of something else. If you are ever confronted by an erect cobra with expanded hood (it is, admittedly, a fearsome sight!), keep your nerve. Don't panic. Don't run. Stay completely still, and the snake will leave you alone.

For any living creature to survive, it must be able to "communicate" with the outside world. You and I do this by means of our five senses – hearing, sight, touch, smell and taste. The bat does it by means of his built-in "radar". How does the snake communicate, if he cannot see properly, hear properly, or smell? He does it by means of his tongue, but not in the way of taste. The snake's tongue has no taste-buds. But it is, nonetheless, a marvel of ingenuity. When the snake protrudes his long, forked tongue, the two small tips pick up tiny, air-borne particles of whatever the snake is investigating. The tongue is then drawn in, and the tips are inserted into two small cavities, known as Jacobson's Organ, situated in the front part of the roof of the mouth. The adhering particles are then brought into contact with nerve cells in the cavities, the message is carried to the brain by nerve cells, and there analysed. In this way the snake investigates his environment. Disturb a snake, and watch how he flicks out his tongue. He is investigating where, and what, the danger is. It is even said that an egg-eating snake will be able to tell in this way whether the egg is fresh or not, or whether the embryo is too far developed for his liking.

Most snakes feed on frogs, toads, lizards, birds and their eggs, and on a number of the smaller insects and mammals, such as snails, slugs, grasshoppers, rats and mice. Some snakes are cannibals, and will eat other snakes. Many a youthful herpetologist has collected a boxfull of snakes, only to find next morning that one or two are missing, although the breathing holes he had drilled in the lid of the box were far too small to allow of a snake crawling through. When I was a very small boy, a mischievous uncle used to tell me the story of two snakes left hanging on a clothes line. Each snake seized the tail of the other, and started swallowing, until each snake had eaten the other and there was nothing left! I used to puzzle my little head for long hours, trying to work out just what had happened to the two snakes!

Snakes will often swallow rats, mice or frogs much larger in circumference than themselves. This is only achieved through muscles, ligaments and skin being able to be stretched to an amazing degree. Even the bones in the head are movable, and the jaws can be stretched in any direction. One very necessary adaptation which is needed to make this possible is the structure of the windpipe. Swallowing could cause suffocation through pressure on the windpipe. But the position of the snake's windpipe can not only be shifted, but it is reinforced with a series of annular rings of cartilage, to prevent its collapse by pressure of the prey. After such a gargantuan meal the snake becomes completely torpid, and it takes him several days to sleep it off.

Broadly speaking, snakes may be divided into two main types, front-fanged and back-fanged. Amongst front-fanged Drakensberg snakes we have the rinkals and the adders, while the skaapsteker is a typical back-fanged snake. There are no true cobras in the Drakensberg. The rinkals, *Hemachatus haemachatus*, which is also called the Ring-necked cobra, or the South African Spitting cobra, is not a true cobra, though it does have a hood which it expands. True cobras (the *Naja* species) have smooth scales, while the rinkals has keeled dorsal scales. Two other differences between the two species are the absence of solid teeth on the maxilla in the case of the rinkals, and the fact that it is ovoviviparous, i.e. it gives birth to live young, while the cobras are oviparous, i.e. egg-laying. The rinkals is found throughout the Drakensberg, up to an altitude of 2 750 metres. The Cape cobra, *Naja nivea*, is never found on the Natal side of the Drakensberg, while the Black-necked Spitting cobra, *Naja nigricollis*, is found only in the lowermost foothills, and never at any great altitude.

The rinkals is, perhaps, better known by its Zulu name, *Mfezi*. He is a little smaller than the true cobra – 120 cm to the cobra's 200 cm and over. When approached suddenly in the open he will rear up and face his enemy, with his hood expanded. You will notice that he has white cross-bands on his throat. But he is only really aggressive if he is disturbed in the mating season. He seldom actually bites with deliberation, and after taking stock of the intruder he will glide away into the grass, head still erect and swaying from side to side.

He does, however, have the ability to eject his poison for a considerable distance, for anything up to two and a quarter metres. This is his first line of defence. The venom is practically colourless, and of the consistency of glycerine, and he will always aim for the eyes. It comes out first as a single stream, and then this breaks up into a fine spray. When his escape is cut off he will sham death with remarkable efficiency. His whole body becomes limp, he will turn on his back, and his jaws will gape open. Like the puff-adder, the young are brought forth alive, anything from 15 to 60 in number. They are marked like adults, can rear up and expand their hoods, and can bite from birth.

Just why does the rinkals spread his hood in this strange way? Several reasons have been suggested. It obviously has very strong survival values. The erect position of the snake, especially in long grass, gives it a point of vantage from which to view its enemy. The expanded hood is certainly a protection to the vulnerable neck. The neck is much broader, and thickened, making it more difficult for a small carnivore to obtain a grip with its teeth. A bite merely on the edge of the hood would not be disabling. Whatever the purpose, the sight of a rinkals with hood expanded and sharp, menacing eyes, sailing through the long grass, is certainly a terrifying one, and likely to deter the most vicious enemy.

One of the commonest snakes in the Drakensberg is the Berg adder, *Bitis atropus atropus*. It is a small snake, with an average size of only 40 cm, though I once came across a huge brute on the slopes of the *Injasuti Buttress*, at least 70 cm long. It is uniformly dark grey in colour, with a double series of black sub-circular markings down the length of the body. He is often to be found lying in the footpath you are following, at dusk, as you head for home after a long hike. Like most adders they are sluggish, but react violently if annoyed. Unlike other adders, however, their venom is more neurotoxic, with a lesser proportion of haematoxic elements. Although this is a small snake, its venom is very potent, and it must always be treated with respect.

I think that possibly the most dangerous snake one is likely to meet is the puff-adder, *Bitis arietans*. As we have said, most snakes are sensitive to ground vibrations, and will get out of your way long before you are upon them, but for some reason this does not seem to apply to the puff-adder, and it is all too easy to tramp on him. He is short and thick and sluggish (I recently put my hand on one in the darkness of my lighting-plant engine-room, and he hardly moved). But tramp on him, and he will strike like lightning. He is often found curled up on the side of a path, or underneath old rubbish. He can reach a length of about 100 cm, but specimens up to 160 cm have been recorded. On the forest slopes of *Mt. Kenya* is a giant type of puff-adder, up to 185 cm in length, and weighing well over 10 kg, a truly fearsome brute.

There are more fallacies about puff-adders than about any other snake. We have already mentioned some of them. Another fallacy is that in the face of danger the mother will temporarily swallow her young. This is quite impossible. Apart from anything else, a snake's gastric juices are so strong that a baby snake could hardly survive a single minute in its mother's stomach. This fallacy was first recorded by Holinshed in his famous *Chronicles*, in the 16th Century, and has persisted ever since.

Front-fanged snakes are more dangerous than back-fanged snakes. This is because the fangs are longer and penetrate deeper into the wound, and because the back-fanged snake finds it difficult to get its fangs into a flat surface.

Snake venoms are of two types, the Neurotoxins and the Haematoxins, the former belonging to the cobra family and the latter to the adders.

Neurotoxins are nerve poisons. They act mainly on the nervous system, and produce paralysis of heart and lung muscles, the respiratory system being the first to suffer. Immediately after a bite, a strong, burning pain is felt round the area of the bite, and there is a limited degree of swelling and numbness. Paralysis of tongue and larynx then follows, accompanied by dryness of the throat. The victim finds progressive difficulty in speaking, eyesight becomes blurred, and there is a loss of balance. Heart-beats increase at first, but these slow down in the final stages, and violent seizures indicate the approach of the end.

Haematoxins are blood poisons. They act principally on the blood system, sometimes as a blood-clotting agent, producing thrombosis, and sometimes as an anti-coagulant. This causes a breakdown in the cell structure, and profuse bleeding. In the case of the adder, blood-clotting appears to be the principal action, whereas anti-coagulant symptoms appear in the venom of the boomslang.

In the case of a puff-adder bite, there is, first of all, the usual intense burning pain, followed by inflammation and swelling of the limb, which becomes extremely painful. Many of the subsequent symptoms are the same as in the case of the neurotoxins – blurred vision, loss of balance, nausea, and difficulty in speaking, due largely to the drying up of mouth and throat, Final symptoms are excessive bleeding, blood oozing from mouth, stomach, bowels and bladder, followed by a short period of unconsciousness, and finally death from respiration and cardiac failure.

People often ask how long it takes to die from the bite of a snake. It is impossible to answer this question with any degree of certitude. It depends on so many factors – age, type and size of snake, locality of the bite, and the degree of immunity of the victim. Obviously a bite into a vein would result in more rapid death than a bite elsewhere. Here the ankle is particularly vulnerable, because of the mass of veins located there, and the main artery. There have been several recorded instances of people dying within a few minutes from a mamba bite in the neck. A few months ago a snake-handler at a Johannesburg snake park died within five minutes of being bitten by a puff-adder, in spite of immediate treatment, but here the cause of death could not have been the poison. Puff-adder venom could never act as rapidly as this. The woman probably died from some form of shock. Cases of such rapid death are rare. Anything between one and six hours would be a safe answer. Generally speaking, haematoxins act more slowly than neurotoxins, but recovery is much slower, and after-effects are much more serious, permanent damage often being inflicted on some organs.

What should one do if one is bitten by a snake? The treatment of snake-bite, especially first-aid treatment, has undergone considerable modifications in recent years, and to-day it is a case more of what one must *not* do rather than what one *should* do. In the first place, don't panic, and don't run. This simply speeds up your heart action, quickens the circulation, and increases the rate at which the body absorbs the poison. Remember, you have plenty of time! Don't take brandy, or any alcoholic drink, as this may speed up the absorption of the poison. Don't *under any circumstances*, cut the flesh around the bite, or in any way interfere with the bite punctures. Not only will it not help, but it will make the wound and the pain very much worse. Unless it is a known cobra bite, don't use a tourniquet. In the case of a cobra bite it may be of some help to put on a *tight* tourniquet, provided it can be done within five minutes of the bite. About one metre of 5 cm wide rubber strip is the best sort of tourniquet, but in an emergency a handkerchief, twisted tight with a stick, will do. The tourniquet can be released ten minutes after giving antiserum. If no serum is available the tourniquet *must* be released after 40 minutes, to prevent gangrene setting in. Tourniqueting, however, is painful and of debatable value.

What, then, should one do, if one is out with someone who gets bitten? First, calm the patient and give him confidence. Remember, there is never any cause for desperate panic. His chances of dying are remote, and he must be told this. Incidentally, remember to kill the snake if you can, and bring it in for identification. The treatment your patient will receive is partly conditioned by the type of venom that has been injected by the snake. Then, of course, get him in to a doctor or a hospital as quickly as possible. You have at least an hour for this, and probably much longer. Keep the limb cool, in ice if you can, for this slows down circulation. If the pain is intense, a pain-killing drug such as codeine can be useful. If the bite was from a cobra, artificial respiration may be necessary if signs of asphyxia set in.

If one is going right into the heart of the Drakensberg, more than, say, two hours from medical help, one should carry a hypodermic syringe and a supply of polyvalent anti-snakebite serum, as supplied by the South African Institute of Medical Research in Johannesburg. But make sure you know how to use it. Half an hour spent with a medical friend, plus a little practice in the use of the hypodermic, might well save a life. Remember that four ampoules of serum, each of 10 cc, should usually be given. Remember, also, that if your patient is a child, the dose must be *increased*, rather than lessened. This is because in a child the ratio between venom injected and body mass is greater than in the case of an adult.

One should also carry injectable antihistamine and synthetic cortisone. With a poisonous bite by an unknown snake, and with the bites of puff-adders and cobras, first inject antihistamine and cortisone, and then 40 ml of antivenom in divided doses into large muscles. (Intravenous injections are more effective, but must be given *very slowly*.) Berg adder, night-adder and boomslang victims (the boomslang does not occur in the Drakensberg) should be given only antihistamine and cortisone, and then transferred to a hospital. The usual antiserum available to the public is ineffective against these bites, but the medical officer can get the correct serum from the S.A. Institute of Medical Research in Johannesburg. Incidentally, the patient should *always* be taken to a hospital, even though you think the snake was non-venomous. (Two puncture wounds usually indicate a poisonous snake. If there are four or more from a single bite you can be fairly sure the snake was non-venomous.)

Remember that the "golden rule" is to know what to do, but to do *nothing* unless the patient shows actual symptoms of poisoning, or unless you have positively identified the snake as poisonous.

The cobra and the rinkals which are spitting snakes, will sometimes eject poison into the eyes. This can cause permanent blindness and even death. Here the easiest remedy is simply to wash the eyes out with cold water, and then with antiserum diluted with ten parts of water. If water is not available, use any non-irritating liquid, such as milk, cold tea, or even urine – a well-tried African remedy.

Incidentally, when you kill a snake, first break its back, and then go for the head. Once its back is broken, it cannot strike at you. In the case of a large snake, such as a mamba (not found in the Drakensberg) or a large puff-adder, it is safer to use a shot-gun. And finally, remember that by law all cases of snake-bite whether fatal or not, must be reported to a magistrate.

In all my experience I have heard of only one death from snake-bite in the Drakensberg. On Sunday morning, April 10th, 1955, three men set out to climb *Champagne Castle*. They were Ian Muller, a brilliant Natal University student, 22 years of age; Peter Newman, who was on the architectural staff of the University; and his brother-in-law, John Burrows, also a student, and son of Professor H. R. Burrows of the University. That evening, in heavy mist, at an altitude of 2 400 m, they camped down for the night. Ian went to a small waterfall nearby to fetch water, and as he was filling his billy-can, he was bitten in the wrist by what was probably a rinkals. He was immediately put to bed, with warm sleeping bags around him (by then it was bitterly cold, and rain had set in) and given an injection of anti-snakebite serum. As the night wore on, however, his condition grew steadily worse. By midnight he could only talk with difficulty. His two companions managed to find some wood and lit a small fire, but the dank mist pressed heavily in around them, and Ian's breathing became difficult. In the early hours of the morning he asked for artificial respiration, and this was applied by Peter Newman.

As the dawn broke it was raining heavily, and Ian's condition was deteriorating rapidly. It was decided that John Burrows should go for help, and he set off immediately at 6.30 a.m., heading for Champagne Castle Hotel, 16 km away. With Ian sinking fast, Peter Newman continued applying artificial respiration, but to no avail. At 8 a.m. he sank into a deep coma, and died shortly afterwards.

In the meantime John Burrows was speeding down the mountain side. At 11 a.m. he reached the Hotel, and raised the alarm. Three rescue parties immediately set out for the peak, one of them from the Durban Ramblers Club which was holidaying in the area. They were led by John Burrows, and the first party reached Peter Newman at 5 p.m. on the Monday, but by then, of course, Ian was already dead. At 3 a.m. on the Tuesday morning the first news reached the Hotel of the tragedy. Peter Newman and John Burrows, exhausted after their long ordeal, reached the Hotel at lunch time on the Tuesday. They were both given sleeping draughts and put to bed. Late that afternoon Ian's body was brought in to the Hotel.

This death from snake-bite is disturbing. Why did Ian Muller die, after being given all the orthodox treatment, including an injection of anti-snakebite serum? Dr. Sherman Ripley, son of "Doc" Ripley and an experienced climber, has made a special study of the treatment of snake bite. I put the question to him, and this is what he says:

"In the absence of specific knowledge of the species of snake which bit Ian, and the lack of detailed post-mortem findings, it is impossible to state with any exactness why he died. From a knowledge of his past medical history and the imperfections of the anti-venom which was available at the time, the possibility of fatal anaphyllactic shock cannot be ruled out. The modern anti-sera are much improved, and are treated chemically so as to greatly reduce the possibility of their causing any adverse shock reaction. However, even with these modern improvements, one should never resort to the use of anti-serum unless one is *certain* that the person has actually been poisoned."

Snakes have many enemies, in addition to man. Large birds of prey, such as the Martial Eagle, and of course the Secretary Bird, find snakes a juicy morsel. I once watched a large eagle with a snake in its talons. I was high on a mountain peak at the time, close on 3 000 metres. The eagle was flying round in great circles above me. Every now and then it would release the snake, swoop down and under it, catching it as it fell, and then soaring up again. Eventually it flew off, with the snake still firmly clutched and writhing in its talons.

The Secretary Bird, *Sagittarius serpentarius*, is an expert snake-catcher. When the Secretary Bird spots his prey, he first of all performs a sinister ballet dance around his victim, just why, no-one seems to know. Then, in a flash, the bird leaps in, and the snake has little chance. With wings outstretched, he uses two powerful weapons with deadly effect, striking swift blows with his feet and ripping the snake to pieces with his beak. He seems to know the difference, too, between poisonous and non-poisonous snakes. If the snake is poisonous, he uses his wings as a shield, and goes warily about his business. If it is non-poisonous he simply holds the snake down with his claws and climbs right in.

Perhaps the snake's most vicious enemy, however, is the mongoose. There are three species of mongoose in the Drakensberg, the Cape Grey Mongoose, *Herpestes pulverulentus;* the

White-tailed Mongoose, *Ichneumia albicauda*; and the Water Mongoose, *Atilax paludinosus*. And of a certainty this little chap must surely pack as large a chunk of sheer, naked courage in his little body as any other creature of the wild. He is a restless, alert little chap, full of grace and cunning, with a perky little tail always carried aloft like a triumphant banner, and his attacks on snakes are legendary. He usually selects cobras, mambas or non-venomous snakes, leaving the adders severely alone. This is because the mongoose is able to build up a certain immunity against cobra venom, but not against adder venom. When the cobra is devoured, its venom enters the blood-stream and gradually produces immunity. The venom of the adder, however, is destroyed by the mongoose's digestive system, and produces no immunity. The mongoose is clever enough to know this. He is not however completely immune. Mr. R. M. Isemonger, an authority on South African snakes, describes an experiment in which a Cape Mongoose was injected with 20 mg of Cape cobra venom, a hundred times the dose required to kill a guinea-pig of comparable size. The mongoose took 18 hours to die.

When he attacks, the mongoose makes a series of feints from all directions, causing the snake to strike out over and over again. When the snake is tired, and its strength exhausted, the little mongoose leaps in like lightning, seizes the snake behind the head, and sinks his teeth into the soft neck, killing it instantly.

But it is time to say farewell to all these fascinating dwellers in the wilds – yes, fascinating, and always lovely in their innocence, even the rapacious baboon, the slavering jackal, and the snake whose bite means death, for are they not all part of Nature's complex pattern, and do they not all possess that mystic gift of life. I think Albert Schweitzer, with his philosophy of "Reverence for Life" has reached further into the heart of things than many of us. All life, to him, was to be reverenced and jealously guarded. Schweitzer could never bring himself to kill any living creature, no matter how repellent it was. As he strolled in the grounds of his hospital at Lambarene he would even go out of his way to avoid treading on the humble ant, for to him all life, no matter how humble, was the gift of God. To Tennyson Nature was "red in tooth and claw"; to Schweitzer it was sometimes a puzzle, often incomprehensible, but always altogether lovely, and he loved the little scurrying creatures of the forest this side idolatry. "Up to now," he once said, "we have only included man in our ethics. We must extend them to include the animals who are our kith and kin – our little brothers and sisters."

CHAPTER XVII

LAMMERGEYER

He clasps the crag with crooked hands
Close to the sun in lonely lands,
He watches from his mountain walls,
And, like a thunderbolt, he falls.
— TENNYSON: THE EAGLE

Our photographing of the African Lammergeyer, the first pictures ever to be taken of this mighty bird, was an event which caused considerable interest amongst ornithologists, while Press reports spoke of it as a "once in a lifetime story". It all started away back in December 1958.

Godfrey Symons, Don Morrison and I had set out on a ten-day trip into the Mnweni area. Godfrey Symons we have already met in the pages of this book. I have often climbed with him: no-one could have had a finer climbing companion. Don, slighter in build, was the English Master on my Staff at the Estcourt High School, and what a climber! Never have I seen a man with a cooler nerve, a steadier eye, a surer sense of judgment than Don Morrison. On a sheer rock face he was magnificent, and always a joy to watch. And what a tremendous mass of energy he packed into that lithe young body of his! I have seen him, at the end of a long day's climb, when the rest of us were stretched out exhausted, high on a mountain crag, filling his lungs with the thin air of the heights, and letting it out in sheer exuberance of spirits, one long joyous call after another flung out to the echoing crags. I remember one evening, when we had only just made our cave in time, with black, menacing thunder-clouds rolling up over the peaks, and Don, 20 metres above us, roaring defiance at the approaching storm. For many years he was a member of the Natal Mountain Club Rescue Team, and more than one man probably owes his life to him. I would have trusted him with my own anywhere.

We had climbed up the lovely Mnweni Valley, through a land of flowers, ascended the Mnweni Pass, and were spending a few days in Mponjwana Cave, under the shadow of mighty *Mponjwana Peak*. One golden afternoon we were lying on a sun-warmed slab of rock, with the peaks all about us. Over all was a great stillness. Suddenly a shadow fell over us, and looking up we saw a huge bird with out-stretched pinions, gliding with smooth precision, in ever tightening circles, in the clear mountain air, its plumage a brilliant gold in the afternoon sun. "Lammergeyer!" breathed Godfrey, and fascinated, we watched it as it circled lower and lower over us, until we could see its bristly beard and its red, staring eyes. We vowed, then and there, to be the first to photograph this beautiful, mighty bird.

For never before had the African species, *Gypaëtus barbatus meridionalis*, been photographed, although the European species, *Gypaëtus barbatus aureus*, had fallen to the lenses of two photographers, Eric Hosking, the world-famous bird photographer, in southern Spain in 1959, and Bengt Berg in the Himalayas in 1942.

It is a mighty bird, with a wing-span of two and a half to three metres, and is easily recognised in flight by its tapering wings and its wedge- or diamond-shaped tail, which is unusually long. The white head, which shows up plainly as the bird glides along the ridges of the Drakensberg, is another characteristic. The wings and tail are slate-black with white shaft-streaks, the underparts are slightly off-white, while the throat and neck are a rich orange colour. The ruff and the neck, when raised and reflected in the sunlight, look almost like a golden mane, a magnificent sight. The feet are an ashy colour, legs well-feathered; the beak is black, with a black patch extending around the eyes, and a black bunch of bristles protruding from the base of the beak. This gives the bird its common name of Bearded Vulture. Very noticeable are the red, staring eyes, which give the bird such a ferocious appearance. We subsequently discovered, however, that this colour varied. The red glare only appeared when the bird was alarmed or disturbed. Normally they were almost devoid of any colour.

The Lammergeyer chooses a pothole, or shallow cave, high up on a cliff face, where it constructs a large nest some one and a half to two metres in diameter. It is lined with sheep's wool, goat's hair, and even old sacking and grass ropes picked up near some Basutho kraal.

Often two nests, close together, are used in alternate years by the same pair, and these appear to be occupied for long periods of time. Some authorities believe that as one bird dies the other seeks out a new mate, and so the occupancy of the same nest continues.

In flight it is a truly magnificent bird, and it has been known to range over hundreds of kilometres in its search for food. Meinertzhagen, writing in 1930, said "Few birds surpass the Lammergeyer in powers of flight, and their great prowess as soarers is probably unrivalled. The bird has been observed floating over *Mount Everest*, the greatest recorded height for any bird."

The diet of the Lammergeyer is mainly carrion. In fact the bird is a link between the true eagle and the vulture, having the feeding habits of the vulture and the graceful flight of an eagle. (The beak, also, is that of an eagle, while the flat feet are more like those of a vulture.) Farmers have often maintained that the Lammergeyer takes lambs, and this is one reason for the rarity of the bird, for farmers have tried to exterminate it. They are, however, quite wrong. From 1959 to date we have made a very careful study of the bird, and never once have we seen it bring in a fresh "kill". It was always some portion of the body of a sheep or an antelope, which the vultures had finished with. Once one of us saw a Lammergeyer with a dassie in its talons, but we believe this to be an exception. Roberts describes the food as "carrion and dassies".

The egg of the Lammergeyer has only once been taken in South Africa, by Graham Hutchinson, at Bushman's Nek, in August 1883. It is now in the Bell-Marley Collection in the Transvaal Museum. Another egg was taken by permit for the Coryndon Museum in Nairobi by Mr. Miles North, several years ago, at *Mt. Kenya*. As far as we know these are the only two specimens to have been taken in Africa.

To-day the bird is on the brink of extinction. At one time it could be found in a broad belt in Europe, stretching from the Pyrenees, the Alps, Sardinia, Austria, Turkey and on into the Himalayas and the mountains of China. To-day it is only found rarely in the Pyrenees, Corsica, Sardinia, the Balkans, the Middle East, Arabia and the Himalayas. It disappeared from Bavaria in 1855, and from the Swiss Alps in 1886, the last bird being shot in Graubunden. In the Carpathians the last birds were killed by poisoned bait in 1935. In Africa the African species, *Gypaëtus barbatus meridionalis*, was once known in the Atlas mountains, Abyssinia, the mountains of Central Africa, and in South Africa all the way from the Drakensberg to the Cape Peninsula. To-day in South Africa there are only a few pairs left, probably not more than twenty-five, in the Drakensberg, Lesotho, and the Barkly East area. There is one nesting pair at Golden Gate in the Free State. In the rest of Africa it occurs sparingly in the Kenya Highlands, *Mt. Kenya*, Abyssinia and the Atlas Mountains.

Some ornithologists describe the Lammergeyer as a fierce and very rapacious bird. It certainly looks it. Bury says: "The Lammergeyer has a very nasty habit of attacking animals in difficulties on a precipice, or even man." Dresser gives a circumstantial account of a small child being carried off by a Lammergeyer, and Wolf's famous picture depicts a Lammergeyer attacking a chamois with young. General Sir Ian Hamilton records how he was attacked by a Lammergeyer when crossing a moving scree, and Sir Alfred Pearse also records being attacked while in difficulties on a slope in Baluchistan. From our own experience we entirely disagree with these records. We would say that the Lammergeyer is a shy and retiring bird, and we have certainly never found any evidence of its attacking human beings. Subsequent to our first sighting of the bird in 1958, we visited, and climbed down to, several nests. Not once were we attacked.

For many months after that memorable afternoon we hunted the bird with our cameras. We were joined by Bill Barnes, the genial Warden of the Giant's Castle Game Reserve, a keen ornithologist, mountain climber and wild-life photographer. We explored the whole mountain range, from *Giant's Castle* to *Mont-aux-Sources*, camping out in all weathers. We penetrated westwards, down into the valleys of Lesotho, watching the skies with our binoculars. Equipped with compass and map, we worked our way into the remoter fastnesses of the Drakensberg, and when a speck appeared in the sky, we followed it in our glasses until we could be sure that it was only a vulture, and not a Lammergeyer. Only very rarely did we strike gold. When we did, we tried to locate the nest. Actually we managed to find two or three nests, but in each case photography was impossible, for they were located high up on impossible precipices, and when Bill or Don descended from the top by rope, their presence so disturbed the bird, that it had already flown off before they reached the nest. We began to despair.

And then one day early in 1961 we had our break. Bill remembered seeing in the faded pages of a Game-Ranger's Logbook a reference to a Lammergeyer's nest in the Mokhotlong area of Lesotho. Although the reference was nearly sixty years old, Bill and Godfrey both reckoned that there was at least a sporting chance of the nest still being there, for, as we have said, it is a known fact that the bird nests in the same place for many years. We decided to go in and look for it.

Mokhotlong, recognised at the time as one of the remotest outposts in the British Commonwealth, is a tiny mountain village in the heart of Lesotho. At one time it was almost entirely cut off from the outside world, and the only means of access to it was by mountain pony and pack-horse over the Sani Pass, a three-day journey. Then came an enterprising mountain-transport company, which blazed a trail for four-wheel drive vehicles over the Pass, and later an airstrip was laid down. When we visited it in 1961 it was still a very isolated little spot.

We decided to go in via the Sani Pass, by Land Rover, but to hike back over the Lesotho mountains, down the Drakensberg, and so back into Natal. Sunday morning, July 2nd, 1961 saw us all assembled at the Mokhotlong Mountain Transport Company base, just outside Himeville. We were equipped with two Terylene-blue light patrol tents, double sleeping-bags, warm, wind-proof clothing, climbing gear, and a whole battery of cameras, lenses and film. There was a nip in the early morning air, and the mountains shone clear and blue in the distance.

The Sani Pass is a spectacular piece of mountain engineering. It climbs the majestic wall of the Drakensberg from 1 350 metres to the lofty Lesotho plateau, 2 875 metres in a little over 8 km. So steep and sharp were the hair-pin bends that at several places the Land Rover had to reverse before it could negotiate them. Old-timers in the bar at the Himeville Hotel will tell you with a twinkle in their eyes, that in the early days, before the track was improved, even the horses had to bend themselves to get round! At one more than ordinarily sharp corner our Basutho driver, Benjamin, remarked that it was called "Gray's Corner". When we asked him why, he replied, "I guess, Sir, it is because you can only get round by the grace of God!"

It certainly was a bracing and exhilarating climb. With gears screaming, the Land Rover battled its way upwards. At some places two of us had to get out and travel on the bonnet to give added weight to the front wheels. Far below, down in the valley, we could see the wrecks of vehicles that had not been able to make it. The air became noticeably thinner and more bracing, and behind us the vast panorama of the plains of Natal opened out in a vista of limitless hills and valleys.

At last we levelled out at the top. A brief rest to stretch our cramped limbs and to admire the view, and then off we set again, bucketing over a wide-stretching plain, and then climbing up to the summit of the Black Mountains, 3 350 metres high. Here we again called a halt to admire the magnificent view – range upon range of majestic mountains and wine-dark valleys, over which marched long cohorts of cumulus cloud, white and glistening. We could just see *Thabana Ntlenyana*, 3 482 metres, the highest point in Southern Africa. The sun shone crisply, and it was bitterly cold. Snow lay on the sides of the mountains. Then on again, down the spectacular Masenkeng Pass into the valley of the Sehonghong River, "the river which twists and turns".

Basutho riders in their bright, colourful blankets came riding past, mounted on their sturdy mountain ponies. We also began to pass trains of pack-mules on their long journey from the highlands of Lesotho down into the plains of Natal, carrying their bales of wool which they would barter for wheat and grain for the return journey. After a quick picnic lunch beside a mountain stream, where rainbow trout swam lazily in the dark pool at our feet, we skirted the gorges of the Orange River on our left, and at 4.30 p.m., tired and smothered in dust, we entered Mokhotlong under a red sunset.

We drove first of all to the residence of Mr. Douglas Stenton, the District Commissioner, where we reported our arrival and were introduced to his charming wife and little boy. Though we had never met before, and were complete strangers to him, no-one could have given us a warmer or more kindly welcome. After inviting us to hot baths and dinner that evening, Mr. Stenton took us over to the Government Rest House, which was to be our base during the next few days while we were searching for the Lammergeyer's nest. There followed a delightful evening with the Stentons, during which Mr. Stenton, an enthusiastic radio ham, called up Dennis Milligan in Estcourt, a mutal friend and also a radio ham, and we were able to keep in touch with our families.

Next morning we all gathered in the District Commissioner's office, and Mr. Stenton listened to a brief account of why we had come to Mokhotlong.

"Well," he said at length, "it's going to be like looking for a needle in a haystack, you know. The Mokhotlong area covers more than 2 000 square miles, and the nest could be any-where. Still, we'll see what we can do."

He called for his orderly, and asked him to send for four of his senior police officers, who knew every corner of their two thousand-square-mile territory.

"Mohlala," said the D.C. to the first man, "I want you to tell these gentlemen if you know of any place where the great birds which you call *Ntsu* fly around."

No, he did not know, nor did the next two, and our hearts sank. But the fourth man, his face lighting up, said, "Yes, Morena, I know of such a place".

"Are you sure?" asked the D.C. "How do you know this is the great bird these gentlemen want, and not just a vulture, a *Lenong*?"

"Morena," replied the man, "we always call this great bird the *Ntsu*, and these birds, they drop the bones of animals from a great height, and break them on the rocks, and then eat the marrow."

At these words a gleam of excitement flashed into Godfrey's eyes, and Bill suddenly stared at the man, for here was the old legend of the Lammergeyer, half as old as time, but never scientifically established.

"Are you sure of this?" asked Godfrey.

"I am sure, Morena," replied the man.

"And where do these birds build their nests?"

"Morena, they build their nests high in the face of a cliff."

"And of what do they make them?" asked Bill.

"Wool, Morena," replied the man, "and sticks and pieces of hide, but chiefly wool."

"This is it, chaps," said Bill excitedly, and then, turning to the police officer, "and can you take us to this place?"

"I can, Morena," the policeman said.

"Come on," said the D.C., almost as excited as we were, "into the Land Rover with all your kit. We'll leave right now."

We piled in with all our gear, and with Douglas Stenton at the wheel and the police officer behind, we set off with a roar, down into the valley of the river, across its clear waters, and up the other side, heading roughly in the direction of the Orange River. It was a wild and lovely country through which we travelled, a country of lofty hills, steep inclines and dark-shaded valleys. It did not take us long to reach the spot as indicated by the police officer, a few kilometres above the junction of the Orange and the Mokhotlong. Anxiously we scanned the cliffs, but to the practised eyes of Godfrey and Bill there wasn't the vestige of a sign of a Lammergeyer's nest. However, three quarters of a kilometre away were some even larger cliffs, and leaving the Land Rover behind, we headed for these on foot.

Ten minutes later Godfrey suddenly stopped dead in his tracks. "What's that?" he said, pointing to the cliff face half a kilometre away, "a little bit off to the right!" "That" was a small cavity in the rock face, 90 metres from the top and about the same distance from the bottom, and in the cavity was an orange dot. Thirty seconds later and the binoculars confirmed the fact that the orange dot was indeed a Lammergeyer, and that our search was almost certainly at an end.

Arrived at the foot of the precipice, we made a swift reconnaissance of the cliff face with our glasses. Roughly level with the nest and about 25 metres away was a narrow, steeply-sloping grass ledge. Between the nest and the ledge was a deep gash in the cliff face, and the nest faced directly on to the ledge, across this gap. With growing excitement we realised that if only we could reach this ledge we could aim our cameras directly on to the nest, across the gap, and so obtain the pictures that we wanted. We decided to try and climb the 90 metres of rock face which lay below the ledge, and the job of route-finding was over to Bill and Don, the two rock experts.

Equipped with pitons, snap-links and 60 metres of nylon rope, the two men set off, while Douglas Stenton, Godfrey and I watched from down below. At first they made good progress, but half way up the attempt nearly ended in disaster on the slippery rocks of a half-dried waterfall, and the men had to return.

We next considered the feasibility of climbing to the top of the precipice via a steep grass slope at the back, and then climbing *down* to the ledge. A wide detour and a stiff scramble brought us out on to a projecting spur of the cliff, from which both the nest and the grass ledge could be seen, 120 metres away, and 90 metres below us. Here we took our first pictures of the orange-breasted bird with the 400 mm lens.

But the range was too great for good photography. It was essential to reach that grass ledge if our efforts were to be crowned with success. We examined the rock face again with our binoculars, and soon Don announced that a 70 metre abseil down the cliff face was feasible at a point midway between our projecting spur and the nest. From the foot of the abseil a steep slope led down to the grass ledge which would present no real difficulty.

Bill and Don immediately set about the preliminaries. Pitons were driven into cracks in the rock above the abseil point, snap-links attached, the rope threaded through and firmly secured. Don went over first, watched with awe by a couple of Basutho herd boys far below, and he was followed by Bill.

Soon they were sitting on the ledge, in a concealed recess, out of sight of the bird, but peering round the corner they could see the hole in the rock face and the great bird sitting on the nest. They watched, fascinated. Few people in the world, if any, had ever been as close to the bird as this. They could clearly see the bristly beard under the beak, and the great red staring eyes which gave the bird such a fearsome appearance. When she flew off the nest as she did when she was disturbed they could see a single egg lying on the sticks and wool. It was about twice the size of a hen's egg, and was creamy white in colour, with patches of light purplish-grey and brownish-yellow. The binoculars revealed fine, dark-brown dots here and there.

The ledge on which they were sitting was less than a metre wide, and below was a sheer drop of 90 metres, but the men were soon hard at work with their cameras, getting a second batch of priceless pictures.

The return of the two men presented no small problem, for they had insufficient rope to rope down the 90 metres to the foot of the cliff. They decided to try and climb the vertical cliff face between the abseil point and the nest, where the rock was a little more broken. Godfrey and I anchored ourselves firmly to the rock face at the top of the proposed climb, from where we let the rope down and belayed Don. He made it, and then he brought Bill up. Bill is a man of few but expressive words. As he flopped down beside us and wiped his brow, he said, "Hell, never again!"

So ended the first day, with success beyond our wildest dreams. But this was only the beginning. The light had been bad, time had been short, and we felt that we could do better. We decided that on the following day all four of us would attempt a descent to the ledge via the broken rock face which Bill and Don had ascended, and spend the day there, using our cameras at our leisure.

Neither Godfrey nor I had had very much experience on the rope, but we were quite willing to give it a bang. Once again the pitons were driven in and the snap-links attached. This time we brought up a reserve supply of rope. Godfrey went first, belayed by Don, his descent punctuated by some of the most lurid language I am sure those ancient crags had ever heard! Then I roped up and went over. I cannot say I enjoyed it, but at the bottom Godfrey was waiting for me. As I unroped he thrust a bottle of brandy into my hands, and said laconically, "Thought you'd need it, old man." But I noticed that the bottle was already two thirds empty, and that his hands still shook! Then came Bill, and finally Don, cool and steady as always, belayed by the three of us already down below, with the double rope running freely through a snap-link at the top of the climb.

We were soon hard at work. We had with us four cameras, two 400 mm telephoto lenses, one 240 mm lens, one 135 mm lens, a battery-operated solenoid device for controlling the shutter of a camera at a distance, a good supply of both black and white and colour film, and, of course, our lunch packs.

It was not easy. There was only room for one man at a time on the ledge, and the position was cramped. Our hands were freezing. One camera jammed and two rolls of film snapped, possibly due to the extreme cold. Every time we left the recess and turned the corner to get a better shot, the bird would fly off the nest. Then at last our luck turned. The late afternoon sun came out strongly. Not only did this give us better light, but the rays of the level sun, shining directly into the eyes of the bird, seemed to blind it to our presence, and she did not fly off when we turned the corner. Tense with excitement, we spoke in whispers, the only other sound being the sigh of the wind and the steady clicking of our cameras.

Then came the climb back. By this time the weather had again deteriorated. Sleet came drifting down the valleys, and a covering of snow began to appear on the higher peaks. It was bitterly cold, and each man carried a heavy pack. In order to get the rest of the team up with the maximum of safety, Don went up first, belayed by the men below. I went up next belayed by Don, followed by Godfrey and Bill. It proved to be one of the stiffest climbs I had ever made. Whipped by driving rain, in a freezing gale, I nearly petered out. Half way up I found myself under an overhang, with my fingers frozen and empty space below. I called up to Don that I didn't think I could make it. His voice came floating down from far above: "*Climb*, you beggar, *climb*!" But the word wasn't beggar! That did it. "What right has he to talk to his Headmaster like that," I thought savagely, and eventually I made it. When Godfrey reached the final slab, his shins raw and his hands bleeding, he hung there and gasped out "Rope climbing! Not on your ruddy life!"

But at the top to welcome us were our good friends Mr. and Mrs. Stenton, with the Land Rover, a thermos of hot tea, and, wonder of wonders, a magnificent steaming ham-and-egg pie! They had watched the weather worsening, and, like the good friends that they were, had hurried out to our rescue. It was then that Godfrey, waving a huge piece of pie in one hand, insisted on knighting the D.C. and his wife – "Lord and Lady Lammergeyer Stenton"! Then, with the sleet hammering on the windows and a rising gale outside, we relaxed, warm and safe in the shelter of the Land Rover, content with the knowledge of a dream fulfilled.

That night, sitting round our camp fire after the rain had passed, we took stock of our results. We had succeeded far beyond anything we had ever dared to hope for, but the job was still not complete. A properly-constructed hide on the grass-ledge would simplify enormously the job of photographing the bird, and though the two 400 mm lenses had done us well, we wanted to return with a 600 mm lens. We also wanted to get pictures of the chick when the egg hatched. It was also necessary to work out a better method of climbing down to, and back from, the nest. The rope climb was far too dangerous and time-consuming for regular use. With all these ideas in our minds we snuggled down into our sleeping bags, while the light of our camp fire slowly flickered out.

Next day we set out on our return. In many ways our journey home across one of the most mountainous regions in the world was perhaps the highlight of the whole trip. Our route lay up the valley of the Mokhotlong River, which twisted and turned through the mountain mazes. It was a country of lofty peaks and clear mountain streams. Douglas Stenton had very kindly provided us with a pack-horse and driver, but even so our packs were heavy, for in addition to all our photographic and climbing equipment, we had to carry extra warm clothing, the two terylene tents, and of course all our food for four days, and our bedding.

We did not hurry unduly. There were frequent halts to consult map and compass, for we were in unknown country, and many a stop for morning and afternoon tea brewed by the wayside.

It was four o'clock on the evening of the first day before we arrived at the junction of the Mokhotlong and the Sanqebethu Rivers, where we proposed to camp for the night. The temperature was well below freezing by the time darkness fell, and we were glad to snuggle down into our warm sleeping-bags.

Next day we left the Mokhotlong River, and turned left up the Sanqebethu. Our route lay through pleasant valleys and steep gorges, climbing higher and higher. At first we found the valleys fairly well populated, and we passed a number of Basutho kraals, perched on the valley sides. Whenever to-day I see the blue-grey smoke, and smell the tang, of a cattle-dung fire, it brings back to me those four care-free days and the lonely Basutho kraals.

On the second night we camped, in bitter weather, on the banks of the Sanqebethu, at a temperature far below freezing point. That night our medical supplies, packed in a ruck-sack and kept inside our tent all night, froze solid, and next morning our eggs were also frozen as hard as a rock. We had to break through the ice of the frozen Sanqebethu to get our water.

And now the country became bleaker and more mountainous as we approached the 3 000 metre level. Kraals were few and far between, until at last there were none, and we were alone in the silence of the great peaks.

At length, at midday of the fourth day, we came out at the head of the Langalibalele Pass, with all Natal below us, and our journey was nearly over. To right and left stretched the massive ramparts of the Drakensberg Mountains, blue, remote, cloud-hung, with the *Injasuti* on our left and *Giant's Castle*, towering up into the clouds, on our right. 1 800 metres below, just beyond the foot of the Pass, gleamed the white walls of Bill's house. With the mists gathering behind us, we

Head of the Lammergeyer, showing the red staring eyes and the bristly beard.

The Lammergeyer chick, about three weeks old.

A juvenile Lammergeyer, two to three years old. The prevailing colour is brown. It is not until full maturity that the rich golden colour appears.

The bird alighting on the nest.

The African Lammergeyer.

5.

1.

6.

1. *Protea multibracteata.*

2. *Protea subvestita (cream).*

3. *Kniphofia brevifolia.*

4. *Schizostylis coccinea.*

5. *Cyrtanthus contractus.*

6. *Brunsvigia radulosa.*

7. *Cyrtanthus breviflorus.*

8. *Greyia sutherlandii.*

2.

7.

3.

4.

8.

made a quick descent of the Pass, and by 5 p.m. we were sitting round a cheery log fire in Bill's lounge, with generous supplies of beer beside us.

We now lost no time in preparing for our new arrangements. The problem of transport was happily solved through the generous offer of Eddie and George Brokensha, two Estcourt business men, to fly us and our new equipment in in their light Cessna plane. A portable hide was made out of hessian, the Natal Parks Board generously came to our assistance with the loan of a 600 mm lens, and most important of all, Bill and his Game Rangers made a light 60 metre chain ladder for the descent of the cliff face.

A week later all was ready. Owing to the weight of the chain ladder it was possible to take only two passengers in the plane, and the choice naturally fell on the two rock climbers, Bill and Don. They took off from the Estcourt aerodrome at first light on July 16. Half an hour later they were soaring over the mighty ramparts of the Drakensberg, and by 8 a.m. they were having breakfast with Mr. and Mrs. Stenton. The gear was all stowed in the Land Rover, taken out to the site, and by late afternoon the chain ladder was in position, the hide erected, and the men back in Mokhotlong. Before they left for home, arrangements were made for Mr. and Mrs. Stenton to keep a watch on the nest for the hatching of the egg.

On August 14th Mrs. Stenton reported to us by radio that the egg had hatched the previous day, and a month later arrangements were made for a final visit to the site, for it was time to photograph the fledgling. On September 17 Godfrey Symons, his wife Norah, and Bill flew in with Eddie Brokensha, and secured a final set of photographs with the 600 mm lens. Amongst them was one of the chick, the second in the world ever to be taken of a Lammergeyer fledgling. (Mr. Bengt Berg had photographed the chick of *Gypaëtus barbatus aureus* in the Himalayas in 1942.)

And it was on this trip that Bill and Godfrey were able to establish the truth of the old legend of the Lammergeyer dropping bones on to a rock slab, a legend which has come down to us from ancient Greek times, but which has often been scoffed at by ornithologists. Pliny was the first to describe it, and it was Pliny who accused the Lammergeyer of having caused the death of the poet Aeschylus by dropping a tortoise on the bald head of that unfortunate gentleman! It is mentioned twice in the Bible (Lev. xi. 13 and Deut. xiv. 12) where the name *ossifrage* is used, a word which means bone-breaker. But Meinertzhagen states: "I have lived with Lammergeyers in the Himalayas, and at Quetta, for years, and have seen them in Crete, the Pyrenees, on *Mt. Kenya*, and in Arabia, but have not yet witnessed this bone-dropping. It is certainly not a regular habit."

Bill and Godfrey actually watched it happening. The bird would come swooping in, like a great bomber, a piece of bone in its claws. When it reached the rock (it always used the same one) it would release the bone which would splinter on the rocks below. Then the bird would swoop in and collect the fragments, always hotly pursued, though at a safe distance, by the ever-present crows.

This rounded off, and completed, our enterprise. But now, before the final curtain rang down, disaster nearly struck. They were late in leaving Mokhotlong. For the last time the gum trees, the tin roofs and the dusty roads of the little outpost appeared below the wingtips of the plane as they took off from the airstrip. The sky was already darkening, and the tiny plane, a speck in the sky, flew on into the gathering dusk.

Bill has often told me what happened. "We flew straight into the Bafali valley," he said. "After a few minutes it became obvious to all that the little plane was labouring under the heavy load. Godfrey's large bulk occupied the front seat with Eddie Brokensha, the pilot, while Norah and I sat behind, smothered in a conglomeration of photographic equipment. The pilot was hugging the cliffs in the hope of making use of any air currents there might be. Around the corner the valley broadened slightly, and Eddie did a tight circle in an effort to gain more height, as the ground ahead was rising steeply. South Africa's second highest mountain, the snow-capped *Makheke*, was just to our right, and the high Injasuti ridge, over which we had to fly, came up rapidly into stark relief.

"Moments later the circling act was repeated. And now the slopes of Injasuti, sinister and bleak, were right below us. I remember looking at the tufts of grass which had made crab-like holes in the snow-drifts as they waved around in the wind. We could almost touch them with our hands. Then we were over, with only feet to spare.

"Any hope of relaxing there might have been, however, was soon dispelled when we saw what lay before us – solid white cloud as far as the eye could see. Undaunted we flew on, as the 5 p.m. weather report from Estcourt, given us by radio ham Dennis Milligan, had been favourable. The minutes fled by, but no break in the sea of cloud could be detected. Around us the dark immensity of night was closing in rapidly. To add to our troubles, the fuel gauge became a matter for concern: 45 minutes flying time left. Durban might have been a possibility, but it was probably shrouded in cloud. An overshoot would mean a watery grave. Bloemfontein, across mountainous country, was just beyond reach. Mokhotlong, from where we had taken off, was the only possible landing strip, ringed by mountains, with no lights, a difficult enough landing strip in daylight, but at night a death-trap. We were all conscious of a vague sense of uneasiness, and the tension was mounting. I was even too frightened to smoke, let alone utter a word.

"Suddenly Eddie broke the silence. 'One more minute, and we must return to Mokhotlong,' he said. Looking back, all we could see were the tips of *Giant's Castle*, *Cleft Peak* and *Mont-aux-Sources*. Below us the same white sea of cloud.

"Suddenly, far below, a single hole appeared, and three distant pin-points of light. Without a moment's hesitation Eddie put the nose of the plane down. Down, down into the blackness we went, the lights getting brighter and brighter. Then, at last, away to our right we spied the glow of a town – Ladysmith, perhaps? But no – the familiar lights of Estcourt. A perfect landing brought us safely back to earth, and to the end of the trip, thanks to the cool courage, the perfect judgment, and the expert handling of the plane by a great pilot. A post-mortem revealed that only six short sentences had been spoken in the plane from take-off to breaking through the cloud."

There is not much more to be said. If it did nothing else, our series of pictures did at least something to draw the interest of the people of Natal and of South Africa to this beautiful bird, and to start a movement for its greater protection. The Pan African Ornithological Conference, held in Pietermaritzburg towards the end of 1961, made special reference to the Lammergeyer, and to the fact that it would become extinct in South Africa, like the dodo, unless special steps were taken to protect it. Godfrey Symons was accorded the honour of addressing the Conference. In 1962 the Transvaal Provincial Administration proclaimed the Lammergeyer a protected bird, a step which had already been taken by Natal. In 1964 the Natal Branch of the Wild Life Protection and Conservation Society of South Africa brought out a well-produced pamphlet, illustrated with our photographs, and designed mainly for distribution amongst the farming community of Natal. This pamphlet made a strong plea for a greater understanding of the bird, and for greater efforts to be made in its protection. It pointed out that its slow rate of reproduction (only one egg each year), and the fact that many farmers were trying to poison the bird, in the mistaken belief that it preyed on their lambs, was resulting in the gradual extinction of the bird. It suggested that if traps were set, or poison laid, for jackals, such carcasses should be covered from view, and that the traps and poison-bait be removed before daylight, as the Lammergeyer, due to its lack of a sense of smell, was very easily trapped or poisoned.

Finally, in September 1967 the Gilbert Handley Memorial Hide was opened on the slopes of *Giant's Castle*, in an effort to create an even greater interest in the bird, and to ensure that it could obtain adequate supplies of food. This was a joint effort by the Natal Parks Board and the Wild Life Protection and Conservation Society of South Africa.

202

These efforts are now being rewarded with success, and Bill Barnes, Regional Warden of the Drakensberg, is of the opinion that the number of Lammergeyers in the Drakensberg is slowly increasing. Even so, it is going to be a long hard battle, and the bird is still on the danger list.

And so, with this mighty bird photographed at last, we leave the Lammergeyer, Lord of the African Skies, to his mountain home and to the freedom of the great peaks and the lonely skies. Long may he survive!

CHAPTER XVIII

THE WILD ONES

Prim little scholars are the flowers of her garden,
Trained to stand in rows, and asking if they please.
I might love them well, but for loving more the wild ones –
O my wild ones – they tell me more than these.

— GEORGE MEREDITH

When Dr. Otto du Plessis, Administrator of the Cape, opened the Caledon Wild Flower Show in September 1958, he said that the Caledon district had more wild flowers to the square mile than any other spot on earth. In the opinion of Professor H. B. Rycroft, Director of Kirstenbosch, South Africa as a whole has possibly the richest flora of any country in the world.

The Republic certainly is unique for the richness and variety of its wild flowers. England possesses about 1 500 flower species. South Africa has no fewer than 16 000. Of course, pride of place must go to the Cape. Ever since those early days when storm-tossed sailors put ashore under the grey crags of *Table Mountain*, and took back with them seeds and bulbs of the strange new flowers they found there, the Cape has been world-famous for the range and the beauty of its wild flowers.

But I believe the Drakensberg comes a close second. Certainly this is so if you consider the number and variety of the flowers to be found here. There are, roughly, about 200 known natural plant orders in the world. About 150 occur in South Africa, and 120 of these are to be found in the Drakensberg. Dr. D. J. B. Killick, in 1950 and 1951, made a detailed study of just one small area of the Drakensberg, the Cathedral Peak area, and found no less than 1 000 species there, 30 of which were new to science. Unfortunately, botanically speaking, the Drakensberg as a whole is still largely unknown, and very little has been written about its floral wealth. Apart from Dr. Killick's *Account of the Plant Ecology of the Cathedral Peak Area*, and W. R. Trauseld's *Wild Flowers of the Drakensberg*, there are only a few monographs in scientific Journals, such as J. W. Bews' *Plant Ecology of the Drakensberg Range* (1917); E. E. Galpin's *Contribution to the Knowledge of the Flora of the Drakensberg* (1909); and E. A. Schelpe's *Plant Ecology of the Cathedral Peak Area* (1946). The rest is silence. The first complete and definitive study of the flora of the whole Drakensberg Range has still to be made.

It will be a rewarding task for someone. There must be few areas in the world which offer a wider range of flowering plants, from lowly ground Orchids to the prehistoric Cycad, from the tiny *Scillas* to the proud and stately *Kniphofias*, from the drought-resistant succulents such as *Kalanchoe thyrsiflora* to bog and water-loving plants such as *Aponogeton junceus*. Habitats range from the warm, sun-lit valleys of the Little Berg to the cold summit areas at over 3 000 metres, where snow can lie for months on end; from hot, north-facing slopes, where the soil rapidly dries out, to the cooler, moister south-facing slopes, where you find the rich, deep *podocarpus* forests; while rainfall can vary between 850 mm per annum and 2 025 mm and over.

Admittedly you will not find here, except in rare instances, those great splashes of colour that make the mountains of the Cape, or the great plains of Namaqualand, blaze so magnificently. The poet* who wrote:

The army of the flowers
In beautiful battalions! Lo, I saw
Their ranks of coloured uniforms appear
And march in splendour down the singing hills

* Charles Hanson Towne.

was not thinking of the Natal Drakensberg! Here in the Drakensberg you will have to search diligently for these lovely gems, and at certain seasons of the year, as in winter, there will be little to delight the eye. But in spring the slopes of the Little Berg and their sun-filled valleys can be a joy beyond telling. Here you will find the soft foam of the *Buddleias*, the clear azure of the *Scillas*, and the scarlet flame of the Bottle-brushes, with their brilliant, water-green leaves. And in the wet grass beside a mountain stream you will find the dainty blue *Lobelia*, and the pure white of the *Schizochilus*. In summer the summit is a riot of colour, rich yellow *Moraeas*, rose-red *Dieramas*, scarlet *Nerines*, and the Red-hot Pokers standing proudly on the edges of their rock-girt pools. In autumn you have the deep yellow of the *Athanasias*, and the even brighter yellow of the Canary Creeper, festooning the trees of the forests.

Never are they lovelier than in their natural setting. To experience the real beauty of these wild flowers one should see them, not in a formal garden, but on their mountain slopes, opening their dew-drenched petals to the sun beside a tumbling stream, gracing a moss-covered rock in the rich gloom of the forest, dotting the green hillsides of the Little Berg after a night of rain, or clinging to the grey summit rocks of some mountain peak. To come suddenly on a patch of dwarf *Dieramas* shining in the wind at the head of a mountain pass, after a stiff climb, or a group of sky-blue *Scillas* and snowy *Anemones* in a hollow of the hills, is to know a joy that makes the heart ache with its loveliness.

And it is not difficult to get to know their names. Of the many delights of wandering in the Drakensberg, I would place the recognition of the wild flowers as amongst the most rewarding. Very little botanical knowledge, if any, is required, and it is surprising how quickly you will learn the names of the flowers, and with what joy you will greet their discovery.

The *Scillas* you will easily recognise. *Scilla natalensis*, the commonest of them, blooms round about October. It is a flower rather like a hyacinth, pale blue in colour, about 35 cm high, with a large bulb, half of which protrudes out of the ground. It is usually found growing on the steep sides of small gullies and ravines. The flower-head consists of a spike of small, misty-blue flowers, with the youngest at the top of the spike. It has two Zulu names, *Ubulika* and *Inguduza*. The Zulus use the plant for a variety of medicinal purposes. The leaves of the plant, when dry, are ground up and mixed with pumice stone. This is given to a child who is late in learning to walk. The bulbs, which are large, are sometimes mixed with food, and this acts as an aperient. In addition to their purgative properties, they are used in the treatment of cattle for lung sickness, and the women-folk even cut them up and use them as soap in the washing of clothes. The well-known expectorant, Syrup of Squills, is made from a species of *Scilla*. In addition to *Scilla natalensis* there are several dwarf varieties, one of them, *Scilla krausii*, being a particularly dainty little flower, with the petals a darker blue and only about six cm high.

Flowering at the same time, and often associated together, is a creamy-white flower with a yellow centre, known as *Anemone fanninii*. It is larger than *Scilla natalensis*, growing to a height of 60 to 70 cm. The flowers are about eight centimetres in diameter. It was named after Mr. George Fox Fannin, of the Dargle, one of Natal's earliest plant collectors. The Zulus make an infusion from the roots, which is black in colour, and this is used as a purgative, and also as a cure for gall-sickness. Their name for it is *uManzamnyama*, which means black water.

Another flower which is quite easy to recognise is the *Dierama*. Dierama flowers are bell-shaped and are borne on slender, arching, grass-like stems, with a series of drooping spikes near the tip, each bearing several pendulous flowers. These range in colour from pure white, through mauves and pinks, to purple, magenta and crimson. Most Dieramas are tall plants, growing in grasslands, usually singly, to a height of 100 cm. They have a number of common names, amongst them Wand Flower, Fairy Bell, Grassy Bell, Grasklokkie, Wedding Bell and Flowering Grass. For many years they have been popular in the gardens of Europe. On one occasion South Africa sent seed over to Ireland as a gift. It was planted in County Down, where, if you remember, "the Mountains of Mourne sweep down to the sea", and here the plants flourished. Dieramas like a rich, moist soil, and apparently they found just what they wanted in the soils of Ireland. Spikes of up to 280 cm have been measured there.

*Dierama robustum** is one of the commonest and tallest of the Drakensberg Dieramas. Much more interesting, however, and very beautiful, is *Dierama igneum*. This is a dwarf variety, only about 20 cm high, and it usually grows on the summit, at an altitude of 3 000 metres. There are two colour varieties, a rose-red and a deep purplish-magenta. It grows in colonies, and I have often seen the hillsides on the summit covered in a rich carpet of crimson and purple. Why this species should be so different to the other Dieramas is something of a puzzle to botanists. At the high altitudes at which this flower grows there is an increase in the intensity of ultra-violet light, and it is believed that these rays inactivate the growth-promoting hormones, resulting in dwarf characteristics. The same phenomenon has been observed in several other Drakensberg flowers.

One of the most beautiful of the spring flowers is the *Watsonia*, very similar in appearance to the *Gladiolus*. Here in the Drakensberg we have two species, *Watsonia densiflora* and *Watsonia meriana*, and they are very easily distinguished. *Watsonia densiflora* is magenta in colour, and you will find it growing singly in the lower grasslands, usually in the month of October. It appears to be more common in the northerly parts, around the Royal Natal National Park. As one proceeds south it becomes more scarce, and only isolated specimens are to be found in the Giant's Castle area. The flower consists of a very distinctive spike of bright magenta flowers, as many as 22 to a spike, and all opening at the same time. The Zulu name for this flower is *uTshumo*, and the flower stem is used by the Zulus to *tshuma* with when smoking *insangu*, or dagga. *Tshuma* means literally to spit through a reed. Amongst the Zulus dagga is smoked through an *igudu*, or smoking horn, while the men are sitting round in a circle on the floor of a hut. The horn is passed round from one to another, each man taking a deep draw and filling his mouth with smoke. He then blows spittle through the stem of a *Watsonia*, on to the floor of the hut, the spittle forming patterns of tiny bubbles full of smoke. The game is to see who can form the most intricate patterns.

Watsonia meriana is a particularly beautiful flower – deep orange in colour, and growing at a somewhat higher altitude to *Watsonia densiflora*. Again in contrast to the latter species, it does not grow singly, but in colonies, and always amongst stones and rocks. I have never seen it growing in open grasslands. On the stony hillsides of the Little Berg it makes a brave show in early spring, with its bright orange flowers against the grey of the rocks. I believe that in Australia it has been declared a noxious weed.

I think that of all the wild flowers in the Drakensberg the easiest for the beginner to start off with is the Protea, for they are easily recognized and easily identified. Drakensberg Proteas are of the summer rainfall type, and we have five species to consider.

The one that is most easily identified is *Protea roupelliae*. This is a fairly large tree, up to four metres in height. The leaves are covered with a woolly down, which gives the young leaves their typical silvery sheen. Take a close look at the flowers, which are usually a bright red. They are saucer-shaped, and about 10 cm in diameter. Round the rim are what appear to be petals, but these are not petals. They are called bracts. The centre of the flower is made up of a mass of closely-packed tiny flowers, each with a stamen protruding from its centre. Notice that the bracts are spoon-shaped, and that the stamens are shorter than the bracts. It is these two features which distinguish *Protea roupelliae* from the other Drakensberg Proteas, together with the fact that the tree itself is of a particularly graceful shape. This Protea was named after Mrs. Arabella Roupell, a lady of the Cape, who published a beautifully illustrated book on South African wild flowers early in the 19th century.

*There is a doubt regarding the specific names of the various Dierama species. Dr. K. D. Gordon-Gray points out that the genus is badly in need of revision and that "any specific names that are applied at present are open to question".

206

The only other tree-type Protea in the Drakensberg is *Protea multibracteata*, and you can easily distinguish it from *Protea roupelliae*. To begin with, it is not a graceful tree. The branches are gnarled and twisted and black, and the tree is often of an irregular shape. The flowers, too, are different. They are still saucer-shaped, but the bracts are oval, and the stamens are now much longer than the bracts. This gives the flower its typical "spiky" appearance. There are two colour varieties, a cream and a rose-red. *Protea multibracteata* was once classified as *Protea caffra*, a Transvaal Protea, the flower which was used for the design of our old "tickey" coins, minted round about 1931. It was only recently discovered that what was thought to be *Protea caffra* was in reality *Protea multibracteata*. *Protea caffra* does not occur in the Drakensberg.

Our third Protea is *Protea subvestita*, which means "partly clothed", a reference to the woolly covering of the leaves. This Protea is smaller than the other two, seldom growing to a greater height than two metres. The trees are more closely packed together than the two other species we have discussed, and while *Protea roupelliae* and *Protea multibracteata* are rounded in shape, *Protea subvestita* is more slender. The flowers also differ, those of *Protea subvestita* being campanulate, or bell-shaped, with the bracts curling outwards. There are two colour varieties, a rose-pink and a cream. And finally, this Protea grows at a higher level to the other two, seldom occurring below 1 850 metres.

The two remaining species are very different from the first three we have considered, for they are dwarf bush types, only about 30 cm high. *Protea dracomontana* is a particularly lovely flower, usually deep salmon in colour, with saucer-shaped flowers, and it grows at a higher level than any of the others we have discussed, usually at about the 2 100 metre mark.

Protea simplex is easily distinguished from *Protea dracomontana*, for the flowers are usually a pale yellow, and are very similar to *Protea multibracteata*. Its range and habitat is also very similar to the latter Protea, and there is obviously a close relationship between the two species. The stems of *Protea simplex* are unbranched (that is what *simplex* means), while the stems of *Protea dracomontana* are branched.

Pollination of our Drakensberg Proteas is usually by birds, and one of the sights you will never forget is that of a Malachite Sunbird, with its flashing wings, visiting one of these lovely flowers. But pollination is also brought about by a metallic blue beetle, *Melyris natalensis*, and you will often find the flower-heads, especially of *Protea multibracteata*, infested with this little chap.

In the Franschhoek Valley of the Cape the men have a delightful custom. Whenever they see a *Serrurier florida* they doff their caps to it, for *Serrurier florida* is one of the rarest of the Cape Proteas. And can we not too pay a similar tribute to our Drakensberg Proteas, as they stand, peaceful and proud, on their mountain slopes!

You will easily be able to recognise the Bottle-brush, of course, with its scarlet flowers and bright green leaves. It flowers in early spring. Like the Proteas, this handsome bush, growing sometimes to the size of a small tree, is found on the slopes of the Little Berg, usually at the foot of steep krantzes. Its botanical name is *Greyia sutherlandii*. It was named after Dr. P. C. Sutherland, a man who played a prominent part in the development of the infant Colony of Natal. He was born at Lateron, Caithness, in 1822. As a boy he accompanied his parents to Nova Scotia, and while there witnessed the arrival of the *Royal William*, the first steamship to cross the Atlantic. This event must have fired the youngster's imagination, because for the rest of his life he had a deep love of the sea, and an insatiable curiosity in all matters scientific. Back at Caithness, he graduated in medicine at the Royal College of Surgeons in Edinburgh, spent a vacation in West Africa, and then visited Greenland in 1845, while still only 23 years old. Here he joined an expedition to try and find Sir John Franklin, who was missing in the Arctic; had an island named after him (he has been called the Sir Vivian Fuchs of early Victorian times); and then in 1853 he decided to emigrate to Natal. He was one of the first medical men to come out to this country. From this point his career reads almost like a fairy tale. Three years after his arrival, in 1856, he became Surveyor-General, a position he held until 1887. In 1857 he undertook charge of the whole public works of the Colony. He became Chairman of the Harbour Board, was appointed Government Geologist (he discovered the renowned Dwyka series, one of the oldest rocks in South Africa); in addition to all this, he became a botanist of repute, and was one of the founders of the Pietermaritzburg Botanical Society, having several plants named after him. Cecil Rhodes, as a young man of 16, was placed in his charge. He must have known the Drakensberg well, for both his geological and his botanical work must often have brought him into this mountain region. *Greyia sutherlandii*, with its whitish-grey wood, its bright green leaves and even brighter red flowers, is a worthy memorial to this most unusual man.

Burchellia bubalina, named after another fascinating character, the traveller W. J. Burchell, is also worth noting. This is a small tree with glossy green leaves, and you will find it growing on the forest edges along the banks of streams. It has red or orange trumpet-shaped flowers, growing in clusters, and you cannot mistake it. It is a great favourite with the birds, and the Zulu name for it is *uTshwala bezinyoni obukhulu*, and it means "beer for the birds – the large one". According to the Zulus, if you make a cold water infusion from the pounded roots, it will cure you of all your bad dreams!

There is another shrub in the Drakensberg which also has the Zulu name *uTshwala bezinyoni*, but with the additive "*obuncane*", "the small one," this time. This is the well-known *Leonotis*, a flower you cannot miss in the autumn time, round about Easter. The stems are long and tough, growing to a height of 1½ metres, and the flowers, which are a rich orange in colour, are produced in dense rosettes at intervals on the stem. It grows at the lower levels, in the valleys of the Little Berg, and is sometimes called the Wild Dagga. This is because its dried leaves are smoked by the Zulus, and are shaped rather like the leaves of the true Dagga, *Cannabis sativa*. It is, however, entirely unrelated to *Cannabis sativa*, nor has it any narcotic properties. It does, however, have many medicinal uses. It appears to possess purgative properties, and is also used as a cure for skin diseases. It is reported to enter into the composition of a patent medicine sold in England. The Zulus use it as a remedy for colds, and also as a reputed cure for snake-bite. The whole plant, except the roots, is used in a decoction as a tonic for calves. The plant is boiled in water until the decoction is the colour of brown sherry, and the dose is half a litre twice or three times a week.

There is one other small tree, growing in the bush, which we might notice. This is the Christmas Bush, *Pavetta cooperi*. Its heavily-scented, snow-white blooms appear about Christmas time, hence its common name, and the long, delicate white styles make identification easy. The Zulus use it in a strange way. They call it the *Isanyana*, and when any members of a kraal have a grudge against men of another kraal, they make an infusion from the roots of the tree. This is then used to "phalaza"* with before a beer drink, and this, it is believed, will cause the death of the children of those they hate!

When spring comes to the valleys of the Little Berg you will find the hillsides a rich treasure-store of flowers. Here you will find the Ox-eye Daisy, *Callilepis laureola*. The flowers are of the daisy type, the petals creamy-white, with black centres. They are about six centimetres in diameter, and the stems run to a height of 30 centimetres. They are, indeed, a lovely sight, nodding in the breeze and spangling the young green grass of early spring with white. They are especially prolific in the Cathedral area. *Laureola* means a small laurel crown or garland, while *calli* is the Greek word for beautiful. The genus consists of three species, all indigenous to the

* To 'phalaza' is one of the oldest customs of the Zulus. Certain herbs, or the bark of trees, or sometimes roots, are pounded and then mixed with hot or cold water. To 'phalaza' the Zulu first drinks a quantity of this liquid. He then takes up a kneeling position and tickles his throat to cause vomiting. This is supposed to cleanse the stomach and, as we have just seen, it has many other magical effects.

Transvaal. Only one is found in Natal, *C. laureola*. The Zulu name is *Ihlamvu*, possibly also *Impila*, which means "good health". An infusion is made from the pounded roots and given to barren women to aid conception.

Here, too, you will find the *Aristeas*, dainty little flowers with a blue that rivals the blue of the summer sky. They have six petals, and they belong to the family of the Iridaceae, named after Iris, Goddess of the rainbow, because of the many beautiful colours of the flowers in this particular family. The flowers are only about 2 cm in diameter, and if you pick them they quickly twist up into a spiral and turn black. In some species the stems are about 40 cm long, each stem bearing several flowers. In other species, such as *Aristea cognata*, the stems are only about 6 cm long, with a single flower at the tip of the stem. The Zulus use this flower in a variety of ways. When a young man goes courting he will make an infusion from roots and leaves and bathe his body with the mixture. This same infusion, when heated, is used as a fomentation for sprains, and it is also used to sprinkle kraals with as a protection against storms.

On the banks of streams you will find two very charming flowers. *Schizostylis coccinea*, commonly known as River Lily, or Kaffir Lily, blooms in the early autumn. The flowers are a deep crimson in colour, and have a satin-like sheen to their petals. You will not easily forget them as they nod their heads in the autumn sunlight over the clear waters of a hurrying stream. There is also a pink variety, somewhat rare. I have seen it only twice in the Drakensberg, once in the Setene Valley, below *Mt. Oompie*, and once on the Free State slopes of the Drakensberg, above Caverns Guest Farm.

The second is *Cyrtanthus breviflorus*, a bright yellow flower growing in clusters on stream banks in the spring with long green slender leaves, about 15 cm long. The flowers have six petals, like a small lily, and they are only about two to three centimetres in length. In the past there was considerable **uncertainty** as to the correct name of this flower. It was originally classified under *Cyrtanthus*, but *Cyrtanthus* flowers have long, pendulous trumpet-shaped flowers, while the flowers of this species were much shorter and more wide-spreading. It was therefore given a special classification, and called *Anoiganthus*. But botanists were still not sure of this, and the whole question was further bedevilled by the fact that there appeared to be a number of sub-species, shading one into another. At one time two separate species were recognised, *Anoiganthus breviflorus* and *A. luteus*. Finally Dr. K. D. Gordon-Gray of the University of Natal, and Dr. F. B. Wright of the Natal Parks Board, made an extensive study of the plant in the early 1960's, and they came to the conclusion that the original name, *Cyrtanthus breviflorus* should be reverted to, and that only one species, *breviflorus*, should be recognised. This suggestion has now been adopted.

But perhaps, after all, the flower itself has the last word, for its Zulu name is *Uvelabahleke*, which means "the happy, laughing flower". And what lovelier name could one wish for, as it laughs happily away in the sun, on the banks of the streams of the Little Berg, as the botanists wrangle over its scientific name!

There are many other *Cyrtanthus* flowers in the Drakensberg. Writing in 1855, Rev. William C. Holden remarked: "Two or three days after the fire has blackened the earth, countless numbers of a little (scarlet) leafless flower . . . shoot up, whose bowed heads seem to supplicate heaven's mercy for the scorched earth, and whose glorious beauty is enough to entice the treasures of the clouds to their feet." He was thinking of that lovely red flower, *Cyrtanthus contractus*, popularly known as the Fire Lily. I have never been quite sure whether the popular name derives from the fact that it is often found on the blackened veld after a grass fire, or whether it comes from its flame-like colour. It always flowers before the leaves appear. The Zulu name is *Umpingizane*, and it is used by the Zulus as an *Intelezi*. An *Intelezi* is a protective medicine or charm, designed to render evil ineffective. It is supposed to ward off all forms of evil and sickness. In the case of *Cyrtanthus contractus* the bulbs are crushed, a concoction is made from them, and the mixture used to sprinkle yards and huts to prevent evil entering.

Two other species of *Cyrtanthus* are worth noting. *Cyrtanthus flanaganii* is a rich yellow in colour, with dark-green, sword-like, glabrous leaves. It grows to a height of about 40 cm, and is found in damp places on the summit plateau, at about 3 100 metres, often growing below moist basalt cliffs and in shady places.

And finally, *Cyrtanthus erubescens*, a strikingly beautiful pink species shading to pure white. It is only rarely seen, and is again found in sheltered places on the summit plateau, though I recently found a white, pink-tipped variety at the foot of *Amphlett's*.

The name *Cyrtanthus* comes from a Greek word meaning "curved flower". This makes its identification very easy, for the flowers are long, slender and trumpet-shaped, and always hang downwards in a graceful curve.

One of the most showy of all Drakensberg wild flowers is the *Brunsvigia*. These handsome lilies bloom in December and January, and are to be found in open grasslands, but sometimes under the sandstone rock ledges of the Little Berg. They consist of a large, fleshy stalk, about 30 cm high, which terminates in a cluster of scarlet flowers of the lily type, branching out in a large sphere from the tip of the fleshy stalk, each flower having its own smaller stalk from 15 cm to 20 cm long. There are two types of leaf. In one case the leaves lie flat on the ground, and are fleshy and heart-shaped. These belong to *Brunsvigia radulosa* and *Brunsvigia cooperi*. Then there are two species where the leaves are long and strap-shaped. These are *Brunsvigia josephinae* and *Brunsvigia grandiflora*. Eventually these flower heads with their long thick stalks dry out and go whirling away across the veld. You will often find them caught up in fences at the sides of roads. The plant has a large bulb, full of water, and this often makes a layer of wet mud round the bulb, with a strong, rotten odour. Hence comes the Zulu name, *Umbolo*, which means something rotten.

One interesting creeper, which you will sometimes find on the edges of forest margins, is the flower known as the Climbing Bell, *Littonia modesta*. The flowers consist of pendulous, orange bells, and the leaves are thin, slender and tapering. It was named after Dr. Samuel Litton, Professor of Botany for 21 years in the Royal Dublin Society. The Zulu name is *Uhlamvu lwentombazane*. A decoction is made from the bulb of the plant, and the bulb of a somewhat similar climber, *Gloriosa superba*, great care being exercised, as the bulbs are poisonous. When a young Zulu, courting a girl, finds she is indifferent to his advances, he will first of all "phalaza" with the liquid. He then walks slowly past the girl, making sure his shadow falls on her. This is supposed to cause the girl to appear pregnant, and this condition will persist until she returns his affections. If, however, she is still reluctant, her father must consult an Inyanga, or witch-doctor. He then prescribes a concoction for *her* to "phalaza" with, consisting of the bulbs of both these plants, together with a few others as well to add a little "kick" to it!

No account of the flora of the Drakensberg would be complete without a reference to the Blue-bells, known to botanists as *Wahlenbergia*. There are at least ten species in the Drakensberg, and their blue, bellshaped flowers nodding in the wind on the slopes of the Little Berg, are a familiar sight to the hiker. One of them is known to the Zulus as *Uqaboza*. They make a liquid from the pounded roots and this is used to wash the body with before going into battle. It is supposed to act as a protection against the assegais of the enemy. It is also used as an eye-lotion. Perhaps one of the finest is *Wahlenbergia grandiflora*, with its Zulu name *Umnqantula*. An infusion is made from the roots of this plant, and this is given to young pups after the removal of the worm from under the tongue. When a young pup is ailing and refusing its food the Zulus remove the sinew or bridle under the tongue. They believe that this cruel practice is a certain cure. There is a white variety of this flower, known to the Zulus as *Ushayindoda omhlope*. Herd-boys who have carelessly allowed their cattle to stray chew the roots of this plant to make themselves invisible to their wrathful fathers who come after them with a sjambok!

The blue of the blue-bells reminds us of yet another blue flower, the lovely little *Lobelia*.

210

As we contemplate their shy and dainty little faces, lifted to the ardent gaze of the sun, we recall those words of Mary Boyd, who won the Bardic Chair in 1921:

While here the blue Lobelia must have spun
Her azure robe from fragments of the skies
Brought by the dew that on her bosom lies.

These dainty little flowers, only a few centimetres high, are a common sight in the Drakensberg, especially along the bridle paths that thread the mountain sides. They have a narrow throat which ends with three broadly spreading petals and two smaller ones. Their colour is an intense blue, and they have small yellow centres. The genus was named after Mathias de l'Obel, physician to William the Silent, and later Botanist to James I of England, the first professional botanist to illustrate South African wild flowers, in 1603.

Then, of course, there are the Everlastings and the many varieties of wild heaths. Everlastings are known to botanists as *Helichrysums*, and they form a very large group of plants. Dr. Killick found no less than 46 species in the Cathedral area alone, and there must be many more along the whole line of the Drakensberg. In the spring and early summer their brittle, bright beauty is a memorable sight on the summit of the Little Berg, while their colours range from white to golden yellow, deep scarlet, rose pink and whitish-pink. *Helichrysum sutherlandii* is not an Everlasting, but is found extensively amongst the grey basalt rocks of the main Drakensberg. It has masses of foam-white flowers, and blue-grey leaves, and is such a prominent feature of these mountain crags that it cannot be mistaken.

There is one other *Helichrysum* that is worth noting, and that is *Helichrysum trilineatum*, a plant to which we have already referred. This is a tough, hard, woody shrub, about 30 cm high with small yellow flowers, growing on the summit plateau, mostly in sheltered gullies at about the 3 000 metre level. Its dried branches, 2 cm to 3 cm in diameter at most, provide the only firewood for the camper at these high altitudes. It makes a good fuel, as it has a very strong oil and resin content.

The Heaths or *Ericas* form a large family of plants in South Africa. Altogether we have almost 600 species. They range from tiny plants growing to a height of only a few centimetres, to tall shrubs up to three metres in height. Heaths may be recognised almost at a glance, from their leaves. These are generally short and needle-like, and arranged in little tufts. The flowers, which are small, are usually clustered very close together, and may be shaped like little bells, long, curved trumpets, or puffed tubes.

Perhaps the most showy and best known is *Erica cerinthoides*. It is one of the most widely-spread of our Ericas, being found throughout South Africa, Lesotho, Swaziland and on into Central Africa, and it flowers throughout the year. The colour is usually a brilliant flame-red, but in the Drakensberg there is a rather rare colour variety, which has pinkish-red flowers, paling to white at the base of the tube. I once found a fine specimen in the Lower Ndedema Gorge, the only one I have ever come across. A white variety is reported from Swaziland. *Erica cerinthoides* grows to a height of 40 cm, and the flowers are in the form of scarlet tubes, covered with downy red hairs. The tubes are slightly constricted at the mouth, and the flowers droop downwards. This plant is another which seems to thrive after winter fires. It was introduced into cultivation in England in 1774 by Francis Masson, a well known Cape botanist.

Erica oatesii is often to be seen in the sheltered valleys of the Little Berg, sometimes just above the sandstone layers. It has pink, bell-shaped flowers, and was named after Frank Oates, English traveller and naturalist, who first collected the species in 1873.

Let us now visit the deep, rich forests of the Little Berg before taking a trip to the summit. Here you will find the shade loving plants, which like a damp, moist atmosphere. And you will find them everywhere. Around you stand the immemorial trees, in silent dignity, reaching up their mighty evergreen crowns to the open sky. The lichen hangs in tessellated profusion from their boughs, and everywhere are the ferns, deep, and rich, and soft. Over all hangs the stillness of a great cathedral. No one who has stood entranced in these green solitudes will ever forget, first of all, those huge mossed boulders, and the rich tapestry of orange and purple which festoons their sides, an abiding memory for the lover of flowers.

The orange flowers are *Begonias*, the full name *Begonia sutherlandii*, another flower which enshrines the name of Dr. P. C. Sutherland. They love wet, dripping ledges, and the south sides of rocks. The purple flowers are *Streptocarpuses*, and the particular species which you will find in the Drakensberg is *Streptocarpus gardenii*. The Streptocarpus belongs to the same family as the Gloxinia. The name *Streptocarpus* comes from the Greek and means a twisted seed-pod. Their seed-pods have a twisted spiral in them, and when they dry out, the spiral relaxes like a spring, and shoots out the seed ensuring its wide dispersal.

Growing on the sides of waterfalls you will find two flowers which you cannot mistake. *Vellozia talbotii* is a small blue flower, about $1\frac{1}{2}$ cm in diameter, with six petals, and long, slender green leaves. The stem structure is a tough, slim central shoot, encased in old leaves and wiry roots, while the leaves are crowded at the top, giving it a plumed appearance.

Similar in size and shape to *Vellozia talbotii* is a red flower, *Hesperantha longituba*, which you will also find on the sides of waterfalls and on wet rock ledges. *Hesperantha* means evening flower, and its common name, Aandblom, or Avond-blommetjie, is really an Afrikaans translation of this Greek word.

The summit is entirely different from anything we have seen so far. In fact it is a typical tundra region. Soils are turfy and shallow, and derived entirely from basalt, dark in colour. They seldom exceed 40 cm in depth. In the rainy season they become boggy, and in winter are frozen hard for long periods. The surface of the soil is often covered with a litter of small stones. Flat rock pavements abound, and small, boggy vleis are very common. The climate is severe. Snow lies for months on end in the winter, though it must be remembered that this blanket of snow actually protects plants from excessively low temperatures, and prevents the soil beneath from freezing. Harsh winds blow in late winter, spring and early summer, and drought is by no means unknown. Rainfall on the summit is less than on the east-facing slopes of the Drakensberg, and decreases progressively as one leaves the escarpment edge and penetrates inland into Lesotho. Atmospheric pressure is decreased, and there is an increase in ultra-violet rays, which, as we have seen, is believed to be the chief cause of dwarfness in alpine plants. There is also a very wide range in soil temperature, from very hot during the day to very cold at night. Temperatures generally are colder, and long periods of bitter cold have been experienced even in the height of summer. Humidity, also, varies tremendously, being very high in the wet, misty months of summer, and very low in winter.

The vegetation, of course, has had to adapt itself to these harsh conditions. Much of it consists of low, woody species of *Erica* and *Helichrysum*, and short, tufty grasses. Many of the plants have grey or whitish leaves, another of the protective devices of Nature, for this reduces the amount of radiation absorbed.

To me it is a perpetual wonder that in the face of these harsh conditions Nature can produce such a lavish display of colour as she does on the summit of the Drakensberg. Justus Thode, one of the early plant collectors in the Drakensberg, called the summit area "a veritable flower paradise". There may not be the wide range of species that you find at lower altitudes, but here you do find great splashes of jewelled colour which you will not find lower down.

Perhaps the most striking plant on the summit is *Moraea spathulata*, or the Yellow Iris. Growing to a height of 90 to 100 cm, it covers the hillsides and valleys with glorious splashes of golden colour. It is frequently found associated with the blue Forget-me-not, *Myosotis sylvatica*, a delightful combination. Its Zulu name is *Ihlamvu elincane*. When a woman fails to conceive, the corm of this plant is ground up with two or three seed mealies, and from this three small cakes are made. The woman eats two of them, her husband eats one, and, hey presto, in no time you hear the patter of little feet!

The plants are poisonous to stock (farmers know it as Tulp) but in spite of intensive work on the plant, lasting for many years, the exact nature of the poison has never been discovered. Strangely enough, the plants are eaten in large quantities by rodent moles without any ill effects.

An amazing coincidence occurred in the naming of this genus. A botanist gave it the name *Morea* in honour of a man named More. It was later discovered that Linnaeus had already named the genus *Moraea*, after his wife, the pronunciation being the same in both cases. In accordance with established procedure the later name had to be dropped in favour of *Moraea*, the earlier, and original, one.

The Red-hot Pokers, known as *Kniphofias*, also make a fine show on the summit, and I have seen acres and acres of them, their proud heads standing like crimson and yellow banners against the blue of the sky. *Kniphofia caulescens* is the species that you will find growing around the small vleis and streams that are so common on the summit. It has bright orange to red tips, shading to yellow at the base, and grows to a height of 90 cm. Three other species of Red-hot Pokers found on the summit are *Kniphofia northiae, K. porphyrantha,* and *K. ritualis.* The genus was named after Johann Hieronymus Kniphof, Professor of Medicine at Erfurt University in the latter part of the 18th century.

A very striking flower on the summit is *Gladiolus cruentus*. There are many species of Gladiolus in the Drakensberg, those magnificent "Sword Lilies", as they have been called. "From their native fortresses on *Table Mountain*," says M. James, F.R.H.S., "they have stormed the floral citadels of the world." And he is right, for the horticultural hybrids, derived from our South African gladiolas, seem to grow more magnificent every year. *Gladiolus cruentus* has a brilliant scarlet colour, and it is popularly known as the Suicide Lily. This is because it grows on the sheer rock faces of the basalt cliffs, is most difficult to reach, and is only very rarely seen. One Christmas, however, I found the cliffs of *Little Saddle*, in the Ndedema area, simply ablaze with them.

There are many other species to be found on the summit – *Cyrtanthus, Dierama, Rhodohypoxis,* the *Nerines* and the *Ericas,* but we have no time to mention them here. These lonely heights can be harsh and forbidding, but their harshness is tempered by the soft beauty of the mountain flowers, growing in peace amongst the mountain crags, with only the wind for company.

*   *   *   *

To-day, in the Midlands of Natal, you will find the smoke of factory chimneys, the roar of machinery, the highways and byways filling up with hurrying crowds of men and women, as the great Tugela Basin begins to flex its muscles. And if you are the sort of person I think you are, there are times when you will want to get away from it all, and sit beside a mountain stream, and contemplate the simple beauty of a wild flower. You can do this easily, for it is all only 50 kilometres away. And you will be in good company! Two thousand years ago there was Another, who also saw the toiling crowds, and felt them pressing in upon Him. He called a few of his friends, and climbed with them the green hillside that rose serene above the Lake of Galilee. He sat there among the flowers on a summer's day. "Consider," He said, "the lilies of the field. *They* toil not, neither do they spin, but I say unto you that even Solomon, in all his glory, was not arrayed like one of these."

CHAPTER XIX

THE MEN WHO GUARD THE TREES

Under the greenwood tree
Who loves to lie with me
Come hither . . .
— SHAKESPEARE: As You Like It

Tuesday morning, 25th July 1967, was a black, wet, dripping morning. The dawn was still two hours away. Heavy mist blanketed the mountains and the valleys of the Little Berg. The night pressed heavy on the land. Over the deep snow-drifts which choked the ravines of *Cathkin Peak*, dark shadows lay. In the bedroom at the Monk's Cowl Forest Station Steve Rossouw, the Foreman-in-Charge, was awake. His wife, Joyce, was still asleep. Steve always woke early these days. It was a good time to plan the work of the day. If only the mist would lift he could burn that fire-break down from *Ndanjane* past the forests of the Upper Makuruman. It was 4.30 a.m. and too early to make the coffee. He drew the blankets up close around him, for it was cold. From outside came the only sound, the steady drip – drip – drip of the dank mist from the Liquidambar trees.

Suddenly the silence of the night was shattered by a frantic hammering at the back door. It woke Joyce, but Steve was first at the door. On the steps outside was a young man, haggard, exhausted, on the point of collapse. Quickly he told his story. He was Peter Keen. He and his brother, Dr. Anthony Keen, had set out along the contour path four days ago on a traverse from Cathedral Peak to Champagne Castle. The previous afternoon, at Base Camp in the Mhlwazini Valley, Dr. Anthony Keen had suffered a heart attack. The two men had attempted to descend the mountains to Champagne Castle Hotel, but Anthony had collapsed for the second time. His brother had placed him in two sleeping bags, and laid him on a stretched-out tent alongside the path, and had then gone for help after Anthony had written down his diagnosis on a slip of paper. Peter had arrived at the Hotel about 9 p.m., and with an African boy and an Indian waiter had returned up the Little Berg to where he had left his brother down in the Mhlwazini Valley. Together they had tried to carry the stricken man down, using the sleeping bags as a make-shift stretcher, but had found it impossible. Through the night, in the bitter winter weather, Peter had again descended the Little Berg, and this time he had pitched up at the Monk's Cowl Forest Station.

Steve and Joyce (a trained nurse) immediately swung into action. A cup of steaming tea and food for the exhausted man, while Steve phoned the Hotel three kilometres away, alerting them to the emergency, and asking for a stretcher and a rescue party to be assembled immediately. Then another call to the Estcourt Telephone Exchange, with an urgent request that they attempt to locate a helicopter. The reply fifteen minutes later: two local helicopters were unavailable, so a third call to an Estcourt doctor, to whom Peter first read his brother's diagnosis. The doctor promised to alert the Defence Department, with a request to them for a helicopter from either Bloemfontein or Durban, and he also promised to send an ambulance out. Yet another call to Durban, to the parents of the two men. In between the calls Steve despatched an advance party of African forest guards up the mountain, with food and blankets. Then Steve and his wife drove Peter Keen over to the Hotel. Here he was immediately put to bed, and was asleep within five minutes. Steve collected the stretcher and then returned to the Forest Station, where Joyce swiftly packed a ruck-sack with hot tea and sandwiches. Then, with Peter's last words ringing in their ears: "Hurry, for God's sake: he may not last long," they sped off, taking a short-cut up the mountain side, while the stretcher-party took the longer route up the bridle path. It was now 6.45 a.m., and the light was just breaking. Behind they left their daughter, Caroline, a child of 12, in charge of the Station, to look after their four younger children and to man the telephone for any incoming calls.

Through heavy mist they climbed up, and reached the summit of the Little Berg at Breakfast Stream in 25 minutes, the usual time for the climb being an hour. Then swiftly along the summit plateau and on to Hlatikulu Nek. An icy wind began to blow off the snow, and the mist was still heavy, but at Hlatikulu Nek it grew lighter, and when, at 8.55 a.m. they reached the stricken man, the sun was just beginning to break through.

They found Dr. Anthony Keen beside the path, half-way down the Mhlwazini Valley. He was conscious, his pulse was strong and steady, and he said he felt better. Soon after that the stretcher party arrived, and arrangements were made for the return trip.

In the meantime, little Caroline, down at the Forest Station, had been kept busy. Competently, she handled all incoming telephone calls – from the parents of the two men, from eager newspaper reporters, from the Estcourt doctor, and from Defence Headquarters. At about 7.30 a.m. came a call with news that an Air Force helicopter was on its way from Bloemfontein. Caroline's younger brother, Stephen, a young lad of 10, immediately offered to climb up the mountains which tower above the Forest Station, with the news. Alone, barefoot, with only a single thin pullover, the boy made the journey of over 12 kilometres in less than two hours, along treacherous footpaths shrouded in mist, and covered in places with snow and ice. He arrived just as the stretcher-party was about to set off.

Down below the mist became thicker, and Caroline took another telephone call to the effect that the helicopter could not get through because of the mist. She realised that the rescue party might be waiting in vain for the machine, and she decided she must go herself to warn them that they would have to depend on themselves to get the sick man down. She did not hesitate a moment. Leaving the three younger children in the charge of an African servant, she set off immediately, taking with her only her father's three dogs, Mutt, Luxy and Toasty, for protection. Up through the mountains she, too, climbed, delivered her message, together with one from the Estcourt doctor urging them to press on, and immediately returned to her post at the Station to prepare food and hot drinks for the return of the rescue party.

All this time the stretcher party was toiling on, manoeuvring the stretcher over mountain streams and along steep krantzes and narrow footpaths. As they climbed up out of the Mhlwazini Valley the mist came down again, heavier than ever, thick, black, wet and dripping. It turned bitterly cold, the wind gusting down from the snow-fields in bitter blasts. Little Stephen, still barefoot, was visibly frozen, even though Caroline had given him her own pullover before she had left home. The little fellow was almost in tears. By the time they reached Blind Man's Corner they were all wet through. They battled on.

At last, when they reached the Sphinx, the huge sandstone rock just below the summit of the Little Berg, the mist began to lift. Down below the Alouette helicopter had by now arrived at the Forest Station, together with the ambulance and oxygen. As soon as the pilot saw the rescue party at the Sphinx, far above him, he took off, landed just below the rock, picked up Dr. Keen, and flew him down to the Forest Station. There his father was waiting for him. A brief halt while the patient's condition was checked, and then the whirling blades began to turn again as the machine took off for Grey's Hospital in Pietermaritzburg. Steve and his wife watched the plane growing smaller and smaller until it was a speck against the drifting clouds. Then they turned to their work. There was dinner to prepare for five hungry children, and it was still early enough to start that fire-break down from *Ndanjane*. Steve called to his labourers. Just one more day in the life of a Government Forester.

The Drakensberg has two priceless treasures, its forests and its water. The water is everywhere, the purest, clearest, most sparkling water you will find anywhere in South Africa. It spouts, it trickles, it gushes and gurgles on all sides. Even after heavy rain it is still as clear and limpid as a washed diamond as it tumbles down the mountain side. The rivulets join to form the most delightful of mountain streams, while rapids foam and splash into sparkling pools, green and translucent. Hurrying on their way, tossing their white sprays into the sun-drenched air, the streams expand and grow, and then their pace slows down until they broaden out into the great rivers that feed the Tugela Basin and the mighty sinews of industry and agriculture, far below in the plains of Natal.

Equally lovely, and closely associated with the hurrying streams, are the forests. Here great Yellow-woods, *Podocarpus latifolius* and *P. henkelii*, tower up in lonely valleys, the gloom is green and cool, and always there is the sound of rippling waters. Here you will find the stately Without, or Cape Holly, *Ilex mitis*, with its shiny, dark-green leaves and white bark; the Wild Peach, or Spekhout, *Kiggelaria africana;* the Black Ironwood, *Olea capensis;* the White Stinkwood, *Celtis africana;* and the Cape Chestnut, *Calodendron capense*, with its bright clusters of pink and mauve flowers that make such a glory in the spring. Smaller trees are *Dais cotinifolia*, the Pompom tree; *Halleria lucida*, with its richly golden, heavily scented flowers in the spring; *Curtisia faginae*, the Assegai tree, and the Cabbage Tree, *Cussonia spicata*. And in autumn you have the yellow flare of the Canary Creeper, *Senecio tamoides*, clambering up the forest trees in a blaze of colour.

I have been in love with forests for as long as I can remember. As a boy I used to venture, timorously at first, because of the silence, into the cathedral gloom of the great forests of the Dargle, and wonder at their mystery and their sense of ageless time. Stretched out, chin in hands, on the floor of my bedroom, oblivious to all else, I used to pore over Longfellow's "This is the forest primeval, the murmuring pines and the hemlocks". The sonorous lines would drift through my mind even as the wind drifted through the leaves of the forest itself. And later, as a young man, I wandered through the Forest of Arden with the spritely Rosalind, and fell hopelessly in love with her. I spent long nights under the pines with Robert Louis Stevenson, while his donkey cropped the short nearby grass and the night wind whispered in the trees, and we dreamed together of far-off lands. And in later life I came to know and to love the forests of the Drakensberg.

It was to protect these two priceless treasures, the water and the forests, that the first Forest Reserves in the Drakensberg were proclaimed in 1922.

Our Drakensberg indigenous forests are found mostly in the deep valleys of the Little Berg, especially on their south-facing slopes. This is partly owing to the greater shade and moisture found there, but also because of the direction of the autumn and winter fires which sweep across the land. These fires burn from north to south, owing to the prevailing north-westerly winds, and are much fiercer on the drier north-facing slopes, where they race *upwards*, than on the moister south-facing slopes, where they burn slowly *downwards*, and cause little damage to forested areas. Only occasional trees occur above these river valleys, and apart from *Leucosidea sericea*, the well-known *Mtshitshi* bush, the tree line ends at about the 1 980 metre level.

In the early days very little had been done to protect these indigenous forests on Crown land. Their control was vested in the Magistrates of the districts in which the forests occurred. Various enactments were made under Ordinance No. 4 of 1853, but these were unsatisfactory and there were no means of enforcing them. In fact the only control appeared to be the issue of permits to sawyers who wished to cut timber. This system dates from 1855. These permits cost £1 per month for each saw, but there was no control over the number of trees a man cut down or the damage that was done in the process, and the sawyers did pretty much as they liked. The police were supposed to make periodical patrols of the forests in their areas to check that no unauthorised persons were cutting wood, but in practice little appears to have been done. In the early 1880's a limited system of employing local farmers, called variously Supervisors of Crown Forests, or Honorary Foresters, was tried out. These men worked at a salary of £36 per annum, and were given the right to arrest people who were cutting timber illegally.

One of the first of these was George Leonard Coventry, who was given control of the forests in the Mont-aux-Sources area. G. L. Coventry was the father of Walter Coventry, who started the first Hostel at what subsequently became the Royal Natal National Park. The system, certainly in its early stages, proved to be of little value. In 1902 the Lister Report stated: "The forests of Natal and Zululand are now being wrecked and plundered." Fortunately problems of transport meant that the Drakensberg forests suffered less severely than those in other parts of Natal.

Both the Bulwer Commission of 1880 and Dr. H. G. Fourcade's Report* of 1889 had urged the establishment of a Department of Forestry, but nothing seems to have been done until the end of 1902, when Mr. T. R. Sim was appointed Conservator of Forests as a result of the Lister Report.

One of Sim's first tasks, after he had created and staffed the new Forestry Department, was to extend the system of Honorary and Part-time Foresters. These men were required to protect patches of indigenous forests by burning breaks round them, and to report cases of illegal cutting, poaching etc. Probably owing to their remoteness, however, nothing seems to have been done in the case of the Cathkin-Cathedral area until 1922.

In July 1910, at the age of 21, young Carter Robinson bought the farm *Benjamin*, under the shadow of *Cathkin Peak*, from Jan Koos van der Merwe, and erected the first buildings which were later to grow into the Monk's Cowl Forest Station of to-day. Early in 1922 he made strong representations to the Government, and as a result of these, in April 1922 the Cathkin Forest Reserve was proclaimed in terms of Section 122 of the South Africa Act, 1909. The Reserve stretched from the Injasuti to the Umlambonja Rivers, and was 40 468 ha (nearly 100 000 acres) in extent. The system of issuing permits for tree-felling was stopped, and the only source of revenue was leasing selected areas of the Reserve to farmers for grazing purposes.

In January 1924 Robinson was appointed Honorary Forester, and in September of the following year he became Stipendiary Part-time Forester at £5 per month, but from November 1933 he reverted to the position of Honorary Forester, a post which he held until the end of 1934, when he resigned, and was succeeded by Mr. Otto Zunckel. On 4th February 1935 the Department of Agriculture and Forestry wrote to Mr. Robinson thanking him for "the excellent service" rendered by him. "Forestry officials," said the letter, "speak very highly of the enthusiasm and able way in which you have guarded the Department's interests during the past 11 years, and I can assure you that the work which you have done is very much appreciated."

But in spite of all Robinson's efforts little was done to make the Reserve the viable concern it is to-day. In 1931 the District Forest Officer in Pietermaritzburg recommended that the Reserve be declared a National Park, or handed over to the Provincial authorities as an extension to the Giant's Castle Game Reserve. He considered it quite useless as a Forest Reserve. The revenue from grazing only just covered Robinson's salary, plus the small current expenditure on paths. To give an indication of the scope of the Reserve in those days we might mention that total expenditure for the seven years 1926 to 1932 was only £1 030, while revenue for the same period only came to £936.

In 1932 a new post of Forest Watcher appeared to have been created, and S. G. Streit was employed in this capacity, as from 1st January 1932, at a salary of £1 per month. Early in 1934 Streit was drowned in the Tugela River while searching for the body of one of the Zunckel family who had perished in the disastrous floods of that year.

* Dr. H. G. Fourcade was a brilliant scientist, at one time Assistant Conservator of Forests in Natal. He always used to maintain that 'no landscape is complete without woods and water'. It is not generally known that he was amongst the first to suggest a method of using stereoscopic aerial photographs in the production of maps. The Fourcade Stereogoniometer, designed and built according to the principles he laid down, was in use for many years in aerial map-making.

In 1934 the Government bought Robinson's farm *Benjamin*, and converted it into the first fully-equipped Forest Station in the area, and two years later Mr. J. van Heyningen was appointed to the Station as the first full-time Forester in charge of the Reserve.

To-day the present area of the Cathedral Peak Forestal District is 48 600 ha, and it is managed by four white Foresters and upwards of 70 African Forest labourers. These men are constantly on patrol, protecting bird life, game and plants, arresting miscreants, and controlling poaching and veld fires, in addition to the supremely important research work being done at the Cathedral Peak Forest Research Station, which we shall deal with shortly.

Ever since Louis VI of France issued a decree entitled *"Le fait des eaux et forêt"* 780 years ago, forest lands in most countries have been protected, controlled and managed by men trained in forestry. To-day the control of a forest reserve is a highly specialized profession, and South Africa is fortunate in having a number of dedicated men whose work is acknowledged and respected not only in South Africa but in overseas countries as well.

The management of a State Forest embraces, amongst other things, the conservation of all indigenous vegetation; the planning and application of protective measures against fires, pests, animals, and the intrusion of alien vegetation and undesirable plants; control of poaching; planning and regulating access to the State Forests by the public, and sometimes supplying accommodation; the dissemination of popular, semi-popular and scientific information on the Reserve and on forestry matters generally; and Catchment Management.

In order to cope with this enhanced programme, it was decided early in 1935 to expand and to re-organise the whole State Forest area. The headquarters of the area were transferred from the Monk's Cowl Forest Station to the Cathedral area, and it was decided to establish there a Forestry Research Station.

What actually triggered off this move was the controversy which arose during the first three decades of the century on the effects of afforestation on water supplies. The opening shots in what was to develop into a battle royal were apparently fired in 1915 by Mr. O. B. Miller, a Forest Officer in the South African Forestry Department. Writing in that year he said: "I have observed that after their surroundings have been planted with fast-growing exotics, there is a tendency for springs to dry up." Soon there was quite an uproar. Others joined in. Letters appeared in the Press. On several occasions the matter was raised in Parliament. It was discussed by Farmers' Congresses and similar organizations throughout the country. On the one hand were those who agreed with Mr. Miller. These protagonists maintained that there was abundant evidence that trees used up an enormous amount of water, and desiccated the land. On the other side were an equal number who argued that trees brought moisture and rain to the land. They pointed to the rain forests of Central Africa, and to the fact that the forests of Natal and Zululand were always damp and moist. Farmers in the Natal Midlands claimed that wattle plantations had dried up springs which flowed again when the trees were felled. But against this Mr. Hunt-Holley, for instance, maintained that "springs running out of wattle plantations" were seen "where none were ever seen before". Dr. Hans Merensky claimed to have shown by extensive scientific experiments at *Westphalia* how streams in the Duiwelskloof area, dry and dusty below plantations, could be made to flow again by bringing back indigenous bush. It seemed incontrovertible that stream flow had diminished over the years. Many elderly farmers will tell you to-day that they caught fish when they were young in streams which cannot now support fish. It is, of course, notorious in South Africa that there are many farms named after springs, streams and vleis, but to-day you look in vain for the particular stream or vlei after which the farm has been named. But was it fair to blame afforestation for this? Could not other factors be involved, such as urban, industrial or agricultural development, plus of course climatic changes? And was there a difference between indigenous forests and

218

exotic plantations? It was obviously a very complex problem, and when the experts were approached they could give no clear answer.

Then in 1935 the British Empire Forestry Conference was held in Cape Town, and the Government asked the Conference to pay special attention to the problem, and in particular to concentrate on the effect of afforestation on climate, water conservation, stream-flow and erosion. The Conference appointed a Committee to study the problem and to make recommendations, and the Committee suggested that "a comprehensive scientific investigation on the effects of tree-planting upon local water supplies would be of value, not only to South Africa but also to other parts of the Empire. South Africa" they said, "has a unique opportunity of carrying out such an investigation."

The Government lost no time in acting on this suggestion. It was decided to establish two research stations in South Africa, one in the winter rainfall area and one in the summer rainfall area. That year a site was chosen for the Jonkershoek Research Station, near Stellenbosch in the Cape, and later it was decided to establish a similar Research Station in the Drakensberg.

Late in 1935 Dr. I. J. Craib, Chief Forest Research Officer, and Mr. S. St. C. Ballenden, Conservator of Forests in Pietermaritzburg, selected the site for the Station at Cathedral Peak, together with 2 500 acres (1 000 ha) which were to be set aside for research purposes. This area comprised part of the farm *Gewaagd* and part of the existing Forest Reserve. The farm was originally owned by a Mr. Salmon Scholtz, and he erected a building which to-day forms the nucleus of the Research Station. Later Mr. I. J. M. Buys ('Ryk Isak Buys') farming at Kransfontein in the Free State, bought the farm, and he sent Jan P. Roux down as his foreman to run the place. Round about 1928 Jannie Roux bought Ryk Isak out, and in 1938 the rest of the farm was incorporated in the Cathkin Peak Forest Reserve.

The man selected to launch the infant project was Mr. A. M. ('Mike') de Villiers, a young Assistant District Forest Officer at George in the Cape. He paid a flying visit to the area in June 1938, before proceeding to Pietermaritzburg for a month in order to organise materials and equipment. He came to a wild and almost inaccessible country. The Hotel had not been completed. The road into the area from Winterton was in places so bad that it often degenerated into a series of tracks across the veld, hopelessly mixed up with sledge trails branching off in all directions. On his first visit he got hopelessly lost. With dusk coming on, he took a wrong turning a few kilometres before the Mhlwazini crossing, and had to spend the night in his car.

Conditions in those early days, too, were primitive in the extreme. Jannie Roux had recently lost his wife, and could not bear living in the old homestead at *Gewaagd*. But he had been given the contract to build the bridge over the Mhlwazini. So de Villiers found temporary quarters in the old house, while Roux camped out at the bridge. At first there were no bridges at all over the rivers, and the roads, especially after heavy rains, were quite impassable. Often his supplies ran out, and, unable to get into Winterton or Bergville to replenish them, he had to fall back on the mealie-meal of his African labourers. Pulling cars out of the mud with teams of oxen became a regular occurrence. H. B. Stephens, who had taken over as Conservator of Forests in 1938, and who often visited the new Station in those early days, remarked caustically on one occasion that instead of the road being lined with an avenue of trees it was lined with an avenue of Africans and oxen!

But the work went steadily on. A start was made on the buildings, roads were built, and a topographical survey of the research area undertaken. The first rain gauges were installed.

Then World War II intervened. The work was not considered vital for the country's war effort, the Station was closed down, and the gauges dismantled. Mike de Villiers joined the Survey Company of the South African Engineering Corps. He was away 'up north' for six years.

But with the war over, he was back at his post in June 1945, with undiminished enthusiasm.

The first full research programme was soon drafted, rain gauges were sited and re-established, and the first stream-gauging weirs constructed.

From the start it had been realised that a motor road to the summit of the Little Berg, where the research catchment areas lay, was essential, but this was a formidable project, for the slopes of the Little Berg are not only steep, but are surmounted by a layer of vertical sandstone cliffs, often 30 metres and over in height. Nowhere, in the whole length of the Natal Drakensberg, from *Giant's Castle* to *Mont-aux-Sources*, had this barrier ever been broached by a road. Although a start had been made in 1938, it was now realised that expert assistance would be required if this barrier were to be surmounted. It was eventually put out to contract, and this was secured by Mr. Monzali, an Italian road construction engineer, a lovable old gentleman who had made his money, and his fame, in fantastic road and railway constructions. These included the Gouritz River Railway Bridge. He was now living in retirement just outside Pietermaritzburg. Unfortunately, on Mr. Monzali's first day on the job, he overturned his truck on a steep portion of the road, and broke his back, an injury from which he suffered for the rest of his life. But he stuck gamely to his task. The first excavations were started in 1947, and the road was completed to the top by 28 May 1949.

This road, now known as Mike's Pass, is one of the most spectacular roads in the country. Ten and a half kilometres long, it climbs up over 600 metres to the summit of the Little Berg, 1 830 metres high, one of the highest motor roads in South Africa. For sheer magnificence and grandeur of scenery it rivals even the famous Hout Bay Drive in the Cape Peninsula.

From the end of the war Mike de Villiers had close on seven years at the Station. When he left, in March, 1952, most of the buildings had been completed, together with the weirs in four catchments. One catchment had been almost wholly afforested, and a Meteorological Station had been established at a height of 1 860 metres.

From the middle of December 1951 to the middle of January 1952 Mr. U. W. Nänni had relieved de Villiers. He was now appointed as head of the Station on a permanent basis.

If it had been de Villiers' job to build the Station, from a physical point of view, it was Nänni's task to initiate the research investigation. This he did, and he and Mike de Villiers will always be remembered as the joint fathers of the Cathedral Peak Forest Influences Research Station. Both men built wisely and soundly.

In 1963 Nänni was transferred to the Forest Research Institute in Pretoria, but the work went steadily on. To-day the Cathedral Peak Research Station is world-famed, and research of immense importance has been going on there for the last 25 years. It is one of the most important centres for Hydrological Research in the Southern Hemisphere. It is even more important than the two experiments in the Northern Hemisphere, those at Wagon Wheel Gap in Colorado, in the United States of America, and at Immenthal in Switzerland, as the basic research facilities at Cathedral Peak are better and more extensive, and it is better equipped. It was founded by a band of highly trained, dedicated men, who were content to know that they would never live to see the final results of their labours. It would take a hundred years to collect, and then to correlate and assess the significance of, the masses of data that would be produced day by day. This they did not mind: it was the effort that counted, and not the distant goal which they would never see. The results could wait. They were content to know that posterity would eventually benefit from their work. So valuable are the data they are producing that all recorder charts are housed in a fire-proof strong-room, and as an additional precaution against loss, they are all photographed and the negatives kept in Pretoria.

The work goes steadily on. The original project was to test the effects on water supplies of afforestation, and to compare these effects with, firstly, controlled veld burning with no grazing, secondly, controlled veld burning with grazing, and finally with total protection of

220

the native vegetation. *Pinus patula* was selected for the afforestation, as a relatively fast-growing tree. It comes from Mexico.

Of prime importance is the measurement of stream-flow. Concrete weirs were built across all streams at suitable points. In the wall of each weir is a V-shaped notch. Through this gap all the water in the stream has to pass. The height of the water in the gap is measured by an ingenious instrument which consists mainly of a slowly-revolving drum on which graph paper is affixed. A stylus pen traces on this moving graph paper a continuous line giving the height of the water at all times. The first such gauge was installed in 1948, and has been recording continuously ever since. To-day stream-flow is measured at 10 permanent stream-gauging sites.

The catchments have been selected and surveyed for a carefully designed investigation on the effects of afforestation on stream-flow. There are ten of them altogether. Eight are to be afforested at eight-year intervals, the last in 1991. Two will be kept as control areas, with no afforestation, one of these to be burnt every second year, and the other totally protected from fire.

In the year 2 000 A.D., when the results of all these experiments have been collected and computerised, it should be possible to answer finally, and with assurance, the vexed question as to the effect of afforestation on water supplies.*

In addition to stream-flow, daily measurements are taken of rainfall, evaporation, air temperature, hours of sunshine, wind, humidity and radiation. Altogether about 25 rain-gauges have been established, scattered over an area of 750 ha.

Tentative results so far have shown that afforestation, of exotics at any rate, *was* having an adverse effect on stream-flow. In 1961 an interesting experiment was carried out to examine the effects of ordinary vegetation on the banks of streams on stream-flow. Two weirs were erected in series in a small stream, i.e. the one further up the stream than the other. The stream-flow was measured at both weirs for two weeks. Then all the vegetation on the banks of the stream, on both sides, between the two weirs, was removed in one day. Immediately, the stream-flow at the lower weir increased by 10 litres for every metre of vegetation removed.

There is much else that is being studied, much that will be learnt in time, at this fascinating research centre. One of these is the question of South Africa's climate. Is the climate of South Africa changing? Is the country drying up? John Bird, writing in 1891, claimed that the rainfall had decreased since 1845, and that "the growth of grass is no longer so luxuriant nor so brightly green as it was then", and no-one who reads Dobie's *Journal* can fail to be impressed by the long periods of continuous rain, day after day, in the 1860's, a phenomenon almost unknown to-day. You will hear this question debated at every Farmers' Congress, and at every village pub where farmers foregather after a thirsty day in the lands. Of course, every pundit has his theory. But, as in the case of the argument on whether trees dry up streams, few opinions are based on any real scientific facts. No-one *really* knows. But opinions are legion. Hendrik Maartens, the founder of Champagne Castle Hotel, who farmed in the Cathkin area for many years, was quite emphatic that changes had occurred in his life-time. Shortly before he died he told me that the mountains were much wetter 60 years ago than they are to-day. Hail was never known in the early days, and the winds were much stronger. From his house under the shadow of *Wostyn* he would hear them roaring up in the mountains. Snow, too, was much heavier in those early days, he said. In those days you could sometimes scale the 20-metre vertical sandstone cliffs of the Little Berg by climbing the snow packed against them. This would be unheard of to-day. Maartens claimed that sometimes the snow used to reach right down to the Sterkspruit where the Champagne and Cathkin Park roads meet. In sheltered places at Cathkin Park Hotel the snow would lie all winter. To-day it falls there, a mere

*Since writing the above this programme has expanded, and the emphasis today is more along the lines of conservation of the whole Drakensberg environment.

sprinkling, once in ten years. Sheep used to be dug out alive after seven to ten days. Their breath had melted a small breathing hole in the snow. Old inhabitants of the Witzieshoek area seem to confirm this. Snow was much heavier in the early days, they say; it lasted much longer, and often fell even in summer.

Carter Robinson, father of the Forest Reserve, confirmed all that Hendrik Maartens said. He was quite certain that snow was far more frequent then than now in the Drakensberg. He also confirmed that hail was unknown in the early days. Old residents still talk of the Great Blizzard of 31st May 1905, when the snow stretched well down into Natal. Steenbokkies and birds crowded on to the farmers' verandahs for shelter, and the Africans still tell of buck which came right into their huts in the storm. As a boy of five years of age I have vivid recollections of my mother telling me how trains on the main line had been snowed up, with passengers marooned, foodless, in their carriages. This never happens to-day.

As one pages through the early records of the Colony, especially the early Magistrates' Reports, the evidence that snow-storms in the Drakensberg were once much more severe than they are to-day mounts up.

On 3rd August 1849 a strong force of police and military, under the command of Lieut. Milles, left Bushman's River Drift for the Cathkin area in pursuit of cattle that had been raided by Bushmen. They left in delightful weather, prepared for an absence of twenty days. But on the third day of their march, while following a clear trail underneath the Drakensberg, they were overtaken by a tremendous snow-storm which compelled them to deviate from their track and seek shelter. The whole country, as far as the eye could see, was completely covered in snow. The cold was "intense" and "insupportable". They only had three tents with them, and the officers shared their tents with their men and with the Africans. For three days it snowed. They were at least 50 km from their base at Bushman's River Drift. Milles suggested marching for headquarters, but James Howell, second in command, refused. His men, he said, were not clad warmly enough, and it would have been death to move. Milles and two farmers with them did leave, but they were soon back. It was impossible to get through.

Next day the weather broke: it was fine, and they struck tents at daybreak, heading for home. For hours they floundered through the snow for most of the way, sometimes up to their knees, and they only reached headquarters at dusk. Howell had experienced a bad snow-storm in the Sneeuberg ten years previously, when he had lost one of his men and suffered himself for nine days from the effects of the snow. It was nothing compared to this, he said.

Another tremendous snow-storm lashed the Drakensberg in 1869. In August of that year the military were busy organising one of the most elaborate expeditions against the marauding Bushmen that had yet been mounted. This is the expedition we have already described in Chapter III. Allison was to go in with a large force up the Namahadi Pass into Lesotho, and Giles, with an equally large force, was to march from Fort Nottingham, climb the Drakensberg south of *Giant's Castle*, and meet Allison somewhere near the sources of the Orange River. But Giles found it impossible to move from Fort Nottingham on time. On 22 August a storm accompanied by tremendous winds, which "exceed in severity anything hitherto experienced in this locality" burst upon them. For three days it raged. Even on the flats at *Meshlynn* the snow lay half a metre deep, and in places was four metres deep. A messenger who was sent to Estcourt had to struggle through snow-drifts up to his middle. For sixteen days the expedition was held up, unable to move, and it was not until 7th September that they were able to march out of Fort Nottingham. These two storms are typical of many others which appear again and again in these early records. The majority are far more severe than anything known to-day.

But still the experts are not so sure that the climate has changed. The Inter-Departmental Committee set up in 1966 to study the problems of afforestation and water supplies could find no evidence that rainfall in South Africa was progressively decreasing. And Nänni, writing in the S.A. Forestry Journal of March 1969, said: "There is no reliable evidence that the climate of South Africa has changed markedly in historic times." But again, no-one *really* knows. The research scientists working at Cathedral Peak Forest Station, will know in a hundred years' time!

Another contentious subject that is being studied at the Research Station is the question of grass-burning. The effects of burning on vegetation are still not fully understood, but almost all informed opinion regards it as desirable to burn the grassland on the escarpment occasionally. There is still considerable difference of opinion, however, as to when, and how frequently, fires should occur. The generally accepted view is that burning of the veld should take place only after the first spring rains, and this has been incorporated in the Soil Conservation Act of 1969. But there is another school of thought which holds that occasional autumn burns, especially for forest regions, are better. Once again, the experts differ.

It has even been suggested by some that fires are unnatural, and man-made, and that every effort should be made to eliminate them altogether. They are certainly *partly* man-made, but this has been going on for thousands of years, and the vegetation has adapted itself to periodic burning. Archaeologists believe that man has inhabited South Africa for at least half a million years, but when he first learnt to use fire is not known. In the dim and distant past fires must often have been caused by man – a sudden gust of wind, and the coals from the cooking fires would in a few seconds cause a huge conflagration. In those early days, with no roads, railways, cultivated lands and fire-breaks to stop them, these fires must have raged for many days over vast areas.

But even without the hand of man, fires must have occurred in the Drakensberg for many thousands of years. It is incorrect to say that fire is not a natural phenomenon. It is often caused by lightning. I have seen this myself. Twice in recent years I have seen the lightning strike high up on the face of the mountains, to be followed by the smoke of a fire. On the first occasion the fire burnt for two days across the face of *Cathkin Peak*. The same thing has been observed at the Cathedral Peak Forest Station. It is also known that rock-falls sometimes start fires.

We must remember, too, that grasslands that have not been subject to fire for some time always deteriorate. Litter accumulates, stifling the good grasses. These are replaced by inferior species, and by herbs and small shrubs. Fire is a cleansing, regenerative agent. Anyone who has seen the wealth of wild flowers in the Drakensberg after a spring burn will realise the truth of this.

But fire is also a vicious killer, and must be controlled. This is one of the main tasks of the men who staff the Forest Reserve and who guard the trees. On Tuesday, 5th August 1958 two bad fires broke out in the Cathedral Peak area, and on the same day extensive fires were reported from the Transkei, the Natal Midlands, and as far north as the north-eastern Transvaal. For many it was a day of terror, as the raging fires swept down upon them. In the Natal Midlands they roared on for 80 kilometres, completely out of control. At least ten lives were lost. Two years earlier a similar fire had broken out on the Research Station at Cathedral Peak. The home of the Research Officer came within an ace of being burnt down, three African huts and the cottage of an African driver went up in flames, and 485 ha of grassland were destroyed. On August 17, 1970 five Forestry labourers in the Cathkin area, burning breaks only a few kilometres from our home, were trapped in a raging, run-away fire. All five men, gravely burned, had to be evacuated by helicopter, and one subsequently died in hospital.

One of the worst fire tragedies in the Drakensberg occurred in the Royal Natal National Park on 3rd September 1966. That morning a lady staying at the Hotel attempted to light her cigarette on the slopes of the Little Berg, above the Cascades. The grass was long and tinder-dry, and a high wind was blowing. She threw her lighted match down, thinking it was out, but it was not, and in a split second a roaring sheet of flame started to race up the mountain side.

Down at the Parks Board office, three kilometres away, the Warden,* was sitting at his

* He has asked me not to mention his name.

desk. He looked up, saw the smoke, and dashed immediately for the African compound, where he quickly rounded up a gang of six African Game Guards. Then together they raced for the hill slopes. It was quite impossible to extinguish the fire, but they managed to put in a back burn and so save the camp site, the Fisheries Office, and a Staff house. Then, after watching the fire carefully to see in which direction the wind was consistently blowing, they raced up the hillside in an attempt to put in a break ahead of the advancing fire. But suddenly the wind changed, and the fire swept down upon them.

In one leap it cleared a gap of 100 metres. The flames were 15 metres high. Ahead of the seven men was a single high rock, and the Warden realised it was their only hope. Towards it the men raced, but one man panicked, and, ignoring the Warden's shouts, ran in the wrong direction and was swallowed up in the flames. The other five, together with the Warden, reached the rock at the same time as the fire. They leapt on to it and started to scramble to the top. Three of the Game Guards managed to reach the summit, and promptly lay down flat, but with the flames all around them two of them again panicked. One jumped off the rock. The Warden leapt down after him, and, fighting desperately for his own life and the life of the man he held, managed to hold him down while the flames swept over them. ("How do you hold down a young, fear-crazed panic-stricken African!" he asked me afterwards.) The three men who lay down flat on top of the rock without moving escaped almost unscathed, in spite of the searing heat, but the other three, the Warden and the two young Africans who panicked, were gravely burnt with third degree burns.

When they were able to descend they started to look for the first boy who had panicked. They found him. He was dead. So fierce had been the heat of the flames that only five paces separated the point where the fire caught him to where he fell. Eventually the rest of the party staggered back home, and three of them, including the Warden, were rushed off to Ladysmith Hospital, where they spent many months in agony, undergoing a series of skin-grafts.

But the fierce hunger of the fire had still not been appeased. Up the slopes it tore, and round the corner to Tendele, the Hutted Camp run by the Natal Parks Board. On its way it caught another African, swept over him, and left him a smouldering, charred trunk. At Tendele upwards of 100 campers were out walking on the hillside, but mercifully, at the last moment, the wind swung round and the fire passed them by.

And the tally? Two dead and six burnt, three of them seriously. The Warden paid in full for his gallant act in saving at least one boy for he has never fully recovered and never will. And all because of one carelessly-dropped match!

What should you do if you are caught in a run-away fire such as the one I have just described? Ignite the veld. It will burn away from you rapidly. Its windward front will move slowly. Step across this slow fire, and follow behind the hot front. By the time the fire approaching you joins your own fire, you will be safe in your own burnt veld. If you have no time for this, or lack matches, run *into* the advancing flames, not *away* from them. By doing this you reduce the time your body is in contact with the flames. Then, when you are through, *roll*. Your clothing will almost certainly be on fire, and rolling is the best method of putting the flames out. If for any reason you cannot do even this, your only hope is to lie flat on the ground, and let the flames sweep over you. By doing this you reduce the area of your body which will be in contact with the flames, and of course heat always rises. Never, under any circumstances, run away from a fire unless you are sure you can out-pace it.

There is one final problem which often exercises the minds of trained foresters, as well as the general public. Should the Drakensberg be afforested with exotic trees, as a commercial proposition? There are some who advocate this. They point out that the land is entirely suitable, that it is too steeply sloping for agriculture, that there is a high rainfall, which is essential for any commercial forestry scheme, and that South Africa is greatly in need of more extensive timber resources. They also point out that soil erosion and flood damage are perennial problems in the Drakensberg, and that it has been proved that afforestation is an excellent protective measure against floods.

These people maintain that afforestation is one of the most gainful methods of utilising land and water resources. They remind us of what Dr. G. J. Stander said in Durban in 1963. At a Symposium organised there by the South African Water Catchments Association he said: "I would like to give you my answer to the controversial question as to whether water should be made available for afforestation rather than for irrigation purposes. The answer is plain and simple. Every 1 000 gallons of water that is used for afforestation in the pulp and paper industry produces a gross income of 160 cents, whereas the gross income from products from an irrigation project such as the Orange River scheme, will be of the order of 10 cents per 1 000 gallons."*

And I entirely, and most emphatically, disagree – not with Dr. Stander's figures, but with the *application* of those figures to the Drakensberg. Can we not keep one small corner of God's earth free from the abrasive profit motive, free from the searching, uprooting, despoiling hand of man, free in all its untouched pristine beauty and grandeur? Let Rosalind have her Forest of Arden. Let her wander foot-loose and fancy-free, hand in hand with her Orlando, under the whispering trees. But in heaven's name, let it be a natural, indigenous forest, and not a forest made by the hand of man.

* * * *

And so, patiently, painstakingly, with their eyes on far horizons, the men who guard the trees in the Drakensberg, at Cathedral Peak, at Cathkin and on the majestic slopes of the Drakensberg go about their business. Wars and rumours of wars will come and go, the busy tide of life will pass them by, the years and the centuries will roll on, but the work will continue, "unacclaimed", said Schiller of a similar project in Europe, "unacclaimed, but free from the tyranny of egoism. Truly," he added, "if I were not a poet, I would like to be a forester!"

---

* Quoted in the Report of the Inter-Departmental Committee of Investigation into Afforestation and Water Supplies in South Africa, 1968.

CHAPTER XX

SMOKE ON THE PASS – 1

"That was the day of the smoke on the Pass"
— WITNESS MAHOIZA, AT THE TRIAL OF
LANGALIBALELE, JANUARY 1874

It was only a minor skirmish in the long story of Britain's Colonial wars, but before the dust of the conflict had finally settled, a popular Lieutenant Governor had been recalled with his career in ruins, Natal's system of native administration under Sir Theophilus Shepstone had been shaken to its foundations, the movement towards Responsible Government in Natal had been set back twenty years, and a gifted and saintly priest, once the most loved man in Natal, had become overnight, in the words of the *Natal Witness*, the most unpopular man in the Colony. And on the summit of a lonely pass in the Drakensberg men had fought and died in the smoke of battle.

His name was Langalibalele. The irreverent British Tommies called him "Old Longbelly', while *Punch* added his own inimitable contribution:

"Some men may praise and some denounce you,
But tell me, how shall I pronounce you?
There's something of a southern sea
In soft Lan-gáli-bále-lé."*

Ten years before he hit the world's headlines, in 1863, John Shedden Dobie, the traveller, had visited him, and had described him as "a big pudding-headed-looking beast, as like a king as any lout of a porter". But nine years prior to this Bishop Colenso had described him as "In appearance rather a young man, of perhaps 26 years" (actually he was nearer 36) "tall, and in good condition – you would hardly call him stout – with that dignity and grace in his actions which so commonly, amidst the most savage nations, proclaim the King." What had happened in the nine years? Was this yet another example of the bitter prejudice and partisanship which bedevilled the whole affair from its very start? Or was it, perhaps, that nine years of "uTshwala", "intombis" (Langalibalele admitted to Bishop Colenso that he had 80 wives!) and "jabuler-ing"† (wine, women and song!) had taken their inevitable toll? Whatever it was, Langalibalele certainly aroused the most heated emotions, and a controversy the echoes of which have, even now, hardly died down.

Langalibalele was born round about 1818, the son of Mtimkulu, Chief of the Amahlubi tribe, who had been slaughtered in the year of Langalibalele's birth by the marauding Matiwane (see p. 17). He was first named Mthethwa, after Dingiswayo, and then later Langalibalele. The name means "The sun is boiling hot" (*Ilanga*, the sun, and *libalele*, it is killing, or hot). Amongst his many other claims to fame, he was a noted rain-maker, and his services in this direction were in constant demand. There is a legend that when John Ross, the fourteen-year old boy hero, called at Shaka's kraal in 1827 on his 960 km journey to Delagoa Bay, Shaka gave him an escort of 30 warriors under the command of Langalibalele, but this can hardly be correct, for Langalibalele himself would only have been a boy of nine years of age at the time.

---

* The correct pronunciation is Lánga-lee-ba-lé-le, with the main accent on the penultimate syllable, rhyming with 'fair'.

† uTshwala, (beer); intombi, (girl); jabula, (to rejoice) (Zulu).

By 1848 he had become Chief of the Amahlubi tribe in their ancestral home on the left bank of the Buffalo River. The Amahlubi, of course, had fared badly over the years. It will be remembered that Matiwane had fallen upon them thirty years before, and had broken them up. Some had fled to the Orange Free State, some to the Cape, some to Lesotho, and some into the Drakensberg. These had later been driven out by Matiwane. Many of those who fled into Lesotho settled under a Chief Molapo, whom we shall meet again. A small remnant had remained behind in Zululand under Langalibalele. By this time they had been reduced in number to about 7 000 men, women and children.

In 1848 further trouble arose for them. In that year Mpande, King of the Zulus, summoned Langalibalele to appear at the royal kraal. Langalibalele refused to come, exhibiting thus at an early age the recalcitrance that was later to result in his complete undoing. He alleged that he was afraid to come, as on a previous occasion his brother, Dhloma, had been murdered when summoned by Dingane to appear before him. Truly, coming events were casting their shadows before! Mpande, in his wrath, fell upon him, and Langalibalele, together with the neighbouring tribe of Putini (Putini was his uncle, and the two tribes were inter-related) fled across the Buffalo into Klip River County, where they appealed to the Lieut. Governor, Mr. Martin West, for help. The Government decided to move the two tribes down into the Midlands of Natal. Once again, Langalibalele exhibited the same stubborness he had already shown, and refused to move, and it was only the skill and diplomacy of Shepstone, who was sent up specially to handle the matter, that finally brought the Chief to heel without bloodshed. In April 1849 the Amahlubi were established on the banks of the Bushman's River, just north of *Giant's Castle*, in 36 450 ha of good arable country, which is to-day known as Drakensberg Location No. 1, while Putini and his tribe were similarly established due north of the Amahlubi, along the banks of the Little Tugela. This is the Drakensberg Location No. 2 of to-day. Part of the idea of the Natal Government was that these two tribes would act as a buffer between the marauding Bushmen in the mountains and the settlers.

Here, in their mountain fastnesses, under the shadow of the mighty Drakensberg, the two tribes prospered and grew, their very isolation tending to increase their spirit of independence. By this time Putini was an old man, with "a soft, wily eye and a slow, drawling utterance", according to Bishop Colenso who visited him in 1854. He was "weak and childish". He even asked the good Bishop if he did not have a medicine for old age! But Langalibalele was young and in his prime, still in his early thirties, and on his mountain slopes, sunwashed in summer but grim and forbidding in the days of winter, he brooded darkly. By the time our story opens, his tribe had grown to 94 000.

Even before the rebellion he was regarded by those in authority as a *mauvais sujet*. In 1869 new Marriage Regulations had been promulgated. Langalibalele's tribe resisted these. The tribe was fined and warned of the consequences of any further trouble. Then came the series of events that precipitated the final catastrophe.

In 1870 diamonds had been discovered at Kimberley, in Griqualand West, and soon the great diamond rush was on. It soon became the practice for the diggers to pay their native labour in the form of guns. In the Cape this was not illegal. Any native could purchase a firearm merely on production of a note from his employer, but in Natal this was not so. Here, no gun could be acquired without registration and a permit from the Lieut. Governor. Langalibalele saw his chance. He made sure that his young men working at the diggings chose their payment in the form of guns instead of cash, and he persuaded Putini's people to do the same. Arrived home, his men refused to hand the guns in for registration.

Early in 1873 John Macfarlane, the Magistrate at Estcourt, ordered Langalibalele to hand in all guns in the possession of his tribe for registration. Langalibalele at first hedged. He did not know the names of the culprits, what guns they had, nor where they were kept. At length he bluntly refused. After several further attempts to induce him to come to heel, Macfarlane eventually told him that "as the vessel in which he kept his offences was full to overflowing", he had reported him to Mr. Shepstone, the Secretary for Native Affairs.

In April a message was despatched to Langalibalele by the Government summoning him to appear in Pietermaritzburg to give an account of himself. Langalibalele promised the messenger that he would come, but he did not keep his promise. Instead he sent Mabuhle, his Head Induna, to say that he could not come because of an old wound in his leg. The Secretary for Native Affairs replied that the matter was urgent, and that it was imperative that he come down, if necessary by ox-wagon. The messenger was treated with disrespect, and was sent back with a message that Langalibalele was too ill to come.

Then occurred an unfortunate delay. Cetewayo, the new Zulu king, was due to be crowned, and Shepstone, with an imposing entourage, left on July 31st for the Royal Kraal. He only returned on September 16th.

In the meantime, Langalibalele had not been idle. He went right ahead with his plans for open rebellion. Even before Shepstone left for Zululand, Colonel Griffiths, the Governor's Agent in Lesotho, had informed the Cape Government of the arrival among the Basutho, at Molapo's kraal, of messengers from Langalibalele inquiring whether Molapo would be prepared to offer a safe refuge in his territory for Langalibalele's cattle and his women and children, in the event of open hostilities. The Cape Government immediately passed this information on to Natal. Actually, Langalibalele had numerous relatives in various parts of the country. He was reputed to have 54 sons and 68 daughters (we have already noted his 80 wives!) He had relatives in Lesotho, Griqualand East, where his brother was a Chief, Swaziland, Zululand, from amongst the Fingoes, who were in large part Hlubis themselves, and as far afield as the Caledon and Fish Rivers. Many of these pledged themselves to help him. Messages and gifts were exchanged with Cetewayo. Langalibalele's regiments were drilled and prepared for battle, many of the troops being sprinkled with an *intelezi* to protect them from the bullets of the white man. Food was prepared and stored in caves in the mountains, gunpowder was manufactured, and the cattle all sent into the Upper Injasuti area (Little Tugela) where it was, at first, planned to defend them. (Later the Chief decided to take the cattle with him into Lesotho.)

Soon after Shepstone's return, on October 4th, a third deputation was sent to Langalibalele. It was decided to add weight to the deputation by sending Mahoiza and Unyembe, two indunas attached to the Magistrate at Pietermaritzburg, as the messengers. They carried with them a final ultimatum. The messengers were treated with complete disrespect, and even insulted. They had arrived at the Chief's kraal, Pangweni, on October 11th. They were kept waiting fourteen days, and only then, at another kraal, 16 km from Pangweni, were they granted audience. Before being brought into the Chief's presence they were subjected to the indignity of being stripped naked. Langalibalele's answer was yet another blunt refusal to go to Pietermaritzburg. This was open defiance. The cup of his offences was indeed full! It was war.

At his subsequent trial Langalibalele alleged that his repeated refusals were motivated by fear. He quoted in his defence what has become known as the Matyana affair. Apparently sixteen years earlier John Shepstone, brother of the Secretary for Native Affairs, had been ordered by the Ladysmith Magistrate to effect the arrest of Matyana on a charge of murder. Matyana arranged to be always surrounded by armed men, but eventually he was induced to come to an *indaba** unarmed, the arms of his men being piled some 200 metres away. John Shepstone is alleged to have concealed a gun under the mat at his feet, and then to have drawn it and fired at Matyana. He had missed Matyana, but had wounded a man sitting next to him. In the turmoil which had followed thirty Africans had been killed. Langalibalele had been present at the action. W. R. Guest, who has made a detailed study of the Langalibalele

* indaba: a council, or meeting.

228

Rebellion, holds that the Matyana affair of 1857 was the key to the whole Langalibalele affair of 1873.

It was time to act. So far a series of unforeseen events had precluded any direct action – Shepstone's absence in Zululand, and the fact that there had been no Lieut. Governor in Natal from the departure of Sir Anthony Musgrave early in 1873 to Pine's arrival the following July, a delay which undoubtedly had its effect in encouraging Langalibalele. Pine admitted as much in his despatch of 13 November, 1873, to the Earl of Kimberley, Secretary of State for the Colonies, when he said that part of the cause of the disaster was that energetic steps had not been taken twelve months earlier. Now the Government could no longer allow open defiance such as Langalibalele's to go unpunished. The whole of Zululand knew of his defiance, and all were watching to see what action the Government would take. To make matters worse, the Government now received information that Langalibalele was preparing to flee the Colony, into Lesotho, via the Bushman's River Pass, with all his tribe and his cattle. This they could never allow. Sir Henry Barkly, Governor of the Cape, and High Commissioner of Lesotho, to whom Pine was accountable, would inevitably require an explanation, and this could lead to a probing of Shepstone's jealously guarded native policy in Natal. It was decided to seal the passes over the Drakensberg, to apprehend Langalibalele, and to bring him to trial.

It was high time. On Wednesday, 29th October 1873, instructions were issued to the Natal Frontier Guard at Ladysmith, the Weenen Yeomanry Cavalry, the Weenen Burgher Force, the Karkloof Carbineers, the Natal Carbineers, Pietermaritzburg, and the Richmond Rifles, all mounted Volunteer Regiments, to report for active service. The Magistrates at Ladysmith, Weenen, and Richmond, and the Border Agent at Oliviershoek, also received instructions to call out a large African armed force. Behind these were the military.

By this time alarm and near panic had spread rapidly throughout the Colony. In order to assess clearly the events that followed, it is necessary to understand the situation in which Natal found herself, in that year of 1873. Memories of the Boer massacres of thirty-five years ago were still vivid in the minds of men. Poorly garrisoned by Imperial troops, Natal felt completely isolated from her nearest help, the Cape, 1 500 kilometres away. The only forces she could rely upon, apart from the pitifully small garrisons of regular soldiers, were a few Volunteer Regiments, as yet completely untried and inexperienced. With a population of only about 16 000 whites, thinly spread, she faced the growing might of 300 000 Zulus. There was clear evidence of collusion between Natal natives and Moshoeshoe's successor in Lesotho, Letsie. With this, and Langalibalele's numerous contacts in other parts of the country, a general uprising, in which the whole country would go up in flames, was an ever-present eventuality. All farming operations in the Midlands were suspended, women and children were sent into laagers in Pietermaritzburg and Mooi River, and two public meetings were held in Estcourt to discuss the defence of the town. Many Boer families trekked over into the Free State. The Government's decision to act swiftly and decisively was widely welcomed.

The plan of operations decided upon was originally proposed by Macfarlane, the Resident Magistrate at Estcourt, a colourful character who played a notable part in the development of the Natal Midlands. Macfarlane handed his plan over to the military authorities, and there it was finally knocked into shape by Lieut. Col. T. Milles, Commandant Natal, who in turn submitted it to the Lieut. Governor, Sir Benjamin Pine.

Although designed as a police action rather than a military one, it was based on sound military tactics, and on paper at any rate was a good one. Its purpose was to prevent the escape of Langalibalele into Lesotho across the Drakensberg, and to effect his capture with the minimum loss of life. It failed because it was based on faulty and inadequate military maps (mainly the one produced ten years earlier by Major Grantham), and by a complete lack of knowledge of the terrain. It is hard to understand this latter point, because, although maps at the time certainly left much to be desired, there were a few men, especially hunters, who had a good working knowledge of the area. They do not appear to have been consulted.

The map on page 231 will make the whole plan of operations clear. Briefly, it envisaged, first of all, throwing a wide cordon of troops, stretching from *Champagne Castle* to *Giant's Castle*, around the two Locations, hemming them in from the rest of Natal, and secondly, sending two flying columns to converge along the summit of the Drakensberg on Bushman's River Pass, thus sealing the tribe off from Lesotho. The following troop dispositions were to be made:—

1. Captain Allison, with 500 armed loyal Africans, was to seize Champagne Castle Pass before 5 a.m. on Monday, 3rd November 1873, and to communicate with the detachment converging on Bushman's River Pass from the south, which would be on his right, and with Captain Lucas' party on his left. He was to watch any possible approach up the mountains between *Champagne Castle* and Bushman's River Pass. Captain Allison, an ex-Carbineer, was the Border Agent at Oliviershoek, near the present Royal Natal National Park.

2. Captain Barter, with one troop of Karkloof and half a troop of Pietermaritzburg Carbineers, was to advance up Giant's Castle Pass, leaving the half troop of Pietermaritzburg Carbineers at its head so as to protect his rear, and then to proceed north along the summit with the Karkloof troop to the head of Bushman's River Pass. He was to be in position by 6 a.m. on Monday, 3rd November, hold the Pass, and was to communicate with Allison's party to the north, which would be on his left. The men were to carry provisions for 24 hours. Charles Barter was the son of an Oxfordshire Rector and a Fellow of New College, Oxford. He had first emigrated to Canada, where he had tried lumbering, had not liked it, had returned to England, and then had come out to Natal on the *Globe*. In Natal he did well. He became farmer, horse-breeder, Magistrate, Member of the Legislative Assembly, Author (he wrote *The Dorp and the Veld* in 1852, and several subsequent works), and Newspaper Editor (he was Editor of the *Times of Natal*). He was greatly beloved and respected, and did much for the infant Colony. He was a keen Carbineer, and his account of the Langalibalele affair is one of the best we have.

3. Captain Lucas, with 500 armed Africans, supported by the Frontier Guards, was to be posted at David Gray's farm, *Cathkin*. He was to be in position by 8 a.m. on 3rd November, his right at the foot of Champagne Castle Pass, his left on the Little Tugela, "feeling the right of Captain Macfarlane's party". Lucas was the Resident Magistrate at Ladysmith, and, as we have seen, had been a survivor from the wreck of the *Birkenhead*.

4. Captain Macfarlane with 500 Africans, supported by the Weenen Yeomanry and the Weenen Burghers, was to be posted with his right feeling the left of Captain Lucas' party, and his left on the left bank of the Bushman's River, near *Ntabamhlope*. He was to be in position by 8 a.m. on 3rd November, and to communicate with the Pietermaritzburg Africans on his left.

5. A contingent of Pietermaritzburg Africans was to be posted with their right on the right bank of the Bushman's River, in communication with Captain Macfarlane's left, their own left resting on the Giant's Castle Pass. Again, they were to be in position on the 3rd.

6. Her Majesty's troops, together with half a troop of Pietermaritzburg Carbineers, were to remain at *Meshlynn* farm in support of Captain Barter at either Giant's Castle Pass or Bushman's River Pass, as might be required.

In addition to the above, Captain Arthur C. Hawkins, Resident Magistrate of the Upper Umkomanzi Division (Richmond) was to take command of the Richmond Mounted Rifles and a force of 500 Africans, and to occupy the country to the south of *Giant's Castle*, between the Umkomaas and Umzimkulu Rivers, so as to prevent any escape in that direction.

Tactically, and on paper, the plan was a good one. In practice it was quite unrealistic. It failed to take account of the nature of the country. The whole area is not only large, but is so broken by great hills and valleys that communication between the various commanders in the field would have been difficult, if not quite impossible.

Altogether 200 British troops, 300 Natal Volunteers and about 6 000 Africans were

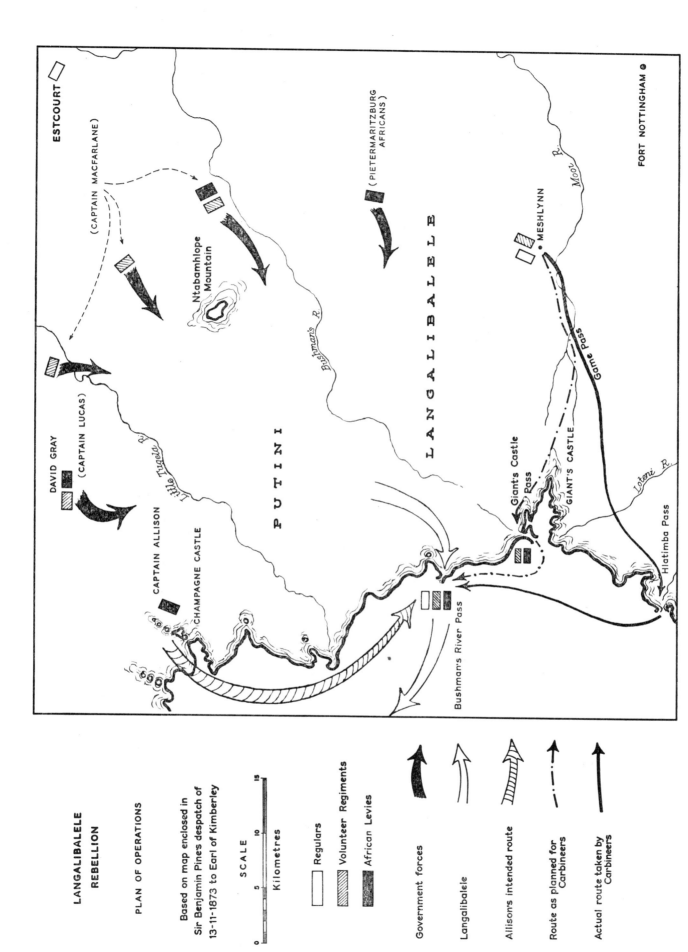

LANGALIBALELE
REBELLION

PLAN OF OPERATIONS

Based on map enclosed in
Sir Benjamin Pines despatch of
13-11-1873 to Earl of Kimberley

SCALE

Kilometres
0   5   10   15

Regulars
Volunteer Regiments
African Levies

Government forces
Langalibalele
Allisons intended route
Route as planned for Carbineers
Actual route taken by Carbineers

ESTCOURT

(CAPTAIN MACFARLANE)

Ntabamhlope Mountain

(PIETERMARITZBURG AFRICANS)

FORT NOTTINGHAM

MESHLYNN

Moot R.

DAVID GRAY

(CAPTAIN LUCAS)

CAPTAIN ALLISON

Little Tugela R.

CHAMPAGNE CASTLE

Bushmans R.

P U T I N I

L A N G A L I B A L E L E

Giant's Castle Pass

GIANT'S CASTLE

Game Pass

Loteni R.

Hlatimba Pass

Bushman's River Pass

involved. The spear-head of the whole operation was obviously the thrust by the Carbineers to occupy the head of Bushman's River Pass.

On Thursday, 30th October, the troops moved out of Pietermaritzburg and commenced the long haul up the Town Hill. They consisted of about 150 men of the 75th Regiment, the Corps of Royal Artillery with their two guns, and the Natal Carbineers. They reached the rendezvous, Fort Nottingham, on the Saturday afternoon.

Fort Nottingham, to-day, is a tiny little hamlet, just off the road from the Dargle to the village of Nottingham Road, nestling under placid, age-old oaks. It had been established in 1850 as a military post to check Bushman raids and for several periods had been almost abandoned. Seldom, if ever, had it seen such busy times as these first few days of November 1873.

Lt. Col. Milles, Commandant Natal, made a point of being there on Sunday, 2nd November, to ensure that all was in order. In his evidence, at the subsequent Military Enquiry, he said that he had not been altogether happy at the idea of Captain Barter, who was not a professional soldier, being in command of the Bushman's River Pass party. At that point Major Durnford, R.E., a professional soldier and Milles' Chief of Staff, volunteered to command the party, and this offer Milles gratefully accepted. Volunteer Law permitted a regular soldier not under the rank of Captain to be in command of a Volunteer Regiment. This superseding of Barter at the last moment sowed the seeds of the subsequent ill-feeling between the two men, which played no small part in the subsequent course of events.

Durnford was a Royal Engineer, Chief of Staff to Commandant Milles, a man of experience and undoubted courage. We shall subsequently have to consider how he shaped up to the strains of command. He had been born in Ireland in 1830, and after service in India and Gibraltar, had arrived in South Africa in 1872, being posted to King William's Town. At the end of May 1873, only five short months before he was caught up in the Langalibalele affair, he was sent to Natal. He was a tall, spare man, with steady, observant eyes, a balding head, and a magnificent moustache which dangled down to his collar-bones. Ascetic and reserved, J. A. Froude, the historian, who knew him, thought highly of him, but Sir Garnet Wolseley, Pine's successor, could not stand him. "I wish I could get rid of him," he wrote. One important point affecting his future actions must be noted here. On assuming command, the Lieut. Governor, Sir Benjamin Pine, told him personally that on no account were the British troops to fire the first shot.

Sir Benjamin Chilley Campbell Pine had only recently arrived in Natal, in July 1873, but he was not new to the country. In fact, this was his second term as Lieut. Governor. His first term had lasted from the end of 1849 to 1855. He returned as Sir Benjamin in July 1873. A man of considerable ability, he had held high office as Acting Governor in Sierra Leone, with great distinction. He was energetic and independent, with ideas of his own, although inclined to be a little unbalanced and impulsive. Some of his actions were certainly somewhat indiscreet. David Dale Buchanan, controversial Editor of the *Natal Witness*, clashed violently with him, and although during his first term of office he got on well with Shepstone, a coolness developed between them after the Langalibalele affair, possibly because Shepstone, now twenty years older, had by then developed a mind of his own. Pine was essentially a man of action. During his first term of office he happened to be at Bushman's River Drift (the present Estcourt) at the moment when a punitive expedition was about to set out in pursuit of a gang of raiding Bushmen. He insisted on taking personal command of the expedition himself. Now true to nature, he did the same again, and decided to take the field himself. Although not in the best of health at the time, he set out from Pietermaritzburg for the front at 2 p.m. on the Friday, together with his Private Secretary, Sir William Beaumont, and Sir Theophilus Shepstone, a brilliant native administrator, but withal cold, withdrawn, an autocrat, and decidedly self-opinionated. Pine was later censured for this action of his by the Secretary of State for the

Colonies, the Earl of Kimberley, who told him he should have remained at his post in Pieter-maritzburg. He was also censured for not having kept the Governor of the Cape, Sir Henry Barkly, fully informed of developments prior to the actual outbreak.

Fort Nottingham, nestling peacefully under pleasantly-wooded hills, was a colourful scene of bustling activity on that Sunday morning of November 2. Mingling with the red coats and white helmets of the British Tommies were the blue uniforms, the white facings, and the jaunty forage caps of the Carbineers, booted and spurred, with their long side-burns and bushy beards. Quartermasters were busy checking stores, the armourers were portioning out the ammunition, while Non-coms. drew supplies from the hard-pressed commissariat. Over to one side the smoke curled up from the cooking fires where the cooks toiled over their great pots of skilly and stew. Men were attending to their horses, checking bridles and harness, and preparing the midday feed of good, ripe oat-hay. Others were preparing the loads for the pack-horses. Small groups sat around under tarpaulins, for it was a drizzly, wet day, with their pipes and tobacco, discussing the latest news, while others, wiser than most, were snatching a few minutes of quiet sleep in their tents, for the word had gone round that they were to ride through the night. Over in one corner was a group of aged *khehlas*,* with their head-rings and grizzled beards, wisely taking snuff and watching with cool indifference the doings of the white men, the "abelungu". Busiest of all was Captain Charles Barter, Officer Commanding the Natal Carbineers. With his massive beard, more imposing even than those of the others, he looked more like a benevolent Father Christmas than a Captain of Carbineers. A little way off from the main tents were the quarters of Sir Benjamin Pine.

Half-way through the morning, after Divine Service taken by Rev. Prichard, a parade was held and the men inspected by Lt. Col. Milles. The contingent consisted of Major Durnford in command; two officers, Captain Barter and Sgt. Major Taylor; six Non-commissioned officers; 47 troopers of the Natal and Karkloof Carbineers; 25 mounted Basutho, and Elijah Kambule, the interpreter, one of Shepstone's key men.

Then, at 7.30 p.m., as the light began to drain from the fading sky, the trumpets sounded for the saddle-up, and at 8 p.m. the men moved out of camp to the steady clip-clop of the horses' hooves and the jingle of their harness, headed by Major Durnford, Captain Barter and the Basutho.

Their destination had been kept secret. Only Major Durnford and the handful of Basutho guides from Chief Hlubi's kraal, and possibly Charles Barter, knew to what point they were headed. Each man had been supplied with 40 rounds of ammunition and provisions for three days, but contrary to Durnford's instructions, these provisions instead of being carried by the men individually, had all been loaded on to four or five pack-horses, which brought up the rear. In the darkness Major Durnford failed to realise that his orders had not been carried out.

Soon after leaving Fort Nottingham instructions were passed down the line that silence was to be maintained, but the men were allowed to ride at ease, and soon a good many pipes were going. Heavy mist blanketed the land. Each man's world consisted of the dim figure of the man in front, and the glow of his own pipe. But the spirits of the men were high, and when the order came that each man was to have two cartridges loose in his pockets, so that they could be easily got at, excitement and eager anticipation reached fever pitch.

On through the night they rode, crossing the Mooi River, and at 1 a.m. in the morning they reached William Popham's farm, *Meshlynn*. Here they off-saddled and rested for two hours. And it was here that the first of many set-backs came. Two pack-horses, they found, were missing, pack-horses carrying some of the ammunition and all of the provisions; and secondly, the farmer, William Popham, was away from home. They had relied on Popham putting them on the right course for Giant's Castle Pass. Now they could only depend on the Basutho guides.

---

* khehla: Zulu for 'old man'.

Two Basutho were sent back to look for the missing pack-horses, but they could not be found, and at 3 a.m. they started up again, this time placing the remaining pack-horses between the two Corps of Carbineers, instead of leaving them in the rear. With scouts on either side to protect their flanks, and in a dripping mist heavier than ever, they rode up the valley of the Mooi River, with guns loaded now, and to the words of their commanding officer: "Fire slow, and fire low, if you are attacked."

Then, just as the light was breaking, they entered Game Pass, which leads up the slopes of the Little Berg to the fine, open grasslands that lie below *Giant's Castle* itself. The mist was breaking, too, and suddenly all the world was alight with the freshness of a dawn that only the Drakensberg knows. The spirits of the men began to rise, and, emerging at the top of the Pass, and seeing the green sun-lit slopes before them, they broke into a spirited canter and jogged merrily along in the morning light. They knew that this was 6 a.m. on the morning of Monday, 3rd November, but they could not know that this was the very moment they were supposed to be at the summit of Bushman's River Pass, twenty-five kilometres away and 1 250 metres above them. Nor could they know that they were already on the wrong trail, and that the series of events that were to lead inexorably to the final tragedy, had already been set in train. Durnford realised the former, and was vaguely troubled: he could not know the latter.

That they were on the wrong trail was soon very evident to him, however. His military maps had shown a level plateau between *Meshlynn* and Giant's Castle Pass. But here, in front of him, lay mile upon mile of the most rugged terrain imaginable, rocky outcrops, steep mountain slopes, hill on distant hill, the whole intersected by a maze of deeply-cut river valleys, and capped by the mighty Drakensberg, still sixteen kilometres away, and still to be scaled. And *Giant's Castle* was on their *right*, instead of on their *left*, as it should have been!

A hurried consultation, but their Basutho guides still assured Durnford that they would get him and his men up the Drakensberg, though by a different pass to the one originally planned, and probably at least 24 hours late.* There was nothing for it but to push on. A drop of rum was issued to each man, and then off they set again.

Urging his men to speed up, Major Durnford galloped ahead. And soon the long column of men became longer still, as the heat increased, and the ground became rougher and more broken, and some of the men, all of whom had been in the saddle now for twelve hours and more, began to drop behind with fatigue.

At midday they came out on the heights overlooking the tremendous valley of the Loteni, six hundred metres below. To the weary men it seemed impossible that any horse could ever stumble down those sheer slopes, but it had to be done, it *could* be done, for there at the bottom was the Major, already beginning to ford the stream. By the time the last stragglers arrived at the bottom, they could see the rest of the troop, a thin, wavering line, struggling up the opposite slope, with Major Durnford still in the lead. So weary and exhausted were the men by this time, that several actually gave up at the river, six of the town troop including Sgt. Maj. Taylor finding their way back to *Meshlynn* from here at their own pace. The rest battled on up an almost impossible slope, dragging the horses up by sheer force when persuasion failed. Some of the remaining pack-horses, heavily laden, simply failed to make it at all, and never reached the top, one being seriously hurt, if not killed. "Never before," says Sir John Robinson, in *A Life-time in South Africa* "had those mountain flanks been trodden by civilised man."

Barter was one of the last up. At the top he found Erskine lying down, "miserably tired". A little way off the rest of the troop had dismounted near a small stream, attending to Durnford. A couple of the men were bathing his head in the clear water. He was in a bad way. Rejecting the advice of the experienced colonials to take a zig-zag route up the slope, he had attempted

* It has always been held that the Carbineers ascended the Drakensberg by the Pass already decided upon by the military authorities, the Giant's Castle Pass. I do not believe they did. My reasons for thus reversing the verdict of history, and taking them up a pass *ten kilometres to the south* of Giant's Castle Pass, are given in Appendix 1.

to go straight up, in accordance with British Army traditions. The hind legs of his horse, unable to bear the strain, had given in, and he had rolled over a precipice and down the slope for some distance. A tree had broken his fall, but he had dislocated his shoulder, put out his collar-bone, injured two ribs, and his head had been cut open.

Here they arranged for Lieut. Parkinson, Sergeant Major Otto and a few of the more tired men of the town troop to remain behind to bring up stragglers and collect pack-horses. Major Durnford also sent on six of his Basutho scouts to climb the Drakensberg and to proceed to the Bushman's River Pass to report on the situation at the Pass. The rest, reduced now to 32 rank and file and about 18 Basutho, pressed on at 2 p.m.

Then came the crossing of the Bohle River, a comparatively easy descent into the ravine at the bottom, but another terrible climb out on the other side, enough, said Sgt. A. R. Button later, to appal the stoutest heart. Slipping, struggling, gasping for breath, lying down exhausted every few yards in the grass, they eventually reached the top. It was here that Captain Barter nearly gave up, and it was only the help and encouragement of his men that kept him going.*

Now at last they came in sight of the main pass which was to take them to the summit. Rounding a corner of one of the spurs of the Drakensberg, they entered upon a scene savage in the extreme. It was a huge amphitheatre of sheer cliffs and towering pinnacles, down which hung ribbons of water, "the very birthplace and nursery of rivers" as Barter described it. Dripping moss and hanging grass and the innumerable waterfalls in the black chasms "gave a sombre and malignant aspect to the scene." To the left, full in view, lay the pass they were to ascend.

By now dusk was coming on. They were already twelve hours late for the rendezvous at Bushman's River Pass, still twenty-three kilometres away, and they still had the mighty Drakensberg to climb. Durnford, utterly exhausted and faint with pain, rested here, but the men, weary though they were, tackled the climb immediately. It soon got dark, and a cutting wind howled dismally in the Pass. "How we slipped and struggled," says Charles Barter, "fell, to get up, and struggle again, or lay panting on the ground, despairing of accomplishing the task, it would be tedious te tell." A few got to the top by 8 p.m., but most of the men climbed the Pass through the early part of the night. They had been in the saddle now for twenty-four hours, with no sleep and no food. The Pass was a grim and forbidding place, choked with great boulders, and so steep it seemed impossible for either man or beast ever to make it. Swearing, cursing, gasping, stumbling over loose rock in the darkness, clinging to tufts of grass, the men battled to get themselves and their horses up to the 2 867 metre summit of the Pass in the darkness of the night. Meredyth Fannin was the first man up, followed by Andries Otto, Tom Day and T. B. Varty in that order, all Karkloof men. Some bivouacked in the Pass itself, but as the night wore on men in ones and twos began to arrive at the top.

After resting a while, Durnford commenced the long climb, accompanied by Erskine and Kambule, and a few of the Basutho, but half way up he collapsed completely. Erskine and Kambule made a bed for him on a ledge under some rocks. After a brief rest he dictated written orders for the senior Volunteer officer ahead, and then watched the sunset. Often in the years that followed he spoke of that brief hour. Far below the country lay spread out below him, "a frozen sea of hills", as he afterwards described it, "glowing in the last rays of the setting summer sun". Slowly the vast panorama of hills and valleys changed from fiery red to deep purple. And slowly, inexorably, the shadows marched across those perfect hills. The wearied and exhausted man must have wondered whether he would ever see that sun again, and what the morrow

---

* In a burst of euphoria the Editor of the *Natal Witness*, in his issue of November 11th 1873, wrote: 'Mr. Barter says little of himself (in his account) but we can see him over every inch of the ground, well-mounted as usual, always in the front, with clear and cheery voice, putting fresh vigour and energy into the tired men, and even the jaded horses'!

held in store for him. His comrades had gone on ahead. He was alone, in a savage and unknown land, gravely hurt, and with a well-armed and unseen foe around him, who might strike at any moment. Then his tired eyes closed, and he slept the sleep of utter exhaustion.

Those who reached the top of the Pass found themselves on the lip of a shallow, saucer-like basin, several kilometres across, and stretching into Lesotho. Riding a few hundred metres over level country, they found a stream "which tasted better than any nectar could have done," said one of them. Here they off-saddled, had a drink of water, "and smoked our pipes as our dinner". None of the pack-horses carrying the rations had arrived. Out of the 82 men who had set out, only 27 had made it so far.

Then Sgt. Clark came riding up with orders that they were to return to the top of the Pass. Here they picketed the horses, placed guards, and tried to get what sleep they could, but so bitterly cold was it that sleep was out of the question for most of them.

During the night young Erskine made it his job to attend to the Major. With a devotion which won the praise of all, exhausted as he was himself, he twice climbed down in the darkness with water and brandy scrounged from the men on top. Of food there was none. "He tended me as my brother might have done," said the Major later.

At 11 o'clock the moon rose. The rocks and the shadows in the Pass stood out starkly. The weary, pain-racked man on the ledge half way up the Pass stirred in his sleep, awoke, and said immediately that he would climb to the top. How they ever got him up will always remain a mystery. The intense cold had stiffened his wounds. He climbed on foot, with a blanket passed round his body, the two Basutho in front holding on to either end, and slowly pulling forwards. Erskine and Kambule supported him from behind as best they could. Every two or three steps they had to halt and lay the wounded man down on the ground to give him a chance to rest. Nine months later he revisited the spot, and did the same climb in fifteen minutes. This time it took him three hours.

He reached the top at 2 a.m., and immediately gave the order to saddle up. He would go on, he growled, even if he only had two men to accompany him. Then he sank to the ground and again fainted. He allowed himself a bare half-hour's rest, and then was lifted on to his grey Basutho horse, "Chieftain", and led the advance over rough, broken country, at 2 900 metres. By now 32 men had assembled at the top, and Captain Barter had also arrived, one of the last to make it.

Just before they left, one of the six Basutho scouts whom Durnford had sent on ahead from the Loteni, returned with the news that all had been quiet at Bushman's River Pass the evening before, but that when he had left some tribesmen were beginning to come up with their cattle. Durnford's only response was to urge his men on.

As they left, one or two late stragglers joined them. The force now consisted of one officer, one Sergeant, 33 Carbineers carrying 40 rounds of ammunition per man, and 25 Basutho, 17 of whom had old guns, some of them muzzle-loaders. They rode in half-sections over a spongy and rocky country, due north. Fortunately the rain held off, and they rode under clear, frosty starlight, to the jingling of their horses' bits, the rough male scrape of leather against leather, and the steady clip-clop of their horses' hooves.

CHAPTER XXI

SMOKE ON THE PASS – 2

"They gave their bodies to the Commonwealth, and received, each for his own memory, praise that will never die, and with it, the grandest of all sepulchres."

— FROM PERICLES' FUNERAL ORATION FOR THE
FALLEN IN THE PELOPONNESIAN WAR.

Three hours later, as they approached the head of the valley leading down to the lip of the Bushman's River Pass, the dawn was just breaking. To their left lay the limitless hills and valleys of Lesotho, stretching mile upon mile into the distance. On their right was the Drakensberg escarpment, and its sheer drop of 1 225 metres into the plains of Natal. High up on this lofty plateau, they looked far down on to a land of wrinkled hills, touched with the fresh glory of the rising sun. Patches of morning mist clung to the sides of the higher peaks. Now they managed to screw a canter out of their horses, and away they went, through bogs and over stones and down a steep hill to a small spruit. Here they found the five remaining Basutho scouts whom Durnford had sent on ahead.

They halted at the spruit for a brief moment, while Durnford explained that he would go on ahead with the Basutho and a few of the Carbineers, while Sgt. Button was to remain behind with the rest of the men as a support group. Arrived at the head of the Pass, Durnford surprised a few tribesmen there, whom he disarmed and forced down the Pass, and then he signalled for the rest of the troop to join him. There were still a few stragglers, and Barter rode to the top of a small rise from where he waved his sword for the men to come on. In five minutes all had assembled at the head of the Pass. It was 6.30 a.m. on the morning of Tuesday, November 4th, instead of Monday, the 3rd.

To right and left of the Pass the ground sloped upwards – on the right, as one faced the Pass, gently, with broken stones and tussocks of grass; to the left, rather more steeply in a series of krantzes. Beyond, on each side, was the vast escarpment of the Drakensberg, with the Pass in front leading down into the depths below. Behind them open grasslands sloped gently down in a saucer-like depression to a small stream at the bottom, the headwaters of the Lakalebalele. Beyond the stream, still further to the west, was a series of hills, rising to a height of 3 200 metres.

At first it seemed to the weary and jaded Carbineers that their delay of 24 hours was not to be important. A few tribesmen hung about the high ground to left and right of the Pass, but looking down the Pass they could see a black mass of hundreds of cattle and their African drivers streaming upwards. Down at the bottom of the saucer-like depression behind them, on the banks of the stream, were a few more Africans with some cattle. Durnford first of all despatched six of his Basutho to these men, ordering them to return down the Pass, but the Basutho soon came back saying that the tribesmen had refused, and that they had been treated with contempt. In the meantime, Durnford had drawn his men up across the lip of the Pass, at one yard intervals. They were dismounted, their horses being tethered nearby.

But there was no sign of Allison and his force, which, it will be remembered, was supposed to rendezvous with them there from the north. It later transpired that the Pass at *Champagne Castle*, up which they were supposed to go, was non-existent. Throughout the previous day, the Monday, Allison had probed right and left, and though supplied with an African guide, he had been unable to find a way to the summit.

The next most important thing was the hunger of the men, for they had been without food now for 34 hours. Durnford ordered the Basutho to kill one of the cattle grazing down near the stream, but not to use a fire-arm. Unfortunately five were stabbed before a cow was killed, and so ravenous were the men that some of them fell on the meat immediately, without waiting for it to be cooked, eating portions of the paunch raw. Durnford proposed paying for the beast, but this was opposed by Barter and some of the men. It was the African's duty, they said, to feed any Government forces in the field. Any payment would be looked upon as a sign of weakness. Durnford deferred to this, but Dunbar Moodie, later Resident Magistrate at Lady-smith, said afterwards that nothing would have been more calculated to rouse the fury of Langalibalele's men than the killing of the animal.

They had just finished skinning the beast when the few tribesmen in their rear were augmented by a large party coming down from the hills to the west. Durnford immediately proposed going down to parley with these men, but they were obviously well-armed and in a truculent mood, and Barter, alarmed for his safety, tried to dissuade him. Failing in this, Barter then offered to go down with him, but Durnford insisted on going alone. Taking with him only Kambule, the interpreter, he rode down the 300 metre slope to the men gathered on the banks of the stream.

Here he found from fifty to a hundred of Langalibalele's men, half of them armed with guns. In the background was a group of younger men, sullen, angry and menacing, fingering their assegais, but in front were several older men, obviously elders and indunas of the tribe, dignified "khehlas" with their ebony head-rings, and with Mabuhle, Langalibalele's chief headman, in obvious command. These men immediately recognised Kambule as one of Shepstone's men. This produced a favourable reaction, and Durnford was able to start talking. Briefly and incisively he offered his terms – surrender, and a return down the Pass to the location, with a promise that their lives would be spared. Otherwise, he said, he and his men would sweep them off the face of the earth. After a long consultation amongst themselves, Mabuhle and the indunas agreed to the terms, on condition that Durnford and his men first left the Pass. To this, of course, Durnford could not agree, and they were discussing the point when there came an angry growl from the young men in the rear. One particularly aggressive man pushed his way to the front and brandished his assegai in Durnford's face. He was promptly struck down by his own head man, but others pressed forward, gesticulating fiercely, and the old man "had to lay about him vigorously with a stick amongst the disorderly youths".

Up on the higher ground, at the actual Pass, Barter and his men, alarmed, watched anxiously. Some urged the Captain to ride back in support of his Chief, but he respected his Chief's wishes, and refrained. He did, however, ride half-way down the depression with Trooper Bucknall, their guns at the ready, in case they should be needed. Then Mabuhle begged Durnford to leave: he could not, he said, be responsible for the behaviour of his young men, who were becoming unmanageable. Mabuhle, however, immediately afterwards sent a messenger down the Pass to urge all his remaining fighting men to come up as quickly as possible.

Back to the head of the Pass rode Durnford, where he found that the situation had deteriorated. Langalibalele's men were now coming up the Pass, pushing past the Carbineers, openly jeering at them, brandishing their assegais and sharpening them ostentatiously on the stones. They began to take up positions behind the rocks on the right, and up on the heights to the left, and they left no doubts as to their menacing attitude.

Durnford first of all re-grouped his small force. He placed the Basutho on the rising ground to his right. To his left he placed the men from the Karkloof, while the Pietermaritzburg troop was held in the centre to guard the actual mouth of the Pass. In his rear he placed Captain Barter with six or seven men.

Then he sat down on a near-by stone and hurriedly wrote a short despatch to Headquarters, saying that Allison had failed to turn up, and asking for reinforcements. He also wrote a note to Parkinson, who had been left behind, ordering him to send on the ammunition at any cost, together with any of the stragglers he had been able to collect, and the remaining pack-horses.

But in the Pass itself conditions were rapidly approaching a crisis. The troopers were trying to force the tribesmen back down the Pass, riding their horses on them and holding their revolvers at their heads. The high ground above, on both sides, was now occupied by a well-placed and well-armed enemy, some two hundred strong, armed men were still coming up the Pass, while away in the distance, on their left rear, the hard-pressed Carbineers saw another large force of Africans approaching. At first these were thought to be Allison's men, but it was soon apparent that they were a large force of Langalibalele's men who had already ascended the Pass and gone down into Lesotho, but who were now returning. They were surrounded.

First Kambule, and then many of the colonials, repeatedly begged Durnford to take resolute action and to open fire, but he refused. At one stage a group of experienced Carbineers approached Captain Barter, pointing out the position, and urging him, as second in command, to reason with Durnford. Barter felt himself unable to do this.

It was at this stage that two things suddenly occurred which triggered off the final tragedy. Barter at last decided to approach Durnford. Striding up to him, he told the Major curtly that the Carbineers were mostly young men, inexperienced in battle, and could not be depended on. Many of them were already saying that they were surrounded and would be massacred.

"Do you mean to report to me officially that you cannot depend upon your men?" asked the astonished Major.

"I do," said Barter, and urged an immediate withdrawal.

Durnford immediately ordered the Corps to be drawn up in front of him, and, addressing them, said, "Gentlemen, I am sorry to inform you that your Captain tells me he cannot place confidence in you."

Barter indignantly denied this in a loud voice, but in the uproar that followed he was not heard.

And then Sgt. Clark, the regular soldier who had been appointed to stiffen the Carbineers, suddenly lost his nerve. He cried out in panic that the end had come: they had been betrayed and all were about to be murdered. (He later claimed, at the Military Enquiry, that he had tried to rally the men, but the evidence was too strong against him, and he was dismissed.) Military order and discipline were on the point of cracking.

Durnford had to act now, and he had to act swiftly. He rode rapidly to the head of the Pass. The Carbineers were on the verge of panic. "Will no-one stand by me?" he called out. "I will, Major," said Erskine. Erskine then rode out from the ranks, and addressing Durnford, said "Will you allow me, Sir, to ride down the Pass with Mr. Bond to show these men there is no cause to fear?" Durnford refused.

But the men had passed the point of no return, and Durnford knew it. He had no option but to sound the retreat. Resolute action at the outset would have saved the situation. It was now too late. Rapidly he called in his outlying parties and made preparations for the withdrawal. It was 9.30 a.m.

And high up on the cliffs to his left, Mabuhle lay crouched behind his rock, and Jantjie, son of Selile, and Maohla, son of Luhoho, their guns at the ready, their fingers itching on the trigger, staring down at the white men below. But like Durnford, they too had been ordered by their Chief on no account to fire the first shot. The time was not yet.

Then Durnford gave the order to retire. At first he had proposed retreating down the Bushman's River Pass, as being the one closest at hand, but the men objected. They said it would be better to go back the way they had come.

They formed fours and set off in orderly fashion. After a few paces they began to form half-sections, and it was then, as this operation was being carried out, that Mabuhle's fingers tightened on the trigger, and Jantjie, son of Selile, chose his man and took careful aim. Some accounts say it was Mabuhle who fired the first shot, and some Jantjie, son of Selile. It is more likely to have been Mabuhle. Both men claimed to have killed their man. Whoever it was, one single shot rang out and startled the silence of those mountain solitudes. And then all hell was let loose. Horses reared and screamed, men were thrown, sporadic firing broke out from both sides of the Pass, puffs of smoke appeared from behind the rocks on the high ground and drifted slowly away in the clear mountain air, and the wild roar of battle spread like an April tide over those quiet slopes. The Carbineers, in wild panic, were off, streaming pell-mell down into the depression, and then turning left up a small gorge. At the first shot Kambule cried, "Ride, Sir, for your life," and Durnford turned to see the Carbineers in full flight.

Erskine was the first to fall. His saddle-girths must have been loose, for as he leapt for his horse, the saddle turned, he fell, was immediately surrounded, and stabbed to death. As his horse fell, Sgt. Button's horse leapt over it, and he was away.

Katana, one of the Basutho, was dropped as he was returning from the stream. He was dead before he reached the ground.

Varty's horse was shot under him. He pitched headlong, but as he fell, Erskine's riderless horse came galloping past. He leapt for its back, gained his seat, but two seconds later this horse also fell with an agonised scream, badly wounded. In a trice Fannin, Speirs and Bucknall were at his side. Fannin shot down one native who was coming up, and then, while he helped Varty transfer the saddle from the dead horse to another (the Major's led horse), Speirs, kneeling down, held the enemy off at 150 metres until the other two had mounted. Then the three galloped away.

In the meantime, Bond had fallen, shot through the head.

Charles Davie Potterill's horse was killed under him. He raced off on foot, with three tribesmen after him. They caught him, and Latyinga, son of Tulisa, was on him in a flash. The two men grappled, but the Englishman had drawn his pistol, and Latyinga took the bullet in his guts. Before he died, however, he managed to drive his assegai deep into the Englishman's side. As Potterill fell, the other two leapt upon him, and finished him off with their assegais.

Durnford found himself completely cut off, but with Elijah Kambule at his side, the two men started to smash their way through the press. Kambule's horse went down, and as it fell Kambule himself was stabbed by an assegai. Durnford turned, leaned down, and attempted to assist the wounded man to mount behind him, but as Kambule lay on the ground, Puluzamati drew his gun and shot him through the head. Durnford raced on, but by this time two of the tribesmen were on him. Running on each side of him, they seized "Chieftain's" bridle. Two assegais flashed. One pierced the Major's left arm, already helpless from the fall on the previous day, the other struck him in the side, but not deeply. Without his sword, which had been damaged in the previous day's fall, he drew his pistol and shot dead the two men at his side. Then on he galloped, only to be confronted by a man with ice-cold eyes and levelled gun.

But now it was time for "Chieftain" to take a hand. With flaring nostrils, bared teeth, ears back and a fearful scream, the beautiful animal reared up and smashed into the man, who went down under flailing hooves. Then they were through, and riding hard for open country, with Durnford firing right and left, and Kambule dead on the ground behind them. And through it all, the hoarse shouts of men caught in the lust of battle, the screams of wounded animals, the frightening rhythmic clash of spear on shield, and the still more frightening "*Usuto! Usuto! Babulaleni abelungu!*"*

By now the main body of Carbineers was well beyond the curve of the hill. As soon as Durnford caught up with them he called out to Barter, "For God's sake, rally your troop!" Barter sent a messenger after his fleeing troopers, but none returned. Durnford, however, was more successful with the Karkloof troop and some of the Basutho. The Basutho had behaved

* Kill the white men.

240

magnificently, many of them staying behind and covering the flight. Now they rallied, and together with some of the Karkloof men, they turned at bay and a volley from them checked the pursuit for a moment. But suddenly they saw a group of tribesmen running up a hill to their left, attempting to cut them off, and they had to abandon the position and gallop away.

Sgt. Clark was well up with the foremost men when a bullet spat into the ground at his feet and kicked up the dust, "and," says Trooper Bucknall in his account of the fight, "he never stopped again until he got to the head of the Pass".

For three kilometres the pursuit continued, but as the tribesmen were on foot and the Carbineers were mounted, they managed to outdistance their pursuers. Then the main body turned back, all except Hlanzi, the son of Magonzi, Umhashi, the son of Mabudaza, Zitshozi, the son of Ngatyana, and a fourth whose name is not known. These four followed the fleeing men right to the head of the Hlatimba Pass.

Singing a triumphant war-song, the main body returned to the Bushman's River Pass. Here a scene of wild exultation and savagery took place. The bodies of Durnford's five men who had been killed were all mutilated, and the men danced round them singing a savage war-chant. The Imfihlweni Regiment was despatched northwards along the line of the Drakensberg to deal with Allison's force in case they should reach the summit. And then the quietness of the high places descended once again, with only the desolate song of the sorrowing wind to break the silence.

Durnford and his men reached the Hlatimba Pass at midday after a two and a half hour ride. The last of Parkinson's men, twelve of them altogether, were just reaching the top of the Pass as they arrived.

And now at last the spirit of the Carbineers began to revive. Apart from Durnford's initial stand, no attempt had been made so far to check the enemy. But now Barter and most of the men proposed making a stand. Durnford, however, would not hear of it. "No!" he said, "get down off this cursed mountain as soon as you can." From now on there are clear signs that even his iron nerve was beginning to crack.

Soon after they left the top of the Pass, on the way down, Parkinson, who was ahead, gave the order to off-saddle. When Durnford caught up with them, he asked angrily who had given the order, and immediately countermanded it. There was an edge to his voice.

At the bottom of the Pass, just before they got to the river, Durnford assembled his men and spoke to them about retrieving their honour. He was in a highly emotional state, and was actually in tears.

Just before they crossed the river, when some form of order had been restored, they heard shots from above. It was Trooper Tainton. He had gone back for a haversack which had been left behind. Two of the four men who had pursued them had followed the troopers right into the Pass, and Tainton had suddenly found himself confronted by them. He had let fly, and one of them, Zitshozi, son of Ngatyana, had pitched headlong down the krantz.

At the river Troopers Fannin and Speirs, who knew the country well, suggested a better route home, and together they led the party down the Hlatimba, proceeding first through "an extraordinary tunnel", then down a long and deep valley, and so out into open country.

Soon after they started down the valley Parkinson was again reprimanded by Durnford for halting without permission, and a few minutes later Sgt. Clark also caught it, for the same reason. Clark had stopped to rest his horse, and as Durnford rode past he shouted at him, saying that he (Clark), an old soldier, should be ashamed of himself setting such an example of mutiny. Durnford seemed to be obsessed with the danger of their being at the bottom of this steep valley, through which the Hlatimba flowed, with heights on each side which could be commanded by the enemy. Parkinson later resigned from the Carbineers. Although he never said anything, nor did he give this as the reason, there is no doubt that he felt keenly his humiliation in front of his men.

Finally, at 1.30 a.m. on Wednesday morning, November 5th, jaded and weary, they reached *Meshlynn*. Out of 52½ hours, 41½ had been in the saddle.

But there never was a time when knights in armour did not have fair ladies to succour them in their hour of peril. The news of the disaster caused consternation amongst the girls of St. Mary's College at Richmond. Many of the girls had relatives and friends amongst the Carbineers. At the end of Study Hour on the evening of the day the news broke, one of the older girls, Ada Knight (later Mrs. Anderson, M.B.E.), sprang to her feet, made a short speech, and then, seizing the hat of the smallest girl, took up a collection. The girls, starry-eyed, asked that the money be used to buy pipes, tobacco, food and comforts for the "starving" Carbineers. This was done, and the goods sent off immediately by two runners recruited from the African staff of the College. They were amongst the first to get through to Fort Nottingham after the news of the disaster had become known. When the packages arrived, we are told, the Carbineers set up such a mighty cheer for "The Girls of St. Mary's", as those wooded hills had ever heard!

But it was defeat, utter and final, a more serious defeat than the casualty list indicated. Shepstone had failed, Langalibalele's tribe had defied the Administration, killed three white men, got clean away, and Langalibalele himself had escaped into Lesotho. He had started his flight, together with his sons, on Sunday, November 2nd. That night he had slept at the foot of Bushman's River Pass, and he commenced the ascent of the Pass the following morning, while the Carbineers were climbing Game Pass, twenty-five kilometres away. Riding up the lower slopes, he then dismounted and walked up the latter portion. Throughout the same day, and during the following night, the bulk of his cattle were driven up the Pass. That night he slept twenty kilometres beyond the Pass, well into Lesotho. On the Tuesday, the day of the action, he pushed on another full day's journey, and is supposed only to have heard of the action at the Pass on the Wednesday evening. On the other hand, there are indications that he was not far off, and that he was actually communicated with immediately prior to the action. Umyovu, one of the accused at the subsequent trial, said that Langalibalele was very near at hand at the time of the action, and he had heard several remarks as to the narrow escape Langalibalele had had, as he had only just left the Pass when the Carbineers arrived. It is quite possible that this is correct, for his tribe as a whole would have been out to "cover" their Chief, and exculpate him, as far as they could, for any possible blame for what had happened at the Pass.

What, we may well ask, were the causes of the disaster?

First and foremost was the lack of knowledge of the terrain, and the faultiness of the military maps available. This made the plan of action completely unrealistic. Captain Allison was unable even to reach the summit, because the Pass he was to use was found not even to exist. Even if he had made the summit, he could not have made contact with Durnford in the time available. It might have been possible for mounted men to proceed up Game Pass, turn right and skirt *Giant's Castle* with the mountain on their left, climb to the summit and reach Bushman's River Pass via the summit plateau in the time allowed (ten hours), but I rather doubt it, especially as the men would be riding through the night. And further, as we show in Appendix 1, Giant's Castle Pass is not a pass capable of being negotiated with ease by mounted men, if at all. But they took, in error, and in ignorance of the terrain, a much longer route, going miles out of their way, over impossible country, with the result that they arrived at their rendezvous twenty-four hours late. Lieut. Col. Milles, reporting to the Assistant Military Secretary, Cape Town, on December 5th, said that the Drakensberg was not known to a dozen men in Natal. That is probably true, but these men were available: they appear not to have been consulted. And why did the military, on that Saturday and Sunday at Fort Nottingham, make no reconnaissance of the ground to be covered by the Carbineers? It could easily have been done. It *should* have been done.

Secondly, we might consider the order not to fire the first shot. Here, the blame must rest squarely on the shoulders, first of all, of Sir Benjamin Pine who gave the order, but ultimately on those of Major Durnford. No-one has ever questioned Durnford's personal courage. The *Natal Colonist* said of him, on November 14th, 1873: "For cool daring and manly endurance, for humanity and every quality which can adorn an Englishman and a gentleman on the field of battle, he is one of whom his countrymen may well feel proud." But one may well ask whether he had those qualities that fit a man for command. The order not to fire the first shot had been given to him personally by Sir Benjamin Pine. Sir Benjamin should never have given him the order in the first place, and Durnford should never have accepted the command, and taken the field, with his freedom of action limited in this way. But, having accepted it, he should surely have had the moral courage to disregard it, and use his common-sense, should the circumstances warrant it.

And they did warrant it. There is no doubt whatever that resolute action, even after the parley, would have resulted in a very different outcome from what eventually happened. According to Zulu custom, the superior army always fires first. The inferior army only fires in self-defence. The failure of Durnford's men not to open hostilities produced a most unfortunate impression on the men of Langalibalele. They expected action. When it did not come, they were at first mystified, and then came the jeers, and the taunts, and the laughter. The commander in the field may not have the *legal* right to disobey orders; but he *does* have a duty to use his discretion. Even Nelson, at the Battle of Copenhagen, put his telescope to his blind eye, and disobeyed orders. It was here that Durnford failed, and he was severely, and rightly, criticised for it afterwards. In the nature of things, he could not defend himself. But his report to Sir Benjamin Pine, soldierly, brief and incisive, ends with these simple words: "The orders I received were 'not to fire the first shot'. I obeyed." He may have thought that this exonerated him. It did not.

And he seemed to lack in other particulars, too. Barbara Buchanan, in *Natal Memories*, remarks that his refusal to accept advice from those who knew the country (remember that he had only just arrived) and his conduct at the Pass "roused burning indignation throughout the Colony".

Then there is the break-down of his own morale when they arrived back at the head of the Hlatimba Pass, and during their return march to *Meshlynn*. Granted his endurance must have reached breaking point, but commanders in the field are not supposed to break!

There is no doubt, too, that there was an undercurrent of hostility between the Major himself and his men throughout the whole affair. His assumption of command over the head of Captain Barter has already been noted. This may have been necessary at the time, but a more tactful man would have found ways of softening the blow, and even of winning Barter over. Instead, he made matters worse by giving orders direct to the men, and to Sgt. Clark, instead of through Barter – and yet, like a good soldier, Captain Barter speaks no word of disparagement of his Commanding Officer in the account he has left us. Parkinson's resignation from the Regiment has been noted, and we might also recall the extraordinary way in which Durnford repeated Barter's warning about the unreliability of his men in front of the men themselves.

To return to the order not to fire the first shot, why was the order given in the first place? It is possible that Pine was actuated by his wish that the whole affair should be regarded as a police action rather than a military one. W. R. Guest suggests that Pine probably had in mind the fact that the three days of grace granted by the Government to the Amahlubi in which to surrender would not have elapsed by the Monday morning, when it had been planned for the Volunteers to reach the head of the Pass. Whatever the reason, Pine was wrong to ham-string his commander in the field in this way, and Durnford was equally wrong in accepting it.

And finally, there is the inexplicable break-down in morale of the Carbineers, a break-down completely foreign to this fine Regiment. But let us not be too hard on them. Most of the men were young lads, scarcely out of their teens. They had had no previous experience in battle. For 36 hours they had been in the saddle, with no food and little sleep, battling their way over some of the most difficult country imaginable. They were in an unknown land, savage in the extreme, surrounded by an implacable and well-armed foe, abandoned, it would seem, by Allison's promised support column, and with their own numbers badly depleted through the inability of some of the men to stay the pace. Added to which is the peculiar and unnerving sense of loneliness and isolation that the summit of the Drakensberg produces on even the most experienced men. It is felt by some mountaineers even to-day. What must it have been like in those days, when the country was *totally* unknown, and communications, such as we know to-day, simply did not exist?

And let us always remember that it was, after all, only a small group of men, in the Pietermaritzburg contingent, who panicked and started the rot. Many of the rest of the Pietermaritzburg men responded promptly to Durnford's call for loyalty, and it was Pietermaritzburg men who died. On their part the Karkloof men acted magnificently. Losses would have been much heavier had it not been for their skill and coolness. We have already noted the dramatic rescue of Varty by Speirs and Fannin, both Karkloof men. Panic is a dreadful thing, unreasoning, unpredictable, frightening. The best can succumb to it: no-one can claim exemption. I saw it once: I do not wish to see it again. It is obvious that the nerves of a few men broke, and there was no-one to steady the rest.

The whole affair was the subject of a Military Court of Enquiry twelve months later, held at the request of the Carbineers themselves. The judgment of the Court, given on 12th December 1874, was that the Volunteers were guilty of a "disorganized and precipitate retreat, with, however, mitigating circumstances".

And let us always remember, in the final analysis, that Isandhlwana, a short five years later, made up gloriously for any possible shame at Bushman's River Pass. There Colonel Durnford himself, together with Lieut. Scott and twenty two men of the same Regiment that had let him down at the Pass, fell in action together, side by side. They could have escaped. They preferred to remain and die fighting. When their ammunition was finished they threw down their guns and drew their pistols. They used these as long as they could, and then they formed a line, shoulder to shoulder and back to back, and fought with their knives until the last man fell.

Much of the blame for the panic at the Pass must go to Sgt. Clark, for what Sir Benjamin Pine called his "shameful and mutinous conduct". He was a Regular Army pensioner, who had been appointed Sgt. Major to the Carbineers by Lieut. Col. Milles to stiffen the inexperienced Carbineers. He had been through the 1851–2 Kaffir War in the Cape, and had served for 17 years in the C.M.R., ten of these as Troop Sgt. Major. Experienced in native warfare, his sudden cry that they had been betrayed and were about to be murdered would be believed, and it undoubtedly triggered off the initial panic. On their return to *Meshlynn*, at 1.30 a.m. on the Wednesday morning, while on their way to their base at Fort Nottingham, he promptly packed up and went home, because "he did not like the way Major Durnford had treated him"! He was later dismissed, and though he demanded an enquiry before the House of Assembly, this was not granted.

Perhaps the man who came out best from the whole affair was Robert Henry Erskine. He was the son of Major Erskine, Colonial Secretary at the time and a former Regimental Commander of the Carbineers. Born in 1846 in India, he was a great-grandson of the well-known Lord Chancellor, under Pitt. He was educated under William Calder at the infant Pietermaritzburg High School, later Maritzburg College and at the time of his death was a rising Advocate in the Supreme Court. Twenty-seven years of age, he was one of the men who found the early ride from the top of Game Pass particularly exhausting. Sgt. Button, it will be remembered, found him at the top of the climb out of the Loteni Valley, stretched out on the grass, "looking miserably tired". And yet he never thought of himself, and gave himself completely and utterly to others. It was Erskine who twice, in the ensuing night, climbed down to his Commanding Officer in the Pass with brandy and other comforts, in spite of his own weariness. He was the first to stand by Durnford at Bushman's River Pass, and he was the first to fall. Throughout he displayed those very qualities of steel-like courage and compassion for others that have made the Natal Carbineers the fine Regiment they are to-day, and it is a pity that the Regiment has not been able to perpetuate, in a fitting way, the memory of this young man, the first Carbineer ever to fall in action.

* * * *

And so the smoke on the Pass drifted away, and the cries of man and beast were stilled. It was defeat, total defeat, as we have said. But once again the inscrutable Drakensberg Mountains spelt out, in letters of gold this time, their ancient story, that the goal itself is less than nothing, fit only to be cast into the limbo of forgotten things. What *is* to be remembered, and told down the years with pride, is the striving, the agony, and the tears, the selfless courage, yes, even the bitter shame of broken men, pushed beyond the limits of human endurance. For even this adds richness and compassion to the long story of man's unending journey.

CHAPTER XXII

AFTERMATH

*"Old, unhappy, far-off things
And battles long ago."*

— WORDSWORTH

The dust and the smoke that arose on that quiet Drakensberg Pass on a summer's morning in 1873 was as nothing to the uproar that followed. Fears of a general native uprising spread rapidly, and men throughout the Colony looked to their guns. Martial Law was proclaimed on November 11th.

According to Hattersley the whole of the Midlands were seething with unrest. The story is told of two young girls, each 20 years old, living in the Nottingham Road area, who had to go to Pietermaritzburg on urgent business. All their menfolk were away subduing the rebellion, and such was the state of the country that they dared not travel by day. They travelled down alone, at night, riding down one night and back the second. David Gray, at Cathkin, was raided on the night of 16th April 1874. A group of rebels broke into their home and stabbed two of their sons, David and Walter. David was 29 years of age, and Walter a lad of 15. David Gray senior, in an adjoining room, heard the noise and ran for his gun. The rebels left, but that same night they burnt down the Nest, (now the Nest Hotel) a kilometre or so away. Both David and Walter recovered from their wounds, though David's was serious. Several other houses in the Cathkin area were also attacked, including those of Sclanders, J. Maree and Florey, the latter's being burnt down.

But it was not only in Natal that the alarm was sounded. For the first time in the history of South Africa it was suddenly realised that what touched one touched all, and help was immediately offered from the Cape to the Limpopo. The Governor of the Cape, Sir Henry Barkly, immediately ordered *H.M.S. Rattlesnake* to sail for Natal with 200 officers and men of the 86th Regiment and a small reinforcement of Royal Artillery. The ship sailed on November 20th and reached Durban on the 25th. The troops were landed and went into camp, but were not required. Sir Henry also ordered the Commandant of the Frontier Armed and Mounted Police, stationed at King William's Town, to move a detachment of 200 men into Lesotho. Orders were sent to Col. C. D. Griffiths, the Governor's Agent in Lesotho, and to Mr. J. M. Orpen, British Resident in Griqualand East, to assist in the apprehension of Langalibalele. Orpen collected a strong force to prevent the retreat of the rebels into Griqualand East. Later he crossed into Lesotho, as we shall see, to assist Captain Allison's flying column. Commandant Bowker, with another detachment of 200 of the Frontier Armed and Mounted Police, was sent to the sources of the Caledon River in support of the Natal authorities. The Governments of the Orange Free State and the South African Republics offered help, as also did the diggers on the Diamond Fields. President Burgers of the Transvaal Republic mobilised a force of 200 men on the Republic's eastern border to prevent Langalibalele from seeking asylum with Cetewayo via the Transvaal. For the first time it was realised that South Africa was one indivisible whole, and the movement towards some form of federation or union was born.

As soon as the military authorities had recovered from the shock of the disaster, it was decided that Langalibalele must be pursued and apprehended at all costs. It was not until November 13th that it became known that he, together with the bulk of his tribe and cattle, had fled over the Pass into Lesotho. But no-one was quite sure what he would do after that. All that was known was that he had disappeared into the heart of Lesotho, a wild and desolate

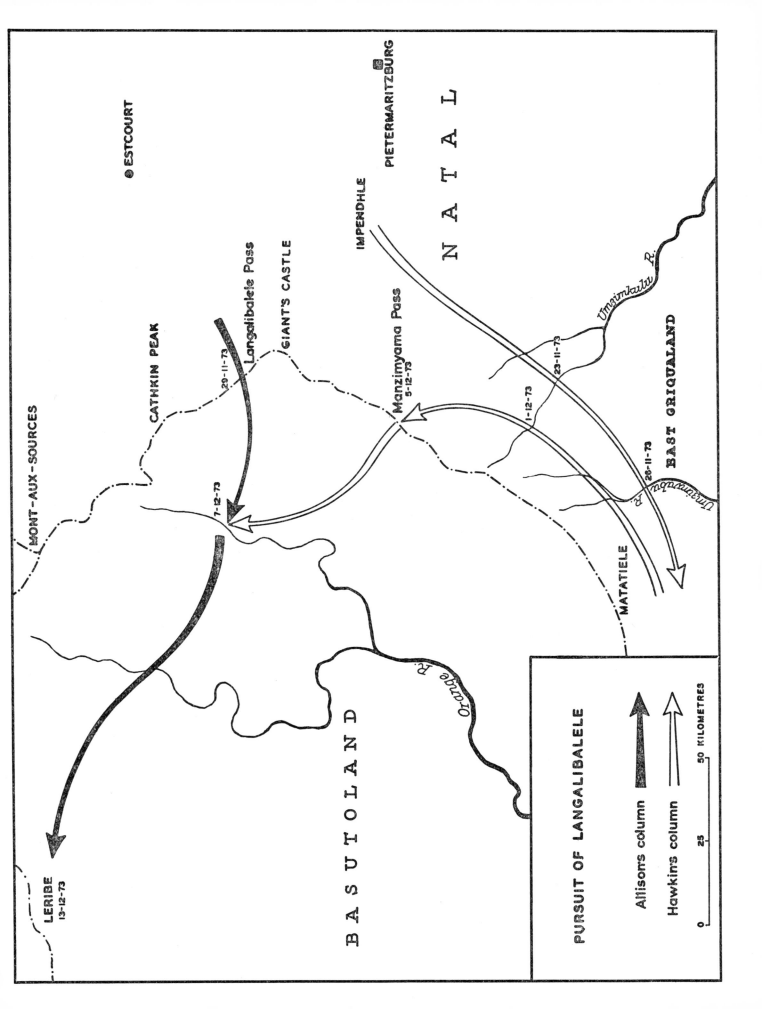

ESTCOURT

PIETERMARITZBURG

IMPENDHLE

N A T A L

Langalibalele Pass

CATHKIN PEAK

GIANT'S CASTLE

20-11-73

Manzimyama Pass
5-12-73

Umzimkulu R.

23-11-73

1-12-73

MONT-AUX-SOURCES

7-12-73

28-11-73

Umzimvubu R.

EAST GRIQUALAND

MATATIELE

B A S U T O L A N D

Orange R.

LERIBE
13-12-73

PURSUIT OF LANGALIBALELE

Allison's column

Hawkin's column

0   25   50 KILOMETRES

country, unmapped and unknown. It was thought that he might head south-westwards in the direction of Griqualand East, or Nomansland, as it was then known, where he had a brother. On the other hand, he had been in close touch with the Basutho Chief Molapo, whose domain was near Leribe in the north-east. He might head there. It was decided to send two flying columns after him, one under Captain Hawkins and one under Captain Allison.

Captain Hawkins had in his column 50 Europeans, members of the Richmond Mounted Rifles and the Natal and Karkloof Carbineers. His object was a thrust south-westwards, along the foot of the Drakensberg, to head Langalibalele off in case he should decide to go in that direction. Assembling at the Impendhle mountain, they crossed the Umzimkulu on November 23rd, and reached the Umzimvubu on the 26th. There they found Adam Kok, the Griqua Chief, with 600 to 1 000 mounted men, together with Mr. Orpen and Mr. Grant with 200 of the Cape Frontier Armed and Mounted Police. There was no sign of Langalibalele, but it was obvious that he would be well cared for in case he should head in that direction. Hawkins therefore decided to return and to link up with Allison's force, which had ascended the Bushman's River Pass on November 29th, and were heading for Leribe. He re-crossed the Umzimkulu on December 1st, and on the 5th ascended the Drakensberg by the Manzimyama Pass (the present Sani Pass). On December 7th he effected a junction with Allison on the east branch of the Orange River. By that time he had 46 Europeans with him and 350 Africans; 280 of these Africans were now sent home and Hawkins proceeded with his 46 Europeans and 70 Africans.

Allison's force consisted of about 50 Europeans from the Natal Frontier Guard and the Weenen Yeomanry Cavalry, together with about 1 600 Africans. They were provisioned for one month, had ascended the Bushman's River Pass on November 29th, and had headed North-west, hot on Langalibalele's trail.

The story of this epic trek across the wilds of Lesotho has never been told, and it never will be told fully, for few records of it were kept. The country was completely unknown and mountainous beyond all telling. A military map compiled and lithographed at the Intelligence Branch of the Quartermaster General's Department in June 1879 shows the area as almost completely blank, and merely marked "Deep rocky valleys infested by Wild Bushmen. Little-known Country."

Sir John Robinson, in *A Life-time in South Africa* says: "The story of this expedition has never been properly told . . . No 'special' correspondents accompanied it, no postmen or runners bore back news of it . . . They disappeared from sight and hearing after sending to Maritzburg an assurance that the objects of the mission would be accomplished 'handsomely and well' – a promise that was fulfilled to the letter. And practically nothing more was heard of the expedition until it had done its work. It groped its way amongst the precipices and defiles, skirting the edges of brawling torrents, camping at times under the eaves of overhanging crags, scaling nameless mountain heights, or scrambling into the depths of rock-strewn valleys – all void, silent and lifeless – ever on the alert for a hidden foe. After each day's hard march they slept the sleep that follows as of right dutiful fatigue, and they rose at dawn, refreshed and confident, to resume the chase."

Allison himself paid a high compliment to his men. The Volunteers, he said, had behaved splendidly, and were a fine body of men. Throughout the expedition he had no occasion to reprimand a single man, and from the African levies, who suffered severely from the cold, there were no complaints at all, and only one case of punishment for neglect of duty.

The Orange River was crossed by an improvised punt made of raw bullock hides sewn together, the Maluti Mountains traversed, and soon the freshness of the trail began to show that the rebels were not far ahead. On the evening of December 11th a spot was reached where there were clear signs that the rebels had only recently left, and were in a hurry. As the fugitives could not now be very far ahead, Allison decided to abandon his heavy baggage and to push on immediately with a smaller and lighter force, provisioned for three days. The final leg of the pursuit started at dawn on the 12th. By noon they began to pass many exhausted cattle and horses, and at 4 p.m. they came up with a large herd of cattle in a valley 40 kilometres north-east of Leribe.

But Langalibalele had already been captured. A few days before a large force of armed Basutho, supported by 120 Frontier Armed and Mounted Police under Griffiths, had moved out from Leribe, heading north-east. In the meantime Langalibalele had surrendered, actually on December 11th, to his reputed friend Molapo, who had lured him towards his kraal, 15 kilometres outside Leribe. With him he had 24 of his men. Molapo promptly handed him over to Griffiths, who was waiting for him. Ever after this the Bantu have never trusted the Basutho.

On the following day 200 more surrendered, but the main body refused to capitulate, and took up a position in the mountains. Here a short, sharp engagement took place, in which ten of the rebels were killed and the rest dispersed. Amongst the dead was Jantjie, son of Selile, who had claimed to have fired the first shot at the Pass. Mabuhle was captured, but a few nights later he slipped his handcuffs, and together with one of Langalibalele's sons, he escaped.

On the following day, December 13th, Allison and Hawkins arrived, and Langalibalele was handed over to them, together with all his men. Nine days later, on December 22nd, Orpen and 200 Cape Frontier Armed and Mounted Police also arrived, after a long and arduous journey through the heart of Lesotho.

Allison, with Langalibalele, five of his sons, four headmen, six to seven thousand captured head of cattle and some hundreds of horses, started their long trek home on December 21st. They travelled through the Witzieshoek area and down Van Reenen's Pass, but owing to the large number of cattle, their progress was slow. Even so, they entered Natal on Christmas Day, and reached the Capital on the last day of the year. Langalibalele's arrival in Pietermaritzburg, in chains, so soon after his open defiance of the Government, produced a most salutary effect on the rest of the population.

In the meantime it had been decided that it was necessary to deal with the rest of the Amahlubi and Putini tribes. Langalibalele had left all the women and children, together with the older men, behind in the Location. These unfortunate people had taken refuge in the caves of the mountains, and they had to be ferreted out. It was decided to break up both the Amahlubi and the Putini tribes, for although the Putinis had not taken part in the rebellion, it was felt they had at least been in collusion with Langalibalele. The cordon which had been thrown round the two tribes was first strengthened, and then heralds were sent into the two Locations calling upon all remaining members of the two tribes to give themselves up. Then the cordon moved in, and started a sweep through the Reserves.

For the next six weeks the work went on. Although the Natal Government later tried to defend itself, there is no doubt that excesses were commited. Durnford himself had spoken about "avenging" the "murder" of his men at the Pass, and had to be gently reprimanded by his friend, Bishop Colenso. Two field guns were brought up, and the forests on the southern slopes of *Ntabamhlope* shelled. The Carbineers spoke openly of "potting niggers", as if it were a national sport. On one occasion a man hid behind a large rock in a cave, and held his attackers at bay for a long time. He eventually surrendered, was brought out, and promptly shot! Many letters boasting about these savage reprisals appeared in the Press. One paper, the *Natal Colonist*, whose Editor was a man by the name of Sanderson, a close personal friend of Bishop Colenso, said, "We have hitherto refrained from publishing (these letters) because they seem to us a disgrace to humanity". Altogether, something like 200 men, women and children appear to have been killed. These things, of course, cannot be excused, although they seem to be inseparable from a war against a savage people. But it is equally certain that many of the reports were deliberately exaggerated.

What started as a mild controversy soon developed into an uproar. Overseas the Anti-

Slavery Society, the Peace Society, and the Aborigines Protection Society, piled in with all their guns. As far back as 1843, J. C. Chase had described this latter Society as "a body of respectable and benevolent individuals, but lamentably ignorant of Colonial affairs, and grossly imposed upon by designing men." In Natal most of the furore centred around the figure of Bishop Colenso and his family.

The Bishop was a prominent figure at this time in the history of Natal. A brilliant mathematician and scholar (his Mathematics text-books were used for many years in England) he had been appointed the first Bishop of Natal in 1853. He arrived in Durban on the 23rd January 1854, and on his first day in Natal was told by leading men in his white congregation "You must never indulge a kaffir". He at once devoted himself to acquiring a sound knowledge of the Zulu language, into which he translated the New Testament. He became an advanced thinker, and his liberal theological views were far in advance of the time. The subsequent controversy which raged around him in the fifties and the sixties, his trial before an ecclesiastical court, and his subsequent excommunication are too well known to need repeating here. Now, at the age of 60, probably at the height of his powers, a much-loved and saintly man, he championed the cause of Langalibalele and his tribe. He was ably supported by his two daughters, Francis and Harriet. Brookes and Webb, in their *History of Natal*, sum him up in the following words: "As a missionary he was outstanding, as a theologian, highly controversial". And may we perhaps add, "as a priest, distinctly 'turbulent'."

Meanwhile, as time went on, the uproar in Natal showed no signs of abating. Angered at what they felt was distorted and unfair criticism, the colonists, almost to a man, rallied to the support of the Government, the military and the Carbineers. The Press was sharply divided. A small section of the Natal Press, notably the *Natal Colonist*, together with the *Cape Argus*, championed Langalibalele. The rest were 100% pro-Government and anti-Colenso. A mass meeting of citizens was held in Durban, which affirmed their faith in the measures the Government had taken to put down the rebellion, and protested against the methods employed by the Peace Society. (The wrathful Editor of the *Natal Witness* advised the Peace Society to change its name!) They were supported by the inhabitants of Alexandra County in a numerously-signed memorial testifying to the correctness of the methods employed by the Government, while 74 ministers of religion, and a number of missionaries, dissociated themselves from Bishop Colenso, and signed a manifesto stating that "we feel and affirm that the action of the Natal Government was throughout humane, lenient, just and urgently necessary." The Bishop became the most detested man in Natal.

What, for want of a better term, we may call the humanitarian point of view, is always a valid one, and there must always be a voice for it. It is a thousand pities that its protagonists so often allow themselves to be led into wild exaggerations, the distortion of some facts and the ignoring of others, for by so doing they weaken their case. It was so in Colenso's day: it is the same to-day, when the mantle of the Colenso's, father and daughters, has fallen upon the shoulders of the Canon Collins's, the Father Huddlestone's and the Dick Shephard's of the 20th Century.

The Colenso's had a good case. They came near to losing it by overstatement and blind prejudice. This was especially so in the case of Francis and Harriet. There is a bitterness, a deliberate distortion, about so many of their statements that is hard to understand. "It is no secret," said Harriet in one of her letters, "that two of the foremost runaways were Mr. Charles Barter, the Captain of the Troop, and his factotum, Sgt. Clark," – a statement, justified, perhaps, in the case of the latter, but certainly, at the very least, unkind in the case of the former. Later she says, "The volunteers ran away, trying to throw all the blame on Major Durnford, whom they so coolly left in the jaws of the enemy." And talking of Governor Pine, Frances called him "weak and vacillating", and expressed the hope that he would soon be recalled. This is certainly not the verdict of history! One looks in vain, in their outpourings, for any note of pity or compassion for any of the *dramatis personae* except the 'down-trodden savage'.

If the mopping-up operations provided good ammunition for the Colenso's, the circumstances of the trial, when Langalibalele was finally brought to judgment on January 16th, 1874, gave them more than they could ever have hoped for. And it must be admitted that it was a most extraordinary trial, and a disgrace to British justice.

It was decided to try the Chief under Native Law, and here the very first of the many anomalies appear, for under Native Law he would never have been tried at all! He would have met his death immediately on the field of battle, for to the African the penalty for treason was automatic, and instant, death. For his two chief judges he had his two chief accusers, Sir Benjamin Pine, the Lieut. Governor and Supreme Chief of the Zulus, and Theophilus Shepstone, Secretary for Native Affairs. They were assisted by four Magistrates and six "loyal" African Chiefs, all nominees of the Government. No Judge of the Supreme Court was invited to sit on the Bench, although legally the charge of treason could only be heard in the Supreme Court. The Prosecutor was John Shepstone, brother of the Secretary for Native Affairs. The prisoner was found guilty on the first day of the trial, evidence was heard against him on the second day, he was only allowed Counsel on the third day, but Counsel was not allowed to interview the prisoner! Nor was the prisoner allowed the right of cross-examination! Finally, the sentence of banishment, which the Court pronounced on him, was in itself illegal, as no Native Court was competent to impose such a sentence. When the Lord Chancellor described the trial in the House of Lords, he was greeted by loud laughter from his assembled Peers.

This was all, and more, than the good Bishop could stomach. He sailed in, with guns blazing! Two years previously another, and still more famous, Oxford mathematician had written, in *Through the Looking Glass*: "He's in prison now, being punished; and the trial doesn't even begin till next Wednesday; and of course the crime comes last of all!" I hope the reverend prelate had noted the appositeness of these words, and had had the wit to use them!

Langalibalele was sentenced to banishment for life. The Cape Government came to the rescue of the highly embarrassed Natal Government by offering Robben Island as the place of his detention, for Natal had nowhere to send him. And to Robben Island he was sent, with the intention that he would end his days there.

But Bishop Colenso continued relentlessly his long fight to see that justice was done. He went over to England to plead his case personally, and eventually he was successful in getting the sentence quashed. The British Government intervened, and in August 1875 Langalibalele was allowed to return to the mainland, first of all to the farm *Uitvlugt* in the Cape, and later to Oude Molen, where he was given very comfortable quarters. Here, in 1881, he was visited by Dr. J. W. Matthews, Vice-President of the Legislative Council of the Cape, who found him sitting on the trunk of a tree at the side of a brick-built cottage, "blear-eyed, old, decrepit, and almost in rags". In 1887 he was allowed to return to Natal. He was confined to the Swartkop Location, near Pietermaritzburg, under Chief Teteleku, and there he died in 1889, a shadow of his former self. He was buried in a secret grave in the foothills of the Drakensberg. For 61 years the place remained a closely-guarded secret until, in October 1950, his grandson, by then Chief of the Amahlubi tribe, revealed the site to Mr. C. J. van Schalkwyk, Native Commissioner of Estcourt. It is on the farm *Eland's Park*, adjoining the Giant's Castle Game Reserve.

He is still remembered in Natal, and in Lesotho, by the African people. Many years ago, while mountaineering in Lesotho, I came across an old man who told me that Langalibalele had passed that way on his long retreat. In Natal he is remembered as the great rain-maker, as the man who, for a brief while, defied the might of the British Empire, as the sun that is always boiling hot. They still talk of the strange eclipse of the sun on April 16th, 1874, immediately after sentence had been passed on him, and they still talk of the violent floods in the

Transkei in the same year. Of a truth, he was a great rainmaker, a mighty man, an "Inyanga"*
of note, even in the bitterness of defeat!

As we have already said, the Langalibalele affair had a profound effect on the future of
South Africa, and even had its echoes overseas, where it played a small, but not unimportant,
part in the downfall of Gladstone's Liberal Government. It brought about extensive consti-
tutional reforms in Natal, which we need not go into here. "The year 1873", said Sir John
Robinson, "marked the turning-point of Imperial policy in South Africa". In particular, the
Shepstone system of native administration was shaken to its foundations and reformed. From
it stemmed the Native High Court, established in 1875, which for 80 years dispensed justice
with fairness, impartiality and humanity. The Langalibalele affair marked the termination of
Shepstone's long rule of 30 years over the African peoples of Natal. The establishment of the
Native High Court deprived him of his judicial functions. From 1876 onwards he was more
concerned in Imperial and Transvaal affairs, although, as Brookes and Webb have pointed out,
"Shepstonism" lived on, right up to the time of Union. Above all, it emphasized the necessity
for a uniform native policy for South Africa, a policy which could only be achieved through
some form of federation or union.

And it is also to be noted that it probably saved Natal at the time of Isandhlwana. The
pitiful under-garrisoning of the Colony in the face of the growing Zulu menace now came
searchingly under the spotlight, and remedial measures were immediately taken. When, five
years later, the storm broke, Natal had a sizeable body of seasoned troops on whom it could
rely, and she was able to ride out the storm. Without Langalibalele she might have been over-
whelmed and, to quote C. J. Uys in *The Era of Shepstone*, "drowned in a sea of human blood".

Finally, it affected profoundly the lives and careers of a number of personalities implicated
in it, and shattered a number of fine friendships. Sir Benjamin Pine, a popular and energetic
Governor, was recalled and put on pension. He was replaced by Sir Garnet Wolseley, one of
the most colourful administrators Natal has ever known. It was the end of a potentially great
and promising career. It was also the end of the friendship between Shepstone and Colenso.
During his earlier ecclesiastical troubles Shepstone had stood loyally behind the Bishop. He
had accompanied the Bishop on the latter's initial tour of his new Diocese, and the two men had
become firm friends. It was Colenso's invariable custom to have Sunday lunch with the
Shepstones after the morning service at St. Peter's Church. One Sunday at the height of the
controversy they met as usual, but a heated argument arose. As Colenso left, he was seen to
stand on the front steps of the house, and say: "I shall never enter this house again". And as far
as we know he never did.

This break in their friendship was a deep hurt to two very fine men, and neither of them
ever got over it. Colenso himself said: "the light has gone out of my life", and writing to
Shepstone from London he said: "I longed for the time when I might see you and speak with
you again as of old." Harriet, also writing to Shepstone, said: "I know that he (her father) has
loved you better than any other man in the world, has reverenced and looked up to you as the
embodiment and realisation of all his own ideas of what a man should be". But it is to be noted
that Colenso was the more bitter of the two. Though the breach was never healed, Shepstone,
on several occasions in later years, acted more than generously towards his old friend.

If Colenso became the most hated man in Natal, Durnford must have come a close second,
for in outlook and ideals, especially on the native question, the two men were very close. The
colonists, almost to a man, turned against him, and blamed him for the fiasco at the Pass.
Abusive letters began to appear in the Press, including a ribald poem which became immensely
popular in the pubs of the city. Only the Colenso's and Sanderson, Editor of the *Natal Colonist*,
stood by him. Always an ascetic, he largely withdrew from social life, and the only home that

* Inyanga: an expert witch-doctor (Zulu).

252

was open to him was that of Bishop Colenso. Even his favourite dog was poisoned. The wounds he had received in the engagement had been serious: he never regained the use of his left arm, which he always kept hidden inside his jacket, but not once in the days following the action did he report sick. The Government gave him a disability pension of £100 per annum, but after his death it was discovered that he had never touched a penny of it.

To add to his troubles, he and Fanny Colenso now fell hopelessly in love with each other. As a young man of 24 he had married the daughter of a retired Lieutenant Colonel, but the marriage had not been a success, and after a carefully hushed-up scandal involving his wife, the couple had separated. Divorce was out of the question for a man who held the Queen's commission, and Durnford solved the problem by simply taking his postings abroad, while his family brought up his daughter. He was now forty-four years old and he had not seen his wife for ten years. Fanny was a frail and lovely girl, just turned 25, but already showing signs of the tuberculosis which was eventually to carry her off. Natal in those days, like any small provincial community, thrived on gossip and tittle-tattle, and who could have wished for a juicier bit of scandal than something connected with a Colenso or a Durnford! But so closely did the two guard their secret that no inkling of it ever leaked out, and there was never even a breath of suspicion. Confined as they both were in the strict Victorian morality of the time, there was no solution to the problem except the death of Mrs. Durnford, and she was to outlive them both. Durnford fell at Isandhlwana, in 1879. Poor little Fanny carried her pathetic secret with her to her grave in 1887. It was only after her death, when her letters were published, and when the authorship of the biographical sketch she had written on the life of the man she loved, under the pseudonym of Atherton Wylde, was revealed, that the story leaked out.

Throughout Natal, for the next five years, the controversy continued to rage. When the ladies gathered on the green lawns of Government House for the Governor's tea-parties, when the officers assembled in the Mess up at Fort Napier, when the transport riders relaxed round their camp fires after the day's trek, when the gossiping farmers' wives from the Dargle met under the syringa trees on the Market Square while their husbands attended Ferreira's open-air market, or downed their beers at the "Plough", the main talking-point was always Langalibalele, and poor Sir Benjamin Pine, and the "wicked" Bishop and that "scoundrel" Durnford. Until one day there came the thunder-clap of Isandhlwana, and all the talk was swept away.

*   *   *   *

On November 17th, 1873, a fortnight after the action, Bushman's River Pass was visited once again. Major Durnford had been despatched with 60 men of the 75th Regiment, 30 Basutho and a force of 400 Africans, to occupy the Pass and to bury the dead. They were accompanied by Sir William Beaumont, Private Secretary to Sir Benjamin Pine, and by the Rev. G. Smith, minister of St. John's Church, Weston, who was to conduct the burial service. Five years later Smith was to fight gallantly, shoulder to shoulder with the men of the 24th Foot, in the defence of Rorke's Drift. They ascended the Pass on the 18th. Very little had been disturbed. Round the lip of the Pass still lay the scattered debris of a deserted battle-field — abandoned shields, broken assegais, items of equipment, three dead horses, and the bodies of the slain. Erskine and Bond were found lying close together. Potterill lay a little farther off. High up in the blue sky a couple of vultures wheeled, and the wind sighed in the short, tufted grass.

The Burial Service took place the next day with military honours. The two men whom Durnford had shot were buried under one cairn of stones. The other five were buried under another, larger, cairn, under which they lie peacefully sleeping to this day. Over the stones a large wooden cross was erected. The haunting notes of the Last Post floated over the desolate crags, and the men moved away.

But one man remained. For several moments he stood with bowed head, a lonely figure, looking down on the cairn and the grave of the men whom he had commanded. Then he stooped, dug up some white everlastings growing near by, and reverently planted them amongst the stones. A few of the flowers he saved, and these, together with some locks of hair he had cut from the dead, he sent later to the relatives of the men who lay below. Then he, too, turned and left.

*   *   *   *

Ninety years rolled by, and on May 5th, 1963 those mountain solitudes were again invaded, and the Pass was once again climbed, by men of the same Regiment, Carbineers past and present. Under the command of Lieut. Col. Bob de Carle, Regimental Commander, they carried with them a new and a stronger cross, made of aluminium, for over the years the old cross had broken down. Ribald jokes and gay chatter accompanied the men as they toiled up the Pass, but at the top a silence fell as they approached the cairn. The working party was soon busy, the new cross erected, and then, with bowed heads, the men gathered round for the Dedication Service. To-day it remains one of my most abiding memories of the Drakensberg, for I had been asked to take it. A short reading and then a prayer, and then came the last words of the dedication:

> "*They shall grow not old as we that are left grow old,*
> *Age shall not weary them, nor the years condemn.*
> *At the going down of the sun, and in the morning,*
> *We will remember them.*"

Once again the notes of the Last Post rang out, sounded this time by Sergeant Bugler Gerrit Booyens of the Estcourt High School Cadet Band. The echoes died away amongst the peaks. The men left, and once again the Pass was wrapped in silence. In the nooks and crannies of the stones there still grew a few white everlastings.

CHAPTER XXIII

WHAT OF THE FUTURE?

"It should be our proud tradition to defend it to the limit."
— GENERAL SMUTS, SHORTLY BEFORE HIS DEATH,
SPEAKING OF TABLE MOUNTAIN.

The Drakensberg is in danger.

Mr. A. R. Willcox, the well-known authority on the Rock Art of South Africa, is a great lover of the Drakensberg. In 1956 he wrote these words:–

> "Here is one of the finest playgrounds left in this overpopulated planet: here one can still walk fifty miles and see no other human being, except by chance a forester or game ranger, and no mark of man upon the face of nature save the footpaths and the relics of the Bushman race . . . But you will see superb scenery and a wealth of wild life . . . and the bird-lover and the botanist will find as much to enchant him as will the lover of animals. For good measure there is mountaineering and rock-climbing, and perhaps the largest number of unspoilt rock-painting sites to be found anywhere in the world in an equivalent space."

Sixteen years have passed since he wrote these words, and already much of what he said is out of date! In another sixteen years *very little of it will be true*! Even the mountaineering will be largely a thing of the past, except for a few selected peaks, for our rights of way will have gone if we continue as we are doing to-day.

Why is this? For two very simple reasons. I am afraid that many South Africans could not care less about the beauty of their country: they despoil, they ravage, they exploit, and they go on their way, uncaring. And secondly, because you and I, who *do* care, and who would not do these things, are too unmindful of our heritage to lift a finger to save it.

Let me tell you some of the things I have seen in the Drakensberg.

The summit of the Amphitheatre, the Plains of the Pofung, used to be a place of matchless grandeur, beauty and peace. To-day a mountain road has been built from Witzieshoek to the base of the *Sentinel*, to within an hour and a half of this place of peace, and at times these high solitudes simply swarm with people. I have seen as many as 200 at a time there, and no amenities are provided, nor is there any control. The whole area is strewn with beer cans, tissues, filth and garbage. There are no toilet facilities whatever. Let me be frank, and say that it is a national disgrace.

Last September 24 students, all members of the University Mountain Club from Pieter-maritzburg, disgusted at what was happening, went up to the top. They cleared the tins away from the immediate vicinity of the Hut alone. It took them three hours to flatten the tins, and to pack them into fertilizer bags. Each man carried a fertilizer bag down the mountain, con-taining 150 tins and weighing 12,5 kg – 24 of these bags! It was impossible, said the leader* of the party, to walk more than a metre without stepping on a tin. The bottles they could not cope with. They were broken, and they had to leave them there. Before they left they pinned a notice on the wall of the Hut: "These mountains are yours and mine. Please keep them clean." There has been little response.

I long ago gave up sleeping in this once-charming Mountain Club Hut. In the early days it was beautifully equipped with wooden tables, bunks, comfortable mattresses, blankets and

*The leader, Alan Palmer, was killed a few months later while descending the cliffs of *Champagne Castle*.

primus stoves. To-day it is nothing but an empty shell. Its doors and windows have been smashed in, most of the woodwork used for firewood, and the cattle have left their dung on the floor. I have preferred to sleep out under the clean heavens. In the wooden floor of another Hut, the Transvaal Mountain Club Hut at the summit of Organ Pipes Pass, used to be a huge hole, a metre wide. Someone had lit a fire there, and burnt right through the wooden flooring. To-day the whole Hut has collapsed.

A few kilometres away from my home below *Cathkin Peak*, on the road to the Forestry Station, there used to be a most delightful picnic spot, a babbling stream in a natural kloof, set in deep, shady trees. It was part of the property of one who loved and cared for this beautiful countryside, but he was glad to share it with others. A couple of years ago he had to fence it in with an eight-strand barbed-wire fence. I could not blame him.

The Little Berg has many lovely caves, each with its priceless heritage of Bushman paintings. One after another these caves which fall within the area administered by the Natal Parks Board have had to be fenced in with barbed wire. Others are being left to their fate.

Why must the hand of man despoil all that is beautiful in nature? Why must he leave his litter behind wherever he goes? Not even the creatures of the wild do this. Their environment is never despoiled by their presence. They do not desecrate the ground with their rubbish. The steenbuck digs a hole in the ground to urinate in, and buries it, and the wild cats cover their dung.

Not only does man leave his litter behind, he exploits all that he touches. Big business has suddenly awoken to the fact that here, in the Drakensberg, is an untapped source of wealth, and the business tycoon is moving in with his deeds of sale. At times he seems completely indifferent to the unspoilt beauty of the mountains. Two or three years ago a Johannesburg company bought 50 acres (20,23 ha) of untouched, virgin countryside in the Drakensberg. They cut the 50 acres up, and planned to erect 48 "chalets" on the land, all in straight rows, plus an administrative block and service roads. The "chalet" owners (incidentally, they would not even have owned their "chalet": they would merely have owned shares in the company) instead of looking out on the glories of the Drakensberg, would have looked out on their neighbour's washing! To their eternal credit, the Natal Town and Regional Planning Commission moved in and put a stop to it. But it was a near thing, and since then other developments in the area have caused grave concern.

One man bought 365 ha of land on the mountain slopes of the Little Berg, commanding the sources of several powerful tributary streams of the Little Tugela, and lying contiguous to land held by the Forestry Department. The main part of it lay above the 1 370 metre contour level. It was land which obviously ought to have belonged to the State, and at one time had actually been offered to the State, but the offer had not been accepted. The owner, using his legal rights, cut it up into 50-acre plots, and to provide access to the higher areas he blasted and bull-dozed a road through a sandstone rock-band, which had been a natural barrier against erosion. He gouged out the soil to the basic rock, creating a huge scar, visible for miles, and irremediably hastening erosion. The houses which are being built on these higher areas are visible for miles down the valley, and some are unsightly blots on the beautiful face of the Little Berg. The original owner has, of course, done no more than exercise his rights, but it is questionable whether any owner should have such rights. This is typical of what is certain to happen in the Drakensberg with increasing frequency unless we take action now.

One recent scheme that went through is another of these "Chalet" schemes. (Incidentally, it is quite a misnomer to call the buildings "chalets". At best, they are cottages.) This scheme is situated at Cathkin Park Hotel, and is financed by a Durban-based company. It has been severely criticised in the Press. Its estimated final cost is to be R5 million, and it is planned to attract upwards of 3 000 semi-permanent residents to the area. Again, however, owners cannot "own" their "chalets". They merely own shares in the company. The company claims that their scheme is "a tasteful development, blending into the grandeur of the Drakensberg scenery". Not everyone would subscribe to this. Critics claim that the cottages are poorly sited, and hardly "blend into the scenery".

In July and August of 1972 the Gourton Farmers' Association, gravely alarmed at what was happening in this lovely Cathkin valley, appointed a sub-committee of their Association "to ensure the orderly development of the area". They also approached Mr. Percy Fowle, M.E.C., in charge of local authorities, with a request for his advice and help.

Mr. Fowle ordered an immediate investigation by the Natal Town and Regional Planning Commission. The Commission were, to put it mildly, perturbed at what they saw. They found a number of unsightly homes going up. Fifty-acre plot-holders were forming companies whose share-holders could erect buildings, often quite unsuitable, and far in excess of the one building per fifty acres which the law allowed. They were shown one building, euphemistically called a "cottage", on a sub-divided 20 ha holding, which was being built of creosoted poles and odd pieces of reject masonite boards. Instead of being discreetly tucked away in some valley, it was being sited on top of a hill.

Mr. Fowle subsequently admitted that the situation was serious, and that further methods of control would probably have to be introduced before the situation got out of hand. He promised his full support in ensuring that the beautiful approaches to the Drakensberg were not spoilt by "thoughtless or selfish acts by a few individuals". He stated that the Natal Provincial Administration were determined to use whatever legislation there was to prevent "speculation entrepreneurs" from cutting up Natal's beautiful acres and destroying the aesthetic beauty of our landscapes. He also promised to watch, most carefully, the Cathkin "Chalet" scheme, mentioned above.

Let me explain. I am not against the opening up of the Drakensberg. I would like to see *more* people coming to this lovely area, not less. But it must be a *controlled* and an *orderly* coming: it must be *planned*. And the hills and the valleys must retain their natural charm and beauty, and not be despoiled. Above all, this mountain region must, as far as possible, belong to the nation and not to any private individual.

Maurice Sweeney has pointed out that the Swiss and Austrian mountains have far more people living in them than in our Drakensberg valleys. "And yet," he says, "they don't appear to make the place look unpleasant. In fact they add to it. The hand of man lies comparatively lightly on those valleys. I would like to see the hand of man lie lightly on ours." He could not have put it better – that the hand of man might lie lightly on our own Drakensberg!*

The Natal South Coast was at one time a paradise of golden beaches, blue seas, graceful trees and rich green coastal bush. To-day its seas are polluted, its beaches are strewn with rubbish, the lovely coastal bush has gone, and the whole area, from Durban to Port Shepstone and beyond, is an unsightly sprawl of houses. Do we want the same sort of thing in our Drakensberg mountains?

One overriding fact emerges from all this: there is no uniform control over the Drakensberg, no common policy, no statutory body which can plan, and guide, and protect this mountain region, and ensure that it remains for all time in its natural beauty.

And remember, it is not only the Drakensberg which is at stake. It is the whole vast Tugela Basin project which is imperilled if nothing is done. The two are interlocked. The Basin depends on the Drakensberg for its very life-blood, its water-supplies, which come entirely from the area we are considering. If these supplies are endangered, then you can say good-bye to the whole vast potential of the Tugela Basin scheme.

This Basin comprises some 29 000 sq. km. It is bounded on the west by the Drakensberg Range. Its water supplies are immense, but they all come from the Drakensberg. The main

* In Argentina's Nahuel Huapi National Park, Swiss Alpine architecture is *obligatory* for all houses.

river of the area is the Tugela, and this is fed by innumerable streams which have their birth-place in the cloud-capped peaks of the Drakensberg mountains – the Buffalo, the Klip, the Singati, the Mnweni, the Umlambonja (the last two carry more water than the Tugela), the Mhlwazini, the Little Tugela, the Bushman's and the Mooi. These water supplies, according to one authority, are so immense that they would be capable of sustaining six cities the size of Cape Town, six cities the size of Johannesburg, four cities the size of Durban, four cities the size of Pretoria, and there would still be enough water left over to supply a city the size of Greater London at its mouth! It could one day be the Ruhr of South Africa, and according to Mr. George Forder, Founder-President of the Tugela Basin Development Association, could support 44 million people.

Already incalculable damage has been done to these water supplies. Writer after writer amongst the early settlers in Natal speaks of the lovely streams of the Natal Midlands, and remarks on their clarity. You will not find these clear streams to-day. But what you will find is muddy torrents in summer, carrying millions of kilograms of silt with them, and in winter miserable little trickles of dirty water. Many have disappeared altogether.

Fundamental to the whole Tugela Basin scheme is the preservation and control of these water supplies. And preservation must start in the Drakensberg. Without these streams the scheme must wither and die. But when it is realised that the Government is spending R20 000 000 on a plan to pump water from the Tugela Basin into the Free State, and to re-deposit it in the Vaal Basin to help feed the vast Witwatersrand complex, then the problem becomes one of national importance, affecting the economy of the whole country.

Even this is not the whole story, for the giant Ox-bow scheme, on the Lesotho side of the Drakensberg, is also dependent on the streams of the Drakensberg. South Africa is already looking to this scheme to augment its own dwindling water supplies in the future. But as far as I am aware no efforts are being made in Lesotho to protect these streams and the land between the future Ox-bow Lake and the Drakensberg watershed. The Basutho are already herding their cattle there, and are already beginning to plough and rip up the land.

Because of divided control over the Drakensberg areas, there is no uniform policy for the conservation and allocation of these water supplies. Worse still, a glance at the map on page 260 will show that three large African Reserves, Drakensberg Location No. 1, Drakensberg Location No. 2, and the Upper Tugela Location, not only sit astride the headwaters of most of the rivers feeding the Basin, but one of them, the Upper Tugela Location, actually stretches right up to the summit peaks of the Drakensberg. Any scheme for the uniform control of the Drakensberg areas must take account of these three Locations.

None of these are traditional Zulu homelands. They are the artificial creation of the white man. But to-day some 100 000 Africans live in them. They are hopelessly over-crowded and over-stocked. The African regards stock as his wealth, and this inevitably leads to over-stocking. Not only so, but a large proportion of the Africans living in these areas, as high as 60% it has been estimated, spend six to nine months away from their homes every year, leaving the care of the land to women and children. This, again, must inevitably lead to further deterio-ration of the soil. To-day there is the most appalling erosion in these three Reserves. The land is serrated and seamed with large dongas, there is bad sheet erosion especially on the hillsides, and there are huge areas where the ground has turned sour and where grass no longer grows. The effect of all this on the water supplies emanating from the Drakensberg is tragic.

For the sake of these Drakensberg areas, for the sake of the people living not only in the Tugela Basin, but in the whole of South Africa, it is surely imperative that the Africans living in these Reserves should be moved out, and that this watershed should be guarded and placed in responsible hands for all time.

The Natal Agricultural Union has, for many years, headed the agitation for the resettle-ment of these 100 000 Africans in other areas, and has already offered alternative land for this purpose. This removal has now been accepted by the Government in principle, and has been incorporated in the Government's provisional blue-print for the consolidation of the kwaZulu Homeland. Unfortunately the scheme is so vast and complex that this part of the blue-print is being postponed, and could take anything from 25 to 50 years to complete. In the meantime, the damage continues, and soon it will be too late.

I would suggest that if the scheme cannot be implemented now, it be tackled in two stages. Stage 1 could involve only the 60% of men in the Reserves who have employment in the urban areas, together with their families. These people could be moved now nearer to their places of employment. This would solve the over-population problem in the Reserves. Only legitimate farmers would then be left behind, and more land would then be available for them. The authorities would then have to move in with a massive scheme of land re-habilitation and soil-education. Riparian agriculture would have to be prohibited, and large sums would have to be expended on the reclamation of the eroded areas. But it would pay handsome dividends, both in the short-term and the long-term. As the Tugela Basin develops, vast numbers of workers will have to be fed. These Reserves, scientifically farmed, could well be part of the answer. More important, a start could be made on saving our Drakensberg streams and rivers. Later, the second stage, the final removal of *all* Africans living in the area, could be tackled.

Tied up with this scheme, however, I suggest that the higher levels of the Upper Tugela Location should be retained as an African area, and developed as a mountaineering and recreational area. Up to the present Africans have shown little interest in the sport of mountaineering, but this will not always be the case, and provision will have to be made for them. This area, the upper reaches of the Mnweni and the two Ntonjelanes, would be ideal for the purpose, for it is one of the most beautiful in the whole Drakensberg.

I only make one stipulation, and that is that this area should be subject to the Drakensberg Regional Authority, to the suggested establishment of which the whole of this Chapter is moving.

So far little has been done towards achieving some form of uniform control over the whole of the Drakensberg area. A glance at the map on page 260 will show that the whole Drakensberg Range, from *Giant's Castle* to *Mont-aux-Sources*, is at present under the control of three different authorities. Immediately to the north of *Giant's Castle* is the Giant's Castle Game Reserve, under the control of the Natal Parks, Game and Fish Preservation Board, a subsidiary of the Natal Provincial Administration. Then comes an extensive area, from the Injasuti to *Cathedral Peak* and *South Saddle*, which falls under the Government Department of Forestry. Then we have the Upper Tugela Location, embracing the Mnweni area, under the Bantu Affairs Department. And finally, from beyond the Singati River (roughly) there is the Royal Natal National Park, again under the Natal Parks Board. In addition to all this, there is one further complication. Pushing in, at the Cathedral Peak and Cathkin-Champagne areas, and in the Injasuti, are the spear-heads of private enterprise.

These three authorities, plus private enterprise, have no common policy. Policies differ on soil conservation, burning of the veld, attitudes towards tourism, camping facilities, game preservation, afforestation, conservation of water supplies, while private enterprise is being allowed to despoil the countryside, erect unsuitable dwellings, cause soil erosion, introduce alien vegetation, and cancel rights of way.

Efforts have been made in the past to solve the problem, but it has been a story of half-hearted measures and Government procrastination. In 1962 the Department of Agricultural Technical Services decided that all land in the Drakensberg Catchment area should belong to the State, and that every effort should be made to buy out all privately owned land within the ensuing five years. Land bought in this way was to be handed over either to the Natal Parks Board or to the Department of Forestry. During 1963 and 1964 land to the extent of 12 534 ha, and to the value of R277 926 was bought in this way, but this was mostly in the

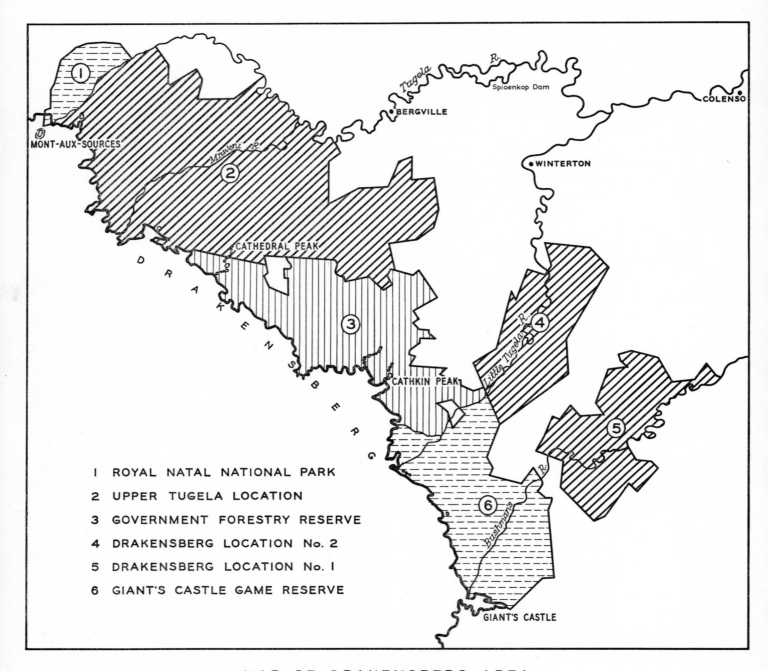

1 ROYAL NATAL NATIONAL PARK

2 UPPER TUGELA LOCATION

3 GOVERNMENT FORESTRY RESERVE

4 DRAKENSBERG LOCATION No. 2

5 DRAKENSBERG LOCATION No. 1

6 GIANT'S CASTLE GAME RESERVE

MAP OF DRAKENSBERG AREA
SHOWING BANTU RESERVES
Note how the three Reserves straddle some of the
most important rivers in the area

area south of *Giant's Castle*. Subsequent to this decision, however, private individuals were allowed to buy land in the area, notably 365 ha of land in the Cathkin area by one man, and "Solitude" in the Injasuti area by another. The former was cut up into 50-acre stands, and re-sold to private individuals. The latter was developed, admittedly into a very fine Nature Resort, by a dedicated conservationist.

At a meeting of the Prime Minister's Resources and Planning Advisory Council on 2nd October 1967, Dr. P. W. Vorster, Secretary for Agricultural Technical Services, submitted a Memorandum, in Afrikaans, to the Council. In it he said: "Die tekens is reeds daar dat beplanning van die hele aangeleentheid aandag verg," and he ends with the words: "Om te verhoed dat botsende belange ontwikkeling strem en mekaar in die wiele ry, is dit uiters belangrik dat beplanning nie vertraag moet word nie."

The Council decided to appoint a subsidiary committee to investigate the whole problem, and to make recommendations. In 1970 this Committee produced its report, entitled "A Guide Plan for the Optimum Utilization of the Natural Resources of the Drakensberg Catchment Reserve".

This is a useful document, though the Committee did report in favour of "Chalet" schemes (admitting, however, that the stringing of chalets along approach roads to the Drakensberg should cease). But they also reported in favour of a cable-way to the summit of a Drakensberg peak! Even worse, they advocated the flood-lighting of some of the peaks! They also turned down the suggestion of any form of uniform control over the whole area.

The Report was immediately relegated to a convenient pigeon-hole in Pretoria, and promptly forgotten. It was only by chance, and through the kind offices of a friend, that I came across it.

I believe that the Committee was wrong in voting against any system of uniform control. If it can be done in America (*vide* the Tennessee Valley Authority), it can be done here.

Some years ago Cape Town faced a similar problem. The good folk of the Peninsula suddenly realised that their priceless heritage, Table Mountain, was in grave danger. Alien vegetation – the hakea and the cluster-pine – was pushing out the natural vegetation, forest fires were causing grave damage, building developments were steadily encroaching on the mountain slopes, and all this was causing irreparable damage. There was no unified control.

On 31st August 1948 the South African Association of Arts convened a public meeting to discuss the menace and its solution. Twenty-five public bodies sent representatives, including the Mountain Club of South Africa, the National Veld Trust, the South African Institute of Architects, the Cape Tree Society, Rotary, and the Historical Monuments Commission. A unanimous resolution was adopted calling on the Government to appoint a Commission to investigate the whole problem. The Government acted immediately, and appointed a Committee, called the Table Mountain Preservation Committee, under the Chairmanship of the Hon. H. S. van Zyl, to investigate the problem. The Committee submitted its recommendations in September 1951. Special legislation was then passed by Parliament, Table Mountain was proclaimed a National Monument, and in 1952 the Table Mountain Preservation Board came into being. Table Mountain was saved.

I doubt whether an area as large as the one we are considering* could be proclaimed a National Monument. But if the Drakensberg is to be preserved in its present natural state, it is imperative that we do something along the lines that Cape Town did in 1948, and that we do it immediately. I suggest that some form of Co-ordinating Regional Authority be established,

---

* So far we have been thinking only of the area from *Giant's Castle* to *Mont-aux-Sources*, but we must not lose sight of the fact that the Drakensberg recreational potential stretches south-west as far as the Natal-East Griqualand border, and even beyond. I am leaving this stretch of country out of the discussion only because this book deals exclusively with the *Giant's Castle-Mont-aux-Sources* section of the Drakensberg, but any form of unified control such as I am suggesting would almost certainly have to take account of this further region.

which would have overriding control over the whole area. It could take over the mountainous section of the Upper Tugela Location, and develop it as an African Recreational Area and Game Reserve. It would, of course, have control over all private enterprise. It would have to be completely divorced from all political influences and local parochialism, and would have to have full statutory powers. Its main function would be the harmonious development of the whole Drakensberg area for the well-being, happiness and contentment of *all* South Africans for all time. The following public bodies, I suggest, could be represented on it:

Natal Parks, Game and Fish Preservation Board
Natal Town and Regional Planning Commission
Department of Forestry
Department of Bantu Affairs
Department of Water Affairs
Mountain Club of South Africa
Botanical Society of South Africa
Wild Life Protection and Conservation Society

National Veld Trust
South African Archaeological Society
Institute of Government Land Surveyors
South African Institute of Architects
National Monuments Council
Natal Agricultural Union
Federated Hotels Association of Southern Africa
South African National Society
South African Tourist Corporation
Rotary

Such an Authority, if established, would have to concern itself, amongst others, with the following matters:

1. The control of vital sponge areas and the protection of water supplies generally

Water is our very life-blood. Agriculture, Forestry, Industry and Tourism are all staking their claims for it. And, though vast supplies exist in the Drakensberg, they are limited. The main task of the Authority would be the protection of our Drakensberg water supplies, and their fair allocation, especially as between the demands of Tourism and Industry. It is important to ensure that this potentially rich recreational area is not irreparably ruined by unsuitable engineering works designed to meet the demands of Industry.

2. Control of indigenous forests

This is mainly the task of the Department of Forestry, but it must be remembered that many of our Drakensberg forests fall outside the proclaimed Forest Reserves. Uniformity of policy is essential here. Much of this we have already dealt with in Chapter XIX.

3. Development and control of exotic plantations, and control of alien vegetation

This is a complex subject, and again demands expert, uniform control. A growing menace in the Drakensberg is the spread of the wattle, both the Black and the Silver, *Acacia decurrens* and *A. dealbata*. Not only does the wattle desiccate the ground and deprive it of ground cover, but it makes access to fishing streams difficult. *Pinus patula*, another exotic species, is also taking a hold in some areas. Professor Brian Rycroft, Director of Kirstenbosch, has said that three quarters of the natural vegetation of the south-western Cape is doomed unless the spread of alien plants is arrested. This process has already started in the Drakensberg.

4. Access roads and buildings

This is a vital matter. A clear policy should be laid down from the start. First of all, I suggest, there should be a minimum of access motor roads leading into the Drakensberg. One road to each of the main areas should be sufficient. Periodically suggestions appear in the Press for a motor road along the summit of the Drakensberg, or for a road through the Little Berg, running north and south. At all costs these suggestions should be resisted. Motor roads, picnic sites, caravan parks and hotels should be restricted to the lower levels. No houses should be allowed above the 1 525 metre (5 000 ft.) level, except for the traditional mountain huts. Only simple bridle paths should be allowed in the middle levels, and these should be well-maintained. The present contour path at the 2 000 metre level should be extended and improved. In places it is in a shocking condition. With a little imagination it could become a South African version of the famed American "Appalachian Trail", extending from the Golden Gate Highlands National Park in the O.F.S., along the whole length of the Drakensberg, and down to the borders of the Cape Province, a magnificent mountain trail 800 km in length. It would have to be provided with simple mountain huts, as in the Giant's Castle Game Reserve, every 25 kilometres. The upper levels and the summit area should be left completely undisturbed, in their wild and natural state, except for the occasional mountain hut, tastefully built and suitably tailored to the surroundings. All attempts to build motor roads to the higher levels *must* be resisted. Cable-ways should be forbidden by law.

5. Recreational use

Every effort should be made to expand and develop the recreational facilities of the Drakensberg, but it is essential that there be close control and supervision. Vandalism of all sorts is increasing at an alarming rate. Beer cans, bottles, cartons, tins and tissues are left in careless abandon at picnic spots and in the sandstone caves. It should be axiomatic that all unburnable litter *must* be carried home. Penalties should be heavy, and particularly heavy for those who deface rock slabs and cave walls with their names and initials.

6. Game and fish preservation and propagation

Here the Natal Parks Board has done particularly fine work, but much still remains to be done, especially in the re-introduction of species that have died out. Fishing rights, and control of fishing, would obviously fall under the Authority.

7. Veld control, veld management, control of fires, and prevention of erosion.

This, especially erosion, is vital to the Tugela Basin. The badly eroded areas in the three African Reserves should be rehabilitated if the great dams envisaged for the Basin are not to silt up. Here, again, policies differ. It is essential that there should be one unified policy, and one central fire-control authority.

8. Rights of way

These should be jealously guarded. As the country fills up these rights of way, and access to the mountains generally, are going to be progressively threatened. Energetic action is required *now* if they are to be preserved for posterity. Since we came to live at *Emkhizweni*, seven years ago, several rights of way to favourite picnic spots have already been closed.

9. Hotels, caravan parks, picnic spots

The whole complex of hotels, caravan sites and picnic spots needs careful study and revision. What type of hotel does the Drakensberg require? Are four and five star luxury hotels what the public wants? Where should these hotels be situated? Should they be allowed on the higher levels? Do they need such facilities as golf-courses? Should they be privately owned or State-owned? Where should you site your caravan parks? What facilities do picnic spots require? How many of each of these amenities should be allowed in each area? Should "chalet" schemes be allowed? These, and many more, are all questions waiting to be answered. While in some areas there is a plethora of hotels, there is a lamentable lack of picnic sites with the necessary facilities. In the whole stretch of country between the Royal Natal National Park and *Giant's Castle* there is only one official picnic site, run by the Natal Parks Board at the Royal Natal National Park. Increasingly people living in the Midlands of Natal like to run out to the Drakensberg for a day's picnic, and this demand is growing. There is an urgent need for a number of selected sites to be levelled, planted with trees, lawned, and provided with rubbish and toilet facilities. But at present nothing is being done.

10. Flora

Apart from the Wild Flower Protection Act (inadequately administered because of lack of Staff) nothing is being done to preserve, and to study, one of the richest flora in all South Africa. Why cannot we have our own "Kirstenbosch" here in the Drakensberg? I know that a Drakensberg National Garden has recently been established at Harrismith, and that the Director, Mr. A. van der Zeyde, is doing a wonderful job, but this is in the Free State, at an altitude of 1 622 metres. There is need for another, on the *Natal* side of the Drakensberg, which would cover the rich flora of the Little Berg, at about the 1 375 metre level.

11. Private encroachment

The desire to own a holiday cottage in the Berg is a very worthy one, but if we had been wise in the past we would have legislated to keep all private ownership of land out of any area above the 1 375 metre (4 500 ft.) level. It is too late now. There should also have been some measure of control to prevent the erection of some of the monstrosities I have seen. But let us at least stop these things for the future. The loophole in the law, whereby a group of people can form a company, buy a 50-acre plot, and then erect as many as one dwelling to every two or three acres, must be closed. I feel that the Drakensberg Regional Authority such as I envisage should be given full powers to say what land is to be sold to private ownership, and what should be State-owned. Every effort should be made to buy back privately-owned land in the higher areas for the State. The Authority should also have an Architectural Division which would lay down certain minimum specifications for the type of dwelling to be erected. Some that I have seen are little better than shacks.

12. The summit of the Amphitheatre

And finally, one of the first things that the Drakensberg Regional Authority should tackle is what I have already called a national disgrace, the desecration of the summit of the Amphitheatre. There is, I understand, a dispute as to who owns the land, whether it is part of the Royal Natal National Park, or part of the Upper Tugela Location, and that this is why nothing has been done to put matters right. This dispute must first be cleared up – it should not be difficult – and then the solution to the present shocking state of affairs should be fairly simple. I suggest, first of all, that the old Natal Mountain Club Hut should be rebuilt, something along the lines of the delightful chalet at the summit of Sani Pass, and that comfortable African quarters should be part of the complex. Then I suggest that a staff of four good African Forest Guards should be recruited to look after the area. Two at a time would live for a fortnight on the summit, while the other two were resting down below. They would change over at fortnightly intervals. Life at these high altitudes, especially in winter, is too harsh to permit of longer periods on the summit. The task of the two on the summit would be to administer the Hut, keep it clean, keep the whole summit area free from rubbish (a system of rubbish bins at strategic points is the obvious answer), and act as servants to any tourists occupying the Hut. The Hut would have to be well-furnished, and provided with gas-cooking, beds, blankets etc. Tourists would bring their own food. At the end of each fortnight the relief team of two men would come up with fresh supplies of gas, and with food for themselves for two weeks. At R2 per night per person the Authority would make a handsome profit, for there would be few periods of the year when the Hut would not be occupied. Later, as the demand grew, more Huts could be built. The damming of the Tugela to make a frozen lake for skating in winter would be a simple matter.

Man has a deep psychological need to keep in close contact with nature and periodically

The sound of many waters.   *The Mnweni River.*

Sunrise over the distant Cathedral Range from Mponjwana.

*Evening clouds gather around
the face of Cathkin Peak*

to renew his spirit. Without this, the quality of life deteriorates. In the face of our population and technological explosion this need is going to grow in the future. It is essential, if we are to preserve our sanity and our integrity, that we strike a balance between the demands of economic development and the deeper demands of man's inner spirit. In the Drakensberg we shall fail to meet *both* these demands unless we scrap our present piecemeal methods of control and go all out for one central and all-embracing Authority.

I hope I have said enough to indicate the urgency of the problem, and how great the need is for something along the lines I have suggested. I believe that if our Drakensberg is to be saved, action must be taken immediately, and taken at the very highest level. We are the guardians of the heritage of future generations: we dare not fail them.

I have written this book with one object, and one object only, in mind – to rouse the conscience of my fellow South Africans to what is happening in this mountain region, in the hope that they will say, and say now: "Enough! This must stop! Tomorrow we turn a new page!"

Shortly before he died (it was one of the last things he did) General Smuts wrote an impassioned plea for the preservation of Table Mountain. "To interfere with it," he said, "is to desecrate what should be our national temple, our Holy of Holies. We, as a nation, valuing our unique heritage, should not allow it to be spoiled and despoiled, and should look upon it as among our most sacred possessions, part not only of the soil, but of the soul, of South Africa. For centuries to come, while civilisation lasts on this sub-continent, this national monument should be maintained in all its natural beauty and unique setting. It should be symbolic of our civilization itself, and it should be our proud tradition to defend it to the limit against all forces of man or nature to disfigure it."

These are noble words. They could have been said, with equal relevance, of our own Drakensberg.

*　　　*　　　*　　　*

As I sit at my desk, writing the last words of a book that has taken me close on twenty years to complete, I can see, through my study window, the nearer peaks of the Drakensberg, with grand old *Cathkin Peak* dominating all. The clouds are gathering about its brooding crags, the evening shadows are beginning to drift across its mighty face. My task is done. We have dealt in this book with a multitude of things, with tragedy and high drama, with man's frailty and with his selfless courage. We have watched the climbers as they set their faces towards the high peaks, and seen their unquenchable determination in the face of tremendous odds. We have watched the wild game on their mountain slopes, feeding in peace and contentment, we have seen the flowers by the wayside, and we have looked into the heart of things and found beauty and compassion there.

Over it all stands the Drakensberg itself, timeless, aloof, inscrutable, but with a wild beauty of its own that tugs at the heartstrings. It is a world of indescribable and ever-changing splendour, a world of basalt giants that stand as sentinels on the roof of South Africa; a world of unspoiled nature, where the cry of the Martial Eagle breaks the silence of distant peaks, where the thunder roars and winds shriek through lonely crags like dragons in torment; where giant yellow-woods dream away their age-long sleep in hidden valleys, and where man, in all this vast loneliness, can find himself.

L'ENVOI

I have enjoyed writing this book, not the least of its pleasures being the many charming people I have met who have responded so willingly and so generously to my requests for information. It is impossible to thank them all individually, but I would like to express my gratitude to some of them here.

Rev. Ernest R. Ball, Archivist of the Sacred Mission at Kelham, Notts., was able to give me details of the later life of Father Kelly; Mr. Raymond Brand, of Witzieshoek, put me on to the early history of *Rydal Mount*; Mr. H. J. Commons, Headmaster of Maritzburg College, and Mrs. Joan English, Parish Secretary of St. Peter's Church, were able to clear up the mystery of the identity of Rev. C. C. Bates; Mr. J. C. Coventry, Mr. Charles Gray and Mr. Anton Zunckel supplied most interesting details of their respective families.

Especially valuable was the helpfulness of the various Forestry Department officials, whose help I sought. All of them gave generously of their time – Mr. C. W. Marwick, Natal Regional Director of Forestry; Mr. A. M. de Villiers, Deputy Director of the Forest Research Institute in Pretoria; Mr. Philip Boustead, Research Officer and Officer in Charge, Cathedral Peak Forest Influences Research Station; Mr. U. W. Nänni, former Forest Hydrologist, Department of Forestry; Mr. W. R. Bainbridge; Mr. H. B. Stephens, former Conservator of Forests, Natal; and Mrs. S. W. Rossouw, wife of a former Forest Officer at the Monk's Cowl Forest Station.

Officials of the Natal Parks, Game and Fish Preservation Board have been equally helpful and generous of their time. I am afraid some of them did not quite realise how importunate my demands on them would be when they offered their help! I am particularly grateful to Mr. P. R. Barnes, Regional Warden of the Drakensberg; Mr. W. R. Trauseld, Warden of the Royal Natal National Park, and to his predecessor, Mr. T. G. Fraser; and to Dr. F. B. Wright, Warden of the Kamberg Nature Reserve.

I have naturally relied heavily on the information that members of the Mountain Club of South Africa could give me, and I am most grateful to the Secretary of the Cape Town Section, Mrs. J. B. Quail; Mr. Vic van Reenen, of the Natal Section; and to Mr. Brian Godbold; Mr. Doyle Liebenberg; Dr. W. James and Dr. Sherman Ripley of the University of Natal; Mr. J. Poppleton; Mrs. Mary Park-Ross; Mr. Martin Winter; Mr. Malcolm Moor; Mr. Harry Barker; and Mrs. Joy Halliday (née Joy Surgeon), who was able to clear up a number of doubtful points in connection with that fantastic climber, George Thomson. All are climbers of repute. Mr. Edward Pyatt, Editor of the *Alpine Journal*, allowed me access to previous copies of the *Journal*, and has also allowed me to re-print from his *Journal* the map on page 53.

I am particularly grateful to Mrs. E. E. Thomson, of Sinoia, Rhodesia. She was able to supply me with details of the recent life of her late husband, the famous climber, George Thomson, and to correct several inaccuracies in connection with his later life, which have even found their way into print.

Mr. Arthur Bowland of the *Natal Mercury* and Mr. W. M. Faill, the *Mercury* Science Correspondent; Mr. Jose Burman; Mr. J. K. Whyte, Manager of the *Friend*; Mr. James Clarke, Assistant Editor of the *Star* were all most helpful, and so too were Mr. R. W. Kent, formerly on the Staff of Maritzburg College, and Mr. G. N. Jenks of Hilton College. Professor A. F. Hattersley, Emeritus Professor of History at the University of Natal, the acknowledged authority on early Natal history, placed his wide knowledge at my disposal, and I found my contacts with Mr. J. B. Wright, also of the University's Department of History, both stimulating and immensely helpful. He allowed me access to the results of his own researches into the life of the early Bushmen.

Mr. Leif Hellend, Vice-Consul for Norway, was able to give me authentic and hitherto unpublished material in connection with the Norwegian boat episode, and Mr. H. C. Lugg, well-known retired Magistrate, Zulu linguist, and historian, was able to supplement this from his own researches. To both these men I am most grateful.

There are many others also who must be mentioned. Amongst them are Mr. A. M. Wood, former M.E.C., Natal Provincial Council; Mrs. Mildred Bush; Mr. B. Christopher of the Ladysmith Historical Society; Mr. A. R. Ferguson of the Town Clerk's Department, Kloof; Dr. G. W. Gale, former Secretary for Public Health; Mr. Ryle Masson, Retired Chief Magistrate of Johannesburg; Mr. B. D. Malan, Secretary of the National Monuments Council; Mr. C. F. Shuter; Mr. Bryan and Mr. Roden Symons; Mr. A. W. van der Riet, well-known Drakensberg Hotelier and Proprietor of the Cathedral Peak Hotel; and Dr. Gordon-Gray of the Department of Botany, University of Natal, who was most helpful in connection with my chapter on the wild flowers of the Drakensberg. Mr. Frank Hume placed his fine collection of maps at my disposal.

I owe a very special debt of gratitude to two gentlemen who did invaluable research work for me, Lt. Col. A. C. Martin, who unearthed a mass of hitherto unpublished material on the Langalibalele Rebellion; and Mr. James Byrom, of the *Natal Daily News*, who, in addition to several other topics, did most valuable work for me on early Natal maps.

Then, of course, there are all those equally helpful Librarians of Public Libraries. I would, in particular, like to thank Mr. R. A. Brown of the University of Natal Library, and his Staff; Miss E. M. van der Linde, Chief Librarian of the Killie Campbell Library, Durban, and her Staff, particularly Mrs. E. P. V. Tedder; the Chief Librarian, Natal Provincial Library, and his Staff, particularly Mrs. E. Yule, Mrs. du Plessis, Miss L. Percival and Mr. M. C. Martin; the Cory Librarian, Grahamstown; and the Chief Librarian, Natal Society Library, and her Staff. Here I owe a very big debt of gratitude to Mr. D. J. Buckley and Mr. T. Lowe, who were indefatigable in responding to my many requests for material.

The Natal Archives are well-known for their helpfulness to the public, and I am deeply grateful to Dr. B. J. T. Leverton, Chief Archivist, for his assistance and advice at all times, and, of course, to his staff.

Dr. J. A. Pringle, Director of the Natal Museum, and Mr. B. R. Stuckenberg, Deputy Director, gave generously of their knowledge, particularly in respect of the latter portion of the Prelude. I am deeply grateful to them both.

Officials of the various Trigonometrical Survey Offices were equally helpful, and here I must mention Mr. W. C. Watson, Chief Cartographic Officer of the Trigonometrical Survey Department, Mr. P. W. Thomas, and Mr. J. Tale, the latter from the Lesotho Government. Mr. Watson, especially, gave most generously of his time, and in addition, was kind enough to check Appendix 3 for accuracy.

Dr. D. W. Bandey; Mr. Harry Barker; Mr. P. R. Barnes; Mr. Philip Boustead; Mr. G. A. Chadwick, member of the National Monuments Council; Mr. U. W. Nänni; Mr. A. R. Willcox, noted authority on the Rock Art of Southern Africa; Mr. B. R. Stuckenberg of the Natal Museum; Mr. Godfrey Symons; Professor G. M. J. Sweeney of the University of Natal, Mr. W. R. Bainbridge, have all read the MS, either in whole or in part, and all have made invaluable suggestions and corrections. It is difficult to thank them adequately for all they have done. I hope they know how grateful I am. Professor Sweeney, especially, has earned my deepest gratitude. He has read the whole MS through, and has brought to his task his unrivalled knowledge of and love for the Drakensberg, his ripe wisdom, and a balanced judgment that have saved me from many a costly error and have added immeasurably to any success this book may achieve.

My debt to Mr. Sigurt Bourquin, Director of Bantu Administration, Durban, is tremendous, and this has been acknowledged on page ii.

In preparing the maps and diagrams I have been greatly assisted by Mr. H. Thomas, of the Anglo-American Association of South Africa, and I am deeply indebted to him.

Without the constant encouragement and help of my son, Malcolm (Rev. M. L. Pearse of the Methodist Church, Primrose, Germiston,) I doubt whether this book would ever have been written. His finely-developed critical sense, and his wide knowledge of the Drakensberg, have proved invaluable to me, and I have relied on him more than he probably realises. He has read the MS through many times. In addition to all this, he has supplied most of the illustrations for the book from his magnificent set of colour pictures of the Drakensberg. For these alone I am deeply grateful. They are a tribute not only to his skill and sensitivity as a photographer, but also to his deep love of the mountains.

In the final stages of the launching of the book Mr. John Tungay was an inspiration, and I am also deeply grateful to Mr. George Forder, an old and valued friend, and to the Rotary Clubs of Estcourt and District 230 for all their encouragement, advice and solid support.

The typing of the MS was all done by Mrs. Cynthia Daniels, and I owe her a very sincere debt of gratitude, not only for all the time she put into her task, but also for the excellence of the work she turned out.

And finally, to Edith, my wife, a very deep, sincere and understanding 'thank you', for she was the one who had to stay at home, alone, and await, often with ill-concealed anxiety but with never a word of complaint, my many returns from the mountains. *Te amo ab imo pectore!*

APPENDIX 1

The Langalibalele Rebellion and the Hlatimba Pass

(Note: this Appendix should be read in conjunction with the map on page 231)

Ever since the Langalibalele engagement at the head of the Bushman's River Pass a number of errors in connection with the Rebellion have been perpetuated. Writing in 1895 J. Forsyth Ingram, in *The Colony of Natal*, says:

"Away up amidst the peaks of Giant's Castle there is a spot held sacred by every true Natalian, for there a small party of colonists, sixty in number, held at bay a rebellious mass of natives, five thousand strong."

They were not sixty in numbers: there were only thirty-two. There were not five thousand natives in the Pass: there were only two hundred. And the colonists certainly did not hold the five thousand at bay: they ran away!

One cardinal error has been made by the majority of historians, including Theal. This is to the effect that the Carbineers, in attempting to intercept Langalibalele, rode up the Giant's Castle Pass. They did not. I believe that they rode up the Hlatimba Pass, 11 miles (17,8 km) away.

In an attempt to clear up the matter I have gone over every inch of the ground covered by the Carbineers. I know it thoroughly, and I have studied all the accounts left by Colonel Durnford, Captain Barter, and many others. The evidence that the Giant's Castle Pass was *not* used is overwhelming, although every contemporary account says it *was* used.

The position is as follows:

There are only four passes in the area that the Carbineers could have ascended. They are as follows:

1. The Bushman's River Pass, now called the Langalibalele Pass. This is the Pass where the actual engagement took place, and was the Pass ascended by Langalibalele and his tribesmen in their flight into Lesotho. Some historians have named this as the Pass ascended by the Carbineers, but this is impossible, as in that case they must have climbed side by side with the rebellious tribesmen, when their object was to *prevent* Langalibalele's men from climbing the Pass. Also it is quite clear that the Carbineers rode for a number of kilometres along the summit of the Drakensberg, after they had ascended their Pass, before they reached the scene of the engagement.

2. The Giant's Castle Pass, exactly five miles (8 km) south of Bushman's River Pass in a straight line, situated at the spot where *Giant's Castle* abuts on the main Berg. Apparently this was the Pass which the military had planned to use. I give below my reasons for thinking that the Carbineers did not use this Pass.

3. The Hlatimba Pass, 11 miles (17,8 km) south of Bushman's River Pass, and 6 miles (9,8 km) south of Giant's Castle Pass. I believe that it was up this Pass that the Carbineers climbed.

4. The Lahlingubo Pass, a couple of kilometres still further south of the Hlatimba Pass. This would be accessible to horsemen, but there would be no point in the Carbineers using this Pass. They were already 12 hours late, and too far south. Nothing would be gained by going *still* further south, when a Pass suitable in every way, and accessible, (the Hlatimba Pass) was at hand.

These last two passes look down on a number of rivers, including the Loteni, the Bohle and the Hlatimba, all of which flow into the Umkomaas. At the time of the Langalibalele Rebellion they were all called, loosely, "the sources of the Umkomaas". The Loteni was known by its present name, but not apparently the Bohle nor the Hlatimba. Neither of these last two names are to be found in contemporary records.

We may now note the following points:

1. Durnford's military instructions were to go up the *Giant's Castle Pass*.

2. Barter, Household, Sgt. Clark, Parkinson, Button, Varty, John Otter Jackson, Bucknall, Jaffray and Durnford himself, all of whom took part in the expedition, left personal accounts of the action at the head of the Pass, and of the ride there and back. (The first two pages of Varty's account, describing the ride to the Pass, are missing, but the rest of the account is complete.) All accounts *say* they went up Giant's Castle Pass.

3. But an examination of these accounts shows quite clearly that (*a*) after climbing the Little Berg *via* Game Pass and proceeding a little way, they had *Giant's Castle* on their *right*: if they had been heading for Giant's Castle Pass it should have been on their *left*; and (*b*) after leaving Game Pass they turned *left*, went down into the sources of the Umkomaas, crossed the Loteni, and then headed south-west into the Pass they eventually climbed. This is quite definite. Not one account describes the country between Game Pass and Giant's Castle Pass, country which is not characterised by the steep slopes and tremendous valleys which the Carbineers negotiated. I have checked this; I have been over the ground. Button, for instance, says: "We descended into the Umkomaas". Bucknall says: "We went down into the valley of the Umkomaas." Jackson says: "(From the summit of Game Pass) we worked our way through the kloofs of the sources of the Umkomaas, in order to get into Giant's Castle Pass." Jaffray says: "We turned down towards our left . . . and descended into the Umkomaas, crossed the Loteni, and went up the other – (side? word undecipherable)." The others are equally definite, with the exception of Barter, who is a little vague, but who still does not describe the country between Game Pass and the Giant's Castle Pass.

4. Sir John Robinson, in *A Lifetime in South Africa* (1900) says quite clearly: "They ascended by the sources of the Umkomaas". This statement alone, if it can be accepted, definitely rules out the Giant's Castle Pass.

5. Charles Barter gives a vivid description of the approaches to the Pass they climbed. It was "the very birthplace and nursery of rivers". Waterfalls streamed down the face of the Berg. Huge krantzes frowned above, with masses of unburnt grass and moss hanging down the rocks, "a sombre and malignant scene". This description fits the approaches to the Hlatimba Pass exactly. By no stretch of the imagination could it fit the approaches to any of the other passes.

6. Apart from the approaches, the Pass itself (the Hlatimba) is exactly as described by the men who climbed it – *just* negotiable by horses, but choked at the top with masses of great boulders. None of the other passes are choked at the top with boulders.

7. Among contemporary references (Magistrates' Reports, accounts of Bushman raids, etc.,) I cannot find a single reference to the Giant's Castle Pass ever having been used. It was not a recognised route into Lesotho. But there are innumerable references to a pass sometimes called "Proudfoot's Pass" about five miles south of *Giant's Castle*.

8. On the night of July 24, 1869, four years prior to the Langalibalele affair, William Popham, farming at *Meshlynn*, had been raided by Bushmen. The stolen cattle had been driven up a pass "to the south of *Giant's Castle*". Charles Barter, in his account of the Rebellion, says the Pass up which they climbed was the one up which Popham's cattle had been driven in the raid of 1869, i.e. a pass *south of Giant's Castle*.

9. Durnford estimated the distance they rode from the top of the Pass they climbed to the Bushman's River Pass as about 12 miles (19,3 km); the distance from the Hltatimba Pass to the Bushman's River Pass, in a straight line, is 11 miles (17,8 km), while the distance from Giant's Castle Pass to the Bushman's River Pass is only 5 miles (8 km). The time taken to ride from the head of the Pass they climbed to the Bushman's River Pass (about four hours) again makes it clear that they did not ride from Giant's Castle Pass. This is a ride of only 1½ hours at most.

270

10. All accounts of the Langalibalele affair agree that after the engagement the Carbineers followed the same route home as they had taken on their ride to Bushman's River Pass. They certainly went home down one of the tributaries of the Umkomaas. Therefore they must have ascended via one of the same tributaries.

11. And finally, I doubt very much whether a troop of horsemen would have been able to ascend the Giant's Castle Pass, especially at night. It is too difficult. Dr. F. B. Wright, Warden of the Loteni Game Reserve, who knows the Pass well, is of the opinion that a man mounted on a wiry Basutho pony might, alone, negotiate it with a good deal of difficulty, but not a troop of mounted men. I agree with him.

The conclusion is, therefore, inescapable that the Carbineers did *not* ride up Giant's Castle Pass, but up another Pass which can only be the Hlatimba Pass.

What, then, had happened?

There are only two possibilities.

Either the Hlatimba Pass was called, loosely, in those days, the Giant's Castle Pass (it is, remember, in the *Giant's Castle* area) and the military had planned all along to use it, or the military had planned to use the more northern Pass known to-day as the Giant's Castle Pass, and somewhere along the line a mistake had been made, and the men had gone up the wrong Pass.

The first possibility is quite untenable. Firstly, I can find no contemporary map which calls the Hlatimba Pass "Giant's Castle Pass", while there is at least one map, the Stocker Map (1888) which has the name "Giant's Castle Pass" in its correct, present-day, position. Secondly, an examination of Grantham's Map, which the military were using at the time, shows fairly level country between *Meshlynn* and Giant's Castle Pass (which Durnford had been told to expect), and very broken country between *Meshlynn* and the Hlatimba Pass. (Incidentally, neither Pass is actually marked in this map.)

But an examination of the military map enclosed in Sir Benjamin Pine's despatch of 13 November 1873 to the Earl of Kimberley finally disposes of the matter. Even this map does not actually name Giant's Castle *Pass*, but *Giant's Castle* is named, and all the lines indicating the proposed military movements prior to the action at the head of Bushman's River Pass converge, in this map, on the present Giant's Castle Pass, and not on the Hlatimba Pass.

The conclusion is, therefore, inescapable: the military had planned to use the Giant's Castle Pass. A mistake was made, and instead of using this Pass, the Carbineers, on their march, diverged *left* instead of *right*, and went up the Hlatimba Pass, 6 miles (9,8 km) *south of Giant's Castle*. This mistake was the prime cause of the disaster that ensued.

I believe that what happened was that William Popham, as mentioned on page 233, was away from his farm, *Meshlynn*, when the Carbineers arrived there at 1 a.m. on the morning of November 3. It was at *Meshlynn*, roughly, that the two routes (to Giant's Castle Pass and to the Hlatimba Pass) diverged, and it would have been up to Popham to put the men on to the correct route. In his absence, Durnford must have turned to the Basutho guides for help. They did not know Giant's Castle Pass – it was not a normal route into the interior of Lesotho. They *did* know the Hlatimba Pass (Proudfoot's Pass), often used by them and by the Bushmen, as contemporary records clearly show. It was up this Pass, therefore, that they elected to lead the Carbineers.

APPENDIX 2

Climbing Techniques

The general reader sometimes finds it difficult to follow the accounts of rock climbs, owing to a lack of knowledge of the techniques employed, and it might be helpful if these were briefly explained.

Mountaineers usually climb in teams of two or three. Three gives a maximum of safety. Four or more can be cumbersome and slow.

Let us assume that the team consists of three men. All three are roped together, one at each end of a length of rope, and one in the middle.

The first man on the rope is the leader. He is the most experienced man in the team, and must be capable of negotiating the route to be climbed. The next man is the "second". His position is about the middle of the rope, and he is sometimes called the "middle man". The third man ties on at the other end of the rope, and is sometimes known as "last man".

The leader starts off and climbs the first "pitch" until he reaches a suitable ledge. A "pitch" is a single section of the ascent which can be climbed without stopping. As the leader climbs, the second man pays out the rope for him.

When the leader reaches a suitable stance, he stops and anchors himself to the rock face. A "stance" is some sort of ledge where a man can stand, easily balanced, and with his hands free. He anchors himself by tying a separate length of rope round his waist and then round a projecting piece of rock, in such a way that he cannot be pulled off his "stance".

No. 2, or the "middle man", now climbs up to the leader. As he climbs, the leader keeps pulling in the rope so that there is no slack between himself and the man who is climbing. (He does not, of course, *haul* the man up.) This is known as "bringing up" the second man. If this second man should slip, or fall, the rope should be able to hold him.

The two men are now standing on the ledge, or "stance", and they now bring up the third man in the same way, until all three are standing on the ledge.

No. 2 (and sometimes No. 3 as well) now anchors himself, and the leader now climbs the second pitch, No. 2, as before, paying out the rope for him. If the leader falls, No. 2 will be able to hold him.

Once again, the leader finds a suitable stance, anchors himself, and brings up No. 2 and then No. 3. Thereafter the same manoeuvre is repeated until the three men reach the top of the climb.

The action of holding the rope, and hauling it in as a man climbs (in other words "bringing him up") is also known as "belaying".

It is to be noted that only one man at a time climbs. The rest of the team waits, safely anchored to the rock face, and the men give their full attention to the man who is actually climbing.

The three men who are now at the top of their climb, then "abseil" down.

Abseiling has undergone a number of refinements in recent years, but fundamentally the procedure is as follows: A piton (see below) is hammered into a crack in the rock at the top of the climb. Through this a metal ring, called a "karabiner" (see below) is threaded, and the rope is passed through this ring until the half-way point is reached. This doubled rope is now passed between the legs of the first climber to descend (he is usually No. 3), passed back over the thigh, across the front of the body, and over the opposite shoulder, hanging loosely behind the back. The two ends of the rope are now thrown down the rock face. The climber now grasps the doubled rope above him with his left hand, to keep himself upright, and with his right hand held below waist level, he grasps the rope dangling behind his back. He grips this tightly, and then steps off the rock face, his body held in the coils of the rope. As he slackens the grip of his right hand, the weight of his body will cause it to slide down the rope, the rate of his descent being controlled by his right hand. He reaches a suitable stance, and the same rope is used by his two companions. When the last man is down, the rope is pulled through the ring, to be used again, if necessary, for the next pitch. The piton and the karabiner are left behind.

Glossary of Climbing Terms

Arête – A ridge running down the side of a mountain.

Belay – To secure a man either by holding the rope to which he is attached, or by fixing the other end of the rope to a firm projection. It can also apply to the projection itself.

Chimney – A narrow crack in the rock face into which the climber can insert his body.

Exposure – Has two meanings, 1. the effect of exposure to cold, harsh weather conditions, etc., and 2. the feeling of empty space below the climber's feet on a cliff face.

Gendarme – A small rock spire.

Karabiner – Sometimes called a snap-link. It is an oval, metal ring, with a spring-loaded gate, which allows a rope-sling (see below) to be clipped into it.

Pitch – A section of a rock climb between succeeding stances or belays.

Piton – A steel spike about 20 cms long, with a flattened blade at one end, which can be driven into rock cracks or ice. The other end has a 15 mm hole drilled through it, through which a rope can be threaded or a karabiner clipped.

Sling – A length of rope about 150 cms long, with the two ends tied together.

Snap-link – See karabiner (above).

Stance – A ledge where the climber pauses to make his belay.

Classification of Rock Climbs

Climbs are graded in difficulty as follows:

A – Very easy. No rock work involved.

B – Involves very easy rock work, but is mostly on grass.

C – Involves moderate rock work. A rope is not necessary, but is sometimes advisable.

D – Involves difficult rock work. A rope should be used, especially in the case of novices.

E – Involves severe rock work.

F – Involves very severe rock work.

G – Borders on the limit, almost unclimbable. Involves exceptionally severe rock work.

APPENDIX 3

Drakensberg Maps

To say that maps are of supreme importance in the development of a country, and that they are also profoundly interesting and equally indispensable to the historian, is, of course, a truism. It is remarkable, therefore, that South Africa was so slow in realising this. It is only within recent years that the country has been mapped scientifically; as late as the early 1930's the Director of Trigonometrical Surveys could still say that South Africa was the only civilised country in the world without maps; and no comprehensive study of early maps has yet been made.

This Appendix will give, first of all, a brief outline of the history of mapping in South Africa, with special reference to the Drakensberg, and secondly an equally brief survey of Drakensberg maps that have been produced in the past and which are available to-day.

1. History of Mapping in South Africa

The making of maps depends primarily, of course, on accurate and scientific surveying. The history of South African survey work dates from 1879, but the surveying of any country is a long and painfully slow business, and the first maps based on this work only appeared at the end of the century. This was the I.D.W.O. 1223 series, 1897, (19 sheets), covering portions of Natal round the Biggarsberg, north of Ladysmith. Virtually all other maps which appeared before the beginning of the twentieth century were either inaccurate sketch maps, such as those of Barrow, Sparrman, Le Vaillant, Gardiner and others, or maps compiled from unco-ordinated and individual farm surveys in the offices of the various Surveyors-General.

As in so many other spheres, it was the exigencies of war that stimulated, more than anything else, the making of maps in this country, for one cannot wage war without accurate maps. From 1860 onwards the War Office in London was engaged in bringing out various military maps of specific regions in South Africa. These were compiled from whatever information was available at the time. Typical of these was the Imperial Map Series of South Africa which was issued in 1900. The whole country was covered to a scale of 1 : 250 000, each sheet being about 25" x 20". These maps, though inaccurate, were used extensively by the British forces in the Anglo-Boer War. The Drakensberg, however, is only very cursorily covered.

A later coverage of similar best-available-compilation style maps was Major Jackson's Transvaal series of 1901-1904. The title is misleading, as both the Transvaal and Natal were covered. Only four or five names are given on the Drakensberg, but the topography has been roughly sketched in. This information was possibly copied from Buller's map of 1900 (see below).

The Anglo-Boer War brought home to the British Government the paramount importance of a series of reliable and accurate topographical maps* covering the whole country, and in 1904 a Congress was held in the Cape to discuss the whole problem. It was decided that a co-ordinated topographical survey of all British Colonies and Protectorates south of the Zambesi should be undertaken. Land for the erection of a Head Office was purchased, and the necessary survey instruments ordered, but almost immediately the whole scheme foundered as one after another of the various colonies withdrew for financial reasons.

So anxious was the British Government to obtain accurate maps of South Africa, however, that about the same time the War Office made a request to the High Commissioner in South

---

* Topographical Maps are generally accepted as being maps with a scale greater than 1 : 250 000 but smaller than 1 : 10 000. They are based on accurate surveys, and show the exact position of the most important physical features. Cadastral Maps show farm boundaries as well as the siting of important buildings. A combination of the two types is known as a Topo-cadastral map.

274

Africa that either the Transvaal or the Orange Free State should be mapped, and the War Office offered to bear half the cost. The Transvaal, again for financial reasons, declined, but the Free State agreed, and from 1905 to 1911 the Colonial Survey Section undertook a topographical survey of the whole Colony. The result was the map known as the O.F.S. Topographical Survey Map (G.S.G.S. 2230). This was the first accurate and extensive topographical map of any British area in Africa. It consisted of 55 sheets, was drawn to a scale of 1 : 125 000, and was an outstanding piece of work. Only that section of the Drakensberg lying between 27 degrees 15 minutes and 28 degrees 45 minutes south latitude (i.e. from Charlestown to *Mont-aux-Sources*) was, of course, covered.

Two other important map series affecting the Drakensberg, which were published during this period, must also be noticed here. These were the Reconnaissance Series of Cape Colony and Basutoland, 1907-1914, consisting of 33 sheets to a scale of 1 : 250 000 (G.S.G.S. 1764), and the Basutoland 1 : 250 000, 1911, Series (G.S.G.S. 2567), known familiarly as Dobson's Map. This map was produced by plane table survey, with 100 ft. form lines, and consisted of four sheets. It included, of course, the Drakensberg from *Mont-aux-Sources* to *Giant's Castle* and beyond, but very few details are given.

Up to the time of Union, therefore, the impetus for practically all serious mapping in South Africa had come from the military.

Union, in 1910, meant the unification of most State Departments, but this, unfortunately, did not include the various Survey Departments. The Surveyors-General of the four Provinces worked independently of each other, and organised and co-ordinated topographical mapping of the country ceased almost altogether.

By 1921 dissatisfaction caused to a great extent by the lack of accurate topographical maps was so acute that the Government appointed a Commission to study the whole problem and to make recommendations. These recommendations led eventually to the Land Survey Act of 1927, which not only placed the profession of Surveying on a sound basis, but made provision for the appointment of a Director of Trigonometrical Survey and the establishment of a Survey Board which from then on was to be responsible for the official surveying and mapping of the whole country. In 1930 three topographers from the newly-established Trigonometrical Survey Department were appointed to form a Topographical Division of the Department, with a view to starting a series of topographical maps of the country. Their first product – the 1 : 25 000 map of the Cape Peninsula – marked the promising start to the work of the Trigonometrical Survey.

In 1934 a Central Mapping Office, as a separate unit from the office of the Surveyor-General of the Transvaal, was established as the official map drawing office. The unit was absorbed by the Trigonometrical Survey Office in 1936.

In the meantime, various Government Departments were crying out for good, sound, reliable topographical maps. Defence, Water Affairs, Transport, Agriculture, to name but four, all found their work hampered through lack of the necessary maps. Individual Departments began to compile their own maps, independently of each other, and thousands of pounds were wasted through over-lapping.

This did, however, result in one very good map, the one produced by the Department of Water Affairs, known then as the Department of Irrigation. In 1934 Mr. A. D. Lewis, Director of the Department, took the initiative, and between 1934 and 1937 topographers from his Department mapped the whole of South Africa in a series of ten sheets, to a scale of 1 : 500 000. These maps were of inestimable value, especially as they were published on the eve of World War II. For many years they remained the only reasonably trustworthy topographical maps covering large areas of South Africa. It was on this map that Professor Sweeney based his celebrated map of the Natal Drakensberg.

But by 1936 it was obvious that something drastic had to be done to relieve the situation.

South Africa was away behind most other developed and developing countries in the matter of its map coverage. In that year the Minister of Lands appointed an Inter-Departmental Committee to assist the Director of Trigonometrical Surveys with a detailed programme of scientific mapping for the whole country. 1936 became a turning point in the mapping history of South Africa.

The greatest single factor contributing to this turning point was the fact that by now air photography had developed to such an extent that accurate maps could be produced by this method relatively quickly and cheaply. Actually the first surveys from air photographs had been made by Laussedat as far back as 1858, using photographs taken from captive balloons or kites, but the development of air-mapping had been a long and painful business, beset by many pitfalls. It was only the development of gyroscopic forms of control in the 1930's, and of precision aerial cameras that made air photography a reliable, accurate and economical method of mapping a country.

By 1936 air photography was being used effectively in South Africa. The Trigonometrical Survey Office was completely re-organized at that stage, and from now on it was to be solely responsible for all topographical mapping and air photography. In 1949 a National Advisory Survey Council was established, which had the important function of advising the Director on what areas were to be photographed, which were to be mapped, and to what scale the mapping was to be done.

Since then the following map series have been published:

1. *The 1 : 25 000 and 1 : 100 000 Topographical Series*

    During the war only those areas important from a defence point of view were mapped. The Drakensberg does not figure in them. The sheets of this series are now out of print, and the series itself has been discontinued.

2. *The 1 : 250 000 Topographical Series*

    Immediately after the Irrigation Department's 1 : 500 000 maps appeared, and as an interim defence measure, a start was made with a 1 : 250 000 topographical series. The Irrigation Department maps were enlarged and rapidly revised in the field. At the moment, however, this coverage is being rapidly superseded by one based on the most recent 1 : 50 000 mapping material (39 of the 71 sheets have either been published or are in preparation).

3. *The 1 : 250 000 Topo-cadastral Series*

    After 1936 a Cadastral series to the scale of 1 : 250 000 was compiled, consisting of 49 sheets. These have now been mostly replaced by the *new* 1 : 250 000 Topo-cadastral Series of 71 sheets. The first sheet of this new Series appeared in 1956. See below for the Drakensberg coverage of this Series, and of the ensuing two Series.

4. *The 1 : 500 000 Topographical Series*

    In 1945 a start was made with the present 1 : 500 000 Series of 21 sheets, to replace the Irrigation Department's maps, which by now were rather old. By 1953 the whole country had been covered. There are three editions of this Series, namely, a topographical map, an aeronautical chart and an administrative map in which magisterial districts are shown.

5. *The 1 : 50 000 Topographical Series*

    This is the standard map of the Republic, and the official mapping policy is to cover the whole country in this series, to this scale. The series is not quite complete yet, but it is hoped to complete it by the end of 1976. The Drakensberg area from *Giant's Castle* to *Mont-aux-Sources* is fully covered, and these maps provide the best and most accurate maps of the Drakensberg that we have to-day. See below.

In 1954 the Lesotho Government commenced work on a similar series of 1 : 50 000 topographical maps, covering the whole of Lesotho. This series is important, for it includes a strip of several kilometres to the east of the Drakensberg escarpment, and again gives excellent coverage of the Drakensberg region. Code numbers are identical with the South African maps, and the series is now complete.

Apart from the 1 : 25 000, the 1 : 100 000 and the *old* 1 : 250 000 topo-cadastral series, all maps which have been produced by the Trigonometrical Survey Office are obtainable from the Government Printer, Bosman Street, Pretoria (Private Bag 85). Full particulars concerning price, availability and code numbers appear in the Map Catalogue of the Trigonometrical Survey Office, priced at 10c per copy. Lesotho maps are obtainable from the Public Works Department, Maseru, Lesotho. The older maps may be consulted in the Archives of the four Provinces, but at the moment these are inadequately catalogued, and to trace them is a time-consuming business. In the case of the various Surveyors-General offices, the position is even more unsatisfactory, because the maps have either been destroyed in order to gain office space, or are stored away in back rooms with no attempt at classification. The only place where availability is reasonable is in the Map Library of the Trigonometrical Survey Office, Visagie Street, Pretoria.

2. Drakensberg Maps

We trace in this section the development of maps covering the Drakensberg, from the first crude sketch maps of Gardiner and Fynn, to the sophisticated and beautifully-produced maps of the Trigonometrical Survey Department of to-day. Section (i) deals with maps of Natal, where the Drakensberg appears only incidentally, and Section (ii) deals with specific Drakensberg maps.

Section (i): *Incidental Drakensberg Maps*

Apart from the Gardiner and Stocker maps, all the maps detailed in this check list and the next are large wall maps. No account is taken of smaller maps appearing in published books.

The first known maps of Natal are those of Gardiner and Fynn. The Fynn map, by H. F. Fynn, appears in the Fynn Papers, and was presumably drawn by Fynn himself about 1830. It only covers the eastern areas, and the Drakensberg does not appear at all.

The Gardiner map appears in Capt. Allen Gardiner's *Narrative of a Journey to the Zoolu Country*, published in 1836. It is only a rough sketch, and the Drakensberg is merely delineated as a straight line, running roughly north-east by south-west, with no names at all except "Saddleback" (See p. 44). Gardiner's map formed the basis of all Natal maps up to the early 1850's.

In 1846 William Stanger, Surveyor-General of Natal, complained that all available maps were full of mistakes. The coastline was correctly drawn, for this had been surveyed by the Admiralty, but the Drakensberg Range to the north-west was invariably indicated some 70 miles (113 km) too far east.

Subsequent maps are as follows:

1. *Wyld*.
   Date: 1850
   Size: 40,6 cm × 55,9 cm
   Scale: 1 inch = 8⅓ miles
   Details: The present Amphitheatre, in the Royal Natal National Park, is given as *Saddleback*. The height is given as 5 000 feet. (Correct height close on 10 000 ft.)

Giant's Castle is marked as the source of the "Umzimcooloe", and is sited at the present *Garden Castle*.*

2. *Stanger (Land Grants 1843 and 1848)*
   Date: 1850
   Size: 63 cm × 48 cm
   Scale: 1 inch = 9 miles
   Details: No Drakensberg names at all.

3. *Alfred Watts*
   Date: 1855
   Size: 86,5 cm × 66 cm
   Scale: 1 inch = 6 miles
   Details: No Drakensberg names at all, but names of a few farms in the area are given.

4. *Masser and Cullingworth*
   Date: 1862
   Size: 71,1 cm × 99,1 cm
   Scale: 1 inch = 6 miles
   Details: Drakensberg is still given almost as a straight line. Only one name is given, that of *Giant's Castle*, and the peak is now in its correct, present position. A number of farms in the Drakensberg area are shown.

5. *Major Grantham*
   Date: 1863
   Size: 96,5 cm × 167,6 cm, in four sheets.
   Scale: 1 inch = 3,8 miles
   Details: Surveyed by Captain Grantham, R.E., F.R.G.S., Assoc. In. C.E. in 1861, with additions from Surveyor-General's Office, Natal. Lithographed at the Topographical Dept. of the War Office in 1863. For the first time an attempt was made to delineate the Drakensberg in shading, but only one or two place-names are given. The map is still very inaccurate, and was the one used by the military in the Langalibalele Rebellion.

6. *Alexander Mair*
   Date: 1875
   Size: 121,9 cm × 162,6 cm
   Scale: 1 inch = 4 miles
   Details: Compiled by Alexander Mair, a Land Surveyor, from information supplied by Surveyor-General's Office. Line of the Drakensberg much more accurate than previous maps. Only names are Tugela Waterfall, Losonjo River (Umlambonja?) *Cathkin Peak or Champagne Castle*, Injasuti or Little Tugela River, Bushman's River Pass, Bushman's River, *Giant's Castle*.

7. *Natal Colonial Engineer*
   Date: 1879
   Size: 94 cm × 58,4 cm
   Scale: 1 inch = 8 miles
   Details: This map was prepared in the Colonial Engineer's Department, by direction of his Excellency the Lieutenant Governor, for purposes of Colonial Defence. Drakensberg names as in the Alexander Mair map.

* This siting is also given in a map which appears in R. J. Mann's 'Colony of Natal' published in 1859. It is the original siting as given by Capt. Allen Gardiner, and these are the only two maps which give it.

8. *Military Map*
   Date: 1879
   Size: 46 cm × 58 cm
   Scale: 1 inch = 10 miles
   Details: A military map, compiled and lithographed at the Intelligence Branch of the Quartermaster General's Department. Many of the details are based on Grantham's map of 1863, but names in Drakensberg region much more numerous, 10 altogether. Lesotho area a complete blank except for the words: "Deep Rocky Valleys infested by Wild Bushmen" and "Very Wild and Little Known Country inhabited by Bushmen".

9. *Natal Education Department*
   Date: 1893
   Size: 160 cm × 99 cm
   Scale: 1 inch = 5 miles
   Details: Only five Drakensberg names, but Mnweni River appears for first time.

10. *Military Map of Colony of Natal, compiled for General Sir Redvers Buller*
    Date: 1900
    Size: 152,4 cm × 167,6 cm
    Scale: 1 inch = 2,35 miles
    Details: Though claiming to be a map of the Colony of Natal, it only covers north-western Natal – the war area. Only six names in the Drakensberg, but *Cathedral Peak* is called *Sikali's Horn*, the Mnweni area is called Cathedral, and the *Mnweni Needles* are called "*The Pegs*".

11. *Masson*
    Date: 1904
    Size: 83,8 cm × 99,1 cm
    Scale: 1 inch = 4 miles
    Details: Like Buller's map, the Mnweni (Rockeries) area is called "The Cathedral". *South Saddle* is called "*The Prop*", and Organ Pipes Pass is called "Old Bushman's Pass".

There is little point in re-listing the other maps referred to in the History of Mapping in South Africa, and we come now to the three series of maps produced at the present time by the Trigonometrical Survey Department. These, together with the Lesotho 1 : 50 000 maps, offer the most reliable and up-to-date maps of the Drakensberg that we have to-day. They are as follows:

12. *Topographical Series 1 : 500 000 (TSO 500)*
    Date: First published 1936, with subsequent, amended, editions.
    Size: 82 cm × 44 cm
    Scale: 1 : 500 000 (approx. 1 inch = 8 miles)
    Details: There are three editions of this map, as noted on page 276. The whole of the Republic is covered in 21 sheets. Sheets Durban SE 31/28 and Kroonstad SE 29/26 cover the Drakensberg. The scale is too small for the maps to be of any practical use in the Drakensberg.

13. *Topocadastral Series 1 : 250 000 (TSO 404)*
    Date: First published 1956, with subsequent, amended, editions.
    Size: 77 cm × 44 cm
    Scale: 1 : 250 000 (approx. 1 inch = 4 miles)
    Details: Whole of Republic has been covered in 71 sheets. The Drakensberg is covered

in Sheet Harrismith 2828 and Drakensberg 2928. The great value of this Series to the mountaineer is the fact that farm names and boundaries are given, information not included in the maps of the 1 : 500 000 Series.

14. *Topographical Series 1 : 50 000 (TSO 200)*
   Date: The Series was started about 1938, and it is anticipated that full cover of the Republic will be provided by the end of 1976.
   Size: 49 cm × 55,5 cm
   Scale: 1 : 50 000 (approx. 1 inch = 1 mile)
   Details: These maps are unquestionably the finest maps of the Drakensberg available to-day, but they should be studied in conjunction with the similar series of 1 : 50 000 maps issued by the Government of Lesotho, for they complement each other. The maps of each Government cover the same area, and carry the same code numbers. To cover the whole Drakensberg Range from *Mont-aux-Sources* to *Giant's Castle* the following sheets will be required:

2828	DB	Witzieshoek
2828	DD	Mont-aux-Sources
2829	CC	Cathedral Peak
2929	AA	Champagne Castle (West)
2929	AB	Champagne Castle
2929	AD	Giant's Castle

   The Index Map on the opposite page will give a clear idea of the full coverage. For instance, if a map of the Cathkin area is required, the sheet to order is 2929 AB. The South African Series is obtainable from the Government Printer, Bosman Street, Pretoria, and the Lesotho Series from the Public Works Department, Maseru, Lesotho. The cost is 60c per sheet, the maps are beautifully produced, and the 50 ft. and 100 ft. form lines make them invaluable to the mountaineer.

Section (ii): *Specific Drakensberg Maps*

1. *The Stocker Map*
   This map has already been dealt with in Chapter V. It appeared in the *Alpine Journal* for 1889. It is such an important landmark that we reproduce it on page 53, with the kind permission of the Editor of the *Journal*.

2. *Map of Drakensberg, Mont-aux-Sources to Giant's Castle.* G. M. J. Sweeney.
   Date: 1927, with many subsequent editions.
   Size: 52,5 cm × 73 cm
   Scale: 1 inch = 2 miles
   Details: For many years the standard map of the Drakensberg. Professor Sweeney based his map on Holmden's Map of Natal, which in turn was based on the Irrigation Department's 1 : 500 000 map.

3. *Cathkin Area.* J. E. L. Peck and R. O. Pearse.
   Date: 1946
   Size: 52 cm × 65,5 cm
   Scale: 1 inch = ½ mile
   Details: Mapped by plane table and air photographs. Published by *Cape Times* in five colours. This and the next map are the only specific Drakensberg maps to have been published. All the others have been reproduced by office copying machines.

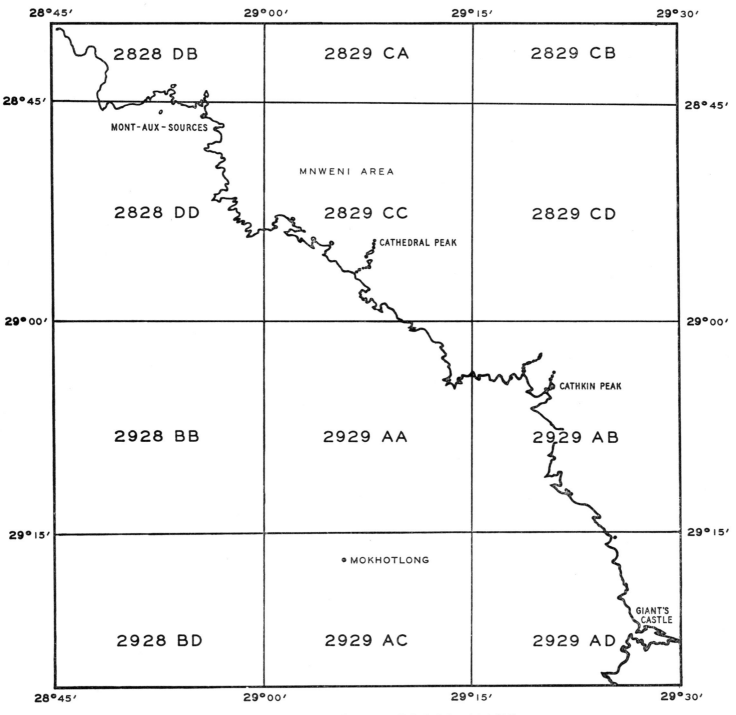

28°45′		29°00′		29°15′		29°30′

2828 DB

2829 CA

2829 CB

28°45′

MONT-AUX-SOURCES

MNWENI AREA

2828 DD

2829 CC

2829 CD

CATHEDRAL PEAK

29°00′

CATHKIN PEAK

2928 BB

2929 AA

2929 AB

29°15′

• MOKHOTLONG

GIANT'S CASTLE

2928 BD

2929 AC

2929 AD

28°45′   29°00′   29°15′   29°30′

CODE INDEX OF 1:50000 MAPS
COVERING DRAKENSBERG AREA

4. *Cathedral Area*. R. O. Pearse.
   Date: 1948
   Size: 62,5 cm x 48,5 cm
   Scale: 1 inch = ½ mile
   Details: A companion map to the last. Mapped by plane table and air photographs, and
            published in five colours by the *Cape Times*. This map, and the last, are now out
            of print.

5. *Mont-aux-Sources to Giant's Castle*. K. E. Fulton.
   Date: About 1948
   Size: 78,5 cm × 55 cm
   Scale: 1 inch = 2 miles
   Details: Compiled from G. M. J. Sweeney 1927 and 1947, R. O. Pearse and J. E. L.
            Peck 1946, R. O. Pearse 1948, and information supplied by the Trigonometrical
            Survey Office.

6. *Mont-aux-Sources Area*. K. E. Fulton.
   Date: 1945
   Size: 117,5 cm × 66,5 cm
   Scale: 2¾ inches = 1 mile
   Details: Map surveyed by K. E. Fulton, using plane table.

7. *Giant's Castle Area*. J. C. Simpson.
   Date: 1957
   Size: 60 cm × 68 cm
   Scale: 1¼ inches = 1 mile
   Details: Compiled by J. C. Simpson from 1 : 50 000 Topographical Survey, air photos
            and local assembly. This map was revised and amplified in 1962 by P. R.
            Barnes and R. O. Pearse.

8. The Natal Mountain Club issues a series of maps of the Drakensberg, based on the
   1 : 50 000 Topographical Survey maps, but these are only available to club members.

APPENDIX 4

List of Drakensberg Peaks in Order of Height together with Record of First Ascents

The majority of Drakensberg peaks standing on the edge of the escarpment can be climbed either from the summit (Lesotho) plateau, the easy way, or from the Natal side, always a much more difficult task. An asterisk indicates a climb via the summit plateau.

All heights are according to the latest survey figures from the Department of Trigonometrical Survey. † Indicates height approximate to within 50 feet.

Peak	Height		Date of first ascent	Climbing party	Standard of climb
	Feet	Metres			
Injasuti	11 350	3 459†		No record*	A
Champagne Castle	11 079	3 377	1888	Rev. A. H. Stocker, F. R. Stocker, *via* the High Route	D
			1861	Major Grantham (traditionally) but route not known	
				via Gray's Pass: no record	B
Popple Peak	10 908	3 325		No record*	A
Giant's Castle	10 878	3 316	1864	Bob Speirs, Augustus Bovill, Henry, Edgar and Fred Bucknall	A
			1941	G. M. J. Sweeney and party, *via* S.E. Gully	C
Mont-aux-Sources	10 768	3 282	1836	Rev. T. Arbousset and Rev. F. Daumas*	A
Cleft Peak	10 765	3 281	1936	D. P. Liebenberg, Dr. L. P. Ripley and party*	A
			1941	D. P. Liebenberg, Else Wong, A. S. Hooper, *via* Diagonal Route	C
			1946	O. B. Godbold, Mr. and Mrs. A. Millard, *via* the cleft	E

Peak	Height		Date of first ascent	Climbing party	Standard of climb
	Feet	Metres			
Indumeni Dome	10 680	3 255†	1925	H. G. Botha-Reid and party*	A
Monk's Cowl	10 611	3 234	1942	J. Botha, E. Ruhle, A. S. Hooper, H. Wong	F
Ifidi Buttress	10 560	3 219		No record*	A
Injasuti Buttress	10 523	3 207	1935	G. M. J. Sweeney, M. Frank	C
Western Triplet	10 455	3 187	1951	R. F. Davies, D. Bell	G
Eastern Triplet	10 400	3 170†	1950	E. Scholes, R. Forsyth, D. Watkins, Lorna Pierson	G
Sentinel	10 385	3 165	1910	W. J. Wybergh, Lieut. N. M. McLeod	D
Middle Triplet	10 350	3 155†	1950	D. Watkins, Gillian Bettle, Lorna Pierson	F
North Saddle	10 346	3 153	1924	O. K. Williamson, D. W. Bassett-Smith	C
			1968	R. Fuggle, C. Fatti, B. Manicom, A. Dick from Ntonjelane Valley	F
Cathkin Peak	10 330	3 149	1912	G. T. Amphlett, W. C. West, Father A. D. Kelly, T. Casement, Tobias, Melatu	E
Mt. Amery	10 311	3 143	1920	D. W. Bassett-Smith, R. G. Kingdon	B
			1955	E. M. Winter, M. C. Moor, R. M. Moor, from Singati Valley	D
Elephant	10 300	3 139†	1936	O. B. Godbold and party*	A
Beacon Buttress	10 240	3 121		No record*	A

Peak	Height		Date of first ascent	Climbing party	Standard of climb
	Feet	Metres			
Cockade	10 210	3 112†	1936	O. B. Godbold and party*	A
South Saddle	10 200	3 109†	1947	J. de V. Graaff*	D
Inner Mnweni Pinnacle	10 170	3 100	1949	J. de V. Graaff, G. R. de Carle, R. Buckland, Phyllis Goodwin	E
Outer Mnweni Pinnacle	10 158	3 096	1948	G. Thomson, C. Gloster	G
Abbey	10 134	3 089		No record*	A
Mbundini Buttress	10 131	3 088		No record*	A
Mponjwana	10 120	3 085†	1946	G. Thomson, K. Snelson	E
Little Saddle	10 089	3 075	1935	D. P. Liebenberg, S. Rose, Dr. L. P. Ripley, H. J. Barker	B
Windsor Castle	10 055	3 065	1935	D. P. Liebenberg, S. Rose, Dr. L. P. Ripley, H. J. Barker	B
Ndedema Dome	10 050	3 063†	1935	O. B. Godbold, E. S. Field*	A
Witch	10 045	3 062	1935	O. B. Godbold, E. S. Field and party	C
Castle Buttress	10 015	3 053		No record*	A
Eastern Buttress	9 996	3 047	1914	Father A. D. Kelly, G. J. Miller	D
The Ape	9 990	3 045		No record*	A
Inner Tower	9 986	3 044	1913	Father A. D. Kelly, G. J. Miller*	C
North Ifidi Pinnacle	9 950	3 033†	1959	E. M. Winter, M. C. Moor	F
South Ifidi Pinnacle	9 950	3 033†	1952	E. M. Winter, Gillian Bettle	D

Peak	Height		Date of first ascent	Climbing party	Standard of climb
	Feet	Metres			
Rockeries Peak	9 930	3 027†	1953	R. F. Davies, J. de V. Graaff, J. Slinger, D. Williamson	F
Mbundini Fangs	9 920	3 024	1953	T. C. Norcott, H. A. Cockburn, M. Allan	E
Mitre	9 919	3 023	1938	O. B. Godbold, L. Bybee and party	E
Outer Horn	9 860	3 006	1934	D. P. Liebenberg, Dr. L. P. Ripley, H. G. Botha-Reid, T. Wood, F. S. Brown	D
Inner Horn	9 858	3 005	1925	H. G. Botha-Reid and party	C
Cathedral Peak	9 856	3 004	1917	D. W. Bassett-Smith R. G. Kingdon	C
Ntonjelane Needle	9 800	2 987†	1934	O. B. Godbold, F. E. Ellis, N. Hodson	D
Old Woman Grinding Corn	9 798	2 986	1937	O. B. Godbold, C. E. Axelson, N. Hodson	E
Sterkhorn (South)	9 755	2 973	1888	Rev. A. H. Stocker, F. R. Stocker	E
Amphitheatre Wall	9 750	2 972†	1935	D. P. Liebenberg, Mary Lear, Aimée Netter, M. Frank	E
Saddle (Centre)	9 750	2 972†	1934	O. B. Godbold, F. E. Ellis	C
Cikicane	9 700	2 957†	1958	Dr. S. H. Ripley, E. M. Winter, J. Grindley	E
Devil's Tooth	9 650	2 941†	1950	E. H. Scholes, D. Bell, P. Campbell	G
Bell	9 612	2 930	1944	H. Wong, Else Wong	E
Column	9 610	2 929†	1945	G. Thomson	F

Peak	Height		Date of first ascent	Climbing party	Standard of climb
	Feet	Metres			
Pyramid	9 600	2 926†	1936	K. F. Howes-Howell, O. B. Godbold, H. C. Hoets, C. Axelson, S. Rose, Naomi Bokenham	E
Inner Mnweni Needle	9 532	2 905	1943	A. S. Hooper, P. B. Fenger, Elizabeth Burton	D
Twins	9 510	2 899†	1931	G. M. J. Sweeney and party	C
Outer Mnweni Needle	9 483	2 890	1921	K. Cameron, D. W. Bassett-Smith	D
Mt. Oompie	9 418	2 871	1930	H. A. Liddle, C. Heron A. G. Bird	C
Amphlett	8 597	2 620	1933	O. B. Godbold, F. E. Ellis and party	C
			(1912)	(Possibly ascended by G. T. Amphlett)	
Turret	8 585	2 617†	1933	O. B. Godbold, F. E. Ellis and party	B
Eastman's Peak	8 466	2 580	1935	H. A. Eastman and party	C
Litter	7 970	2 429	1935	D. P. Liebenberg, S. Rose, Dr. L. P. Ripley, H. J. Barker, Mary Lear, Rene Hodson	D
Gatberg	7 900	2 408	1910	W. Carter Robinson, M. E. Robinson	B

The following two peaks have not been included in the above list. They are on the Lesotho side of the watershed, and are, therefore, not true Drakensberg peaks.

Peak	Height		Date of first ascent	Climbing party	Standard of climb
	Feet	Metres			
Thabana Ntlenyana (highest peak in Africa south of Kilimanjaro)	11 425	3 482	1951	D. Watkins, B. Anderson, R. Goodwin and party*	A

Peak	Height		Date of first ascent	Climbing party	Standard of climb
	Feet	Metres			
Makheke	11 355	3 461	1938	J. van Heyningen, Col. Park Gray* (But height had already been computed, presumably by aneroid, in 1888, so this could not have been a first ascent.)	A

BIBLIOGRAPHY

1. Official Manuscript Sources

A. *Secretary for Native Affairs (SNA)*
   1/3/19 Deposition of W. Popham 31/7/69
          Allison to Macfarlane 23/11/69
          Giles to O.C. Expedition 12/9/69
          Giles to Macfarlane 13/9/69
          Giles to Allison 22/9/69
          Macfarlane to Shepstone 27/8/69 & 28/8/69
   1/6/9 Allison to Shepstone 15/6/68 & 18/6/68
          Statement of Jagarta 17/6/68
   1/3/2 Howell to Shepstone 10/8/49

B. *Colonial Secretary's Office (CSO)*
   44(1) No. 8 Melville to Shepstone 22/12/48
   49(1) No. 65 Ditto 4/1/49
   84 No. 92 St. George to CS 12/3/56
   85 No. 4 Allen to St. George, enclosed in St. George to CS 24/3/56

C. *PRO Colonial Office Series 179/112*
   Official Despatches on Langalibalele Rebellion from Sir Benjamin Pine to Secretary of State Lord Kimberley

D. *Govt. Notice No. 37 of 1853*

2. Unpublished Papers

1. Preliminary Draft of Research Programme for Cathedral Peak Forest Hydrological Research Station, P. G. Boustead. 1970.
2. Cathedral Peak Guide, U. W. Nänni. N. d.
3. Sundry Papers, Cathedral Peak Forest Hydrological Research Station. N. d.
4. Evidence before the Military Court of Enquiry into the Langalibalele Rebellion. 1874.
5. Diary of a Natal Carbineer (A. R. Button) from papers of the late Samuel Marriott. 1873.
6. James J. Hodson Diary. 1873.
7. Jaffray Papers (Diary). 1873.
8. Account of Langalibalele, Sgt. T. B. Varty. 1874.
9. The Engagement at Bushman's River Pass, Charles Barter. 1873.
10. The Langalibalele Rebellion, Sgt. John Otter Jackson. 1874. (Also published in *The Pictorial*, April 27, 1911).
11. The Langalibalele Rebellion, Tpr. Bucknall's Account. 1873. (Also published in the *Natal Mercury*, 11 November 1873).
12. Judgment of Justice A. A. Kennedy in Supreme Court, Pietermaritzburg, 9 August 1956, in case of Regina v. Mandolozane Ndaba and 25 others.
13. Memorandum submitted by the Estcourt Farmers' Association on Drakensberg Locations Nos. 1 and 2. 1971.
14. Report of Water Symposium, Durban, May 1970.
15. Log Book, E. Martin Winter. N. d.
16. The History of the Gray Family, I. M. N. Mudie. 1956.
17. Fannin Papers. N. d.
18. Underberg-Himeville, J. S. Little. 1971.
19. History of Mooi River and District, E. J. Shorten and A. H. Young. 1939.
20. Zunckel Papers. N. d.

21. Garden Papers. N. d.
22. John Shepstone Papers. N. d.
23. Statement of Nonqala Ndhlovu, (type-written document in possession of Dr. F. B. Wright). 1957.
24. Encyclopaedia Britannica Research Department: Notes on *Gypaëtus barbatus aureus* and *G. b. meridionalis*. 1962.
25. A Guide Plan for the Optimum Utilization of the Natural Resources of the Drakensberg Catchment Reserve. Department of Planning, August 1970.

3. Published Papers

1. Report of International Symposium on Forest Hydrology, ed. William E. Sopper and Howard W. Lull. 1967.
2. Report of the Interdepartmental Committee of Investigation into Afforestation and Water Supplies in S. Africa. 1968.
3. Forestry and Water Supplies in South Africa, C. L. Wicht. 1949.
4. Report on Natal Forests, H. G. Fourcade. 1889.
5. Natal Regional Survey, Vol. 1, 1951: *Archaeology and Natural Resources of Natal*, O. Davies.
6. Report on the Geology of Basutoland, G. M. Stockley. 1947.
7. South African Archaeological Bulletin, 22 : 27-30: *The Brotherton Shelter*, Peter Beaumont.
8. Parliamentary Papers re Kaffir Outbreak in Natal, 1873-4, C-1025, 1864, XLV; C-1121, 1875, LII.
9. Bantu Studies, Vol. VII, No. 2, 1933: *Archaeology of Cathkin Peak Area* (Wits. Univ. Archaeological Expedition, Dec. 1931).
10. Ethnological Publications, Vol. VII, 1938: *History of Matiwane and the Amangwane Tribe*, N. J. van Warmelo.
11. Annals of the Natal Museum, Vol. 20(3), Feb. 1971: *A Bushman Hunting Kit from the Drakensberg*, Patricia Vinnicombe.
12. Botanical Survey of South Africa, Memoir No. 23: *Vegetation of Weenen County, Natal*, Oliver West. 1951.
13. Botanical Survey of South Africa, Memoir No. 34: *An Account of the Plant Ecology of the Cathedral Peak Area of the Natal Drakensberg*, D. J. B. Killick. 1963.
14. Stone Age Art from Cantabria to the Cape, A. R. Willcox. 1969. (Reprint from *Optima*, June 1969).
15. Third and Final Report of the Geological Survey of Natal and Zululand, W. Anderson. 1907.
16. Natal's Part in the Langalibalele Rebellion, Sir William Beaumont. 1874.
17. History of the Zulu and Neighbouring Tribes, A. T. Bryant. (Pub. in *Inzindaba Zabata*, 1911-13, reprint 1964).
18. Natal Archaeological Studies, O. Davies. 1952.
19. Souvenir Guide Book issued in connection with the visit of members of the British Association, August 22 to 27, 1905, in particular *Cave Hunting in the Drakensberg*, Maurice Evans.
20. Pioneers of Underberg, P. McKenzie. 1946.
21. The Kaffir Revolt in Natal in the year 1873, pub. Keith & Co. 1874. (Includes the official record of the trial of Langalibalele and his tribe).
22. Twentieth Century Impressions of Natal: *The Bushmen and their Art*, A. W. Squire. 1906.
23. The Thousand Years before Van Riebeeck, Monica Wilson. 1970. (Raymond Dart Lecture No. 6).
24. South African Journal of Science, May 1971: *Size and the Hunter*, A. R. Willcox.
25. University of Witwatersrand Department of Archaeology: Occasional Papers 8, June

1971: *Report on Excavations in Rock Shelters in the Ndedema Gorge, Cathedral Peak Area, Natal, 1967-68*, A. R. Willcox.
26. South African Archives Journal 12 (1970): *Topografiese Kaarte van Suid-Afrika*, E. C. Liebenberg.
27. Trees in South Africa, 1958: *Proteas of the Summer Rainfall Area*, Dr. J. S. Beard.

4. Unpublished Theses

1. Natal and the Annexation of Basutoland, 1865-1870, E. V. Axelson; (M.A. Natal-South Africa, 1934).
2. The Establishment of the Location System in Natal, 1846-1850, M. E. Dreyer; (M.A. Natal-South Africa, 1947).
3. The Langalibalele Rebellion and its Consequences, W. R. Guest; (M.A. Natal, 1966).
4. The Matyana Affair, E. C. Leandy de Bufanos; (B.A. Hons. Natal, 1965).
5. A Figure of Controversy: the First Bishop of Natal, H. K. H. McCallum; (B.A. Hons. Natal, 1966).
6. Colonel Anthony William Durnford in the History of Natal and Zululand, 1873-1879, J. St. C. Man; (B.A. Hons. Natal, 1969).
7. David Dale Buchanan, the *Natal Witness*, and Discontent under the Government of Benjamin Pine, F. Ovendale; (B.A. Hons. Natal, 1963).
8. The Langalibalele Rising, B. C. Janse van Rensburg; (M.A. Natal-South Africa, 1930).

5. Published Theses

1. The Shepstones in South Africa, R. E. Gordon; (Ph. D. Natal, 1965).
2. In the Era of Sir Theophilus Shepstone, K.C.M.G.: 35 Years of British Expansion in South Africa, 1842-1877, C. J. Uys; (D. Litt. Pretoria, 1932).
3. The Mountain Bushmen and their Neighbours in Natal, 1840-70, J. B. Wright; (M.A. Natal, 1966).

6. Published Books

ACUTT, A., The Simple Chronicle of a South African Family (the Acutts). 1926.
AHRENS, F. W., From Bench to Bench. 1948.
ARBOUSSET, T., Narrative of an Exploratory Tour to the Cape of Good Hope. 1846.
BAKER, H. A. & OLIVER, E. G. H., Ericas in Southern Africa. 1967.
BARTER, C., Dorp and Veld. 1852.
BATTISS, W. W., The Amazing Bushman. 1939.
BERG, B., Den Slygande Braken. 1965.
BIGALKE, R., What Animal is it? 1958.
BIRD, J., The Annals of Natal, 1495-1845. 1888.
—— Natal, 1846-1851, By an Old Inhabitant. 1891.
BLEEK, D., Cave Artists of South Africa. 1953.
BLEEK, W. H. I., A Brief Account of Bushman Folklore. 1875.
—— The Natal Diaries of Dr. W. H. I. Bleek, ed. O. H. Spohr. 1965.
BLEEK, W. H. I. & LLOYD, L. C., The Mantis and his Friends, ed. Dorothea Bleek. 1923.
BREUIL, H., Beyond the Bounds of History. 1949.
BROOKES, E. H. & WEBB, C. DE B., History of Natal. 1965.
BROOKS, H., Natal, A History and Description of the Colony, ed. R. J. Mann. 1876.
BROOME, F. N., Not the Whole Truth. 1962.
BRYANT, A. T., Olden Times in Zululand and Natal. 1929.
—— The Zulu People. 1949.

BUCHANAN, B., The Pioneers of Natal. 1934.
—— Natal Memories. 1941.
BULPIN, T. V., Natal and the Zulu Country. 1966.
—— To the Shores of Natal. N. d.
BURMAN, J., A Peak to Climb. 1966.
—— Great Shipwrecks on the Coast of Southern Africa. 1967.
BYROM, J., Field Guide to the Game Animals of Natal and Zululand. N. d.
BYRON, E., What We Did in South Africa in 1873. 1874.
CAMBRIDGE HISTORY OF THE BRITISH EMPIRE, Vol. VIII. 1936.
CHAPMAN, J., Travels in the Interior of South Africa, Vol. I. 1868.
CHASE, J. C., Natal Papers. 1843.
CLOETE, H., History of the Great Boer Trek. 1900.
COLENSO, F. E. (pseudonym "ATHERTON WYLDE"), My Chief and I, or Six Months in Natal
       after the Langalibalele Outbreak. 1880.
COLENSO, F. E., The Ruin of Zululand, Vols. I and II. 1884.
COLENSO, F. E. AND DURNFORD, LIEUT. COL. E., History of the Zulu War. 1881.
COLENSO, J. W., Ten Weeks in Natal. 1855.
—— Langalibalele and the amaHlubi Tribe. 1874.
COOKE, C. K., Rock Art of Southern Africa. 1969.
COX, REV. SIR G. W., Life of Bishop Colenso. 1888.
DE KOK, K. J., Empires of the Veld. 1904.
DOBIE, J. S., South African Journal, 1862-1866, ed. A. F. Hattersley. 1945.
DRAYSON, CAPT. A. W., Sporting Scenes Amongst the Kaffirs of South Africa. 1858.
DREYER, A., Die Kaapse Kerk en die Groot Trek. 1929.
DURNFORD, LIEUT. COL. E., A Soldier's Life and Work in South Africa. Memoir of Col. A. W.
       Durnford. 1882.
DU TOIT, A. L., The Geology of South Africa. 1926.
ELLENBERGER, D. F., History of the Basuto, Ancient and Modern, tr. J. C. MacGregor. 1912.
FANNIN, J. E., The Fannin Papers. 1932.
FITZSIMONS, V. F. M., Snakes of Southern Africa. 1962.
GARDINER, CAPT. A., Narrative of a Journey to the Zoolu Country in South Africa, undertaken
       in 1835. 1836.
GREEN, L. G., Tavern of the Seas. 1947.
—— In the Land of Afternoon. 1954.
—— Karroo. 1955.
—— Where Men Still Dream. 1956.
—— These Wonders to Behold. 1959.
—— On Wings of Fire. 1967.
HATTERSLEY, A. F., More Annals of Natal. 1936.
—— Portrait of a Colony. 1940.
—— The Natalians: Further Annals of Natal. 1940.
—— The British Settlement of Natal. 1950.
—— Carbineer: The History of the Royal Natal Carbineers. 1950.
—— Oliver the Spy, and Others. 1959.
HAUGHTON, S. H., Geological History of Southern Africa. 1969.
HINCHCLIFF, P., John William Colenso. 1964.
HOLDEN, REV. W. C., History of the Colony of Natal. 1855.
HOLLIDAY, J. D., Dottings on Natal. 1890.
HOLT, C. P., Mounted Police of Natal. 1913.
HOPE, A., Yesterdays: The Story of Richmond. 1969.

How, M. W., The Mountain Bushmen of Basutoland. 1962.

Hulme, M. M., Wild Flowers of Natal. 1954.

Hurst, G. T., Volunteer Regiments of Natal and East Griqualand. 1945.

Ingram, J. F., The Colony of Natal. 1895.

Isaacs, N., Travels and Adventures in Eastern Africa, ed. L. Herrman. 1937.

Isemonger, R. M., Snakes of Africa. 1968.

Johnson, T., Rock Paintings of the S.W. Cape. 1959.

King, L. C., South African Scenery. 1942.

Klein, H., Land of the Silver Mist. 1951.

Lee, D. N. and Woodhouse, H. C., Art on the Rocks of Southern Africa. 1970.

Lückhoff, C. A., Table Mountain. 1951.

Lugg, H. C., Historic Natal and Zululand. 1948.

—— Zulu Place Names in Natal. 1968.

—— A Natal Family Looks Back. 1970.

Maberly, C. T. A., The Game Animals of Southern Africa. 1963.

Mackeurtan, G., Cradle Days of Natal. 1930.

Mann, R. J., The Colony of Natal. 1859.

—— Physical Geography and Climate of the Colony of Natal. 1866.

—— Emigrants' Guide to the Colony of Natal. 1868.

Marais, E., My Friends the Baboons. 1939.

Marsh, J. W., A Memoir of Allen F. Gardiner. 1866.

Matthews, J. W., Incwadi Yami, Twenty Years Personal Experience in South Africa. 1887.

Moodie, D. C. F., The History of the Battles and Adventures of the British, the Boers, and the Zulus in Southern Africa. 1879.

Morris, D. R., The Washing of the Spears. 1965.

Nathan, M., The Voortrekkers of South Africa. 1937.

Page, J., Captain Allen Gardiner, Sailor and Saint. 1883.

Pager, H., Ndedema, 1971.

Palmer, E., Plains of Camdeboo. 1966.

Peace, W., Our Colony of Natal. 1883.

Phillips, E. P., The Genera of South African Flowering Plants 1951

Preller, G S., Voortrekker Mense: Dagboek van Erasmus Smit. 1920.

Rees, W., Colenso Letters from Natal. 1958.

Ritter, E. A., Shaka Zulu: The Rise of the Zulu Empire. 1955.

Robinson, Sir J., Notes on Natal: An Old Colonist's Book for New Settlers. 1872.

—— A Lifetime in South Africa. 1900.

Rogers, G. M., I . . . Alone. 1937.

Ross, J. J., Die Sending te Witzieshoek, Paulus Mopeli, en Andere Sake. 1928.

Rossouw, F., The Proteaceae of South Africa. 1970.

Russell, R., Natal, the Land and its Story. 1904.

S.A.R., Descriptive Guide to the Province of Natal. 1910.

Schapera, I., The Khoisan People of South Africa. 1930.

Schoeman, P. J., Hunters of the Desert Land. 1957.

Shepstone, S. W. B., A History of Richmond, Natal. 1937.

Shuter, C. F., Englishman's Inn. 1963.

Smail, J. L., With Shield and Assegai. 1969.

Stalker, J., The Natal Carbineers, 1855-1911. 1912.

Stow, G. W., The Native Races of South Africa, ed. G. McCall Theal. 1905.

Stow, G. W. and Bleek, D. F., Rock Paintings in South Africa. 1930.

Taljaard, M. S., A Glimpse of South Africa. 1949.

THEAL, G. M., History of South Africa from 1873 to 1884, Vol. X. 1919.
TOWN AND REGIONAL PLANNING COMMISSION, NATAL, Towards a Plan for the Tugela Basin. 1960.
TRAUSELD, W. R., Wild Flowers of the Natal Drakensberg. 1969.
VOGTS, M. M., Proteas, Know Them and Grow Them. 1958.
WALKER, E. A., The Great Trek. 1934.
WIDDICOMBE, J., In the Lesuto. 1895.
WILLCOX, A. R., Rock Paintings of the Drakensberg. 1956.
—— The Rock Art of South Africa. 1963.
WILSON, M. AND THOMSON, L., Oxford History of South Africa, Vol. I. 1969.
WOODHOUSE, H. C., Archaeology in Southern Africa. 1971.
WRIGHT, J. B., Bushman Raiders of the Drakensberg, 1840-1870. 1971.
WYLDE, ATHERTON, My Chief and I. See Colenso, F. E.
YOUNG, A. H., Hathorn Family History. 1967.

7. Newspapers, Periodicals and Magazines

Natal Mercury
Natal Witness
Natal Daily News
Sunday Times
Rand Daily Mail
Natal Colonist
Times of Natal
Natal Guardian
The Patriot
Alpine Journal
Journals of the Mountain Club of South Africa
Natal Mountain Club Journals
Pax
Panorama
South African Forestry Journal
African Wild Life Magazine
Natal Wild Life Magazine
South African Journal of Science
Cape Monthly Magazine
Natal Agricultural Journal and Mining Record
Grahamstown Journal
Hilton College Magazine

8. Maps

See Appendix No. 3.

Index

(The figures in heavy type indicate Map pages)

Abatwa 3, 4
Abbey **110**, 109, 159, 160, 285
Abbott, Professor C. W. 156
Aborigines Protection Society 250
Acton Homes 29, 97
Acutt family 75
Adelson, Pip 105
African Recreational Area 259, 262
Air crash, slopes of *Gatberg* 135 *et seq.*
Aliwal, S. S. 28
Allan M. 286
Allen, Captain 33, 152
Allerston, William 40
Allerston (photographer) 98
Allison, Captain Albert 33, 34, 95, 97, 222, 230, 237, 238, 239, 241, 242, 244, 246, 248, 249
Alpine Club, British 48, 65, 67
    Journal 49, 50, 54, 266, 280
Amachunu 20
Amahlubi i, 16, 17 *et seq.*, 32, 226 *et seq.*, 243, 249, 251
    Arrival in Northern Natal 17
    Attacked by Matiwane 17
    Invasion of Drakensberg 17
    Flight from Drakensberg 18
    As buffer against Bushmen 32, 227
Amangwane 17 *et seq.*, 28, 32, 33, 46, 109, 112 *et seq.*, 122, 123
    Arrival in Northern Natal 17
    Attacked by Dingiswayo 17
    Attack on Amahlubi 17
    Arrival in Drakensberg 17, 122
    Flight to Free State 19
    Involved in Wars of Mfecane 19, 20
    As buffer against Bushmen 32, 227
Amanzana River **110**, 54, 109
Amapondo 20
Amatheza 13, 18, 92
Amazizi i, 3, 6, 11, 12 *et seq.*, 39, 109, 112, 144
    Origin 12
    Arrival in Natal 12, 17
    Attacked by Amahlubi 17
    Flight to Free State 18
    Life and customs 12 *et seq.*
    Burial sites, Cathkin area 12, 144
Amery, Col. L. C. 65, 95, 101
Amphitheatre (*Saddleback, Horse-shoe*) **88**, 23, 25, 52, 54, 57, 59, 65, 66, 78, 79, 87, 89, 91, 95, 100 *et seq.*, 255, 264, 277, 286
    Visited by Arbousset and Daumas 44
    Visited by Dr. J. W. Matthews 97
    First ascent 70, 100, 286
    Second ascent 73, 100
Amphlett **132**, 67, 144, 210, 287
    First ascent 287
Amphlett, G. T. 67, 69, 75, 89, 91, 138, 139, 144, 284
    Mrs. G. T. 67, 91, 138
Anderson, Barry 56, 102, 111, 287
Anderson, William 111
Angus-Leppan, Pam and Peter 101, 102
Anti-Slavery Society 250
Ape, The **148**, 285
Appalachian Trail 263
Arbousset, Rev. T. 21, 44, 100, 283
Archbell, T. H. 135, 136
    Rev. James 135
Armstrong, R. Stuart 135, 136
Arnold, Emily 75
Arthur's Seat (*Mpimbo*) 19, 26
Askanya Nova 155
Australopithecus africanus ix

Axelson, Charles 128, 153, 286, 287
Ayres, Col. W. A. E. 114

Baboon Rock **120**, 62, 128
Bafali River 55, 201
Bafukeng 18
Bahalanga 93
Bainbridge, W. R. 266, 267
Bakoni clan 22
Bakwena tribe 18
Bale, Sir Henry 50
Ballenden, S. St. C. 219
Ball, Rev. Ernest R. 266
Balule, chief 21
Bandey, Dr. D. W. 267
Bantu, origin 12
    Arrival in Natal 12
Bantu Affairs Department 259, 262
Barber, Charles 129
Barker, H. J. (Harry) 70, 71, 142, 143, 174, 266, 267, 285, 287
    Mrs. H. J. (Margot) 70
Barkly, Sir Henry 229, 233, 246
Barnes, Philip 151, 152
    Mrs. P. (Rosie) 151, 152
Barnes, P. R. (Bill) 51, 105, 149, 151, 152, 154, 156, 174, 196 *et seq.*, 266, 267, 282
    Mrs. P. R. (Leila) 152
Barnes, Sydney 147, 149, 150
    Diary 149
Baroa 4
Baron, Terry 167
Barrett, Mike 116
Barrow, John 274
Barry, R. V. M. (Dick) 70, 71, 72, 140 *et seq.*
Barter, Charles 17, 31, 40, 173, 230 *et seq.*, 269, 270
Basalt vi *et seq.*
Base Camp 48, 136, 142, 143, 214
Bassett-Smith, D. W. 55, 63, 65, 68, 72, 80, 101, 111, 112, 123, 284, 286, 287
    Mrs. D. W. 72, 111
Basutho, origin 23
Basuto Caves (Gray's Cave) 48, 49, 55
Basuto Gate (Gordon's Pass) **88**, 13, 18, 19, 23, 91, 92, 93, 97, 99, 105, 169
    Pass (farm) 98
Basutoland Mounted Police 50
Basuto War of 1866 41, 93, 101
Bates, Rev. C. C. 149, 150, 266
Batlokwa 18
Battiss, Walter 9, 37
Battle Cave **148**, 153
Bazley, William 7
Beacon Buttress **88**, 78, 101, 284
    Gorge 79
    Gully 99, 106, 107
Beaumont, Sir William 232, 253
Beevers, A. 138
Bele tribe 20
Bell **110**, **120**, 59, 69, 76, 102, 119, 123, 129, 286
    First ascent 70, 71, 286
Bell, David 70, 102 *et seq.*, 153, 284, 286
Bell-Marley Egg Collection 195
Benjamin (farm) 217, 218
Bennett, Cynthia 105, 106
Berg, Bengt 194
Bergville n, 29, 50, 59, 64, 75, 98, 109, 113, 114, 117, 128, 134, 136, 219
    Naming of 98

Bergvliet (farm) 40
Berlin Missionary Society 28
Berrisford brothers 67
    Frank 100
Bettle, Gillian 112, 115 *et seq.*, 142, 154, 284, 285
Bews, Dr. J. W. 204
Bezuidenhout, Daniel 41
    Pass 25
Bhulihawu, see Giant's Castle
Big Game Fishing International 122
Bird, A. G. 287
Bird, John 39, 221
Birds 155
    Black Eagle 100, 109, 150, 182
    Cape Robin 182
    Cape Rock Thrush 182
    Chorister Robin 182
    Crowned Eagle 181
    Golden Bishop 182
    Hadedah 182
    Jackal Buzzard 146, 150, 182
    Lammergeyer 100, 150, 182, 194 *et seq.*
    Lanner Falcon 182
    Malachite Sun-bird 182, 207
    Martial Eagle 22, 150, 151, 182, 192
    Red-winged Starling 182
    Secretary Bird 192
    Yellow-billed Kite 151
    Yellow Fly-catcher 182
Birkenhead, H.M.S. 33, 230
Bishop, H. 48
Bisschoff, A. 56
Blaaukrantz River 25
Blackburn, Tpr. E. R. 50
Black, Mally 159 *et seq.*
Black Mountains 196
Bleek, Dr. W. H. I. 3, 5, 7, 40
Blind Man's Corner **132**, 215
Bloemendal 24
Boast, H. C. 42
Bohle River 235, 269, 270
Bokenham, Naomi 65, 128, 287
Bollen, Ralph 128
Bond, Edwin 239, 240, 253
Boonstra, Dr. L. D. v
Booyens, Sgt. Bugler Gerrit 254
Boshoff, Sgt. J. G. 125
Botanical Society of South Africa 262
Botha, Jackie 70, 71, 143, 284
Botha-Reid, Hubert 63, 70, 72, 101, 123, 284, 286
    Mrs. H. 101
Bothma, Dr. J. du P. 179
Bourquin, Sigurt ii, 140, 267
Boustead, P. G. 266, 267
Bovill, Augustus 147, 283
Bowker, Col. T. H. 8, 246
Bowland, Arthur 105, 106, 266
Boyd, Mary 211
Brand, President J. H. 93
Brand, Raymond 266
Breuil, Abbé H. 11
Bridge Hotel (Mooi River) 28, 29
Bridger, F. L. 48
Brighton, W. G. 98
Bright, Tom 70, 71, 102
British Association for the Advancement of Science 45
Brockbank, Bill 116
Brokensha, A. E. (Eddie) and G. M. (George) 201
    A. E. (Eddie) 51, 201
Brookes and Webb 12, 250, 252
Brooks, Henry 45, 111, 174

Broom, Dr. Robert ix, x
Broome, Judge William 63
   Broome Hill 63
Brotherton 121, 134
   Shelter 12
Brown, F. S. 70, 123, 286
Brown, Mike 106
Brown, R. A. 267
Bryant, A. T. 12, 14, 22
Buchanan, Barbara 243
Buchanan, David Dale 232
   and see Natal Witness
Buckland, Roy 111, 285
Buckley, D. J. 267
Bucknall brothers: Edgar 147, 283
   Fred 35, 147, 238, 240, 241, 270, 283
   Henry 27, 147, 283
Buffelshoek 26
Buffelshoogte 144
Buhl, Hermann 166
Bulpin, T. V. 101
Burchell, W. J. 4, 208
Burgers, President T. F. 246
Burman, Jose 266
Burrow, G. 71
Burrows, Professor H. R. 192
   John 191, 192
Burton, Elizabeth 70, 102, 111, 123, 287
   Mike 70, 123
Bury, H. 195
Bush, K. F. H. (Keith) 139
   Professor Frank 139
   Mrs. F. (Mildred) 267
Bushman Raids 26, 30 *et seq.*, 133, 147, 152, 222, 227, 232, 270
   Against Boschoek (Cedara) 32
      Bushman's River area 31
      Cathkin area 33
      Dargle 32, 34
      Lotter, C. P. R. 31
      Mondisa 33
      Nel, Philip 31, 32
      Ogle, Henry 32
      Popham, W. 33
      Pretorius, P. G. 31
      Speirs, Robert 32
      Upper Polela 36
Bushman's Nek 195
Bushman's River and Valley (Mtshezi) **148**, 8, 12, 13, 26, 31, 40, 52, 54, 55, 121, 147 *et seq.*, 227, 230, 258
   Area 25, 31, 32
   Drift (Estcourt) 28, 40, 222, 232
   Military Post 31, 32, 40
   Pass, see Langalibalele Pass
Bushmen 3 *et seq.*, 12, 13, 16, 17, 22, 23, 28, 30, 35 *et seq.*, 39, 42, 89, 92, 124, 131, 144, 154, 255, 266
   Origin 3 *et seq.*
   Arrival in Southern Africa 3, 4
   Physical characteristics 5
   Life, customs and beliefs 5 *et seq.*
   Mythology 6
   Arrows and poison 8, 9, 39, 41, 133, 154
   Paintings 4, 6, 8, 9 *et seq.*, 75, 97, 129, 153, 155, 255
   Poetry 6
   Discovery of hunting kit 133, 134
   Fight on *Eastman's Peak* 133
   Inoculation against snake-bite 7
   Reported on by John Shepstone 5, 31
   Seen by Kelly's 97
   Bushman boy captured by Speirs 35
   Kalahari Bushmen 7, 37
   Museum, Giant's Castle 154
   Last stand 37
   Present numbers 37
Button, Sgt. A. R. 235, 237, 240, 244, 270
Buys' Cave 187
Buys, I. J. M. (Ryk Isak) 121, 219

Groot Isak 121
Bybee, L. 286
Byrom, James 267

Cairns, G. 142
Calder, William 244
Caledon River 13, 18, 22, 44, 93, 228, 246
Camel 120, 126
Cameron, Ken 55, 67, 68, 69, 73, 111, 287
Campbell, Peter 102 *et seq.*, 286
Cannibalism 20, 21
   Cannibal Caves 20, 97
Cape Argus 250
Cape Tree Society 261
Carbutt, Capt. Noel J. O. 135
Carr, Len 64
Carroll, Lewis 251
Casement, Tom 66, 69, 75, 89, 91, 92, 102, 139, 284
   Sir Roger 66, 89
Castle Buttress 124, 126, 285
Cat Cave 174
Cathedral Peak (Zikhali's Horn) **110, 120,** 10, 50, 54, 59, 62, 68, 71, 73, 74, 76, 119 *et seq.*, 131, 161, 259, 279, 286
   First ascent 72, 123, 286
   Area 12, 22, 28, 33, 50, 55, 57, 71, 76, 78, 81, 112, 116, 119 *et seq.*, 134, 153, 163, 167, 181, 185, 204, 208, 211, 214, 218, 223, 259
   Forest Influences Research Station, *see under* Forests and Forestry
   Hotel **110, 120,** 57, 61, 62, 64, 74, 77 *et seq.*, 115, 116, 121, 122, 123, 125, 128, 129, 131, 159, 161 *et seq.*, 168, 219, 267
   Range 49, 57, 59, 60, 61, 79, 80, 109, 115, 121, 129, 167
   Transposition of name 123
Cathkin Peak (Mdedelolo) **132, 148, 247,** iii, 3, 18, 19, 29, 47, 48, 49, 52, 54, 55, 67, 69, 70, 74, 81, 115, 131, 135 *et seq.*, 174, 214, 217, 223, 256, 265, 278, 284
   First ascent: S. Gully 66, 67, 68, 75, 139, 284
      North face 139
   Area 19, 21, 26, 29, 33, 49, 81, 131, 151, 174, 181, 187, 221, 222, 223, 246, 257, 259, 261
   Attempts at climbing 138 *et seq.*
   Braes 29, 139
   Cathkin Park Hotel **132**, 12, 28, 56, 57, 135, 140, 142, 145, 221, 256
   Farm **231**, 29, 42, 45, 46, 48, 139, 230, 246
   Meaning of Zulu name 140
   Naming of 44, 45, 139
   South Gully 49, 50, 67, 69, 138 *et seq.*
Cato, C. J. 26, 40
Cave Art of France and Spain 4, 5, 9
Caverns Guest Farm 98, 209
Caves, fencing in of 256
Cedara district 32
   Agricultural College 32, 73, 156
Cetewayo 228, 246
Chadwick, G. A. 267
Chain Ladder **88**, 87, 99, 100, 101, 104 *et seq.*, 169
Chalet schemes 256, 257, 261, 263
Chalmers, William 98
Champagne Castle **132, 231,** 34, 47, 48, 51, 52, 54 *et seq.*, 111, 136 *et seq.*, 164, 168, 174, 186, 191, 230, 255, 278, 283
   First ascent 45, 48, 283
   Area 48, 159, 214
   Hotel **132**, 82, 136, 143, 144, 145, 180, 187, 192, 214, 221
   Naming of 44, 45, 139

Pass (assumed) 230, 237, 242
Chapman, James 173
Charlet, Armand 72
Charlie (Maqadi Ngcobo) 75, 76
Charters, Major S. 17
Chase, J. C. 250
Chessmen (Needles, Saw-tooth Ridge) **110, 120,** 54, 57, 59, 112, 124
Christensen, Peter 106 *et seq.*, 163
Christopher, B. 267
Churchill, Senator Frank 98
Cikicane, first ascent **110**, 286
Cinnabar claims 134
Clarke, Ian 56
Clarke, James 266
Clarke, Lieut. Col. Sir Marshall 47
Clark, Sgt. 236, 239, 241, 243, 244, 270
Clayton, Hon. W. F. 98
Cleft Peak **120**, 55, 57, 65, 124 *et seq.*, 168, 202, 283
   First ascent 283, 125
   Cleft Peak Frontal ascent 74, 125, 126, 283
Cleopatra's Needle see Devil's Tooth
Climate, changes in 221 *et seq.*
Climbing techniques 272
   Why do men climb? 82, 83
Cloudland's Col **148**, 55, 153
Cockade **120**, 79, 124, 285
   First ascent 285
Cockburn, H. A. 286
Colenso, Bishop J. W. 46, 95, 123, 226, 227, 249 *et seq.*
   Break with Shepstone 252
   Championship of Lan alibalele 250 *et seq.*
   Visits Zikhali 123
      Francis (Fanny) 250, 253
      Harriet 250, 252
Column **120**, 75, 102, 112, 124, 125, 127, 128, 153, 286
   First ascent 77, 78, 286
Commons, H. J. 266
Compensation 55
Conquering Hero, S.S. 28
Contour Path **120, 132, 148,** 65, 131, 136, 263
Cooke, C. K. 10
Corner **148**, 153
Coryndon Museum 195
Couch and de Barth Store (White Mountain Inn) 145, 149
Coventry family: Cecil 266
   Doreen (Mrs. Chalmers) 98
   George Leonard 217
   John 29, 97
   Walter 29, 75, 92, 93, 97 *et seq.*, 217
   Mrs. Walter 99
"Cowards' Bush" *see* Magwaleni
Cowie, Dr. Alexander 41
Craib, Dr. I. J. 219
Craigieburn 34, 35
Cronje, Dr. Andries 92
Cross, Arthur 105
Crow's Nest Cave 89
Curle, Bill 102, 127

Dagga *(Cannabis sativa)* 206, 208
   Police raid, Mnweni 113 *et seq.*
   Smoking 206
Dale, Sir Langham 8
Daniels, Mrs. Cynthia 268
Dargle 27, 31, 41, 147, 205, 216, 232
Dart, Professor Raymond ix
Daumas, Rev. F. 44, 100, 283
Davie and Gibbons 173
Davies, Professor O. x
Davies, R. F. (Bob) 70, 103, 112, 153, 284, 286
Davis, Neville 106
Dawson, I. W. 129

Day, Tom 235
De Barth 145
De Beer's Pass 25
De Carle, Lieut. Col. G. R. (Bob) 111, 254, 285
Deelpunt 134
De Lange, Sgt. S. J. D. 113 *et seq.*
De l'Obel, Matthias 211
Department of Agricultural Technical Services 259, 261
De Perthes, Boucher 8
De Villiers, A. M. (Mike) 219, 220, 266
Devil's Hoek (farm) 98
Devil's Tooth (*Cleopatra's Needle*) **88, 110,** 58, 59, 91, 102, 112, 153, 286
    First ascent 71, 102 *et seq.*, 286
    Attempts at climbing 102
    Cave 103
    Gully 102, 103
Dew Drop Inn 29
De Wit, Mr. 104
Dhloma 227
Diamond 98
Dick, A. (Tony) 112, 284
Dick, Col. 98
Dicks, Henry 35
Dillon, Capt. Patrick 114
Dingane 22, 23, 26, 43, 122, 227
Dingiswayo 17, 18, 226
Dinosaurs in Drakensberg v, vi
Dobie, John Shedden 27, 40, 45, 46, 47, 147, 174, 226
    Journal 27, 46, 147, 221
Dobzhansky, T. iv
Dodds, Mr. 29
Dooley 95, 98
Dornan, Rev. S. S. v
Dragon Peaks 146
Dragons, mythical 40
Dragon's Back **132,** 48, 54
Drake, Capt. Spencer 174
Drakensberg: Access roads and buildings 262, 263
    First ascent of 32
    First sight of 41
    Future control and development 255 *et seq.*
    Geographical position i
    Geology of iv *et seq.*
    Highest peaks 55 *et seq.*
    Origin of name i
    Passes, blowing up of 27, 42
    Picnic sites, lack of 263, 264
    Private encroachment 256, 257, 259, 261, 264
    Proposed African Recreational Area 259, 262
    Proposed Regional Authority 259 *et seq.*
    Proposed National Garden 264
    Recreational use of 263
    Rights of way 263
    Spelling of name i
    Vandalism 255, 256, 263, 264
Drakensberg Boys Choir School **132,** 146
Drakensberg Club 63
Drayson, Capt. A. W. 7
Dresser, H. E. 195
Driemeyer, Ivan 29, 46
Duga clan 20
Dumisa, chief 36
Du Plessis, Dr. Otto 204
Du Plessis, Mrs. 267
Durnford, Maj. A. W. (later Col.) 42, 147, 232 *et seq.*, 252, 269, 270, 271
    Mrs. A. W. 253
Du Toit, A. Leeb 139
Dwyka series ix, 208

Eagle Cave 49, 55
East Coast Fever 50

Eastern Buttress (Outer Tower) **88, 110,** 54, 58, 59, 65, 66, 74, 75, 95, 102, 103, 115, 285
    First ascent 91, 92, 285
Eastman's Peak **120, 132,** 133, 287
    First ascent 287
Eastman, H. A. ("Grandpa") 67, 133, 287
Edgerton, John 106
Eiger, North Face 69
Eland Cave (Makambi Cave, Lombard's Cave) **120, 132,** 131
Eland Domestication Unit 156
Eland River **88,** 24, 44, 87, 89, 93, 97, 99, 100
Elandskop district 31
Eland's Park 251
Elenge, see Job's Kop
Elephant **120,** 124, 284
    First ascent 284
Ellenberger, D. F. 4, 9, 19, 20, 22, 23
Ellis, F. E. (Tom) 111, 144, 286, 287
El Mirador Hotel **132,** 146
Els, Brig. C. J. 114
Embo Nguni people 6, 12, 13, 17
Emkhizweni **132,** iii, v, 46, 162, 169, 263
Emmaus M. S. 28, 40, 42, 47
English, Mrs. Joan 266
Enslin, Mrs. 92
Erasmus, Keith 105 *et seq.*
Erskine, Robert Henry 234, 236, 239, 240, 244, 245, 253
    Major D. (Colonial Secretary) 244
Estcourt High School iii, 28, 119, 194, 254
Esterhuizen, Elsie 67
Eugenie, Empress 34
Evans, Maurice S. 37
Express (newspaper) 40

Faill, W. M. 266
Fannin family 27, 31
    Emily 27
    George Fox 27, 36, 205
    John Eustace 27, 42, 147
    Marianne 27
    Meredyth 27, 235, 240, 241, 244
    Tom 27, 32
Farewell, Lieut. F. G. 20
Farrington, Kip 122
Fatti, Carl 112, 284
Federated Hotels Association of S.A. 262
Fenger, P. B. 111, 287
Ferguson, A. R. 267
Ferguson, S. 104, 105
Ferguson, Sgt. I. 153
    Fergy's Cave **148,** 153
Field, E. Stanley 67, 68, 285
Field, John Coote 174
Fires: Control of 223, 263
    Fire tragedy of September 1966 223
    Ditto August 1970 223
    Precautions against 224
    Veld burning: policy 223, 263
Fish preservation and propagation 263
    Hatchery, Royal Natal National Park 100, 224
    See also under Trout
Flora, S.S. 27
Florey, C. 246
Forder, G. D. B. 258, 268
Forests and Forestry 214 *et seq.*
    British Empire Forestry Conference 219
    Bulwer Commission 217
    Cathedral Peak Forest Influences Research Station **120,** 218 *et seq.*, 266
    Control of alien vegetation 262
    Department of Forestry 157, 217, 256, 259, 262, 266

Exotic plantations 224, 225, 262
    Effects on water supplies 218 *et seq.*
    Forest Research Institute, Pretoria 220
    Forestry Road (Mike's Pass) **120,** 220, 131
    Foresters: Hon. Part-time 145, 216, 217
        Work of 218
    Fourcade Report 217
    History of control measures 216 *et seq.*
    Jonkershoek Research Station 145, 219
    Lister Forestry Report 217
    Management of Forests 218
    Proclamation of Cathkin-Cathedral Reserve 145, 216, 217
    Trees, individual, *see under* Trees
    Woodcutting Concessions 95, 144, 216, 217
Forsyth, R. 70, 71, 154, 284
Fort Durnford 31
Fort Napier 253
Fort Nottingham **231,** 32, 33, 222, 232 *et seq.*, 242, 244
Fourcade, Dr. H. G. 217
Fowle, E. Percy, M.E.C. 247
Franklin, Sir John 207
Frank, Mark 65, 100, 284, 286
Fraser, Col. J. 63
Fraser, T. G. (Jock) 266
Freer, Carlos 129
Freiburg 20
Froude, J. A. 232
Fuggle, Roger 112, 284
Fulton, K. E. 280, 282
Fynn, H. F. 19, 28, 277

Gabela, Const. 113 *et seq.*
Gale, Dr. G. W. 267
Galpin, E. E. 204
Game 155 *et seq.*, 173 *et seq.*, 184 *et seq.*
    Conservation and Management of 157, 263
    Decimation of 173, 174
    Discipline amongst 181, 182, 185
    Profusion in early days 173, 174
    Springbok treks 173
        Baboons 100, 184 *et seq.*
            as a fighter 185, 186
            Family life 184, 185
            Fear of leopards and snakes 186, 187
            Destructiveness 185
            Intelligence 186
            Love of honey 184
            Reluctance to attack man 186
            Sense of humour 187
        Blesbok 40, 155, 156, 178
        Bushbuck 100, 177, 178
        Caracal 181
        Common Reedbuck 175, 176, 177
        Dassie 59, 100, 178
        Eland 149, 155, 156
        Elephant 174
        Genet 181
        Golden Mole 178
        Grey Duiker 176, 177
        Grey Rhebuck (Vaalribbok) 100, 155, 175, 176, 177
        Grysbok 178
        Ice-rat 178
        Jackal 149, 151, 179, 180
        Klipspringer 155, 176, 177
        Leopard 149, 174, 186
        Lion 29, 47, 174
        Lizard 178
        Mongoose 192
        Mountain Reedbuck (Rooiribbok) 155, 175, 177
        Natal Mole-rat 178
        Oribi 155, 173, 177
        Otter 178, 182

Porcupine 178, 182
Quagga 10, 174
Red Hartebeest 155, 156, 178
Serval 180
Steenbok 177
Vervet monkey 181
Vlei-rat 178
Wild dogs 151
Wildebeest 100, 155, 156, 157, 174, 178
Game Pass 231, 234, 242, 244, 270
Game Reserves and Recreational Areas 157, 158
Proposed African Game Reserve 259, 262
See also Giant's Castle Game Reserve
Ganapu Ridge **110**, 61, 62, 112, 128
Garden Castle 43, 70, 152, 277
Gardiner, Capt. A. F. 42, 52, 152, 274, 277
Gatberg (Ntunja) **132**, 42, 54, 134, 135, 136, 145, 187, 287
First ascent 145, 287
Gebhardt, Colin 140 *et seq.*
Geology of Drakensberg, *see under* Drakensberg
Gerneke, Major R. A. 114
Gewaagd 121, 219
Giant's Castle (Bhulihawu, Phosihawu) **148**, **231**, **247**, 31, 32, 33, 40, 42, 43, 46, 50, 52, 54 *et seq.*, 131, 147 *et seq.*, 180, 200, 202, 222, 227, 230, 234, 242, 259, 261, 269 *et seq.*, 277, 278, 283
Meaning of Zulu name 152
First ascent 147, 283
First frontal ascent 71
Area 42, 57, 206
Game Reserve **148**, vi, 129, 147 *et seq.*, 173, 174, 177, 178, 179, 196, 217, 251, 259, 263
Hutted Camp **148**, 42, 152
Main Caves **148**, 10, 42, 147, 154
Pass **231**, 55, 71, 147, 152, 230, 233, 234, 242, 269 *et seq.*
Transfer of name from *Garden Castle* 43, 152
Giant's Cup (Hodgson's Peak) 36, 43
Gibson, Alexander 46
Gilbert Handley Memorial Hide 202
Giles, Major 33, 34, 222
Globe, S.S. 230
Gloster, Charles 55, 70, 82, 102, 111, 285
Godbold, O. B. (Brian) 65, 68, 74, 111, 112, 124, 125, 128, 144, 153, 266, 283, 284, 285, 286, 287
Mrs. O. B. 74
Gold Badge, Mountain Club of S.A. 64
G. T. Amphlett 67
E. S. Field 68
D. P. Liebenberg 70
D. Robbins 64
G. M. J. Sweeney 74
W. C. West 67
Golden Gate Highlands National Park 195, 263
Gondwanaland iv, vii
Goodoo **88**, 29, 65, 97, 98, 100, 111
Pass 99
Valley 105
Goodwin, Phyllis 74, 111, 127, 285
Goodwin, Roy 56, 287
Gordon-Gray, Dr. K. D. 206, 209, 267
Gordon-Smith, Miss 91
Gordon's Pass, *see* Basuto Gate
Gould-Adam's Pass, *see* Namahadi Pass
Gourton Farmers' Association 257
Graaff, J. de V. (Jannie) 67, 78, 80, 102, 111, 112, 285, 286
Grahamstown Journal 174
Grant, Mr. 248

Grantham, Major 44, 45, 52, 138, 147, 229, 283
Gray, Bishop Robert 40
Gray family: Andrew 45, 49
Bill 64
Charles 45, 266
David (Jnr.) 246
David (Snr.) 26, 28, 42, 45, 46, 48, 49, 55, 139, 144, 146, 246
David (grandson of latter) 146
Mrs. David (Snr.) (Isabella Park) 28
Mary 29
Park, Col. 55, 288
Walter 246
Gray's Cave, *see* Basuto Caves
Farm, *see* Cathkin Farm
Pass **132**, 42, 45, 48, 136, 186, 283
Peak, see Makheke
Green, Benjamin 41
Green, Charles 29
Green, Lawrence 8, 11, 180, 185
Green, Rev. James 40
Greystone 28, 32, 46
Griffiths, Col. C. D. 228, 246, 249
Grindley, J. 286
Griqua's Hoek 47
Guest, W. R. 228, 229, 243
Guy, Robin 10
Gyrindae 182

Halliday, Mrs. Joy (née Surgeon) 266
Hamilton, Gen. Sir Ian 195
Hardbies huts 26
Harding, Walter 31
Harker, Canon A. J. S. 142
Harkins, G. L. 104
Harries, F. B. ("Tiny") 169
Harte, N. D. 139
Harwin, John 56
Hathorn, Kenneth Howard 46
Hattersley, Professor A. F. 20, 35, 246, 266
Haviland, Dr. 145
Hawkins, Capt. A. C. 230, 248, 249
Heartsease 47, 67, 139, 145
Hellemans, Auguste 128
Hellend, Leif 266
Henkel, Dr. J. S. 63
Henning, Peter 57, 79
Heron, C. 287
Hey, Dr. D. 158
Hills, Tpr. 50
Hilton College 33, 72, 266
Himeville 196
Historical Monuments Commission, *see* National Monuments Council
Hlanzi, son of Magonzi 241
Hlatikulu Nek **132**, iii, 47, 54, 136, 215
Hlatimba Pass (Proudfoot's Pass) **231**, 33, 34, 147, 235, 236, 241, 243, 269 *et seq.*,
River 241, 269, 270
Hlongwane, Chief Ndungunye 114
Hlubi, chief 233
Hodgson ("Old Man of the Berg") 144
Hodgson, Thomas 35, 36
Hodgson's Peak, see Giant's Cup
Hodson, Norman 153, 286
Hodson, Rene 287
Hoets, H. C. 65, 128, 287
Hoffenthal M. S. **110**, 42
Hofmeyr, Hon. J. H. ix
Holden, Reg 124
Holden, Rev. W. C. 40, 209
Holinshed 190
Homeward Bound, S.S. 93, 94
Hooper, A. S. (Tony) 70, 111, 123, 124, 143, 283, 284, 287
Hopeton 121
Horites (Hurrians) 4
Horns **110**, **120**, 54

Inner **110**, **120**, 59, 123, 128, 286
First ascent 123, 286
Outer **110**, **120**, 59, 71, 74, 123, 128, 286
First ascent 70, 123, 286
Horse-shoe, see Amphitheatre
Hosking, Eric 194
Hotels and Hotel Industry 28, 37, 158, 263
and see also under individual Hotels
Hottentots 4, 5
Household, D. T. 270
Howell, James 222
Howes-Howell, Ken 67, 68, 71, 74, 128, 287
Hume, Frank 267
Hunt-Holley, Mr. 218
Hutchinson, Graham 195
Huts, mountain 153, 154, 157, 263
Bannerman **148**, 153
Giant's Castle **148**, 153
Keith Bush **132**, 48, 139
Mountain Club, Mont-aux-Sources **88**, 89, 101, 104 *et seq.*, 163, 167, 169, 255, 264
Official opening 101
Present state of disrepair 101, 255, 256, 264
Transvaal Mountain Club 256
Policy 153, 154, 157, 263
Hypothermia 164 *et seq.*
Hyracium 10, 178

Icidi River **110**, 109
Ifidi Buttress **110**, 15, 109, 284
Pinnacles **110**, 109, 112
South Pin. 112, 115, 285
First ascent 285
North Pin. 112, 285
First ascent 285
River **110**, 109, 112
Imfihlweni Regiment 241
Impendhle **247**, 32, 36, 248
Indumeni Dome **120**, 119, 124, 126, 284
First ascent 284
Inglis, Colin 67
Ingram, J. Forsyth 31, 269
Inhluzana Mtn. 34
Inhoek 121
Injasuti Buttress **148**, 153, 154, 189, 284
First ascent 284
Meaning of name 129
Area 12, 23, 63, 67, 71, 131, 144, 149, 151, 153 *et seq.*, 200, 228, 259, 261
Caves: Lower **148**, 153
Upper **148**, 168
Dome **148**, 55 *et seq.*, 283
Ridge 202
River (Little Tugela) and Valley **148**, **231**, 19, 25, 42, 46, 52, 54, 55, 111, 129, 144, 153 *et seq.*, 217, 230, 256, 258, 278
Triplets **148**, 71, 153, 154
Eastern 71, 153, 284
First ascent 154, 284
Middle 71, 153, 284
First ascent 154, 284
Western 71, 102, 153, 284
First ascent 153, 284
Inner Tower **88**, **110**, 102, 103, 285
First ascent 75, 91, 285
Ravine 68, 97, 104, 105
Insinga River 34
Institute of Government Land Surveyors 262
Intelezi 209, 228
Inyanga 210, 252
Isandhlwana 244, 252, 253
Isemonger, R. M. 193

Jackal Hunt Clubs 180

Jackson, John Otter 270
Jacob's Ladder: Cathkin area 135
    Mont-aux-Sources area 89
Jaffray, J. L. 270
Jagger, Miss 91
James, Dr. W. 266
James, M. 213
"James" (Rock Dassie) 179
Jansen, Joy 105, 106
Jantjie, son of Selile 239, 240, 249
Jeans, Sir James iv
Jengis Kahn 22
Jenks, G. N. 266
Job's Kop (Elenge) 20, 21
John (Zulu guide) (Mtateni Xosa) 76
Johnson, Sir Harry 15
Johnson, Townley 10
Jonkershoek Research Station, *see under*
    Forests and Forestry
Joyce, T. A. 21
Julia, S.S. 28

Kaltenbrun, Nick 105
Kamberg Nature Reserve 155, 177, 180,
    266
Kambule, Elijah 233, 235, 236, 238, 239,
    240
Karroo System v, vii
Katana 240
Keen, Dr. Anthony 214 *et seq.*
    Peter 214 *et seq.*
Kelly, Father A. D. 66, 69, 75, 89, 91,
    92, 102, 139, 140, 266, 284, 285
    Father Herbert 66
Kelly, Fred 95, 96
    Mrs. F. (Edith Pickering) 95, 96
Kennedy, Mr. Justice A. A. 115
Kent, R. W. 266
Kerkenberg 24
Kerr, Brian 106
Khoho 22
Khubedu Rivers, Eastern and Western
    88, 44, 100
Kilfargie 46, 47
Kilgobbin (Buffel's Bosch) 27, 32
Kilimanjaro 56, 67, 69
Killick, Dr. D. J. B. 204, 211
Killie Campbell Library 12, 267
Kimberley, Earl of 229, 233, 271
King, Dick 43
Kingdon, R. G. 63, 65, 68, 72, 101, 111,
    123, 284, 286
    Mrs. R. G. 72
King Louis VI 218
King Sobuza 122
Kirstenbosch 68, 204, 262, 264
Klein Waterval 98
Klein Winterhoek Frontal 69
Klip River 40, 258
Knight, Ada (Mrs. Anderson) 242
Kniphof, Professor J. H. 213
Knox, Joan 71
Kok, Adam 248
Kolonyama 22
Koorts, Lance Sgt. J. 113 *et seq.*
Kranskop (Ntunjambili) 134, 135
Krugerbos, *see* Makuruman
Kruger, Const. T. 113 *et seq.*
Kruger National Park 157
Kruger, Sawyer 144

Lahlingubo Pass 269
Lakalebalele River 237
Lake District 66
Land Survey Act, 1927 275
Langa, chief 3, 12
Langa, Sgt. 113 *et seq.*
Langalibalele 17, 23, 226 *et seq.*, 269
    Birth and early life 226
    Appearance and character 226

Meaning of name 226
Attains chieftainship 227
Moves to Giant's Castle area 32, 227
Prepares for war 227, 228
Preparations against him 229 *et seq.*
Flight, pursuit and capture 242, 246 *et
    seq.*
Trial and banishment 242, 251
Death 251
    Pass (Bushman's River Pass) **148,
    231, 247,** 32, 42, 50, 52, 54, 111,
    147, 168, 200, 226, 229 *et seq.*,
    252, 253, 254, 269 *et seq.*, 278
Langalibalele Rebellion i, 27, 147, 150,
    226 *et seq.*, 269 *et seq.*, 278
    Events leading up to 227 *et seq.*
    Preparations at Fort Nottingham 233
    The ride to the Pass 233 *et seq.*
    Action at head of Pass 239, 240
    Causes of disaster 242, 243, 244
    Pursuit of Langalibalele 246 *et seq.*
    Mopping-up operations 249
    Results 226, 252
    Military Enquiry 232, 239, 244
Langmore, John 70, 143
Laplace iv
Lathrop, Dr. Theodore G. 165
Latyinga, son of Tulisa 240
Lausedat 276
Lava eruptions, *see* Basalt
Leafmore 121
Lear, Mary 100, 124, 286, 287
Lee, D. N. 10
Leribe **247,** 248, 249
Leslie's Pass **148,** 154
Lesobeng Pass 47
Letsie 229
Letuele River, *see* Tugela River
Le Vaillant, Francois 274
Leverton, Dr. B. J. T. 267
Lewis, A. D. 275
Liddle, H. A. ("Oompie") 67, 70, 101,
    287
Lidgetton 27, 28, 32
Liebenberg, D. P. (Doyle) 70, 71, 75, 100,
    123, 124, 125, 128, 266, 283,
    285, 286, 287
Lightning and lightning hazard 127, 128
Likhoele 22
Linden, Rob 167
Linnaeus (Carl von Linné) 213
Lion (Injasuti area) 154
Litter **120, 132,** 287
    First ascent 287
Little Berg, geology of v *et seq.*
Little Saddle **120,** 124, 126, 131, 213, 285
    First ascent 285
Litton, Dr. Samuel 210
Livingstone, David 5, 187
Lloyd, Miss L. C. 3
Locations, Bantu 32, 113
    Resettlement of 258, 259
        Drakensberg Nos. 1 and 2 **260,** 23,
        26, 32, 227, 230, 249, 258, 259,
        263
        Quathlamba Reserve 26
        Upper Tugela Reserve **260,** 23, 26,
        32, 98, 109, 122, 155, 176, 258,
        259, 262, 263, 264
        Swartkop Location 251
Lombard, Anton 121, 133, 135
    J. S. Lombard 133, 134, 187
    Cave, *see* Eland Cave
Londt, G. T. 67, 69, 71, 100, 139, 140
Lord Haddo, S.S. 29
Loskop 25, 50
Loteni River and Valley **231,** 31, 32, 33,
    34, 41, 147, 152, 234, 244, 269,
    270
    Nature Reserve 155, 156, 177, 271
Louw, Mr. and Mrs. 125

Louw, Tobie 70, 102, 127
Lowe, T. (Natal Society Library) 267
Lucas, Capt. G. A. 33, 230
    Rt. Hon. Edward 33
Lugaju, chief 32, 34
Lugelezana 46
Lugg, H. C. 152, 266
Luphalule, chief 20
Lytton 95

Maartens, Hendrik 136, 143, 145, 174,
    180, 221, 222
    Gert 136
Mabuhle 228, 238, 239, 240, 249
McCormick, Pat 145
Macfarlane, John 33, 227 *et seq.*
Macingwane 20
Mackeurtan, Graham 43
Maclear's Beacon 129
McLeod, Lieut. N. M. 89, 90, 101, 284
Madolawana 135
Mafadi 55, 56
Magangangozi stream 19
Magonondo 46
Magwaleni ("Cowards' Bush") 20, 23
Mahlaphahlapha 20, 21
Mahoiza 228
Main Caves, *see under Giant's Castle*
Mair, Alexander 54, 278
Makambi Cave, *see* Eland Cave
Makheke (Gray's Peak) 48, 55 *et seq.*, 202,
    288
    First ascent 55, 288
Makholokoes 93
Makonosoang 20
Makopo 15
Makowski, M. 143
Makuruman (Krugerbos) **132,** 8, 144,
    214
Makwela 117
Malan, B. D. 267
Malan, Eddie 116
Mallory, George 67, 82
Maluti mountains 18, 37, 43, 63, 70, 87,
    248
Manicom, B. Q. 112, 284
Man, emergence of ix *et seq.*
Mann, Dr. R. J. 152, 277
Mann, John S. 138
Mantatisi, Queen 18
Mantish (forest guard) 136
Mantsunyane River 47
Manzimyama Pass, *see* Sani Pass
Maohla, son of Luhoho 239
Maphetla (Pioneers) 13
Maps: Cato 26, 40
    Gardiner 52, 274, 277
    Grantham 44, 45, 52, 147, 229, 271
    Holmden 57
    Mair, Alexander 54
    Masson 123
    Military 1879 52, 248
    Military 1900 123
    Pearse: Cathedral 57 *et seq.*
    Pearse-Peck: Cathkin 57
    Stanger 52
    Stocker 50, 53, 54, 55, 57, 266, 271,
    277, 280
    Sweeney 57, 60, 74, 275, 280
    Trigonometrical Survey 123
    Wyld 52, 277
    and see Appendix 3
Marais, Eugene 7
Marais, Thys 174
Marble Baths Stream 154
Marcus, Hans Otto 128
Maree, J. 246
Maritzburg College 72, 244, 266
Maritz, Gert 25, 154
Marriott, W. E. (Bill) 63, 73
Marsh, Sub-Inspector 50

Martin, Lt. Col. A. C. 267
Martin, M. C. 267
Marwick, C. W. 266
Masenkeng Pass 197
Masongwana River **120**, 54, 121
Masopha 23
Masson, Francis 211
Masson, Ryle 267
Matiwane 17, 18, 19, 22, 32, 39, 122, 226, 227
   Death 23
Matsheni 46
Matthews, Dr. J. W. 20, 97, 99, 251
Matyana affair 228, 229
Maze 145
Mbeka, acting chief 123
Mbendse, Const. 113, *et seq.*
Mbundini Buttress **110**, 285
   Fangs, first ascent 286
   Pass 97, 159
   River **110**, 54, 109
Mchesana River **148**, 153, 174
Mdavu 20
Mdedelelo, see Cathkin Peak
Mdlaka 19
Meiklejohn, Keith 152
Meinertzhagen, R. 195, 201
Melatu 66, 75, 76, 89, 91, 92, 139, 284
Melville, Lieut. 32, 35
Melyris natalensis 207
Merensky, Dr. Hans 66, 218
Mesaga 69
Meshlynn **231**, 33, 222, 230, 233, 234, 242, 243, 244, 270, 271
Mfecane, wars of 18 *et seq.*, 93
Mhlangana 22, 23
Mhlwazini River and Valley **110, 120, 132**, 8, 12, 18, 19, 42, 48, 54, 121, 133, 135, 136, 138 *et seq.*, 174, 187, 214, 215, 219, 258
Mike's Pass **120**, 220
Millard, Mr. and Mrs. A. 125, 283
Miller, G. J. 91, 102, 285
Miller, O. B. 218
Milles, Lieut. Col. T. 222, 229, 232, 233, 242, 244
Milligan, Dennis 197, 202
Mills, D. Gordon 65
Millward, Tim 169
Mitre **110, 120**, 59, 80, 112, 124, 162, 286
   First ascent 74, 286
Mnweni River and Valley **110**, 12, 54, 109 *et seq.*, 117, 194, 258, 259, 279
   Area 13, 15, 18, 19, 23, 42, 47, 49, 50, 65, 68, 80, 81, 109 *et seq.*, 176, 194, 259
   Cut-back 109, 111, 160, 161, 162, 167
   Needles **110**, 54, 60, 111, 279
      Inner 68, 109, 287
         First ascent 111, 287
      Outer 58, 59, 109, 287
         First ascent 68, 73, 111, 287
   Pass **110**, 160, 162, 163, 180, 194
   Pinnacles **110**, 109, 111, 160
      Inner 74, 111, 285
         First ascent 111, 285
      Outer 111, 285
         First ascent 82, 111, 285
Moe brothers 156
Mohlala 197
Mohlezi Pass 56
Mokapakapa 21
Mokhotlong 32, 56, 116, 196 *et seq.*
   Mountain Transport Company 196
   River 198, 200
Molapo, chief 227, 228, 248, 249
   Jonathan and Joel 36
Mole Hill 112
Molema 4
Molteno Beds v *et seq.*

Moncrieff, Robert Hope 46, 123, 145
   Col. Sir A. 46, 145
Mondisa 33
Monk's Cowl (Inkosana) **132**, 54, 66, 71, 72, 102, 138 *et seq.*, 284
   Attempts to climb 140 *et seq.*
   First ascent 71, 143, 284
   Forest Station **132**, 131, 136, 214, 215, 217, 218, 256, 266
   Monk's Ravine 66, 67, 69, 138, 139, 140
Monontsa 93
   Pass, *see* Namahadi Pass
Mont-aux-Sources **88, 247**, 24, 25, 34, 40, 47, 54 *et seq.*, 69, 70, 75, 76, 87, 89, 97, 100 *et seq.*, 127, 202, 283
   Area 13, 20, 29, 36, 63, 66 *et seq.*, 71, 75, 78, 95 *et seq.*, 159, 163, 167, 217
   Naming of 44
   Hut, *see under* Huts, mountain
Mont Blanc 72
Monzali, G. R. 220
Moodie, Dunbar 238
Moodie, D. C. F. 123
Mooi, Little 33
Mooi River **231**, 28, 29, 31, 40, 121, 229, 233, 234, 258
Moor, Sir Frederick 28, 46
   M. C. (Malcolm) 101, 112, 143, 266, 284, 285
   R. M. (Robert) 101, 284
   Moor Park 28
Mopeli, Paulus 93
   Bridle Path 47, 50, 51
   Pass, *see* Namahadi Pass
Morgenrood, S. B. 48
Moriah M. S. 44
Morija vi
Morrison, D. D. (Don) 194 *et seq.*
Moshoeshoe (Mosesh) 22, 23, 36, 41, 89, 93, 124
Moth Organisation 144
Mountain Club of S.A. 63, 65, 67, 68, 261, 262, 266
   Hut, *see under* Huts, mountain
   Journal 112, 165, 265
      Cape Section 48, 67 *et seq.*, 138, 150, 266
         Transvaal Section 70 *et seq.*
      Natal Section 57, 63 *et seq.*, 77, 82, 101, 124, 129, 140, 266, 282
         Formation of 63
         Annual July camps 63 *et seq.*, 124, 133, 144, 145, 154, 174
         Code of ethics 63
         Jubilee 63
         Rescue Team 129, 168, 194
   Drakensberg Club 63
   Natal University Mountain Club 255
Mount Amery **88**, 65, 68, 101, 111, 168, 284
   First ascent 101, 284
Mt. Karisimbi 176
Mount Memory, see under Sterkhorn
Mt. Mikeno 176
Mount Misery 34
Mt. Oompie (Ntaba Ndanyazana) **88, 110**, 70, 74, 109, 209, 287
   First ascent 70, 287
   Ridge 112
Mount Park 28
Mount Qua-qua 87, 92, 93, 94
Mpande 227
Mpangazita 17, 18
Mpimbo, see Arthur's Seat
Mponjwana (Rockeries Tower) **110**, 49, 54, 59, 60, 75, 80, 81, 109, 111, 112, 115, 116, 117, 123, 160, 163, 194, 285
   Cave **110**, 80, 81, 109, 115 *et seq.*, 160, 194

   First ascent 80, 81, 285
   Incorrectness of name 123
   and see Rockeries
Mthethwa 17 *et seq.*
   Arrival in Northern Natal 17
   Attack on Amangwane 17
   Absorbed by Zulus 18
Mtimkulu 17, 23, 226
   Death 17
Mtshezi, see Bushman's River
Muller, Ian 191, 192
Musgrave, Sir Anthony 229
Mzania (game guard) 151
Mzilikazi 22

Nagazana 46
Nahuel Huapi National Park 257
Namagari River (Vaal River) 44
Namahadi Pass (Mopeli's, Monontsa's, Gould-Adam's) **88**, 34, 41, 50, 87, 89, 90, 91, 92, 93, 97, 99, 222
Nandi 19
Nanga Parbat 166
Nänni, U. W. 157, 220, 222, 266, 267
Natal Agricultural Union 179, 258, 262
Natal Archives 123, 267
Natal Colonist 243, 249, 250, 252
Natal Daily News 146, 267
Natal Mercury 32, 36, 105, 135, 266
Natal Mountain Club, *see under* Mountain Club of S.A.
Natal Museum 20, 133, 134, 267
Natal Parks, Game and Fish Preservation Board 57, 100, 107, 129, 131, 152, 155, 156, 157, 180, 201, 209, 223, 224, 256, 259, 262, 263, 266
Natal Town and Regional Planning Commission 256, 257, 262
Natal Unicorn Company 41
Natal Witness 226, 232, 235, 250
   and see Buchanan, David Dale
National Advisory Survey Council 276
National Monuments Council 261, 262, 267
National Veld Trust 261, 262
Native High Court 115, 252
Native Reserves, *see* Locations, Bantu
Ncibidwane **148**, 55
Ndanjane **132**, 214, 215
Ndedema Dome **120**, 56, 121, 124, 131, 285
   First ascent 68, 74, 285
   Area 213
   Forest 131
   Gorge 131, 211
   Pass 74
   River and Valley **120, 132**, 10, 19, 54, 68, 124, 131, 134, 136
Ndema forest **132**, 145
Ndwandwe 17 *et seq.*
   Arrival in Northern Natal 17
   Attack on Amangwane 17
Nefdt, Gustav 77
Negenya 55
Nel, Philip 31, 32
Nelson, Sawyer 144
Nest Hotel **132**, 26, 29, 46, 64, 146, 246
Netter, Aimée 100, 286
Newman, Peter 191, 192
Newnham, Rev. W. O. 33
N.G.R. Photographic Team (Tatlo Watkinson, Allerston) 98
Nicholls, Cyril 70
Nilsen, Ingvald and Bernhard 93
Nkentshane Hill **148**, 151
Nkosazana River and Valley **132**, 54, 134
Nkwakwa stream **132**, 145
Nomlalazi 122
Nongale 67, 138
Norcott, T. C. 142, 286

North, Miles 195
Norwegian boat episode 93, 94, 266
  Settlement at Port Shepstone 93
Ntaba Busuku, see Saddle
Ntaba Mabutho, see Rockeries
Ntabamhlope **231**, vi, vii, 50, 111, 145, 149, 153, 230, 249
Ntabamnyama, see Sentinel Peak
Ntaba Ndanyazana, see Mt. Oompie
Ntonjelane River and Valley **110**, 8, 18, 49, 58, 60, 68, 112, 117, 124, 174, 179, 259, 284
  Ntonjelan' ephumalanga **110**, 49, 54, 59, 60, 61, 62, 109, 112
  Ntonjelan' eshonalanga **110**, 49, 54, 59, 109, 111
  Cave **110**, **120**, 59, 109, 112, 179
  Needle 74, 112, 286
    First ascent 112, 286
  Pass **110**, **120**, 49, 58, 109, 116, 167, 179
Ntshaba, Xungu 125
Ntunja, see Gatberg
Ntunjambili, see Kranskop
Nunn, Colin S. 139
Nxaye stream **110**, 62

Oates, Frank 211
Oetse, chief 93
Ogle, Henry 28, 43
Old Bushman's Pass, *see Organ Pipes Pass*
Old Woman Grinding Corn **148**, 149, 153, 154, 286
    First ascent 74, 153, 286
Olivia 121
Oliviershoek 33, 42, 95, 229, 230
  Pass 28, 65, 99
  Police Post 121
Olsen, Zefanias 93
Oosthuizen, Willem J. 121
Openshaw, Sgt. A. H. 50, 51
Opperman's Kraal 26, 29, 144
  Mr. Opperman 26, 29
Oqalweni **120**, 8, 121, 162
Orange River (Sinqu) **247**, 33, 34, 41, 44, 47, 116, 197, 198, 222, 225, 248
Organ Pipes (Cathedral area) 109, 119, 124, 126, 127
  Pass **120**, 22, 42, 79, 119, 123 *et seq.*, 131, 256, 279
  Cave 126, 127
Organ Pipes (Mnweni area) **110**, 109
Orpen, J. M. 9, 246, 248, 249
Osborn, A. 40, 41
Osborn, Ross 104
Ostack, Mr. 92
Otto, Sgt. Major 235
Outer Tower, see Eastern Buttress
Oxbow scheme 105, 258

Pager, Harald 10, 131, 134
Paisley 29
Palmer, Alan 255
Pan African Ornithological Conference 202
Pangweni 228
Parker, Douglas 49
Park, Isabella, *see under Gray family*
Parkinson, Lieut. 235, 239, 241, 243, 270
Park-Ross, Dr. A. H. 63, 73, 100
  Mrs. A. H. (Mary) 73, 266
  Mungo 100
Passes, blowing up of 27, 42
Pasture Research Station 46
Pastures, The 98
Paton, Dr. Alan 56
  David 56
Peace Society 250
Peake, Hugh 56
Pearse, Rev. M. L. (Malcolm) 15, 112, 113, 115, 179, 268

Lost in blizzard 159 *et seq.*
  Joan 168, 169
  Mrs. R. O. (Edith) iii, 159, 268
Pearse, Sir Alfred 195
Peck, J. E. L. 57, 60, 280
Peete, chief 22
Percival, Miss L. 267
Pfenning, W. Gulden 28
Phalaza (Zulu custom) 208, 210
Phosihawu, see Giant's Castle
Pickering, Edith, *see under* Kelly, Fred
Pierson, Lorna 71, 154, 284
Pietermaritzburg Botanical Society 208
Pine, Sir Benjamin C. C. 226, 229, 232, 233, 243, 244, 250 *et seq.*, 271
Pinkney, Tom 57, 78
Pliny 201
Plowman, Hon. G. T. 63
Pofung (Empofeni) 44, 100, 101
Police Dagga Raid, Mnweni area 113 *et seq.*
Police Patrol, Giant's Castle to Mont-aux-Sources 50, 51
Politzer, Willie 102
Pope-Ellis, Peter 57, 78, 100, 105
Popham, William 233, 270, 271
  J. K. 42
Popple Peak **148**, 57, 283
Poppleton, J. 266
Posselt, John 156
Posselt, Rev. C. W. 28
  Mathilda, *see under* Zunckel family
Potterill, Charles Davie 240, 253
Preller, Carl 28
Pretorius, A. W. J. 31
Prichard, Rev. 233
Prime Minister's Resources and Planning Advisory Council 261
Prince Alfred 174
Pringle, Dr. J. A. 267
Proudfoot, Capt. William 34, 35
  Pass, *see Hlatimba Pass*
Puddings, Three **110**, **120**, 60, 61, 62, 112
Puluzamati 240
Putini, chief 32, 227
  Tribe 227, 249
Pyatt, Edward 266
Pygmies, 4, 5
Pyramid **120**, 74, 78, 124 *et seq.*, 287
    First ascent 68, 74, 78, 128, 287

Qacha's Nek 56
Qalo vi
Qing 9
Qolo la Masoja, *see Organ Pipes Pass*
Quail, Mrs. J. B. 266

Rainbow Crag 69
Rainbow Gorge 129
Rainfall, changes in 221
Ralfe, Robert 40
Ramblers' Club 192
Rattlesnake, H.M.S. 246
Red Beds v *et seq.*, 134
Reed, Dick 105
Rees, Dorothy 105
Regiments: 7th Dragoon Guards 50
  24th Foot 253
  45th Regiment 32
  73rd Regiment 33
  75th Regiment 42, 147, 232, 253
  86th Regiment 246
  Cape Mounted Rifles 31, 33, 244
  Corps of Royal Artillery 232
  Durban Volunteer Guard 32
  Frontier Armed and Mounted Police 246, 248, 249
  Natal Carbineers 30, 32, 34, 124, 229 *et seq.*, 254, 269 *et seq.*
  Natal Frontier Guard 229, 230, 248

Natal Police 50
  Richmond Mounted Rifles 229, 230, 248
  S.A. Engineering Corps 219
  Weenen Burgher Force 229, 230
  Weenen Yeomanry Cavalry 229, 230, 248
Reserves, Native, *see Locations*
Retief, Piet 20, 24, 25
  Deborah 24
Reynish, D. O. 138
Rhodes, Cecil 208
Ribbon Falls 44
Richmond 43, 229, 230
  St. Mary's College 242
Rinderpest Patrol 42
Ripley, Dr. L. P. ("Doc") 63, 70, 73, 123, 125, 192, 283, 285, 286, 287
  Dr. Sherman 73, 129, 192, 266, 286
Ritter, E. A. 19, 22
Rivulette **110**, 113 *et seq.*
Roads: Estcourt-Loskop 25, 46
  Forestry road (Mike's Pass) **120**, 131, 220
  Freeway, Natal-Witwatersrand 39
  Mountain road to *Sentinel* **88**, 93, 100, 101, 159, 255
  Old Main Road, coast to Natal border 39
  Rookdale-Mnweni road **110**, 109, 112
  Winterton-Cathedral Peak **120**, 122, 136, 219
  Giant's Castle 151
  Road policy in Drakensberg 157, 262, 263
Robben Island 29, 251
Robbins, Dorothy ("Robbie") 64
Roberts, Ven. Archdeacon 27
  Dr. Austin 27, 195
Robinson, Margery 124
Robinson, Sir John 40, 234, 248, 252, 270
Robinson, W. Carter 69, 134, 145, 151, 155, 174, 180, 187, 217, 222, 287
  M. E. 69, 151, 287
  Robinson Jun. 69
Rockeries (Ntaba Mabutho) 19, 54, 60, 78, 109 *et seq.*, 115 *et seq.*, 123, 160
  Peak 109, 112, 286
    First ascent 112, 286
  Tower, see Mponjwana
  Pass **110**, 42, 49, 54, 60, 80, 81, 115, 116, 117, 161, 163
Rookdale M. S. 109, 112
Roosevelt, Theodore 155
Rorke, Madge 128
Rorke's Drift 253
Rose, Stan 74, 78, 102, 128, 285, 287
Ross, J. J. 87
Ross, John 226
Rossouw, Mr. and Mrs. S. W. 214 *et seq.*, 266
  Caroline 215
  Stephen 215
Rotary 261, 262, 268
Roupell, Mrs. Arabella 207
Roux, Jan P. 121, 219
Royal Natal National Park **260**, 20, 46, 63, 65, 79, 95 *et seq.*, 98, 109, 111, 112, 115, 152, 153, 157, 168, 206, 217, 223, 230, 259, 263, 264, 266, 277
  Hotel **88**, 29, 64, 75, 92, 97, 98, 100, 102, 105, 217, 223
Royal William, S.S. 207
Rudolph, G. 31
Rugged Glen 100
Ruhle, Emil 70, 143, 284
Rycroft, Professor H. B. 68, 204, 262
Rydal Mount 66, 87 *et seq.*, 139, 266

Saddle (Segwana Cirque, Ntaba Busuku) **110**, 54, 60, 80, 109, 111, 116, 161, 286
First ascent 74, 286
North Saddle **110**, 49, 60, 109, 111, 112, 116, 284
First ascent 112, 284
South Saddle **110**, **120**, 58, 59, 60, 109, 111, 112, 116, 162, 179, 259, 279, 285
First ascent 111, 285
Stream 60, 111
Saddleback, see Amphitheatre
Safety measures in Drakensberg 107, 127, 129, 163 *et seq.*
St. Andrew's College 72
St. George, Lieut. Col. 32
St. Mary's College, *see under* Richmond
Sanderson, J. 249, 252
Sandlulube 13
Sandstone iv *et seq.*
Sani Pass (Manzimyama Pass) **247**, 43, 196, 248, 264
Sanqebethu River 55, 200
Santo Alberto, S.S. 41
Saw-tooth Ridge, see Chessmen
Scaley Peak 154
Schaapkraal 121
Schaeffer, Derek 115 *et seq.*
Schapera, I. 4
Schelpe, Dr. E. A. 204
Schiller, Friedrich 225
Schoeman, Professor P. J. 3, 6, 9, 30
Scholes, E. H. (Ted) 70, 71, 102 *et seq.*, 152, 154, 284, 286
Scholtz, Salmon 219
Schoongezicht Cave **120**, 131
Schweitzer, Dr. Albert 193
Sclanders, Andrew 29, 156
Patrick Campbell 29, 246
Scott, Captain 107
Scottfield 55
Scott, George 139
Scott, Lieut. 244
Seate River 47
Segwana Cirque, see Saddle
Sehonghong River 197
Cave 47
Semena River 47
Sentinel Peak (Ntabamnyama) **88**, 24, 25, 54, 65, 66, 67, 75, 87, 89, 90, 91, 93, 95, 99, 101, 102, 103, 105, 106, 107, 159, 169, 255, 284
First ascent 67, 284
Cave 106
Gully 72, 75, 91
Setene River **110**, 70, 109, 112, 173, 209
Shaka 17, 18 *et seq.*, 26, 39, 43, 109, 124, 226
Shepstone, Sir Theophilus 5, 17, 31, 34, 226 *et seq.*, 242, 251, 252
John 5, 31, 228, 251
Ship's Prow Pass **132**, **148**, 54
Shuter, C. F. 267
Sibayeni Cave **120**, 131
Sidinane, chief 20, 97
Sikwate 21
Simpson, J. C. 282
Sim, T. R. 217
Singati River and Valley **88**, **110**, 12, 54, 65, 101, 112, 258, 259, 284
Area 23
Gully 68
Wall 73, 74, 101
Sinqu River, *see* Orange River
Sinqunyana River 34
Sitole, Const. 113 *et seq.*
Slinger, J. 112, 286
Smit, Ds. Erasmus 24, 25
Smith, Herbert 87, 89, 92
Smith, Rev. G. 253

Smith, Sir Harry 26
Smous 26
Smuts, General xi, 66, 67, 129, 156
Snakes 186, 187 *et seq.*
Enemies 192, 193
Eyesight 188
Feeding Habits 188
Hearing 188
Method of communication 188
Popular misconceptions 187, 189, 190
Snake-bite and its treatment 190, 191, 208
Venom 189, 190
Berg Adder 189
Black-necked Spitting Cobra 189
Boomslang 191
Cape Cobra 189, 193
Cobra 189
Puff-adder 189
Python 186, 187
Rinkals 189, 192
Skaapsteker 189
Snelson, Kenneth 80, 81, 109, 285
Snow conditions and precautions 159 *et seq.*, 212
Severity and frequency of snow-storms 221, 222
Great Blizzard of 1905 222
August 1849 snow-storm 222
August 1869 snow-storm 33, 222
see also Hypothermia
Soil Conservation Act 223
Solar Cliffs 121, 133, 135, 187
Soldaten Pas (*sic*) see Organ Pipes Pass
Solitude **148**, 261
Somerset, Colonel 22
South African Archaeological Society 262
South African Association of Arts 261
South African Institute of Architects 261, 262
South African Institute of Medical Research 191
South African National Society 262
South African Tourist Corporation 262
South African Water Catchments Association 225
Sparrman, Andries 274
Speirs family 31
Alexander 28
Charles 28, 34, 36
James 28, 34
Robert (Jnr.) 28, 34, 35, 36, 147, 240, 241, 244, 283
Robert (Snr.) 27, 32, 34 *et seq.*
William 35
Sphinx (Cathedral area) **120**, 124, 131
Sphinx (Cathkin area) 48, 187, 215
Spioenkop Military Post 32
see also Fort Nottingham
Spitzberg stream 49, 55
Springfield, *see* Winterton
Stander, Dr. G. J. 225
Stanger, W. 42, 52, 277
Stanley, H. M. 4
Stanton, Joe 105, 107
Stark, Dr. A. C. 65, 66
Steatopygia 4, 5
Steenkamp, Dr. W. J. 29
Stegner, Professor Wallace 182
Stenton, Mr. and Mrs. Douglas 197 *et seq.*
Stephens, H. B. 128, 219, 266
Michael 128, 129
Step Pass 25
Sterkhorn (Mount Memory) **132**, iii, 48, 54, 67, 74, 144, 145, 286
First ascent 49, 286
Sterkspruit (Impofana) River and Valley **132**, 12, 18, 42, 45 *et seq.*, 54, 134, 136, 144, 145, 146, 221
Gorge 48, 174
Stevenson, R. L. 216

Stocker brothers 48 *et seq.*, 54, 55, 109, 111, 112, 124, 138, 139, 140, 144
Rev. A. H. 48 *et seq.*, 283, 286
F. R. 48 *et seq.*, 283, 286
Stockley, G. M. v
Stokoe, T. P. 67, 68
Stone Age man x, 3, 5, 10, 37
Stone, W. J. 42
Storm over Organ Pipes 126, 127
Stow, G. W. 3, 5, 9, 37
Streit, S. G. 217
Stuckenberg, B. R. 267
Suai's Cave 89
Sugar-loaf **120**, 124, 131
Sunday's Kloof 33
Sungabala Pass 46
Sutherland, Dr. P. C. 35, 152, 207, 208
Swart, Hon. C. R. 115
Sweeney, Professor G. M. J. (Maurice) 8, 57, 63, 72, 74, 124, 127, 128, 144, 257, 267, 275, 283, 284, 287
Mrs. G. M. J. ("Snib") 8, 74
Symons, Roden 150, 156, 267
Bryan 151, 267
Leslie 267
Symons, H. G. (Godfrey) 51, 115, 150, 194 *et seq.*, 267
Mrs. H. G. (Norah) 201

Table Mountain 70, 129, 204, 213, 261
Preservation Committee 261
Preservation Board 261
Sandstone iv, ix
Tainton, Tpr. 241
Tale, J. 267
Tamma's Tower, see Turret
Tatlow, Mr. 98
Taylor, Sgt. Major 233, 234
Tedder, Mrs. E. P. V. 267
Tekoane vi
Tempest, George 106
Tendele **88**, 100, 224
Tennessee Valley Authority 261
Tent Hotel 29
Teteleku, chief 251
Teyateyaneng vi
Thabana Ntlenyana 56, 197, 287
First ascent 56, 287
Thabantshonyane see Thabana Ntlenyana
Thaba Ntshu 18
Theal, Dr. George McC. 20, 269
The Climb (farm) 135
Thembu 20
Thode, Justus 212
Thomas, H. 267
Thomas, P. W. 267
Thomson, George 57, 76, 77 *et seq.*, 109, 111, 127, 266, 285, 286
Mrs. E. E. 266
Thrash, Edward 152
Through the Looking Glass 251
Times of Natal 230
Tinley, Mr. and Mrs. K. B. 152
Tobias (Amphlett's servant) 139, 284
Tobias, Professor P. V. x, 37
Torday, E. 21
Tourism 154, 262
Clash with Game Preservation 157, 158
Toverkop 77
Trauseld, W. R. 51, 204, 266
Trees: *Acacia dealbata* 262
A. decurrens 262
Calodendron capense 100, 216
Celtis africana 216
Curtisia faginae 216
Cussonia spicata 216
Dais cotinifolia 216
Ilex mitis 216
Kiggelaria africana 216

Leucosidia sericea 216
Olea capensis 100, 216
Pinus patula 221, 262
Podocarpus henkelii 100, 216
P. latifolius 216
Trigonometrical Survey Department 267, 274 *et seq.*, 283
Trout 121, 145, 154
Tryme 121
Tseketseke River **120**, 77, 121
Tshani, chief 122
Tsikoane vi
Tugela River (Letuele) and Valley **88**, i, 17, 19, 21, 25, 26, 32, 39, 41, 44, 52, 54, 65, 90, 91, 95, 100, 102, 105, 107, 112, 144, 159, 174, 217, 258
  Gorge **88**, 72, 79, 89, 91, 92, 95, 97, 100, 102, 105
  Waterfall **88**, 54, 79, 89, 95, 97, 101, 278
  Tugela Basin Development Scheme 100, 213, 216, 257 *et seq.*, 263
  Little Tugela, *see* Injasuti
Tungay, R. W. 146
  John 146, 268
Tunnel Cave **88**, 105
Turret (*Tamma's Tower*) **132**, 144, 287
  First ascent 74, 144, 287
Turret Arête, Orange Kloof 69
Tutumi stream **120**, 131
Twins **110**, **120**, 57 *et seq.*, 116, 124, 287
  First ascent 124, 287
  Cave **110**, **120**, 57, 59, 60, 61, 78, 80, 112, 115, 124

Ubutswane 55, 56
Udibi 19
Umgeni River i, 27, 32, 34
Umhashi, son of Mabudaza 241
Umhlonhlo River and Valley **120**, 119, 121, 126, 131
Umkomaas River i, 20, 28, 31, 32, 41, 43, 147, 230, 269, 270, 271
Umkomozana River 43
Umlambonja River and Valley **110**, **120**, 12, 19, 23, 33, 54, 57, 58, 68, 115, 116, 119, 121, 124, 125, 126, 128, 129, 135, 187, 217, 258, 278
  Buttress 57, 119, 121, 124
  Meaning of name 129
  Pass **120**, 42, 80, 115, 161 *et seq.*
Umyovu 242
Umzimkulu River **247**, i, 17, 20, 31, 32, 35, 41, 43, 230, 248, 277
Umzimvubu River **247**, 20, 34, 41, 43, 248
Underberg 43
Ungiyeza 100
Unicorns 40, 41
University of Natal 104, 139, 156, 191, 209, 266, 267
  Medical School 73
  Mountain Club, *see under* Mountain Club of S.A.
Unyembe 228
Upper Hilton 33
Uys, C. J. 252

Van der Linde, Miss E. M. 267
Van der Merwe, Jan Koos 217
Van der Riet, A. W. (Albert) 57, 62, 64, 77, 116, 119, 121, 128, 267
  Mrs. A. W. (Doreen) 121
  Philip 121, 122
Van der Schijff, Professor H. P. 157
Van der Zeyde, A. 264
Van Gruening, Sawyer 144
Van Heerden, Col. R. de Wet 114
Van Heerden, Dr. 117

Van Heyningen, J. 55, 82, 131, 145, 218, 288
Van Reenen's Pass 22, 24, 249
Van Reenen, Vic 266
Van Riebeeck, Jan vii, 12
Van Rooyen (butcher) 98
Van Rooyen, Stoffel 121
Van Schalkwyk, C. J. 251
Van Vuuren, Stephanus 31
  Military Post 31, 32
Van Zyl, Flelette 121
Van Zyl, Hon. H. S. 261
Varty, Sgt. T. B. 235, 240, 244, 270
Veld and Vlei Organisation 28
Vemvaan **88**, 98
Vermeulen, Mr. and Mrs. Sybrand 121, 135, 136
Visser, Commd. 101
Volunteer movement 32, 34, 229, 232, 248
Voortrekkers i, 20, 23, 24 *et seq.*, 41, 93, 100, 144, 168
Vorster, Dr. P. W. 261

Wagon, Cape 39, 40
Walton, Isaac 59
Warren, Dr. Ernest 133
Water supplies, protection of 262
Watkins, D. (Des) 55 *et seq.*, 71, 102, 111, 142, 143, 152, 154, 284, 287
  Mrs. D. (Jean) 102
Watkinson, Mr. 98
Watson, W. C. 267
Watwoa 4
Wellington 48
West, Lieut. Gov. Martin 227
West, W. C. 67, 69, 75, 138, 139, 284
Weston 28, 29, 253
Whelan, Capt. H. C. 145
White Mountain Inn 145
White, Paul 67, 68
Whymper, Edward 39, 67, 82
Whyte, J. K. 266
Wilderness Areas, *see* Foreword
Wilderness Trails 154
Wild Flowers 204 *et seq.*
  Amaryllis toxicaria 9
  Anemone 205
  A. fanninii 27, 62, 205
  Anoiganthus, see Cyrtanthus
  Aponogeton junceus 204
  Aristea 209
  A. cognata 209
  Asclepias gibba 10
  Athanasia 205
  Begonia sutherlandii 212
  Boophane disticha 8
  Brunsvigia 24, 210
  B. cooperi 210
  B. grandiflora 210
  B. josephinae 210
  B. radulosa 210
  Buddleia 205
  B. salvifolia 155
  Burchellia bubalina 208
  Callilepis laureola 208
  Cotyledon paniculata 10
  Cycad 204
  Cyrtanthus 209, 210, 213
  C. breviflorus (Anoiganthus breviflorus) 209
  C. contractus 209
  C. erubescens 210
  C. flanaganii 210
  Dierama 71, 205, 213
  D. igneum 206
  D. robustum 206
  Disperis fanninii 27
  Erica 71, 211, 212, 213
  E. cerinthoides 211
  E. oatesii 211
  Eulophia hians 10

Euphorbia arborescens 9
Euryops multifidus 10
Gladiolus cruentus 71, 213
Gloriosa superba 210
Greyia sutherlandii 61, 62, 119, 205, 207 208
Halleria lucida 155, 216
Helichrysum 62, 211, 212
H. sutherlandii 211
H. trilineatum 164, 168, 211
Hesperantha longituba 212
Kalanchoe thyrsiflora 204
Kniphofia 204, 205, 213
K. caulescens 213
K. northiae 213
K. porphyrantha 213
K. ritualis 213
Leonotis 208
Littonia modesta 210
Lobelia 71, 205, 210, 211
Moraea 71, 205
M. spathulata 9, 212
Myosotis sylvatica 212
Nerine 205, 213
Parapodium castatus 10
Pavetta cooperi 208
Protea 206
P. caffra 207
P. dracomontana 207
P. multibracteata 207
P. roupelliae 206
P. simplex 207
P. subvestita 207
Rhodohypoxis baurii 213
Schizostylis coccinea 209
Schizochilus 205
Scilla 204, 205
S. krausii 205
S. natalensis 62, 205
Senecio tamoides 205, 216
Serrurier florida 207
Streptocarpus gardenii 212
Vellosia 71
V. talbotii 212
Wahlenbergia 210
W. grandiflora 210
Watsonia densiflora 206
W. meriana 206
Wild Life Protection and Conservation Society 202, 262
Wilkes, Ben 48
Willcox, A. R. x, 4, 255, 267
William of Orange 155
Williams, F. C. 65, 75, 98
Williamson, D. 112, 286
Williamson, O. K. 112, 284
William the Silent 211
Wilson, Professor Monica 12
Wilson, R. W. 42
Windsor Castle **120**, 124, 126, 285
  First ascent 285
Winter, E. M. (Martin) 64, 101, 105, 107, 112, 115 *et seq.*, 143, 152, 266, 284, 285, 286
Winter, Hon. H. D. 122
Winterton (Springfield) 50, 59, 114, 115, 122, 134, 219
Wintervogel 4
Witch **120**, 131, 285
  First ascent 68, 74, 285
Witches **88**, 102, 105
Wits. University Archaeological Expedition 21
Witzieshoek 13, 19, 22, 41, 47, 50, 66, 87 *et seq.*, 101, 107, 113, 222, 249, 255, 266
  Mission Station 87, 93
Wolf, Joseph 195
Wolseley, Sir Garnet 232, 252
Wonder Valley **132**, 49, 55

Wong (Wongchowski), Hans 70, 71, 102, 140, 143, 284, 286
  Else 70, 71, 124, 283, 286
Wood, A. M. 267
Wood, Robert 159 *et seq.*
Wood, T. 286
Woodhouse, H. C. 10
Woods, Col. J. P. S. 67, 138, 139
Wood, Wilson 46
Wostyn iii, 145, 221
Wright, Dr. F. B. 209, 266, 271
Wright, J. B. 266
Wybergh, W. J. 67, 69, 89 *et seq.*, 101, 138, 139, 284
  Mrs. W. J. 91, 138
  Betty 91
"Wylde, Atherton" 253
Wyld, James i, 52, 277

Wylie, Gen. J. S. 98

Xaba, Const. 113 *et seq.*
Xameb 3, 6, 9, 30
Xan-xeib 3, 11, 16, 17

Yellow-woods, *see under* Trees, Podo-carpus
Yosemite National Park 157
Yule, Mrs. E. 267

Zikhali 23, 32, 46, 122, 123
  Zikhali's Horn, see Cathedral Peak
Zimbabwe Tower 70
Zitshozi, son of Ngatyana 241
Zondo 113
Zulu place names i, 123
  Orthography i

Zulus 17 *et seq.*
  Arrival in Northern Natal 17
  Rise to power and conquests 18 *et seq.*
Zunckel family 29, 64, 217
  Anton 28, 266
  Carl 113 *et seq.*
  Fred 116
  Gerald 28, 142, 145
  Mathilda (née Posselt) 28, 99
  Otto 28, 64, 92, 99, 101, 121, 135, 142, 145, 217
  Rev. K. E. 28
  Ruth 28
  Udo 28, 142, 145
  Walter 28, 92, 99, 100, 101
  Wilhelm 28
Zunckel's Cave 28
Zwide 17

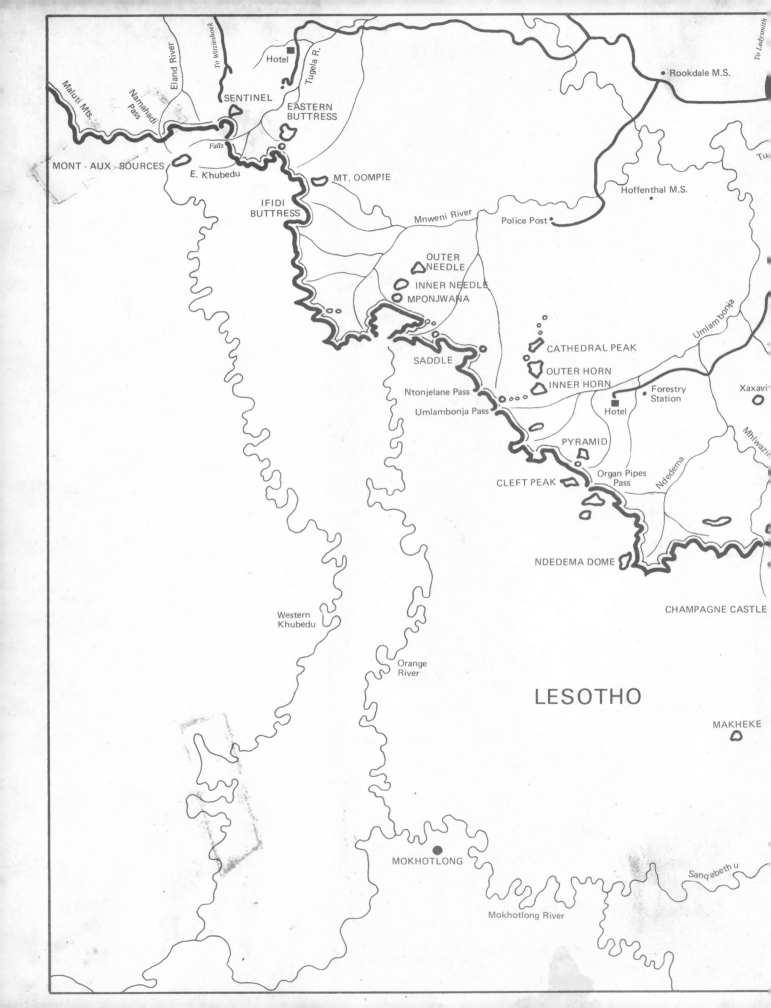